D0065004

SOCIOLOGICAL THEORY AND RESEARCH

Other Joint Publications of The Free Press
and
The American Sociological Association

Peter M. Blau, *Approaches to the Study of Social Structure*

In this concise and definitive work, some of the world's foremost sociologists present differing, at times opposing, sociological conceptions of social structure.

The 1974 meeting in Montreal

Lewis A. Coser and Otto N. Larsen, *The Uses of Controversy in Sociology*

A critical assessment of some of the major controversies in sociology today. Twenty-three distinguished sociologists examine several areas of concern: trends in American society, cleavages in the social structure, individual and societal modernity, conflict and revolution, the resurgence of ethnicity, the links between knowledge and policy, and theoretical and methodological problems.

The 1975 meeting in San Francisco

J. Milton Yinger and Stephen J. Cutler, *Major Social Issues: A Multidisciplinary View*

Thirty-six authorities in the fields of sociology, economics, psychology, anthropology, history, philosophy, law, and biology present a number of different approaches to such topics as poverty and civil rights programs, crime, the impact of contemporary trends in the family on socialization, the quality of life, fertility, and social change.

The 1977 meeting in Chicago

Amos H. Hawley, *Societal Growth: Processes and Implications*

Eminent sociologists, demographers, and economists present fresh and divergent outlooks on the complexities of growth within social systems and examine such topics as the causes and consequences of population change, the evolutionary perspective of societal growth, social stratification and the division of labor, structural differentiation within the nuclear family, the limits of societal growth, and future projections of current processes.

The 1978 meeting in San Francisco

SOCIOLOGICAL THEORY AND RESEARCH

A Critical Appraisal

Edited by

Hubert M. Blalock, Jr.

A Publication of
The American
Sociological Association

THE FREE PRESS
A Division of Macmillan Publishing Co., Inc.
NEW YORK

Collier Macmillan Publishers
LONDON

The Free Press
A Division of Macmillan Publishing Co., Inc.
866 Third Avenue, New York, N.Y. 10022

Collier Macmillan Canada, Ltd.

Library of Congress Catalog Card Number: 80-754

Printed in the United States of America

printing number

1 2 3 4 5 6 7 8 9 10

Library of Congress Cataloging in Publication Data
Main entry under title:

Sociological theory and research.

    "A publication of the American Sociological
Association."
    Papers presented at the annual ASA meeting in
Boston, Aug., 1979.
    Includes bibliographical references and indexes.
1 1. Sociology--Congresses. 2. Sociological
research--Congresses. I. Blalock, Hubert M.
II. American Sociological Association.
HM13.S56   1980   301   80-754
ISBN 0-02-903630-5

Contents

About the Contributors

CHARLES E. BIDWELL, Professor of Sociology and Education and Chairman of the Department of Education at the University of Chicago, received his Ph.D. from the University of Chicago in 1956. Recent works include "The Structure of Professional Help," published in *Explorations in General Theory in the Social Sciences,* and "The Ecology of Organizations," written with John Kasarda and to appear in *New Approaches to Human Ecology.* From 1973 through 1978, Bidwell edited *The American Journal of Sociology.*

HUBERT M. BLALOCK, JR., Professor of Sociology at the University of Washington, served as President of the American Sociological Association in 1979. He has been elected Fellow in the American Academy of Arts and Sciences and in the American Statistical Association and is a member of the National Academy of Sciences. His books include *Social Statistics, Causal Inferences in Nonexperimental Research, Theory Construction, Toward a Theory of Minority-Group Relations,* and *Intergroup Processes* (with P. H. Wilken).

PETER M. BLAU is Quetelet Professor of Sociology at Columbia University and Professor of Sociology at the State University of New York at Albany. He received his Ph.D. at Columbia University in 1952. He is a fellow of the American Academy of Arts and Sciences and a Past President of the American Sociological Association. His first book was *The Dynamics of Bureaucracy;* his latest is *Inequality and Heterogeneity.*

BURTON R. CLARK, Allan M. Cartter Professor of Higher Education, Graduate School of Education, and Professor of Sociology, University of California, Los Angeles, received his Ph.D. at the University of California, Los Angeles, in 1954. He is a member of the National Academy of Education and was awarded the AERA-ACT 1979 Research Award for significant research on American higher education. Among Dr. Clark's books are *Adult Education in Transition* (1956), *The Open Door College* (1960), *Educating the Expert Society* (1962), *The Distinctive College* (1970), and *Academic Power in Italy* (1977).

JOHN A. CLAUSEN is a Professor of Sociology and Research Sociologist at the Institute of Human Development at the University of California, Berkeley. He received his Ph.D. from the University of Chicago in 1949 and is the co-author of *Socialization and Society, Medicine and Society,* and *Explorations in Social Psychiatry.*

JACK ELINSON, Professor of Sociomedical Sciences at Columbia University, received his Ph.D. from George Washington University. He has been a senior study director of the National Opinion Research Center and an assistant Professor of Sociology at the University of Chicago. He is an elected member of the Institute of Medicine of the National Academy of Sciences, and has served as Chairman of the Section on Medical Sociology of the American Sociological Association and as President of the American Association for Public Opinion Research. He is co-editor of *Sociomedical Health Indicators* and of *Health Goals and Health Indicators.*

WILLIAM FORM is Professor of Sociology and Labor and Industrial Relations at the University of Illinois, Urbana–Champaign. He received his Ph.D. at the University of Maryland in 1944. His recent books include *Blue-Collar Stratification: Auto-Workers in Four Countries* and *Income and Ideology* (with Joan Huber). Currently he is studying the internal tensions within the United States and French working classes as well as problems of economic equity in the world of work and in the larger society.

KENNETH E. FRIEND received his doctorate in social psychology from Carnegie–Mellon University in 1973. After spending five years at the University of Chicago's Graduate School of Business, he is now on the organizational behavior faculty of the School of Management at Clarkson College in Potsdam, New York.

W. PARKER FRISBIE, Associate Professor of Sociology and Research Associate at the Population Research Center at the University of Texas, Austin, received his Ph.D. at the University of North Carolina in 1972. Among his recent publications are two papers reflecting comparative demographic studies of racial and ethnic groups (in Bean and Frisbie, eds.), *The Demography of Racial and Ethnic Groups* (1978), and "Technology in Evolutionary and Ecological Perspective" (with Clifford Clarke, *Social Forces,* December, 1979).

PHILLIP E. HAMMOND, Professor of Religious Studies and Sociology, University of California, Santa Barbara, received his Ph.D. at Columbia University in 1960. He is presently the Editor of the *Journal for The Scientific Study of Religion.* His most recent book is *The Structure of Human Society,* and he is co-author (with Robert Bellah) of the forthcoming *Varieties of Civil Religion.*

AMOS H. HAWLEY is Kenan Professor Emeritus, University of North Carolina, Chapel Hill. He received his Ph.D. at the University of Michigan in 1941, was the President of the Population Association of America in 1971, and served as President of the American Sociological Association in 1978. Professor Hawley is the author of numerous books including *Ecology* (1950), *The Changing Shape of Metropolitan America* (1955) and *Urban Society* (1971) and was the editor of *Societal Growth* (1979).

GEORGE C. HOMANS received his undergraduate education at Harvard. Later he was a member of the Society of Fellows there, whose rules forbade his receiving the Ph.D. His highest degree is an MA from Cambridge University (1955), where he served as Visiting Professor. He has been Professor of Sociology at Harvard since 1953 and was President of the American Sociological Association, 1963–1964. His best-known books are *The Human Group* (1950) and *Social Behavior* (rev. ed., 1974).

BENTON JOHNSON received his Ph.D. from Harvard University. Since 1957 he has taught at the University of Oregon, where he is currently Professor and department head. From 1971 to 1974 he was Editor of the *Journal for the Scientific Study of Religion* and is currently President of the Society of the Scientific Study of Religion. Among his published works are *American Mosaic* (co-edited with Phillip E. Hammond) and *Functionalism in Modern Sociology: Understanding Talcott Parsons.*

NATHAN KEYFITZ is Andelot Professor of Sociology and Demography at Harvard University. His doctorate is from the University of Chicago (1952), and he served on the faculty of the universities of Toronto, Chicago, and Berkeley. He has taught at the universities of Moscow, Costa Rica, and Indonesia. He is a member of the American Academy of Arts and Sciences and of the National Academy of Sciences. His *Applied Mathematical Demography* appeared in 1977.

LEWIS M. KILLIAN received his Ph.D. at the University of Chicago in 1949. He has taught at the University of Massachusetts, Amherst, since 1969. Before that, he taught at the University of Oklahoma, Florida State University, and the University of Connecticut. In 1975 he was awarded a Guggenheim Fellowship for research on race relations in England. He is co-author (with Ralph H. Turner) of *Collective Behavior* (1957, 1972) and is author of *The Impossible Revolution: Black Power and the American Dream* (1968, 1975).

JAMES D. LAING, Professor of Public Policy Analysis at the University of Pennsylvania, holds a Ph.D. in political science from Stanford. His scientific papers on research methods, authority systems in formal organizations, bargaining and coalition behavior, collective decision-making, and game-theoretic analysis have appeared in various symposia and professional journals. He is a member of the Public Choice Society and of the editorial board of the *Journal of Conflict Resolution* and is associate editor of the *Journal of Mathematical Sociology*. He is co-author of *Prediction Analysis of Cross Classifications* (1977) and *Analysis of Ordinal Data* (1977).

ROBERT K. LEIK is Director of the Minnesota Family Study Center and Professor of Sociology, University of Minnesota. He obtained his Ph.D. from the University of Wisconsin and has held faculty positions at the universities of Washington, Bergen (Norway, visiting), Alberta (Canada, visiting), and Massachusetts. He is a member of the Family Impact Seminar, a national policy group. His publications include *Mathematical Sociology* (with B. F. Meeker) and *Methods, Logic and Research of Sociology*.

GARY T. MARX, Professor of Sociology in the Department of Urban Studies and Planning and Humanities at the Massachusetts Institute of Technology, received his Ph.D. from the University of California, Berkeley. In the area of collective behavior, he has written on police behavior in riots, issueless riots, majority involvement in minority riots, urban vigilantes, and agents provocateurs and is currently involved in work on social control and social movements. He is the author of *Protest and Prejudice*.

JOHN W. MEYER received his Ph.D. from Columbia University in 1965. He is currently Professor of Sociology at Stanford University. He is the author of a number of papers in comparative sociology and the sociology of education and has recently published (with Michael T. Hannan) *National Development and the World System* (1979).

WILBERT E. MOORE, Professor of Sociology and Law at the University of Denver since 1970, received his Ph.D. from Harvard in 1940. Previously he taught at Pennsylvania State University and Princeton University and was a sociologist at the Russell Sage Foundation from 1964 to 1970. Moore is a Past President of the Eastern Sociological Society (1953) and of the American Sociological Association (1966). Among his numerous books, two recent publications are *Social Change* (rev. ed., 1974) and *World Modernization: The Limits of Convergence* (1979).

LEONARD I. PEARLIN, who received his Ph.D. from Columbia University, is a Research Sociologist in the Laboratory of Socio-environmental Studies of the National Institute of Mental Health. He is the author of *Family Relations and Class Context: A Cross-National Study* (1971) and of a number of articles seeking to identify various social structural links to psychological functioning.

ALEJANDRO PORTES is Professor of Sociology at Duke University. He is Chairman of the Council on Latin American Studies and director of the graduate training program in Comparative Studies of Migration and Ethnicity at Duke. He received his Ph.D. from the University of Wisconsin and has taught at the University of Illinois, Urbana–Champaign; University of Texas, Austin; and University of Brasilia. His recent publications include *Urban Latin America* (with John Walton) (1976).

MATILDA WHITE RILEY, who is on leave from Bowdoin College, is Associate Director for Social and Behavioral Research, National Institute on Aging. She is a former Fellow, Center for Advanced Study in the Behavioral Sciences; senior member of the Institute of Medicine, National Academy of Sciences; and emeritus professor of sociology, Rutgers University. Her books include *Sociological Studies in Scale Analysis* (1954), *Sociological Research* (2 vols., 1963), and *Aging from Birth to Death* (1979).

PAUL ROCK received his B.Sc. in sociology at the London School of Economics and Nuffield College, Oxford (D. Phil. [Oxon]) and is currently Senior Lecturer in Sociology at the London School of Economics. Among his books are *Making People Pay* (1973), *Deviant Behaviour* (1973), and *The Making of Symbolic Interactionism* (1979).

NORMAN B. RYDER, Professor of Sociology at Princeton University, received his Ph.D. from Princeton in 1951. He was a member of the Department of Sociology, University of Wisconsin, Madison, from 1956 to 1971, and in 1969 was named Thorstein Veblen Professor of Sociology. Dr. Ryder served as Editor of the *American Sociological Review* (1965–1969) and as President of the Population Association of America (1972–1973) and is a Fellow of the American Academy of Arts and Sciences. He has been co-director of the National Fertility Study since 1965.

NEIL J. SMELSER, University Professor of the University of California, received his doctorate from Harvard University in 1958. He is a former Vice President of the American Sociological Association. His publications include *Social Change in the Industrial Revolution, Theory of Collective Behavior,* and *Comparative Methods in the Social Sciences.*

GUY E. SWANSON, Professor of Sociology at the University of California, Berkeley, received his Ph.D. from the University of Chicago in 1948. Some of his publications include *The Birth of the Gods* (1960), *Religion and Regime: A Sociological Account of the Reformation* (1967), *Rules of Descent: Studies in the Sociology of Parentage* (1969), and *Social Change* (1971).

JACKSON TOBY, Professor of Sociology and Director of the Institute for Criminological Research at Rutgers, received his Ph.D. from Harvard in

1950. A former student of Talcott Parsons, Toby edited Parsons and Platt, *The American University* (1973), and Parsons, *The Evolution of Societies* (1977). His introductory textbook, *Contemporary Society* (1971), attempted to explain the Parsonian perspective on modern societies to undergraduates. As one of three literary executors of Parsons, Toby is helping to prepare for publication Parsons' unfinished manuscript, *The American Societal Community*.

STANLEY H. UDY, JR., received his Ph.D. from Princeton University in 1958 and is now Professor of Sociology at Dartmouth College. His principal publications include *Organization of Work* and *Work in Traditional and Modern Society*.

ROBIN M. WILLIAMS, JR., Henry Scarborough Professor of Social Science at Cornell University, received his Ph.D. from Harvard. He has been President and Secretary of the American Sociological Association, President of the Eastern Sociological Society and of the Sociological Research Association, and Editor of the Arnold and Caroline Rose Monograph Series of the American Sociological Association. Among his several books are *American Society: A Sociological Interpretation, Strangers Next Door,* and *Mutual Accommodation: Ethnic Conflict and Cooperation.*

WILLIAM JULIUS WILSON, Professor and Chairman of the Department of Sociology at the University of Chicago, received his doctorate from Washington State University in 1966. He has been named a Sydney Spivack Fellow by the American Sociological Association in recognition of his writings in intergroup relations. His publications include *Power, Racism and Privilege: Race Relations in Theoretical and Sociohistorical Perspectives* (1973), *Through Different Eyes* (1973), and *The Declining Significance of Race: Blacks and Changing American Institutions* (1978).

Preface

This volume contains thirty essays selected from papers delivered in the plenary and thematic sessions at the 1979 Annual Meeting of the American Sociological Association held in Boston. Panelists in these sessions were asked to respond to a series of questions oriented to the theme of the meetings: the relationship between theory and research. They were requested to identify the most important theoretical and methodological problems, including conceptualization and measurement issues and data or knowledge gaps. In addition, they were urged to discuss the reasons underlying any difficulties, disputes, or deficiencies they may have noted, as well as possible resolutions. In the plenary sessions the focus was on general sociology, whereas each of the sixteen thematic sessions dealt with a specific substantive field of sociology.

The chapters that appear in this volume thus focus on *issues* in the field and are not intended to represent reviews of the literature or summaries of all important developments. Not all substantive fields of sociology have been covered. For instance, the field of family and kinship had to be dropped from the program. Three of the remaining sixteen substantive fields are not represented in this volume because not all of the participants submitted their chapters for inclusion, and because space considerations required necessary selectivity.

In no sense, therefore, can it be claimed that the volume "represents" the field, or that all substantive areas have been equally covered. Instead, the reader should approach this work as a reasonably adequate sampling of appraisals of sociologists who are looking at a diversity of substantive fields from a number of different viewpoints. All, however, are recognized scholars in their fields, and have addressed themselves to what they consider to be highly important issues within their fields. The four chapters in Part I, all taken from plenary sessions, are addressed to highly general issues. The remaining chapters, in Part II, are more narrowly concerned with specific substantive fields.

The reader will discover that many of the issues addressed in these chapters are perennial ones. Some deal with matters relating to theoretical or ideological biases, value premises, and difficulties standing in the way of achieving "value-free" science. Others are concerned with the advantages and disadvantages of macro-oriented approaches and microapproaches. Still others involve the conceptual confusions and debates in which scholars appear to be talking past one another, sometimes because members of rival "schools" have vested interests in one or another approach. Several authors talk about boundary problems, or what topics should or should not be included within a field, as well as those that have been neglected because they appear to be beyond the scope of that field. Other authors deal with questions relating to static versus dynamic theoretical formulations and the pros and cons of cross-sectional and longitudinal research designs.

Most of these issues apply in varying degrees to *all* fields of sociology, and therefore their implications are of import to general sociology. Presumably, some such issues can be resolved by constructive means. Others, perhaps, should be forgotten or at least should not be permitted to consume too much of our time. Unfortunately, it is often difficult to decide, in advance, which specific issues belong in which category. Most certainly, we may safely assume that all such issues will remain with us for a long time to come.

Since very few readers will have substantive interests in all of the fields covered in this volume, the editor's recommendation—based on his own reading and rereading of these chapters—is that it may be most fruitful to approach each chapter with a series of questions concerning the implications of the discussion for one's own field(s) of interest. This assumes, first of all, that many of the problems faced in one field of our discipline will also occur in another. And, second, it recognizes that the particular authors discussing any given field have necessarily selected, in accord with their own interests and biases, a small subset of the problems and issues that confront sociologists in that field. Thus it would be a mistake if one were to conclude, for example, that problems outlined by authors discussing the field of occupations and professions are very different from those encountered in the field of deviance or that of race and ethnic relations.

Readers might ask some or all of the following questions of each chapter. Do the issues cited apply to my own field of specialization? If so, what different forms do they take and why? What are some of the reasons why these issues occur across fields, or (perhaps) why are they more common in one field than in another? What can we learn from the formulations or corrective steps that have been taken in other fields of sociology, or perhaps in other disciplines? What common issues arise because of missing data, factual inaccuracies, or "weak" findings? Which types of problems and disputes are most likely to involve matters of conceptual confusion or ambiguities in theoretical formulations? Which ones seem to result primarily from the use of common types of data-collection strategies (e.g., survey research or participant observation)? Which ones involve problems of micro–macro gaps, improper aggregation, or missing information on one or the other level?

Why do some fields or subfields seem to progress more rapidly than others? Are there phases of development or "plateaus" that are easily reached but difficult to surmount? If so, what kinds of strategies can be applied to enable fields to move along? What mistakes have been made in a given field that can be avoided in others? Are there apparent "dead ends" in one field that seem to have counterparts in others? By what mechanisms are we sucked into giving too much attention to issues that cannot possibly be resolved? What strictly methodological issues seem to require a specific "break-through" to achieve a resolution? To what extent do we need new data-collection techniques or new types of data-collection organizations?

No doubt, the answers to many such questions can be achieved only through hard work and concerted efforts to achieve consensus on basic theoretical and operational definitions. Some will involve technical problems, whereas others will be more theoretical or conceptual. But still others will probably involve issues falling within the province of the sociology of sociology. For instance, several authors refer to disputes between rival "schools" or orientations to sociology. To what extent are disputes kept alive, or even deliberately obfuscated, merely to preserve or augment one's status within the field? How many of our debates stem primarily from efforts to treat theories as simplistic alternatives to each other, rather than searching for a more complex synthesis? How many disagreements result primarily because some of us are willing to accept, as evidence, a set of data that others reject as inadequate? How often are intellectual double standards applied in evaluating evidence, in the sense that weak evidence in support of one's own theoretical position is accepted, whereas sharp methodological attacks are made on studies that provide counterevidence?

How often are we hampered as a result of someone's having posed a "big question" that has not been broken down into simpler ones that can more easily be answered? And, where this occurs, does it result primarily from the fact that we tend to reward those who pose the big questions, even where they have been stated in such a fuzzy fashion that they are almost guaranteed to result in endless disputes? Conversely, how often is it that we address ourselves to trivial questions, merely because they can be answered simply and because they can lead more easily to a journal publication? Do we have two almost totally distinct reward structures in the field, one for "theorists" and the other for "researchers"? Do "theorists" tend to have high standards of scholarship on the theory side, but very loose ones in connection with data analysis, whereas the reverse is the case for "researchers"? And do any of these possible tendencies vary by field or subfield within the larger sociological enterprise? If so, why?

It is hoped that the essays in this volume will help to stimulate thought on these and other questions—and perhaps to point the way toward some eventual answers.

I

General Theoretical and Methodological Issues

1

For General Sociology

Guy E. Swanson

THE SUBJECT IS general sociology. Fifty years ago there would have been less to say. Sociology was one effort to foster the good in society. The workings of every society were complex. The strains on solidarity and meaningfulness were often severe. Polities and policies needed to be informed by facts as well as by yearnings. As Durkheim (1888: 47–48) said of France:

> We live in a country which recognizes no master but opinion. In order that this master not become a mindless despot it is necessary to enlighten it.

Sociologists understood, of course, that there were other contributors to social enlightenment. There were anthropologists, economists, and political scientists, and the contribution of sociologists was complementary to theirs: the understanding of industrialized and secularized societies and, especially, of those whole systems comprised of societies, organizations, institutions, and social currents. To provide this understanding, sociologists believed that they would have to study the general features of human association and also societies of many types.

Was sociology a form of history? Fifty years ago, most sociologists said that, unlike history, sociology was an analytical enterprise. Its job was to develop conceptualizations and principles that would subsume great ranges of events and thereby make them understandable. It would not, however, be a merely formal discipline. Its analyses would deal with phenomena distinctive to social life and would be developed and modified to fit empirical observations. As an analytical undertaking, and one disciplined by observation, sociology would qualify as a science.

The promise of a scientific account is, in fact, what sociologists understood it to be: the promise that empirical events which seem diverse can be understood on the basis of a relatively small number of assumptions and that the account can gradually be perfected by improving the fit between interpretations and evidence. Our predecessors were less likely to appreciate that all empirical subject matter does not lend itself to this sort of analysis. The possibility of accounting for much from little rests on the fruitfulness of interpreting many things as instances of a few and also of assuming that these more general entities relate to one another according to a relatively small number of principles. Whether the subject matter of sociology lent itself to that kind of analysis was an empirical and a formal problem.

In declaring for a new science, the sociologists of the 1920s, and before, suggested that their subject matter required an analytical framework that would not readily be subsumed within the concepts and principles of other scientific accounts. This, too, required some justification.

Fifty years ago, it seemed to most leading figures in the discipline that these questions about the possibility and distinctiveness of a science of sociology were answered, and answered satisfactorily. The answers, as we use them today, derive especially from Mead (1934) and Durkheim (1895). They can be expressed in this way: Sociology is the analysis of collective relations and collective relations are a form of social relationship. Social relations are relations among people as persons: that is, relations in which people take account of whatever is on their own minds and the minds of others and seek to articulate the two (Swanson, 1965). Social relations are collective to the extent that persons are engaged, whether knowingly or not, in a common undertaking: taking account of concerns, capacities and potentialities for joint action: trying to make use of the common life or to promote or change it.

A special value of Mead's formulation, or of Durkheim's, is their distinguishing of a subject matter by the process through which entities relate. The premises of an explanation give the principles that govern the relations among entities. The essential step in justifying a new science is that of showing that those relations are distinctive and that those premises help one to interpret many variations in those relations. That is the step for which Mead and Durkheim lay the groundwork.

The warrants, both formal and empirical, that justify the suitability of sociology's subject matter for a distinctive and scientific analysis have often been reviewed (Parsons, 1937; Swanson, 1965, 1968) and need not detain us. They are not fully adequate, but neither are the comparable warrants for any field of science (Bernstein, 1976; Hesse, 1974). They do seem a sufficient basis from which to work and the promise they offer is borne out by developments in theory and research.

Or is this true?

Randall Collins (1975) thinks that it is, but that the accomplishment has been lessened and obscured by our pursuit of "practical, ideological, or aesthetic aims" (p. 37). He says (p. 2) that "we now have a solid framework

of a scientific sociology,'' indeed (p. 1), ''the elements of a powerful explanatory theory.'' All will come right, he suggests, ''if we set our minds . . . on
building an explanatory science'' (p. 37). ''I believe,'' he writes (pp. 37–38),

> that a considerable number of advances have been made in theory and re-
> search. The task of putting them together into a generalized explanatory theory
> has simply been held back by the implicit dominance of non-scientific orienta-
> tions. In particular, we know a great deal about stratifications [*sic*] and organi-
> zations; and these areas provide the core of a general sociology.

And then, across 550 pages, he gives us a theoretical integration of much of
macrosociology replete with 17 postulates and 27 major causal principles.

I take Collins' book to be important for many purposes. His conclusions
frequently do not follow from his premises, his belief that it is ''realistic''
(p. ix) to integrate the discipline from a focus on conflict strikes me as irrational, and the data on which he relies—it is not his fault—are usually inadequate for his purposes. Nevertheless, his is a powerful contribution and one
that documents both the active pursuit among us of problems in general
sociology and the low salience of this activity in our professional debates and
curricula. As Collins asks, why are there so few efforts to identify the key
problems of general sociology or to effect even partial integrations?

To make immediate what Collins has in mind, consider a typical graduate
curriculum in sociological theory. It is a pastiche of social history, social
thought, metatheory, philosophy of science, the sociology of knowledge, and
the sociology of sociology. It includes an exposition of the thought of selected
founders of the discipline. It is heavy with prolegomena to sociology but light
on the general contents of the discipline. What is missing is any sytematic
presentation of questions about the fundamentals of collective relations, of the
ideas and findings on which our understanding of these matters turns, and of
the potentialities for drawing these materials into larger syntheses. There is
lacking a comprehensive vision as found, for example, in Park and Burgess'
(1921) *Introduction to the Science of Sociology* or Sumner and Keller's (1927) *The
Science of Society*. At some point after the 1920s, this sort of effort disappeared.
(Parsons' *The Social System* [1951] might be taken as a partial exception, but it
is more a hermeneutic system than an attempt at the whole of a scientific
account.)

It is true, of course, that a systematic treatment of problems in general
sociology can be had in courses on particular topics. Norms and normativity
are likely to be treated in courses on religion or law; group growth and
development are covered in courses on collective behavior or on small groups;
bargaining and negotiation may be dealt with in a generalized fashion by
ethnomethodologists, by students of complex organizations, and by many
social psychologists. What is rare is an education in sociology that makes clear
the similarities in the principles of stratification as exemplified in small
groups, industrial plants, whole societies, and all other collectivities or the
similarities in the principles of justice or legitimation that operate in all social

relations. Even rarer is an education involving efforts to address problems in which these phenomena must be handled simultaneously.

The problem, then, is the obscuring .of general sociology. There is something to what Collins says. Conflicts are at work. Some colleagues actually "struggle" against a science of sociology. I think, however, that Collins passes too quickly over genuine obscurities concerning the nature of general sociology: what it is and what it is not. I also think we need to consider more seriously some arguments that general sociology is impossible or undesirable.

What General Sociology Does and Does Not Mean

As I have pictured it, general sociology consists of problems that depend for their solution on an understanding of general and distinctive features of collective life and of the ideas and procedures required to attain that understanding. In practice, no one studies collective life as such. We work on specific problems, and all of this work draws to some extent on general considerations. Whatever the collective relations we have under study, they are, to some extent, aspects or variations of phenomena found in all collective relations and they operate according to principles at work in all collective relations. Thus we can see Lipset (1960) drawing on general considerations when he declares in *Political Man* that the stability of a political order, like that of any social relationship, depends upon its effectiveness and legitimacy, and when he interprets several forms of extremist politics as variant combinations of these and other common underlying considerations.

Some studies of specific topics go further. They enlarge our grasp of the general characteristics and principles of collective life. We can see Durkheim (1912) working quite directly on general properties of collective relations when he concludes that religious experiences result from encounters with societies, or other embracing groups: encounters with these groups in their capacities as collective actors. He struggles to distinguish between a collectivity's acts and its purposes and vision, claiming that the religious encounter involves these latter realities. The enlargement of general sociology is contained in the distinction he is trying to make between collective acts and collective vision and in the relations he describes between the two. Again, we can find direct contributions to general sociology in Mills' (1967) and Slater's (1966) studies of the steps and processes in the careers of small groups as they emerge from social aggregates and in the formally similar work on societal evolution as found in Parsons (1977) or Bellah (1964). As a final example, we can appreciate that general sociology is being expanded through the efforts of Cicourel (1973) and others to uncover the principles that govern all instances of communication.

It is against this characterization of general sociology, and these illustrations, that I want to consider some enterprises with which it is often confused.

First, general sociology is not general theory. The heart of the matter is a concern for problems and not for ideas as such. Just as research is an aid to thought, so thought—or theory—is an aid to life and one expression of it. General sociology is sterilized unless we keep foremost the problems that ground it in life.

But the theory relevant for general sociology *is* general theory in the sense I have described. It is not metatheory and it is not what Merton (1967) called "total" theory.

Metatheory refers to the bases for characterizing some field of knowledge, including any distinctive epistemological problems associated with it, and for placing it in relation to other fields. That is what we find in Mead's discussions of the foundations of social psychology or in Durkheim's essay on social facts. It is the focus of most discussions of the meaning for sociology of hermeneutics, existentialism, or phenomenology. Work in a science goes on within metatheoretical warrants but scientific theory is not metatheory.

Merton's discussion of total theory has two parts. The first deals with total theory as an objective; the second with examples of that objective from the history of sociology. Theory, he says (1967: 39), consists of "logically interconnected sets of propositions from which empirical uniformities can be derived." Total theories are those "in which observations about every aspect of social behavior, organization, and change promptly find their preordained place" (p. 45). They are theories by which "all of the observed uniformities" (p. 39) in these phenomena can be explained. Since nothing approximating a total theory exists in any field of knowledge, Merton can cite as illustrations only the aspirations of sociologists who sought to create a total theory. Merton thinks that this was true of Comte, Gumplowicz, Marx, Pareto, Simmel, Spencer, Sorokin, and Parsons.

Interestingly, Merton does not object to the aim of total theory as long as it functions as a goal toward which sociology or any science moves. What he decries, as is only realistic, is the belief that total theory can be developed at a single stroke. He assumes it is never fully achieved, and that it is approximated only by the piling up of accretions to knowledge and by syntheses of accretions.

Merton's discusssion has been understood in ways that impede our understanding of general sociology. First, he is taken as identifying work on general theory with grandiose claims that a comprehensive analysis has been achieved. This charge has turned many sociologists from efforts to deal with general questions about collective life. Second, he has been taken to mean that the aim of general theory is to derive, or to make derivable, all aspects of all instances of collective relations from general considerations. An elementary consideration in logic—namely, that every derivation about particulars must have premises about particulars as well as premises about more general properties—makes it clear that this would be impossible were anyone to desire it. What one might hope would be that general theory could supply ideas helpful for the understanding of specific cases. Third, Merton himself does not help us to characterize the questions and studies that would expand general knowledge. Rather, he says that all theories that are not total theories are theories of the middle range, and he includes within this middle range every argument, whatsoever, from which "empirical uniformities can be derived." Many of these would, of course, be quite limited in scope and trivial in importance. By contrast, the work having priority in general sociology concerns problems that seem to elude existing conceptualizations and existing principles, and the aim is to see whether new interpretations that are grounded in general considerations will aid in solving these problems.

General sociology has also suffered from claims that it is the only, or for all purposes the most important, analytical enterprise in the discipline. That is certainly false. For example, the power of important analyses such as Barrington Moore's (1966) treatment of the social origins of dictatorship and democracy or Morris Janowitz' (1978) interpretation of social trends of the last half-century comes mostly from principles far less general than those I have been describing.

Finally, there is nothing intrinsic to the conception of general sociology that excludes hermeneutic, semiotic, or other interpretative analyses in favor of causal explanations. The interpretation of systems of meanings or symbols takes its place along with causal explanation as an aspect of any scientific account of collective life. The only requirement is that the interpretation be analytical and that empirical observations be used to help us judge its adequacy. I appreciate that this will seem to some sociologists only a declaration of faith, and that it assumes a favorable outcome of some epistemological issues that are as yet unresolved. I will return to these matters in considering whether general sociology is possible.

Is General Sociology Possible?

Is it? Not if we share the view of George Homans (1961) and some other behaviorists that sociology can be reduced to psychology, at least in the principles from which explanations must be built. Not if we hold with Clifford Geertz (1973) that, to be *usefully* understood, any instance of collective relations must be understood in its full uniqueness. Not if we believe with historicists that the very principles by which collective relations operate vary in kind from one historical period or situation to another. Not if we take seriously Herbert Blumer's (1969) injunction that individual and collective acts are intrinsically unpredictable. Not if we believe with some ethnomethodologists, ethnographers, and historians that systems of meanings cannot profitably be analyzed according to any general categories or principles;

that they are not amenable to any analytic formulation, be it mathematical, semiotic, or whatever. Not if we conclude with some hermeneuticists, phenomenologists, and others that reasons and causes, or interpretations and explanations, cannot be brought within a common analytical frame (Bernstein, 1976; Brown, 1977; Giddens, 1976).

Each of these arguments deserves attention because each points to possible excesses in our claims or to omissions in our work. None, I think, has the consequence for general sociology that its advocates claim. Although it is not possible to examine any of these positions in the way it deserves, three conclusions seem reasonable. First, the behaviorists, and other reductionists, seem involved in a simple "category" error (Swanson, 1965). Second, there are many successful interpretations of the rise and functioning of social relations, of social currents, and of social organizations, and many validated interpretations of the structure, meaning, and sources of ideologies, myths, rituals, and styles of art and science. All of this suggests that principles can be defined that have explanatory power, that deal effectively with both meanings and causes, and that meet empirical tests for adequacy. Third, I agree with Bernstein (1976), Harré and Secord (1972), Giddens (1976), and Strawson (1959: 81–113) in one conclusion from their examination of arguments that causal and interpretative accounts are incompatible, or that only one of these accounts is appropriate in the analysis of collective relations. They conclude that these arguments are mistaken and, specifically, that the "impossibility theorems" invoked in these arguments are formally and empirically unjustified.

Epistemological and other metatheoretical questions are important. If we work from the wrong answers we can go astray. On the other hand, recent developments in the philosophy of science (Hesse, 1974) underscore the formal as well as the empirical importance of our taking seriously any proven ability that we have to pursue our objectives. We can talk and communicate while lacking anything like an adequate grammar of speech or communication. Existing semiotics for the arts are grievously incomplete and their major principles are flawed (Culler, 1975), but artistic accomplishment is a fact. As with speech and art, so with general sociology. Any argument that it is impossible or that its epistemological supports are insufficient is of little importance beside its actuality. And it seems to me that general sociology does exist. We are able to define problems that are clearly social and collective in nature, and to see that the relationships involved cut across historical and cultural boundaries and across many features of the collectivities concerned. We are able to treat many crucial variations in collective relations as but variations in properties general to such relations. We do, on many occasions, take suitable account of meanings and structures, reasons and causes, persons and collectivities, and of the interrelations among all of these. Collins (1975) conveniently assembles material that displays these analytical features. So does Blau (1977) in his recent synthesis of work on inequality and heterogeneity, and so do Kelly and Thibaut (1978) in their theory of interdependence. It may be objected, however, that these particular volumes give too little place to problems dealing centrally with meanings and persons or reasons and rules. An assessment would take us too far afield. Let me, instead, sketch five problems that do make such matters central and that seem to meet the other criteria I have listed for work in general sociology. (These problems can serve as further examples of questions in general sociology, and they may also help to focus discussion.)

PROBLEM 1.   RELATIONS AMONG DEVELOPMENTAL LEVELS WITHIN A COLLECTIVITY

We are well aware that levels of supervision, or of jurisdiction, exist in collectivities but we have come only recently (Gibbard, Hartman, and Mann, 1974) to see that there are, *in organizations,* levels of relationship analogous to the ones that developmental psychologists claim to find in individuals. When a group begins to develop out of a human aggregate, relations consist at first of interpersonal ties centered by some vague sense of people's interdependence. Later on, some leaders emerge, and any elaborate division of labor tends to wait upon the appearance of these leaders. Still later, a sharp distinction may be drawn between the "persons" of the leaders and the broad purposes of the group which all participants are supposed to serve (Swanson, 1970). Five or six such steps have frequently been identified both in studies in the laboratory and in research on large-scale instances of elementary collective behavior: crowds, social movements, and the like.

The new appreciation is that the forms of relationship found in the earlier stages in this sequence do not disappear when new steps are taken but come instead to be organized under the new arrangements. This is an argument of the sort we find in Piaget or Freud when they suggest that children do not stop using the skills associated with sensory–motor behavior or orality but combine these with other skills and orientations in the course of development. Of special importance is the developmentalists' proposal that the earlier skills and orientations persist and constantly interact with those that come later.

How is this idea to be applied to collectivities? We catch something of the continued existence, and separate organization, of several levels of relationship when we observe that interpersonal relations in a family are close and supportive but that there are grave problems of coordinating specialized roles. Or when we say that an athletic team works well as a formal organization but that, interpersonally, there is distance and distrust.

We can appreciate that each of these levels of organization has its own structure and normative priorities and its own requirements for support. Thus, solidarity in interpersonal relations turns especially upon personal trust and dependability and some measure of diffuse dependency, whereas solidarity in a division of labor requires the honoring of abstract differences in function and a set of limited responsibilities. As we know from studies of complex organizations, these bases of solidarity are not just different from one another but are competitive and conflicting. Are there, then, procedures and standards for moderating and adjudicating this special set of conflicts? Or are relations among these levels almost anormative, operating more as a shoving match tempered by available resources and by prudence? Are there means by which the collapse of relations at one level is repaired or taken into account at others? Are there special norms or organizational structures that express the whole set of layers of relationship and their independence and interdependence?

PROBLEM 2. COLLECTIVE LIFE AS DRAMATIC ACTION

The idea is developed most fully by Kenneth Burke (1941, 1968) and Orrin Klapp (1962, 1964). Whenever people undertake something together, some or all will serve as heroes, villains, or fools: as heroes insofar as they overcome threats to collective action, as villains insofar as they block or attack that action, as fools insofar as they prove incompetent to carry their share of the effort. We have, then, a distinctive set of roles and the usual questions about the degree to which they become institutionalized.

A coding of families that have been studied at Berkeley since 1929 (Block and Haan, 1971) shows that about a quarter of them present themselves as if they were a cast of characters in a real-life drama. These dramatistic families tend to be small in size, cohesive in spirit, and egalitarian in polity. One also finds that, in samples of nonliterate societies, those that are small in population, and cohesive and egalitarian in organization, devote extraordinary amounts of time and resources to the public dramatization of their lives. Is it, then, that dramatic forms become salient when people lack managerial roles and a task-oriented division of labor and yet must act collectively? Are these roles also essential when management and a division of labor are present, essential perhaps for representing collective struggle and for mobilizing people into that struggle? If they are essential, the production and nurture of these forms cannot be left to chance. How is it accomplished and how are dramatic role systems related to others? Or, turning again to families and other small, personalized groups, does a person's being cast in a dramatic role have especially potent consequences for his personal identity, forging a limited but especially vivid self-image? Attribution theory suggests that this is likely (Goffman, 1967; Shaver, 1975).

PROBLEM 3.   VARIATIONS IN POLITY AND IN OTHER
ASPECTS OF COLLECTIVE LIFE

Where there is collective action, there are means for mobilizing people
and for allocating costs and benefits. Basic forms of collective decision making
embody these procedures (although "decision making" is too formal a term
for the amorphous processes we often find). If we confine ourselves to forms
of decision making that are familiar (perhaps the varieties given by Aristotle
or by Weber), we find that the main variations number from three or four to
nine or ten. Perhaps there are principles in the theory of coalition formation
that would account for the variations reported. In any case, much the same
range of forms can be found in samples of societies from classical antiquity, in
samples of nonliterate societies, in samples of societies in early modern
Europe, in samples of advanced industrial societies, and in samples of families
in complex societies (Swanson, 1967, 1969, 1971).

Whatever this means, it suggests that variations in these arrangements are
not drastically limited by historical period, by level of societal complexity, by
cultural matrix, or even by group size. In societies at all levels of complexity,
the form of decision making is strikingly associated with religious or other
cosmological beliefs. In nonliterate societies, there are strong associations
with rules of residence and descent. There are, however, only slight relations
with the structure of economies. (And, indeed, this has become a topic for
contemporary reflection on the part of Marxists and other analysts of political
economies [Giddens, 1976].) In families, patterns of decision making are not
associated with socioeconomic indicators and only slightly with family size.
There is some evidence that they are related to the personalities of husbands
and fathers (Swanson, 1979). They have a significant relation with the ability
of the children to solve formal problems and with the likelihood that they will
be hypnotizable or lose themselves in imagined worlds as when reading a
novel, seeing a movie, scuba diving, skiing, partying, or listening to music
(Swanson, 1974, 1978a, 1978b).

We have all too many questions here. To focus on one that seems
strategic: if variations in polity are indeed so independent of other indicators
of collective complexity, and are independent of economic arrangements in
particular, what does produce them and how do they then relate to economic
arrangements, and vice versa? Is there a real hiatus here in collective systems,
or has the whole question been misconceived?

PROBLEM 4.   STRUCTURAL AND FUNCTIONAL
EXCHANGE

Structural and functional relations are given together in collective life and
are intrinsic to it (Swanson, 1971). Most theories of exchange deal with struc-

tural relations. This means that the parties are seen as having their own interests and that the parties' relationship to one another is only one among
their similar relations with still other parties. This is the case, for example, in
Homans' (1961) theory of exchange or Lévi-Strauss' (1967) or in John
Rawls' (1971) treatment of the social contract. In functional relations, on the
other hand, the parties are creatures of a common enterprise—their
character, their objectives, and their powers being delegated to them by it.
This is true, for example, of people acting as husbands and wives, as parents
and children, or as officers and enlisted men. What difference does this make
in exchange?

In Book 5 of the *Ethics*, Aristotle distinguished corrective justice from
distributive justice. *Corrective justice* seems to refer to problems in structural
relations—problems of independent actors' striking fair bargains and carrying them out. These relations involve the kind of standards of justice that
Homans and Rawls describe (although Homans terms this ''distributive''
justice). In current experimental studies (e.g., Berkowitz and Walster, 1976:
Thibaut and Walker, 1975: 102–116), corrective justice is associated with a
criterion of equality.

Distributive justice seems to catch one of the features of functional relations:
that of people being rewarded according to their contributions to a collective
enterprise. The experimentalists discuss this under the term ''equity.'' Note,
however, that it is those social theorists who come from Marx, and who
therefore focus on functional relations (Sztompka, 1974), who most advocate
equality.

There are conceptual confusions here, but there are also indications that
exchange is different in these two settings. Even the mechanisms and processes may be different. The functionalist treatment of exchange by Parsons
and Smelser in *Economy and Society* (1956) highlights considerations not found
in structuralist accounts. These points need clarification and so, also, does the
nature of exchanges and the operation of justice across the structural–functional boundary. If exchange is an elemental process in collective life, we are
only at the beginning of understanding the elements.

PROBLEM 5.   FIGURATIVE SYMBOLS;
FIGURATIVE DISCOURSE

Here I want only to state a problem and a direction for work. There is, in
social science, a lively interest in the principles that might render myths,
dreams, and rituals intelligible. More generally, there is interest in what is
sometimes called the ''grammar'' or ''logic'' of figurative symbols and
figurative discourse. Many studies claim to show what it is that some aspect of
a myth or dream, or, perhaps, the whole plot, has as its referent. This kind of
understanding may not have the range or the detailed grasp of any particular
case that Clifford Geertz (1973) has urged on interpreters of cultures, but it

does suggest that the nature and intelligibility of figurative discourse may be rooted importantly in its referential or semantic position. I proposed in one earlier paper (1974) that the logic of functional relations may be the one we seek and, in another paper (1976) I presented an interpretation of the plot dynamics of two myths employing that assumption and using materials from a sample of more than fifty primitive societies. I mention this only to suggest a possible direction for work on a problem of great complexity. I need not expand upon the fact that the phenomena concerned are collective universals.

Is General Sociology Desirable?

Whatever one concludes about the possibility of a general sociology, there are sociologists who consider it undesirable. Some associate it with a mad *esprit de système:* a flight into total explanation. That certainly is not inherent in the enterprise. Many sociologists want simply to work, as some always have (Matthews, 1977: 90–91), on questions that deal with collective events in all their empirical richness and to take some account of phenomena that lie outside a sociological level of analysis: of technology, perhaps, or genetics, or the physiology of perception. With all the things of this sort that need so urgently to be understood, who could wish them anything but the best? And one can feel similarly about people who are gripped by metatheoretical problems, by issues in social thought, or by questions concerning some one institution or society or historical epoch. But these interests do not seriously challenge the prospect of a general sociology.

There are, however, arguments that do pose such a challenge. Consider these examples: (1) Nothing worth studying can be understood simply within a sociological level of analysis. (2) Only the metatheoretical questions deserve a grown person's time. (3) Until those questions are answered conclusively, no general scientific analyses are warranted. (4) The inherent rooting of general scientific questions in one or another framework of social values makes it essential to solve the value questions first, or suggests that no dependable knowledge in sociology can be had because all is fatally tainted by considerations of value. (5) When the questions about social values are resolved those that remain will be trivial.

Once again, I think we have claims that present at least important qualifications for work in general sociology and even for the possibility of science of any kind. And, once again, I think that most of these claims are hard to sustain, if only against the record of large accomplishments. But I think that many of these claims will survive all manner of argumentation and evidence. This is especially true of arguments in favor of metatheoretical or ethical or social philosophical concerns. On an intellectual level, this order of question is the one familiar to Galileo (Clavelin, 1968; De Santillana, 1955).

The Church applauded his work but was uneasy about its meaning for doctrine, authority, and institutions. Substitute for the religious terms those appropriate to social or political positions, and the similarities to past and current debates about social science are evident. Did Galileo (read "social science") claim that science was as important as salvation (read "emancipation," or "meaningful existence," or what you will)? Did he claim that science could answer questions treated by theology? Did not the claims of science spring from a rejection, or intransigent ignorance, of revealed truth, or from the inspiration of devils or a desire for plaudits and wealth or from overweening pride (read "bourgeois values," "alienation," or whatever)?

No demonstration of the power of theory to order data, or of science to serve human interests, and no delineation, however careful, of the special spheres of faith and values as contrasted with science, can, of itself, conclude debates of this sort. The parties are contending for resources and legitimation and, especially, for hearts and minds, and only a process of institutional differentiation that provides a place of honor for each will resolve the differences.

How Can We Foster General Sociology?

I have begun to answer this question in talking about the possibility or desirability of general sociology. What remains are some suggestions that may deserve exploration. They vary greatly in scope:

1. As things now stand, the annual meetings of the American Sociological Association are devoted every dozen years to a general appraisal of the discipline. This appraisal might usefully include a focus on general sociology.

2. The Association's Section on Theory might reasonably conceive its charge as that of fostering general sociology and might sponsor working groups to clarify the problems, prepare relevant materials, and propose methods for educating sociologists in this kind of work.

3. As to materials, we urgently need some high-level texts or monographs dealing with basic problems and puzzles in general sociology and with theoretical and empirical materials important for their solutions. I would stress a focus on problems and empirical phenomena and, only in that context, on theory and research.

4. As to education, we need methods and organizational structures that encourage sociologists to formulate research so that, when appropriate, it illumines general questions as well as specific issues. We need an education in which sociologists learn so to formulate general questions as to make them amenable to scientific work. We need a style of education that enables sociologists to observe collective relations and systems of meanings, as such, and that enables sociologists to take the several aspects of these phenomena into account when studying any one of them. Sociologists need also to be

equipped to think and work in a comparative framework. As it is, too many of us feel incapable of getting at the relevant literature, or making the required judgments and observations, if a problem extends beyond a type of organization, institution, or society that we know well.

5. Finally, if we do envision a clearer differentiation between social thought and social science, we must be sensitive to a problem confronted by every sociologist, the problem of finding a calling in sociology. A distinctive legitimation and inspiration for sociology as science is a part of that differentiation. I do not doubt that it will come or that it will undergird a scientific, and not merely a technical, vision (Nisbet, 1976: 4), but I also do not doubt that there will be struggles before it is articulated. The urgency of the problem, and our inarticulateness, are heard in Gouldner's essay "For Sociology" (1973: 150). He writes:

> . . . we who have lived our lives *for* sociology . . . are convinced that sociology is terribly important; and it is therefore greatly worthy of the most profound criticism of which we are capable. . . . a criticism of sociology is inevitably a criticism of our *existence* . . . a challenge to our lives. . . . our *lives* are important to us and we do not want to *waste* them.

My own aspiration is both broader and narrower. I hope that we will find ourselves called to human life, which is always life in community, and will find in sociology as science one vehicle for that larger calling. Then, in those periods when sociology lies stagnant or in disarray, both it, and we, can be renewed.

2

Discovery and the Discovered in Social Theory

George C. Homans

OUR SUBJECT IS the nature of theory construction, but a difficulty faces us at once. Though we use no word more often or more reverently than we do *theory*, we do not agree on what a theory *is*. How can we agree on how to construct something, when we do not know what that something is? It is conceivable that we must use different methods to construct different kinds of theory.

Let me consider just two examples of the many things sociologists have called theories. Blalock (1979: 119–35) would certainly include *causal chains* among theories. A causal chain or network I take to be a statistical construction by which the effects of certain initial conditions are traced through intermediary variables, often with many feedback loops, to selected dependent variables, a number being assigned to the correlations between the variables in the chain.

We talk of theory construction as if it were analogous to building a house. From its plans we know what the completed house should look like, and from the experience of craftsmen, contractors, and architects we usually know how to build it according to plan. A causal chain does not altogether fit the analogy, because we cannot tell in advance what the chain will look like in detail, except that it will be a chain. Yet it does fit the analogy, because I am told that sociologists can be taught the procedures for constructing the chain, and that some of them are highly skilled in doing so.

Unfortunately, there is another kind of thing which is also called theory, but which, unlike causal chains, no one can fully teach us how to construct—a fact that many persons who talk about theory construction do not seem to understand. I hope I can show you the difference between this kind of theory and causal chains by going back to a single link in the latter, a relationship between cause and effect. For example, people knew for millennia that the motion of the moon and to a lesser degree the sun caused the ocean tides, but they had no explanation, though they had myths, why these causes had these effects until Isaac Newton invented—and I really mean invented—his laws of motion and showed how the proposition that there are approximately two high and two low tides a day followed by logical deduction from his general laws applied to certain given conditions in the relative motions and other properties of the earth, moon, and sun. Under different given conditions Newton could deduce many other propositions, such as Kepler's laws of the planetary orbits.

This is the kind of thing *I* mean by theory (Homans, 1967b). It consists of a set of propositions, each stating a relationship between properties of nature. Some of the propositions in the set are more general than the others in the sense that they cannot be deduced from the others. Instead, from the general propositions, when applied to propositions stating the given conditions, we can deduce the propositions that are to be explained, such as the tidal phenomena. Such a theory is powerful to the degree that other empirical propositions may be deduced under different given conditions from the same general propositions. Such a theory can never be completed, because both the general propositions and the given conditions may turn out themselves to be explainable deductively. In using an example from physics, I do not in the least imply that I want to construct a social science on the model of a physical one. The propositions of sociology are different from, and usually much less exact than, those of physics. All I imply is that this classical definition of theory—the "covering law" or "deductive system" view of theory—applies to both.

Nor by defining theory in this way do I in the least wish to disparage causal chains. They can be great intellectual achievements and great technical contributions to social science. All I want to argue is that, if both are theories, they are theories of different kinds. True, they can and sometimes do merge. The condition for merger is that the various links in the causal chain can themselves be shown to follow as the *explicanda* of deductive systems. Sometimes sociologists can do this, but often do not, and for perfectly good reasons. It takes a long enough time to construct a complicated causal chain, without taking still more to explain each link.

Since the two are different kinds of theories they are constructed differently. As I have said, I believe good sociologists can specify the procedures by which they construct causal chains. But we cannot fully specify how to construct the other kind of theory, though we know what it ought to look like once constructed: it ought to look like a deductive system. We call the process *induction,* but that is just a word: no person can teach another how to induce.

No one could have taught Newton how to get from the empirical phenomena—the tides, Galileo's rolling balls, and Kepler's planetary motions—to the laws of motion from which the empirical phenomena could be deduced. He had to invent them. What was required was "a leap of the imagination," and unfortunately no one knows how to produce such a leap at will (Holton, 1978: 96-97). "Intimate, habitual, intuitive, familiarity" (Barber, 1970: 67) with the empirical phenomena is necessary but not sufficient. The philosopher Whitehead (1949: 61) used to distinguish between "the logic of discovery and the logic of the discovered." The former may use logic but always requires a nonlogical element. The latter is certainly logical. What is discovered by a leap of the imagination can sometimes become the principle of organization of a deductive theory. An investigator often moves from one to the other and back.

But sociology may not be required to produce its own Newtons and Einsteins to invent its general propositions. We may not have to make our own leap of the imagination, or at least not have to leap so far. Sociology, I have often argued, has already had its general propositions—or many of them—discovered for it by another science, from which it can borrow them. I believe that science to be psychology. Some think it is economics, but I am persuaded that the propositions of at least microeconomics, or as it is sometimes called "rational choice theory" (Heath, 1976), can be derived from psychology. I do not wish to specify what *kind* of psychology, as I believe the distinction between, for instance, behavioral and cognitive psychology has been made much too sharp. It is not just the acts but the perceptions of people that are shaped by reinforcement. Nor do I believe that psychology, more than any other science, is a finished product and will not continue to grow.

Nor will sociology be alone in this fate. The general propositions of all the social sciences will be the same and psychological, in the sense that they will be propositions about the behavior of members of a species, about what the behaviors of human beings have in common. I do not mean propositions about particular personalities, for I believe these could be shown to follow from the former, if we knew enough about the past histories and present circumstances of the personalities in question.

Another way of saying the same thing is that our general propositions will be individualistic and not holistic (Vanberg, 1975). Let me be very careful here. Sociology has made and stated many propositions that apply to social wholes: aggregates, structures, organizations, and societies. It will and certainly should continue to test such propositions, and I do not argue for one moment that such social wholes do not really exist. All I argue is that propositions about social wholes have failed as the general explanatory propositions of sociology. On the other hand, the limited holistic propositions can often themselves be explained by individualistic ones, provided we remember that the individuals in question may be many in number, acting at cross-purposes, creating structures no one of them intended to create, and that these structures once created change the contingencies under which the individuals or their successors act. Provided also we remember that the deductions will require what the philosophers call "bridging propositions" between the micro and the macro concepts. Indeed, I think the chief theoretical task of sociology in the near future will be to show—to use the title of a recent book by Tom Schelling (1978)—how micromotives produce macrobehavior. If we do not undertake the job—and I am glad to say that some of us have already undertaken it—representatives of the other social sciences will be delighted to do it for us. Schelling, for instance, is an economist. In any event, we cannot do it all ourselves.

If what I have written above were accepted—and I have no confidence that it will be, for I have made the point often but gained few converts—it might just help put an end to the present condition of sociology, which I would call scandalous if it were not so ridiculous. For a time in the fifties it looked as if sociology might be united under the paradigm of structural-functionalism. I call it a paradigm because it was never a real theory, and it was largely holistic. When that unity broke down, as it was bound to do, it was not replaced by a new unity but by a number of named schools: symbolic interactionism, ethnomethodology, phenomenology, conflict theory, and various forms of Marxism. I have not listed all the schools. I myself contributed, though unintentionally, to the chaos. I wrote a paper called "Social Behavior as Exchange" (1958). It was simply a preliminary effort to use psychological propositions to explain social phenomena, but someone picked up the word *exchange* and labeled persons like Peter Blau and myself as members of still another school, that of "social exchange theorists."

Now the implicit assumptions of many of these schools are individualistic. The fact does not become clear, because the schools do not spell out their general propositions but leave them implicit. Let me take one example, that of ethnomethodology. John Mitchell (1978: 148) says that "ethnomethodological research is for the communication processes that lead to a sense of common understanding among people." Now I do not have to argue that "common understanding" is rewarding to people. Of course there are some that "just will not understand," but most people find social life impossible without some degree of common understanding. Not only is common understanding rewarding, but ethnomethodology assumes that the communication processes lead to, that is, are successful in, attaining this common understanding. This means that ethnomethodology accepts implicitly, at least for acts of communication, two main propositions of psychology. First, the one I call the *value proposition,* which says that a person is more likely to perform an action, the more rewarding he or she finds the result of the action; and second, the one I call the *success proposition,* that a person is more likely to perform an action if it is successful in getting the reward. What makes the behavior social is that the reward and success of an action are provided by the action of at least one other person.

As far as I understand them, I believe the same sort of thing to be true of the other individualistic sociologies. I suspect it to be true even of the Marxists. What assumptions, indeed, do Marxists make about human psychology, apart from economics and sociology? If human beings make their institutions and in turn are made by them (E. P. Thompson, 1978: 29)—a statement with which I fully agree—by what mechanisms do these processes occur? It is not enough to make the statement as a matter of ontology. For theory, the formal propositions must be made explicit. Again, Jim Coleman (1975: 79) is quite wrong to reject behavioral psychology as incompatible with purposive action. What behavioral psychology shows is that human purposes are learned like other actions and by the same mechanisms. Coleman is a great contributor to "rational choice theory" but does not understand that it is a branch of behavioral psychology. I do not despair of his conversion.

We have been asked to discuss the relation of theory to research. In the old days, there were wiseacres who told us that theory should guide research. I am not so sure. If a science has a good theory, then much research tests the new empirical deductions that can be made from the theory. But first one must have a good theory, and that, it seems, is just what we sociologists do not have, or at least cannot agree we have. Under these circumstances, I believe a researcher should simply acquire by whatever means seem natural "intimate, habitual, intuitive, familiarity" with the phenomena that happen to interest him or her. Then test out some empirical propositions about the phenomena. Nothing is more precious than a tested proposition. But do not worry about theory. Since we cannot produce it at will, let it come when it will. Sooner or later, the leap of the imagination will suggest what general propositions must be invented or borrowed to explain the empirical ones.

Theory has another function besides guiding research, and that is organizing a science. If it is to do this, the practitioners must make explicit the general propositions—if they have any—that they use in explaining their findings. With some exceptions, the members of the different schools of sociology do not do this now. If they took the trouble to do it, I think they would find that they were, in the main, using the same ones. I make allowances for differences in vocabulary that make little difference in meaning. Perhaps they refrain from doing this because they unconsciously fear they would lose their cherished identities. If so, their identities cannot be very robust. What they do not seem to appreciate is that, from the same general propositions, but applied to different given conditions, a wide variety of empirical findings—indeed, whole different fields of findings—may be explained (Heath, 1976). I myself try to show how the emergence of relatively enduring, though small, social structures can be explained by psychological propositions under particular given conditions. But my chosen field is only one of many of which this is true.

If they followed this strategy, the various current sociologies would not be robbed of their special empirical subject matters. If they treasure their names, they would not need to lose even them. More important, we sociologists might cease our squabbling, which often seems more a matter of words than of substance, and reach that theoretical unity within empirical diversity which is the mark of a self-confident and progressive science. Tom Kuhn (1962, 1970) tells us that this condition seldom lasts forever in any science. But it is what sociology needs now.

3

Biography, the Structure of Explanation, and the Evaluation of Theory in Sociology

Neil J. Smelser

ONE OF THE MAXIMS that my teacher and friend, Talcott Parsons, was fond of repeating, was this: In dealing with any theoretical topic, it never fails to repay one's efforts to go first to the great classical thinkers on that topic. Parsons himself observed that principle repeatedly, revisiting and recasting the original insights of Durkheim, Weber, or Freud as he continued his lifelong struggle to conquer the mountainous obstacles to systematic sociological theorizing.

In considering once again—at the request of Tad Blalock—the relation between theory and research in sociology, I decided to attend to this principle as well. And the classic that beckoned first and foremost was the pair of essays written more than three decades ago by Robert Merton—"The Bearing of Sociological Theory on Empirical Research," and "The Bearing of Empirical Research on Sociological Theory" (1968). I daresay that these essays constitute the most widely read methodological statements in the history of sociology. And consulting them again, I became convinced why they should be regarded as classic. They remain unsurpassed in crispness, clarity, and soundness of thinking. And Merton captured the essential *mutuality* between the two facets of scientific knowledge, as he traced the data-organizing capacities of different orders of sociological ideas, ranged in a scale of explicitness and formality, on the one hand, and the stubborn power of empirical data to divert, recast, refocus, and clarify sociological ideas, on the other.

23

In my restudy of Merton's essays I developed three distinct reactions, which taken together constitute the point of departure for the few ideas and distinctions I want to develop in this brief essay. My reactions were these:

1. In introducing his first essay, Merton distinguished between *sociological theory*, "which has for its subject matter certain aspects and results of the interaction of men and is therefore substantive," and *methodology*, which deals with "the logic of scientific procedure" (1963: 86). While based on a true difference, this distinction between substantive theory and methodological canons, if regarded as mutually exclusive, begs for correction and reformulation. Methodology—or the application of the canons of correct procedure—surely pervades the entire structure and process of scientific thinking, and one can be as rigorous methodologically in assessing the clarity, consistency, and elegance of substantive theory as in evaluating the design and execution of empirical research. Moreover, the theorist's substantive preoccupations surely condition if not dictate his use of research methods and procedures.

2. In many respects, Merton's essay struck me as more nearly a statement of *scientific ideals* than as an effort to describe how social investigators *actually* proceed. Or, to put the point more precisely, he set apart those two facets of the scientific enterprise from one another only incompletely. While from time to time Merton pointed to deviations from the ideal of scientific explanation—for example, in his sensitive account of the limitations of post factum interpretations—his essays stand more firmly as a statement of how theory and research ought to affect one another than as a statement of the way they do in practice.

3. My last reaction is most impressionistic of all. Although Merton stressed the interplay of theory and organized factual knowledge, I found his account to be more precise and compelling with respect to the power of discovered or established facts to influence substantive formulations than with respect to the influence running in the opposite direction. I believe that Merton's statement can best be further developed by deepening and sharpening our understanding of the power of our sociological ideas to shape what we try to know about the empirical world.

These three reactions lead me to a formal statement of departure: the need to press further and specify the actual operations of bringing general sociological explanations (or theory) to bear on the organization of empirical research.

An Illustration from Ongoing Historical Research

I wish to base my explorations on historical research, not necessarily because I am convinced that historically based sociological explanations are really that different from any other explanations, but rather because I am currently engaged in an effort to generate a systematic understanding and explanation of certain historical processes. For the past two years I have been residing part time once again in the British Museum Library, in an effort to generate a sociological account of the vicissitudes of British primary education in the nineteenth century, particularly in comparison with developments in the United States during the same period.

My main points about the research will be methodological. But to make them I must write a little about how I am thinking—or, if you wish to dignify it, the model I am using—in approaching this problem.

Several features of the spread of primary education in Britain are striking and fascinating to the historical observer. The first is its *sluggishness.* Both contemporaries and historians stress this, forever comparing it unfavorably with educational development in Prussia, the United States, Holland, and to some extent France. The second is its *unevenness,* building by episodic bursts in the Sunday school period of the late eighteenth century, the Bell–Lancaster period of the early nineteenth century, the fifteen years following the period of government initiative in 1846, and the fifteen years following the parliamentary legislation of 1870; between these episodes could be observed signs of floundering and stagnation. And the third remarkable feature of the century was the tendency of primary education to *proliferate* in separate, almost exclusive streams along certain lines of primordial division; British schools were neither common nor universal, but were consistently segregated by class, religious grouping, nation (i.e., England, Scotland, Ireland, and to some extent Wales), and sex.

As my research on British educational development has proceeded, a certain explanatory scheme has been crystallizing. Its origins are diverse, being based in part on other theoretical statements of social change, and in part on my own theoretical predilections and knowledge, and in part on what is being suggested by the historical record. The central feature of this scheme is as follows: The political and economic pressures to educate the British population were enormously strong in the nineteenth century, as they were elsewhere. But the precise pattern of educational development itself can best be accounted for by a pervading principle: British primary education developed in the way it did—with the remarkable features I have mentioned—*because it was prevented by a context of social structure and group conflicts from developing otherwise.*

Lest this principle seem both simple-minded and circular, let me say immediately what it meant historically. Through a series of political battles in the early and middle nineteenth century it became clear that the Church of England could not enforce its avowed historical monopoly on the education of the young; the Nonconformist and later the Catholic protests effectively beat down the Church's efforts along these lines. Yet the Church was sufficiently powerful to enforce its argument either that the state should stay completely out of education or, if it should tax to support education, its management should be by the Church; Nonconformists and others, however, protested against supporting a system—either by paying taxes or sending their children to it—based on a religion they rejected. Ireland's Catholics refused to support established Church of Ireland schools, and the Church beat down state support for Catholic schools. Segregation by class and sex was so deeply rooted early in the century that providers and clientele alike assumed that education should be stratified and segregrated along both lines; reformers scarcely suggested otherwise until the end of the century and later.

Faced with this kaleidoscope of structural and group rigidities, the state and others interested in educational reform navigated precariously among them, and evolved minimalist policies that were barely acceptable to all; such were the structural origins of the principle of *voluntarist* growth that characterized British education for so long—a matching-fund system that left management of the schools in the hands of competing religious and national groups, who pressed educational development forward through a process by which each strove aggressively to expand or defend its turf. Only after these structural rigidities and group relations had shifted significantly, later in the century, could other kinds of educational development occur, and even then their influence on that development continued to be important.

So much for an indication of the kind of theoretical framework I am attempting to bring to bear on my historical subject. One day I shall write a whole book on the topic, and expose the explanatory potential of this scheme to critical appraisal. But in the meantime I would like to present a few ideas about what appears to have gone on, at several levels, in the development of what I have sketched.

Three Levels of Process in Social Science Scholarship

THE BIOGRAPHICAL LEVEL: MEANDERINGS

The first level of process to be identified in the research enterprise is the biographical one. A biographical story would include an account of how I first approached the problem of primary education from the perspective of age grading and age stratification, as it has recently developed in American social science literature, but found myself being pulled increasingly toward other perspectives, especially religious and other group conflict. It would include an account of my encounter with various revisionist and Marxist writers on British primary education, and the complicated pattern of my acceptance and critical rejection of their explanations. It would include perhaps a dozen encounters with audiences of sociologists and British historians who listened to what I had to say—at various stages of my thinking—and who applauded, qualified, and shot down various ideas and thus further shaped my thinking. It would include an account of the moments of frustration over time spent in false starts, moments of euphoria as new interpretative insights flashed into my mind, and moments of disappointment as I later discovered how limited were these insights.

But, above all, the biographical story is an unsystematic, even untidy one. It cannot be readily ordered into a progression of refinements that ultimately result in a more scientifically adequate statement. It cannot be chronicled as any inductive movement from facts to theory or any deductive movement in the opposite direction; rather, it is a somewhat chaotic bouncing around among fantasies, hunches, hypotheses, factual accounts, and disputations and debates among other scholars about facts and interpretations. Certainly it cannot be assimilated, as process, to any formal account—for example, that of Walter Wallace (1971)—of the ingredients of the scientific method.

THE LEVEL OF BUILDING EXPLANATIONS: OPERATIONS REQUIRED

In building up the explanatory sketch about British primary education in the nineteenth century, the first thing to acknowledge is that it is necessary to *select* certain problems and certain ranges of data and to *exclude* others. The perspective I outlined selects and highlights specific sociological categories such as institutional arrangements (especially those with ascriptive salience), group conflicts that swirl around those arrangements, as well as individual and collective adaptive strategies that take those arrangements and conflicts into account. It also selects and highlights historical events and situations subsumable under those categories. At the same time it diminishes interest in, even excludes, other problems and facts. My perspective generates little interest in the marginality of the nineteenth-century schoolmaster and his striving for respectability; little interest in government account-keeping and budgeting; and no interest whatsoever in the state of health of the children or the ventilation of the schools—all facts which were important in the minds of some historical actors and which would be important to me if I were bringing another kind of explanatory framework to bear.

This process of selection and exclusion is, moreover, necessary if we are to strive for any kind of general and determinate theoretical explanation. Theoretically based explanation calls for ruling out all but a few potentially interesting problems, all but a few explanatory factors, and all but a few types of potentially available data. Anything does not and cannot pass as fair game for study and analysis. Insofar as we become less discriminatory in identifying problems and explanatory variables, the more we permit theoretical structure to melt away, and the more nearly we approach shapeless eclecticism on the explanatory side and vacuum-sweeper description on the factual side. In sum, to bring theoretical explanation to bear is simultaneously to select, exclude, and thereby distort the whole historical record.

The next operation involved in theoretically based explanation is that, for the range of historical facts selected and highlighted, *we as investigators endow those facts with special meanings for the historical actors involved.* This process of endowment is seen clearly in the special psychological assumptions and assertions contained in my explanatory sketch. To illustrate: In my presentation I revealed a number of psychological generalizations. I assumed, for example, that location in a given corner of the social structure (e.g., membership in a church) carries with it a jurisdictional interest in that corner; I also assumed that educational reformers and government bureaucrats had a historical memory of what had failed as reform in the past, and what was possible and not possible; and, more generally, the "image of human nature" that emerges from the sketch is of the historical actor as a purposive, goal-seeking, adaptive, compromising, more or less "satisficing" individual—not maximizing, but doing what can be done. All these psychological assumptions and images are fair game for criticism and rejection; and certainly one family of assumptions may prove more useful than another in generating historical explanations. But we cannot forget the general point that systematic explanation necessarily requires *some kind* of meaning to be endowed, or else we do not have an explanation.

We cannot deny this truth, however Durkheimian or positivistic we strive to be in relating social regularities to other social regularities in law-like fashion. For example, to link fluctuations in the price of wheat to fluctuations in rates of collective violence—both eminently qualified social facts—is possible as a matter of empirical association without recourse to some kind of psychological or meaning connection. But to *explain* the association requires reference to a principle of absolute deprivation, a principle of relative deprivation, or some other intervening psychological connection.

By pointing to the centrality of the meaning–endowing operation as essential to explanation, moreover, I have brought us to the point of being able to identify a fundamental basis of difference and conflict among several interpretative styles in the social sciences. A strict phenomenologist would assign meaning to historical facts as nearly as possible as the historical actors themselves appear to assign meaning to them; so might a symbolic interactionist. Likewise, an investigator with an emphasis on *verstehen* might wish to honor the historical actors' own endowment of meaning to events, but he or she might wish to amalgamate these meanings into more general, ideal-type categories. Others might seek to be faithful to a degree to historical actors' meanings—as, indeed, my own sketch seeks to do—but may wish to transcend those actors' renditions and seek a somewhat grander logic. Still others may regard the assignment of meaning to historical actors as a matter of convenience or heuristic assumption; the endowed meaning (e.g., economic or political rationality) may or may not have anything to do with actors' own accounts, but may be admittedly relied upon as a simplified conceptual device to render consistent wide ranges of behavior. Still others may regard the historical agents' assignment of meaning to their actions as positively erroneous or false; the nineteenth-century debates over Bible reading in schools, for example, may be interpreted as distorted renditions of positions that are really dictated by the agenda of class or national interest.

These intellectual postures differ from one another with respect to the *source* from which explanatory meaning is derived; but all alike are forced to resort to the operation of endowing *some kind* of meaning to weld the selected facts of history into a consistent explanation. The issue of assigning meanings to others' minds will forever be with us in the search for sociological explanations. But at the same time, it seems erroneous to chase this truth to fruitless philosophical ends, and imagine that really knowing others' minds (especially when those others are now in the historical past) is a goal that is achievable or even to be striven for. The operation of knowing others' minds, from the standpoint of social-scientific explanation, is a matter of the active imposition of some perspective by the investigator, and this operation is to be assessed not in terms of some kind of "correspondence" between the investigator's perspective and the mind of the other, but rather in terms of the utility of this operation in generating adequate explanations.

I also believe that at this point I have reached the heart of the group of issues that George Homans raised fifteen years ago in his presidential address entitled "Bringing Men Back In" (Homans, 1964). In that address, he scolded various functionalists—he included me among them—for focusing on functional exigencies and on regularities at the social system level. These efforts, he argued, were misguided because they left out the real engine of individual and institutional behavior, which is men and women acting according to definite psychological laws. On the basis of what I have observed, it is possible to weigh the merits of this argument. Insofar as Homans was asserting the necessity of taking some stand on the psychologies of human beings in the construction of sociological theories, he was absolutely right. I would go even further; it is impossible for it to be otherwise—even for the most abstract and unreconstructed functionalist—and still to have any kind of theoretical explanation. It is possible, of course, to downplay and obscure those essential psychological ingredients. But as is often the case, the carrier of a valid observation often, in enthusiasm, runs too fast and too far with it, and in the process overshoots the limits of validity. Homans went too far in his presidential address in two respects:

1. He argued that an essential part of reasserting the importance of the psychology of the human being was to insist that social regularities are *derivations from, if not reducible to,* psychological laws. Certainly psychological assumptions and assertions are essential ingredients of sociological explanations, but they are not the sole basis of their construction.

2. He argued that the basis of this derivation is a *specific type of learning*

theory resting on rewards, costs, and resultant valued behavior patterns. Such a theory is not without its merits, but surely not the exclusive ingredient of all valid explanatory theories in sociology at all levels.

THE LEVEL OF EVALUATION: METHODOLOGICAL QUESTIONS

During the process of research, the investigator engages in—or should engage in—a kind of constant monitoring process, in which he continually asks questions of himself, questions that are generated by the methodological canons of social science research. Are the historical facts authentic? Are they appropriately to be considered as representative instances of the general categories (social groups, social forces, etc.) that are being employed? How is it possible to assign causal priority to one of several co-occurring historical facts or trends? Are the causal propositions being invoked rooted in, or, better yet, in some way derived from a general theoretical scheme? Is that scheme specified and is it theoretically consistent internally (Warner and Smelser, 1976)? After the research is completed and written up in book or journal form, others comb it over and assess it—or should assess it—with the same order of questions. By posing these kinds of questions the adequacy of the operation is assessed, and its worth as a social scientific product is established.

A Concluding Remark

In these few pages I have attempted to review some of the processes and levels of activity that transpire in the execution of social science research. I conclude by observing that much confusion has been created in the literature on the methodology and philosophy of the social sciences in compressing the several levels to some statement of *the* scientific process and thus failing to acknowledge that each of these levels has an independent and legitimate place in that execution. The most common reduction is the overformalization or overrationalization of the process, imagining that the biographical flow of research should somehow correspond to formal posing of some methodological question (e.g., asking whether a proposition is supported by the available facts), and then imagining that the biographical flow of activity is, say, deductive or inductive in character. Such reductions obscure the complexity of the research process itself, and often lead to misdirected philosophical questions, such as "What is the process of deduction or induction?"—misguided because they confound the process of methodological criticisms of research with the flow of the research process itself. Both processes would probably be better understood if their separate character were acknowledged and honored.

4

Measurement and Conceptualization Problems: The Major Obstacle to Integrating Theory and Research

Hubert M. Blalock, Jr.

IN ONE SENSE, the theme of this chapter is obvious. Sociologists face extremely tough intellectual and practical tasks owing to the ambitious nature of our common objectives and the complex reality with which we deal. These tasks will require a *concerted* effort of scholars with diverse substantive, theoretical, and methodological interests and persuasions. Yet in many respects we seem badly divided into a myriad of theoretical and methodological schools that tend to oversimplify each other's positions, that fail to make careful conceptual distinctions, and that encourage partisan attacks.

Rather than dwelling on these divisive issues, it is crucial that we learn to resist overplaying our differences at the expense of common intellectual interests. There will obviously be disagreements over appropriate strategies, as well as ideological and subdisciplinary differences. But an idealization of dissensus is self-defeating. Some conflicts will inevitably occur and, if constructively resolved, may result in benefits to the discipline. But I think there has been too great a tendency to exaggerate these benefits, without recognizing the inherent dangers of endless theoretical and methodological debates and a further fractionating of our field.

One particularly disappointing feature of our discipline is that we have not

☐ Adapted from the presidential address, American Sociological Association, September 1979. The unabridged version was published in the *American Sociological Review* 44 (December 1979): 881–894.

had the productive interplay between theory and research called for so eloquently by Merton (1968). This interplay will require us to grapple with a number of extremely complex problems that I shall merely list before narrowing my remarks to two issues that illustrate the need for analyses that are simultaneously theoretical and methodological. My abbreviated list is as follows:

1. Reality is sufficiently complex that we will need theories that contain upward of fifty variables if we wish to disentangle the effects of numerous exogenous and endogenous variables on a diversity of dependent variables.

2. Many social changes are either very rapid compared to intervals of observation or are continuous rather than discrete, so that temporal sequences cannot easily be inferred or linked to given historical events.

3. Realistic models of naturally occurring social phenomena must be nonrecursive or contain highly specific assumptions about lag periods or distributed lags.

4. Many important theoretical variables are highly intercorrelated, though perhaps the empirical associations among them will be underestimated due to random measurement errors. Resolving this multicollinearity problem will require a *combination* of large samples and good measurement.

5. Human actors and social systems tend to be nonhomogeneous with respect to parameters in structural equations, implying that they will not respond similarly to changes in other variables. This will have major implications not only for our theories but also for measurement decisions, whenever effect indicators are being used, and for macroanalyses where aggregation decisions are needed.

6. Many groups and contexts have fuzzy boundaries. Standards, such as group norms or role expectations, also tend to be imprecise. Measurement that depends in some essential way upon these fuzzy boundaries or standards thereby becomes exceedingly difficult.

7. The linkage of micro and macro theories involving different units of analysis is problematic unless simplifying assumptions can be made. In particular, aggregation—disaggregation problems are made difficult whenever there are non-negligible contextual effects, nonlinearities, or unknown measurement errors.

8. All measurement is to some degree indirect and therefore requires untested assumptions of a causal nature, but this problem is especially serious whenever one-to-one linkages between constructs and indicators cannot be assumed, whenever replications under standardized conditions are impossible, whenever homogeneity properties facilitating indirect measurement cannot be assumed, and whenever the ratio of unmeasured variables is high.

9. Given the practical roadblocks to data collection that will continue for the foreseeable future, any piece of research will necessarily involve large amounts of missing information, thereby requiring either implicit or explicit

assumptions and the neglect of numerous variables thought to be theoretically important.

Although the development of theory is important in its own right, I believe that the most serious and important problems that require our immediate and concerted attention are those of conceptualization and measurement. I have reached this conclusion coming at the matter from two very different perspectives. The first is through an examination of the implications of measurement errors for data analysis and theory testing, and the second is through frustrating efforts to make sense of the theoretical and empirical literature in one of our substantive fields, that of race and ethnic relations. Both these endeavors leave me with the realization that these conceptualization and measurement problems are so complex, and their implications for analysis so serious, that I believe that a really coordinated effort in this direction is absolutely essential.

Given the limitations imposed by our meager resources and missing data, it is crucial that we examine carefully what these imply in terms of linkages between theory and research. Missing variables force us to use highly indirect measures, improper aggregation operations, and crude background factors as indicators of experience variables. For practical reasons, many of these missing variables must remain unmeasured. Thus, we must substitute a series of implicit or explicit assumptions about how these variables operate. But assumptions can either be made blindly for convenience or after one has carefully tried to identify the missing variables and think through their implications. The latter course is much more frustrating and disillusioning, but it is the surest way to make progress in pinpointing inadequacies in existing theories and data.

In the sections that follow I shall discuss two very different problems that illustrate the complexity of the type of analysis I believe is needed in the face of such missing information. These problems are: (1) the plethora of theoretical definitions of generic behaviors and their implications for measurement, and (2) the confounding of measured and unmeasured variables when individuals are aggregated in macro-level analyses.

Both types of problems illustrate an important kind of temptation, namely, that of substituting relatively simple operational indicators for theoretical constructs without paying careful attention to the underlying measurement model. In the case of behaviors, we shall note a tendency to define variables to facilitate generalizability at the expense of realism with respect to simplifying assumptions. In the case of aggregation by spatial criteria we encounter the need to specify unmeasured variables linking location in physical space to whatever dependent variable is being investigated.

The researcher, constrained by serious data limitations, usually finds it convenient to sidestep these issues. The theorist, trying to make sense of diverse empirical studies, is then confronted with an almost hopeless task and may be tempted to use the empirical information either selectively or anecdotally—or even to ignore it.

The Measurement and Conceptualization of Behaviors

We have recently made considerable progress with respect to data *analysis* but relatively little with respect to data *collection,* and in particular with respect to our ability to observe, categorize, and measure behaviors. Even if one does not accept this assertion, I assume there is consensus on the need to improve our measurement of behaviors. There will inevitably be numerous practical obstacles to observing behaviors as they actually occur, but the problems I shall discuss are conceptual or theoretical and would occur even under the most ideal circumstances.

Human behaviors are extremely diverse, so much so that if we were to try to explain each one separately the situation would become hopeless. One way to resolve this problem would be to limit ourselves to a very restricted number of behaviors, but this is obviously not the course we are following. In a few instances behaviors pose no special measurement problems aside from observability. For the most part, these revolve around simple biological or economic needs.

Many behaviors of greatest interest to sociologists, however, are not of this nature. We recognize that there are many different "forms" of these behaviors, which are often very different in terms of manifest or directly observable characteristics. Thus one may achieve status in a variety of ways: by killing enemies, by saving lives on the operating table, or by tackling opponents on a football field.

How do we get a theoretical handle on these diverse behaviors so as to group them into a much smaller number of conceptual ones? I am aware of four strategies, all of which rely on theoretical assumptions that usually remain implicit. These are as follows: (1) a linkage is assumed between the behavior and some motivational state, which usually appears in the theoretical definition; (2) there is an assumed causal linkage between the behavior and some consequence, which is an integral part of the definition; (3) the behavior is defined in terms of some general social standard with which it is compared; and (4) there is an assumed linkage between the behavior and other variables that cause this behavior to be repeated, with replication being an essential component of the definition.

Each of these definitional strategies thus requires simplifying assumptions that will be more or less realistic, depending upon the complexity of the setting, the motivations of the actors, and the reactions of other actors who may also affect outcomes or ways in which behaviors are repeated. We should, therefore, not be surprised to find each definitional strategy being accompanied by certain theoretical biases that help the social scientist to justify whatever simplifying assumptions are most convenient for that strategy. The more complex the behavior, the more crucial it is to uncover such biases and to state assumptions explicitly.

BEHAVIORS DEFINED IN TERMS OF INTERNAL STATES

The lack of a perfect correspondence between attitudes and behaviors has been well documented. But it may not be so obvious that many general types of behaviors are *defined* in such a way that some internal state becomes an essential ingredient in the definition, so that measurement requires assumptions about these internal states. For instance, aggression may be defined as behavior intended to injure another party or altruistic behavior as any form of behavior intended to benefit someone other than the actor. Avoidance may be defined as any behavior the purpose of which is to reduce contact with another actor.

What simplifications seem necessary in using this definitional strategy? Let us illustrate with the aggression example. *If* there were a closed set of behaviors that could be listed, each of which is clearly linked to the injury of another party, one could supply the observer with the names of these familiar behaviors. Two kinds of difficulties are encountered, however. First and most important, many behaviors serve several ends at once. In fact, human beings are remarkably adept at creating situations in which actors can kill several birds with one stone. Aggression may be instrumental in weakening the competitive position of an opponent or in attaining status among one's peers. This means that the same behaviors can be classified in different ways if the theoretical definition is stated in terms of a postulated internal state. One theorist may refer to aggression, a second to exploitation, and a third to competitive behavior, all "observed" in the same way.

The second obvious problem is that the relationship between the internal state and the behavior may be more or less direct, may involve differing time delays, and may be subject to distortion by either the actor or the observer, whose theories of social causation may differ. Some forms of aggression are very overt, immediate, and nonsubtle. Others are very delayed. Still others may be subtle and disguised as behaviors of a different type.

Given these difficulties, what kinds of simplification are we tempted to make? First, we may confine ourselves to simple laboratory settings in which actors' choices are restricted to a small number of alternatives, each of which is assumed simply linked to a postulated internal state. Aggression, altruism, or avoidance may thereby be identified with relatively simple operations such as that of pushing a blue rather than a red button. The measurement-conceptualization problem is then transformed into one of assessing "external validity" or generalizability.

A second simplifying strategy uses a restricted subset of behaviors most simply linked to the assumed internal state. If some forms of aggression are subtle, indirect, or delayed, these are excluded from the operational definition because they are difficult to interpret. The result is a nonrandom selection of behaviors biasing the findings in unknown ways.

A third strategy is closely linked with the second. One may limit oneself to a small number of "master motives" that underlie nearly all human behaviors, so that whenever a behavioral form can be located that supports one's theory, this master motive is invoked in labeling the behavior to confirm this theory. Thus if one believes that an intent to injure others is present in almost all human interactions, then nearly every form of behavior can be considered as a subtle form of aggression. Those who see status-seeking as a prime motivator may define whatever behaviors they see as instances of status-seeking, and to some degree they will probably be correct. Since most behaviors involve mixtures of motivations, there is a wide-open opportunity to label any given behavior as an instance of many different kinds of generic behaviors defined in this fashion.

A fourth way to simplify the classification of behaviors is to accept the actor's word for his or her own motivation. Rarely are we so naive as to believe a respondent who claims a pure motive, but in effect this may be what actually occurs whenever we ask a respondent or witness to recall what has taken place. To do so, one must rely on popular vocabulary and common definitions, rather than scientific usage. The social scientist wishing to give precision to behavioral concepts that have popular meanings is thus faced with a dilemma. Either one must rely on popular definitions when events are being reported, or one must develop a more precise terminology that does not correspond to this popular usage. If one wishes to generalize across cultures or languages, these problems become even more serious.

BEHAVIORS DEFINED IN TERMS OF CONSEQUENCES

One may sidestep the problem of identifying internal states by focusing entirely on the consequences of the behaviors. *Someone* must assess the consequences since a causal theory is being invoked to link the behaviors with some set of outcomes. But whose theory? The actor's? Other parties' in the situation? The supposedly neutral observer's? And which outcomes and using what time span? If there are both short-term and long-term consequences that are not identical, which should be used? And what if these outcomes are conditional on the behaviors of *other* actors in the setting?

Once more, there will be pressures to simplify. One possibility is to confine oneself to very simple situations. Another is to dichotomize consequences as either occurring or not, thereby ignoring variations in degree. Still another is to ignore multiple consequences and to look only at those consequences that are obvious and immediate in a temporal sense. Taking the example of aggression (now defined as behavior that results in injury), this would rule out many forms of delayed aggression or subtle types where the consequences seemed to be highly indirect.

Whenever the consequences are *conditional* on the responses of other actors, it will be especially tempting to simplify one's causal theory to obtain an unambiguous measure. Suppose one defines discrimination as behavior that results in unequal consequences for classes of actors defined in certain ways—as for example by age, sex, or race. Suppose an employer makes a set of judgments that result in the hiring of disproportionately few blacks. Was the lack of hiring *solely* a consequence of the employer's action or also of the behaviors of the applicants for the position? It is tempting to try to get off the hook by crudely matching blacks and whites on "relevant" variables, as defined by the investigator, usually in accord with data-availability considerations.

Furthermore, if the discriminatory behavior leads to some sort of response that jointly affects the outcome, then how does one define or measure the behavior without taking this response into consideration? How does one measure teaching effectiveness or leadership quality? The most tempting resolution is to assume away the problem by taking the second actor's behavior either as being totally dependent on that of the first or as having negligible consequences in its own right. Thus we often assume that minorities, children, and other *relatively* powerless actors are *totally* powerless, so that their own responses can be ignored.

Basically, this measurement strategy may tempt one to ignore all sorts of intervening and conditioning variables by grossly oversimplifying the causal connection between the behavior in question and the consequences that are being identified. There will be a vested interest in simplifying this set of consequences, just as the prior strategy creates one in simplifying the actor's motivational structure.

BEHAVIORS DEFINED IN TERMS OF STANDARDS

Certain kinds of behavior are defined theoretically in terms of some social standard, which is often either rather vague or differently defined by actors having contrasting interests. For example, deviance is defined in terms of departures from social norms, which may be subject to dispute. In the case of criminal behavior, the norms may be clearly stated in the form of laws that are enforced by official sanctions, but the laws themselves may vary from one jurisdiction to the next. Similarly, the notion of exploitation in an exchange relationship may be defined in terms of some standard by which equity can be evaluated. There are also a number of popular terms such as "mentally disturbed," "addiction," or "antisocial" behavior that presumably imply some sort of implicit standard.

In all of these instances, an investigator who attempts to measure the degree of departure from such standards is faced with a dilemma. If reality is fuzzy, how is it possible to obtain precise measures? We have, it seems, a kind of sociological Uncertainty Principle that places an upper limit on the accuracy of measurement of such behaviors. How can one measure degree of conformity to imprecise norms? What if actors define a "fair" rate of exchange differently? Is there, any meaning to a notion such as exploitation? The terms "conformity" and "exploitation" can be used in ideological writings, but can they become a legitimate part of a scientific vocabulary?

I believe it is possible to retain the essential features of the theoretical arguments that use such concepts, provided we make careful distinctions and somehow build the *degree* of fuzziness into these theories, as a separate variable. Whenever there is dissensus on group norms or what constitutes a fair rate of exchange, this in itself becomes a datum of relevance to actors. Perhaps a measure such as a standard deviation can be used as a measure of such dissensus whenever the issue is unidimensional. When it is not, this in itself requires analysis because it will constitute an additional source of fuzziness for the actors concerned. Where the standards for a given subgroup are clear-cut but distinct from those of another, two separate variables can be delineated, as for example degrees of deviance from group A norms and from group B norms.

The temptation, here, is to substitute more precise standards for the true but fuzzy ones. One way to simplify the situation is to substitute some measure of *average* behavior for the norm, thereby giving it a definite meaning, although one that may differ from its meaning to the actors themselves. As is well known, there are two meanings to the word "normal," namely, some measure of central tendency, on the one hand, and some idealized value, on the other. Insofar as these may differ according to the situation, our theories will then need to make the necessary distinction between the two types of standards.

Another alternative is to confine our operational measures to absolute values, using zero as the comparison point. Thus one may take suicide rates as a measure of deviance, but only if *all* suicides are socially defined as contrary to normative expectations. If certain suicides are not defined in this fashion, however, and if normative standards vary across the units being compared, then clearly suicide rates will not be an appropriate indicator of deviance. Unfortunately, many of our theories of deviance are not very precise as to the standard about which deviance is to be measured, or whether the norm is to be defined in terms of a measure of central tendency or some legal or ethical standard.

BEHAVIORS DEFINED IN TERMS OF REPLICATIONS

The fourth strategy, that of relying on replications, seems most common among behavioral psychologists and social psychologists who rely heavily on experimental designs involving repeated measurements. Given very simple settings and assumptions about motivating factors, such a strategy indeed does make sense. In generalizing beyond the laboratory setting, one obviously cannot rely so heavily on operational definitions of behaviors that require such replications. For example, if one defines reinforcing behaviors as those that are followed by later instances of the behaviors they are supposed to reinforce, one must rule out *other* causes of the replicated behaviors. Perhaps the behaviors are repeated because they are constrained or influenced by factors unknown to the investigator.

The more general point is that whenever several variables jointly affect a behavior, a reliance on the replication operation to measure a behavior will lead to both theoretical ambiguities and empirical irregularities that make measurement much more difficult. In short, the research operations cannot be generalized readily to more complex situations in which replications occur under much less controlled circumstances. In making comparisons across such situations, both the measurement operations and the situations themselves will vary, so that theory and measurement become hopelessly confounded.

Whenever manifestly similar behaviors are rarely repeated in real-life situations, we are faced with another kind of dilemma the resolution of which will require theoretical assumptions. The observation period, being arbitrary in most instances, may in part determine the relative frequency of occurrences within a given population. If this proportion is very small, one will be confronted with a highly skewed response variable. This may be countered by defining the behavior in question as merely an instance of a larger class of behaviors that occur more frequently, but then problems of aggregation and homogeneity will arise. That is, the diverse behaviors that have been lumped together into the class may have different sets of causes or consequences.

Another alternative is to aggregate over individuals assumed to be similar in certain respects, so that one then works with behavior *rates* as estimates of probabilities of engaging in the behavior. Obviously, this requires a well defined theory as well as data sufficient to classify such individuals into categories that are homogeneous with respect to the parameters of the equations and not merely a set of "objective" attributes of individuals, such as age, sex, or SES. Often, these aggregation decisions are made on the basis of convenience or convention, with the theoretical rationale being only implicit.

To conclude this section on behaviors, in considering the implications of each of these definitional strategies the essential point is not that assumptions can or should be avoided but that they need to be made explicit. Further-more, we see that each *measurement* strategy requires the use of *theoretical* assumptions, only some of which can be tested. Our own experience (Blalock and Wilken, 1979) in attempting to analyze selected basic concepts in the field of intergroup relations is that an apparently simple form of behavior, such as discrimination, aggression, or avoidance, requires for adequate concep-tualization auxiliary measurement theories containing as many as twenty or thirty variables. I would be surprised if the same does not hold for other reasonably general social behaviors.

The Confounding of Variables in Aggregating by Geographic Proximity

The literature on aggregation and disaggregation is both technical and discouraging in its implications, if one takes seriously the goal of integrating micro- with macro-level studies.[1] Ideally, theories on the one level should be consistent, in some sense, with those on the other (Hannan, 1971: 18–23). Furthermore, since some groups are nested within larger ones, and since in many instances group boundaries are fuzzy and therefore arbitrarily defined, it is also desirable to pass systematically from one aggregate level to another, as, for example, from counties to states.

In discussions of aggregation in the econometrics literature, it is assumed that those who do the aggregating have a theoretical rationale for grouping in-dividuals into behaviorally homogeneous aggregates. In most instances where sociologists use aggregated data, however, the grouping operation has already been done, usually with another purpose in mind. In these instances, ag-gregation can hopelessly complicate one's analysis, unless the criterion for ag-gregation can be fitted rather simply into one's theory.

Sometimes we may aggregate over a territorial unit that for certain pur-poses may be considered a corporate group (e.g., a state or county), but where the corporateness may not be an essential feature of the theory in ques-tion. For example, we may be studying crime rates in various counties, where county-level policies have virtually no impact upon these rates. Or our theoretical interest may be on the micro level. Yet the data may be available only in aggregated form, as, for example, census tract data. In no sense can these territorial units be said to constitute true "groups," nor is there any pretense that we are interested in highly coordinated behaviors.

[1] For three very different, though complementary, perspectives on the aggregation problem, the reader is referred to the works of Firebaugh (1978, 1979); Hannan (1971) and Hannan and Burstein (1974); and Irwin and Lichtman (1976) and Langbein and Lichtman (1978). These sources also contain numerous additional references.

In such instances, we use the aggregated data because they are the only ones available. What can we say about the problems created when individuals are aggregated by spatial criteria? The answer depends upon the causal connections between the criteria used in grouping and the variables that appear in our theories (Blalock, 1964; Hannan, 1971).

The usual assumption is that the aggregation criterion, which we shall call A, is an independent variable in the model and that it is not operating to confound the effects of the independent variables under study. When we acknowledge the myriad ways in which spatial location may be linked to the variables of interest to sociologists we can anticipate the complications that such aggregation may produce. People are influenced by what goes on around them in the immediate present, but also in the past. They may have moved from one community to another, carrying with them those effects in the former residence that we refer to as "background influences." Furthermore, not all individuals are affected in the same ways by the variables in their immediate environment. Some may have lived in the area all their lives. Others may have moved into the area because of its local traditions, whereas others may have entered and resisted them.

To come to grips with the problems that such complexities create, it will be helpful to examine several models that are themselves oversimplifications of the actual processes at work. We begin with a model in which it is presumed that the territorial units are closed to migration and that contextual effects operate entirely within the boundaries that have been operationally defined.

A CLOSED-SYSTEM EXAMPLE

Suppose we are willing to assume that our criterion for aggregation, here a spatial one, operates only as an independent variable. Of course we do not imagine that location, per se, affects the variables of interest. Instead, one's spatial position may be taken as a cause indicator of the unmeasured variables that are presumed to be the true causes of the variables in question. Take the model of Figure 1 as an illustration. Perhaps X_1 represents educational achievement, assumed to be a constant property of the individual once the process has been completed. Suppose X_2 represents a relatively constant type of personal value (say, "egalitarianism") that has been developed over time as a result of socialization experiences linked closely with one's spatial location. Let X_3 represent another kind of attitudinal variable (say, one's attitude toward a specific minority) that is readily modifiable and therefore subject to changes in one's immediate environment. Finally, suppose X_4 represents a contextual variable (such as a set of sanctions) that operates in the immediate locale.

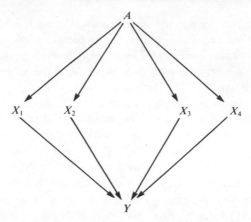

Figure 1. Closed-system Model, with Location *(A)* Affecting *Y* Through Intervening Variables

Now suppose that all these X_i affect a certain form of behavior Y. To simplify we shall assume that the effects are additive, so that the behavior Y may be represented by the equation

$$Y = \alpha + \beta_1 X_1 + \beta_2 X_2 + \beta_3 X_3 + \beta_4 X_4 + \epsilon \qquad (1)$$

In the model of Figure 1 we have drawn causal arrows from A to each of the X_i representing the argument that one's location in space in part determines the levels of these X_i as intervening variables.

In any realistic situation, an investigator will be unaware of or unable to measure many of the X_i that affect Y. Suppose, for example, that only X_1 and X_4 have been measured and used in an incorrectly specified equation for Y. The least-squares estimates b_1 and b_4 of the parameters β_1 and β_4 will then be biased to the degree that the omitted intervening variables are correlated with X_1 and X_4. In the model of Figure 1 the intercorrelations among the X_i are due solely to A, implying that a control for A (if perfectly measured) would wipe out these interrelationships. Thus if we were to examine the data *within* a single territorial unit we would find no association among the X_i, implying that even in the incorrectly specified equation

$$Y = a + b_1 X_1 + b_4 X_4 + e \qquad (2)$$

the estimates b_1 and b_4 would be unbiased estimates of β_1 and β_4.

Of course this is a highly oversimplified model in which there are no other arrows connecting the X_i, whereas in actuality we would expect intercorrelations within each area. But this prototype model is presumably illustrative of more complex ones and involves the kind of assumption needed to justify controlling for residential area. The essential notion is that many causal factors are generally confounded together because of common residence. Therefore a control for residence is expected to weaken these associations, if not to do away with them altogether.

What is less obvious is that when we *aggregate* by location we do the very opposite of controlling for A. In grouping by A we put together people who are similar in their X_1 levels. But they will also be similar with respect to their X_2, X_3, and X_4 values. Suppose the X_i are labeled so that the relationships with A are all in the same direction, so that we may represent them by positive signs. Then persons who reside in a location where the X_1 values tend to be high will also have high X_2, X_3, and X_4 values. If we shift our analysis to the macro level, using the estimating equation

$$\overline{Y} = a^* + b_1^*\overline{X}_1 + b_2^*\overline{X}_2 + b_3^*\overline{X}_3 + b_4^*\overline{X}_4 + e^* \qquad (3)$$

where the $\overline{X}_i$ represent mean values for the same X_i as represented in Figure 1, we may ask how the new least-squares estimates b_i^* may be expected to compare with estimates that would have been computed on the basis of individual-level data.

What happens in this case is that the $\overline{X}_i$ will be more highly intercorrelated than the micro-level counterparts X_i. If we have specified the model perfectly and if there is aboltely no measurement error in any variable, this will not lead to any systematic biases in the macro-level estimates of the parameters. But because of the increased intercorrelations we encounter a multicollinearity problem that tends to increase sampling errors.

It is more important, however, to consider the implications of this confounding of intervening variables in instances where there are specification errors. Suppose we do not know all the X_i that cause Y and that are intercorrelated because of location. To be specific, suppose we have included only $\overline{X}_1$ and $\overline{X}_4$ in the equation for $\overline{Y}$. Our biases in parameter estimates will now be much more serious than in the micro model discussed earlier. In effect, if we shift to group means but ignore certain of the causes of $\overline{Y}$, the effects of these omitted variables are even more confounded with those of the intervening variables we have been able to include. Put another way, our aggregated model is more sensitive to at least these types of specification errors than is the micro model, even where the location variable A has been ignored.[2]

For the model of Figure 1 we thus have three analysis possibilities. Our best option is to use micro data and to control for A. Our second best bet is to use micro data and to ignore A. In doing so, if we happen to leave out any of the intervening X_i we will confound their effects with the remaining X's. The third option is to obtain between-area data by aggregating, in which case we

---

[2] Irwin and Lichtman (1976) stress that the essential criterion in deciding between a micro and a macro model is that of the relative degree of specification errors involved. Here, this criterion implies that the micro model is to be preferred. Firebaugh (1978) discusses this kind of situation in terms of a general criterion for avoiding aggregation bias, namely, that the association between Y and $\overline{X}$, *controlling for* X, must be zero if bias is to be avoided. In other words, $\overline{X}$ must not belong in the equation for Y, a criterion that will not be satisfied if $\overline{X}$ is a surrogate for other variables that have been omitted from the equation because of specification errors.

increase the intercorrelations among the intervening variables (Hannan and Burstein, 1974), thereby confounding to an even greater degree the effects of the omitted $\overline{X}_i$ with the causal variables in which we are explicitly interested. We cannot say that aggregation will *always* have this effect, but to the degree that reality approximates the model of Figure 1 this will hold.

AN OPEN-SYSTEM EXAMPLE

Now consider the somewhat more complicated but also more realistic situation in which persons are immigrating into and emigrating from each of the areal units. Here we must take A as a dependent as well as an independent variable. Of course, the "area" is not "dependent" upon its residents. What we mean is that since our micro units of analysis are individuals or families, the particular area in which they are located is dependent upon their decisions. To study this kind of situation we now must bring in the time dimension and try to distinguish between contemporary and past influences, as well as internal states that we are willing to assume are stable over time as contrasted with those that may change as a result of immediate stimuli.

Consider the model of Figure 2. Here we distinguish between an individual's location at time 1, namely A_{t_1}, and his or her location at time 2. Migration may or may not have occurred in the interim. Following Stinchcombe's (1968) discussion of historical explanations we may draw an arrow linking A_{t_1} to A_{t_2}. What one does today, or where one is, influences tomorrow's behavior or location, if only in the sense that once a given pattern of behavior has been learned there is a vested interest in not changing it unless

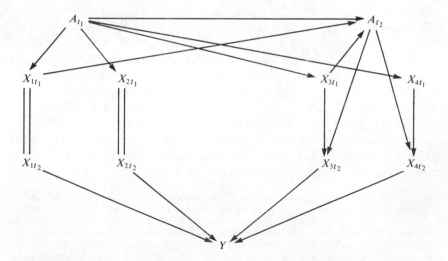

Figure 2. Open-system Model, with Two Locations and Two Time Periods

there are specific pressures to do so. For those who have not migrated, A_{t_1} and A_{t_2} will be identical. The degree of association between these two variables will depend on the proportion of migrants.

Suppose X_1 and X_2 represent variables that do not change over time. Therefore, the change in location has not affected either of these variables. I have represented this by drawing in double lines without arrowheads to indicate that X_1 and X_2 remain identical at the two points in time. Suppose, however, that X_3 and X_4 may be affected by the new location as well as the old. Therefore, I have drawn arrows to X_{3t_2} from both X_{3t_1} and A_{t_2} (and similarly for X_{4t_2}), making the assumption that the changes produced by the change in location are almost immediate. Finally, the behavior Y at time 2 is taken as dependent upon the contemporary values of the X_i, as was also true in Figure 1.

Now suppose both migrants and nonmigrants are lumped together, as is practically always necessary for aggregated data. Again, if we have perfect measures of the contemporary values of all the X_i, we may estimate their separate effects without bias, though if they are too highly intercorrelated we shall have large sampling errors. But suppose there are specification errors, either in the form of poor measurement of some of the X_i or their omission from the equation. Previously, we noted in Figure 1 that a control for A would remove all the intercorrelations among the X_i, so that if some were inadvertently omitted the estimates of the structural parameters for the others would remain unbiased. This will not be true, however, for the more complex model of Figure 2 unless *both* A_{t_1} and A_{t_2} are simultaneously controlled. If we looked only within A_{t_2} we would expect to find a correlation between X_1 and X_2 that would be some function of the proportion of immigrants, since these variables depend only on the factors operating during the earlier period. Presumably, X_1's correlation with X_3 and X_4 would be somewhat weaker, owing to the contemporary factors affecting the latter two variables. The correlation between X_{3t_2} and X_{4t_2} will depend on the relative importance of contemporary influences as compared with earlier ones.

What happens when we aggregate using only the *present* location A_{t_2}? Once again, we do the very opposite of controlling for location and thereby tend to confound the effects of the four X_i. But now we are also grouping by a variable that may be dependent upon certain of the X_i. In Figure 2, I have drawn arrows from X_{1t_1} (say, education) and X_{3t_1} (say, attitude toward a minority) to A_{t_2}, presuming that these two X_i have influenced the decision to migrate. But if we aggregate by A (at time 2) we are manipulating a *dependent* variable in terms of the relationship between X_1 and X_3, and this will distort their relationship in an unknown way.

The models with which we have been concerned are grossly oversimplified, merely illustrative of the problems one encounters when aggregation operations are poorly understood. In a sense, aggregation by spatial units is "understood" in that the criteria for aggregation are clearly operationalized. But what we generally lack is a *theoretical* model connecting spatial location with the other variables in the system. Thus, we achieve operational simplicity at the expense of theoretical clarity. The result is that we are unable to link our macro-level aggregated data with the micro-level causal processes that may have produced these data. Put another way, if we wanted to insert the aggregation criterion into the causal model we would find that the model would have to be highly complex because one's spatial location is not simply related to the other variables in these models.

Concluding Remarks

These are but two among many possible illustrations of the need for careful conceptualization and attention to measurement problems and of the fact that theoretical and methodological issues are closely interconnected. They also suggest the importance of bringing implicit assumptions out into the open, even where the added variables in the model may have to remain unmeasured in any given piece of research. Unless this is done, many of these variables will remain confounded with measured variables. It will then be difficult to decide rationally as to the relative merits of alternative design strategies needed to unravel their interrelationships. In particular, it is important to reemphasize how crucial it is to avoid the temptation to sidestep theoretical and conceptual issues by resorting to very simple operational procedures.

Initial efforts to specify models more completely and to theorize explicitly about linkages between measured and unmeasured variables are almost certain to have discouraging implications. We shall realize how many missing variables and hidden assumptions tend to be ignored in empirical data analyses, as well as theoretical interpretations of empirical results. Obviously, this carries with it the danger of inhibiting further work and encouraging a hypercritical appraisal of the sociological literature. I believe this is a risk we must take, however, if we are to create a really cumulative knowledge base.

This, in turn, leads me to one inescapable conclusion. Sociologists need to work *together* on these problems. We can ill afford to go off in our own directions, continuing to proliferate fields of specialization, changing our vocabulary whenever we see fit, or merely hoping that somehow or other the products of miscellaneous studies will "add up." The plea, then, is for a sustained effort to clarify our theoretical constructs and self-consciously to ask ourselves how different strategies of conceptualization relate to problems of data collection and measurement.

There will still be plenty of room for differences in terms of the kinds of propositions we wish to state and test, the assumptions we are willing to make, the problems we study, the courses of action we recommend, and the theoretical and ideological biases with which we operate. In the proposed joint effort, there is a need for many different kinds of skills, interests, and knowledge bases to help solve technical issues, bring out implicit assumptions, and try to reach a working consensus on our conceptual apparatus and epistemic correlations.

If nothing else, such a concerted effort will better enable us to comprehend what we are all trying to say and to appreciate more fully the complexity of the theories and analyses needed to understand a very complex reality. If we do not make this concerted effort, I fear that sociology in the year 2000 will be no more advanced than it is today, though perhaps it will contain far more specializations, theoretical schools, methodological cults, and interest groups than, even today, we can readily imagine.

II

Issues in Specific Substantive Fields of Sociology

5

Contexts, Units, and Properties in Sociological Analysis

Peter M. Blau

THE STUDY of formal organizations as closed systems is often unfavorably compared with their study as open systems. The original villain in this scenario is Max Weber, who is criticized for treating bureaucracies as closed systems and for ignoring their interdependence with the broader society, that is, the influences of the external environment on organizations and their influences, in turn, on the society of which they are a part. I have never understood this criticism, since a major concern of Weber's is the analysis of the historical conditions in societies that led to the bureaucratic form of organization, and since another major interest of his is the study of the profound changes widespread bureaucratization has wrought in modern society. To be sure, Weber also presents a theoretical scheme analyzing the interrelated characteristics that constitute the typical bureaucracy, confining himself at this point to bureaucracy's own attributes, as a first step for examining the relationships between these bureaucratic attributes and conditions in society. It is hard to see how else he could have proceeded, inasmuch as a prerequisite for systematically investigating how society affects, and is affected by, a certain institution is first to clarify the properties and structure of that institution.

Quantitative research on organizations, including my own, has concentrated attention on their internal structure. It, more than Weber, can be justifiably criticized for neglecting the connections between organizations and their wider social context, although these connections have not been entirely ignored by quantitative research, as illustrated by comparative studies of organizations in different societies (Hickson et al., 1974), markets (Pennings, 1975), and communities (Blau and Schoenherr, 1971: 205–37). However, implicit in the distinction between closed and open systems in conceptualizing organizations is a deeper issue of generic significance in sociological inquiry. The issue is what our unit of analysis is. Once we no longer consider it a matter of course that the cases being analyzed are persons—a notion foreign to classical sociological theory and made popular by sampling surveys—the choice of the unit of analysis is problematical, and it governs the substantive questions that can be raised and possibly answered.

In the sociological studies of social structures, the unit of analysis may range from small groups to entire societies. Larger social structures encompass smaller ones, and the concepts and variables relevant for their investigation are not the same. Formal organizations can be the units of analysis in one investigation, but they may be the social context in another investigation of a narrower unit, such as departments or work groups, and they are the properties that help define the social structure of still another investigation's broader units, such as communities or societies. I shall deal with these general conceptual problems here using formal organizations as main illustrations.

Hierarchies of Structural Complexity

In an influential paper, Simon (1962) explicates the nature of complexity, which is characteristic not only of social systems but of all systems, be they physical, biological, psychological, or social. A complex system is one composed of many different interrelated parts. Simon's central thesis is that complex systems consist of interdependent subsystems which in turn comprise interrelated subunits, with the substructuring recurring on successively narrower levels until one gets to the interdependent elements whose substructure is unknown or irrelevant in terms of the theoretical framework. He calls this feature of a complex system a hierarchy, emphasizing that he uses the term not in the conventional sense of levels of subordination but to refer to successively less inclusive sets of interdependent units. In the physical realm, for example, galaxies consist of planetary systems, these of satellite systems, and one can move on down to the microscopic level of molecules made up of interrelated atoms, which consist of interacting elementary particles, which may be composed of quarks. In biology, similarly, there is a hierarchy of increasingly encompassing systems as cells build up tissues, tissues combine into organs, and various related organs constitute organisms, which make up species and genera.

The hierarchical character of complex systems—their consisting of successive levels of systems of interdependent subunits—is an essential factor in their development. Simon uses the analogy of two watchmakers, Tempus and

Hora, to illustrate this hypothesis. The watches made by both had 1,000 parts each, but the procedures for assembling them were different. To construct a watch, Tempus had to fit all pieces together, so that every time he was interrupted—by a customer, for instance—he had to start again from scratch. Hora, in contrast, made first subassemblies of ten parts each; then she put about ten of these into larger assemblies; and finally she constructed a watch out of the ten larger assemblies she had made. Consequently, any interruption required Hora to redo merely a small part of her work on a watch, the assembly or subassembly just worked on. With a chance of interruption of one in a hundred, Simon calculates that it would take Tempus 4,000 times as long as Hora to complete a watch.

The implication is that the evolution of a complex system of many interdependent elements is much more likely if it occurs as the result of the emergence of successive subsystems than in the absence of such hierarchical structuring. The chances that ten elements with some affinity combine into an interrelated unit before a disruptive event pulls them apart are evidently much greater than the chances that a thousand elements combine, and so are the chances that ten units combine into a system and ten of these into a larger system. Complex systems involving thousands or even millions of elements probably exist only because they have hierarchical structures of successive levels of subsystems. Simon uses this theoretical principle to explain biological evolution, problem solving, large empires, and complex systems generally.

The relations between elements within substructures are generally stronger than those between different substructures, since the stronger connections within are what distinguishes the various substructures. Simon notes that the weaker interdependence among subunits makes the larger system nearly decomposable and justifies treating the subunits as independent cases and restricting an investigation to their internal properties and structures, realizing, of course, that doing so ignores the external influences on them and the larger system. The significant relations within substructures may be different in kind as well as in degree from those among substructures. The forces that govern the relations between elementary particles in atoms differ from those governing the links between atoms in molecules, and sociable interaction affects the network structure of work groups but economic transactions, not sociable ones, are most relevant for the structure of relations between firms or between nations. In the study of macrosystems, it is naturally impossible to trace the relations and properties of all elements in subsystems, and neither is it necessary, because the components and relations among components of macrosystems differ from those within their subsystems. These emergent properties of macrostructures are the focus of the study of them.

In a recent paper, Wallace (1979) defines social phenomena as "interorganism behavior regularity" and suggests that Simon's concept of hierarchies of expanding structuredness can be applied to all three aspects of this definition. Sociology is concerned with *regularities* in the *behavior* between *organisms,* and each of these terms has a hierarchical structure. For organisms, the scope of the collectivity under consideration can range from a dyad to a society. The behavior being examined can range from elemental acts—a greeting, a vote—to molar syndromes of social action—a marriage, a strike, the manufacture of cars. Regularities, finally, may differ in the wavelength of recurrence and the complexity of the rhythm; interaction patterns in discussion groups exemplify brief regularities, economic fluctuations in societies longer ones. Wallace raises the question of how the levels of structure in these three dimensions are related.

Whatever the units of sociological analysis under investigation, two concepts can be distinguished from these units themselves: the larger social contexts in which the various units exist, and the properties that characterize their internal structures. *Social context* refers to the more encompassing level of structure. As a matter of fact, contexts on several levels and in more than one dimension can often be distinguished. Thus, the contexts of local government offices are their district agencies, state departments, and state governments; and, in another dimension, their local communities, metropolitan areas, states, regions, and the entire country.

Social structures on every level have emergent *properties,* by which I refer to attributes that characterize the unit of analysis as a whole and not its separate subunits. One of these is the pattern of social relations among subunits. For instance, sociometric networks are attributes of group structure and not attributes of the individual members of groups. Similarly, the interdependence among specialized departments in an organization characterizes the organization itself, not individual departments. A second set of emergent properties of social structure results from the differences among subunits and the population distributions among them, which find expression in various forms of heterogeneity and inequality. For instance, communities differ in ethnic and religious heterogeneity, in educational and economic inequality. Obviously, social heterogeneity and inequality cannot characterize individuals, only collectivities. A third emergent property of social structure is the degree to which differences in several dimensions intersect or overlap, as indicated by their correlation. Are the best swimmers in summer camp also the best ball players? How different are income distributions of men and women? What are the educational differences among ethnic groups? Is a community's religious composition related to its division of labor? These, too, are questions that can only be answered for collectivities, since one cannot compute the relationships between variables for an individual.

The expanding compass of social structures involves a shift in units of analysis from one perspective, as just noted, but it involves a change in the conceptual relevance of the same phenomenon from another perspective. The same entities—say, cities—can be part of the social context, the units of analysis, and properties of units of analysis in three studies with different substantive concerns and units of analysis—for example, an investigation of ethnic neighborhoods, one of American cities, and one of urbanization of American states. Government agencies are the social context in studies of career patterns of civil servants; they are the units of analysis in studies of centralization of public bureaucracies; and their features and interrelations are properties of societies in comparative studies of nations. New theoretical issues become apparent with these shifts in focus.

Expanding Compass

The unit of analysis in most social research is the individual person, which is not a design well suited for developing and testing theories of social structure, because the focus on individuals diverts attention from the systematic study of properties of social structure, which are those properties of collectivities that do not characterize individual members but only their combination and relations. To be sure, social research, in contrast to psychological investigations, generally examines the influences of various social conditions on the attitudes or behavior of individuals, which indicates that conditions in the social structure are not ignored. Although not ignored, neither can social structures be explained in such studies that treat them as social contexts of other units of analysis. For in the investigation of contextual influences—whether on individuals or on social units—the contextual characteristics are conditions assumed to be given and not the object of explanation. Whereas social contexts have a structure, the analysis of that structure requires a new study design in which the compass is enlarged and what had been the context is now the unit of analysis.

The narrowest social unit is the small face-to-face group, as illustrated by Cooley's primary group, whether family, friendship clique, or work group. Its components are individuals, and the basic property defining the group structure is the network of relations among them. Actually, this is a set of properties rather than a single one, because numerous aspects of social relations can be distinguished, such as liking, respecting, consulting, helping, arguing, contact frequency. The study of group networks has advanced far beyond Moreno's (1934) sociometry in several directions—network analysis (Barnes, 1954; Mitchell, 1969), graph theory (Harary et al., 1965), and block models (White et al., 1976). A second set of group properties involves the composition of the group, notably the differences in attributes individuals bring to the group and the different roles that develop in social interaction. A third set pertains to the extent to which various relevant attributes of individuals are related—for example, whether differences among members in ethnic background and bowling skill are related or unrelated.

Although background attributes of members influence their roles in the group, they do so primarily by influencing their social relations, which are the source of role distinctions of group members. The internal psychological states of members are not properties of group structure and are thus ignored in analyzing that structure, even though they indirectly influence it by affecting the behavior that is involved in social interaction. Taking what motivates the partners to engage in social relations as given, structural inquiry analyzes the patterns of these relations, their connections with the group's composition and role structure, and their significance for collective action. Whereas a group consists of nothing but its members in the literal sense, it has observable properties that refer to the group as a whole and cannot be observed when its members are examined separately, namely, the relations among members, the differences among them, and the relationships between the various differences among them; these emergent properties are what characterizes the social structure.

Small groups exist in a great variety of social contexts, and the same group is often affected by several contexts. The composition of a group is governed by its social contexts. In schools that are ethnically homogeneous, few friendship groups will be ethnically mixed; and in cultures with strong ethnic prejudice, there will be few mixed friendships even if the schools are ethnically integrated. The relations in a group depend on the context. In traditional communities where only kinship bonds are trusted, the relations among co-workers will rarely be close. A group's survival chances are affected by the context. Small firms are more likely to go bankrupt in some industries than in others, owing particularly to differences in markets among industries. The context imposes limits on groups. Thus industrial organizations determine the size and composition of the work groups within them. The context may also influence groups indirectly by provoking them into counteraction. Work groups frequently react to organizational pressures to raise productivity by enforcing in their social interaction standards of fairness that restrict output. Such tracing of contextual effects helps explain the group structures but must take the contextual conditions exerting the effects as given and cannot explain *them,* as already noted, because explaining them is possible only in another study in which the former context is the unit of analysis.

There are several directions in which small groups can be aggregated into more and more encompassing social structures. The formalized arrangements of organizations clearly delineate how work groups are combined into increasingly larger organizational segments and into the total organization, from which one could proceed, at least in the economic realm, to markets of autonomous organizations and economic systems of interdependent markets. Evans-Pritchard (1940) describes two lines of growing compass among the Nuer. Families are combined into narrower and these into broader lineages, which compose the twenty clans in Nuer society. This kinship system does not have a parallel in industrial countries, where kinship is not a society-wide institution, but the geographical–political system of the Nuer does. Villages, which comprise hamlets with several huts in each, are organized politically by territory into four levels of tribal sections of increasing scope, the largest of which combine into the twelve Nuer tribes. This is similar to our towns, which are composed of neighborhoods and which compose counties and states. Another illustration for industrial societies is occupation, which ranges from narrow specialties, such as neurosurgeon, to the broad dichotomy of manual–nonmanual. The social structures on every level have emergent properties, which have been defined as the relations among subunits, the differences among them, and the overlap of the differences in various dimensions. We shall not examine the properties and contexts of every level but turn to those of the highest levels of structure, communities and societies, reserving the discussion of organization—an intermediate level—for later.

The major subunits of a society or community are the large groups and strata into which its population can be divided, such as ethnic groups, educational strata, religious groups, and socioeconomic strata. As the examples illustrate, a population can be divided into groups on the basis of numerous different dimensions. Groups generated by any and all of the dimensions that are socially recognized and used to make distinctions among people are considered subunits.[1] Since social relations, as I conceive of them, depend on actual social interaction between persons, groups cannot, strictly speaking, have social relations, only their members can. By social relations between groups I refer, accordingly, to the rate of association between their members, including the rate of intermarriage, the average number of dyadic social contacts of any kind (greeting, gossiping, kissing, coitus), and the average amount of time persons in one group spend in contact with those in the other. Hence, the first type of emergent property of the structure of a society are the rates of intergroup relations, remembering that these can refer to numerous dimensions of group division and to various criteria of social relations. In-group relations are not so relevant for the analysis of the structure of societies or communities as intergroup relations. One exception is the variation in the density of in-group relations, which is indicative of group differences in social cohesion and in-group pressures.

The differences among groups in a community or society are a second type of emergent property of its structure. One such difference has just been noted. In many respects, however, the same groups are found in most communities of the same country and in most societies, at least those that are similar in economic development. Some members of all major religious

---

[1] Evidently, I refer by group here not to a collectivity all of whose members are in direct social contact with each other but to much larger groupings of people that are socially distinguished. In-group relations are taken into account in my concept of group, since I would not consider a category of persons a group unless in-group relations were more prevalent than out-group relations. Although the term "group" is sometimes confined to collectivities whose members have direct social relations with one another, doing so makes all groups small groups. Those who do not like my usage may substitute the term "significant social category" whenever I use "group."

groups live in all likelihood in nearly every American city, and all major occupational groups are undoubtedly represented in every highly industrialized society and probably in most less developed ones too. But this does not mean that there are no structural differences. While all societies have professionals, some have much fewer than others. A generic difference among groups of all kinds in all societies and communities is that they vary in size. Moreover, the size distribution of a population among various groups in a given dimension indicates the degree of heterogeneity in this dimension. If most people are farmers, there is little occupational heterogeneity. The more evenly the labor force is distributed among many different occupations, the greater the occupational heterogeneity, and the same principle applies to ethnic heterogeneity, religious heterogeneity, and any other form of heterogeneity.

Whereas important differences among nominal groups are reflected in the population's heterogeneity, the important issue about differences among hierarchical strata is how much inequality they manifest. If most of a country's wealth is concentrated in few hands, inequality is great. Generally, the more unevenly a resource—wealth or power or income or education—is distributed among ranked strata, the greater is the inequality.[2] In short, various forms of heterogeneity and inequality are emergent structural characteristics of societies and communities, characteristics that represent the two generic differences or kinds of social differentiation among groups and strata.[3]

A third type of emergent property of a community's or society's structure is the extent to which the groups and strata distinguished by different criteria for partitioning the population overlap or intersect. If every criterion for classifying people yields the same subunits—empirically an impossibility—overlap is perfect and all differences among people are perfectly correlated. If group membership in terms of any one criterion is completely independent of group membership in terms of any other criterion—also an impossible extreme—intersection is maximal and group differences are uncorrelated. For example, education and occupational status are highly correlated, whereas sex and ethnic affiliation are virtually unrelated.[4] This means that there is much overlap between educational and occupational strata but that sex differences intersect ethnic differences. Strong correlations of several dimensions, which find expression in much overlap, consolidate social positions, reinforce social distances, and inhibit intergroup relations. Multiple intersecting dimensions, in contrast, imply that people in different groups

---

[2] The boundaries between strata are usually arbitrary. The arguments in the text hold wherever the boundaries are drawn and, indeed, without drawing any boundaries but simply working with a status ranking or continuum.

[3] Measures of dispersion are operational indicators of these structural characteristics.

[4] The correlation between education and occupational status is positive, of course. Hierarchical differences, as distinguished from nominal ones, can be negatively as well as positively related, though such negative correlations are empirically very rare. A negative relationship between two hierarchical social differences would indicate a low, not high, overlap.

and strata share other memberships and interests, which promotes intergroup relations.

The social context of communities is their society, which exerts much political and economic influence on them. National societies are here considered the most encompassing units of sociological analysis. This seems to conflict with Wallerstein's (1974) historical study that stresses the importance of the world system of interrelated nations, which occupy three distinct positions: a core of economically dominant nations, a periphery of weak nations dependent on the core ones and exploited by them, and a semiperiphery of countries whose dependence on the core is not so great. The world system constitutes the social context of national societies, and I fully agree that a nation's position there governs how this context influences it, for instance, what influence international trade has. Thus, recent research indicates that economic growth is substantially more likely for nations at the core than for those at the periphery or semiperiphery (Snyder and Kick, 1979). Yet there is only one world system, whereas sociological analysis requires numerous cases to derive generalizations about their social structure, which is the reason I think it appropriate to treat the world system as a given social context but do not think it an appropriate unit of sociological analysis.

Organizations as Contexts, Units, and Properties

Most earlier organizational research involved studies *in,* not *on,* organizations. Whether primary concern was with decision making, promotion patterns, attitudes toward combat, productivity, work satisfaction, or absenteeism, the unit of analysis was the individual in her or his role as member of an organization. There were also many studies of the informal organization of workers, with work groups as the units of analysis. Investigations in which individual members or work groups are the units of analysis contribute to our understanding of internal processes in organizations but cannot explain the overall structure of organizations. They can only treat the organization as the context of the work groups and employees under study.

Actually, however, investigations of contextual influences were rarely undertaken in this research tradition, and those that were were limited to the influences of variations in conditions within one organization and generally ignored effects of differences among organizations, because studies usually collected data only in a single organization. To analyze the influences on individuals of attributes characterizing the organization as a whole—say, its hierarchy of authority—requires a different research design which examines a sample of persons working in different organizations. An illustration is Kohn's (1971) study of the contextual influences on employees of more or less bureaucratized organizations, as indicated by differences in their hierarchies. He finds that people working in multilevel bureaucracies are, surprisingly, less rigid and more intellectually flexible than those employed in less bureaucratic organizations.

Large organizations constitute the context of their organizational subunits as well as of their individual employees. Major subunits of organizations—divisions of corporations, schools of universities, bureaus of government departments—usually have considerable autonomy without being completely independent, the degree of autonomy depending on the extent to which authority is decentralized. Two examples of contextual influences of universities on their professional schools are (Blau et al., 1979): the more affluent a university, the greater is the emphasis on research in its professional schools; and universities with better libraries have professional schools that obtain more grants and other external funds than schools in other universities. The two findings can be interpreted together. Ample libraries imply superior academic investments, quite possibly not only in books but also in other equipment, and affluent universities can undoubtedly afford superior scholarly and scientific facilities, which attract better faculties and students than are attracted to poorer universities with inferior libraries and other academic facilities. Superior academic conditions and colleague climates in their university context foster emphasis on research in professional schools and improve chances of success in soliciting outside funds for research and training.

The study of the structure of formal organizations requires that they be the unit of analysis. It is hardly more than a score of years that quantitative research with such a focus has been carried out, although Weber and Michels treated organizations as units of their theoretical analysis. One set of emergent properties of organizations consists of the various dimensions of differentiation of the work force. Examples are the division of labor, vertical differentiation into hierarchical levels, horizontal differentiation into major functional departments and sections within departments, geographical branches, ratio of supervisory to nonsupervisory personnel, ratio of staff to line.

Another kind of emergent property refers to the interrelations among components, such as interdependence and, particularly, centralization of authority and decision making, including autonomy of subunits and closeness of supervision. Thompson (1967: 54–59) distinguishes three types of interdependence of increasing complexity: pooled interdependence, when the performance of the organization depends on that of all its parts but the performance of any part does not depend on that of any other, as in a retail business with branch stores; sequential interdependence, when the output of any unit is a necessary input for another, as on an assembly line; and reciprocal interdependence, when groups are mutually dependent, as nurses and physicians in a hospital. In my own work, I have been especially concerned with the connections between an organization's size, structural differentiation, and administrative ratio. Although size and differentiation are positively related, they have opposite effects on the administrative ratio; large size reduces whereas a differentiated structure increases the ratio of administrative personnel in organizations. I have suggested a theory to explain these and related empirical regularities in terms of administrative investments and feedbacks engendered by administrative problems (Blau, 1974: 297–348).

Formal organizations are nowadays not only the social context in which most people spend their working lives, and major institutions the understanding of which requires treating them as units of analysis, but also important properties of communities and societies which help shape their structure. To study the problems this poses, it is not sufficient to consider organizations as open systems and take external influences on them into account. It is necessary to extend the compass to larger social structures as units of analysis, of which organizations are subunits in one (though not the only) dimension and the interrelations and differences among organizations are emergent properties. Beginnings along these lines have already been made. Some students of organizations adopt the view of population ecology and conceive of populations of organizations as interdependent systems in competition for resources, with the growth and survival of organizations being governed by natural selection (Hannan and Freeman, 1977; Aldrich, 1979). Research on interlocking directorates of corporations (summarized in Aldrich, 1979: 340–50) also deals with the network of social relations that tie organizations into a larger system. Although analyzing numerous organizations, from the perspective of the system of organizations all these are case studies of a single structure of interdependent organizations.

Systematic knowledge about the role of organizations in contemporary societies must be based on comparative studies of nations as units of analysis, with various aspects of each country's organizations, notably their interrelations and differences, as the properties of nations. There are no such studies, because the data needed for them do not exist. Collecting these data would be difficult, though not impossible. A few organizational properties of nations may be mentioned.

Initially, work organizations with employees would be distinguished from voluntary associations with participants. Work organizations would be classified by type, perhaps on the basis of industry. Examples of their emergent properties are: the differences in average size among types and the total variation in the size of work organizations; the differences in average wage among types and the total variation in wages; the differences in average annual budget among types and the total variation in budgets; the share of the market of the largest organizations of every type for which this is applicable. A basic question to be answered by the research envisioned is how different aspects of a nation's organizational structure are related to other properties of its structure, as manifest in various forms of heterogeneity, various forms of inequality, and the degrees of intersection of various dimensions of social differences.

Voluntary associations should not be ignored either, because they help integrate the people in a society by directly linking the participants in the same organizations and indirectly those belonging to different organizations that have some members in common. McPherson (1980) suggests that the average number of links necessary to connect any two persons can serve as index of the contribution of organizational participation to social integration, which depends on the number, size, and heterogeneity of voluntary associations as well as on the average number to which a person belongs and the size of the population. Another important issue is the role of organizations in society's power structure, which is the final topic to be discussed.

Organizations and Power Structure

Domination in modern society is largely exercised by and through formal organizations. This idea is implicit in Weber's analysis of traditional, charismatic, and administrative authority, except that in the contemporary world bureaucratic structures are the roots not only of authority but of both basic types of social power he juxtaposes, "domination by virtue of a constellation of interests (in particular: by virtue of a position of monopoly), and domination by virtue of authority" (Weber, 1968: 943). Before explicating this point, the difference between two kinds of organizations just alluded to needs to be specified.

There are fundamental distinctions between work organizations, whose members are employees, and voluntary associations, most of whose members are not, though they often employ a staff. A formal difference that affects the procedures of analysis pertains to the number of affiliations. All persons in the labor force, and an increasing proportion of the total adult population, belong to one and only one work organization, at least as far as their major job is concerned. Thus, the labor force can be classified by work organizations. In contrast, individuals may belong to no voluntary association or a considerable number. Hence, people cannot be classified in a single dimension by their voluntary association membership, but they can be characterized by the number and kinds of these associations to which they belong. A crucial substantive difference for modern power structures is that work organizations are a major source of power whereas voluntary associations are important means for implementing power.

The two main types of power, according to Weber, are economic control and administrative authority, both of which have their source today largely in top positions in formal organizations, particularly in industrialized societies. The case of authority is self-evident. Most employees exercise no authority but are subject to the authority of others; middle managers in large and bosses in small organizations have some authority over subordinates; and top executives of large organizations have a great deal of command authority. Even domination through coercive force—illustrated by army coups and military dictatorships—is exercised, not by waving a gun, but by occupying senior positions in military organizations, which enables a person to command large-scale use of arms.

Economic power entails control over great resources, the allocation of which affects the lives of many people, and most of such power in industrial societies is also exercised by senior officers of big corporations and government departments. This assertion is often criticized in the false belief that the substantial wealth of most senior corporation executives is counterevidence, and under the misapprehension that Marxist theory needs to be defended by insisting on the position that economic power can rest only on ownership (Zeitlin, 1974). But the question is not whether rich people are more likely than poor ones to become top executives of large corporations, which is taken for granted; the point is that in such a position they exercise much more power than their own wealth would command, and without such a position they exercise much less.

A simple indicator of authority is the sheer number of persons under the jurisdiction of a manager. Of course, this is a crude measure, leaving out various sources of authority, such as the legislator's, the bishop's, and the welfare worker's; and it ignores variations in the extent of compliance and discipline, for example, the greater authority over subordinates of the general than the university president. The basic measure might be weighted to take at least part of these differences into account. A possible index of economic control is the amount of organizational resources that a manager is authorized to allocate at his discretion without consulting a superior (Jaques, 1956). It is expected that administrative authority and economic control are highly correlated, not merely within organizations, but for entire societies. If this is the case, an even cruder indication of power may suffice, based solely on an executive's position and the size of the organization, however measured. Power is greatly concentrated, and the growth of organizations concentrates it further. Which form of government reduces the concentration of power? Does diminishing income inequality reduce it? How does ethnic heterogeneity affect it? Has it decreased or increased in this country during this century? There are no data to answer these questions, which leaves plenty of room for ideological disputes.

Although most people have very little power, there are so many of them that they together have much potential power, but realizing this potential necessitates becoming organized for collective action. Powerful individuals also join in organizations to implement their strength in power struggles. Many voluntary associations have the explicit purpose to further the interests of their members by engaging in collective action and participating in the political process. Political parties and unions are not the only examples; others are the National Association of Manufacturers, the American Medical Association, Common Cause, and the National Association for the Advancement of Colored People, to name just a few. Participation in voluntary associations that have no political objectives, like religious organizations, may nevertheless contribute to political efficacy by providing opportunities for mutual influence and collective action, as illustrated by the role of churches in the civil rights movement. A major reason is that nonpolitical associations are linked with political ones through common memberships. A procedure for analyzing these linkages of voluntary associations has been suggested by Breiger (1974).

A rectangular matrix is generated with different persons in the rows and different voluntary associations in the columns. The binary entries in the cells indicate whether an individual belongs to an organization (one) or not (zero). The matrix reveals the number of organizational memberships of every person (in the row sums), the size of the various organizations (in the column sums), and the number of links between any two organizations (by matrix multiplication). In contrast to conventional sociometry, a link is not a social relation but a person, whose memberships in two (or more) organizations link them. Of course, such a matrix can be constructed only for a limited number of persons and organizations—for example, an elite's formal participation or the interlocking directorates of a country's largest corporations.

Whereas it is impossible to produce this kind of matrix for a large city or a total society, which would entail millions of rows, important features of the network it represents can be estimated from survey data, as McPherson (1980) shows. Specifically, the total number of links between organizations can be estimated from the size of the population and the average rate of participation in organizations; this can be done for various subpopulations on which data are available, such as social classes or ethnic groups; and network distances can be calculated, which indicate to how many others a person is linked through organizational affiliations and how densely linked organizations are.

Substantial class differences in organizational participation have existed for at least half a century, as numerous studies reveal (Lynd and Lynd, 1929; Williams et al., 1973). Poor people belong to few if any voluntary associations—usually only their church and possibly their union—while persons in the middle class tend to belong to several, often including some political organizations. Many voluntary associations, though not all, are socioeconomically homogeneous, containing mostly members within a limited range of economic circumstances. Class differences in organizational participation have a multiplicative effect on organizational linkages, owing to the class homogeneity of most voluntary associations. A middle-class organization has more extensive links to other organizations, and these, being also largely middle class, have in turn more extensive links to one another and to still other organizations, than is the case for a working-class organization and the fewer organizations with which it is linked and which are mostly working class.

Middle-class organizations are much more densely linked than working-class organizations. Fewer steps of organizational linkage are necessary to connect most members of the middle class or any two of them than to connect most members of the working class or any two of them. Not so many persons in the middle as in the working class are isolated from the organizational network. These statements apply if the two classes are of equal size, and a fortiori when the middle class is smaller. The small size of an elite greatly enhances the density of the connections among its organizations. To be sure, if working-class organizations are larger than those of higher strata, it would reduce these differences, but large organizations would simultaneously attenuate the ties common membership engenders.

Strong organizational connections facilitate mobilizing resources in political contests, economic conflicts, and power struggles. Dense organizational networks give the middle class and, especially, the elite great competitive advantages in the political arena and in the economic markets by enhancing their power. Note that this conclusion is reached purely on the basis of a formal analysis of organizational participation and without taking into consideration the larger economic resources an elite can muster.

Conclusions

In my view, the prime objective of sociology is the study of social structure and the processes that generate and change it, which implies that our units of analysis are collectivities, not persons, because only collectivities have social structures. Collectivities range in compass from small groups to total societies, and which ones are selected as units of analysis for research or theory depends on the substantive problems of concern. Smaller collectivities combine into larger ones in repeated steps, so that there are successive levels of more encompassing social structure. The structure on every level has emergent properties, which term refers to variables that do not characterize the component subunits separately but only their combination in the larger collectivity under investigation.

The three main kinds of emergent property are the relations among subunits, the differences among them, and the relationships of their differences in various dimensions. For a small group, the three are illustrated by the network of interpersonal relations, differences in roles among members, and the correlation of relevant background characteristics of individuals. Illustrations for an entire society are rates of ethnic intermarriage, religious heterogeneity or income inequality, and the degree to which differences in occupation intersect or overlap with race differences. Whatever the units of analysis, the encompassing collectivities are their social context. Tracing contextual influences can clarify the structure of the units of analysis but cannot explain the social context, which requires a shift in focus to make what was the context the new unit of analysis.

Formal organizations can be treated as social context in some studies, units of analysis in others, and properties of societies in still others. Workers or work groups are the units of analysis in most organizational research, which means that organizations themselves—their properties and structures—are merely the social contexts assumed as given and not the objects of explanation. Organizations are clearly the units of analysis to be explained in Weber's theoretical study of bureaucratic structure, as well as in recent quantitative research on organizations and their structure, as exemplified by my work and that of the Aston School (Pugh et al., 1968). Systematic investigation of the important role of organizations in societies, however, requires further expanding the compass to nations as units of analysis and treating organizations and their interrelations as properties characterizing nations.[5] As an illustration of this approach, I noted the significance of some organizations for the concentration of power and that of others for class differences in the potential for organizing collective action in power conflicts.

[5] Special provisions for multinational corporations would have to be made.

6

Institutional Control Over Education: Origins and Effects

John W. Meyer

MODERN EDUCATION is usually studied as a system of organized interaction—a network of differentiated positions and relationships. Here is the language of the modern sociology of education: there are school organizations and their student and teacher role incumbents. The students are seen as a socially organized interacting group, progressing through the system and affected by the instruction and interaction it formally and informally provides.

With this perspective, educational effects on student learning and attainment are studied well. The organization itself is studied—the student, teacher, and administrator roles and their linkages. But one crucial topic is faced less well—discussions of the *origins* of the system and its components lapse into theoretical clichés, hypotheses at odds with the available data, and anecdotal forms of evidence.

This failure occurs partly for methodological reasons—studies of educational origins and changes often require difficult historical and comparative research designs. The failure is also theoretical: conceptions of education as only interactional or organizational neglect the institutional or societal components of its structure and history. In this chapter, I discuss education as an institutional system rather than as an organizational one, and show how an institutional view would improve research on educational origins and

☐ The research for this project was supported by funds from the National Institute of Education (Grant No. OB-NIE-G-78-0212). The analysis and conclusions do not necessarily reflect the views or policies of this organization.

changes. Finally, I suggest how an institutional perspective would alter our notions of educational organization and effects.

Education as an Institution

The distinction between interaction systems, organizations, and institutions is partly artificial and certainly relative—the issue is which levels of social life are seen as central. If education is mainly an interaction system, central characteristics and effects depend on the interdependent activities of students and teachers. It is also implied that the activities are chosen by these local actors as decision makers. Calling attention to education as an interaction system emphasizes both the choices of actors and the impact of these choices on each other. For instance, teachers' classroom choices and their efforts on students become research problems.

Conceptions of education as an organizational system depict these choices as defined and constrained by organizationally structured roles: the roles of students and teachers in various subjects, for instance. Now the system is one, not simply of interaction, but of interaction within a formal or informal structure. American organizational thought tends to assume that the important effects of this structure still come from actual activity that it creates. We study, for instance, the effects of school organizational resources or decisions on student outcomes. There is a more cynical line in theories of educational organization—that decisions may be structured organizationally, but that the formal decisions or labels used are more important than the actual interaction and activity they affect. Here the organizational system is a system of authority in its own right, disconnected from ongoing interaction and activity: schools are seen as creating graduates rather than learning.

Seeing education as an institution involves two changes. First, the idea is used that the crucial decisions are established in the wider society. (Local actors may not even approve or disapprove, but simply take for granted the binding social reality of the roles [Berger and Luckmann, 1967].) Second, the notion is employed that main aspects of education lie in the societal labeling or classification of activities and actors, not only in these elements as part of a system of interaction. In an institutional view, education is centralized in its controls, and also involves much formal authority or ritual meaning. This point of view emphasizes the shared meaning and value of education—and their legitimation and objectification in society.

Both of these aspects of the institutional view of education are valid, and it deserves more attention in the research literature. First, decisions are highly centralized in modern societies and states (Ramirez and Rubinson, 1979). The whole structure of levels of education and degrees is nationally standardized. All elementary schools have third grades, and completion of any one is given standard meaning. So is the list of authoritative curricular topics, although some local or state variation exists in the United States. The legitimate types of schools, and the accreditational standards defining each, are nationally defined in most modern systems. Societal rules define teacher roles, the functions of these roles, and the credentialing standards applicable to each. General rules assign young persons to particular student roles, and define the conditions under which they may receive occupational credentials. The term "education" itself is given great cultural meaning and value, and a standardized interpretation.

Second, institutional definitions in the system are more crucial in their consequences than are particular activities or interactions. The survival of a school and the success of its students depend more on proper accreditation in the eyes of all relevant constituents than on any activities or interactions. A student desiring to enter college needs proper completion of the twelfth grade more than any particular knowledge or activity. In completing the twelfth grade (or a college major), it is more important to have completed courses in the required categories than to have experienced or learned from particular activities or interactions. To be a teacher, it is more important to have the proper educational labels leading to formal certification than to have learned how to teach well. From inspecting activity or interaction, there is no way to be sure a given person is a student, a graduate, or a teacher. One must know the institutional label itself, not the properties or competencies of the actor.

Institutionally, education is a set of rules defining categories and linking them together, and a set of organizations and interactions that apply the categories in particular instances. There are rules defining types of students, legitimate passage from one type to the next, proper curricula and teaching personnel for each type, occupational certificational eligibility for students completing each type, and accrediting schools. These rules or understandings make up a society-wide ideology about the sources and processing of personnel for the modern order (Meyer, 1977).

Research on Factors Affecting Emergence and Change of Educational Systems

Where do these systems come from ? What produces change in their components or organization? There are few careful explanations for the most obvious facts about education in our own society. Why did mass education develop so early in America? Why did so many forms of professional education develop in the late nineteenth century, and why did these expand so rapidly?

Most of the available explanations are social organizational and interactional in character. They explain national institutional change in three steps, analogous to what Stinchcombe (1968) called "demographic explanation" at the individual level:

Step 1. Large-scale social changes generated a set of specific interests for more training or socialization of the young to meet a new need.

Step 2. These interests, often copying each other, succeeded in constructing local schooling organizations that met the need. Sometimes they built these through national or state action.

Step 3. As more and more local schooling organizations were created, pressures for standardization and unification along more institutionalized lines developed and triumphed, generating national rules.

Consider some recent research along these lines:

1. One line of research treats educational expansion, especially at higher levels, as resulting from status group competition (Ben-David, 1977; Ben-David and Zloczower, 1962, 1963–64; Collins, 1971, 1977, 1979). The idea is that as education becomes required for entry into positions in society, various status groups compete for access to the system to improve the life chances of their children. In systems with more such competition, education tends to expand.

In a related argument, the modern expansion of education in so many countries results from their elites' competition in a wider world system (Cohen, 1970, 1975). Competition is not inevitably involved here; nations may simply be attempting to join the wider system.

Linked to this tradition is the recent work at Yale by Clark and his associates (Clark, 1977; Van de Graaff et al., 1978) on the ways different higher educational systems respond to pressures for expansion. Organizational attributes of the extent system are seen as restricting and channeling its ability to respond to competitive (and other) pressures.

2. Another body of work treats educational expansion and organization as a reflection of capitalist social organization and structural forms, or as—in contemporary Marxist phraseology—a means of reproduction of the class structure (Bowles and Gintis, 1976; Field, 1976; Katz, 1968, 1975; Tyack, 1974). This discussion has been developed mainly by historians, but sociologists have tended to take it quite seriously.

3. The lines of thought above are not devoid of functionalism, though the functions involved tend to be those of special subgroups, not of society itself. A broader functionalist line—probably the most common one in the field—is that societal modernization and complexity create requirements for a more highly socialized population, which are met by the creation of a specialized and extended educational system. The correlations between societal development and educational expansion are indeed very high, both historically and at present. Most of the thinking about the links involved (especially in economics) has emphasized economic manpower requirements as the main

factor. But some theories have emphasized other modern requirements for broader socialization, including political and cultural as well as economic factors (Bendix, 1964). Other theories have called attention to social changes in demographic structure (Ariès, 1962) or family organization (Eisenstadt, 1956).

4. Still another theory calls attention to the rise of the modern nation-state and its demand for loyal and participatory citizens: large-scale and bureaucratic state forms directly linked to individual membership outmode more traditional socialization, and make necessary organizations that will tie the socializee directly to the nation and state. Modern educational systems rise with state power (Reisner, 1927) and are usually creatures of the state from the start (Ramirez and Rubinson, 1979).

All of these lines of thought tend to run into evidentiary problems. Economic functionalisms—whether of the right or of the left—ignore the weakness of the association between the modern industrial system and educational expansion. Scotland expanded its educational system long before England—the first industrial society—did. The agrarian United States expanded education long before much industrialization took place (Meyer et al., 1979). Prussia was an early constructor of mass education—again, in a rural economy—and France was relatively early, too. Within the United States, much available evidence has it that mass enrollments were not higher in urban and industrial areas than in rural ones, the South aside (Meyer et al., 1979).

Among the developing countries, narrow economic theories, whether of industrialism or the power of the capitalist class, break down completely. All sorts of nation-states now expand education rapidly, whether they are economically developed or not. Amount or kind of economic development is a minor causal factor (Meyer et al., 1977; Coombs, 1968). The economy in general, or the capitalist class in particular, may affect the *organization* of education, but they cannot easily account for the *rise* and *expansion* of the system.

The status group competition theory has the same problem (Collins, 1977). Systems with more ethnic diversity are, if anything, less likely to generate mass education (Meyer et al., 1977). The competition thesis may explain the later evolution of the system under various conditions, but does not explain its rise well. In reality, the theory does not address this issue. Why would competition determine the selection of *education* over other methods of status allocation? This problem also arises with attempts to generalize from the thesis of Bowles and Gintis (1976) on capitalist uses of American education to an explanation of the rise of the system.

A further evidentiary problem has to do with the *process* by which the system is created and expanded. Specific social interests are usually seen as pressing the issue—interests linked to the economy, the state, or even the family system. This does not explain varying situations in which both strong (e.g., Prussia or France) and weak (e.g., Scotland or the United States) states act in the same way. In the contemporary period, variations in state structure have little to do with rates of expansion (Meyer et al., 1977). States aside, many different economic structures and interest combinations end up pursuing the same general end of educational expansion.

Modern educational systems arose as ideological creations, pursued by modernizing social movements that ultimately used varying organizational forms. These movements were institutional and societal in that they took the stance of representing the future of all of society, not simply past or present immediate interests. The action involved was highly collective action, not only the slow aggregation of interests and local organizations. In America, for instance, education spread less through state or interest organizations than through a nationwide set of linked social movements—often religious in their basis, but organized around a secular millennial future (Meyer et al., 1979; Kaestle and Vinovskis, 1979).

Ideological and social movements have many interest group bases, but the process by which interests construct ideological systems is complex, and highly dependent on institutional availability. In the course of becoming diverted to the ideological or institutional level, interests change and take on new forms. For instance, it is little in the narrow economic logic of capitalism to create expensive mass education which might expand worker expectations and unrest: capitalism as an *economic* system can find easier and more docile solutions to the problems of labor control and labor socialization than universal education (note the restriction of education in southern agrarian captialism, for example). The capitalism that may help create universal mass education is at the institutional level—hegemonic capitalism—and may well conflict with the interests of members and groups in the capitalist class itself.

In developing countries, the general point is clear. States organize in the world state system around ideological futures filled with progress and equality. Education is part of the generalized and institutionalized national plan for the future, not a response to present needs. To some extent the narrow interests of the state elite in creating a population more loyal to the nation are involved, but the larger choice is for future progress in the world system.

We are discussing, thus, the question of the structure of the broader polity or culture within which collective action building a mass educational system occurs. Leaving aside social organizational factors that might affect such a polity, let us consider what fundamental rules might be involved.

1. *Individualism:* A mass educational system instructing and processing individuals makes much more sense in a society in which action is seen to come from individuals rather than from group structures or exogenous forces. All modern systems—including the most highly socialized ones—are individualist in this sense: action and value are seen to arise from individual choice.

2. *Personality:* Setting aside the early period of life for mass education is more plausible if individuals are seen as having continuity over time, and if in-

dividuals are seen as primordial or constitutive members of society. If individual biography has no continuity, why have early instruction? If the individual is not distinctive or primordial, but is entirely moldable by social exigencies, why not create directly the required social controls?

3. *Rational Universalism:*

   a. At the individual level: before the standardized institutional processing of individuals is justified, they must all be seen as, at bottom, alike, and as subject to the same general (i.e., educational or developmental) laws.
   b. In nature: standardized instruction on action in nature makes more sense if nature is generally lawful.
   c. In transcendental authority: the lawfulness of individual life is sustained by linking all to a common transcendental authority.

4. *Society as Purposive and the Idea of Progress:* Why separate children from ongoing adult institutions and subject them to a special one? Because present institutions are not enough—the children are to live in a new constructed world that is orderly and rational, not in the old and contaminated one. The conception of education as a defensive measure against social control breakdown (Bailyn, 1960) misses the optimism associated with the rise of modern education in both old and new nations. A brave new world is to be built through education.

We are discussing a polity, or cultural system, deeply infused with the logic of the world capitalist system—whether it contains the standard social relations of capitalism or not (e.g., rural America in the nineteenth century, and the developing nations now). This polity is linked to modern rationalized political conceptions of action and progress, whether or not the forms of the strong modern state have been built up. It is linked to universalistic and rationalistic religious systems, whatever the organization of polity and economy (e.g., Scotland).

Research on the origins of modern mass education should attend more directly to institutional considerations. These systems are highly legitimated societal institutions—they are not only the products of some manufacturers wanting education for their workers, some mothers for their children, or some state functionaries for their subjects. They are created by collective actors building for society a broad new structure to be inhabited by all children.

ELITE EDUCATION

We have emphasized mass education above, as it is the most distinctive feature of modern education, but modern systems of elite education have some of the same origins. The component of universal equality is weaker here: the rational universalism of the authority created is not. There is more concern with the rules of allocation at the higher levels, although the justifications of the rules are similar to those at the mass level.

Whatever the roles of elite and professional interest groups, the larger societal legitimating frame is of great importance. The principles are the same as with mass education. The regrounding of traditional authority in modern rational universalistic justifications can, even in the absence of much that we would now call knowledge, produce elite educational systems. The construction of new rationalistic forms of social authority tends to call for specialized elite training programs. This is closely related to the modern polity, whether in the form of a strong state (France, Prussia) or a rationalized and universalistic nation dedicated to progress (the United States).

In the contemporary period, these principles are endemic. To an astonishing extent, new nations build in the same elite training programs that are now standard in world culture; the variations depending on local political or economic circumstances, or other social organizational considerations, are quite small (Ramirez and Rubinson, 1979).

Research here is badly needed. Ben-David, Clark, and their students have done some detailed case studies (Ben-David, 1977; Clark, 1977b). But these have limited comparative frames and concentrate on immediate organizational factors. Many others seem to assume that elements of elite education will spring up as soon as there is some useful knowledge. This is naive: many legitimated fields in education have little that can usefully be called knowledge, and little demonstration that what knowledge they do have is needed.

Much modern authority is propped up, not by technical knowledge, but by a certification system. Understanding the evolution of this system is of the greatest importance. The factors discussed above in relation to mass education also shift elite allocation and socialization to expanded elite education: individualism, rational universalism, and the reconstruction of political society around the purposive attainment of progress. But other factors are involved—unlike with mass education, there are clear alternatives to education in the legitimation and allocation of elites. The spread of the political culture of the modern system, combined with the weakness of structural alternatives, may account for the phenomenon at issue. Thus, beyond modern political culture, elite education, and its use in elite selection, should be greater where

1. traditional methods of elite selection are weak (e.g., ethnic groups);
2. a highly legitimized system of diffuse status of class inequalities is not available;
3. the state is not strong enough to legitimate its own elite selection, and indeed to restrict educational expansion (Ben-David and Zloczower, 1963–64; Clark, 1977b); and
4. such other institutions as the economy are organized in rational bureaucracies, and thus require rationalistic justifications of their personnel selection.

These factors may explain the early flowering of elite education in America, despite what Hofstadter (1963) calls the ''anti-intellectualism of American life.'' Traditional bases of elite selection were weak, and a diffuse stratification system (race aside) was delegitimated. State organizations were too weak either to control education or to legitimate their own personnel selection (e.g., with elaborate testing or career-sequence rules). Other institutions, such as industry, with the breakdown of family capitalism and its more traditional methods of elite selection, were organized bureaucratically. Of critical importance, American society was linked to the most rationalistic and individualistic forms of modern world culture.

In contemporary developing nation-states, rapid expansion has undercut alternative methods of elite selection, and the whole world is committed to modern political culture. However, one might still find effects of the factors discussed above: very strong states may slightly restrict elite educational expansion and its extension to new fields. Rates of autonomous societal bureaucratization may have positive effects. Some recent research suggests the greater use of education in status allocation in larger organizations (Stolzenberg, 1978).

SUBSTANTIVE DOMAINS INCORPORATED INTO EDUCATION

Which social domains are incorporated as bodies of knowledge in education? Fields enter mass education as necessary common knowledge, and elite education as legitimized collective authority. What scheme of ideas can help explain what happens here? Professions and interest groups successfully push for entry, but what are the wider factors—the factors that explain why collective society accedes, not why some groups push?

1. The extension of rational universalistic collective authority and jurisdiction (Swanson, 1971) into a given domain—whether in the state or not—makes more likely its educational incorporation. Sociology, with its approved technocratic form, enters; astrology does not. Sexuality as technical and biological enters; sexuality as emotional and aesthetic does not. Sociology and sexuality enter as society and polity assume jurisdiction over related aspects of life—social problems, reproduction, and disease. With the rise of the nation-state system, many matters of national life enter: language, history, and culture.

2. The rationalization of nature, transcendental authority, and the status of the individual bring related issues into the legitimated body of schooled knowledge. Thus, medicine and science, psychology and economics, civics and religion, all enter the system.

3. The absence of alternative justificatory loci for expanding authority increases the prospects for educational incorporation. Sociology, for instance, is

slower to arise when the legitimate command of the state over society is relatively complete and self-contained: it rises in America, with a strong and rationalized national culture, but a weak state. So also arise the peculiar dominance of technocratic economics in America, and the quick development in America of schooled forms of knowledge relating to business administration. Thus occurs the early rise of highly professionalized education, and the extraordinary American expansion of law and medicine.

RESEARCH DESIGNS

The issues we discuss require comparative evidence, and evidence across long periods of time. Consider some examples:

1. Which societies (and when) develop a rationalized national history and insert it in the elementary curriculum?
2. Which societies elaborate in education such measures of individual personality as ability and personality tests? And which societies build psychology into the curriculum more completely?
3. Which societies, and when, create business schools and the associated principles of personnel allocation?
4. Which societies build into their educational systems rationalized subjects dealing technocratically with social problems?
5. More generally, which societies, and in which domains, incorporate educational criteria most completely in personnel allocation?
6. Historically, what explains which societies expanded mass education first?

SUMMARY

Viewing education as an institutional system changes one's view of its origins. We have emphasized institutional, ideological, or cultural aspects of collective society—broadly, the polity—in suggesting lines of inquiry about the origins of modern educational expansion, both at mass and elite levels.

Research on Educational Effects

Most discussions of the effects of education have also used interactional and organizational perspectives. When education is seen as an institutional structure, alternative conceptions become plausible (Meyer, 1977). We discuss effects at the individual, the organizational, and the societal levels.

THE INDIVIDUAL LEVEL

School effects research often proceeds as if only interactional and organizational variables were relevant. A moment's thought tells us that this is not so. An adult, for instance, cannot easily manage the lives of thirty children for a whole working day: parents have trouble with two or three. Yet a *teacher* can supervise thirty *students* for a day without much difficulty. The transformation of the adult into a teacher and the children into students accomplishes much. This is not accomplished by the individual school: the teacher is an agent of a huge institution in society, and the students are members of a standardized nationwide category that controls the meaning of the present for them and that regulates their access to valued futures.

The central proposition of any real sociology of education has received little investigation: *Changing instruction into education increases its power and effectiveness, and mobilizes much more commitment.* The organization of learning for educational credit (and thus success) maximizes effectiveness. Less institutionalized instructional systems have nonattendance, dropout, and sloth: in schools, young persons stay for years and do surprising amounts of work and learning. All the studies comparing youths in school with those outside show that the former learn much more (Holsinger, 1974). Further, some research shows that the more highly the institutional validation of a program, school, or course, the more students learn (Alexander et al., 1978).

Most simply, the institutional structuring of a decision point has enormous effects. Twelfth graders learn to go to college the next year: eleventh graders, no matter what their personality qualities, rarely do. Has there been some hormonal change, or was advice necessary from friends, teachers, or parents, or did some educationally generated learning occur? No, a simple certificational rule with binding power applied. In America most twelfth graders plan to go to college, while in other societies many fewer do. Is this not directly structured by the wider institutional system?

These factors are left out of research on individuals. College-going is studied only among twelfth graders in one country, missing most of the variance in the world. Learning is studied mostly among schools similarly defined in society (high schools or colleges, in America). Such studies should include broader samples: children not in school; children in schools that are not accredited or not defined as part of the main sequence; children in programs (e.g., vocational) not given regularly legitimized definition; children in courses not given regular labels; and so on. They should examine effects on children in different societies: the institutional structuring of the system may have substantial effects.

Research on teaching in the classroom should also be broadened. The institutional system is in part a ritual form (like a baptism or a communion), and it derives its power from such exogenous institutional sources. Viewing it as an interaction system or an organization leads us to dismiss its most central components as meaningless. The literature thus exaggerates—far beyond the weak research results—the positive benefits of individualized instruction (which may weaken for a child the institutional meaning and generality of the work), or small group instruction and discussion (which may have the same effects). Standardized seatwork is taken as evidence of teacher laziness. Sociologists tend to dismiss all the aspects of the classroom that immerse the student in the wider institutional system of legitimate authority as arbitrary authoritarianism. Disciplinary activities, for instance, are treated as evidence of instructional defectiveness. The research findings run against these prejudices: they are discounted by arguments that measures are defective. But the power of the system lies in its ability to absorb a child into the general societal category of fourth-grade student, to get this child to accept the commitment involved, and thus to mobilize the child to do an enormous amount of otherwise uninteresting work, relevant to adult life not to present circumstances.

We need research, in other words, that investigates the effects of education as a ritual structure that transforms a child into a student—a careerist entry into the modern stratification system. The child becomes a résumé, and socializing power is gained.

EFFECTS ON SCHOOLING ORGANIZATIONS

Similarly, research on schooling organizations has not emphasized their institutional status. Educational organizations are seen as weak and ineffective—the teacher is isolated in the classroom, the principal doesn't know what is going on, and so on (see the classic review by Bidwell, 1965). Moralistic views here are comical, when one considers that educational organizations are among the strongest and stablest and best-funded ones in any modern society. If these schools are so decrepit, how does it happen that they have far more stability and survival value than the business organizations technocrats so admire (Meyer, Scott, Deal, 1979)?

Schools succeed organizationally through their conformity with specifications in the institutional environment (Meyer and Rowan, 1978). They are accredited in such terms, and they survive by their accreditational legitimacy. It is possible to see their outward orientation to institutional legitimacy as both the source of their power and the explanation for their internal lack of integration: ritual systems retain more institutional clarity if technical integration is avoided. Contemporary theorists of organizations as loosely coupled systems are coming to this view (Weick, 1976; March and Olsen, 1976; Meyer and Rowan, 1978).

To counterpoise this argument to the more conventional one, consider the following propositions about whether schools survive and retain stability:

Conformity to institutional standards determines a school's organizational ability and survival more than does technical effectiveness in producing desired student outcomes.

Technically effective internal organizational integration tends to lower actual and perceived institutional conformity, and thus to lower a school's prospects for survival and stability.

Perhaps the instructional and coordinated schemes presently advocated by the moral entrepreneurs of the educational system are likely to lower educational organizational success: for instance, effective instructional evaluation; effective use of evaluational data in program design; effective measurement of outcomes; effective control over the curriculum and teaching methods; and effective systems of accounting and management control.

All this is speculative, because there is little research on school characteristics that predicts success and survival in the environment. Technical innovations in schooling organizations are advocated, but researchers treat with incidental regret that these virtuous schemes ran into environmental trouble and were eliminated, or were not implemented, or led to serious difficulties for the school. We need to take a more objective view: what works in terms of school survival, not our private standards of educational effectiveness?

SOCIETAL EFFECTS

There are few empirical studies at the societal level of the effects of education. Partly this is for methodological reasons—longitudinal and comparative designs are required, and this kind of research is difficult.

Part of the problem is intellectual: we can often only envision educational effects on society that arise from the system as an interactional and organizational one. It is supposed that societal effects arise from the changed properties of the individual students, and research shifts down to the individual level (Meyer, 1977). But education can reconstruct society even if the students learn little: they are changed entries into the societal table of organization, and they have authority that is itself partly produced by the educational system. Similarly, even if individuals were greatly affected by education, there might be few societal effects if these individuals are placed back into a more traditional structure. Societal questions, here, require macrosociological data.

A good way to put this issue is to ask the following question: What does it do to members of society, with their own schooling held constant, to expand by mass education the education of everyone else? And what does it do to authority patterns to have newly certified personnel with new authority? As examples, consider two academic fields that, in technical terms, probably have little that should realistically be called knowledge to offer society: economics and sociology. Assume the actual persons who have studied these fields have acquired little. What effect has their incorporation into legitimized bodies of knowledge had on society? A whole host of economic (especially) and social (less) issues have been technicized: treated as subject, not to citizen or elite opinion, but to the special authority of professionals. To societal ability to incorporate economic and social problems issues as policy issues is enhanced—technocratic schemes that would never be adopted by ordinary political processes are taken under consideration.

The argument is simple:

1. The incorporation of bodies of knowledge and certification in educational systems strengthens their authority in the wider polity, and brings the associated domains of social life under collective jurisdiction.
2. The incorporation of bodies of knowledge in the educational system strengthens the elites that manage these domains in society, and thus tends to legitimize new forms of social inequality. But
3. the incorporation of bodies of knowledge into the mass sectors of education tends to legitimize citizen rights and authority.

These propositions illustrate the utility of an institutional line of thought in a research area that has received little attention. It will be a long time before we are able to assess the effects involved: the best we may be able to do now is show, with the analysis over time of societal data, some societal effects of whatever character.

One example of each of the authority enhancing and equality creating functions of education may suffice. It is generally against the rules for functionaries of the American state to offer prayers to the cosmos on behalf of the collectivity. With an educational rationalization and transformation, this becomes legitimate: the American state now funds academically trained and certified engineers to send all sorts of electronic signals out to the putative Higher Intelligences nearer the center of the galaxy. On the other side, political democracy—from many rationalistic points of view an allocation of social authority that is unjustifiable—is probably sustained by mass education that certifies citizen competence: there is a close association between mass education and all forms of citizen mobilization.

Research can more easily be done on the societal effects of particular elite legitimations. What are the effects on state policies of the presence or absence of educationally legitimated elites in various domains? Does the presence of demography and demographers enhance the capacity of the state to take action in control of reproduction? Do agricultural specialists enhance the expansion of state agricultural policy? Do sociologists legitimize collective action dealing with societal problems?

A NOTE ON STUDENTS

One of the most dramatic effects of the modern educational system is the setting aside of a large proportion of the population in the distinctive status category of "student." Perhaps 15 percent or 20 percent of the people in most societies are primarily students. We know that people placed in this institutional category and in the associated organizational and interactional life act very differently from youth of similar ages not in the system. The students more often make political trouble, and less often engage in ordinary criminal conduct. There is an extended literature on the organizational and interactional sources of such behavior. Investigations into the effects of the whole system on society have yet to be made, but theory suggests that such a restructuring of life around a rationalized, nationalized, and universalistic institution has considerable impact. Most young people have their futures determined by the impersonal rules of a national-level bureaucracy, rather than by their more parochial social and organizational relationships. Whatever this does to the young people involved, it must have considerable effect on society.

Conclusions

We need to take a more institutional view. The child is not only a third grader in a given teacher's classroom or in the organization of a given school—the child is a third grader in society. Much of the power and effectiveness of the teacher and school derive from this: we should not be surprised to find interaction in the classroom and organization in the school responding to it. Taking an institutional view would enable us to consider societal effects of education that escape not only our present methods of evidence but even our theories.

An institutional view also broadens our ability to think about the origins of the educational system, its expansion, and its extension into new domains of social knowledge. We need to look beyond the immediate organizational pressures that create these processes: if education is the institutionalized secular religion of a modern system, a view of its origins is needed that stresses more its bases in collective action and authority, and in the changes in these involved in the modern order.

Macrosociological research is needed, exploring more comparative, historical, and longitudinal data. To understand the effects of institutional variations on children and schools, such variation must be included in our research designs. Studies of high school seniors leave out of the analysis the effects of what it means to be a high school senior. Studies of the career lines of economists leave out what it means to have economics as schooled in society. Looking at the origins of education only through who chooses to go to a given type of school will not help one understand why that type of school arose and expanded in the first place. We need to compare societies, not only to create a comparative sociology of education, but in order to understand education sociologically at all.

There are technical problems here, but fewer than might be supposed. It is relatively easy, for instance, to study curricula cross-nationally and to look for the societal factors associated with their variations. And it would not be difficult to study the effects of variations in higher educational content (e.g., the presence or absence of given fields) on subsequent national policy in parallel domains.

7

Cross-National Study
of Academic Systems

Burton R. Clark

HIGHER EDUCATION may be viewed sociologically as a professionalized social system concerned with the control of advanced knowledge. As a sector of society that is simultaneously and increasingly knowledge-intensive and knowledge-extensive, it connects to other social institutions in diverse, subtle, and contradictory ways. Research on its activities and its interconnections has thus far been highly unsatisfactory in the way that global assertions have preceded open and extended inquiry. Controversy has raged over whether education in its entirety and everywhere is dependent on the will of elites in the economic and political institutions, or passively reproduces the social class structure, or has no important socialization effects, with advocates staking positions without the benefit of research or basing conclusions solely on research done in one country or even a single city or region within it. In the current state of the sociology of education, each global generalization about such connections has a warranted countergeneralization. For example, against the portrayal of higher education as a dependent institution, which dates in sociology from some comments by Durkheim (1922) about all of education, one can claim that its production of new knowledge (Halsey, 1960; Clark, 1962; Machlup, 1962) and its broad certification and legitimation effects (Meyer, 1977) make it active and influential. Much of the confusion results from theorizing without careful attention to time and place and without the careful building of an extended empirical foundation. Two guides for future research may be asserted.

1. Any sought-after relationship between higher education and some

other major sector of society will vary among nations. In a trenchant discussion of the controversy over the relation of education to subsequent individual occupational performance and earnings, and, at the macro level, to national economic development, Dore (1976a, 1976b: 84–97) has emphasized the wide variation among societies in the importance of different mediating links. Against the gross correlational exercises, especially those of economists, that systematically fail to disaggregate systems into their varied parts (e.g., vocational and nonvocational higher education), Dore sets forth ten mechanisms of connection between education and the economy that vary in importance among societies, especially between developing and developed ones. The wide variation in strength of the mechanisms, rooted in different histories and structures of educational systems and employment institutions, rules out any generalization about *the* role of "Education" in the "Economy," or indeed in "Society." Hence, serious inquiry must turn to the study of the histories and structures of the institutions involved, even if it means examination of characteristics not currently measurable and a search for many modes rather than a universal connection.

2. Systems of higher education vary in complexity of relationship to other major institutions according to the extent and form of their internal complexity. As systems become more complex, it is necessary to seek relationships between the parts of each rather than between the whole of the one and the whole of the other. There are likely to be important differences in socialization effects, allocation effects, and legitimation effects by levels and sectors—for example, in the American system, between such levels as the first two undergraduate years and the Ph.D. level, and between such sectors as distinctive liberal arts colleges and urban community colleges. Research on internal differentiation helps to identify important segments that are likely to connect in different ways to external social segments; while research on effects that attends also to the growing segmentation of higher education can, in turn, help identify the parts that are truly different and those that operate in a similar fashion.

Thus, it is imperative in the future development of the sociology of education generally that research be comparative, that is, cross-national; and that it take seriously in each case what is inside the black box, that is, how the system is internally constituted. The latter means particularly that we look at structures of activities and control: how existing structures of work condition behavior and constrain change, and how those structures institutionalize certain biases and group interests while excluding others. For this large effort, we need some modest analytical apparatus, a few cues drawn from general sociological thought and from comparative research done to date that suggest what structures and processes are worth exploring. We need also to turn further to organizational theory, political theory, and educational history.

I shall limit my overview to higher or postsecondary education, which I shall refer to as the academic system—meaning national system in each case, unless otherwise specified. It is important to differentiate higher education analytically from the other levels of education, since it has basic characteristics not shared with secondary and elementary systems. Therefore, I turn first to the nature of the activities of academic systems. Second, I want to highlight the divisions of labor found within academic systems by (1) applying the distinction between profession and bureaucracy and pointing to the fragmented professionalism of the academic world; and (2) maintaining that academic systems are bottom-heavy knowledge institutions and as such are extreme cases of loosely coupled social enterprises. Third, I discuss briefly how academic systems are coordinated by means that vary from state authority to market, with, in most countries, much professional oligarchy included. Finally, I emphasize differentiation as a key process of change, tapping into general sociological thought on differentiation and hopefully sharpening it for application to academic systems.

Throughout, the relevant research materials vary from the heavily statistical to the interpretative essay. Comparativists are in no position to be methodologically proud or fixated on technique. Needing to crawl before they can walk, and walk before they can run, they find that the patient gathering of descriptive materials on various countries, lightly guided and exploited by evolving concepts, is appropriate procedure. Without such homework, without the willingness to master conditions and traditions, country by country, comparativists are prone to pratfalls that make them look silly in the eyes of informed observers and a danger to those who cannot get out of the way, especially in these days when implications for policy are drawn so quickly. Then, too, most sociologists of education who work with materials drawn only from one country are hidden comparativists, since they offer generalizations that supposedly apply everywhere. That easy form of scholarly corruption may be the greatest danger of all, especially when the literature is so dominated by the researchers of one country.

The Activities of Academic Systems

In the long evolution of modern societies, higher education became differentiated as a separate sphere of activity around work that involved the handling of bodies of thought. Its basic organizational forms in the Western world, beginning in the twelfth century, became locations for conserving and refining knowledge; its main workers, socially defined as professors (masters) and bachelors (journeymen), absorbed and sometimes critically assessed written accounts and observations handed down from past generations (Rashdall, 1936; Haskins, 1957; Ben-David, 1968; Reeves, 1970; Baldwin and Goldthwaite, 1972). The largest activity became that of transmitting advanced bodies of ideas and skills in deliberate and wholesale fashion to learners, individuals defined as apprentices or students and socially segregated in a student role. Notably, preparation for the professions became the primary societal task, to the point where the university became the central place for the legitimation of occupations as leading professions (Perkin, 1969).

Then, in the nineteenth and twentieth centuries, most leading academic systems added the commitment of discovering knowledge, as the research imperative entered the university in many countries, turning the professor into a researcher as well as a scholar and teacher and providing science its principal institutional home (Ashby, 1966; Ben-David, 1971; Turner, 1971; Guralnick, 1975). Higher education also sometimes becomes directly involved in applying knowledge to the solution of contemporary problems, when its agents respond to external requests for advice or participate as experts in external councils or carry out applied research called for by government or industry (Kerr, 1963). In discovering, conserving, refining, transmitting, and applying advanced ideas and skills, the handling of knowledge materials has been a common thread in the many specific and diverse activities of academic workers.

A simultaneous intensive and extensive concentration on advanced knowledge distinguishes higher education from other social institutions: economic, political, religious, recreational, and charitable institutions all use knowledge and are involved in aspects of producing and distributing it, but they do not so fully concentrate on knowledge tasks or attempt to encompass a similarly wide range of specialities. No other major institution covers the alphabetical spectrum of fields of knowledge from archeology to zoology, with business management, engineering, French literature, law, medicine, physics, psychology, and dozens of other fields included. And higher education differs in degree from elementary and secondary education in focusing on more advanced, specialized materials; and in kind by including the research imperative and thereby serving as a principal location for science. These differences in tasks constitute an important basis for differences in organization.

A major social institution committed to discovering, conserving, and distributing knowledge faces certain generic problems: What will be the academic division of labor, the distribution of the work of research, scholarship, and teaching to persons and groups? What knowledge, general and special, is to be included? How will the overall system as a set of operating organizations be internally governed and administered? Who will be admitted to the system as learners and how will they be treated and then certified as they leave the system? To what degree will the system as a whole and its major parts be insulated from, or interdependent with, government and other sectors of society? There are responses to these problems in the higher education systems of every country, generally more emergent than enacted, the answers crystallizing over time into patterned arrangements. I shall point to only a few.

The Structures of the Academic Division of Labor

Academic activities and tasks are divided and grouped in two basic ways: by enterprise and discipline. The *enterprise,* or individual institution, is a comprehensive organization, a community of interest linking such disparate specialists as chemists, psychologists, and historians. A state or a provincial or national system is then a set of these comprehensive aggregations. In contrast, the *discipline,* or profession, is an organization of similar specialists, a craft-like community of interest that knits together chemists with chemists, psychologists with psychologists, historians with historians, and thereby links parts of one institution to similar parts in another as this principle of organization cuts across the enterprises. Then a national system of higher education is a set of disciplines and professions, or crafts, however they are linked together. In fact, the reach of the discipline extends even further, since most disciplines do not stop at national as well as institutional and system boundaries. Academic scientists reach readily toward world community, since their shared perspectives and interests can so readily expand across nations along "functional" lines, much as people in specialized lines of industry, commerce, and banking can have more in common with counterpart specialists abroad than with others outside the specialty at home. It is primarily because of its disciplinary organization that higher education is always more international, or metanational, than are elementary and secondary education. The lower levels are more bounded by national culture and national enterprise forms, and have weaker interpersonal ties fashioned by the discipline of the specialty.

That the disciplines organize higher education is a phenomenon widely overlooked by observers of higher education. The enterprise mode of grouping preempts attention. When we seek to describe national systems, we immediately depict universities and colleges. It is a common habit in annual national reports and periodic international data books that describe higher education to list enterprises, describe them briefly, and sum their students, faculties, and resources. With academic statistics everywhere gathered primarily on this basis, only occasionally is some attention paid to the discipline as a prime organizational form. Yet the discipline has enormous underlying strength and even primacy. A simple test suggests its power: give the academic worker the choice of leaving the discipline or the institution, and he or she will typically leave the institution. It is more costly to leave one's field of expertise than to leave one's university or college. The higher the level of one's advanced education, the greater will be the import of one's specialty, one's discipline or profession, in shaping personal identity and commitment.

The discipline and the enterprise converge in the primary working groups of the academic world, making the parts of academic systems unusually strong and central. Compared to organizations in other domains, there is an imposing functional basis for strong departmentalism or bottom-heavy organization. Of course, the operating parts of organizations are always crucial in one sense; but there is wide variation among organizations in how much the parts are authoritative, each in its own way and one from the other. As disciplines crosscut organizations in higher education, the centrality of the parts is enormously enhanced, and even made qualitatively different from that found in nearly all other sectors of society.

Thus, three points are central:

1. *The core membership unit is discipline centered.* As formulated by Swedish researchers: "The most important membership group consists of teachers and researchers. They are organized in subsystems according to disciplines (departments, etc.), and their main competency as well as their professional identity is chiefly connected with the discipline. The discipline also determines their national and international contacts outside of their own department" (Berg and Ostergren, 1977: 102). Thus, the disciplines determine the division of labor within the enterprises and give content to the segments. They are the source of perceived competency of the main workers, confer much identity, and offer channels of contact and communication with others. Professors are resident agents of disciplines in institutions.

2. *Each membership unit has self-evident and acclaimed primacy in a front-line task.* As noted by two English observers: "Underlying the status of the department is its crucial characteristic of being authoritative in its own field of learning" (Moodie and Eustace, 1974: 61). Authoritativeness holds across the great range of knowledge areas identified earlier. No other cluster of people in the institution or the system at large can claim to know as much history, and to know about its operation as a field, as the historians—or as much physics as the physicists.

3. *The nature of the membership group affects everything else in the organization.* The effects of core activities and core groups, in capsule form, include: effects on organizational structure, primarily that of making the departments or equivalent units typically the most powerful organizational units; effects on organizational ideology and purpose, where the overall doctrines must serve as a common denominator for the disciplines; and effects on coordination and governance, where unusual leeway must be left for the initiatives of the prime academic segments and many indirect forms of coordination are brought into play. It is the special nature of the core groups that render universities and colleges something other than unitary organizations; that makes personal and collegial controls so prevalent; that requires an unusual vocabulary of crafts and guilds, federations and conglomerations, to tease out the realities that re-

main hidden when approached by the standard terminology of organizational life. We have an extreme case of loosely coupled organization.

Loose coupling applies to the relation among disciplines as well as the parts of the enterprise, making the academic profession fundamentally different from every other known profession. Other professions—for example, medicine, law, engineering, architecture—are relatively singular. Despite their known internal specialties, they can be more readily unified by a body of values, norms, and attitudes developed over time within the profession itself and considered an intrinsic part of it. It is then the case that an organization loaded with members of the profession, as a hospital is by doctors, can be run in an integrated fashion in part by professional norms as well as bureaucratic rules. Larger sets of organizations, such as those of a health system of a state, region, or nation, may be similarly integrated. But not so in academic institutions and systems. Here we find medical doctors in the medical faculty, lawyers in the law faculty, architects in the architecture faculty, and other professional clusters in a range of professional units that may number anywhere from a half-dozen to two dozen. Which is only the beginning, since the number of specialized clusters is much larger in the physical sciences, social sciences, and humanities. Hence the academic difference is that of fragmented professionalism (Clark, 1963; Baldridge et al., 1978). In place of a closely knit group of professionals who see the world from one perspective, academic systems are loose collections of many professional types.

The principle is this: When professional influence is high within a system *and* there is one dominant professional group, the system may be integrated by the imposition of professional standards. Where professional influence is high *and* there are a number of professional groups coexisting side by side, the system will be split by professionalism. Academic systems are increasingly fractured by expertise, rather than unified by it.

As we follow the lines of discipline and enterprise in various countries, we find that the elemental features that center on discipline have wide currency, flowing across national boundaries and hence shared among national systems—for example, the dividing of the natural sciences into such well known fields as physics, chemistry, and biology. Segmentation by discipline is considerably organic, even internationally organic, with much of the momentum of each field set internally, driven by the research imperative and its knowledge results. But features of differentiation that center on the enterprises vary widely among nations, more subject to particulars of origin and context. The decomposing of academic work by enterprise is more determined by imposition, essentially the accumulation of organizational forms from a history of groups attempting deliberately to organize higher education. Those forms can be analyzed as horizontal and vertical arrangements, within and among the enterprises, what I have elsewhere termed sections and tiers, within institutions, and sectors and hierarchies, within the larger systems (Clark, 1978). Extensive differences among national systems on these dimensions can be suggested briefly here by means of just two examples that will serve also to highlight the U.S. system as a deviant case and hence a poor one in itself upon which to generalize.

SECTION DIFFERENTIATION

The horizontally distributed academic units of universities differ significantly in how they establish authority over production. The basic difference internationally is between chair organization and department organization. The chair concentrates the responsibilities and powers of the primary operating unit in one person, the chairholder (Ben-David, 1971; Clark, 1977a). It is the prime source of personal authority in academic systems. In contrast, the department is an impersonal unit that spreads responsibilities and powers among a number of professors of similar senior rank and more readily allows for some participation by associates and assistants (Ben-David, 1971; Parsons and Platt, 1973; Blau, 1973). It thereby becomes a basis for collegial as well as bureaucratic order at the operating level, while still admitting personal authority.

Chair organization is very old. It has been the traditional form of operational control in European universities, with roots in the original organization of medieval universities as guilds and guild federations of master professors who took unto themselves a few journeyman assistants and a small batch of student apprentices. It was reinvigorated and given modern dress in the German research university that became the most important worldwide model during the nineteenth and early twentieth century (Turner, 1971). It has had extensive influence in Great Britain, where it has been blended, more than on the Continent, with collegiate and departmental units. Most important, chair organization has spread through the world wherever German, French, Italian, Spanish, Portuguese, Dutch, and English modes of academic organization have been implanted by colonial regimes or voluntarily adopted, and has persisted as the normal way of structuring and manning the university. In Japan, where by set formulae each chair is apportioned several positions for assistants, the chair is jokingly referred to as a sofa (Hall, 1975).

Departmentalism is relatively new, a deviant form that has developed most strongly in the United States, where it arose in the context of trustee and administrative control over growing individual colleges and emerging universities in the nineteenth century (Duryea, 1973). The American enterprises were organized from the top down (in contrast to bottom-up in Europe), as external private groups and public authorities delegated authority to boards of trustees, who then obtained campus-level administrative assistance, in the form of the president and his assisting officers, as the enterprises became larger and more complicated. Within such frameworks, bureaucratic models of subdivision could and did predominate over guild models. When the all-inclusive faculty had to subdivide to organize growing and disparate specialties, especially after the common classical curriculum gave way to the elective system—free choice for students *and* more room for faculty experts to pursue their specialties—there was not already in place the guild-like presumptions and forms of faculty control over the operating levels that had come down in Europe from the medieval universities.

Thus, chair organization is a persistent source of personal dominance, as against collegial as well as bureaucratic control, while the department is a less personal form. In addition, chair organization has been a source of faculty control over higher levels of organization, as senior faculty, serving as masters, elect deans and rectors from within their own ranks. However, as enterprises and systems have grown, the chair has become an increasingly inappropriate unit for swollen disciplines. In the 1950s and 1960s, systems that have kept the chair as primary unit while growing much larger have risked extreme fragmentation. Hence an important step in serious reform has been to replace chairs with departments or to absorb them in department-like units. Considered a hopelessly old-fashioned unit by American reformers, the department is one of the primary means of reform elsewhere. It is capable of supporting and integrating modern disciplines within institutions to an extent not normally possible under the hegemony of chairs (Trow, 1977).

SECTOR DIFFERENTIATION

A second example of critical differences in national academic systems in their basic division of labor is the form of horizontal differentiation among institutions, which, in the twentieth century, occurs in at least four patterns. From simple to complex, they are: a single sector of institutions, within a single public system; several sectors, within the one government system; several sectors, in more than one formal public subsystem; and multiple types under private support as well as public system allocation.

The first pattern expresses a double monopoly—of authority and institutional type. The whole of higher education falls almost completely under a unified national system, topped by a national ministry of education, and the system contains essentially only one form, the state university, with 80 percent or more of enrollment in that one type of institution. Italy has been a clear case of this form in Western Europe in the twentieth century.

In the second pattern, higher education remains under the control and financial support of one level of government but the system is differentiated into two or more organizational forms. This is the most common pattern around the world, the dominant arrangement in Western democracies, communist societies, and Third World nations alike. Typically, the main sector is a set of universities, with one or more "nonuniversity" sectors organized around vocational instruction, or teacher training, or both, but occasionally around esoteric functions prized by one or more departments of the central government. France is a striking case of this pattern, with its historic differentiation of universities and *grandes ecoles,* specialized schools that for the most part rank above the universities in prestige. Countries as different as Thailand, Iran, and Poland fall within this pattern of nationalized pluralism.

The third pattern occurs primarily in nations that have a federal structure of government, with higher education falling within a number of state or provincial systems while influenced in varying degrees by national government. There are multiple public systems as well as multiple sectors, with the dispersion of state control generating more variation than does the unified public system. Countries often evolve into this pattern from a background in which the formal organization of higher education took place primarily at the subgovernment level, reflecting provincial differences, with the influence of the national government later superimposed. At the same time, private sectors, if they existed, gradually vanished or became reduced to a small part, 10 to 15 percent or less, of student enrollment. With considerable variation, West Germany, Great Britain, Australia, and Canada fall in this pattern.

The fourth national arrangement consists of multiple institutional types existing under private sponsorship as well as public control, with at least 15 to 20 percent of the students in institutions that receive most of their financing from nongovernment sources and have boards of control selected through private channels. The existence of one or more private sectors increases considerably the division of forms, first by providing a private–public antithesis not available in the first three patterns and, second, by the multiplying of subtypes and unique institutions as the search for competitive advantage among the private universities and colleges leads many of them to different postures. Japan, the United States, and Brazil all fall in this pattern. Japan is the leading case of private sector development, since it expanded rapidly into mass higher education in the 1950s and 1960s by allowing the burdens of that expansion to be picked up by private institutions to the extent of some 75 to 80 percent of enrollment, reversing the private–public proportions found in the United States. A huge system of over 2 million students and one thousand institutions, the Japanese structure has numerous major sectors: a small set of leading national (formerly "imperial") universities; other national universities; universities supported by the municipal level of government; private universities and colleges, numbering in excess of three hundred and varying widely in type and quality; and over five hundred junior colleges, public and private, but mainly private (Narita, 1978; Wheeler, 1978; Cummings et al., 1979). The heterogeneous set of institutions entails great differences in selection, from exceedingly tight, as at the universities of Tokyo and Kyoto, to exceedingly loose, as in some private colleges that are virtually degree mills; and, in job placement, from guaranteed placement to specific offices in government to unspecified entry into a broad band of the total job market, including some blue-collar work, clerical positions, and sales occupations (Ushiogi, 1979).

In sum: All academic systems are segmented by discipline and made bottom-heavy and operationally fragmented by a variety of esoteric clusters of experts at operating levels. However, national systems have grouped and organized the disciplines within and among institutions in different ways. To seek the causes of the national patterns requires inquiry that stretches into historical and contextual roots. To determine the consequences of the patterns requires patient intensive comparison of sets of such systems to determine how the structures condition such outcomes as magnitude and equality of access, competence in professional training, scientific productivity, and system adaptability. An outstanding example of national comparison on a significant outcome is the hypothesis from comparative research by Ben-David and Sloczower (1962) that decentralized and competitive national systems are more productive in scientific research than are centralized and noncompetitive ones.

The Coordination of Academic Systems

The co-ordering of the parts of academic systems takes at least four major forms: bureaucracy, politics, profession, and market (Clark, 1979). The first two can be grouped as "state authority," since most bureaucratic and political personnel work for the state or exercise influence through its political–administrative machinery. The professional form refers to coordination by professors, which generally entails control by small cadres of senior professors operating at national as well as local levels, essentially professorial oligarchy. Market refers to the nondeliberate allocating and co-ordering that comes about through exchange among autonomous or semiautonomous parts pursuing different interests, and, borrowing from political economy, may be studied in such important subforms as labor market, consumer market, and institutional market (Lindblom, 1977).

All academic systems contain all four forms of coordination. In the most state-dominated systems, professors retain some personal and collegial authority, requiring that state officials negotiate and persuade as well as command; students retain some market-like choice of courses and programs and professors some choice of position and task. In turn, in the most professor-ridden systems, some state controls and market choices are operative. And, in the most market-like systems, we can readily find state officials and professional oligarchs roaming the corridors of power. We may posit that state authority, rule by academic oligarchy, and market interaction are all needed for the different functions they perform. The special function of state authority is to articulate a variety of public interests, particularly equity, as these are defined by prevailing groups within and outside of government. The special function of academic oligarchy is to protect professional self-rule, to lodge the control of academic work, including its standards—as Durkheim would put it—in the hands of "a group intimate enough with it to know its functioning, feel all its needs, and able to follow all their variations" (1893: 5). The special function of the market is to enhance and protect freedom of choice for personnel, clientele, and institutions, and thereby also indirectly to promote system flexibility and adaptability. Given the special task structure of higher education, we may hypothesize that it is not possible to coordinate by the market alone, nor can either state or professional hegemony in itself do what must be done. In addition, all three forms have well legitimated ideologies that insist on their usage. Thus, analytically and normatively, what we do not need is fanatical devotion to any one form of coordination because of its obvious advantages (or vested position in scholarly literature!), or a combative juxtaposing of forms whereby the acceptance of one means the exclusion of the others. Needed instead are reconciliation models of state–market–professional relations, the identification of primary combinations and modes wherein these three forms are interpenetrated.

As we trace these forms of coordination in national systems, we encounter radically different combinations. Continental European systems typically have combined state authority and professorial oligarchy—all power to the state bureaucrat and the chairholder—while subordinating the market. The British pattern has exhibited weaker state authority, considerable professional oligarchy, and modest amount of market coordination. The United States has been the leading case of a market system, with very active labor and consumer markets and unparalleled competition among institutions, but now experiencing a major expansion of government authority at both state and national levels.

As we pursue how the forms interpenetrate one another, our basic concepts can be used in new combinations to identify phenomena of emerging and growing importance. One is the evolution of state authority into what may be called a power market. The more higher education comes under state authority—the fundamental trend in the control of higher education in the nineteenth and twentieth centuries—the more does the struggle of its internal and external interest groups have to take place within the government structure as a conflict among ministries, departments, bureaus, divisions, councils, and committees. Given the special complexities of task and interest in higher education, its absorption into government frameworks produces great struggle among a large number of government and quasi-government bodies arrayed in parallel, unclear, and overlapping hierarchies. The situation is a power market in the sense of units struggling against one another to gain and exchange the resources of power.

This, too, is a form of coordination. In a classic essay written thirty years ago, Norton E. Long (1949: 262) gave us an important clue to this phenomenon when he maintained that "competition between governmental power centers" is probably the most effective instrument of coordination in complex government. He noted: "The position of administrative organizations is not unlike the position of particular firms. Just as the decisions of the firms could be coordinated by the imposition of a planned economy so could those of the component parts of the government. But just as it is possible to operate a formally unplanned economy by the loose coordination of the market, in the same fashion it is possible to operate a government by the loose coordination of the play of political forces through its institutions." Recent work in political economy, especially that of Charles E. Lindblom (1977), has further developed this line of thinking. Authority is seen as operationally divided among a plurality of officials and offices; conflicts and reciprocal obligations develop among them. In place of unilateral coordination, we find "mutual adjustment among authorities who practice an extended use of their authority in order to control each other" (1977: 32).

Such reasoning is especially applicable to national systems of higher education, where administrative pyramids have no clear apex but instead at the top are engulfed by a variety of boards, bureaus, commissions, and committees; where the ever more embracing global frameworks are ever more segmented by discipline and institution, and authority is distributed in a host of political, bureaucratic, and professional forms.

Differentiation, Integration, and Power

The study of the division and coordination of academic activities raises the key theoretical issues of the causes and pathways of social differentiation and integration. Observation of academic systems can help clarify and reformulate these fundamental sociological concerns; while in turn general sociological thought on these concepts helps generate potentially powerful perspectives to guide research on higher education. In this concluding section, I wish to pursue one idea raised in recent theorizing which resonates well with my own cross-national observation of academic systems. The idea is that both the structural differentiation and the structural integration of academic systems are better approached and understood as a result of a struggle for power than of a search for efficiency.

In a recent article on "Structural Differentiation, Efficiency, and Power," Dietrich Rueschemeyer (1977) has helped greatly to clarify the advantages of turning from efficiency to power in understanding the causes of structural differentiation. The fundamental problem with efficiency as a concept is that it hinges on preferences, sets of ranked goals. Hence, "what efficiency means is always and inevitably determined by varied interests and value commitments" (Rueschemeyer, 1977: 5). The advantage of turning to conceptions of power is that power by definition (Weber, 1921: 53) is the chance greater than others' to realize one's goals, even against resistance. When we study power we learn whose preferences dominate or have influence—and "efficiency" falls into a subsidiary place as effective action for particular interests. The distribution of power resources and the substance of power interests then move centerstage as determinants of the actual social changes involved in differentiation. Further division is favored by those who thereby gain in privilege, status, and power; for example, in the academic world, the emerging disciplines of psychology, anthropology, and sociology early in the century, and biochemists and historians of science in recent years. Those who will lose oppose such divisions. The results of such struggle between old vested interests and new interests seeking to become vested depend largely on the power resources of the opposing factions and on the interests and the power resources of higher level decision makers (Rueschemeyer, 1977: 13).

The argument that the pursuit of power is a major cause of differentiation becomes stronger as we turn from general societal evolution to concerted subsystems of society, such as academic systems, for then power is more embodied in the immediate structures constraining an arena of action, and participants, even under market conditions, are forced to interact and hence to be subjected to each other's preferences and powers. In addition, the higher the class and status positions of the members of an occupation, the stronger their influence will be on the level and types of specialization. "For this reason, specialization in a profession reflects more closely conditions and interests within the occupational group than it does in lower rank occupations" (Rueschemeyer, 1977: 19). When we recall the inherent fragmentation of the academic profession, the primacy of the discipline and its carrying units (department, chair, institute), and the bottom-heavy nature of academic systems, there is ample reason to turn to issues of power and the pursuit of group self-interest to understand academic differentiation.

This analytical stream of thought has a host of tributaries in traditional and modern sociological theorizing. High among the important contributions in traditional thought is Durkheim's perception that differentiation is promoted by similar units seeking to protect themselves. The bordering units seek to take up different specialties in order to avoid direct confrontation and possible defeat (Durkheim, 1966: 266–75). Both can prosper, as anthropology and sociology found out by giving up joint departments. More recently, Arthur Stinchcombe (1965) has offered an insightful argument on the origin and persistence of different types of organizations in any sector of society, in which persistence is due more to the vesting of interest in different forms, with a related buildup of traditionalized behavior and legitimating ideologies, than it is to competitive advantage and a survival of the fittest. The current array of organizations is then an accumulation of types originating in different historical periods, each preserved by group power. If this argument seemingly applies to the profit-seeking sectors, and Stinchcombe drew his main examples from American industry, it surely applies in greater measure to public and nonprofit sectors, especially academic systems, where it is difficult even to give lip-service to efficiency and effectiveness.

Finally, there is the recent effort by Neil Smelser (1974) to trace the structural differentiation of the University of California system in a period of expansion, in which he postulated six possible structural responses, observed that a particular three occurred during the 1960s which the other three did not, and concluded by likening the situation to the classic one explored by Alexis de Tocqueville in which powerful interests fail to adapt to new demands by sharing power and responsibility, and in that failure help to magnify feelings of deprivation and dissatisfaction that lead to crisis. This pattern of old academic groups clinging to privileges in a period of rapid expansion occurred even more strongly in European systems than it did in the United States, since established powers, fixed in the combination of chair oligarchy and state bureaucracy, could be, and were, more resistant—until crisis responses broke the stalemate and led to many major top-down reform efforts (Van de Graaff et al., 1978).

In understanding the nature and causes of the structural *integration* of academic systems, our best conceptual leads come from modern public administration. Since modern education is typically a part of government, a serious student of the organization and governance of education must study the nature of the government vessels within which it is contained. Those who study modern government now put it bluntly: "Economy and efficiency are demonstratably not the prime purposes of public administration. . . . The basic issues of [government] organization and administration relate to power: who shall control it and to what ends?" (Seidman, 1970: 27). And: "Logrolling is the tactic most appropriate to the ends of small and relatively homogeneous units within a larger system. It is both simple and effective for the leaders of such units to exchange support for each others' demands" (McConnell, 1966: 111). I noted earlier the classic observation by Norton Long that the play of political adjustment through and among the parts of a vast administrative apparatus is probably *the* basic form of coordination in modern government, as well as the analytical point of view developed more recently by Lindblom on government as mutual adjustment among a plurality of semiautonomous officials.

In general, the insightful literature on modern public administration emphasizes complexity of the apparatus, the balkanization of interest in professionalized segments of the many departments and bureaus, the enormous difficulties of forging horizontal coordinating linkages by formal bureaucratic means, and the de facto coordination effected by thousands of exchanges and mutual adjustments made among interested and overlapping parties. This is the nature of the government vessels within which higher education is everywhere increasingly located as the state monopolizes sponsorship, one that clearly calls for detailed research on power. The more socialistic the state, we might say, the more do the crucial power struggles of society move inside the administrative apparatus of the state. In parallel, the more nationalized the system of higher education, the more do we need to seek the realities of control within the administrative superstructure that is elaborated over time—layer upon layer—to "integrate" the system.

The perspectives we draw from the study of government to use in the study of academic government indicate that we have only barely begun to look in the right direction and at the right phenomena. We need new ways to comprehend the superstructures as well as the understructures of academic systems, and we shall find those ways as we tune more finely into power exchanges within these ever more complex and professionalized structures. We move inside the seemingly large impersonal forces of history and understand their dynamics better when we carefully pursue the play of group interest. This old idea can now be a new and powerful analytical imperative in the comparative study of academic systems. As we focus on group interest and its embodiment, we marry the analysis of politics to the analysis of organizations. The analysis of group interest in educational structures can entail research that will relate problems of academic power to the core issues of political as well as sociological theory.

8

The Sociology of the School and Classroom

Charles E. Bidwell

THE BEGINNINGS of modern sociology mark the beginnings of sociological reflection and research on education. In the United States, Lester Ward's *Dynamic Sociology* (Ward, 1883) initiated a body of reformist and pragmatic American writings notable less for its analytical power than for a sunny view of social progress through the cumulative effect of changes induced in individual human beings. Chief among the agents of these changes was education.

By the Depression, sociological meliorism had lost its force, and the interest of American sociologists in education waned. From the 1950s forward, however, the sociological study of education, more analytical but no less motivated by concern for application to social practice, has flourished in this country. A portion of this work has centered on the institution of education. Another portion, to which my remarks are principally addressed, looks within schools to trace the processes of education.

I will argue that these studies, though stripped of the more visible trappings of social meliorism, maintain the traditional American emphasis on social reform by individualist means. I will also argue that this emphasis has directed the avowedly analytical intent of this research away from the very phenomenon that it purports to study: the social processes of schooling. I will

☐ Preparation of this chapter was made possible by National Science Foundation Grant No. SOC 74–24287. Many of the ideas emerged from conversations and debates with John Kasarda and John Meyer. The argument of the paper owes much to the stimulating environment of the Educational Finance and Productivity Center, Department of Education, University of Chicago.

try to show how this research might be redirected toward the analysis of schooling and of relationships between institutional aspects of education and the instructional work of schools.

For guidance in such matters, we can turn, as we do so often, to the European founding fathers. For my purpose, Durkheim's work is central. For Durkheim (1956, 1961), the forms of educational organizations, the varieties of their curricular content and structure, the accessibility of these organizations and curricula to children of different social origins, and the processes of schooling distinctive of each of the varieties of education are all creatures of historical societies. Education performs its paramount function, to act as "the means by which society perpetually recreates the conditions of its very existence," by adapting its organizational form and instructional means to a historical society's characteristic beliefs and structures (Durkheim, 1956: 65).

In modern societies, the re-creative function is specified as the formation of moral consensus, required by the decay of kinship and tradition, the fragmentation of social formations, and the individualization of human consciousness. It is nothing less than to construct the normative basis of the national state: widespread respect for national political and moral authority and disciplined cooperation, balanced against trained, skeptical intellect and specialized scientific and technical preparation.

The extreme differentiation of modern society creates not only the conditions that specify the function of education as moral and intellectual training, but also the conditions of the performance of this function. These conditions are the emergence of the school as a semiautonomous social formation and of teaching as a specialized vocation.

For Durkheim, the content of schooling, the curriculum, is the means of intellectual training and specialization. Even in the common school, the curriculum in the main prepares for specialist roles and the skeptical, rational outlook. It is the social organization of the school classroom that fosters the moral habits that bind the national society together. The simple fact of the child's participation in the organized life of the school class forms the moral habits of the student and, thereby, the moral habits of the citizen.

Age, vocation, and intellectual and cultural superiority, Durkheim said, combine to make the teacher the dominant classroom actor: an "incarnation of duty" who is at once the microcosmic embodiment of the authority of the state and the source and governor of an impersonal, austere order of disciplined classroom conduct. To survive, the child, however willing or unwilling, must comply with the social order of the classroom. Moreover, the school class itself becomes a chief source of social identity for its students. Both the compliance and the identification, heightened and reinforced by the separateness of the classroom and its consequent isolation from child and family life, form in the child habits of group loyalty, acceptance of authority, and disciplined cooperation.

Certain themes in Durkheim's analysis especially merit our attention:

1. that the social organization of the school and classroom itself is shaped by fundamental traits of historical societies,
2. that the conditions of classroom life are formed powerfully by its social organization,
3. that the socially formed conditions of life in schools and classrooms shape the processes of schooling, and, thus,
4. that each historical society inevitably selects from a wide array of theoretical possibilities only certain things that students learn in school.

Contemporary Sociology of the School and Classroom

Among contemporary sociologists of "school effects," the dualistic preoccupation of Durkheim and his American contemporaries with moral commitment and personal liberation has been replaced by a single-minded preoccupation with achievement. Although the reformist impulse continues in this work, the goal is social equality, framed in general terms as the equalization of occupational life chances, though variously specified to opportunity or outcome. The paramount problem of social welfare is the existence of status-based imparities in economic participation; the paramount problem of personal welfare is biased status attainment. The solution of these problems remains an individualistic solution: to give every member of society the means and even the motivation to do well. Evidently, solving the problem of personal welfare cumulates to solve the problem of social welfare.

Intense interest in status attainment led certain sociologists to study the attainment of educational status. Because Durkheim had been most concerned with the formation of social habits, he gave scant attention to the learning of school subjects. Contemporary students of educational attainment profess an interest in cognitive learning, yet they give no more attention to its substance than did Durkheim. Instead, they ask how students acquire years of schooling, school marks, achievement test scores, and diplomas. Thus, school effects research has sought ways to maximize every child's chances of doing well in tests and grades and of staying in school.

The search has involved three steps: (1) to document for the United States the degree of imparity in students' access to schools of varying funding, curricula, staff and student composition, and facilities; (2) to devise a model of student learning that would connect grades, scores, and persistence in school to such attributes of schools as funds, curricula, composition, or facilities; and (3) to determine the relative weights of these school attributes as contributors to school attainment.

The first step was taken with magisterial effect by James Coleman and his colleagues (Coleman et al., 1966). *Equality of Educational Opportunity* stimulated replications and extensions (Jencks et al., 1972; Hauser, Sewell, and Alwin, 1976). These studies have shown that with certain limited exceptions, neither unit nor aggregate properties of schools have much influence on what students achieve either in school or later in the labor force. Although years of schooling may be a powerful predictor of occupational destinations and income, there appears to be a low upper bound on the proportion of variance in academic, occupational, or income attainment that lies between schools.

The second step, to adumbrate a theory of learning as school achievement, has not been taken by any one theorist, but has evolved implicitly in the empirical studies of student achievement. This implicit theory of learning is notable for its individualism. It centers on the individual learner; it treats not only his intellectual and motivational capacities, but also his exposure to the resources and social life of the school as if they were his own personal traits.

Together, the documentation of minimal between-school variance in academic and postschool attainment and this individualist theory of learning have prevented our taking the third step and extending it into an effort to connect analytically the social properties of schools to the substance of students' learning. We have been discouraged by the negative findings on school attendance and attainment, while the individualist theory of learning does not provide the necessary conceptual tools.

The Sociology of Learning in School

A substantial portion of the literature on the sociology of learning in school has been reviewed by Sarane Boocock (1972). As a review, her book, *An Introduction to the Sociology of Learning*, exemplifies the principal characteristics of this literature. For this reason, I have singled out her thorough and competent treatment for attention.

Boocock (1972: 4) defines school learning as "how well [the student] is 'making it' in the school system." The Durkheimian would not have serious reservations about this definition. After all, Durkheim's analysis of the consequences of school for moral learning used survival in the classroom as the principal means of socialization. As it turns out, though, Boocock, like those whose work she reviews, regards "making it" in school entirely as cognitive learning, operationalized to denote test scores, grades, and persistence in school. The acquisition of motives, beliefs, values, and social skills is there, but it is important only to the extent that it fosters or retards academic performance. The social organization of the school or class is significant only as it promotes or retards the acquisition of those habits that in turn foster cognitive attainment.

In the school achievement model revealed by Boocock's review, learning occurs through the interaction of cognitive tasks set by the school with the resources that any one student commands for these tasks. The social organizational properties of the school or classroom are treated only to the extent that they can be seen as a part of this bundle of individual students' resources. It is the student in his or her role, rather than the school or class as a collectivity and the student role in its web of social relations (including relations with the teacher), that is the one social variable in the learning model. The school and classroom are disaggregated into collections of unrelated student actors. The bearing of social relations on social learning or of the school and classroom social order on the distribution and receipt of resources for cognitive learning are questions unasked.

The reformism that lies behind the school effects studies has engendered a preoccupation with the deliberate social control of education: the formation of educational policies designed to equalize students' access to opportunities and means for academic attainment. We have neglected what Durkheim stressed: that such societal forces as the institutional specialization of education and the occupational specialization of teaching foster social properties of schools and classrooms *sui generis*. Comparative studies of historical societies or periods within societies are required to reveal the action of these forces, which may operate independently of or constrain social policy to shape the emergent social organization of schools and classrooms and, thus, to select what students learn in school.

School and Schooling

Neglect of organizational and institutional variables makes the school effects literature inadequate sociologically. I should like to expand on one aspect of this inadequacy: a confusion in the school achievement model of school with schooling. Schools are organizations that conduct instruction. Schooling is the process through which instruction occurs. It is a process that students experience, but as members of the classroom and other collectivities within schools that are the immediate social settings of schooling. Schooling is purposive action by students and teachers, but this action is shaped and its consequences are affected by the social organization of these collectivities.[1]

Students of school effects ignore schooling so conceived. The student is in

---

[1] I will limit my remarks to classrooms because they are principal among these settings, but these remarks can be extended readily to such other settings as curricular tracks.

a school, certainly, but this school comprises a simple collection of resource stocks on which he can draw as he achieves. In this formulation, the relationship between the school and its resource stocks and what and how students learn is unmediated by the social organization of classrooms and the schooling processes that they contain and order. Being in school suffices as an indicator of being schooled. This confusion of school with schooling, I think, has discouraged efforts to conceptualize the social organizational components of schooling. Hence, it has weakened our understanding of the ways schools are organized to instruct, of the consequences of this organization for schooling, and in turn of the consequences of schooling for what students learn and how they differ in what and how much they learn. Equally, it has hampered our understanding of institutional constraints on the school–schooling–learning triad.

Reviewing the school effects studies, I have been struck by the fact that every study that reports trivial effects of school measures school attributes as central tendencies of schools or even of school districts: the average verbal competence of teachers, the number of books in the school library, or per pupil expenditures of a school district, for example.

A few studies have yielded more positive results which are strong and consistent enough over both cross-sectional and longitudinal designs and with extensive controls for extra-school sources of learning not to be dismissed as random events. These studies limited their attention to a narrow range of cognitive learning or attainment, but they measure properties of immediate settings of schooling: the high school curricular track (Heyns, 1974; Rosenbaum, 1976; Alexander and McDill, 1976; Alexander, Cook, and McDill, 1978; Breton, 1972: 229–53; Alwin and Otto, 1977) or the classroom (Murnane, 1975; Summers and Wolfe, 1974, 1977; Rutter et al., 1979).

Although these studies measured intuitively selected schooling resources, such as teachers' experience, the availability of textbooks or counselors, or the complexity and depth of material taught, they found notable partial associations between students' receipt of certain of these resources and their cognitive achievement. These findings imply that when resources involved in schooling are measured in a way that is fairly sensitive to the specific schooling experiences of students, at least some of these resources enter the process as potent forces for learning.

These studies relied on the individualistic model of school learning, even though the attainment process was measured close to the setting of the schooling process. In the absence of such a conceptualization, the resource variables that enter school effects studies, whatever the level of measurement, will continue to be selected intuitively. More important, it will remain difficult at best to pursue any of three topics that a serious sociological analysis of schooling entails:

1. the bearing of the social organization of the classroom on the distribution of educational resources among students,

2. the bearing of the social organization of the classroom on the use that students make of the resources that they receive, and
3. the bearing of the social organization of the classroom on patterns of student conduct.

These three topics in the analysis of schooling place the social order of the classroom in an analytical sense squarely between the stocks of educational resources that schools contain (such as teachers' command of subject matter or the variety or quantity of instructional materials) and the resources they receive and the ways they use these resources. They leave open the possibility that the receipt and use of educational resources are a function not only of students' motives, goals, or capacities, but also of the opportunities and constraints that follow from their membership in a classroom. They leave open as well the Durkheimian question: whether, beyond its possible action as a mechanism for distributing resources and constraining their use, the classroom social order itself is an instructor through the patterns of conduct that constitute the student role.

Instruction

Investigation of these topics should clarify relationships between schooling and learning, which in themselves are a significant object of inquiry. It also leads naturally into the study of institutional sources of variation in the school–schooling–learning triad. I should like to illustrate both of these potential contributions of a social organizational study of schooling by discussing a research agenda that begins with variation in modes of instruction.

In the foregoing pages, I propose a Durkheimian hierarchy, in which what students learn is nested in a broadening array of social contexts, each of them subject to formative influences from contexts higher in the hierarchy: the immediate instructional setting (in my discussion, the classroom), the school organization, the institution of education, and the broader society of which this institution is a part. Modes of instruction are an attractive starting point because they relate explicitly to each of these hierarchical levels. To use this starting point, one follows Durkheim by assuming that a teacher's intentions and actions have a disproportionate influence on the social order of classrooms and are an important link between institutional and micro-level components of the school–schooling–learning triad.

Various kinds of tutorial or individualized instruction are at present common in American classrooms. Such teaching, even in subjects like chemistry or biology in which American high schools and many lower schools routinely provide laboratory experience, is much less common in European and Third World countries where didactic teaching by lecture and recitation dominates.

Of course, it was not always so in the United States. For example, around the turn of the century, when faculty psychology was the core of educational doctrine, teaching emphasized mass drill and practice. This emphasis was found even in scientific subjects in which laboratory teaching had already appeared in the colleges and universities. Not until the 1930s, with growing emphasis in educational psychology on dynamic process and individual differences, did student motivation and variable intellectual capacity appear as problems for instruction, and it is only in the last few decades that this trend has flowered as individualized instruction.

From one side, such historical and cross-national variations raise interesting questions about the ways in which societal forces affect educational organizations and instructional practices. Serious consideration of such questions leads to sophisticated pursuit of the correlations between historical societies and specific forms of school and classroom organization and conduct.

From another side, these variations should lead us to ask about the consequences of modes of instruction for what students learn. Let me first consider this question and then turn to the issues of school, schooling, and the social selection of the outcomes of education.

Investigation of instruction and learning can be pursued through several sets of studies that correspond to issues raised by Durkheim in his analysis of the school class. One first would ask whether variation in a teacher's characteristic instructional mode is associated with such aspects of classroom social organization as the form and nature of ties among students in a classroom: for example, their density and mesh and the degree to which they are cooperative, competitive, or antagonistic. Such an analysis must demonstrate how the consequences of instructional modes are distinctive of or related to other sources of classroom social structure—some of them endogenous, such as the size of the classroom group, others exogenous, such as peer relationships in the neighborhoods from which the classroom draws its students.

This analysis would pose no small task; it might very well reveal an interaction of instructional modes and other sources of the social order of the classroom. However, I wish mainly to suggest that this inquiry would be one interesting way to discern the existence and sources of the separateness of the small societies of classrooms and ways in which the organizational form of schools and the occupational characteristics of teaching combine with such variables as the size and the age and socioeconomic composition of a classroom to shape its social organization.

There is some evidence of an association between instructional modes and the peer social structure of classrooms. Bossert (1979), for example, has found an association between lecture–recitation and the emergence of a highly stable achievement-stratified order of competitive social ties among a classroom's students. He has found an association between tutorial forms of instruction and cooperative, relatively unstratified social ties that ebb and flow in response to temporarily shared interests that result from students' joint engagement in classroom projects.

Accumulated evidence of such associations would suggest two directions for further inquiry. One line of investigation would pursue the Durkheimian problem of the consequences of student life in classrooms for the acquisition of social habits and beliefs. I have suggested elsewhere (Bidwell, 1972, 1973) that one may consider social participation in itself as an opportunity to practice certain habits and infer beliefs, and also as a source of reinforcement for these habits and beliefs. If so, a way is opened for systematic study of this problem of Durkheim's. The notion that classroom social structure is a structure of interpersonal influence (Bidwell, 1972, 1973) complements such a formulation of classroom participation as a progenitor of habituation to forms of conduct in other social settings.

Such questions are to me so obvious and important that I have been surprised and disappointed by our general failure to pursue them. For example, if students are exposed to laboratory instruction in science, what are the consequences of variation in the amount or content of exposure, of success or failure in the work, of fellow students' evaluations of its worth, for commitment to or appreciation of science, or for skepticism and belief in the value of empirical evidence and experimental method? If didactic teaching fosters competitive and instrumental social relationships among students while tutorial modes foster cooperation and consummatory social ties, what are the consequences for orientations toward work or civic participation or for the capacity for intimacy and friendship? These are no small questions, but I find such questions singularly absent in the contemporary sociology of education.

The second line of investigation is closer to the school attainment research, although it need not be limited to cognitive outcomes of schooling or to the conventional indicators of cognitive attainment. It is significantly different from this research, however, because it brings the schooling process directly into view as a prime mediator of students' learning. This line of investigation would ask how the social order of classrooms distributes resources for schooling and thus influences what students have to work with to learn.

Research of this kind would ask whether variation between classrooms in mode of instruction is associated with the stratification of students according to their levels of motivation, ability, or academic performance. It would ask further whether a classroom's stocks of resources for learning are distributed differentially across these strata, with consequent biases in students' opportunities to learn. By way of example, let me use again the lecture–recitation *versus* tutorial dichotomy

Lecture–recitation and tutorial instruction represent different patterns of resource deployment by teachers. So far as the teacher's own time and skills are concerned, lecture–recitation provides a formally equal exposure of each student to whatever content the teacher wishes to present. It does so by making the students collectively into an audience—for the lecture or for questioning–answering exchanges. Thus the entire student group is engaged with the same body of material for as long as the teacher wishes. In recitation, the teacher may involve students serially in the same asking and answering routine—for example, foreign language classes in which students follow one another in translating the same passage until the teacher is satisfied. However, the teacher may also vary the specific activities of individual students within a recitation episode—for example, a teacher who asks certain students more difficult questions than are asked of others. Nevertheless, most of the time students are formally doing the same thing—listening to fellow students recite.

Tutorial, by contrast, divides the teacher's time into shares that can be allotted in different proportions to individual students or subgroups of students. Moreover, the content of tutorial sessions can be differentiated from student to student or subgroup to subgroup on some distinguishing criterion, such as interest, past performance, or estimated ability.

The allocation of materials differs similarly between lecture–recitation and tutorial. In lecture–recitation, of course, the entire student group is engaged with the same body of material—say, the lesson or lecture topic. Most often, this common engagement is coupled with common readings, exercises, experiments, or whatever other student use of instructional materials the curriculum dictates. There may be some differentiation across students, as in the use of different paper assignments or supplementary or alternative readings or exercises. Nevertheless, the possible range of variation is much greater in tutorial because the constraints of common subject matter and common tasks are loosened when the classroom group no longer is an audience and need not work within the same frame of content and time.

Indeed, in lecture–recitation the amount of time spent on each lesson or topic, even if not always on specific tasks, is in the hands of the teacher and is usually allocated uniformly across students. Under tutorial, the student can be more fully in control of his or her own time per lesson or assignment (as well as his or her time per task). Hence, it is possible for students or for subgroups of students to work at their own rates until they decide or the teacher decides that the work is done.

Finally, lecture–recitation differs from tutorial in the degree of uniformity with which students are exposed to such attributes of their fellow students as interests, motives, abilities, and academic performance. In recitation, answering provides information to the student audience about such attributes of other students, but only within the limits set by the teacher's queries. In tutorial, individual or subgroup differentiation of academic tasks may be accompanied by some degree of latitude within which students may select not only tasks but also students with whom to work. Moreover, freedom of movement during time out of tutorial increases opportunities for interaction with other students during time that is allotted to academic activities. As a result, students' exposure to one another should be governed substantially by the complementarity of the varying tasks with which they are engaged and their preferences among their fellows as, for example, work partners, advisers, or friends. In short, there should be substantial differences between lecture–recitation and tutorial in the degree to which teachers' and students' acts are visible to the classroom collectivity and in the variability of requirements for the content and pacing of students' performance.

These two ordering principles in the conduct of instruction—collective visibility and performance requirements—in turn should influence the social structure of the classroom. This influence should appear especially in the degree to which teachers' skills and students' performance are central among the stocks of instructional resources in a classroom, in the degree to which the students are stratified according to performance-centered criteria, and in the degree to which a student's access to instructional resources is correlated with his or her location among these strata.

RESOURCE CENTRALITY

In lecture–recitation, exchanges between teacher and students are the focal elements of classroom activity—exchanges between the lecturing teacher and the student audience or the public exchanges of asking and answering. In either case, the teacher's acts dominate the class sessions. Thus, the teacher's subject matter competence and teaching skills are of necessity central instructional resources when lecturing or recitation is used. Moreover, because of the public nature of recitation and the uniformity of students' tasks in lecture–recitation, the distribution of student performance in the classroom is also a central resource. This distribution provides a comparative reference standard against which students individually can assess their own classroom performance. The pervasive visibility of what students do and the uniformity of the teacher's requirements for the content and pacing of academic tasks encourage a unidimensional ranking of attainment, on which the teacher's and students' evaluations converge.

In tutorial, because the content of student performance is more varied, less closely tied to interaction with the teacher, and less pervasively public, neither the teacher's competence nor the distribution per se of student performance so strongly dominates the stocks of classroom resources as compared, say, with instructional materials. Access to each resource stock will depend primarily on supply relative to the incidence of student demand. Of course, the teacher's ability as tutor and the supply of fellow students' abilities to perform one or another of the tasks set for individual students or student subgroups remain important resource stocks on which a student may be able to draw, but students are likely to use these stocks selectively according to their own predilections and the demands made upon them by other students. Consequently, attainment rankings are likely to be multidimensional, applied with different weights to different students, and less consensual than in lecture–recitation classrooms.

STRATIFICATION AND RESOURCE DISTRIBUTION

At least implicit in a teacher's decision to lecture is his or her assumption that the stock of teacher competence thereby is made equally accessible to all students because lecturing precludes students' decisions to demand unequal shares. However, the intuitive notion that abler and more strongly motivated students attend more to lectures than do others suggests that the lecture as a device for allocating this central resource stock is in fact quite vulnerable to students' decisions about its use. This vulnerability should cause use of the lecturing teacher and such student attributes as motivation and ability to covary.

The decision to teach by recitation may be based on a variety of criteria: for example, to allow each student a temporally equal share of participation, to favor the low performers, or to favor the high performers. Nevertheless, the recitation method, too, is vulnerable to students' decisions about using the teacher through asking–answering exchanges, more obviously so than the lecture. There is clear evidence that whatever the teacher's intentions, the high performing and the more compliant students outcompete the low performers and the less compliant for shares of recitation time (Bossert, 1979: chap. 4).

Consequently, one should observe in lecture–recitation classrooms a sharp stratification of resource receipt and resource use by the students that parallels their equally sharp stratification by achievement. I have argued that in lecture–recitation, teacher competence and the distribution of student performance are central resources. Now I have suggested that those students who rank high on performance-related criteria, which in these classrooms should be subordinated to a unidimensional performance standard, should also rank high on use of the lecturing teacher and on shares of time in recitation. Moreover, because of the unidimensionality of the performance standard, students' performance levels necessarily must correspond to qualitatively different information received and used by these students to assess their own performance.

The covariation of resource receipt and use with performance rankings should be considerably weaker in tutorial classrooms. If my earlier argument is correct, no stock of instructional resources is so clearly central to the activities of these classrooms as are teacher competence or the distribution of student performance in lecture–recitation classrooms. Performance rankings themselves are more complex and less clear-cut, while students use resources in more individually selective ways.

Nevertheless, resource receipt and use by students in tutorial classrooms is not likely to be unbiased. In these classrooms, students have greater control over the distribution of resource shares than they do in lecture–recitation classrooms. Consequently, they should have greater leeway to acquire disproportionate shares. Sussmann (1977) has shown that groups of energetic and aggressive students in "open" classrooms may dominate the social order of the class by becoming brokers of the class's resources. While such energy and aggressiveness may accompany high performance (as academic success rewards predispositions to demand and use instructional resources), it is not clear that such demand for classroom resources is a simple function of academic performance. Moreover, there are certain aspects of schooling that should yield a less performance-stratified resource distribution in tutorial than in lecture–recitation classrooms. This possibility can be suggested by further discussion of collective visibility and performance standards as aspects of classroom activity.

COMPETITION, EVALUATION, AND PEER RELATIONSHIPS

As I have said, in lecture–recitation the pervasive visibility of students' performance means that each student can evaluate his or her performance in relation to the performance of every other student. Invidious competition is less likely in tutorial classrooms because of the lower visibility of student performance, the greater variability and complexity of performance standards, and students' tendencies to become selectively engaged with one another in task-centered subgroups. Invidious competition should reinforce the stratification of students by performance and the tendency of the more highly ranked students, especially those striving for the top ranks, to make intense demands on classroom resources.

Uniform performance standards and public performance also foster evaluation of student attainment by a group-anchored criterion ("grading on the curve"). This mode of evaluation provides positive reinforcement disproportionately to the better performers, negative reinforcement disproportionately to the worse.

The more varied the performance standards and the less visible the performance, the more likely is evaluation to be set against an absolute standard or against a student's own earlier performance. Such evaluation should provide a favorable balance of positive and negative reinforcement for all students in a classroom independent of their performance histories. Here the amount of positive reinforcement should vary more with motivation than initial attainment. As the tie between performance histories and evaluation weakens, so may the association between these histories and demands on classroom resources.

Finally, there is some evidence that compositional effects of student membership on academic performance may be mediated by the degree to which students' performance is subject to common performance standards. I have noted Bossert's (1979: chap. 5) finding of an association between teachers' use of lecture–recitation and stratification of students' classroom friendships according to level of academic performance. The more uniform the performance standards, the more likely were ties among students to center on academic ability and attainment and to form stable networks. The less uniform the standards, the more likely were students' academic interests to undergird peer ties, independently of performance histories, and the more likely were these ties to change as students' interests changed with the ebb and flow of classroom tasks. To the extent that peer networks in classrooms are formed into a stable, performance-centered hierarchy, the performance-based stratification of access to classroom resources and learning opportunities should be reinforced.

The foregoing argument suggests that modes of instruction, through their effects on the social order of the classroom, may shape the centrality of resource stocks and at the same time constrain students' access to and use of these stocks. These constraints arise from the consequences of instructional modes for the distribution of students' demand for the instructional resources that their classrooms contain.

Intuitively, it is plausible that variation in the centrality of instructional resources and the demand-structuring consequences of the visibility of student performance and of the complexity and clarity of performance standards should affect the distribution of rates of learning among a classroom's students. It follows from my argument about the performance-based stratification of resource receipt and use that learning rates (and achievement gains) should correlate more strongly with initial achievement levels in lecture–recitation than in tutorial classrooms. Thus, with consistent exposure over some period of time to didactic instruction, the rank order of a group of students with respect to academic achievement should become increasingly stable and its gradient increasingly steep.

Completing the Triad

I have now suggested certain lines of investigation into the schooling and learning portion of the school–schooling–learning triad. These studies would consider how the social organization of schooling bears on what students learn (e.g., the various normative outcomes of schooling) and how much they learn (e.g., resource stratification and rates of learning). My postulated Durkheimian hierarchy, of course, also directs attention to the relationship between school and schooling. It suggests that the organization properties of the school intervene between society and the microcosm of the classroom to shape the social organization of schooling.

Therefore, if one wished to explore the social selection of what is learned in school, investigation of schooling and learning would be complemented by analysis of association between the social order of the classroom and the organization of schools. On the one hand, one might ask how the organizational properties of schools—for example, their division of instructional labor and devices for distributing students to teachers—shape the social form of classrooms.

On the other hand, one might ask in what ways and to what extent the classroom in fact develops its own distinctive social order, undoubtedly limited in part by the organizational form of schools but also surely in part an emergent social fact in its own right. If classrooms to a degree develop separate social and moral orders, is there system to be found in their emergence? What are the consequences of these emergent social and normative properties for schooling?

It is entirely possible that inquiry of this kind will show that at least in contemporary American society schools as organizations have very little control or influence over schooling and that the principal external constraints on the social organization of classrooms and schooling are to be found in broad societal variations in the institution of education: for example, the differentiation of the occupation of teaching, the degree of separation between family or economy and education, the nature and degree of class bias in access to schools, or national policies that govern investment in education. As I have suggested, such influences will not be revealed by school effects studies conducted without a comparative societal referent. A comparative statics of national systems of education or of notable regional differences within societies and historical and prospective investigations of change in national or regional systems over significant time periods are required.

My skepticism about the potency of the contemporary American school organization as an element in the Durkheimian hierarchy has been stimulated by the variance-partitioning studies that I discussed earlier in this essay, even though they address a narrow range of schooling outcomes. These studies set a low upper bound on the variance in student attainment that lies between schools. This bound does not imply weak cumulative contributions of schooling to students' learning. However, the formal organizational milieus that schools provide for schooling will affect this process only to the extent that they affect the kinds and amounts of resources allotted to classrooms or the use of these resources by teachers and students. Hence, one's attention is directed to organizational policies that govern the differential allocation of resources within schools or the decision rules used by teachers in schooling itself—most notably, perhaps, their decision rules for the selection of modes of instruction.

There is no clear evidence for the contemporary United States that resource allocation at either the district or local school level is consequential for schooling. In our society, the funding, organizational forms, and managerial practices of schools and districts may be too uniform to engender the covariation of school and schooling that would give evidence of such consequences. Indeed, Meyer and Rowan (1978) argue for a "decoupling" of the formal structures of schools and their actual work processes on the basis of broad societal trends toward bureaucratization. As I have in this essay, they press for comparative and historical studies to discover institutional consequences for schooling.

If we are to pursue such arguments or more generally inquire into the social selection of learning, it will be necessary to search out potential mechanisms of organizational control over schooling and the institutional conditions of their varying incidence and effectiveness. In other times and places, perhaps where the funding, forms, and management of educational organizations are more diverse than in our own society, organizational influence on classrooms and schooling may be more palpable.

Nevertheless, it is very possible that to some degree the social organization of schooling is always formed by direct institutional constraint. Durkheim proposed differentiation as the key constraint; Meyer and Rowan follow Weber by proposing bureaucratization. These possibilities call for careful specification and testing, but they need not restrain further search for mechanisms of institutional influence more useful analytically than the neo-Marxian stress on the isomorphism of dominance in the society and classroom (Bowles and Gintis, 1976). Imaginative pursuit of these questions may well lead us into a most interesting articulation of institutional and microsocial analyses, in a return to the earlier sociological concern for the societal selection of the forms, processes, and outcomes of education.

9

Is Group Theory Useful?

Robert K. Leik

TOO MANY YEARS AGO to recall readily and to relate with equanimity, a mythical apprentice sociologist cast about for a dissertation topic. It had to serve many purposes: able to address important theoretical questions about social process and structure, permitting experimental hence causal analysis in spite of a discipline that avoided the concept of cause, allowing precise measurement in an era of recently awakened precision, possibly enabling mathematical treatment at a time when a courageous soul could hope that an integral sign might yet appear in ASR, and above all, capable of producing definite results at a reasonable cost in time and money. With a growing number of other enthusiasts, the MA (mythical apprentice) turned to small group research. It promised to satisfy all these demands. Whether such a daring affiliation was to lead to victory and spoils in the academic jousts or to ignominy if the new enthusiasm proved a false faith could not be foretold, but the adventure was great.

What became of our heroic apprentice? Many chapters of successes and failures, of joys and frustrations, could unfold. There are still some small grouping quests to join, but the ardor seems to have cooled and the excitement of discovery is diminished. In portions of the realm, one can find group research laboratories now divested of their frocked assistants and being used for classes, for meetings, and even, oh woe, for storing dead data. Has the dream failed, or is our hero unable to recognize among current researchers the new standard bearers for the old faith?

Undoubtedly, there will be devotees of small group theory who see no weakness or enervation, yet many seem to feel that there is little new being done. Attendance at small group sessions is noticeably diminished and more

115

than one colleague has spoken of a need to revitalize the field. I do not share Mullins' (1978) contention that small group theory is "the light that failed," but surely the light is dimmed. To ask whether group theory is useful is to imply that there is such theory and that there are criteria of usefulness. As to the existence of theory, there has been and continues to be an impressive array of treatises on groups. The list begins with pioneers such as Simmel (1950), Freud (1960), Moreno (1934), Thrasher (1927), Sherif (1936), and Whyte (1943). It develops into major streams emanating from Harvard via Bales (1950) and his many associates (Hare, 1962; Strodtbeck, 1951; Dunphy, 1972), and from Michigan via Lewin (1951) and his coworkers and followers (Cartwright and Zander, 1960). There have been offspring in fields such as industrial relations (Fiedler, 1967), public relations (Golembiewski, 1962), speech communications (Cathcart and Samovar, 1970), personal growth and human potential movements (Shaw, 1976), family counseling (Olson, 1976), and many other areas. Specialized substantive applications have focused on families (Parsons and Bales, 1955; Turner, 1970; Aldous et al., 1971), on gangs (Cloward and Ohlin, 1960; Short and Strodtbeck, 1965), on sociometric cliques, structures, and related balance problems (Katz, 1953; Hubbell, 1965; Davis, 1967; Taylor, 1970; Hallinan, 1974), on influence and status structures (Hopkins, 1964; Berger et al., 1974), on group productivity (Steiner, 1972), and on a wealth of other emphases. The list seems endless, and only a minute sampling of representative works has been suggested.

Sheer volume of effort does not imply theoretical integration or utility of knowledge. In fact, despite the large volume of work, the major sources of ideas are not necessarily recent. For curiosity, the date of publication of all references in two recent texts on small groups was tabulated. The texts are by Nixon (1979) and S. Wilson (1978). Mean date for references in both books is 1961, and median for both is 1962. The former contains 445 references; the latter contains 263. Each draws about 5 percent of its references from prior to 1940, and 11 or 7 percent, respectively, from prior to 1950. In short, about 90 percent of relevant work, according to these two volumes, was done in the fifties, sixties, and seventies, about evenly scattered over that period. Other subject areas show essentially exponential growth in publishing over the past few decades. Has the field really lost its vigor?

The answer is, of course, both yes and no. There does appear to be less sociological concern with something called small groups. However, there is by no means a loss of interest in the questions of structure and process that have motivated small group research. What seems to have happened is that small group notions have been transported to a variety of applied fields, as cited earlier, while academic researchers have increasingly focused on particular process or structure problems rather than on groups. For example, those dealing with groups as therapeutic vehicles really talk about groups per se, as do those who advise how to have effective committees, how to optimize leadership in business settings, and so forth.

It is interesting to read some of that material in part for its contrast with a standard small group text or collection of readings. The contrast is due largely to an applied field asserting that there are specific goals which can be furthered by using knowledge of how groups operate. The knowledge (which is by no means always correct and dependable) gains an immediacy and vitality because it is potentially useful for some important end. There is an obvious parallel with good evaluation and policy research.

The academic concern with groups often lacks such a focus or sense of purpose. That would not be problematic except that, if groups are seen as armies in the laboratory (Zelditch, 1969), that is, as representing general social systems in more easily observable form, then almost all of general sociology and social psychology is fair game. The field is no longer a field, but a huge collection of only partly related concerns.

As happens in any area, when volume and diversity become too great, subdivisions appear. We have at this time a number of vital areas of inquiry that are studied in a small group manner, but that are not so labeled. A good deal of work on exchange theory is of this type (Cook and Emerson, 1978; Leik et al., 1975). Similarly, equity (Cook and Parcel, 1977), communication networks (Granovetter, 1974), status differentiation (Gray et al., 1968), and so forth are eminently group problems, but are so large scale themselves that they become isolated and researched apart from other group questions.

I do not mean to decry this development. It is unavoidable anyway, and it is also necessary if these more focused areas are to progress. I do believe, however, that the group has been lost as a focus of theory development. Texts still use early small group notions as if they are generally valid and still empirically supported. Yet there is mounting evidence, especially from special application areas, that some of these ideas are either invalid altogether or must be carefully conditioned and qualified. Two examples might help.

Early in their studies of groups, Bales and his associates formulated the dual leadership theory, including reasonable explanations of why such duality should arise and some evidence of its existence in real groups. That theory was transported intact to the area of the family, with the assumption (indeed the prescription in at least one family therapy volume) that the husband–father was instrumental leader and the wife–mother was expressive leader. Even cross-cultural evidence was arrayed.

As Aldous notes, this conception "was widely accepted in the past, but today has been largely discredited" (Aldous, 1977: 117), and Raush et al. (1974) concluded from their work that it was "time to put to rest once and for all the sex-role differentiation theory of Parsons and Bales." A considerable body of evidence shows that ad hoc task-oriented groups, which most small group researchers have preferred to study, simply do not show the same patterns that families show. Again, Lennard and Bernstein (1969) provide evidence that seriously questions the long-standing notion that satisfying or successful groups display about twice as much agreement or other positive behavior as disagreement. Actual families, they found, seldom agree as much as they disagree, let alone twice as much.

Another area of interest is the application of group leadership principles to work settings. In particular, Fiedler's (1967) well known work shows that leadership style must be compatible with conditions of control and task clarity in order to be effective. Different conditions imply different optimal styles. Fiedler's work showed, among other things, that some foremen would get better results from their groups after going through a standard leadership training course emphasizing understanding, communication, and so forth. Other leaders, however, would do worse after such a course. They had changed their styles in the "preferred" direction and the new style became a liability. This line of inquiry was evidently sparked less by academic concerns than by the attempt to apply group leadership theory to the work setting in the form of leader training.

The first example given above says that not all groups operate by the same rules: the rules change because of interpersonal development internal to the group, from stranger groups to primary groups. The second example says that external conditions help specify how the rules shift. Perhaps a single formulation could cover both sources of group differences. I know of no such formulation as yet.

There are many studies which can expand these examples. Richmond (1976) found that wives' resources influence the balance of power in families of Cuban refugees if there is a supportive milieu for equalitarianism. Without that supportive milieu, a wife's resources have virtually no influence on her power. Wish and Kaplan (1977) demonstrate that the type of dyadic relationship (husband–wife, lawyer–client, etc.) and the type of situation (social conversation, settling a misunderstanding, etc.) greatly influence the character of interaction in terms of cooperativeness, intensity, dominance, formality, and task orientation. Yet these dimensions relate closely to the IPA profiles and who-to-whom matrices characterizing much early small group research.

These examples point to a useful critique of most group research. That research, at least in the sociological tradition, has tended to assume that there is one set of rules governing groups. Even though Bales and others were quite clear that they were talking about only one type of group, and even though exchange theorists have clearly enunciated the idea of diverse sets of rules (Meeker, 1971; Cook, 1975), there seems to be blind insistence that all groups are represented by *my* particular study and all groups are encompassed by *my* theory, whatever study or theory is involved.

The use of group theory in applied areas cannot be so insensitive. As Minuchin (1974) or Watzlawick et al. (1974) formulate the therapeutic problem, "any change that does not alter the basic premises governing the system . . . is no change at all." (Bochner, 1976: 388). Watzlawick is concerned with effecting changes in the rules by which the family operates. Similarly, Minuchin, following Jackson (1965), uses therapeutically created crises to force review of current rules and to generate reconstruction of the group's reality. I do not mean to endorse or disagree with such techniques. The point is that all these examples emphasize that the rules change as either internal or external conditions change. There is a vast need to know how and why, and very little to answer that need.

Perhaps the point is clear by now that the need in various applied areas for bringing about results has forced attention to questions that we do not ordinarily ask. Those concerns have, in turn, provided important insights for developing more complete and general theory, if we only attend to them. As it is often presented in sociology, the field of small groups is a large collection of generalizations about idealized and rather isolated groups. The general and the ideal can get pretty dull, at times. One key to revitalization of small group research, it seems to me, is to focus on how rules governing group structure and process evolve and change across the developmental history of the group and within the diverse contexts that real groups experience. The detached, ad hoc, problem-solving group should be only one special case from a more complete developmental theory of situated groups.

There is a quite different point that may appear rather trivial but is potentially important. Because early small group research was the major reason for establishing experimental facilities in many departments, those facilities were typically called "small group laboratories." No matter what went on in those labs, it seemed, that was called "small group research." Even single-person learning experiments have been so labeled because the lab label carried the day. Semanticists could have had a ball.

The proliferation of group-relevant research which was cited earlier is not all small group research, although it may well pertain to small groups. Exchange processes operate in groups, but they operate elsewhere as well. Differentiating processes are general, not just group processes, as is true of most of the kinds of things now being studied. There is a vigorous and growing tradition of experimental sociology which is only partly concerned with groups. Much of it is at best tangential to questions of group structure and process. Yet there is still a tendency to see this body of research as small group research; after all, it is done in a lab.

In the process of such confusion we have lost track, as often as not, of what are group-specific questions versus what are general social structure and process questions. To illustrate the former, one area of early interest in the Harvard "school" was the phases a group passes through as it solves problems. Not much was done with that eminently group-focused concern after an initial flurry of research. However, that concern is still vital to those using groups for treatment or personal growth purposes. People who are going to lead such groups need a good sense of what constitutes progress through desired stages and how to recognize those stages and facilitate their progression. Of course, values have been interjected in words like "good" or "desired," and we may not share those values. Nevertheless, it is easy to find numerous objective studies of group stage development in journals such as *Human Communication Research* (Mabry, 1975; Ellis and Fisher, 1975) or *Small Group Research* (Babad and Amir, 1978). Similarly the emergence of leaders in natural groups is necessarily a group problem, and not just a general problem that happens to be relevant to groups. Such work also continues in the applied literature (Schultz, 1978).

The point of referring to the applied fields so often in this commentary is to emphasize that they must focus on groups per se with all their variability and context-specific or history-specific complexity. We, on the other hand, have tended to lose sight of groups in our search for general principles, but have retained the label of small group research to cover almost anything experimental. If we wish to further theory development in the area of groups, then we must sort out when we are talking group and when we are talking general structure or process. The two are not incompatible, of course, but the emphasis on groups as such leads to concern with real groups in real time and real context. All the general principles, all the general rules, become conditional. If we don't get around to focusing on specific group questions, we never notice the real-world contingencies that give life to the abstract principles.

10

Cognitive Processes, Social Behavior, and Game Theory

Kenneth E. Friend and James D. Laing

THIS CHAPTER PROCEEDS from the fundamental assumption that much social behavior is purposive. People choose their social actions in calculated attempts to achieve objectives they value. We review research indicating that recent advances in the theory of cooperative games can provide one useful basis for analyzing social behavior, and that this analysis can be made substantially more effective by adding explicit assumptions about social and cognitive processes.

The first section argues that game theory is one potentially good basis for analyzing and predicting observed behavior, but certain traditional assumptions in game theory require augmentation or modification if we are to generate effective models of social behavior. The second section reviews research on cooperative coalition behavior among actors competing for status. This review of coalitions in sequential games of status illustrates the range of cognitive and social process models which can be used to improve classical game-theoretic analysis of social choice. Models derived from game-theoretic analysis enjoy greater success when supplemented by assumptions from individual information-processing psychology, when appropriate normative constraints on behavior are included, and when the negotiation process among actors is modeled explicitly.

These results for coalitions in status games have general implications for the study of other social choice behavior. However, coalition research typi-

☐ An earlier version of this chapter was discussed at the ORSA/TIMS meetings in New York, May 1–3, 1978.

cally has focused on bargaining over apportionment of one divisible "good" among coalition members: this emphasis limits the direct relevance of traditional coalition research to many types of conflict situations. The third section discusses this limitation and briefly reviews recent game-theoretic and experimental research designed to overcome this problem. This research on games *without sidepayments* analyzes collective decision making under majority rule by committees that are choosing a multidimensional outcome from an infinite set of alternatives (e.g., choosing a policy from some multidimensional policy space), rather than dividing a single "good." The results obtained already in this research on *spatial games* encourage us to believe that recent advances in game theory of this sort provide a useful basis for analyzing collective choice.

The final section indicates two important directions for future research on collective choice. First, the trends identified in our review of research on status games ought to be applied to current theoretical and empirical work on decision making by majority rule in spatial games without sidepayments. Second, this application should lead to models which more clearly relate to collective problem solving and the creation of decision alternatives. We can increase understanding of the relations between conflict and collective problem solving by incorporating models of human cognitive processes.

Game Theory and Social Behavior

We consider here the relevance of game theory in general as a conceptual foundation for the study of social and organizational behavior.[1] By Max Weber's classical definition,

> Action is *social* insofar as, by virtue of the subjective meaning attached to it by the acting individual (or individuals), it takes account of the behavior of others and is thereby oriented in its course. (Weber, 1947: 88)

The theory of games gives primary attention to the social nature of human behavior, thus defined.

The social and organizational context of human behavior has many crucially important influences on individuals involved in collective action. For example, to analyze a collectivity, one must take into account important features of the social situation, such as the enforcement of various norms of conduct and associated sanctions, patterns of interdependence linking individuals, and relevant institutions that are important sources of constraint on the alternatives, decision processes, and effects of collective action. Social in-

[1] This section follows closely an argument presented by Laing and Ordeshook (in preparation, chap. 5).

puts such as these help to determine important features of the social situation that the theory of games, per se, takes as given, yet these ingredients are absolutely essential to effective game-theoretic analysis of collective action. However, this should not be taken to suggest that all important social aspects of behavior lie outside the theory of games. In fact, few other theories focus more directly on the social nature of human behavior.

The theory of games (Luce and Raiffa, 1957) is a general theory about human cooperation and conflict. It concerns social action among persons who recognize that each person's fate not only depends on his or her own actions, but also depends on the actions of others. The possible actions of others provide contingencies for individual action in pursuit of valued social and personal states. The interdependence among actors is fundamental to each individual's calculus of effective social action, and provides the basis for cooperation and conflict in society. The hallmark of game-theoretic reasoning is the prediction of stable patterns of behavior based on the assumption that each person chooses acts in pursuit of valued outcomes, recognizes the interdependence among people in the situation, takes their calculations into account, and expects that other actors will do the same. Thus, game theory analyzes the way in which each person's social action "takes account of the behavior of others and is thereby oriented in its course," meeting Weber's definition, cited above.

Game theory deserves careful attention as a theory of social behavior. Unfortunately, many early attempts to apply game theory to complex social situations were so simplistic that many social scientists incorrectly concluded that the basic theory was wrong. The primary failure was not with the theory, but rather with the way it was applied. Although simple exercises can illustrate basic concepts of elementary social phenomena in bold relief, a two-by-two game matrix seldom provides a valid representation of complex social situations. We probably should not take seriously elementary textbook exercises such as "Suppose that the USA and USSR each face two alternatives—drop the bomb or don't." Effective game-theoretic analysis is not simplistic. Sophisticated applications of game-theoretic reasoning have appeared in the literature and more are on the way which provide effective scientific models of complex social situations. A later section provides clear instances of this.

However, the classical theory of games does possess important shortcomings which must be corrected if the theory is to provide a sound basis for generating a viable and robust system of scientific propositions about social behavior, rather than providing an only apparently substantive justification for exercises in mathematics. One set of issues relates to substantive assumptions at least implicit in game theory about human cognition, information-processing capacities, and preferences. Almost without exception, classical game-theoretic models assume "unlimited" rationality: actors have well behaved utilities defined for all available outcomes, and they have perfect ability to calculate the possible consequences of all strategies that might be pursued. In many situations, even the analyst, who might spend more time thinking about the actor's situation than does the actor himself, cannot begin to meet this requirement, even with the help of modern computer technology. Another difficulty relates to classical cooperative game theory's almost exclusive attention to payoff allocations. First, this has the effect of directing attention away from the *process* whereby allocations are arranged. Second, this tends to remove the possibility of predicting patterns in cooperative behavior, since the classical theory of cooperative n-person games seeks to identify payoffs that make actors *indifferent* over alternative coalitions to which they might belong (Rapoport, 1970: 287). This can be interpreted to imply that certain coalitions are equally likely, yet systematic patterns of coalition frequencies are often observed.

The next section illustrates how these potential problems in the classical theory may be overcome by introducing certain types of behavioral modifications that permit development of good scientific models predicting social cooperation and conflict. This sets the background for our later consideration of recent advances in the theory of cooperative games that have important implications for analyzing collective decisions.

Modeling Coalition Behavior in Sequential Status Games

Many phenomena have important effects on patterns of cooperation and conflict in ongoing social relations. Sociology has devoted special attention to the importance of social status in human behavior. It is useful to assume that social behavior is motivated in part by status objectives, and status striving by interdependent actors can be subjected to game-theoretic analysis (Shubik, 1971). It is also useful to recognize that social actions in ongoing social relations occur in temporal sequences. Whether motivated by status or other objectives, the history of earlier decisions—and the pursuit of long-term objectives in the sequence of decisions as a whole—can have important effects on behavior in the current episode. In this section we review some research on cooperation and conflict among status-motivated actors in a sequence of collective decisions. This review provides some concrete examples of ways in which behavioral assumptions of game theory may be modified to establish a more effective basis for analyzing social behavior.

Laing and Morrison (1973) designed a laboratory situation in which the same three persons play a sequence of coalition games. On each game in the sequence, two people form a coalition and decide how to split the points won by that coalition between the partners, thus increasing their total point scores. Throughout the sequence, subjects know everyone's current total score, and that each person's monetary payoff for the sequence of games as a whole will be determined solely by a known linear function of his *rank* status in the final scores. For example, players finishing in first, second, and third place, respectively, win $10, $5, and $0.

HEURISTIC DECISION RULES

Rather than treating the entire sequence of decisions as one super-game which might be solved for optimal strategies, known limits on human cognition suggest that actors may calculate options and make choices on a decision-by-decision basis. To form tractable representations of each decision problem, actors may adopt short-term objectives as surrogates for long-term goals, and employ certain heuristics embodied in rules-of-thumb for negotiating each decision. This is consistent with Newell and Simon's (1972) conceptualization of cognitive processes in human problem solving.

Following this general strategy, Laing and Morrison (1973) assumed that each player, unable to calculate optimal paths to the ultimate objective of maximizing his final mark, adopted a surrogate short-term objective for the outcome of the present game such that a player always prefers an outcome giving him higher rank at the end of the trial, and considers actual differences in scores only to break ties between two outcomes giving him the same rank. Laing and Morrison's model also assumed that in forming expectations about the outcomes associated with each potential coalition and in negotiating the agreements, players use, and expect others to use, three bargaining heuristics. The first of these, and one we will return to later, is: a coalition member should outrank his partner in the outcome resulting from their coalition if and only if he also outranked the partner when the coalition formed.

The heuristic rules in this model are sufficient to predict a unique vector of ranks across the three players associated with any two-person coalition in a three-person status game. Given that each player calculates his expected rank from each alternative coalition, and prefers forming that coalition in which he expects higher rank, the model generates predictions about (1) the probability that each coalition forms, and, via an analysis of relative "dependencies" (Emerson, 1962) related to the pattern of preferences for coalition partners, also predicts (2) the exact division of points within the coalition. This heuristic model is well supported by the results of Laing and Morrison's (1973) study and has been replicated in subsequent laboratory studies of status games (Friend, Laing, and Morrison, 1977a) and in the experiments of Vinacke (1962) in which extrinsic rewards were *not* tied to final ranks (Friend, Laing, and Morrison, 1977a, 1978).

CLASSICAL GAME THEORY AND STATUS GAMES

The classical theory of cooperative n-person games can be applied to each game of status in the sequence, given the preferences assumed to represent the players' short-term objectives. Unfortunately, the *core* (Luce and Raiffa, 1957)—perhaps the most prominent solution concept in the theory of cooperative games[2]—is empty in every game of status without a veto player (Shubik, 1971: 124; Friend, Laing, and Morrison, 1977b). Even had a core existed, however, this would imply that every coalition of two or more players would be included in the predicted set. The core is potentially useful for predicting allocations of payoffs; however, neither the core nor von Neumann and Morgenstern's (1947) stable set concept can be used to predict coalitions.

On the other hand, Aumann and Maschler's (1964) solution concept, the bargaining set, identifies coalition structures as well as the associated payoff configurations that are "stable." Therefore, there is some reason to hope that the bargaining set might provide a useful basis for predicting which coalitions form. This hope is not fulfilled in the data on status games (Laing and Morrison, 1974). For most of the status games observed in the laboratory study, the bargaining set's coalition predictions are tautological, since they include all admissible coalitions in the predicted set. In the few instances in which the bargaining set could have been wrong, it usually was. Later in the chapter we discuss recent experimental research on committee decision under majority rule. Here, also, the bargaining set and other classical theory either fails to make predictions or makes incorrect predictions as to which coalitions form.

In welcome contrast, we noted earlier the success attained by a heuristic decision model, predicated on the assumption that actors cope with complex decision problems by partitioning them into manageable components, forming simplified representations of reality, and applying rules-of-thumb, thus reducing the problem into one they can solve. In an important sense, the heuristic model is in the spirit of game-theoretic analysis: it assumes that actors do choose their actions in calculated attempts to attain valued objectives (albeit through a limited rationality), and that in making these calculations they take into account expectations associated with the preferences, strategic positions, and actions available to the other actors, expecting also that others will do the same. Nonetheless, because the heuristic model in many ways represents a substantial departure from classical game-theoretic analysis, the next two subsections review the results of other attempts to make behavioral

---

[2] The basic idea underlying the core of a cooperative game may be explained as follows. A particular alternative belongs to the core of the game if, when that alternative is about to become the outcome of the game, no subset of players can agree to shift, instead, to any other outcome which their coalition could bring about. When no alternative meets this criterion, the core is an empty set.

modifications of game theory in order to predict coalition behavior in games of status.

APPLYING GAME-THEORETIC ARBITRATION OF BILATERAL NEGOTIATION TO COALITION FORMATION

Pairs of potential coalition partners in the three-person status games might simplify their calculations by treating negotiations in each potential two-person coalition as a two-person bargaining game. Nash's (1953) scheme for arbitrating two-person negotiations requires a *reference outcome* (or *status quo* point) which is established by identifying the outcome if two players play "noncooperatively." In three-person games, Friend, Laing, and Morrison (1977b) calculated this reference outcome in terms of potential alternative agreements of each of the two bargainers with the third player. This represents a departure from, but is consistent in spirit with, the general rationale of Nash's approach. Once a reference outcome is determined from considering each player's possibilities in association with the third, the arbitration scheme singles out a unique agreement within the coalition which can be used to generate expectations of outcomes associated with each alternative coalition. These, in turn, can be used to identify preferences for coalition partners and to derive predictions about which coalition forms. Using reference outcomes associated with "threat" strategies involving the third player, predictions from this model perform nearly as well as the heuristic model. In fact, it is intriguing to note that this model typically points to outcomes that are consistent with the heuristic (described earlier) that is a crucially important ingredient of the heuristic model. Consequently, this modification and application of Nash's arbitration scheme offers a game-theoretic basis for justifying and explaining one reasonable, but somewhat arbitrary, assumption of the heuristic model. Game-theoretical analysis was successful in this case when a simpler form of strategic calculation was assumed than in the classical theory of n-person games.

NORMATIVE CONSTRAINTS ON NEGOTIATION

The heuristic rule described earlier as a crucial ingredient in the heuristic model may be considered as a particularization of a general social norm of fairness such as suggested by the concept of distributive justice. It prescribes that members of a coalition should maintain the same ranking *relative* to one another as they had before joining the coalition: even if partners improve their positions vis-à-vis another player, changes in relative status *within* the coalition are "inappropriate."

When players want to obey such a norm or expect punishment for deviation, classical game theory attempts to reflect all such preferences via the
players' utility functions over the possible outcomes. Players then perform
strategic calculations that take into account all possible strategies and outcomes. Thus, the effects of such norms appear only in terms of how changes
in the utility functions affect the results of strategic calculations.

An alternative approach more consistent with cognitive models of social
choice is to assume that social norms act to limit the range of alternatives actors consider. This approach was adopted by Laing and Morrison (1974) in
evaluating the predictions of Aumann and Maschler's (1964) bargaining set
as it applied to predicting negotiated rank outcomes in sequential status
games. The solution procedure associated with the bargaining set can be interpreted as a sequence of screening operations which reduce the total set of
feasible rank outcomes down to the subset predicted by the theory. Use of the
above heuristic rule, so that only outcomes consistent with it were ever considered in the subsequent solution procedure, substantially improved the rank
outcome predictions of the bargaining set. This indicates that game-theoretic
predictions may be improved by assuming that elements of strategic calculations are limited to a set which is acceptable under some social norms of
bargaining. This has the effect of simplifying the decision problem to one
which can be more easily addressed within the player's limited information-
processing capacities.

PROCESS CONSIDERATIONS IN BARGAINING

Virtually all behavioral and game-theoretic models of social choice are
"black-box" input–output theories that do not model explicitly the negotiation process. They relate strategic aspects of the starting conditions directly to
predicted outcomes of negotiations. As examples, Aumann and Maschler's
(1964) bargaining set, based on a fairly explicit conceptualization of the
negotiation potentials of actors, merely sets static conditions indicating
whether a certain proposal is stable. Laing and Morrison's (1973) heuristic
model and Komorita and Chertkoff's (1973) theory both include assumptions
about the bargaining process, but they are designed to predict the end product, not the process through which the outcome is produced.

In contrast, Friend, Laing, and Morrison (1977a) have modeled the
negotiation process explicitly by incorporating assumptions about information processing of individual decisions (Newell and Simon, 1972) with a process model of interacting negotiators. First, a detailed cognitive process model
of each player was designed to predict at each stage of the actual negotiation
process whether an individual actor would make an offer, accept one made to
him, or reject one he had received. These predictions were verified empirically. Second, computer simulations of interactions among three such in-

dividual process models were used to predict outcomes, and these predictions agree substantially with the patterns of results obtained in laboratory research and with the pattern predicted by the heuristic model.

Further work with these process simulations led to predictions *not* available from preexisting theoretical work: (1) Initial proposals of coalition partnerships tend to conform strongly to the predictions of the heuristic model, but as the process proceeds, results move toward an "all coalitions equally likely" pattern. Thus, the average length of negotiations should affect the pattern observed. (2) Payoffs may often start at equal splits (in status games) but, as negotiations proceed, they change toward the asymmetries in allocations predicted by the heuristic model. Thus, any tendency for short or prolonged negotiations affects outcomes in several ways. These and other unique process-related predictions were supported by the data (Friend, Laing, and Morrison, 1977a). Such results indicate that detailed process models, based on information-processing models of individual decisions, can enrich our understanding of social behavior, even when the primary objective is to predict outcomes.

DIRECTIONS FOR ANALYSIS OF SOCIAL BEHAVIOR

The theoretical developments reviewed above suggest some directions for analysis of social behavior. First, this research indicates the importance of investigating strategies in sequences of ongoing decisions in collectivities (e g , "logrolling" in policy-making groups). Analysis that treats each decision episode as a distinct event misses important effects associated with the sequential context. Particularly, the observation that low-status parties tend to coalesce and that they maintain relative status in their agreements may have important implications for status equilibration in ongoing social relations.

Second, this research suggests important specific phenomena to be investigated in research on interpersonal conflict and cooperation: (1) It is useful to incorporate explicit recognition of certain social norms into game-theoretic models of conflict resolution. (2) Process models of social conflict should seek to identify effects related to the intensity (duration) of bargaining, because patterns of decision processes and outcomes on important decisions differ qualitatively from less important decisions where negotiations may have less intensity.

Finally, the success of models more responsive to current understanding of cognitive processes indicates the importance of analyzing social systems in terms of the cognitive properties of their individual members. This, of course, is the primary theme of seminal contributions to organizational analysis by Herbert Simon and colleagues (especially March and Simon, 1958; Cyert and March, 1963). Indeed, the bounded rationality school of organizational behavior had fundamental effects on guiding the research reviewed above. Effective models of formal organizations and other collectivities should recognize that members have partly compatible, partly conflicting motives. This can be analyzed effectively from the viewpoint of the theory of games, once suitable modifications for social processes and human cognition are incorporated. The next section discusses some recent advances in the theory of games per se that greatly extend its relevance for the analysis of collective decision.

Policy Adoption by Committees: Games Without Sidepayments

The research reviewed above and most other coalition research provides subjects with a choice problem that follows quite naturally from the classical theory of n-person cooperative games: the winning coalition has to decide how to divide some divisible "good" among the members of the winning coalition. This procedure follows directly from an important feature of the classical theory that renders it inappropriate for analyzing cooperation and conflict in many social settings. The theory, as originally developed, used a particularly restrictive and often inappropriate set of assumptions to represent social situations. Specifically, the classical theory used a *characteristic function* to assign a single number to each coalition representing its "value" in the situation. Here we will discuss one of several crucial difficulties associated with the characteristic function.[3]

In order to develop a characteristic function, the classical theory requires that we attribute to each actor a utility function of a very special form. Suppose, for clarification, that any person's outcome of social action can be represented appropriately in terms of M dimensions, so that any outcome o can be described by the vector of its M attributes $(o_1, o_2, \ldots, o_M)$. The classical theory of cooperative games requires that each person, i, in the situation has a utility function over the set of alternative outcomes such that the value to him of any outcome o can be expressed in the highly particular form:

$$u_i(o) = a_i(o_1, o_2, \ldots, o_{M-1}) + b_i(o_M)$$

Note that, in this function, the actor's utility for an outcome equals the sum of two components: the first component depends on the first $M - 1$ outcome attributes, the second depends only on dimension M. Thus, this function identifies a "separable commodity" M (read "money") such that the actor is

---

[3] This subsection follows closely one part of the argument presented by Laing and Ordeshook's (in preparation, chap. 5) considerably more general critique of the characteristic function of the classical theory of cooperative games.

willing to trade off various changes in the first $M - 1$ attributes for some amount of M. The classical theory also requires that the separable commodity be infinitely divisible (unless lotteries are considered) and freely transferable among the actors. Moreover, it is assumed that the $b_i(o_M)$ term is *linear* for each actor, at least for the range of O_M values that covers the interesting possibilities in the situation. These assumptions are used in the classical theory of cooperative games to permit linear "transfers of utility" to increase the value to an actor of an outcome which he might otherwise abhor. Thus, the classical theory requires that a medium of exchange be available in the situation which can act as currency for purchasing cooperation through *sidepayments*. On the basis of these assumptions, the classical theory establishes a characteristic function which can be interpreted to measure the "value" of alternative coalitions in dollars.

Clearly, these assumptions can be useful in modeling certain economic situations. This is perhaps an important reason why many of the reasonably effective applications of the classical theory of cooperative games dealt with economic problems. It was no accident that von Neumann and Morgenstern's (1947) seminal book was entitled *Theory of Games and Economic Behavior*.

Nonetheless, in many social situations such sidepayments are unavailable, irrelevant, immoral, or otherwise inadmissible. For instance, ignoring pathological exceptions, collectivities such as curriculum committees, school boards, voluntary associations, ideological political parties, and even committees in business firms make decisions among multiattribute alternatives on the basis of their members' beliefs about which decisions per se are appropriate or preferable, rather than in response to bribes tendered in the currency of a "separable commodity." The characteristic function of classical game theory is inappropriate for modeling such collective decision units. Consequently, it is important that work be done on developing and testing theory that does not require some or any of these assumptions on which the characteristic function of the classical theory rests.

Fortunately, it has been demonstrated that the theory of games can be reformulated without assuming linear transferability of utility (Aumann, 1967; Wilson, 1971) and that the revised theory can be used to generate successful empirical models of real and laboratory social situations "without sidepayments" (Dyer and Miles, 1976; Fiorina and Plott, 1978; McKelvey, Ordeshook, and Winer, 1978; McKelvey and Rosenthal, 1978; Laing and Olmsted, 1978). The "without sidepayments" approach permits a natural and substantively direct representation of social situations that, nonetheless, is tractable to effective game-theoretic analysis. Moreover, the approach can also be used if any or all of the classical assumptions underlying the characteristic function are satisfied. In fact, the theory of cooperative games without sidepayments subsumes the classical theory of cooperative games as a special case.

AN EXAMPLE OF POLICY SELECTION
WITHOUT SIDEPAYMENTS

Before discussing spatial games in particular, we will review an exciting case study of organizational decision that can be related to the theory of cooperative games without sidepayments. Dyer and Miles (1976) analyzed NASA's selection of trajectories to be flown past Jupiter and Saturn in the 1977 Mariner space project. The final decision was to be made through consensus by a Science Steering Group composed of team leaders from each of ten science teams. The teams were divided according to scientific specialties, and each was to study a different set of phenomena. In fact, each team collected data from a different instrument on the spacecraft. Engineers from the Jet Propulsion Laboratory identified the characteristics of feasible trajectories, and the teams developed criteria representing scientific objectives of the flight. Since there were some incompatibilities among these criteria, it was decided that two spacecraft, hence a pair of trajectories, would be needed. On the basis of these criteria, a large number of trajectory pairs could have been generated, but attention soon focused on just 32 alternatives.

Because of the differences in research objectives, the teams had different preferences over these alternative trajectory pairs. Using each team's report about its preference order and von Neumann-Morgenstern utilities for these pairs, Dyer and Miles applied both game-theoretic analysis and normative social-choice analyses to these data. While n-person games without sidepayments typically do not have a core, one of the trajectory pairs constitutes the unique core of the associated simple majority-rule game without sidepayments. In contrast, the social-choice analyses produced results which depended on details of the particular social-choice rule used, thereby failing to provide a clear normative prescription that the committee might have used. It is satisfying to report that the one alternative constituting the core is precisely the trajectory pair that was chosen by the Science Steering Group.

Parallel to this example, one can easily imagine many other organizational policies being selected from some fixed set of alternatives by actors with mixed motives. R and D, production, accounting, and marketing departments, for example, might face this situation in selecting a computer system for the company. Presumably, they would like to maximize the organization's profits (or, perhaps, chances of survival) by choosing the best overall alternative, but this is subject to the constraint that the configuration of the computer selected maximizes ease of operation and other benefits for their own departments, thus providing a basis for conflict. These kinds of situations are likely candidates for application of the theory of cooperative games without sidepayments. Game-theoretic analysis can provide insights into the likely patterns of cooperation and resulting outcomes, and the effects of changes in, say, decision rules or membership on the nature of the resulting outcomes.

SPATIAL GAMES AND POLICY ADOPTION

Very often, policy alternatives can be represented as points in a multidimensional space where the dimensions describe the relevant policy attributes or issues, and policies can vary continuously along these dimensions. For example, an organization deciding to diversify into a new product area might identify three potential varieties (R, S, and T) of products in this area. A policy decision about the production mix for these products could range from producing zero R, S, and T to producing some very large quantities of these products if the organization put all its resources into the new area. All possible points between these extremes in the three-dimensional space would represent policy alternatives.

If the actual policy in such situations is to be selected by a committee composed of differing interests in the organization, then we should expect that their preferences are not completely congruent over the whole space. If all members of the committee care about what outcome is chosen and if sidepayments are generally ruled out, then we should expect each member to act solely on the basis of his outcome preferences, seeking to bring about an outcome that he can endorse.

N-person game theory without sidepayments has been applied usefully to analyze such spatial policy games. Although different preference assumptions can be dealt with, usually in these applications it has been assumed that committee members' preferences are characterized as follows: members have *ideal points* (or "bliss" points) in the space which represent their most preferred alternatives, and their utilities for various policies decrease as a function of the policies' distance from the ideal point. The core, a very well established solution concept in *n*-person game theory, has been well supported (when the core exists) in regard to its predictions of the policy adopted in experimental analogues of this policy game (Berl, McKelvey, Ordeshook, and Winer, 1976; Fiorina and Plott, 1978). However, there are two difficulties with the core in these games. First, since the core can be endorsed by every potential majority, it provides no predictions as to which committee members will belong to the effective majority. Nonetheless, games with a core offer the opportunity to satisfy every effective set of actors. Such opportunities are rare. This leads to the second difficulty. Very special symmetry conditions in the pattern of preferences across the committee members must be satisfied before the core exists (Plott, 1967; Sloss, 1973). Thus, we need other game-theoretic solution concepts to analyze spatial policy games with no core. Fortunately, recent work has produced theory for such situations.

THE COMPETITIVE SOLUTION

McKelvey, Ordeshook, and Winer (1978; McKelvey and Ordeshook, 1978) recently developed a new solution concept in an attempt to deal with majority-rule games (spatial or otherwise) without sidepayments. The core, when it exists, is consistent with a *competitive solution*. However, the competitive solution exists in many games with empty cores. The competitive solution makes nontrivial predictions about coalition structures, unlike much other established n-person game theory. Also, the essence of the logic underlying the competitive solution is relatively simple and intuitively appealing: the "competition" of various potential controlling coalitions for the crucial members that swing or pivot between them is examined in order to identify a predicted set of coalition structures (each with associated payoff proposals) such that the proposals constituting the elements of this set are balanced against each other and cannot be upset by any other viable proposal.[4] Finally, its basic predictions seem well supported in laboratory research reviewed below. All of these observations provide good reason for considering the competitive solution as a basis for game-theoretic analysis of policy adoption in spatial games.

The competitive solution makes predictions about who will cooperate together as well as about what policy will be chosen, unlike the classical theory of cooperative games. The predictions of the competitive solution concerning both decision outcomes and coalitions have been supported in laboratory studies of spatial games without sidepayments under majority rule, while the classical theory of cooperative games appears to fail (McKelvey, Ordeshook, and Winer, 1978; Laing and Olmsted, 1978). These predictions have also been supported in some nonspatial games without sidepayments (McKelvey and Ordeshook, in press). Given this experimental evidence and the further theoretical development by McKelvey and Ordeshook (1978), the competitive solution deserves serious consideration as a game-theoretic basis for generating more robust models of collective decisions.

Cognitive and Social Processes in Policy Formulation

Using the basic approach to studying collective policy selection suggested in the previous section, we consider here the way in which the cognitive approach to studying individual decision makers can increase the predictive

---

[4] Consider coalition C_1 trying to adopt policy p_1 against coalition C_2 trying to adopt p_2. The proposal (p_1, C_1) is said to be *viable* against (p_2, C_2) if, of all the members common to both C_1 and C_2, at least one of them weakly prefers p_1 to p_2. That is, (p_1, C_1) is viable against (p_2, C_2) if *not* all

capacity and theoretical richness of game-theoretic analyses of policy adoption and, also, how the study of cognitive processes can relate the understanding of policy choice to questions regarding problem solving in the creation of policy alternatives.

COGNITION AND POLICY CHOICE

The competitive solution and other solution concepts which can be formulated for *n*-person games without sidepayments promise to give insights into policy adoption. However, the results of coalition research reviewed earlier suggest that effective game-theoretic analysis of collective decisions can be extended greatly by augmenting game theory with models of cognitive and social processes. The several distinct types of such augmentation identified earlier all seem applicable to coalition formation in policy games. For instance, simplified heuristic models can probably be formulated which consider limits on individual decision-making ability as well as effects of social norms that may be relevant in such games. Heuristics and norms identified in research on this problem may also be incorporated in formal game-theoretic models. Similarly, it should be possible to formulate detailed models of the negotiation process and to identify systematic effects of changes in situational constraints or other factors influencing the energy or time devoted to negotiations.

We know of no work which has gone very far in the directions specified above. However, McKelvey, Ordeshook, and Winer (1978) and Laing and Olmsted (1978) have recorded the face-to-face negotiations of subjects in their laboratory committees, thus providing data for future work relevant to questions concerning social and cognitive processes. It is of interest to note that laboratory work on the competitive solution has at least recognized the possibility of incorporating social and process considerations. For example, McKelvey and Ordeshook (in press) state that understanding the competitive solution in games with a core

> necessitates a better understanding of the dynamics of bargaining and the convergent properties of solution concepts. In particular, can negotiations in games with a core get trapped nonetheless in subcycles that are broken only with the fortuitous discovery of the core?

We envision a merging of process and game-theoretic approaches to these

---

the "swing" members prefer p_2. A set of proposals is said to be *balanced* if no coalition represented in the set has more than one proposal in it and if every proposal in the set is viable against every other proposal. A proposal (p^*, C^*) *upsets* a balanced set if it is viable in that set and if, for some proposal (p', C') in that set, every member common to C^* and C' prefers p^* over p'. Given these preliminaries, a competitive solution is defined as a balanced set such that no possible proposal can upset it.

problems which will add to existing theoretical understanding and stimulate further useful research on collective choice.

COLLECTIVE PROBLEM SOLVING

The field of individual problem solving and cognition has been advanced significantly by the development of information-processing psychology (Newell and Simon, 1972). The melding of individual information-processing models and social process models into the study of group phenomena can yield substantial theoretical dividends (Friend, Laing, and Morrison, 1977a). While we expressed this view above in regard to processes of conflict resolution and policy *selection,* it should also apply to processes of collective problem solving and the creation or *formulation* of policy alternatives.

Before expanding on this point, we review some of what is known about the relations between social conflict and quality of problem-solving processes. Several lines of work suggest that conflict among social actors may act to increase the quality of the group's problem-solving process. Laing and Olmsted (1978) observed that "competitive" committees were more likely than "fair" committees to adopt the core when it exists, and also took about 40 minutes less in making five policy decisions. Hall and Williams (1966) found that established groups, in comparison to ad hoc groups, seem more capable of using conflict of opinion to generate new ideas and insights and thus to make decisions more effectively. Hall and Watson (1970) found that a normative intervention instructing group members to confront conflict of opinion and use it to scrutinize reasons and opinions (rather than compromising or otherwise "negotiating" away the conflict) allows even ad hoc groups to improve their performance. This research can be related to Hoffman's (1961) work which views intragroup conflict as one important condition for creativity in group problem solving. These findings suggest that there may be important relations between conflict resolution by coalitions as they adopt certain policies and adaptive processes of collectivities seeking to solve problems.

The game-theoretic analyses discussed earlier in this chapter assumed that all possible alternatives, whether a finite set of policies or an infinite set of points in some defined space, are specified in advance and that all actors have well defined preferences over the set of available alternatives. Thus, we can speak of game-theoretic analysis of policy *selection.* Initially, understanding of policy selection processes might seem to be quite different from understanding of problem solving and policy *formulation* processes in which decision alternatives are created. However, both these sorts of processes have potential common roots in the study of cognitive processes so it is possible, on this basis, to envision a unified study of collective policy formulation and decision.

There does not appear to be much concrete work to point to in this area, so this is largely a task for the future. However, a study which has been in the literature for quite a few years points out some directions and provides some interesting insights. Bower (1965) simulated organizational policy adoption in three-person groups, some operating under simple majority rule and others under a rule for unanimity. Policies were to be selected from a given subset of points in a multidimensional space that represented various attributes of an investment decision. Some of the groups, called *teams,* had complete congruence of preferences: each member received the same payoff as a function of the quality of the group's decision. Other groups, *foundations,* had a group payoff that was a function of the quality of the group's decision, but each member's share of the total depended on the rank order of the distance between the selected policy and his own "ideal" point. ("Ideal" points were established by asking each person to state before interacting in the group his own estimate of the best policy).[5] Each group member initially received information about the effectiveness of a few points in the space. By sharing this information and extrapolating or interpolating in the multidimensional space, groups were to decide on their estimate of the best policy. In Bower's experimental procedure, groups which failed to reach an agreement after a given number of communications automatically received a score (and a payoff) of zero.

If the payoff results for all policies in Bower's study were known by subjects, this would be a trivial decision for the teams and, given some established "ideal" points, this would be a spatial game of policy selection for the foundations. Of course, the consequences for all policies were not known, so the problem becomes more complicated. One might expect conflict in the foundations to have a detrimental effect on problem solving or, alternatively (consistent with the work cited earlier), to lead to more search behavior and better problem solving. That is, actors might be motivated to analyze their own information and to share it in order to justify policy choices closer to their own "ideal" points. Teams, too, might certainly have conflicts of opinion, but these conflicts would not be tied to differential payoffs, so the motivational aspect of opinion conflict would certainly be different in teams. Whatever the effects of conflict under majority rule, we might expect them to be exacerbated under a unanimity decision rule.

Overall, Bower found somewhat superior scores for teams than for foundations. The chief reason for this seems to be that foundations, under unanimity rules, often failed to reach agreement. Teams, under unanimity, surpass foundations nearly nine out of ten times; under majority rule, in con-

---

[5] These are not ideal points in exactly the same sense as that term was used earlier in this chapter since each actor in this study is *not* certain that a policy choice exactly coincident with his own "ideal" point would give him the greatest payoff. The points were optimal only in the sense that the actor *initially felt* it was the best policy and in the sense that a policy close to the "ideal" would maximize an actor's share of the total. However, the actual total might be small for such a policy choice whereas an actor's actual best individual payoff might be at a policy far away from his individual "ideal." To maintain this distinction, we will place the word "ideal" in quotes throughout this subsection.

trast, foundations beat teams and took no more time to make decisions. One of Bower's conclusions:

> Where the problem of reaching a group decision was facilitated by a rule permitting two-man coalitions to decide for the group, foundations made better choices and took no more time than teams to do so. (Bower, 1965: 284)

The observation earlier that Laing and Olmsted's "fair" committees took longer to make decisions and less frequently adopted the core is consistent with Bower's results, since "fair" committees typically sought consensus, while competitive committees operated under simple majority rule.

Further analysis of Bower's communication data showed that foundations exchanged *more* information than teams in the unanimity condition (when the foundation's choice problem was most difficult), while the two kinds of groups hardly differed on the information-exchange dimension under majority rule. Analyzing problem solving into search, analysis, and choice stages, Bower posits that intragroup conflict may have a debilitating effect on the choice stage, but it can improve "rationality" in the first two stages. Moreover, it seems that an appropriately chosen decision rule can overcome this difficulty for foundations, allowing them to surpass teams.

Looking within types of "organizations," we can see the direct effects of various choice rules on problem solving: teams under unanimity were superior to teams under majority rule about seven out of ten times, whereas foundations under majority rule were superior to foundations under unanimity more than nine out of ten times. The first part of this observation leads us to speculate that in teams, because of their relatively low degree of inherent conflict, the unanimity rule encourages effective search and analysis in the problem-solving process. On the other hand, foundations in Bower's study experienced more than sufficient conflict, so they were helped by majority rule which allows choice to occur effectively. As he puts it: "Where an appropriately chosen decision rule ameliorates this difficulty [of choosing], foundations can surpass teams" (Bower, 1965: 284).

Using the hypothesis that unanimity was a detriment to the *choice* aspect of policy adoption, Bower performed exploratory analyses in which the "no decision" cases were eliminated. In the remaining data, foundations were superior to teams on average. Further, the unanimity rule produced superior decisions on average, and it had greatest effect in foundations. These results are only suggestive, but the possibility they suggest is interesting. If foundations, under unanimity, could still find a way of eventually resolving their conflict and reaching a decision, it might tend to be the highest quality decision. Otherwise, as mentioned above, the kind of conflict represented by foundations in Bower's study is most successfully related to problem solving when majority rule prevails. Although his theoretical position is slightly different, Falk (1978) recently has reported that majority rule (as opposed to unanimity) procedures lead to a superior quality problem-solving process in a simulated work group composed of unequal power members with differing interests. Thus, except perhaps for teams composed of peers with no inherent conflicts of interest related to the decision (as in Hall and Watson, 1970), majority rule procedures may lead to the most desirable outcomes.

Bower's study exemplifies one kind of research that may be very fruitful in understanding collective problem solving *and* policy selection. Bower reports no detailed information-processing analyses of actors' decision processes or of the communications. We know of no other study which has done this. Certainly, such analyses are needed.

Similarly, we find no game-theoretic analyses of the choice problem faced by Bower's subjects. One observation he makes is quite interesting, however, as it relates to very simple models of conflict resolution in spatial games:

> Foundations, particularly under unanimous conditions, chose points exterior to the convex defined by [the members' "ideal" points] more often than teams, despite the "naturalness" of interior solutions for bargaining groups. The result is understandable if it is true that a more (relative to teams) intensive process of analysis freed the group from initial positions. (Bower, 1965: 288)

Detailed explanation of this and other phenomena of problem solving in spatial policy games awaits the integration of information-processing models of cognition and problem solving with game-theoretic analysis of social choice.

Some conclusions suggested by the research reviewed in this section are, in their broad outlines, the same as those stated by many analysts of social behavior. For example, the conclusion that "social structures encouraging or permitting differing interests and the consequent formation of coalitions are not necessarily bad since they may lead to superior choices for the collectivity" is essentially the same point made by many organization theorists when they claim that organizational differentiation of attitudes, viewpoints, and goals may be a very adaptive response to certain environments for the organization, rather than being the problem claimed by classical management theories. However, by generating this conclusion from the type of research and analyses discussed above, we are led to a more microprocess view of the value of differentiation in decision making. From this view, for example, implications can be developed about the influence of various decision procedures (e.g., majority rule vs. unanimity) used to resolve conflicts and achieve social coordination. Thus, the approach we have recommended here—augmenting recent developments in the theory of cooperative games without sidepayments with important discoveries about social and cognitive processes in collective choice—promises to add a new dimension to the analysis of social choice and to understanding the creation of social alternatives from which collectivities choose.

11

Resolving Ideological Issues on the Division of Labor

William Form

OCCUPATIONAL SOCIOLOGY IS divided into the study of the occupational structure, specific occupational groups, and the nature of work. The major intellectual problems in all three areas are related to the central concept of the field, the process by which labor is divided. Prior to 1965, occupational sociologists believed that they adequately understood this process and its consequences, but today these ideas are being challenged on the grounds that they merely justify the interests of the economic and political elites in society. New explanations of the division of labor are being proposed.

Two and a Half Questions

To demonstrate the controversies and to evaluate the positions of the antagonists, I will examine two major issues directly and a third indirectly. The first is basic to all of occupational sociology: What causes the division of labor? I will show that Durkheim's approach to this question is more or less ignored; the controversy rages instead on the reasons why managers have extended the division of labor. The traditionalists believe that managers seek to increase productive efficiency while the revisionists think that managers divide labor better to control workers, thereby crushing their creativity and

☐ I am grateful to Joan Huber and Leslie Moch for suggestions that improved the manuscript and Gary Miller for research assistance.

reducing their productivity. I will examine the historical and comparative evidence that both sides bring to this issue, evaluate it, and suggest research needed to reduce the disagreement.

The second question is derived from the first: Does the division of labor reduce or increase the complexity of occupational skills? Traditionalists hold that occupations are becoming more complex because their knowledge base is expanding, while revisionists see a steady erosion of occupational skills. After evaluating the historical evidence on the question, I suggest that the answer is within our grasp. Finally, I pose the question whether occupational specialization inevitably increases worker alienation. While I do not examine and evaluate the evidence, I point to the need to answer related questions before we can attack the question on alienation.

What Causes the Division of Labor?

EFFICIENCY VERSUS POWER THEORIES

Causal explanations of the division of labor derive from two sources: Adam Smith and Karl Marx, on the one hand, and Emile Durkheim, on the other. Though Smith and Marx differed in their moral evaluation of the division of labor, they both felt that it was spurred by the owner's desire to increase the firm's efficiency, thereby reducing labor costs and increasing profits. Durkheim (1964) asserted that the division of labor grows as segmented structures decline. But what causes the process?

Durkheim somewhat ambiguously concludes that population growth and increasing intensity of interaction increase the division of labor which, in turn, promotes societal growth and social interaction. Though increasing commerce or production results from this two-way process, Durkheim disclaims that the division of labor is caused by anyone's desire to increase their happiness, consumption, or power. He opposed Smith's and Marx's view that self-interest, greed, power, or any human motive promotes the division of labor. It grows from the Darwinian struggle for existence, but the struggle is mellowed when units specialize rather than compete (pp. 266–70). Though increasing productivity may result from specialization, Durkheim disagreed with Smith and Marx that this constituted progress. "If we specialize, it is not to produce more, but it is to enable us to live in new conditions of existence that have been made for us" (p. 275). Whatever that means.

Most sociologists curtsy politely to Durkheim, but ignore his ideas in their work (Kemper, 1972). Without acknowledging it, they turn to Smith's or Marx's simpler views that increased efficiency results from the conscious splitting of work into different tasks. For Smith (1937), division of labor grows out of the nature of humans to barter, truck, or trade which, in turn, leads to greater productivity and more goods for everybody. Thus, the division of labor grows naturally in response to self-interest.

Marx's thoughts on the division of labor also reflect Darwinian ideas. Technology and presumably the division of labor represent the human mode of dealing with nature, the process of production by which humans sustain their lives (Marx, 1963: 64). Marx's theory of historical materialism says little about the division of labor, but his descriptive work resembles Smith's in emphasizing that the self-interest of entrepreneurs goads them to rationalize production by dividing labor and introducing machinery.[1] For both Marx and Smith, the division of labor proceeds inevitably and consciously to increase productivity—to make people happy for Smith and to satisfy capitalist greed for Marx.

In short, the prevailing sociological position is utilitarian (Kemper, 1972). Division of labor, whatever its origin, is a conscious process, guided and stimulated by managers to increase labor productivity and organizational efficiency. How surpluses or profits are used depends on the prevailing political economy: to increase the profits of capitalists, the well-being of the people, or the military power of the state. I'll call this view the "efficiency theory" of the division of labor.

The attack on the efficiency theory is based on a power conception of management probably originated by Marglin (1971). Attacking the technological and materialist theories of industrial evolution, Marglin contends that at the inception of the industrial revolution capitalists were motivated more by a desire to control workers than to increase their productivity. The technology, division of labor, and productivity of the early factories were not superior to home production. Machines were not expensive and artisans could have bought them. Capitalists collected workers in factories not to increase their productivity, but to control them better. Employers had flexibility in designing technology and work organization; they could have designed machines that preserved or expanded workers' skills while simultaneously increasing their productivity. Instead, employers designed a technology that simplified skills and increased specialization or the division of labor. I shall call the managerial strategy to forego efficiency for increased labor control, the "power theory" of the division of labor.

Stone's (1974) historical study of the steel industry's job structure amplifies Marglin's thesis. She attacks the view that technology determines the division of labor; rather, it defines possibilities. How work is actually organized is a matter of class conflict. Thus, before the great steel strike of 1892, workers controlled production and even the foremen had little authority. Management introduced the blast furnace to gain control of production.

---

[1] Marx's views on the organization of the bourgeois state should not be confused with his views on the division of labor: in the former, he held a power view; in the latter, an efficiency view.

When the workers lost the strike, management created a flat occupational structure of semiskilled employees by downgrading skilled occupations and upgrading the unskilled ones. In this process, management wrested knowledge about production from workers and appropriated it to itself and to newly created white-collar occupations. The loyalty of the new white-collar class was assured by high pay and physical segregation from manual workers. Management also replaced the worker-controlled apprentice system with one that it could control: workers were trained for skilled manual occupations that were appropriate only for the new technology. To foster an illusion of upward mobility and to instill work incentives, management, along with the CIO, inaugurated an elaborate job hierarchy with small pay differentials. In sum, management appropriated technical knowledge unto itself, created a homogeneous class of semiskilled workers, and created a class of white-collar workers to buffer class conflict. Reversing Marx, the social relations of production determined the force of production.

The power theory of the division of labor fits neither Durkheim's functionalist view nor the utilitarian views of Smith and Marx. How valid is the power theory and how can it be tested? I have selected this question precisely because it provokes ideological controversy. Since sociological questions will increasingly contain such controversies (compare Montagna's 1977 text on occupational sociology with earlier ones), it is important to consider ways that the discipline might try to resolve them. European sociology has long engaged in ideological disputes that often go nowhere because so many sociologists would rather argue than do research.

The efficiency–power dispute pervades other areas of occupational sociology: growth of work organizations (Perrow, 1978), occupational trends (Parker, 1972), occupational alienation (Braverman, 1974), and class conflict in work organizations (Aronowitz, 1973). I will argue that questions like the efficiency–power dispute cannot be resolved by staying within the bounds of occupational sociology. Relevant data are available in other specialties and other social sciences: economic sociology, comparative sociology, economic history, and labor economics. While evaluating the data in these other fields, I will support the efficiency side of the dispute, not only because the evidence tends to support it, but also to highlight the controversy. After reviewing the data, I will suggest ways to reduce disagreements further.

THE ARGUMENTS, BUT WHERE ARE THE STUDIES?

The more broadly theories are stated, the more difficult they are to prove or disprove. So many sociological theories sound plausible because they have a grain of truth. Thus, it would be strange if managers, when instituting new technological and occupational systems, did not consider modifications if they encountered worker opposition. But to design a system primarily with power

rather than efficiency objectives in mind is another matter. Yet neither power ·
theory nor efficiency theory can be rejected on the ground that they appear to
have a promanagement or prolabor bias. Theories with apparent class bias
can be supported or rejected if scholars agree on standards of evidence. For
example, the Marxist or power model of income determination offered by
Wright and Perrone (1977) has stronger evidence in its favor than the functionalist or achievement model.

Studies supporting power theory are few, but they have the advantages of
being grounded in observations of specific industries (Noble, 1979) or in
histories of single industries (Stone, 1974). However, all of them lack productivity measures under different conditions of division of labor. The evidence
favoring efficiency theory at first seems overwhelming: productivity increases
accompanying the division of labor since the industrial revolution have been
enormous. But, strangely enough, few empirical productivity studies have
used the division of labor as a variable—almost limited to the work of Jack
Gibbs and his colleagues. In a 1950 representative study of twelve nations,
Gibbs and Browning (1966) found a correlation of + .91 between technological efficiency (per capita consumption of energy) of nations and their industrial division of labor, and a + .96 correlation between efficiency and
intraindustry occupational division of labor.

Evidence on this question may also be found in studies by comparative industrial sociologists. Research on the industrial convergence hypothesis has
examined the evolution of occupational structures under different sociocultural conditions. In an extensive review of that literature, I found (Form,
1979) sturdy evidence supporting the convergence hypothesis. Moore's
(1964) study of changes in the occupational structures of many nations points
to enormous regularities. Though national variations exist even within the
same industry (Landes, 1966), the more sophisticated the technological level
of nations, the more similar are their occupational structures.[2] Shiba's (1973)
important study of 37 thermal power plants, in seven countries varying in
economic development, demonstrated not only a tight link between technical
and occupational factors but also the skill and type of generating equipment
alone accounted for 90 percent of plant productivity.

Though power theorists have not commented on the above evidence, their
reaction to it is predictable: almost all comparative research has been done in
nations with capitalistic class structures; consequently, all occupational structures reflect management's accumulation of power. Moreover, noncapitalistic
nations borrow advanced capitalistic technology that has been designed to fit
occupational structures that maximize managerial control.

This counterargument has also been applied to the Soviet Union, whose
occupational structure could have been designed to maximize workers' skills

[2] Landes (1965: 75) shows that national variations exist in the labor intensity of industries that
have the same technology, but he doesn't propose that such variation results from a managerial
strategy to maximize labor control.

and productivity. Power theorists claim that the Soviets lacked time to develop alternative technologies and occupational structures. To survive threats of capitalist nations, the Soviets not only had to adopt capitalist technology, they had to operate it with greater efficiency. Moreover, the argument runs, most Soviet nations are not genuinely socialist, but authoritarian regimes that do not permit workers to run the industries. In this sense, they differ little from capitalist regimes (Aronowitz, 1973: 426). In short, data supporting efficiency theorists are unacceptable because they cannot be compared to evidence from "truly" socialist economies.

Efficiency theorists retort that power theorists unreasonably demand that the current reality be tested against an unrealizable utopia. Rather than wait for future history to decide this question, I suggest that we reexamine the available historical and comparative evidence.

EXPERIMENTS TO DECREASE
MANAGEMENT CONTROL

Strangely enough, power theorists seem unaware that their theory is not new and that legitimate experiments have been conducted to increase workers' skills and control over production. The best documented experiment is Stalin's postrevolutionary fight against bourgeois engineers who believed that only engineers should run industry. Bailes' (1978) historical study of the Soviet technostructure thoroughly documents Stalin's purge of these engineers and his successful twenty years' effort to put *praktiki* in charge of industry. The *praktiki* (practicals) were self-taught technicians and engineers who lacked specialized or university training. They increased their authority inexorably until 1941 when they comprised almost 90 percent of the foremen, 60 percent of the shop heads, and 77 percent of the plant directors. Along with the purge of old-line engineers, Stalinists tried to erase credentialism in the university training of engineers. Keenly cognizant of the power ideology of engineering professors, Stalinists introduced courses on communist theory, increased representation of students from proletarian backgrounds, encouraged student participation in curriculum planning, and campaigned to increase worker participation in industrial planning and production. Yet at the end of World War II, engineers were being trained much like engineers in the West—to be efficiency oriented. And today they fill most of the posts in industry, government bureaus, and the politburo. But, more to the point, the engineers have fashioned an occupational structure that remarkably resembles that of the West, and Soviet workers respond to that structure much like Western workers (Land and O'Dell, 1978: 10). Bailes (1978) concludes that the Soviet reversion to the earlier practice of giving engineers control of production was necessary because the *praktiki* could not meet quantitative and qualitative production goals.

A few other critical experiments can be summarized. Communist China confronted the efficiency–power controversy for twenty years (Whyte, 1973; Hern, 1978). Even before the Great Leap Forward and the Great Proletarian Cultural Revolution, official ideology opposed the bureaucratic centralism of the USSR. Mao insisted that greater productivity could be achieved by reducing distinctions between labor and management and loosening occupational boundaries: workers should participate in management and management should engage in menial labor. Though the results of these experiments have not been sufficiently documented, most scholars conclude (Whyte, 1973) that the efficiencies gained, if any, resulted from campaigns to persuade workers to work harder rather than from changes in the division of labor. The proponents of the efficiency ideology now seem to be in power and they are giving managers more power to shape the occupational structure.

Countries in Eastern and Western Europe have also experimented with increasing workers' control of management (Hunnius, Garson, and Case, 1973). No one has reviewed these experiments for evidence of change in the division of labor. My impression is that structural changes have been rarely attempted and, when attempted, have not noticeably increased worker productivity (Sturmthal, 1964). The famous experiment to redesign the automobile assembly line in Sweden's Saab works shows mixed results at best (Goldman, 1976). The Histadrut labor federation in Israel provides a crucial test because it owns and operates a substantial sector of industry, it espouses an ideology of workers' control, it is free of government domination, and it has endured for two or more generations. Derber (1963) and others have compared worker participation in management and productivity in the Histadrut, government, and privately owned enterprises and found overwhelming similarities.

Finally, a natural experiment has been going on in Japan. Okochi, Karsh, and Levine (1974) claim that Japan is the only industrial nation that does not have a stratification system based on occupations. While I will not examine this claim, scholars do agree that the concept of lifetime employment found in large Japanese firms differs from the concept of employee utilization found in the West. When workers are hired with the expectation of lifetime employment, they are not hired for specific occupations but for a future of continuous job changes. Because workers do not have an occupational affiliation in the Western sense, neither they nor management has an investment in a given division of labor. Moreover, since management, staff, and production occupational ladders are not segregated, management has little incentive to monopolize technical knowledge and skill. In short, though Japan has a capitalistic economy, her unique status arrangements permit a wide latitude in designing the division of labor. Given this latitude, do Japanese managers divide labor differently than managers in other capitalistic nations? The few studies that explicitly compare Japanese and Western industries show enormous similarities in technologies and occupational structure (see the bibliography in Form, 1979).

To conclude: The historical and comparative data show that giving workers more power to change the division of labor is not a new idea. Whatever the ideological dedication to the idea, labor remains divided more or less the same way at given technological levels, and managers retain power to design the technology and the division of labor. It seems unreasonable to conclude that all who experimented with changes in the division of labor were insincere, ideologically callous, or overly committed to immediate economic returns.

REDUCING DISAGREEMENT

To reduce theoretical disagreement over the causes of the division of labor, scholars should study it directly in addition to lining up the existing evidence as I have done. The conceptual and methodological requirements for such studies have already been confronted (Land, 1970; Kemper, 1972; Smith and Snow, 1977). Though the efficiency–power dispute cannot be resolved by one crucial study, considerable progress can be made with an intensive historical study of one industry in several nations that have different political economies. The advantages of a one-industry study are impressive. First, industries should be studied as international systems, thereby settling questions concerning the extent that they borrow technology and organization from one another. We can also determine the extent of their past and present economic competition. Second, though we have made progress in defining and measuring concepts, they are necessarily crude when applied to all industries. Measuring crucial variables such as ideology, productivity, occupational knowledge, authority, skill, and technology is sharpened when applied to specific industries. Third, when measurement is under control, new questions can be considered: How do industrial technology and occupational structure become articulated? How does bargaining among managers, workers, labor unions, and the state affect technological change and the occupational structure? Shiba's (1973) study of 37 thermal power stations in seven countries provides us with a good model. To his design we must add a historical dimension, evidence on technological diffusion, and data on bargaining among management, labor, unions, and the state.

Is Occupational Complexity Growing or Declining?

PARSONS VERSUS BRAVERMAN

The second question is an extension of the first. While the first asks whether division of labor promotes efficiency, the second asks whether specialization necessarily reduces the skill content of occupations. Efficiency theorists argue that the growth of job simplification or job complexity depends on what is most economic for the system, but that the long-term trend is increased occupational complexity. Historical evidence shows that the labor force in simple manual occupations declines with mechanization, while white-collar (professional, technical, and administrative) jobs that require extensive education continue to increase. Indeed, Parsons (1968) and others forecast a society in which all occupations, even manual ones (Foote, 1953), will become professionalized because occupational knowledge is constantly expanding.

This view is strongly challenged by power theorists like Braverman (1974). Subtitling his book, "The Degradation of Work in the Twentieth Century," Braverman accuses monopoly capital of using science to simplify all occupations. He interprets the rising educational requirements of occupations as credentialism because most workers are overeducated for their jobs. Rising levels of universal education reflect the desperate effort of capitalism to solve its unemployment problem and not increasing occupational complexity. The white- and blue-collar distinction is meaningless because most manual, office, and sales jobs are simple, menial, and trivial. Professional specialization is simply a euphemism for job simplification. Braverman agrees with Marglin that management deskills workers in order to concentrate production control in its own hands. Automation and mechanization do not upgrade jobs; on the contrary, they turn workers into robots. Finally, Braverman claims that government statistics exaggerate the amount of skilled work in the labor force in order to split the working class.

With few exceptions (Bauman, 1972), most scholars agree with Braverman that the industrial revolution created a homogeneous working class. While Marx recognized the "lazarous layers" of the proletariat of his day, he predicted that machines would erode workers' skills and create a homogeneous class of machine tenders. Since Marx, generations of scholars have elaborated this theme. Even traditional economists hold that rising educational levels increase the job transferability of workers and reduce wage differentials. Students of automation (Blauner, 1964; Harvard, 1969; Shepard, 1971) thought that it would reverse job simplification but radicals disagree. However, both traditionalists and radicals concur that job simplification tends to increase job dissatisfaction and worker alienation. Though the evidence for this is far from conclusive (Form, 1976: 113), to ascertain whether work alienation is increasing, we must first determine whether deskilling is a historical trend. If it is not, the increase in work alienation, if it is occurring, cannot be attributed to job simplification.

HOW SKILLED WERE OUR ANCESTORS?

Whether occupational complexity is increasing is a historical question, but few sociologists have examined the historical evidence. Perhaps the question is unresolvable because the historical data may not be adequate or accurate.

Even census data are troublesome because occupational classifications have been changed constantly. However, scholars have worked hard to make census data since 1900 comparable (U.S. Bureau of the Census, 1975, Series D).

I attempted to reconstruct the skill distributions of U.S. manual workers for 1870–1970 (see Table 1). The most striking trend is the slow rise in male skilled workers since 1900 and the rapid decline of unskilled labor. For women, the percentage of skilled, operatives, and laborers has remained stable, but service occupations have increased as domestic workers declined. Since the occupational classification is relatively consistent for this period, we can conclude that, contrary to received wisdom, skilled work has not declined for over seventy years. Braverman (1974) insists that semiskilled work, which has increased, is not more complex than unskilled labor. If he is correct, the important distinction is that between skilled and all other manual labor. The evidence still points to no change in over seventy years. To sustain his position, Braverman must prove that today's skilled workers are less skilled than they used to be. His attempt is not convincing.

The second conclusion to draw from Table 1 is that the census occupational classification must have changed drastically after 1890. From 1870 to 1900, about 60 percent of males were classified as skilled, but in 1900 only 30 percent were so classified. A 30 percent decline occurred also for women. Since the occupational classification is more accurate and consistent after 1900 than before,[3] we conclude, contrary to Braverman, that the percentage

T A B L E 1. **Distribution of Manual Workers by Skill and Sex: 1870–1970**

YEAR*	CRAFT		OPERATIVES		LABORERS		SERVICE		PRIVATE HOUSEHOLD		TOTAL	
	M	F	M	F	M	F	M	F	M	F	M	F
1870	61	45	27	13	5	1	5	37	3	5	101	101
1880	60	38	27	28	7	1	4	27	3	6	101	100
1890	58	31	30	25	4	1	8	35	1	8	101	100
1900	31	2	25	38	36	4	7	11	1	45	100	100
1910	31	3	28	39	32	3	8	14	1	41	100	100
1920	34	3	30	42	29	5	7	17	—	33	100	101
1930	32	2	31	37	27	3	9	21	—	37	99	100
1940	30	2	35	38	23	2	11	22	1	36	100	100
1950	35	3	38	46	16	2	11	29	—	20	100	100
1960	37	3	38	41	14	1	11	34	—	20	100	99
1970	38	5	35	38	12	3	15	44	—	10	100	100

* Data for 1870–90 from Edwards (1943), tables 9 and 10. Specific trades and occupations were classified as craft workers, while operatives and laborers were entered as separate categories. Data for 1900–70 from U.S. Bureau of the Census (1975: Series D; 182–232).

[3] "Particularly, prior to 1910, there is little information available on the exact definitions used for the several occupational categories" (U.S. Bureau of the Census, 1975: Series D; 125).

of skilled workers was vastly overestimated in the past. This conclusion is supported by the data for women workers. Both conservative and radical scholars agree that women have been traditionally barred from skilled trades. Yet over one-third of women workers were classified as skilled prior to 1900, but only 2 percent since then (see Table 1). One can only conclude that women were not skilled prior to 1900 and that social scientists have perpetuated a myth of skill degradation based on questionable data in the pre- and early industrial eras.

DEMYTHOLOGIZING THE PAST

If skills did not decline among manual workers (a point to be examined later), then the decline in occupational complexity could have occurred only in the expanding white-collar sector. Most scholars agree that professional occupations have become more complex because their knowledge base is expanding (Harvard, 1969; Moore, 1970). Not only have law, medicine, and science become more complex, but many contemporary professions did not exist earlier. The plausibility of the skill degradation hypothesis, then, must rest on evidence that the highly feminized clerical and sales occupations have declined in complexity. Yet the outrage expressed in the skill degradation literature is about male manual workers, not about female white-collar employees. Nonetheless, whether clerical occupations are being deskilled is an important question.

Obviously, the complexity of clerical work varies and better ways must be found to measure it (Temme, 1975). In investigating trends in office work, scholars may confront a historical myth. Most male workers in nineteenth-century offices spent most of their lives copying records and adding figures. Operating a typewriter is not more routine than copying things by hand. Educational qualifications for office work are not lower today than for earlier periods. Though today many people possess the educational qualifications for office work, the supply of skills does not define their complexity.

Most office work is more complex than most unskilled and semiskilled manual jobs. Illiterates can be trained quickly for assembly-line work; they cannot quickly acquire the literacy necessary for office work, no matter how dull or routine that work may be. Task specialization may be at a simple or complex level; work may be routine even though its training requirements are long and arduous. Braverman and others err by equating routine work with unskilled work; the routineness and complexity of occupations are distinct dimensions (Smith and Snow, 1976). In short, occupational complexity must be considered independently of the supply of skills in a society, the repetitiveness of work, and the personal and societal evaluation of repetitious work that varies in its training and educational requirements.

Sociologists think that most workers in pre- and early industrial societies were artisans, and that most manual employees in mature industrial societies are semiskilled operatives. That is, sociologists compare the skills of manual workers in past occupational structures made up largely of manual workers to manual workers in current societies that have a sizable white-collar sector. This is not a very meaningful comparison. It is more appropriate to compare entire occupational structures. Though current occupational *structures* are clearly more complex than earlier ones, it is possible for current structures to have many complex occupations with relatively few incumbents and a few low-skilled occupations to contain the bulk of the labor force (Smith and Snow, 1976). This position cannot be accepted because, as I argued above, professional and clerical occupations today are not only more numerous than in earlier societies, but their work is more complex. The remaining question then is: How do the skills of manual workers in pre- and early industrial societies compare to those in late industrial society?

A cursory examination of the occupational structures of eighteenth- and nineteenth-century cities reveals that most urban manual workers were not skilled. In twelve readily available studies of that era, artisans and skilled workers were found to comprise from 26 to 54 percent of the labor force and laborers, servants, and unskilled workers comprised from 25 to 50 percent (see Table 2). Reconstructing occupational structures is difficult and arduous and we should applaud historians for their efforts. Yet all their studies under-counted low-skilled workers and overestimated the skilled. Most studies counted only the male head of the household, omitting younger family workers who probably had the least skilled jobs, employed women (mostly un-skilled industrial workers and domestics), women and children who worked for their board and room, unpaid family workers, transients, and unemployed. I estimate that these studies missed from 15 to 40 percent of the low-skilled manual workers.

Knapp (1976), reviewing the literature of eighteenth-century European cities, found that the urban poor were unregistered and undetected unless they came into contact with a record-keeping agency such as the police or a charity hospital. The unemployed, transients, vagabonds, and criminals com-prised from 15 to 33 percent of the population of European capital cities. Mumford (1938: 122) estimated that, in 1684 Paris, casual beggars made up 25 percent of the population.

Though the precise skill composition of the working class of late mediaeval, renaissance, and early industrial cities is unknown, we do know that the majority of the bourgeois and working class were not guild members where the crafts were concentrated. A careful reading of the literature on guilds leads to three important conclusions. First, the *ideal* version of the skill ladder of apprentice, journeyman, and master as including *most* workers ex-isted (if it did at all) for a brief period. Second, the main function of the guild system was to restrict the supply of skilled workers so that local monopolies could be preserved. Third, most of what is known about guilds deals with

T A B L E 2. Manual Skills in Preindustrial and Early Industrial Cities

SOURCE	OBSERVATION DATE	LOW SKILLED (%)	SKILLED (%)	OBSERVATION
Aminzade (1977)	Toulouse, 1840	60	40	For working class
Beier (1978)	London 1548–1694	33–50	25	Unemployed 20%
Foner (1976)	Philadelphia, 1771	50		Poor 25%
Garden (1975)	Lyon, 1791	52	20	Excludes most female workers
Geruson and McGrath (1977)	U.S. cities, 1910	31	38	
Hirsch (1978)	Newark, 1800–60	24	54*	Omitted women, 20% employed
Main (1966)	Prerevolutionary America	40		
Moch (1979)	Toulouse, 1906	41	25	Sample of households
Tilly (1977)	Milan, 1880	40		Census omits episodic female employment
Thernstrom (1964)	Newburyport, 1850	25	50	Women, unemployed omitted
Tyree and Smith (1978)	Philadelphia, 1789	29	37	Male heads only
Knapp (1976)	Continental Europe, 1850	50	50	For working class only

* Crafts overcounted by U.S. Census; 20 to 50 percent of "craft workers" were not skilled.

their decline and their abuses. In short, scholars of the early guild system had an idealized version of it and most sociologists cling to that version.

In the idealized version, a master worked with two journeymen and two apprentices. After an apprenticeship of about seven years, apprentices became journeymen, and after a period of perfectionization, they became masters and employed other journeymen and apprentices. In such a system, obviously, the supply of craft workers would expand rapidly: every seven years two apprentices would be trained to be journeymen and four to six journeymen would be released to become masters. But the local market for high-quality goods was limited to the small bourgeois and aristocratic classes. Furniture, silverware, and other goods were passed on to succeeding generations. Long before the commercial and industrial revolutions, the guild system was in trouble (Pirenne, 1934).

To apply the current terminology, the guild system was the very embodi-ment of overcertification. Its main purpose was to monopolize the local market for the masters, to limit the supply of skilled workers, to exploit journeymen and apprentices by extending their training and delaying their certification. Journeying removed trained workers from the local labor market and provided cheap skilled labor to masters in other markets. The years spent in journeying far exceeded the time needed to perfect skills. By the end of the seventeenth century, examinations for attaining the master's status were so expensive that only a small minority could afford them.

Prolonged apprenticeship was restricted to children of privileged families as early as the fourteenth century (Pirenne, 1934). And apprentice training was needlessly long. Older boys could be trained in three or four years, but they were acquired at a younger age to provide the master with an inexpensive pool of unskilled labor. The need for this labor was high: before the invention of modern machines, as much as nine-tenths of shop work was unskilled. In cabinet making, for example, apprentices spent years doing little else than sanding wood, rubbing surfaces smooth, sweeping the floor, running errands for the workers, and even taking care of the master's children (Knapp, 1976: 41). Even before the advent of capitalism and powered machines, most work was unskilled, dull, repetitious, and required little time to learn.

By the eighteenth century, parents began to pay masters to accept their children as apprentices (Garden, 1975: 207). But even this was no assurance that apprentices would become masters because the system had become stratified. Children of masters could expect to become masters by inheritance, but others could rarely achieve that status. As the number of journeymen grew, they organized associations to break the monopolies of the masters. In the United States, the apprenticeship system never became widespread. In some eastern cities where it took hold, journeymen often left the local labor market and later abandoned their occupations (Hirsch, 1978).[4] More typi-cally, skills were learned informally outside of the organized trades. Most of the hand-produced articles of the nineteenth century that survive today (an-tique furniture, tinware, glass, dishes) is of poor quality and not the product of skilled workers. And products manufactured by farm families were of even poorer quality.

When trades were brought into the pre–Civil War factories, an attempt was made to preserve the apprenticeship system. But the trades became quickly stratified. Women and foreigners were typically pushed into low-skilled jobs (Hirsch, 1978; North and Weissert, 1973) which they never left. For example, in 1869, unskilled women in Newark factories comprised 34 percent of the shoemakers and 50 percent of the hatters. Yet the census reported them as regular shoemakers and hatters.

[4] The average age for attaining master's status in 1830 Newark was 40 years (Hirsch 1978).

SO, WHERE ARE WE?

This truncated historical analysis of skilled labor underscores the need for occupational sociologists to do historical research if they want to answer historical questions. Though I have not proved that manual workers are as skilled today as in the past, I have shown that the question cannot be answered unless we shed some myths about the past. Widespread ideas about the degradation of industrial labor may be wrong because they romanticize about the past. From mediaeval times through the appearance of capitalistic manufacturing, most labor was not skilled, but dull, backbreaking, monotonous, uncreative, and unrewarding. Preindustrial systems to train workers had features of credentialism, exploitation, and stratification as highly developed as in modern capitalism. Finally, the historical record unmistakably shows not only that most labor was unskilled, but that it was accompanied by a level of poverty, disease, and disrespect of labor that far surpasses the current scene (Mumford, 1938).

The above analysis is not an apology for today's mindless and inhuman work. It would be wrong to deny that skill degradation is occurring, but it would also be wrong to ignore skill upgrading. The task of occupational sociology is to determine how much skilled labor existed in the past to gauge current trends. Though historical records are insufficient, they are more ample than most sociologists think. Whatever our conclusions about the past, occupational sociologists must measure occupational complexity today—to establish base lines for future studies. The entire occupational structure should be studied and Spaeth (1979) has suggested ways of doing this. To my knowledge, only one national study has measured changes in occupational complexity of the entire structure. Spenner (1979) matched a 5 percent sample of occupations listed in the *Dictionary of Occupational Titles* for 1965 and 1977. He found that work with data, people, and things had become slightly more complex over the period. No evidence for downgrading of skills appeared in any occupational or industrial sector.

Is Work Alienation Increasing?

Resolving the question concerning the trend in work complexity is crucial for attacking the final question on work alienation. Most social scientists assume that repetitious, monotonous, and trivial work is alienating. If such work is not increasing, the basis for the alleged rise in alienation is absent. Current evidence suggests that work alienation varies by worker, situation, and historical period. The satisfactions from creative and interesting work apparently have higher saliency for the more highly educated than poorly educated, for employees in advanced than less developed industrial societies, and for those who already have challenging jobs (Form, 1976: 113). Even automobile assembly-line workers vary greatly in their job adjustment (Deming, 1977).

Many social scientists think that working with simple machines is mindless and alienating. Szymanski (1978), in an analysis of Braverman's work, identifies this as a neo-Luddite view of machine civilization. Though many case studies exist on how workers respond to their machines and technological change, I know of only one national study on the subject (Mueller et al., 1969). It confirms what many sociologists do not want to believe, that the large majority of people working with machines, even those who have little control over them, like their machines and are satisfied with their work. This finding suggests that the alleged link between the spread of machine technology, work routinization, and worker alienation may be a myth waiting to be exposed.

Conclusions

Some questions in occupational sociology seem unresolvable because they are immersed in ideological controversies. I have tried to show that disagreements can be reduced when the antagonists examine related research findings in other sociological specialties and other social sciences. Over-specialization is partially responsible for our failure to consider the historical evidence for the historical issues that we raise. In examining historical evidence, a posture of skepticism concerning conventional wisdom is in order.

But whatever the results of historical research, future trends may differ from past trends. So we must design studies now to establish baselines for future studies. I am impressed with our current intellectual preparation for the task. Durkheim's simple views on the division of labor have been criticized and reformulated, so now we have a better grasp of the phenomenon (Kemper, 1972). Land (1970) has mathematically formalized Durkheim's theory, presenting some findings that support efficiency theory. His analysis needs to be extended to the present and replicated in other societies. Smith and Snow (1976) have also proposed statistical techniques for examining functional differentiation. I have proposed some additional research questions on the division of labor that are not so encompassing but are capable of falsification. This should be the outcome of empirical research in areas immersed in ideological controversy because, after all, the function of ideology is to simplify the world and the function of research is to discover its complexities.

12

The Configuration
of Occupational Structure

Stanley H. Udy, Jr.

OCCUPATIONAL STRUCTURE IS SO central to contemporary society and relates to so many areas of social life that the way it is studied cannot fail to have profound effects on our entire discipline. It is thus perhaps ironic that both the basic conceptualization of most research on occupational structure and the theory lying behind it are rather difficult to apprehend. Occupational structural research has, generally speaking, been empirically and topically inspired. Its conceptual apparatus has been largely emergent, and its theoretical basis, often implicit.

This situation has led at least one recent president of our Association to dub this field "a method in search of substance" (Coser, 1975). I agree with Horan (1978), however, that in the course of its history this research tradition has developed a rather definite conceptual and theoretical structure beneath its surface, although—as will become apparent—I am not wholly in agreement with Horan as to the precise nature of that structure. In this chapter I will try to indicate what I at least think that structure is, and what limitations and possibilities it implies for the field when it is made explicit. Finally, I will try to show how a certain body of very recent research is addressing these limitations and possibilities in what I take to be very promising ways.

The "Edwards Paradigm"

Nobody who carries out even the most cursory historical review of the literature in this field can fail to be struck by its persistent preoccupation with questions of prestige and status. I would argue that this situation did not result from an act of theoretical deduction, but from a succession of acts of empiricist opportunism reflecting a desire to make use of available data in the form in which they were published. The basic paradigm did not originate with Davis and Moore (1945) or with Parsons (1940), but earlier with Alba Edwards (1938), in the form of the famous "Edwards scale."

Although rather crude and seemingly almost offhand, the Edwards scale rendered vast amounts of available census data usable for sociological analysis by classifying them according to a system of occupational categories hierarchically ranked on the basis of presumed differential prestige—prestige explicitly thought by Edwards to be conferred at least partly on the basis of educational requirements and perceived income. Edwards' formulation thus projected an image of occupational categories as rungs on a ladder which everybody, with the aid of education and propelled by a desire for prestige, is trying to climb. Although it has undergone numerous refinements, principally in the course of being adapted to continuous variable analysis, the basic structure of this model has not changed. It has persisted as the central conceptual and theoretical characterization of occupational structure in sociology (Haug, 1977).

I shall therefore refer to the idea of a conceptual arrangement of occupations in a prestige hierarchy, with the accompanying theory that people try to move up the hierarchy, as the "Edwards paradigm." In addition to being simple and politically congenial (it is almost an ideological statement), the Edwards paradigm could be readily assimilated to then developing culturological versions of sociology wherein people are oriented toward goals and trying to realize them by acting in accordance with learned beliefs. Perhaps more important, however, it proved highly amenable to further extension and refinement through the also then newly developing field of survey research. The Edwards paradigm did not require one to penetrate organizations, observe the tasks and constraints of the immediate job, the degrees of authority and control it conveys, or even learn how much the job pays. Rather, it suggested that one could learn what one needed to know simply by taking a survey and asking people some questions.

This suggestion proved to be eminently productive. The North–Hatt–NORC study of 1947 (Hatt, 1950; Reiss, 1961) set the stage by providing prestige data for a sample of 88 essentially representative occupations, in the form of numerical scores conducive to continuous variable analysis. This study engendered a series of replications and methodological refinements (Reiss, 1961; Duncan, 1961; Miller, 1960) and the decade or so following thus saw the entrenchment of the descriptive statics of an improved version of the Edwards paradigm. Although the Edwards framework had been employed conceptually in the study of social mobility (Rogoff, 1953a; Miller, 1960), it remained for Blau and Duncan (1967) to provide a more dynamic treatment, while also using it as a vehicle for methodological innovation, and setting the stage for a subsequent virtual outburst of literature on status attainment and related topics, both national and comparative.

This material has become very extensive and it would be both foolhardy and unnecessary to try to mention it all here (Hauser and Featherman, 1977; Treiman, 1977; Siegel, Hodge, and Rossi, 1974). An excellent summary, particularly regarding methodological development, is provided by Haug (1977). Suffice it to say that this work has not lost its empiricist character, nor has it, by and large, departed significantly from the basic Edwards paradigm. Sometimes different people get to start in different places, and sometimes they try to run up a ramp rather than climb a ladder, but the essential conception remains the same.

Yet, during the past few years especially, a small but growing body of literature, much of it reporting empirical research inspired by the Blau–Duncan formulation, is beginning to depart quite markedly from the Edwards paradigm, and suggests that a major reformulation of the mainstream conception of occupational structure may be in the making. One might contend that this is hardly amazing, since it has long been recognized in a variety of common-sense ways that the Edwards paradigm does not take into account many palpably important aspects of occupational structure. People who enjoy high status but possess little authority suspect that they are being hoodwinked, and if prestige is substituted for pay beyond a certain point they are apt to get mad. Even the strongest motivation to attain status cannot guarantee the actual availability of a suitable job, and women and minorities are discriminated against even when they enjoy relatively high prestige. And you do not have to be either a cynic or a Marxist to be aware that if you can somehow contrive to have a lot of people working for you without having to pay them very much, you have a fighting chance of becoming both rich and famous. (See Robinson, 1970: 1–3, as well as Haug, 1977: 74, for a more systematic and scholarly discussion of these points.)

Perhaps one reason for the seeming lack of attention to such obvious matters is that the theoretical structure of the Edwards paradigm has not generally been made explicit. It has thus not always been clear just what the model is or is not supposed to apply to. We noted earlier that the implied underpinning of the Edwards conceptualization is a highly culturological, cerebral mechanism, which itself refers to a quite restricted range of phenomena. When one further examines the way in which occupational structure has implicitly been operationally defined in most of this literature, it becomes apparent that the implied theoretical mechanisms we are dealing with are even more culturological and cerebral than they seem at first glance. In virtually every empirical study I have seen about American occupational structure, ultimately an "occupation" is implicitly defined operationally as anything the *Dictionary of Occupational Titles* (U.S. Department of Labor, 1965) or the U.S. Bureau of the Census says is an occupation. Occupations, as they have generally been studied, are thus clearly revealed to be components of culture, not components of social structure. They are categories, not roles. This is an important point, because occupational structure thereby becomes essentially a system of beliefs to which people are oriented, not a system of activities that people perform. Occupations are thus quite different from jobs.

A *job* may be thought of as a role ordinarily performed primarily for the purpose of earning a livelihood in a commercial economy. It is a component of social structure. More often than not, it is a specific role in a particular organization, involving a specified range of activities, particular modes of interaction with others, a given degree of authority and control, and a specific amount of pay. An *occupation,* on the other hand, emerges as a more or less publicly recognized cultural category, into which certain people are both popularly and officially classified because they all hold, or in some cases at one time have held, jobs exhibiting that particular set of characteristics which constitute the criteria for inclusion in that particular occupational category. Occupations are thus culturally defined by certain selected aspects of jobs that many jobs have in common.

Problems of Phenomenology and Applicability

Distinctions between "job" and "occupation" are not uncommon in the literature (Moore, 1969: 864). It is not usual, however, for such distinctions explicitly to assign occupations to the cultural realm and jobs to the social realm, an assignment we find implicit in the corpus of occupational structure research. Such an assignment gives rise to two broad sets of considerations.

First, it unfortunately raises a number of complex and rather tangled questions concerning the phenomenological status of occupational structure. In an immediate operational sense, occupations are categories set forth in government publications, but suddenly they come to be "culturally defined," presumably with high levels of public identity on the part of some public. Of course, we know that neither Mr. Edwards nor his colleagues invented these categories out of whole cloth; with varying degrees of deliberateness, they sought to take "judicial notice," as it were, of what they already found to be present, though precisely how, we are not always sure. It would clearly be foolish to say that we believe in the existence of plumbing contractors simply because the government says they exist. However, it is worth noting that the *Dictionary of Occupational Titles* does serve both as a guide for preparing industrial and other job descriptions, and as a standard basis for occupational classifications used in a variety of formal documentary situations. Thus, once an occupational category is officially promulgated, its reality is further reproduced and reinforced.

There has not been much sustained research specifically on the processes by which occupational categories develop public identity as objects of cultural orientation—with or without government assistance. Some material on technological development and on the nature of capitalism indirectly suggests a combination of technical change and political–managerial decisions as moving forces (Udy, 1970; Braverman, 1974), but much more work needs to be done in this area.

A number of other similar kinds of phenomenological problems arise which I shall merely mention, both because there is no time to dwell on them in detail and because I have no very good solutions to any of them. The fact that occupational classification schemes frequently double as scientific typologies and empirical descriptions of real cultural configurations should delight the heart of any ethnomethodologist, since it means that different typologies may not merely reflect different ways of classifying the same data, but may well introduce different data. Real cultural configurations to which people are oriented are hardly exempt from being treated as data themselves.

One should also note that variations in both level of public identity and level of generality of occupational categories—both of which levels, in fact, vary considerably across any extant set of such categories—can affect the causal efficacy of any culturological theory in which they are involved. Finally, since they are simply there, there is no reason to suppose that any set of real cultural categories will be differentiated according to scientifically acceptable or consistent criteria, and occupational categories are no exception. When one varies occupation "experimentally," one may thus in fact be varying a great many variables some of the time, but none of them all of the time, all without knowing exactly what most of them are. Perhaps this is one reason why occupational status turns out to be statistically significantly related to so many things with r always seeming to be equal to about .25. Though I may be laughed out of the Association for saying so, I conclude that the time is ripe for ethnomethodologists to join demographers in studying occupational structure, and I am dead serious about this suggestion.

Assuming we can successfully consign our phenomenological colleagues to the foregoing morass and get out of it alive ourselves, we may face a second set of considerations arising from explicitly conceiving occupational structure as a cultural configuration. Such a conception helps us to clarify the precise range of phenomena to which the Edwards paradigm appropriately applies. It is appropriate to problems involving cultural and personal–attitudinal variables explicable through an action frame of reference. The Edwards paradigm thus produces quite consistent patterns of occupational prestige scores (Tyree and Smith, 1978; Treiman, 1977), and yields relatively good results when one is dealing with characteristics linked closely to culture per se (Vanneman and Pampel, 1977; Otto and Haller, 1979). It is also applicable up to a point in more complex situations where individuals are significantly motivated as a result of being oriented toward occupational categories, the outstanding example being the basic status attainment model.

In contrast, the Edwards paradigm does not, strictly speaking, apply anywhere to the extent that social structural elements are causing or constraining anything. Such situations are of two types. One involves morphological processes such as shifts in numbers of jobs assignable to given occupational categories, or changes in the distribution of jobs over a set of categories. The second type is more subtle, and involves social systems—roles and role structures, such as jobs and organizations and their attributes. Owing to the fact that occupational structure has not generally been recognized as a cultural configuration, but has itself been presumed to be a system of roles, the Edwards paradigm has commonly been applied in many such situations. Its lack of direct applicability has been obscured by the fact that occupational categories are culturally defined in terms of selected job characteristics. It is thus often possible to run occupation against variables which are, in fact, not causally related to occupations at all, but to jobs and other organizational phenomena, and still get statistically significant results, simply because one "picks up" enough relevant job characteristics through at least some of the occupational categories—a possibility enhanced by a lack of uniformity in types of job characteristics used to define different occupations, as previously noted.

One can further enhance one's empirical results along such lines by combining job-related characteristics with occupational characteristics, as in the Duncan Socio-Economic Index (SEI) (Duncan, 1961; Hauser and Featherman, 1977). As one might imagine, my inclination is toward measures of prestige alone (Siegel, Hodge, and Rossi, 1974; Treiman, 1977), even if one can gain a temporary empirical advantage through "hybridization." Strictly speaking, the Edwards paradigm does not apply directly to problems involving causation by social systemic components, because it is a culturological construct.

Some Recent Dissenting Literature

Not all sociological literature bearing on occupational structure over the years has used the Edwards paradigm, but, with the possible exception of the area of occupational mobility, it is only during the past few years that I have been able to detect any consistent pattern of trends away from it that point in an identifiable direction. Furthermore, all of these trends appear to have originated in efforts to cope with morphological processes or social system variables basically extraneous to the Edwards paradigm.

The need to supplement the Edwards paradigm with other models has undoubtedly been recognized for the longest time in the study of occupational mobility, where morphological processes palpably foreign to the Edwards paradigm have obvious relevance. Thus, one finds a long history of efforts to separate the effects of "structural mobility" from those of "circulation" or "exchange mobility," the former referring to morphological processes, and the latter, essentially to the forces embedded in the Edwards paradigm (Hauser, 1978; Hauser et al., 1975; McClendon, 1977).

Such efforts have generated an abundant methodological literature (Boudon, 1973), and in themselves, virtually constitute a disciplinary subspecialty in which there is internal controversy. However, such efforts have largely been seen as supplementary to the Edwards paradigm, the prevailing interest being to get the latter to fit better by controlling out the effects of structural mobility (Boudon, 1973). Furthermore, the relevance of using Edwards-type occupational status categories (or analogous continuous scales) for ordering mobility data in the first place has only very recently been challenged. Horan (1978) explicitly calls attention to the restrictive action theory basis of the Edwards paradigm, and further suggests that its categories do not necessarily portray what people are trying to achieve. Neither do they necessarily portray significant population movements among work positions occasioned by structural constraints, as opposed to action orientations. He suggests exploring alternative formulations based on neo-Marxian classifications.

Horan also calls attention to the morphological relevance of the particular economic sector in which a job is located as a determinant of earnings, quite independently of its occupational classification, noting the findings of Bibb and Form (1977) and Beck, Horan, and Tolbert (1978). There are various ways in which economic sectors can be conceived, ranging from the now almost traditional division of extractive, manufacturing, and service sectors, which is relevant to changes in types of available jobs in the course of economic development, to contemporary conceptions of dual or multiple labor markets (Montagna, 1977). Stolzenberg (1975) argues for an incorporation of this aspect of labor market theory into occupational sociology, and it has indeed been found helpful in explaining variations in earnings or career opportunities that cannot be accounted for by occupational status per se (Stolzenberg, 1975b; Spilerman, 1977; Pampel, Land, and Felson, 1977; Montagna, 1977).

Conceptualizations of sectors that yield measures, however rough, of degree of centrality of industries and jobs to the economy appear particularly promising as adjuncts to the study of occupational structure, and an especially interesting literature regarding women and minorities has recently developed around this theme—a literature that I shall reserve for special discussion later.

It is evident that these morphological concerns are not only important in themselves in drawing attention to the distribution of jobs in the occupational system, but that they also lead to a focus on social systemic, as opposed to cultural, variables connected directly with jobs and organizations and the positions of both in the social structure.

This has been most evident in the recent literature on earnings, an area in which the Edwards paradigm simply does not work very well since earnings are job-connected (McLaughlin, 1978). Efforts to construct models more predictive of earnings usually start from a sector-of-the-economy approach, and, beyond that, have taken two related directions. The first takes its cue from administrative theory, and examines the actual positions of jobs in organizations. McLaughlin (1978), for example, finds that the task-based potential of the job for resource control estimates earnings better than does occupational prestige, accounting partly for the lower earnings of women than men in the same kinds of occupations. Similarly, K. Wilson (1978) is able to predict income attainment better when he adds a measure of power in an organizational context to conventional measures of occupational status. Finally, one should mention a particularly important article by Stolzenberg (1978) in which he demonstrates that size of employing establishment has a very strong effect on SES returns to education.

The second set of efforts goes further and is practiced by a small but growing number of sociologists who combine a Marxist orientation with empirical data and sophisticated statistical techniques to very great advantage, in my view. This group is hampered by the fact that the Edwards tradition has not especially led to the collection of the data they need on a large scale, although Wright (1976) has made heroic efforts to find ways to operationalize Marxian class position independently of occupation using more or less readily available material. Using such measures, which estimate degrees of ownership of the means of production, purchase of the labor power of others, control of the labor power of others, and sale of one's own labor power, Wright and Perrone (1977) find that class differences have substantial effects on income and returns to education when occupational status is controlled. A later paper by Wright (1978) underscores the importance of class by showing that class differences very strongly mediate the effects of race on income returns to education among black and white males. Using a modified version of Wright's scheme, Kalleberg and Griffin (1978) apply it to a different, essentially job-connected component, namely, job satisfaction. They find that both occupational status and class position affect job satisfaction but that class position does so more, particularly when certain subtleties involving class differences in satisfaction expectations are taken into account.

The trend in all this work seems to be toward the development of a typology based on class and perhaps ultimately involving components of organizational positions, alongside the Edwards paradigm. In a paper recently published, Kalleberg and Griffin (1980) explicitly set up an analysis of inequality in job rewards along these lines, attempting to allocate variance between occupational status and class. Barring strained interpretations of Max Weber, the most explicit general statement of this parallelism appears to me to be that of Robinson and Kelley (1979) (see also Robinson, 1979), who show that by combining a class model with a conventional Blau–Duncan model, the amount of variance explained in the income of men in the United States and Great Britain can be increased by about one-half. They conclude that two distinct stratification systems exist—one embedded in the relations of production and in the authority system, and the other based on education and occupational status in the Edwards tradition.

Where does all this leave us? The work of Wright, Kalleberg and Griffin, and Robinson and Kelley in particular is strongly consistent with our own theoretical argument that occupational structure is a materially different phenomenon than the social structure of work. But there is one important difference. Our argument suggests that it is not merely a question of separately using or combining two typologies. Occupational structure is also a real cultural configuration to which people are demonstrably oriented. The social structure of work, at least in our culture, is not, and typologies representing it thus remain merely scientific constructs. It is thus not simply a question of allocating variance to each structure, but also one of exploring their actual interplay.

A possible clue to the nature of this interplay is found in some of the recent literature on the position of women and minorities in the work force—particularly women. It has generally been found that, although women in the same occupations ordinarily earn less than men, they fare just as well as men do in terms of prestige as set forth in the Edwards paradigm, given equivalent degrees of labor force participation (Treiman and Terrell, 1975; McClendon, 1976). To what can one then attribute the earnings differential? Wolf and Rosenfeld (1978), Bibb and Form (1977), and Snyder et al. (1978) find that working women tend to be found in different sectors of the labor market than men, sectors where pay is less. Furthermore, although their occupational statuses may be similar to men, women do not get comparable positions of authority in organizations (Wolf and Fligstein, 1979; McLaughlin, 1978). In short, both men and women benefit equally from mechanisms allocating occupational status, but men benefit from organizational and class position while women do not (Robinson and Kelley, 1979).

Conclusion

Vulgar Marxists to the contrary notwithstanding, there is nothing unreal about a cultural configuration. It is actually there, and it performs important integrative functions in society, as illustrated by the foregoing example. Men and women are equal in culturally visible ways, and women will thus presumably be happy about that, since these ways are visible. The ways in which men and women are unequal in work, however, are limited to social structure, are thus not culturally visible, and hence, in principle, not disruptive. Social integration triumphs.

It seems reasonable to presume that similar mechanisms occur in other areas of social life as well. The Edwards paradigm doubles as a typology and a virtual ideological statement, and in the latter capacity exhibits many properties of an ideology. For one thing, it relates statistically to enough things in the social structure to a sufficient degree to be credible—so credible that it has even hoodwinked sociologists. The study of the interplay between the two stratification systems we seem to have, if we recognize that one is cultural and the other social, would thus seem to be a potentially fruitful way to illuminate some very basic processes in human social life. That is why I think the literature I have tried to review here is important. It can indeed have some profound effects on our entire discipline.

13

Occupational Prestige
and Social Inequality

Wilbert E. Moore

OCCUPATION HAS COME to be recognized as a principal factor or determinant, over a wide band, of other significant social variables: life styles and life cycles (Form, 1976a; Wilensky and Lawrence, 1979), morale and social participation (Blauner, 1964; Form, 1976a), and, especially, social status or rank. Income, power and authority, and prestige are all linked to occupation, not only by correlational analysis and regression equations, but also at least in part by constituting attributes of jobs or rewards for work. Education, which along with occupation and income, is a standard component of combined measures of socioeconomic status (Duncan, 1961), figures primarily as a mode of access to occupations (and occupational careers). Generalized social ranking, if it makes any sense at all except as an analyst's exercise, is likely to reflect all of these modes of differential valuation.

Occupation has also been the key structural component of studies of "social mobility," whether intergenerational or within careers. The chances for sons to exceed the occupational ranks of their fathers constitute a measure of the openness of any institutionalized system of social equality. Thus, in the properly technical sense of the term "stratification"—a concept to which I shall return—a society that permits extensive intergenerational mobility is less stratified than one with a high degree of hereditary social position. Thus, Lipset and Bendix (1959) found little difference in mobility rates among leading industrial societies. Their data permitted only a binary division of occupations into "blue collar" and "white collar." Using a somewhat more extensive array of occupational ranks, Miller (1960) reconfirmed Americans'

166

impression that intergenerational mobility is greater in the "land of opportunity."

The rationalization of social, including occupational, systems—which is the proper definition of modernization (Moore, 1979)—should include a transition from predominantly ascriptive occupational assignments to sorting on the basis of achievement. This transition is amply evident in "developing areas," as documented by the contributors to the volume edited some years ago by Smelser and Lipset (1966b). Form's (1979) more recent review further confirms that generality, even in the difficult cases of Japan and India.

Yet in both newly developing countries and in more advanced industrial societies some complications need to be sorted out. In neither category of countries, in the contemporary world, can the assumption be made that the occupational structure itself remains relatively fixed, with the only significant "stratification" question being whether succession to occupational position is predominantly hereditary or, by the rules of rationality, based on a merit-sorting process.

Several statistically sophisticated studies, using American data, that have held occupational structure "constant," have found almost no change in a period of forty or more years in the amount of intergenerational mobility. The research reports by Rogoff (1953b), Blau and Duncan (1967), Hauser and associates (Hauser et al., 1975b, 1975d) and Hauser and Featherman (1977) are most noteworthy. A later report by Featherman and Hauser (1978), based on a replicated national survey, finds an increase in "universalistic" criteria of mobility, particularly in the broadening of educational opportunities. (See also Wilensky and Lawrence, 1979) As I have previously commented (Moore, 1966: 196):

> Now the analytical separation of mobility accounted for by changes in the distribution of occupations within the socioeconomic structure from that ac counted for by changes in the distribution of opportunity or accessibility is a perfectly legitimate procedure. But there is no reason to say that only the second datum is interesting.

I should now add that without effective mobility aspirations, specialization and upgrading as two of the master processes of changing occupational structures (Moore, 1966: 204–209) would fail to occur. (It is no more automatically true that demand will create a supply than that supply will find an effective demand. Mechanistic thinking can delude us.)

A further comment is relevant to the measurement of occupational mobility. I mentioned earlier that Miller had found more mobility than had Lipset and Bendix by attending to more categories. It has become conventional for mobility studies (particularly those relating solely to the United States) to use some variant of the United States Census classification, with 8 to 15 groups, depending on the number of distinctions within categories. Were the researchers to take account of the more than 22,000 occupations—not counting alternative titles for the same tasks—defined by the *Dictionary of Occupational Titles* (U.S. Department of Labor, 1965) or the somewhat lesser number enumerated in the decennial census, analysis would reveal a great deal more intergenerational mobility.

The rationale behind the groupings, aside from the mechanical problem of data management, is clearly related to notions of ranking and inequality. That is a perfectly legitimate interest, both for scientific analysis and for relevance to social policy (Haug, 1977). Yet this deliberate suppression of details may lead to the impression that the "inheritance of relative occupational position" is the same as occupational inheritance, particularly when the researchers are careless in their language. Since, to my knowledge, no one has actually dealt with detailed occupations in studying intergenerational mobility, I am free to speculate that precise inheritance of an occupation is rare, and inheritance of an unchanged occupation is virtually nonexistent.

Some Conceptual Clarifications

An occupation comprises performance of "a more or less precise *set* of renumerated activities" (Moore, 1969: 864). Although the line is either hazy or arbitrary, I prefer to distinguish occupation from a job or position, and thus implicitly to carry with the term a somewhat more enduring relation between the performer and the set of tasks than exemplified by the succession of jobs held by the casual laborer or the organizational positions held by an itinerant manager or professor. (Laborer, manager, and professor are thus the occupations of such vagabonds.)

The understandable propensity to group such occupations, and then to rank the groups, entails some costs. The honogeneity of the occupations included in any group is by no means perfect, even on those limited criteria used to rank the groups. These are, conventionally, either the income, prestige, and educational levels comprising Duncan's (1961) socioeconomic index (SEI) or the prestige scales alone as exemplified (for the United States) by Siegel, Hodge, and Rossi (1974) or (internationally) by Treiman (1977). It must be added that Treiman, in some instances, has variable scores within groups among the several hundred occupations for which he develops prestige scores. Hauser and Featherman (1977: 27–41) argue for the superiority of the combined SEI, and Treiman (1977: 208–13) defends the tactical and substantive advantages of prestige scores alone. Somewhat offhand, I find Treiman's argument more persuasive, but fundamentally I am disenchanted with both positions.

The heterogeneity within occupational groups on those criteria commonly measured is made much greater if one adds some other significant occupational dimensions. This is true if one confines one's interest to those dimensions that are scalable, that is, relate to inequality. Perhaps the most glaring lack in the inequalitarian aspects of occupational differentiation is the inattention to the (admittedly poorly operationalized) dimension of power, authority, influence. Power—to use a shorthand term for this dimension—is for some an intrinsic reward, and otherwise shares with money (but not with prestige; see Goode, 1978) instrumental utility in increasing other rewards.

In no very orderly fashion (for a somewhat more orderly analysis, see Moore, 1969) let me note some other dimensions of occupations that are likely not to be highly correlated with standard scale criteria: employment security; safety, cleanliness, and comfort; socioecological settings, including freedom to move about; relative autonomy in the actual pursuit of occupational tasks. These are occupational dimensions that Form does include in his four-country study of *Blue-Collar Stratification* (1976a). Perhaps a parochial comment may be permitted: If occupation is your subject, always trust an old card-carrying industrial sociologist over a demographer. (I claim to have been both.) These occupational dimensions have relevance for morale and psychological alienation, the propensity to form craft-oriented or status-oriented labor organizations, matters that are also related to the dynamics of social inequality, especially from a stringently or vaguely Marxist orientation. Other occupational dimensions, such as the preference for things, people, or ideas in the job description, have a much higher variability in space and time with regard to ranking, but misfitting occupational assignments do have implications for work satisfactions.

I turn next to the grievously abused term "social stratification." I have not taken the time to determine the etymology of the term. It was certainly common in 1945 when Kingsley Davis and I perpetrated the notorious (infamous?) brief essay (Davis and Moore, 1945) that enunciated what has come to be known as the "functional theory of stratification." The term "stratification" was misused by our common mentor, Pitirim Sorokin, in his classic *Social Mobility* (1927). In the course of an extensive essay on functionalism (Moore, 1978), I have disavowed the term "stratification" as a synonym for inequality, as I had done earlier in some of the intermittent disputes over the original formulation. Both "class" and "stratification" clearly and *necessarily* imply objectively tenable lines of demarcation across status distributions. Some such exist in advanced industrial societies (e.g., the hereditary rich who comprise some fraction of the rich and the hereditary poor who comprise a minority of the poor), but lines across the undistributed middle (which may be 75 to 85 percent of the total population) are purely and intolerably arbitrary.

The multiplex differentiation characteristic of American society—and to a lesser extent that of other highly modernized societies that still carry the burden of historical feudalism—is well analyzed in Janowitz's career-crowning volume, *The Last Half-Century* (1978: 123–63). No one open to objective truth—and that will exclude the religious Marxists with their eschatological beliefs in an originally flawed and long-outdated creed—can read Janowitz and still use the term "class" in the loose and slovenly way that many sociologists do. But, as demonstration of the power of entrenched semantic error, Janowitz, though explicitly rejecting the "stratigraphic" model, persists in the term "stratification," meaning inequality. (The book's index has "Inequality. *See* Social Stratification.")

To show the ridiculous extremes that semantic silliness may lead to, Featherman and Hauser (1978: 10), citing Duncan (1968), write, "We shall use the term *social mobility* synonymously with *social stratification . . . ,* defining the latter as a dynamic, life-long process." Even if the term "inequality" were substituted for "stratification," that statement remains pure conceptual garbage. It is of course commendable to deal with process as well as results, but not to confound the analysis with conceptual confusion.

As the cited Duncan essay was in a book of which I was a joint initiator and editor, I recalled no such nonsense and, indeed, on review, there is none. Duncan (1968: 681) writes, "Social *stratification* refers to the persistence of positions in a hierarchy of inequality, either over the life time of a birth cohort of individuals or, more particularly, between generations." Thus, it is precisely lack of mobility that, to Duncan, warrants the term "stratification." The use of the term "hierarchy" is, in Duncan's ensuing discussion, clearly intended to include in the concept of stratification the notion of layers or *strata*. As Duncan notes with respect to "class," however, determining the boundaries of strata, and thus their number, is not easy across an entire society's various status distributions. A short excerpt (Duncan, 1968: 694) is to the point:

> The concept of "class" is often used in such a way that it means little more than the imposition of more or less arbitrary intervals on the scale of a status variable. . . . An incredible amount of paper and ink has been wasted in presenting factitious solutions for the artificial problem of where "class boundaries" really belong. "Class" in the sense of a statistical "class interval" is merely a nominal category of greater or lesser analytical convenience. The virtually irresistable temptation to make something more of it is reason enough to forgo employment of the term in a treatment of social stratification.

Goode's (1978) exhaustive (and sometimes exhausting) analysis of prestige as a control system is seriously flawed in his chapter on "class," for he moves injudiciously from systems of institutionalized inequality where strata are objectively distinct (the extreme being the Indian caste system) to highly rationalized ("modernized") societies where they are not.

It is readily possible to determine distinct strata (at times in inconveniently large numbers) in hierarchically organized (bureaucratic), formal organizations. This objective reality partially exempts from conceptual complaint Form's (1976a) work on *Blue-Collar Stratification,* which analyzes increasing differentiation (including status gradations) rather than increasing "class" homogeneity among automobile workers.

I say that Form's work is partially exempt, for I believe that his comparative evidence, particularly with his four countries arranged along an approximate scale of degree of industrial rationalization, exhibits both increasing gradations in terms of skill categories and increasing *occupational* as distinct from rank-oriented commitments of those workers at upper-skill levels. It is increased occupational differentiation that leads to "distinctions without a difference," if the sole difference is arbitrarily limited to status inequalities (Moore, 1965). Since differentiation ambiguously includes both inequality and heterogeneity, Blau's (1977) conceptual clarification of this distinction is to be recommended.

Some Substantive and Methodological Issues

If occupation is to be used as one major component of mapping and measuring social inequality, and *the* critical mode of analyzing social mobility within careers and between generations, a thicket of conceptual and methodological problems hampers procedures. On problems of achieving common meanings for occupations and occupational categories across time and space, Treiman (1977: 46–56) has a sensible and somewhat optimistic discussion. With the worldwide process of increasing structural rationalization, there are both theoretical arguments and some scraps of evidence that occupations become not only increasingly comparable but increasingly uniform in their relative prestige or socioeconomic status rankings (Form, 1976a, 1979; Smelser and Lipset, 1966b; Haug, 1977; Treiman, 1977; Wilensky, 1979). The authors just cited use the overly restrictive term "industrialization." Structural rationalization affects all occupations, and is not narrowly constrained to the technology of manufacturing (Moore, 1979). Yet that same process of rationalization leads to ever increasing occupational specialization. I suggest that this must increasingly produce occupational titles with which the "public" will have no familiarity. This would put in jeopardy sole reliance on prestige scores for occupational rankings, except (as seems to have been the case in prestige scales now used) as "representative" occupations are used from categories established by other technical status criteria such as income and education, and those scores assigned to all occupations not directly ranked. That kind of procedure makes me extremely nervous about the *behavioral* meaning of prestige, for how is either deference or disdain to be expected with respect to an unknown occupational position?

This component of ignorance must figure in some, now unknown, degree in the avid quest for professionalization of new occupations, along with more pragmatic goals such as income and increased autonomy in performance (Goode, 1978; Moore, 1970; Wilensky, 1964). Thus, if a relatively unknown occupation can credibly lay claim to being a profession, the apparently uniform aura of high respectability attached to that category may cover ignorance of particulars. Still, who is making the assignment, the investigator or the lay informant?

What I am reflecting here is considerable unease about the operational meaning of prestige as a variable, and neither Treiman's heroic comparative data nor Goode's "sensitive observer" style of analysis sets that unease at rest. Particularly for occupational positions with extremely limited "publics" (that is, informed judges), educational qualifications and income rewards may be more defensible ranking criteria than prestige. Were some metric for power–authority–influence to be developed, the preference for the more "objective" rankings would be overwhelming.

A Final Note on the "Functional Theory"

I shall not here go through the various conceptual errors and errors of omission by Davis and me (Davis and Moore, 1945) in our brief essay "Some Principles of Stratification," some thirty-five years ago. These are recorded elsewhere (Moore, 1978: 331). Although the original argument was cast in an evolutionary perspective (which assumes a trial-and-accidental-success pattern), it has also been noted as having the rationalistic overtones of a modern labor market. As I have noted in the cited essay:

> A test at the level of generality assumed by the theory would require establishing an ordered array of essential functions, clear data on availability of persons with differential talent and training, and a measure of rewards, financial or otherwise.

None of the various "tests" of the theory has met that set of conditions. Though the research that I have been briefly reviewing here was not explicitly designed as a test of the functional theory, the remarkable (and possibly increasing) uniformity of occupational status rankings in various societies adds some credibility to the original formulation. My own interpretation of the apparent uniformities is consistent with that view, but would put the proximate causal emphasis on contemporary efforts at structural rationalization. Still, some enduring variability cannot be denied, and it is always possible—since no society in the contemporary world is truly isolated and self-subsistent— that a great deal of imitation is going on. Thus, the similarities in social inequality might be simply a consequence of cultural diffusion rather than functional necessity. I do not believe it, but on the evidence so far this alternative hypothesis cannot be rejected.

14

Population: Note
on the Problem of Explanation

Amos H. Hawley

THE QUESTION of the relation of theory and research in population study is in the first instance a question of boundaries. At the core of population study is demography which, strictly speaking, is the study of "human populations as influenced by 'demographic processes': fertility, mortality, and migration" (Glass, 1957: 15). Since such events are discrete, they have lent themselves to quantitative treatment. Accordingly, demography developed as a quantitative analysis of population composition and change. Its theory, best exemplified by the stable population model, is essentially deductive. The theory consists in drawing out the mathematical implications of certain specific measurable processes, the "demographic processes." In the demographic conception, population is an abstraction—it is simply an aggregate of events that can be subjected to quantitative analysis.

In the last few decades, however, demography has undergone an extension of its boundaries. This has occurred as a result of attempts to explain the formal properties of population. To some extent the broadening of the field has been attempted by redefining certain attributes of individuals, such as education, religion, marital status, and labor force membership, as demographic properties on the grounds that, once acquired, such characteristics are relatively unchangeable (Ryder, 1964a: 451–52). They are thus comparable to age and sex. The role of acquired characteristics is not always clear, however. Sometimes they are used to flesh out the demographic description of a population. At others they are treated as independent variables with which to explain the "demographic processes." But as causes

173

the acquired characteristics can be no more than proximate, for as with the "demographic processes" they can be fully understood only as consequences of social, economic, and political processes. In other words, when the population student turns from description to explanation it becomes necessary to draw upon the disciplines of sociology, economics, political science, and others (Gutman, 1960). This is not to say that those fields have a corpus of theory readymade and suited to the population student's needs. Where the theory of a discipline is fairly well developed, the population student has had to adapt it to the problem at hand; where theory has been somewhat inchoate, the student has had to try to fashion a theory suited to the phenomena under investigation from the materials of the appropriate discipline. Thus, in the pursuit of explanations the boundary of demography is progressively blurred.

Population theory—or, better said, theory dealing with population issues—falls into two broad categories. One is social-psychological and microanalytical. It comprises a large accumulation of very specific propositions, some of which have emerged from clear theoretical contexts; others are simply questions posed without any explicit theoretical support. For the most part, the analytical techniques used in testing the propositions are drawn from the corpus of social science methodology and are not, therefore, peculiar to demography. Ryder's (189–202) searching criticism of micro-level theory and its research product leaves little to be said.

The second category consists in theories cast at a macro level. These have originated mainly from the perspective of social economy, that is, they are theories in which systemic properties are the independent variables. Prominent in this class is the Malthusian model from which various equilibrium approaches have been developed. A more recent and currently prominent theory goes under the name of demographic transition theory. Granted that this idea began as a historical observation and was later fitted with a theoretical rationale, it is an explanation that utilizes technological and institutional changes to account for demographic events. It is noteworthy that while both the Malthusian and transition theory derive identical growth curves they proceed from very different assumptions. The one assumes fixed resources with a limited population carrying capacity, while the other assumes a changing resource base and an expanding carrying capacity. Whereas Malthus anticipated an increasing death rate as an important, if not decisive, control on growth, transition theory contemplates a convergence of a declining birth rate upon a declining death rate. A third member of the macro-level category, as yet relatively undeveloped, deals with changing population requirements incidental to technological involution in a system.

Now, since transition theory has replaced Malthusian theory as a point of departure for much current population discussion, it might be useful to devote a little more space to it here. After enjoying a great vogue for a period transition theory has fallen lately on troubled times. Criticisms have been aimed at its failure to specify a definite time frame and at its historical bias

(Teitelbaum, 1975). The first of these is a little bit specious inasmuch as it is not peculiar to transition theory; it is characteristic of all social theories, in fact, of all theories that have access only to necessary conditions as causes. Some progress has been made in treating the temporal factor in change, however, by identifying threshold conditions for demographic events (Kirk, 1971). The determination of temporal surrogates may be the nearest approach to the timing of events that can be realized.

With reference to the historical limitation, Keyfitz (178–88) suggests that the demographic transition may be less of a theory than a loose characterization of a certain epoch in population history. But I think it is more than that, though it may still be a first approximation to a full-fledged theory. As a model of change, it fits nicely with the expected movement of age composition changes incidental to shifts in birth and death rates. Thus, it joins social–economic influences with shifts of formal demographic properties. But the historical question is not unrelated to the timing problem. At issue is whether the time difference in the downturns of death and birth rates in contemporary developing countries is of the same order as that experienced in Western countries during the nineteenth and early twentieth centuries. In other words, is the duration of lag in the trend changes similar and are the underlying structural circumstances comparable? These are empirical questions. But, whatever may be their answers, the course of demographic change seems to have been replicated in general outline at least in virtually all Third World countries. Deviations there have been, yet if a theory is supposed to identify a central tendency, how much dispersion is acceptable without disqualifying it as a plausible theory? And what kind of weight should be given to occasional, short-term historical variations from the model?

The historical question cannot be left without mention of two methodological contributions to its treatment. One is known as cohort analysis, which entails a disaggregation of populations into age groups and systematic observations of their behaviors through their life cycles (Whelpton, 1954; Ryder, 1965). Ryder has proposed the cohort as a key structural component for population analysis. A second contribution comprises the techniques of family reconstruction developed by historical demographers (Glass and Eversley, 1965). It would seem that in this matter population students have made a useful contribution to historical research.

A great deal of the criticism of the demographic transition has concentrated on the character of fertility change. Some historical research suggests that fertility might have increased in nineteenth-century Europe before it entered upon its decline. That has been attributed to a proletarianization of the industrializing population (Tilly, 1978a). There is also the possibility, however, that some increase would be incidental to mortality reduction, inasmuch as the same improvements in nutrition that initiate mortality reduction might also be expected to increase fecundity. Rose Frisch (1978) has brought together a great deal of evidence in support of this possibility.

Whether subsequent fertility reduction comes about through increasing age at marriage or through contraceptive practice provides some commentary on the prospects for family planning program success (Coale, 1973, 1978), but it doesn't gainsay the trend anticipated in the transition model.

But transition theory is not just a theory of fertility change; it is a theory concerning the changing relation of fertility to mortality. The neglect of mortality by the critics is peculiar in view of the fact that there has been no long-term downward trend in fertility without a corresponding, and usually a prior, trend in mortality. Reduced mortality may be the critical necessary condition for a fertility decline. Added years of life would seem to have a displacing effect on births. For example, an increase in life expectancy at birth from 35 to 70 years means that birth frequencies in a stationary population can be reduced by one-half without any loss of person-years of life. And with that kind of change there is improved economy, for more than twice the number of years of productive life can be realized from a single generation than are obtainable from two generations at the lower life expectancy. The theoretical question here, as in all aspects of fertility behavior, is how the effects of structural changes in a society are communicated to and through a population.

The critics also contend that mortality declines in contemporary developing countries have been due to the diffusion of medical and sanitary knowledge and therefore are unrelated to development. Apart from the rather peculiar conception of development implied in such a statement, it overlooks the obvious fact that food supplies in developing countries, in even the poorest among them, have kept pace with population growth. Had that not been the case, it is doubtful that modern medical and sanitary knowledge would have been very helpful. Nor could there have been any increases in longevity. Improvement in food supplies should certainly be counted as an important manifestation of development, whether it results from a simple or a complex technological advance.

It must be admitted, however, that transition theory is in need of considerable refinement. Lacking are explicit assumptions concerning the relation of fertility to mortality, the mechanics through which technological and institutional changes impinge on vital rates, and the prescription of threshold circumstances.

The basic theoretical problem confronting population study, it seems to me, has to do with how a viable relationship between population and a social system is achieved and maintained. No doubt the question must be treated differently for closed and open systems. For a closed system, an equilibrium model is usable (Wilkinson, 1973). In that circumstance, a net reproduction of unity and a stationary age distribution might be expected to be associated with various other equilibrium conditions, such as a complete utilization of existing knowledge, a balance of production and consumption, a regular succession of generations through an unchanging role structure, a consummate integration of the system, and a fixed repertory of ways of dealing with environmental variations. These conditions are apt to be found only in isolated situations, cases of which are few and diminishing.

An equilibrium model is much more difficult to apply, if it is applicable at all, to an open system. For then the system is exposed to frequent information inputs with the consequent changes in structure. Yet it seems very probable that open systems, such as contemporary developed nations, may be brought to zero population growth and some approximation to a stationary age composition. The theoretical question concerns the possibility of a coexistence of population equilibrium and structural disequilibrium in a system. Would the population equilibrium be highly unstable? If so, what form would the interaction take? Of course, what is called an open system may be more appropriately regarded as a unit or subsystem of a more inclusive system. That does not simplify the theoretical problem. It suggests, rather, that a complex system has built-in instabilities and that therefore an equilibrium model may be totally inapplicable.

A possibility referred to in an earlier paragraph concerns the effects of social system change on the system's population requirements. Albert Hirschman (1958: 180) has suggested a three-stage progression in which a changing system is first impeded by population growth, then is able to capitalize on growth, and finally becomes independent of population growth. But he considers the relationship in its production aspect only. Does the same progression apply to population units consumption function? I think not. Even though numbers of a given magnitude may not be needed in production in a highly productive society, they are needed as consumers, for otherwise the economies of scale will be lost. There is, however, the possibility that the production function can continue to grow in the service sector. How far this can be carried is a question of some importance. We cannot all live by taking in one another's laundry. But the consumption function need not be confined to the society in question, nor does consumption have to follow traditional patterns. Considerations such as these open the discussion to the complexities of processes in a world system and to the uncertainties in the course of future change. In any case, the possibility of a shifting effect of population with structural changes in society is an intriguing problem that merits a careful study.

As one pursues the theoretical problem in reference to population movements, it becomes increasingly apparent that he or she is confronted with a much broader question than that with which the inquiry began. What is needed is a theory of social–economic structural change. With that in hand one would be in a better position to entertain questions of how structural changes impinge upon demographic parameters. That would require, of course, a satisfactory operationalization of structural variables, and this, in turn, requires data resources only now becoming available in sufficient quantity and quality.

15

Explanation in Demography and History

Nathan Keyfitz

MODELS ARE USED by demographers to explain past and forecast future population in much the same way as models are used by historians and by other social scientists. We may be better able to understand the demographic transition, and to say where and when it will next occur, if we realize that it involves issues common to understanding the Renaissance or the rise of capitalism. At the very least we will be able to draw on the longer experience of historians, who for many centuries have tried to extract lessons from history. Understanding and skill in prediction come out of errors and failures, and the historian's stock of these is greater than ours.

The question is not a trivial one, but consists in nothing less than the likelihood that the demographic transition will spread to the one-half or more of the world's population in which high fertility rates still exist. And this, in turn, is really a question of how much poverty there will be in the world during the twenty-first century.

The present statement concerning the logic of historical interpretation in relation to the subject matter of population is the fourth in a sequence of contributions intended to illuminate the use of models in demography. I shall begin by summarizing the three aspects of the use of models in demography taken up in my previous papers.

Previous Work

The first paper in the series (1971) showed how the continuing effort of demographers to forecast population forced them to invent models; looking back at the forecasts, proved wrong time and again by unexpected changes in the demographic reality, brought agonized renewal of the search for models that would be more appropriate to that reality. In this way demography went successively from the logistic curve to Whelpton's components method, to cohorts, to a psychological-survey approach. We still fall short of accuracy in forecasts, especially across turning points in the birth curve, but the search for a forecasting method has had a clear positive result, the devising of new models and new approaches, though one incidental to its main purpose.

The second work (1975) dealt with the facts of demography, especially with the great difference between what is revealed by raw data, including correlation and regression of raw data, and the relations incorporated in models. An obvious example is age distribution, in particular the proposition that the fraction of old people in a population is larger, the slower the rate of growth. Attempts to establish this by observation of the countries of the world and regressions among those countries fail utterly to give the quantitative relation. In contrast to such a statistical approach, a simple model, that of the stable population, in which age-specific rates of birth and death are fixed but at various levels, provides the relation exactly. This relation, familiar as the comparative statics of economics, emerges from theoretical comparisons between two populations when all elements are the same except rates of birth. Models provide a certain kind of knowledge—how two variables relate to one another when all others are unchanging—in contrast with the kind of knowledge obtainable by statistical and econometric methods—how two variables relate to one another when other things vary as they do in concrete actuality.

My third paper, given at the 1979 ASA meeting, pursued further the multiplicity of models available to explain a given phenomenon, and examined the bearing of this multiplicity on policy. I argued that a simple incisive model can lead to clear-cut policy advice, and that the greater readiness of economics than of sociology to give policy advice is due to the relative sharpness of its models. Yet, whatever purer purposes models may serve, they are devices of persuasion. They present a condition—say, that ignorance of contraception is what keeps the birth rate high, and this in turn holds up development—in a formal and relatively abstract way that leads to a clear-cut policy indication: in this case, provide contraception to poor countries. Such a model may indeed fit the reality, and hence the policy drawn from it may be effective, but we cannot know that without contrasting with other models (for instance, that poor people have many children because they want helpers in the home and in the fields) that lead to very different policies. Any proposer has an obligation to compare his model with alternatives and to gather data that would ascertain which is the better fit. A model used without such comparison and checking can be merely a way of promoting a policy, closer to rhetoric than to science.

My fourth theme, the subject of this chapter, relates to understanding rather than directly to policy. I shall use as an illustration the leveling off of some populations in our time, a process to which the name "demographic transition" has been assigned, and see whether its existence is explained in a way that enables us to forecast its subsequent appearances.

All demographic materials are part of history. That births in the United States in 1978 numbered 3.3 million is a part of the history of this country, whatever else it may be. And, like historians, demographers assemble such elementary facts into larger entities, entities like the demographic transition, or the baby boom, or the presently rising mortality of the Soviet Union. Once we have created entities of significance, we want to find in what context they exist, what prior events constitute their antecedents, and what natural laws give the prior events the power or force to bring about the events we are trying to explain. These four aspects (the entity to be explained, its context, the prior causes acting on it, and the laws relating the causes to the entity as effect) require some elaboration.

The Entity to Be Explained

The very existence of the larger events or entities that we spend our time trying to explain is constantly under challenge. The demographic transition has been abolished on paper many times—most recently by Peter Kunstadter (1979). Yet the definition of the transitional condition seems simple and unexceptionable: "that in which the decline of both fertility and mortality is well established but in which the decline of mortality precedes that of fertility and produces rapid growth" (Notestein, 1945). Such a definition is backed by statistical observations that many European countries show a decline of deaths, then of births.

Unfortunately, the timing has not always been in accord with the theory, as Notestein points out. In France of the eighteenth and nineteenth centuries the fall in birth rates was simultaneous with, even preceded, the fall in death rates, and both occurred much earlier than in England, despite the fact that in other aspects of modernization England was ahead. In smaller areas within countries a great lack of uniformity appears, as the Princeton study is showing.

All this is troublesome, but no more so than in other fields. Whatever doubts can be cast on the entity or event "demographic transition" can equally be cast on the entity or event "Renaissance." We know that from the mid-fourteenth to mid-seventeenth centuries, in Italy and England and the countries between them, there arose a movement to rescue and study Latin and Greek manuscripts; wealthy merchants like the Medici of Florence and the Sforza of Milan, along with Leo X and other popes, came to be patrons of the arts; a few geniuses like Leonardo lived and worked, along with many artists of talent; universities sprang up; geographical discoveries were made as European sailors went round the globe. A this-worldly humanism came into its own. The movement spread from Italy through France, Holland, and England, and with it are associated writers that include Boccaccio, Rabelais, Erasmus, and Shakespeare.

Did the Renaissance exist? After all, not everyone in the Europe of the time participated, indeed only a small elite even knew what was going on; whole regions were left out. And certainly there have been writers and artists and patrons of the arts in other times and places. The whole thing could be no more than a way of speaking given scholarly respectability by Jacob Burckhardt.

Both the Renaissance and the demographic transition have characteristics that vary somewhat with the writer, and their boundaries are ill defined, as are those of any entity that exists in the matrix of history. Our demographic transition has about the same kind and degree of existence as the Renaissance, the rise of capitalism, or the end of colonialism, which is to say that it is a concept of ill-defined boundaries and uncertain characteristics, yet it still constitutes a useful summary of a phase of history that without the concept would be too complicated to talk about coherently.

The Context

Not every decline of births and deaths is an instance of the demographic transition. The decline must take place in the context of industrialization before it constitutes the transition we are talking about. In general, the fall has been greatest in the countries that were industrially most advanced, and within those countries among the social strata that were most involved in industry, as workers or managers. Yet sometimes fertility fell long before industry came, as in rural Saxony from the eleventh century onward.

The context of the phenomenon is difficult to specify in other regards. Europe had late marriage from the seventeenth century onward; its crude birth rates prior to industrialization, about 35 per thousand in the eighteenth century, were already lower than most preindustrialized populations. Europe had gone through the Renaissance and the Reformation, and had inherited very special legal systems from classical antiquity. One could list many hundreds of items of historical conditions and changes that preceded or were simultaneous with the demographic transition in Europe; which of them were relevant to the transition? The question is answered by each writer in his own way. How one defines and bounds the transition is related to how one plans to explain it.

Antecedents and Laws Needed
for Historical Explanation

We come, then, to the question of what brought the entity into existence. Here again Frank Notestein, in the mature analysis of the demographic transition (1953: 16):

> Mortality dropped rather promptly in response to external changes because mankind has always coveted health. The decline of fertility, however, awaited the gradual obsolescence of age-old social and economic institutions and the emergence of a new ideal in matters of family size. . . . Urban life stripped the family of many functions in production, consumption, recreation, and education. In factory employment the individual stood on his own accomplishments. The new mobility of young people and the anonymity of city life reduced the pressures toward traditional behavior exerted by the family and community. In a period of rapidly developing technology new skills were needed, and new opportunities for individual advancement arose. Education and a rational point of view became increasingly important. As a consequence the cost of child-rearing grew and the possibilities for economic contributions by children declined. Falling death-rates at once increased the size of the family to be supported and lowered the inducements to have many births. Women, moreover, found new independence from household obligations and new economic roles less compatible with childrearing.
>
> Under these multiple pressures old ideals and beliefs began to weaken, and the new ideal of a small number of children gained strength.

Notice that this not only gives the antecedents of the transition but implies a set of natural laws. As a minimum it seems to be saying that urban life, social, geographical and occupational mobility, education, entry of women into the labor market, all tend to reduce family size. They may of course work through one another: education may inspire mobility and that in turn may reduce family size, or education in and of itself may reduce family size—nothing is said about the sequence of causes, but without their effective action the transition would presumably not go through.

Is the statement too informal, mere casual theorizing? Would it not have been better to establish each of the propositions explicitly by means of regressions or other use of statistical data? Much has been done along that line since.

Demographers are often casual in the "laws" that they introduce into their arguments, either implicitly or explicitly. Do couples with more education always tend to have fewer children? Something must depend on the kind of education; that given to Moslem boys in the Koranic schools by no means leads them to have small families. There is indeed a negative correlation between the years children spend in Western schools and the number of children they have later. The contrast ought to be a challenge to find what is the educational content that is associated with small families. Such investigations are not usually undertaken as part of the study of the demographic transition, and the issue is not mentioned in either of the Notestein articles cited.

But historians are even more casual. David Potter (1954) imputes the generosity of the American character to our plentiful resources, plentiful at least at the time that the national character was being formed. People do not rush to grab a seat in a train where there are few passengers. That may be so, but it overlooks a thousand difficulties, first in merely identifying national character, then in the numerous possible causal influences on character.

Other historians impute warlike behavior of a country to its lack of natural resources. Yet imperial Russia was warlike despite extravagantly great resources, and Switzerland, with nothing but mountains, is the most peaceful of countries. Demographers have been properly restrained in such imputations.

Thus, on this scheme the apparatus of historical explanation includes the entity (demographic transition) to be explained, the context (incipient industrialization) in which that entity existed, the antecedent causes (education, urbanization, mobility), and the general laws under whose auspices the causes bring about the effect to be explained.

Such explanation has been known in historical methodology as the covering law model (*Encyclopedia of Philosophy,* Vol. 3: 158, and Vol. 4: 8). It is an apparatus eminently suited to prediction as well as to explanation. In the words of Hempel (1942):

> The explanation of the occurrence of an event of some specific kind E at a certain time and place consists . . . in indicating the cause or determining factors of E. Now the assertion that a set of events—say, of the kinds C_1, C_2, . . . C_n—have caused the event to be explained, amounts to the statement that, according to certain general laws, a set of events of the kinds mentioned is regularly accompanied by an event of kind E. Thus, the scientific explanation of the event in question consists of
>
> 1. a set of statements asserting the occurrence of certain events C_1, . . . C_n at certain times and places,
> 2. a set of univeral hypotheses.

The task of the historian or demographer is to ascertain empirically whether the causes C_1, . . . C_n were actually present, as well as whether the effect E took place. The explanation is more convincing if it can be shown that the quantitative variation of the C's corresponds to that of E in the degree that the explanation requires.

A Sequence of Questions

Any answer to the ''why'' of a historical event must open the door to further questions. Whenever we face one question we face a sequence. The drastic fall of births that has taken place over the past decade is clearly related to the increased entry of women into the labor force. Probably women have fewer children because of their wish to enter the labor force; it is also true that having fewer children frees them for entry. Ask women why they seek employment, and they answer that they need the money. But needing money is a universal constant, and as such it cannot explain a specific happening of the 1960s and 1970s. Married women cannot need the money now more than in the past, since wage statistics show that their husbands are as well paid as ever in terms of real purchasing power. It must be that work outside the home is more attractive than it was.

Any causal inquiry involves construction of models; within any model some questions are answered, while new questions are posed; question follows question, and the trail is traced to the point where it crosses the boundary of the discipline, then abandoned. Why the fall in the birth rate? Because women prefer to take jobs. Why do they take jobs now when they did not before? Because the jobs are more attractive, let us say. How has it been possible to make the jobs more attractive? By the greater productivity of the economy. Sooner or later a point is reached where the trail must be abandoned, at least by the practitioners of the discipline that posed the original question.

Alternatives to Covering Theory

What if the trail goes both ways at once? Women want to be part of the work world, and to this end they avoid having children. But women who have no children to look after are therefore inclined to seek jobs. The empirical materials show no more than that working outside the home is correlated with having few or no children. Does one of these contain the power to cause the other, which is then its effect? Hume showed that we have no way of knowing; at most we can take as cause the one that is prior in time, and then only if the uniformity of the association can be counted on through all places and times. We may say that industrialization causes a decline in the birth rate, just as we may say that the sun's shining on a rock makes it warm, but these are mere ways of talking rather than descriptions of the world. Hume's challenge has never been answered satisfactorily. Observed uniformities make us *think* that one element has the power to cause the other, but that is subjective, for the power in question can never be observed.

In social science the complexity of relations that appear, the number of factors involved, the tendency for simultaneous action, all make matters even more difficult than the question of whether the sun causes the rock to become warm. Because of the subsequently recognized failure of so many hopeful attempts at direct causal explanation functional analysis has come to have a central place in social science. It admits, indeed emphasizes, reciprocal action, multiple causes, circularity, that are embarrassing to covering theory.

Verstehen explains the events of the past by an intimate kind of understanding; one puts oneself in the place of the actors. "What would I do if I were Napoleon trying to decide on that 1812 campaign against Russia—from what he knew then, not what we know now?" *Verstehen* gives the reader a good feeling ("If I were Napoleon"), and it does genuinely help to explain those parts of history in which an elite command structure was in place and whoever stood at its peak exercised arbitrary personal power. That Napoleon had vast ambitions, that Stalin had a paranoiac fear of the Western powers, may well explain the march to Moscow and the treaty with Hitler. But the events with which demographers deal involve masses of people, and aggregating the *verstehen* of many individuals is not straightforward.

Surveys asking women their childbearing intentions have not produced good forecasts of the birth rate. It is as though Mrs. A, asked about her childbearing five years hence, reports to the survey enumerator what her friends and neighbors are doing now rather than what she will do later. Whatever social forces will later influence her are unknown at the time the enumerator calls.

Yet *verstehen* is by no means excluded from demography. Why did the French peasant have so *few* children? For the sake of security in his old age, knowing that the family farm was none too large, he wanted to pass it on to a child who could run it and maintain him when he was too old to work it himself. Why does the Javanese peasant have so *many* children? Because in a regime of largely wage labor, lacking property in land, the more children he has the greater will be his old-age security; each child will earn a pittance, but the sum of these will enable him to live in comfort. In both cases family discipline is assumed. We can easily put ourselves in the skins of such people, and these are perfectly proper explanations.

A more objective psychology refers behavior to hope of reward and fear of punishment, without anyone internalizing the behavior of another, except in the broad sense of accepting that people will seek things of value and avoid things that hurt. George C. Homans sets down some general propositions of behavior not easily challenged: "The more often a person's activity is rewarded, the more likely he is to perform that activity" (1967a: 33); or the principle of satiation: "The more often in the recent past a person has received a particular reward, the less valuable any further unit of that reward becomes to him'' (p. 37).

Application is straightforward in a nonhuman environment. A person will keep fishing in a certain spot if his previous attempts have been occasionally successful; since the value of the fish to him is decreasing, he will not continue fishing indefinitely. But when the person is acting vis-à-vis another person, and that other person is following similar laws, then complications arise, in the theory as in the real world. The interplay of simple theory builds up to the point where it can explain typically complex events of society and history.

Such explanations have been called ''reductionist,'' a term that has been used pejoratively. Durkheim tells us that the essence of the social phenomenon is lost in a psychological or biological explanation. But if a brain physiologist could explain thinking in terms of the chemistry and physics of neurons, he would consider that a complete solution.

A special hazard for the human sciences is the kind of circularity that hides itself in a purely verbal explanation. Great civilizations, wrote Arnold Toynbee, arise when the harshness of the (physical or social) environment is sufficient to challenge, but not so great as to overwhelm, the fledgling society. Apparently, Italy about 500 B.C. and England in Elizabethan times faced such challenges and became great. But for the explanation to be of any use we need an independent measure of the severity of a challenge, independent of whether the society became great or not later. This is not easily available, and without it ''challenge and response'' is a mere verbal expression masquerading as an explanation.

The Problem of Transfer

These considerations apply to the question of if, how, and when the demographic transition will take place in the circumstances of the Third World. If the circumstances, in particular the causes identified as operative, were the same in nineteenth-century Europe and in present-day Asia, we could confidently assert that the transition will occur in the same way and at the same speed. This is far from the case, and analysis of the differences is imposed on us.

Europe's initial density and its birth rate were much lower than Asia's, largely because of much higher ages at marriage, and as a result its dependency ratios were lower. Private property in land was more common in Europe. In these respects Asia is handicapped.

On the other side, Asia has a higher degree of literacy as well as far more institutions of advanced education; it has a large and effective industrial structure, capable of manufacturing automobiles, jet aircraft, and television sets. Asian governments are mostly aware of the need for population control and are actively encouraging it, while Europe's governments, in the shadow of mercantilism, at least until World War II, incited their citizens to have as many children as possible. Artifacts of family planning are being made widely available in Asia, while in Europe modern and convenient means of contraception did not exist, and those means that did exist were withheld from the public as far as governments could withhold them.

To judge the transferability of the phenomenon—drop in the birth rate—from nineteenth-century Europe and America to contemporary Asia, Africa, and Latin America, we have to ask questions on all four of the aspects that covering theory has brought forward.

Is the entity the same, as far as can be judged from birth and death declines to date? Is the context of today the same as that of nineteenth-century Europe? What about the antecedent elements? Are the laws we know that profess to show causal linkage equally valid in nineteenth-century Europe and twentieth-century Asia? The best analysts (Tilly, 1978a) are cautious in answering such questions.

Conclusion

What is to be learned by treating the models of demography as special cases of historical explanation? Incomplete as is the foregoing exposition, it suggests:

1. Definition of the entity to be explained is a problem in itself; all historical objects of interest are constructed—some would say artificially—and their boundaries and even their existence are subject to debate. The demographic transition is as real as the Renaissance or the rise of capitalism.

2. The imputation of cause requires a natural law or universal relation. If that relation is made explicit, it may be tested on material more extensive than the entity being explained.

3. The most successful explanation goes only so far; beyond it is another question; when this is answered there is a further question beyond it; and so on in an infinite regress. The conventional stopping point is at the border of one's discipline.

4. Even if the entity is defined in a way that is broadly acceptable, and some laws relating its parts to their antecedents are established, the question is open as to which of the variables associated with the entity in the course of historical happening is cause and which is effect. History is full of reciprocal action, so the usual recourse for discriminating—that the cause precedes the effect in time—is not clearly applicable. Functional analysis is a refuge in the frequent cases where causal explanation is impossible.

5. As among alternative explanations of a given phenomenon, there is a hierarchy of preferences that is partly conventional. If the crude birth rate

goes up, but not the standardized birth rate, we prefer to say that the cause is changed age distribution rather than people wanting more children.

6. All passive (i.e., nonexperimental) analysis of statistical observations is subject to the difficulties and dilemmas of historical explanation. Correlation, regression, path analysis, tests of significance, and block diagrams are indispensable aids, but they are not ways of circumventing the problem of explanation.

7. The procedures appropriate to demography and other historical study, known as covering theory, provide criteria that are suited to prediction and hence to policy analysis. Unfortunately, any causal system and explanation so extracted from the reality is partial. It disregards the branching chains of causes, the reciprocal influences, the circularities that exist in the real world. Simple causal chains extracted from the reality may provide convincing explanations, especially to a sympathetic audience, but because they are incomplete they fail dramatically in prediction. The strength of functional explanations is their lesser pretension to prediction and policy guidance.

The world and our minds are so made that explanation tends to drastic and inappropriate simplification. With Keynes (1936: 371), we must admire "the brave army of heretics who, following their intuitions, have preferred to see the truth obscurely and imperfectly rather than to maintain error, reached indeed with clearness and consistency and by easy logic, but on hypotheses inappropriate to the facts."

16

Where Do Babies Come From?

Norman B. Ryder

ALTHOUGH MY TITLE IS childlike, I hope it will become evident that the question is not childish. My concern is with research strategy. The stakes are high, whether viewed from the perspective of the social consequences of population growth, the magnitude of the intellectual challenge, or in more profane terms. It would be difficult to name another question in sociology to which an equivalent amount of research time and money has been committed.

When fertility began its systematic decline in the industrializing countries during the nineteenth century, two explanations were initially forthcoming. One was that the transformation of our way of life had weakened our generative faculties through some unspecified physiological nexus. The other was that we were exercising more stringent regulation of fertility. In brief, had the birth rate declined because people were *unable* to bear, or because they were *unwilling* to bear?

The debate was settled in due course: fertility decline was intentional. The next question remains open: Why did people's reproductive intentions change? Again, two levels of answer can be proposed. On the one hand, individuals provide intelligible accounts of their reproductive decisions in terms of their preferences and resources, within what is for them a prescribed normative context. Presuming the normative context to remain fixed, the explanation is forthcoming by microanalysis, based on questions addressed to individuals who may be presumed to have the answers at that level. On the other hand, the normative context may not remain fixed, in which case the

☐ This work is part of the National Fertility Study, 1975. The co-directors are Charles F. Westoff and the present author. The Study is being done under contract to the National Institute of Child Health and Human Development.

individual is an inappropriate source of information and research must proceed to the macro level. The issue is cross-cut by serious questions about the feasibility of successful research at the individual level of analysis.

American Fertility Surveys

Since the predominant research instrument in fertility inquiry is a cross-section of individuals sampled from a national population, a brief account of some of its history may be instructive. At the conclusion of the Indianapolis study, there was much discussion of the appropriate next steps in fertility research. Although that study well deserves its place as a landmark in social science, it was more a failure than a success. On the good side, some progress was made in establishing the links between overt reproductive behavior and the instrumental determinants—in brief, fecundability and fertility regulation. This essentially biometric accomplishment at least specifies more sharply the questions the social scientist must answer. On the bad side, almost nothing beyond the instrumental realm could be shown to be more than feebly linked to variations in reproductive behavior from individual to individual.

The Indianapolis study was designed to test hypotheses at the individual level. In quasi-experimental fashion, much of the variance in the population at large was controlled by focusing on educated WASPs in a midwestern city. On the basis of the outcome of that inquiry, two directions of endeavor were spawned. One, the Princeton Fertility Study, remained within the microanalytic tradition. It attempted to succeed where Indianapolis had failed by making a major investment in concept formation and measurement, and by employing a longitudinal design to come closer to the possibility of causal analysis. But the upshot was the same. Substantial progress was made at the biometric level, but the investigators came up nearly empty-handed in the task of explaining individual variations in reproductive behavior, other than in terms of black boxes like religion and education. No such ambitious attempt of this kind has been undertaken since.

The other direction of endeavor was the Growth of American Families Study, initiated in 1955 by P. K. Whelpton and Ronald Freedman. The design was cross-sectional and the style of analysis was macro and descriptive. Measures of individual performance were submerged in aggregate tabulations; hypotheses were not tested. In one sense, at the macro level, the effort was longitudinal: the venture led to the repeated interviewing of representatives of a succession of birth cohorts. The study was replicated in 1960, 1965, and 1970 by private investigators, and in 1973 and 1976 by the National Center for Health Statistics. The continued commitment of substantial funds and the eventual institutionalization of the enterprise by the federal government attest to the success of these efforts. Beyond our borders, this decade has seen the unparalleled efforts of the World Fertility Survey to conduct studies patterned explicitly on the National Fertility Study in the United States, in dozens of developing and developed countries.

One issue addressed in this chapter is the optimal exploitation of the extraordinary wealth of data being produced by these surveys. One strategy with strong support, judged from the character of pedagogical materials being produced for the guidance of those planning to work on World Fertility Survey data, is to advance beyond macro tabulations and engage in extensive microanalysis of the output. I would argue against this on substantive grounds because success at this level would leave unanswered the central questions of why fertility differs from one country to another, and why it changes over time. That aside, I would argue against the strategy on methodological grounds as well, because the probability of success at this level is very low.

Unreliability of Measurement
of Reproductive Behavior

While investigators in other areas of sociology are not blind to the existence of measurement error, they are continually tempted to assume it is tolerably small because they have no evidence to the contrary. In fertility inquiries, we have frequently asked the same respondent the same question twice; we cannot evade the fact that individual consistency of response is low. Some of this is random, and therefore manageable with an increase of sample size. Some of it is nonrandom, but attributable to defects in our measuring instruments; that can be remedied by more diligent efforts on our part. Of much more concern are two other sources of unreliability, intrinsic to the process of obtaining some kinds of information from individuals. Although the referent here is the *explanandum* of a fertility inquiry, the issues are generic.

The first problem may be called "normative unreliability." Nonrandom error may be expected whenever one seeks information with a high normative overlay. Such questions tend to elicit individual responses which are a compromise between the actual and the respectable, provided the response is plausible and therefore not subject to obvious challenge. The more important a piece of information for the individual and for the society, the more likely it is that particular responses will be approved or disapproved. Not only is the area of sexual and procreative behavior defined as private and intimate, but particular actions are defined as immoral if not illegal, so that a question is tantamount to asking for a confession. Our information about copulation is quite untrustworthy, the reasons reported to us for sterilization are biased, we are almost totally unsuccessful in obtaining believable reports of abortion. In short, the information necessary to appraise the extent to which fertility regulation is practiced, and the efficacy with which it is practiced, is effectively blocked from clear view by a normative shield.

The second problem may be called "stochastic unreliability." "In most topics of demographic study, chance variations are of little importance because the significant measures are for aggregates, sufficiently large for the systematic effects to be overwhelmingly dominant. This is not the case, however, for the aspects of fertility research in which the childbearing performance of the individual couples is relevant." (Barrett and Brass, 1974: 473). If one's dependent variable is defined as the eventual parity achieved by a woman, there is sufficient experience averaged over the individual lifetime, as well as feedback in the form of appropriate response to contingent outcomes, that stochastic variation is reduced to a low, but not insignificant, level. But three aspects of sophisticated inquiry make this scant consolation. (1) There is almost as much interest in the time pattern of childbearing as in its eventual level, and the noise is much louder for the former than for the latter. (2) A cross-sectional survey censors each respondent's history at time of interview, forcing one to be concerned with the relationship between parity attained by a younger and parity attained by an older age. Under plausible assumptions about physiological parameters, it has been shown by simulation that those correlations are low (Barrett and Brass, 1974). (3) Analysts have long since abandoned the superficial level of investigation typified by the birth record for identification of the instrumental variables responsible for that record. This brings stochastic variation dramatically into the forefront.

The question why a birth does or does not occur to a particular woman at a particular stage in her life cycle is answered by the following procedure: (1) total time is classified into segments of copulation and noncopulation; (2) copulation time is divided into segments of regulation and nonregulation; (3) length of segment and type of outcome (conception or otherwise) are used to make inferences about efficacy (from regulation segments) and about fecundability (from nonregulation segments); (4) conceptions are classified by whether or not they end in birth, intentionally or unintentionally.

This procedure establishes the appropriate division of labor among research activities. The biological assignment is to determine the relationship between behavior (copulation and regulation) and the reproductive outcome. The nonbiological assignment is to explain the behavior. More to the point, there is identification of intentional behavior, defined as that behavior for which the individual can be held responsible for an explanation.

The birth record becomes transformed into a set of lengths of segments, regulated or unregulated, closed or open, for each respondent. The variables for which we may have ideas about correlates are not these lengths at all, but rather the fecundability and efficacy which determine the monthly probability of conception. The relationship between the probability of conception and the length of an interval is extremely complex. It may be shown that the correlation between two interval lengths, for a woman with identical conception probability in both segments, is necessarily less than 0.5 and typically much less (Sheps and Menken, 1973). That result is interpretable as a perfect analogy to a correlation coefficient used to measure consistency of response to the same question by the same individuals. The information which is available as evidence for the phenomenon for which we hypothesize correlates consists of a small systematic element and a large random element. Even a potent relationship at the latent level is going to be substantially attenuated at the manifest level by the random element.

This is the essential explanation for the inability of the Princeton Fertility Study to detect any more than trivial relationships between reproductive observations and a host of plausible explanatory variables. It is a sufficient argument for abstaining from proliferating such failures by conducting microanalyses with bodies of data like those provided by the World Fertility Survey.

The Regression Equation

The foregoing account has focused on problems of measurement of the so-called dependent variable in the microanalysis of fertility. The dependent variable designation is derivative from a mode of data reduction epitomized by the regression equation; its counterpart is a list of "independent" variables strung out on the right-hand side of that equation. There are manifold inadequacies in this approach to understanding when the *explanandum* is a behavior pattern like parenthood.

In conceptualizing the research task, it would be most convenient to consider that what is to be explained is an event, which occurs within a particular temporal climate and has antecedents which can be detected in the past. Such a consideration is clearly not the case with the event of maternity, because it casts such a long shadow before it. The parenthood decision is made in the clear understanding that the implications extend over a long stretch, if not all, of future life, and pervade all other areas of life. The same is of course true for such decisions as education, occupation, and residence. Statistically speaking, one anticipates substantial correlation among indices of diverse activities about which information would be collected in a comprehensive study of individual reproductive behavior.

The regression equation is intended as a mode of data reduction in a nonexperimental situation which may set the stage for cause-and-effect considerations. Although it may prove to be a fruitful approach if one wants to evaluate the immediate consequences of a momentary modification of some elements in a system of variables, most of which can safely be presumed to be essentially constant in the relevant interval—and this would help to account for its appeal to such as microeconomists and psychologists—the regression equation has important limitations in the appraisal of the interdependent aspects of a life history.

The problems begin with the requirement that one variable be specified as dependent on the rest. This requirement is ordinarily fulfilled not so much in terms of any direction of causality the investigator is prepared to hypothesize as in terms of the phenomenon in which lies the primary interest. Couples engaging in decisions about parenthood are also involved in other activities. Decisions made concerning the allocation of time and other scarce resources among these activities are made jointly rather than separately. Nor can any one activity be considered as a kind of ultimate goal to which the others are directed. Indeed, it would seem unsatisfactory to posit the activities as goals at all; they are rather alternative ways of achieving some basic kinds of net satisfaction. Now it is trivially true that a larger expenditure in one direction implies a smaller expenditure in another, but it is a mere verbal trick to move from that insight to the assertion that the reason for more of one is that there is less of another.

The interpenetration of variables extends into the set assembled on the right-hand side as so-called independent variables. Although the phenomenon of multicollinearity is well recognized, it seems generally to be regarded as the consequence of failure to measure properly. It seems to me that the information descriptive of the life course is intrinsically multicollinear: an individual life has coherence to it because the actor weaves together the strands of different experiences as time passes. Again, from a statistical standpoint, the existence of multicollinearity robs the regression equation of the capability of identifying some variables as more important than others. Moreover, excluded as well as included variables share this property; they are in the equation implicitly, if they are not there explicitly. This means that whatever description is achieved by one particular regression equation is conditional on the set of variables available for inclusion. If one views the aim of data reduction as the achievement of a parsimonious statement of the relationships among a limited set of variables, it would seem clear that the multifaceted complexity of the individual life course stands squarely in the way of that ambition.

Longitudinal Analysis

If one has a cross-sectional study in the literal sense of the word, providing measurements of various properties at one time for individuals at varying stages of their life course, then the regression equation is the basis for statements of the difference between one variable, measured across individuals, that is associated with a unit difference in another variable, likewise measured across individuals. That may be a useful description of a static pattern but it is unresponsive to the causal question of the relationship between a change in one variable, for an individual, and a subsequent change in another variable, for the same individual. Such answers require longitudinal data.

When the National Center for Health Statistics, early in this decade, assumed responsibility for periodic cross-sectional surveys, Charles Westoff and I took the opportunity to redesign the 1975 National Fertility Study as a cross-section constituted in large part of reinterviews with respondents from our 1970 study. The prose which accompanied our proposal paid the customary homage to the virtues of longitudinal over cross-sectional procedures; the words have a magic to them quite independent of the cogency of the claims.

Now the conventional cross-sectional survey is not confined to measurements as of the moment of interview; it ordinarily contains many questions with a historical referent, that is, datable events in the respondent's past. To that extent it is suitable for longitudinal analysis. One should not confuse observations about the same unit as of two times with observations at two times concerning the same unit. Either are suitable for longitudinal analysis.

Three kinds of information may be distinguished in a cross-sectional survey: (1) measurements, specific to time of interview, and liable to momentary modification in either direction; (2) ascribed statuses, characteristics fixed at birth or at least prior to the relevant range of observations; (3) achieved statuses, intermediate between the first two, in the sense that they constitute temporary residences for the individual. An achieved status can be recognized by the event of change of state, frequently cumulative or irreversible.

If one means by cause and effect a change in one variable that increases the probability of a change in another variable, it is clear that ascribed statuses qualify as neither causes nor effects, since they cannot change. They are the conditions of an individual's life, on which other relationships may depend. Measurements, specific to time of observation, qualify, with respect to the data at hand, solely as possible effects, but not as causes, since there is no observation to which they can be prior. The analysis of cause and effect, in the sense used here, is especially appropriate to the achieved statuses. Since they can be dated by the change of state that produced their value at interview, they may be ordered in time. The causal ordering posited in path analysis, using the output of a single cross-sectional survey, typically relies heavily on just such an explicit or implicit temporal ordering.

By the nature of a cross-sectional survey, individuals are arrayed across the different stages of the life cycle. Since measurements are specific to time of observation, there is no way, within the confines of a single survey, to distinguish variations in measurements attributable to life cycle stage, and those stemming from other sources. Ascribed statuses, at the other pole, are completely independent of time of observation. With respect to the foci of cause-and-effect analysis, the achieved statuses, one has dated events. The process of achievement is censored by interview time. Such variables are prone to stochastic unreliability of the same kind as described above. It follows that the ability to measure a relationship between two variables, each of which is manifested in the outcome of a stochastic process, is hampered by a compound of the problems of unreliability of each. If, as is not uncommon, the achieved status is unaccompanied by a date of achievement, part of the problem is concealed from view, but it remains implicitly active.

Longitudinal analysis is ordinarily considered to be restricted to observations made on the same unit at more than one time. The superiority of this form to the historical records which can be derived from a single cross-sectional survey hinges on the difference between responses at $t2$ to questions about the history prior to $t1$, and responses at $t1$ to the same questions. Inconsistency of response may be random or nonrandom. Random inconsistency probably increases with the lapse of time since the event or condition about which the question is asked. The location of the decay curve depends on the referent of the question, which may be any time between birth and interview, and on the life-cycle stage of the individual at interview. In principle, however, the problem of random inconsistency is controllable by an increase in sample size.

Nonrandom inconsistency arises as a consequence of systematic misreporting at $t1$ or at $t2$ or both. The information obtained is a function of the question asked, and of the characteristics of the respondent at the time the question is asked. The important point is that, in contrast to the case of random error, one cannot infer that a report made at a time closer to the event or situation concerned is less likely to be biased than one made at a more distant time.

The one exception to this general caveat is a measurement, which is specific to the time of interview. In that case, although one cannot assume that the report is free of bias at time of observation, it is at least devoid of modification as a consequence of the passage of time. Moreover, measurements with respect to times prior to interview may not be feasible, if only because of the difficulty of identifying the time for which the measurement is requested. It is likely that the common association of longitudinal analysis with repeated interviewing (rather than exploitation of dated information from a cross-section) derives at least in part from the idea that the interview would consist predominantly of measurements. Yet if the advantage of a second interview is perceived as the capacity to make measurements at more than one time, that gain must be discounted by the consideration that experience with such measurements shows they are highly prone to response inconsistency.

The conclusion of this account is that the marginal advantage of longitudinal analysis requiring two or more interviews with the same person, over longitudinal analysis based on the historical record collected at one interview, is restricted to the reduction of that random error associated with problems of recall, and the capacity to make time-specific measurements of items which typically have low reliability. This must be balanced against not only the marginal cost of a second round of interviews, and the expense of maintaining an interim address file, but also against the inevitable biases associated with attrition of the sample, and a change in one or another aspect of the research apparatus. But, above and beyond this, and in my judgment a sufficient argument against reinterview, is the implicit commitment of the enterprise to analysis at the individual level. On the basis of our experience with the 1975 study, Westoff and I have gone through a process of "agonizing reappraisal," and came to the conclusion that a further round in 1980, long planned, was not worth the expenditure of our time and the taxpayer's money.

Relationships between Micro and Macro Analysis

I have argued that there are severe methodological problems impeding the search for correlates of individual reproductive behavior, problems which shroud real relationships in a dense fog of unreliability, primarily although not exclusively stochastic in origin. The literature abounds in examples of frustration at the disjuncture between plausible hypotheses and statistically puny outcomes. Our will to answer a particular question, at a particular analytic level, is no guarantee of our ability to answer the question, given the state of the art and a no more than reasonable commitment of research resources.

If we persist in the premise that our prime scientific task is the explanation of variance in behavior at the individual level, then we may adopt the position, in light of this account, that the task is bound to be complex, and that we should press on notwithstanding, trying to devise better hypotheses, as well as better measures with which to test them. From this perspective, our customary procedure in the National Fertility Study of presenting averages in cross-tabulations is a simple-minded way of reducing stochastic noise by grouping, but fundamentally unrespectable from a statistical standpoint, since all we can see are the marginals of the underlying individual-specific data, and we are forever on the verge of perpetrating one or another ecological fallacy.

But there is another view. Fertility is a collective property of a system, to be explained in relation to other collective properties of the same system. Far from being an expedient in lieu of individual-level analysis, a macro orientation is theoretically appropriate.

To provide some substance to this position, consider the following characterization of the reproductive process. The dominant model of reproductive behavior at the individual level follows a quasi-economic framework of decision making with respect to the allocation of scarce resources among alternative ends, with the economizing notion extended well beyond objects of the marketplace to encompass time, energy, emotional commitment, and the like. Implicit in the model are conditions, influential variables over which the couple has little or no control, and which are taken as constants in the calculus of decision.

One can explain intentional behavior in terms of a catalogue of ends, means, and conditions, using as an operational definition of intentional behavior those actions for which one can hope to elicit explanations from the individual, in the form of reasons for choice among alternatives. A comprehensive statement might display alternative reproductive possibilities in terms of their implications for quantum and tempo, and the costs and benefits associated with each, extending the concept of cost to embrace foregone alternatives in the form of other activities, and the benefits associated with them. At root, the system is tautological: what one does is what in some sense one prefers to do.

Several categories of conditions underlie this assessment. There are biological conditions. One can manipulate the variables in this probabilistic system to some extent, but the laws of biology cannot be broken. There are also macroeconomic conditions. Although the individual's command over resources depends in part on choices which he or she can make, it depends mainly on characteristics of the local, national, and world economy which must be accepted as givens at the individual level. Beyond these constraints lies the sociocultural context. Each reproductive act may be thought of as an implicit contract. In making a decision to have a baby, the costs and benefits perceived depend on the terms of that contract, because it spells out the rights and responsibilities of parents vis-à-vis children, of the male vis-à-vis the female, and of family vis-à-vis nonfamily members. The contract exists because the occurrence of a child is consequential to others beyond the immediate decision makers, and those others are prepared to administer rewards and punishments to insure that the individual decision corresponds with the collective will. Human society regulates the behavior of members, through norms, in such ways that they perform activities fulfilling societal needs. The individual acquires norms through a process of indoctrination. The norms are not necessarily external rules; they are frequently internalized as part of the personality, automatically expressed in behavior and not regarded objectively at all (Davis, 1949).

The terms of the reproductive contract are conditions in the sense that they cannot be formulated ad hoc by the couple immediately concerned. It is implicitly accepted by them or imposed on them. The contract is clearly a property of the collectivity, explainable only in terms of other properties of the same collectivity. Members of any social group are programmed by the processes of socialization and social control, the intent of the program being to yield a collective outcome satisfactory to the group, by circumscribing the degrees of individual freedom. The evidence for the existence of such conditions is readily detectable in interviews. A couple will choose one mode of fertility regulation over another because it would be wrong to do the other, although they are unable to explain why it would be wrong. A couple will explain their choice of a particular number of children in terms of what is expected of them as parents, but they cannot explain why those are the rights and responsibilities of parenthood. One cannot calculate costs and benefits without knowledge of the nature of the reproductive contract.

The record of fertility surveys is not completely without success in detecting correlates of individual variability. Ascribed characteristics are almost uniformly important. Prominent examples would include, beyond the identification of the population itself, religion, race, ethnic group, farm background, and, during a period of social change, the birth cohort. These characteristics are fixed in value over the relevant lifetime of the individual. In a regression equation they play the role of conditions rather than variables. The strength of these conditions in explaining variance in fertility lies in the circumstance that they identify membership in groups with distinctive systems of socialization and social control. Only superficially can such pieces of information be assigned unequivocally to the individual level of analysis. More appropriate would be the position that the respondent is an agent in the process of inquiry, contributing a description of her reproductive behavior to the construction of a macro distribution, and signifying in response to questions about ascribed status the groups to which she belongs, and thus the aggregates for which it is appropriate to construct such distributions.

As a demographer, my research object is by definition aggregate in character. A population is defined as an aggregate with a property possessed by no individual member. It is a denumerable set of individual elements, each of which must die, whereas the population has the capacity for persistence beyond the lifetime of any constituent, by virtue of its fertility, the creation of new members to compensate for the loss of old members. The basic element of a population is the birth cohort, the set of new members created at any one time. Demographic change, as distinct from changes in the characteristics of individuals throughout their personal life courses, is measured by and produced by differences in the life histories of successive cohorts, viewed in the aggregate.

Given that characteristics of individuals affect their behavior, it follows that the distribution of individuals by any such characteristic, within a cohort, has influence on the performance of the cohort aggregate. The initial distribution of cohort members with respect to any characteristic is created in the period-specific context of time of birth. That initial distribution is the property not of any individual element, but of the cohort to which the individual belongs.

Subsequently, the distribution changes through time, and in two distinct ways. (1) It changes as a consequence of the movement of cohort members from one to another status within the distribution. Two qualifications are important. First, the interest is in net rather than gross movement. Second, the net mobility of individuals within a cohort is itself dependent on other properties of the cohort as an aggregate. (2) The initial distribution is subject to change through time because of selective mortality, itself generally associated with particular statuses within the distribution.

Thus, there are two broad divisions of demographic change: the selective processes of birth and survival, which determine an initial distribution and modify it through time by selective survival; and the processes of net mobility of individuals within the cohort. Both are conceptually autonomous of individual change. The questions which are justification for the magnitude of support for fertility inquiry are in my opinion demographic questions. Why is fertility higher in one population than in another? Why does fertility decline more in one population than in another? One may charge that these questions have not been answered by research at the micro level. Success at the individual level of analysis, typified by a comprehensive and impeccable regression equation, is inherently limited in its scope. There is no explanation for the mean value of each of the independent variables that do the job at the individual level. There is no explanation of the distribution of the population with respect to those independent variables. In particular, there is no basis whatsoever for the study of temporal variations in these aggregate properties.

If one begins with a macro question—why does one population have higher fertility than another, or why does a population have lower fertility than it once did—it seems obvious that one must look for a macro answer. The populations clearly differ or change in some respect, and our task is to determine the relevant respects. With this perspective, it is an interesting puzzle why the answer should be sought at the micro level.

One possible explanation is the stance of the statistician, with substantive specialization not otherwise specified. By definition, the statistician comes to the task without preconceptions, using a common-sense orientation and a disposition to let the facts speak for themselves. Since the facts are responses to questions posed to individuals, and since the sociocultural reality is invisible, it is not surprising that the individual actor would occupy center stage in the analytic design.

Another explanation would be associated with the psychologist or microeconomist. Recognizing that the macroanalytic questions are of interest to others, they are unfortunately unresponsive to technical apparatus with which these specialists are familiar. Accordingly, the investigators exploit the data sets to answer their own kind of question. They can do successful regression analyses at the individual level, by holding other things constant. What they hold constant turns out to be the characteristics of the culture, and changes in them over time. The baby goes out with the bathwater.

Scarcely distinguishable from these are the sociologists who are at root reductionist in persuasion. Possessed of the ineluctable truth that no explanation at the sociocultural level can be complete without a demonstration of an explicit instrumentality at the individual level, and suspicious that properties of the collectivity are myths invented by Durkheimians, and ideologically offensive as a threat to the concept of free will, they proceed directly to the finest level of detail attainable, unaware or uncaring that they will drown in the morass.

But perhaps the simple answer is that the empiricist is embarrassed by the obligation to theorize. The person who evades that responsibility is continually exposed to the risk of allowing the form in which data are created to dictate the concepts to be employed in their appraisal. As an example from a different context, we were limited, in the long stretch of time before we began to collect reproductive information by survey, to the data produced by official registration systems in a year-by-year format. Our response was to develop a complete array of period indices of reproduction, not because that was what we needed but because the data came that way. Only after a long and painful experience could we bring ourselves to restructure those data in cohort form and finally see what it was we needed to explain. In the present situation, I maintain that we tend to look at the results of cross-sectional surveys from the perspective of the individual, again because the data come that way.

In conclusion, I have argued that microanalyses of fertility have been unsuccessful in the past, not because they have been imperfectly executed, but because of formidable obstacles in the way of their success. Principal among these is the predominance of chance over systematic components in reproductive behavior, and in the variables used to characterize those sectors of life which are interdependent with reproductive behavior. I have argued that the regression equation, used to epitomize sophisticated inquiry in the microanalytical mode, is an unsuitable model when the scope of the inquiry encompasses a lifetime of experience. I have further argued that the collection of longitudinal data by reinterview has insufficient advantages over the histories available in cross-sectional inquiries to justify its cost, and quite apart from that, commits one to an inherently flawed microlevel of explanation. Moreover, even if the problems associated with stochastic unreliability and strategies of data reduction could somehow be overcome, success at the micro level would provide no answer to the questions which in fact justify the extraordinary investment in cross-sectional fertility surveys.

The fundamental point is that fertility is a collective property and therefore calls for explanation at the macroanalytic level in terms of other properties of the collectivity. To this end, fertility surveys are necessary but necessarily insufficient. They provide the raw materials for appropriate measurement of the reproductive pattern as an aggregate phenomenon, but they are largely uninformative on the determinants of that pattern because those determinants are institutionalized and therefore inaccessible to the individual respondent. The task of explaining why fertility is higher in one population than in another, and why fertility has declined more in one population than in another, requires sociological analysis at the system level. That assignment is difficult indeed, but at least it is not inherently impossible. If we can overcome our obsession with the explanation of individual deviations, and confront the macroanalytic challenge, some day we may find out where babies come from.

17

Theory and Research in Urban Ecology: Persistent Problems and Current Progress

W. Parker Frisbie

THE QUESTION OF whether there are gaps between urban ecological theory and research conducted on the basis of that theory is scarcely debatable. Of course such gaps exist, as they do in all disciplines. The issue here will be to identify specific instances where the theoretical promise of urban ecology seems notably unfulfilled or where the inconsistencies are great between conceptualization and empirical test. In making this assessment, it seems eminently reasonable to employ as a standard the universe of inquiry delineated by urban ecologists themselves. Ecology offers what is perhaps the most comprehensive macro-level theory of urbanization available. This does not mean that the theory is complete or that it has begun to effect closure, or that it is free of serious ambiguities. It does mean that what urban ecology is, or claims as its essential conceptual problem, offers a sufficiently rigorous criterion for judgment. It also means that little time will be spent relating and responding to criticisms of ecological study for not being something else.

In some respects, urban ecology has come to be almost synonymous with human ecology. One widely cited definition suggests that human ecology is "the study of the form and development of the human community" (Hawley, 1950: 68; 1968: 329). Although "community" is defined generically as a "territorially localized system of relationships among functionally differentiated parts" (Hawley, 1968: 329), the urban community has, from ecology's inception, been the primary locus of attention (Frisbie, 1979). If, as has recently been argued, "(t)he central problem of contemporary ecological inquiry is understanding how a population organizes itself in adapting to a constantly changing environment'' (Berry and Kasarda, 1977: 12), then it is clear that the "community is a generalized form" of collective adjustment based on a division of labor or functional specialization (Hawley, 1971: 11). Phrased slightly differently, "Cities represent an organizational response on the part of a population to the problems of adaptation to a social, economic, and physical environment" (Smith and Weller, 1977: 89).[1]

GENERAL SOURCES OF THE THEORY/RESEARCH GAP IN URBAN ECOLOGY

As portrayed by Hawley (1948: 155), "The special task of the human ecologist" is the "analysis, description, and explanation of community structure," a structure that must be studied in terms of both its static and dynamic aspects (Hawley, 1944). Unfortunately, urban ecologists have paid more heed to Hawley's admonition to describe than they have to his concomitant emphasis on explanation, and have given considerably more attention to statics than to dynamics.

I believe that the gaps which exist between theory and research in urban ecology derive from failings in at least three areas. The fact that one or all of the three might be common to other disciplines does not diminish their applicability in the present case. First, while notable progress has been made in describing and cataloguing structural aspects of urban communities, we have, as just noted, too often been satisfied with description alone and too little interested in explanation. Second, the almost omnipresent use of the variable of city size in ecological research has not given rise to an ability to specify and conceptualize the causal operators linking size to other aspects of urban structure. Finally, we have been content (usually) with essentially static tests of dynamic theory. Each of these issues will be considered in sequence, first in general terms, and then in terms of specific examples.

Description and Explanation

Criticisms labeling ecological studies of urban phenomena as "merely" or "overly" descriptive are certainly nothing new. Much of the early work of ecologists consisted of community studies that "provided detailed descriptions of . . . physical features (and) social, economic, and demographic characteristics" or mapping of certain "social phenomena such as crime rates or mental disorders" (Berry and Kasarda, 1977: 6). As Hawley has pointed

[1] Or as Lampard (1965: 521) states, "Urbanization itself may be regarded as the organizational component of a population's achieved capacity for adaptation. It is a way of ordering a population to attain a certain level of subsistence and security in a given environment."

out, studies of this sort "permitted human ecology to be construed as merely the description of distributions of social phenomena" (1944: 402). The idea of natural areas, for example, or more elaborate models of the form and growth of cities, such as Burgess' Concentric Zone hypothesis, were premised on significant theoretical insights concerning the expansion of ecological units, structural hierarchies, and competition for space as related to land use and value, but, unfortunately, they gave rise to research that was primarily descriptive in nature.

Similarly, Social Area Analysis was based on a rather dynamic conceptualization of growing functional differentiation and organizational complexity (Shevky and Bell, 1955), yet typically eventuated in static descriptions of spatial patterns according to economic, family, and racial/ethnic status. Factorial ecology differs from Social Area Analysis, not only in terms of the sophistication of the methods employed, but also by leaving open the question of the number and nature of the dimensions that best describe urban structure. Moreover, factor analyses of data from cities around the world have contributed a needed comparative perspective to our knowledge of urban morphology. Although not inherently so, most work in factorial ecology has been heavily inductive (Schwirian, 1974: 8–12), and a substantial fraction of this research could, with fairness, be termed atheoretical. There are, as always, notable exceptions (Abu-Lughod, 1969; Hunter, 1971; Berry, 1972); nevertheless, the overall contribution has clearly been more descriptive than explanatory.

AN ILLUSTRATION: FUNCTIONAL SPECIALIZATION

Let us turn from this highly generalized critique of the tendency toward overly descriptive research to a specific illustration taken from mainstream urban ecology. At least from the time of Hawley's classic formulation stating that "the community (from an) ecological standpoint (is) an adaptive mechanism in which all of the parts have or tend to have functional relationships to one another" (1948: 155; see also Hawley, 1944, 1950), few if any ideas have enjoyed greater centrality or generated more interest than the concept of *functional specialization*. In the most fundamental sense, the organization of specialized function, by means of which urban populations extract sustenance from the environment, lies at the heart of how populations survive, for it is through the performance of sustenance producing activities that basic survival needs are met. Hence, numerous studies have been concerned with identifying specialities as a basis for categorization of functional types (see Kass, 1973, for a concise review of the literature).

Other scholars have been more interested in the conclusion that "*inequality is an inevitable accompaniment of functional differentiation*" (Hawley, 1950: 221, emphasis added). Inequality arises out of the fact that certain functions are more "strategically placed" than others in terms of spatial location and in the division of labor and out of the need for greater centralization of control in an increasingly complex system (Hawley, 1950: 221; see also Lincoln, 1979: 917). In other words, functional differentiation has both a horizontal dimension along which cities vary according to types or modes of specialization and a vertical dimension along which cities vary as to position (or degree of dominance) in a metropolitan hierarchy (Wanner, 1977: 535).[2]

Actually, of course, inherent in the recognition of the first two dimensions of functional specialization is the existence of a third. Specifically, functional differentiation implies interdependence.[3] Because

> specialization in an activity by a particular population aggregate is indicative of interdependence with others, the patterning of functional specialization may be used to examine the pattern of interdependence which exists among the various components of an urban system (Weller, 1967: 736).

Identifying a city's modes of specialization and place in the metropolitan hierarchy should be a necessary and useful beginning in the analysis of systems of cities. But empirical investigations of urban systems cannot be said to approach realization of their full theoretical potential unless and until they move well beyond basically static, largely descriptive studies of ecological structure. Among other things, I think this would entail: (1) analysis of the degree of functional interdependence that exists, that is, the study of the volume or intensity of interaction and exchange among cities in a system; and (2) the use of functional variation of cities to account for variation in other ecologically relevant phenomena.[4]

Despite its obvious importance for urban ecological research, the analytical complexity of the concept of functional differentiation remains

[2] It has been noted that "function and location seem like two sides of a coin" (Duncan et al., 1960: 23), which is one way of expressing the close relationship between organization and environment. The spatial location side appears to have been dealt with in a more or less adequate fashion. The familiar notions of break-in-bulk, central place, and industrial location decisions (see Smith and Weller, 1977, for a useful summary) have over the years provided explanations of city location and should require no elaboration here.

[3] Other scholars have identified yet other dimensions of functional differentiation. Stern and Galle (1978), e.g., make reference to the "locus of control," i.e., to the question of whether production is locally or nationally controlled. While this distinction results in a useful interface of conventional urban ecology with community studies, the issue of absentee ownership is not actually a component of functional specialization per se. Another dimension mentioned by Stern and Galle, "General function," is operationalized by recourse to indicators of output in manufacturing and wholesaling variables, which have more commonly been viewed as measures of the vertical or hierarchical dimension (Wanner, 1977).

[4] One may also profitably carry out comparative analyses of the degree of the division of labor *within* cities. In this case, one might also focus on three dimensions (Gibbs and Poston, 1975): (1) *structural differentiation*—the number of functional categories; (2) *distributional differentiation*—the uniformity of distribution across the categories; and (3) again, *functional interdependence*—this time *within* any given city. At present, our interest is in analyses of relationships between or among cities. But in the case of both intracity and intercity division of labor, it is in the area of functional interdependence that the gap between theory and research seems the greatest.

largely unexplored for several reasons.[5] First, most early functional classification schemes, while not unreasonable, were characterized by a fairly high degree of arbitrariness. For example, Harris (1943) selected threshold values which identified as specialized in manufacturing those cities with at least 60 percent of their labor force in manufacturing industry, but selected substantially lower cut-points for identifying cities specializing in wholesaling and retailing (Smith, 1965: 541–42). Later research, although more systematic, remained heavily subjective. Nelson defined as specialized in a given industry any city that was at least one standard deviation above the mean for that industrial category—but there is nothing inherent in the properties of the normal curve that would necessarily suggest that one standard deviation implies specialization. Second, as Kass has pointed out, most "systems for the functional classification of communities use a single function approach" (1977: 221). Such one-specialty typologies have often failed to distinguish clearly among the full range of cities in a system (Berry, 1972: 47). Further, single-function models do not result in mutually exclusive categories thereby precluding comparisons between groups (Kass, 1973, 1977).

A third reason for the gap between theoretical potential and empirical result is that urban classification schemes have, until very recently, been "cast as discrete taxonomies, usually with an unmanageable number of separate city types" (Wanner, 1977: 519). For all these reasons, ecological research on functional specialization of cities has remained heavily oriented toward description and explanatory gains have been limited. As Wanner (1977: 519) puts it:

> The enormous investment in time and effort committed to these functional classification schemes has seldom furthered our understanding of urban structure and process, since few have been utilized to explain or predict other facets of urban social organization.

This comment echoes the earlier criticism by Hadden and Borgatta that "little is gained . . . if a city is identified (as having a given functional speciality) unless this information allows us to predict something else about that city" (1965: 17), as well as that by Duncan et al., who concluded that often little is done with functional typologies after they have been constructed (1960: 3; see also Kass, 1973).

CURRENT PROGRESS

Although these criticisms are well taken, and the theory/research gap which they imply must be acknowledged, the picture is not nearly so dismal as it might appear. An encouragingly large number of urban ecologists usually

---

[5] The author is indebted to Lisa J. Neidert, whose ideas and critical comments acted as direct stimulants for the views expressed in this and the following paragraph.

building on the classic work of Duncan and his associates, have begun to address the problems enumerated above. Research by Kass (1973, 1977) employing location quotients in a "cluster analysis" has produced a classification built on the entire distribution of functions (instead of on single specialities) which results in a categorization of mutually exclusive groups. Relying on Q-factoring of location quotients, Wanner (1977) has developed a continuous variable approach to the measurement of functional dimensions and thereby succeeded in verifying the suggestion by Duncan et al. (1960) that metropolitan specialization varies vertically along a financial–commercial hierarchy and horizontally along a manufacturing–services dimension.

Even more encouraging is the progress made in the utilization of functional specialization as explanation of other urban phenomena. A few early analyses demonstrated that communities in different functional categories evidenced dissimilar socioeconomic characteristics (Duncan and Reiss, 1956). Variation in key function performed has been shown to be associated with variation in the degree of division of labor (Kass, 1977) and in the spatial location of social classes (Schnore and Winsborough, 1972; Kass, 1977). More recently, Stern and Galle (1978) found several dimensions of functional specialization to be moderately effective predictors of the frequency, breadth, and duration of urban industrial conflict (strikes). Thus, even though, by and large, functional typologies have served mainly descriptive purposes, notable instances of the use of the concept as explanation may be cited.

SUMMARY

Since its inception, perhaps the most persistent criticism of ecology has been that it has been inclined toward atheoretical, heavily decriptive research. While this evaluation can probably not be sustained as a sweeping, general indictment, it does appear valid in the case of studies of urban functional specialization. Urban ecologists themselves have time and again bemoaned the lack of analytical payoff from the construction of functional typologies. However, recent research has begun to bridge this particular gap by building on the work of Duncan and his co-authors to develop multiple-specialization models based on continuous measurement, thereby considerably enhancing the explanatory potential of the concept.

The Ecological View of Size

We have just considered a situation in which research in urban ecology has failed to keep pace with theoretical development. Let us now examine the converse, that is, a situation where theory does not seem to have provided an adequate foundation for interpretation of empirical results.

From an ecological point of view, population size has, in general, been regarded as a limiting, rather than a causal, factor. Based on Durkheimian precedent, sheer numbers (or an increase in them) are not seen as "causing" anything. Advancing division of labor, for instance, does not emanate from an increment in numbers, but from an increase in "moral" or "dynamic" density, that is, from an increase in the volume and intensity of interaction among people facilitated by advances in transportation and communications technology. More to the specific point of this discussion is Hawley's comment on the social significance of size of urban centers:

> Virtually every functional characteristic varies systematically with the number of people residing in urban centers. This variation does not imply that size of population is a cause of the properties associated with it. Rather, size is a necessary condition; it is a factor in the absence of which certain things cannot occur. (1971: 135–36)[6]

RESEARCH OPTIONS WHEN SIZE IS VIEWED IN NONCAUSAL TERMS

For a moment, let us consider both the general implications and certain specific results of adherence to the conventional perception of city size as non-causal. One option that has sometimes been exercised is simply to ignore size altogether. However, most scholars have found this an unacceptable alternative, given the often substantial correlations of size with other variables crucial to an understanding of urban form and structure.

A second, more logical alternative, assuming that the number of persons in a city is highly interrelated with other salient variables, but is itself "uninteresting," is the use of size as a surrogate. Berry and Kasarda, for example, based on a comparison of numerous studies in the United States and elsewhere, conclude that city size is a universal latent dimension and the best indicator of a city's hierarchical rank (1977: chap. 15; see also Berry, 1972; Kasarda, 1972b: 174). Thus, "city size has generally been employed as a surrogate measure for hierarchical position," even though "the hierarchy concept implies the measurement of exchanges between cities" (Stern and Galle, 1978: 259). This strategic use of city size is perfectly reasonable and necessary where the unavailability of data thwarts attempts to measure exchange linkages directly. But such analyses tell us little about the effects of size per se. When data *are* available that allow a more direct exploration of in-

---

[6] In turn, size or growth is subject to inherent limitations. As embodied in the principle of nonproportional change, this means that a unit cannot grow beyond a certain point without a change in form (Boulding, 1953). In Hawley's terms, "(a)pplied to an urban system this principle suggests that, with increases in population size, other things remaining constant, costs of communication needed to preserve the integrity of the whole increase more than proportionately" (1971: 137). This principle, as applied in empirical research, is discussed further below.

terdependence in the urban hierarchy, a noncausal view of size often does not offer an intelligible interpretation of the results.

To illustrate, recent research has examined, in ingenious fashion, the relationship between an updated version of Vance and Sutker's index of metropolitan dominance and interdependence operationalized in terms of range and volume of trade (Eberstein, 1979). As expected, a strong positive association was found between metropolitan dominance and the measure of exchange. However, when city size was added to the equation, it alone retained a significant net relationship with trade. Such a finding is not explainable if the role of size is held to be strictly noncausal. However, if size of city is conceived either as a powerful exogenous factor accounting for virtually all the variation in the hierarchical position of cities, or as an intervening variable indirectly mediating the relationship between rank in the hierarchy and trade, a meaningful interpretation emerges. Whatever the appropriate specification of the model, the point is that existing theory fails in this instance to provide the necessary framework for drawing substantive conclusions.

Another option if size is of little or no inherent interest is to standardize for it. Obviously, it would not be correct to conclude that a city is characterized by a higher degree of specialization in a given industry than another simply because the first has 20,000 workers employed in the industry and the second has only 10,000 workers thus employed. In fact, if the first had a population size of 1 million and the second, 100,000, the conclusion, in all likelihood, would be that the latter showed the higher degree of specialization. Hence, the most frequent use of size is as a deflator (denominator) in creating per capita measures for comparative purposes.

This quite general tendency, coupled with a lack of theoretical development, has led to a peculiar impasse in research. If comparative analyses of cities (or other ecological units) are carried out in terms of absolute values unstandardized for size, the fact that a large city may have more of anything (crimes reported, total industrial product, service receipts, etc.) than another smaller city would usually (and rightly) be regarded as a finding that was either trivial or totally predictable. On the other hand, if per capita or percentage measures are employed, one must confront the issue that ratio variables with common terms may create built-in, definitional dependencies thereby resulting in relationships that are partly spurious (Schuessler, 1973; Fuguitt and Lieberson, 1974).[7]

The issue of complex variables and definitional dependency may not be as serious as it first appeared (MacMillan and Daft, 1979; Kasarda and Nolan, 1979). Nevertheless, the question of whether to standardize by size has placed numerous authors in an uncomfortable "damned if you do—damned if you don't" situation.

---

[7] Most of the debate concerning this issue has centered around studies of administrative intensity in formal organizations. It is clear, however, that the problem of definitional dependence can arise in investigations of other substantive questions (Fuguitt and Lieberson, 1974).

For purposes of this discussion, however, the most disturbing aspect of the dilemma is the frequent truth of Fuguitt and Lieberson's comment that, even though spuriousness is not at issue if interest is in the ratio itself and not in the numerator component being standardized, "it is not always easy to determine when the major interest is in the ratio . . . and when it is in the individual components" (1974: 132). Certainly, a substantial portion of this uncertainty in urban ecological research must be attributed to an incomplete conceptualization of size. Where the theoretical role of size is clarified, greater analytical power results, and the problem of definitional dependency is precluded at the outset. For example, Wanner in his (1977) study of the dimensionality of the urban functional system makes quite specific his intention to develop a hierarchical ranking of cities from the point of view of the metropolitan community rather than from the point of view of the entire system of cities. Attention is therefore directed to the intensiveness of activity measured in units per capita rather than to the extensiveness of a function measured in gross figures, and it is clear that what is of interest is the ratio, not the numerator component.

RESEARCH WHEN CITY SIZE IS OF SUBSTANTIVE INTEREST

As sensible and valid as the noncausal view of size may be for many purposes, such an interpretation is often difficult to maintain in light of its relationship to characteristics as diverse as deviance rates, levels of income and income inequality, rate of innovation, and degree of functional specialization (Ogburn and Duncan, 1964; Thomlinson, 1969; Hawley, 1971). Indeed, it is sometimes difficult, if not impossible, to escape Simmel's conclusion that size determines internal structure (Berry and Kasarda, 1977: 338).

Unfortunately, research in which city size has been a major focus has often yielded results that mirror the ambiguity of the theory. A case in point is the findings of studies that relate size to industrial diversification. In a study of 600 communities (circa 1960), size of city was found to have no significant direct effect on industrial diversification when controls were instituted (Clemente and Sturgis, 1972). Another study has reported city size to be positively and significantly related to the same measure of diversification, but to have no significant effect on income inequality (Betz, 1972). Other, more recent research found size to be significantly related to industrial diversification and to have a marginally significant effect on income inequality (Neidert, 1978). Although each of these works was based on somewhat different samples, and thus some differences in results are to be expected, the point is that the conventional ecological approach to size offers rather little help in explaining the differences.

Before moving on, let us add another degree of specificity. It should be clear that size is not the same as growth and that neither size nor growth is the same as ecological expansion. The former distinction may seem so obvious as to be trivial, but one reason for the minimal success enjoyed by urban ecology in dealing with size is that, all too frequently, population size has been the measure when the underlying concept was population growth. The distortion that may arise out of the use of cross-sectional data to test what is essentially a dynamic model will be treated in greater detail below. At this juncture, the intent is mainly to distinguish between the two processual variables. Citing Hawley, Kasarda defines expansion "as a progressive absorption of more or less unrelated populations into a single organization" (1972b: 165). Illustrative of this point is the case of American cities which "grew to be quite large before they began to routinely interact with their outlying settlements to form a single interdependent system" (Kasarda, 1972b: 166). City growth, then, refers to increments in population, while expansion emphasizes centralization of control and integration of the unit.

In recent years, Kasarda has made perhaps the most consistent contribution to our understanding of the effects of size on urban structure (1972a, 1972b, 1974). But even in Kasarda's work, the limitations of the urban ecological perspective on size are apparent. In a study of expansion in 157 metropolitan areas in 1960, he found population size in the periphery (rings) to be directly, positively, and significantly related to the relative numbers of persons engaged in providing professional, managerial, and other similar administrative and coordinative services (1972b). Controls for other variables such as age of city, per capita income, proportion nonwhite, and distance to nearest other SMSA did not diminish the relationship, and the net effects of these controls generally failed to reach conventional levels of significance. Similar conclusions were forthcoming from a later study (1974) of 207 Wisconsin communities. (Actually, there was a treble focus which included school systems and entire societies as well as communities.) Unfortunately, the case for the causal significance of city size is undermined by the limitations of the available theoretical framework.

First, in both instances, cross-sectional data are employed, but often the interpretation is couched in dynamic terms, thereby blurring the distinction made between size, on the one hand, and growth and expansion, on the other. Second, the effects of size are accounted for in terms of the principle of nonproportional change (Boulding, 1953), and it is suggested that large size creates problems of coordination that may be met by allocation of material and human resources to administrative, communications, and transportation functions. While logical enough as far as it goes, it is clear that, from Durkheimian–based ecological theory, neither size nor growth per se is sufficient to create an expansion of control and coordination mechanisms. Rather, as noted above, size is a necessary condition,[8] but it is the increase in the

---

[8] Obviously, a necessary condition may assume causal significance, and, in fact, size approaches such a status in certain portions of Hawley's work cited above. Nevertheless, it is organizational and technological variables, not population size and growth, that are typically assigned causal priority in ecological theory.

volume and intensity of interaction that calls forth technological and organizational changes to preserve the functional integrity of the unit. On the basis of urban ecological theory, the causal mechanisms through which size affects organizational structure cannot be precisely specified.

When causal linkages *can* be delineated, the contribution of the research effort is multiplied. In an investigation of the effect of size of suburban population on central city expenditures on a whole range of public services, Kasarda (1972a) achieves a more complete interface of theory and research. Based on data from 1950, 1960, and 1970, he reports a strong positive correlation between size and expenditures. The explanation is that "forces of expansion" brought suburban populations to the city for work and recreation on a regular basis, thus increasing costs of maintenance and control for the central city. A full elaboration of the causal mechanism would of course be premised on the assumption of heavy inward commuting, and empirical evidence of this is adduced in the form of a significant positive association between expenditures for each category of public services and numbers of commuting suburbanites. The entire investigation is strengthened by the consistency of the relationships over time (including correlation of change scores) as well as in the cross-section.

SUMMARY

To summarize, the conventional conceptualization of size is as a limiting variable—one which itself is limited by and dependent upon organization in accordance with the principle of nonproportional change. Perceived in these narrow terms, the most logical use of size in ecological research is either as a surrogate measure of other concepts that can be assumed highly correlated with size or as a basis for standardization. It should be reiterated that there is nothing inherently amiss in such strategies. The problem is that the perspective offers little or no guidance for analyses in which it is reasonable to accord city population size some causal significance.

Size may also represent the only record of past advantages leading to city growth. Current city size taken as an indicator of historical stimuli to growth and expansion is, in a sense, simply an analytical convenience which may substitute for more detailed, but unavailable, information. Cities emerge and grow for a variety of reasons, some general and some unique to given locales. It is the latter idiographic factors that create problems because they cannot be incorporated into a general or nomothetic framework. In addition to the general prerequisites for large-scale urbanization such as a minimally adequate natural resource base, development of transportation, communications, and other technologies, differentiation of function sufficient to stimulate trade, and so on, individual cities may grow rapidly due to the political/economic prowess of persons who happen to settle there, or because of other fortuitous circumstances. These particularistic influences may be partially reflected by population size. The argument is not that size *ought* to be used in this fashion, but that, desirable or not, current size probably taps some of these particularistic influences and that the implications of this should be taken into account in theoretical models in which size plays a part.

On the other hand, where population size can be reasonably viewed as causal, whether as a labor pool, as an organized aggregate requiring services supplied by the city, or in other respects, the actual mechanisms through which size affects the organizational structure ought to be specified as far as possible.

In any case, it is clear from the work of Kasarda and others that progress is being made. The point is not that size must be seen in every case, or even in most cases, as a primary causal variable. It may well be, as Hawley notes (1968: 330), that "population is for many purposes better regarded as a dependent variable delimited and regulated by organization." Certainly, there is no reason to abandon Gras' conclusion that "what distinguishes a metropolis from a city is not size or shape but the economic function of commercial dominance over a wide area" (as cogently phrased by Weller, 1967: 735). Whether size is conceived of as causal or merely limiting in its effects will depend, among other things, on one's analytical focus, just as the issue of whether to standardize for size must ultimately be a theoretical decision. What is important is that researchers have a firm conceptual foundation on which to base interpretations.

Static Tests of Dynamic Theory[9]

Attempts to make longitudinal inferences from cross-sectional data are subject to serious error (Duncan et al., 1961), as Lieberson and Hansen clearly demonstrate (1974). Such attempts are particularly dissatisfying in urban ecological research. Elsewhere (Frisbie, 1979), I have written as follows:

> From the classical interest in the growth of cities described in terms such as invasion, succession, concentric zones . . . to Hawley's perceptive linking of change and spatial movement . . . as well as his definitive statement on cumulative change and the principle of expansion . . . to the recurrent focus on population redistribution as seen in urbanization, suburbanization, metropolitanization (e.g., Schnore, 1965; Hawley, 1971) and now "nonmetropolitanization" (cf. Beale and Fuguitt, 1976), the emphasis has continued to be on process and the dynamics of society. In particular, it has been suggested that "communal adaptation constitutes the distinctive subject matter of ecology . . ." (Hawley, 1950: 31) and that adaptation, in turn, is "the most important dynamic concept in human ecology" (Klausner, 1971: 27).

[9] A number of the ideas expressed in this section are treated in greater detail elsewhere (Frisbie, 1979).

Even so, relatively little research in urban ecology has exploited the dynamic potential of the theory. Moreover, "specific methods of analysis (have) attempted too often to explore propositions of change by looking at ecological distributions at a single point in time" (Hunter, 1971: 425). In subsequent sections, the advantages and dilemmas of diachronic analyses are discussed, along with a comparison of the results of both static and dynamic research.

ADVANTAGES OF DIACHRONIC ANALYSES

As important for some purposes as change itself is the stability of social structure. A primary goal of all science is prediction, and it is very often the case that the best predictor of a variable at a given point in time is the same variable measured at some earlier point. Farley (1964: 38) reports that over the period 1920–60 "particular suburbs retain their peculiar socio-economic characteristics for long periods of time." Duncan and Lieberson in their sequel, *Metropolis and Region in Transition,* demonstrated that the "relative positions of the established centers with respect to levels of specialization in the manufacturing sector as a whole have changed little since the turn of the century" (1970: 158), a finding reinforced in more current analysis (South and Poston, 1979). Similarly, in his investigation of industrial characteristics in thirty-one metropolitan areas (1950–60), Weller found "little change in the means of the location quotients" and concluded that, if anything, metropolitan areas "have become more alike rather than more differentiated" (1967: 739). Thus, one sometimes overlooked contribution of diachronic analysis is that only by this means can the degree of stability in urban structure be ascertained.

Perhaps the major stimulus to research with a temporal dimension stems from its "theory probing" potential (Campbell, 1963), or, as Hannan and Young note in a slightly different context, the intent is "to exploit intertemporal variation in such a way as to simplify causal inference" (1977: 54). If X and Y are significantly related and X is temporally prior to Y, Y can scarcely be a cause of X. Unfortunately, the methods of diachronic analysis are rarely as clean-cut as the associated logic.

A third benefit, and one highly interrelated with the second, is that much of urban ecological theory is dynamic in nature and therefore requires diachronic analysis for an adequate test. A prime example, of course, is Burgess' hypothesis of city form and development, which early on attracted heavy criticism for its failure to predict accurately spatial patterns in the cross-section—criticisms that, for more than two decades, seem to have been largely accepted at face value. However, Burgess' notion of concentric zone was first and foremost a dynamic conceptualization of city growth (Schnore, 1963), a fact which should have been obvious in his use of terms such as expansion, succession, and zone in transition. Accordingly, any conclusive test of Burgess' theory must be with data collected at more than one point in time. In fact, as Haggerty discovered in his analysis of cities over the 1940–60 interval, the general evolutionary process which, according to Burgess' model, suggests a positive relationship between socioeconomic status and distance from the center finds substantial support "even within cities which show an inverse cross-sectional relationship" (1971: 1084). Obviously, then, not only may relationships measured at one point in time be different in magnitude from those measured over time, but even the direction of the relationship may be different.

Similarly, evidence of ecological expansion of metropolitan areas must depend on longitudinal data. Kasarda's cross-sectional analysis of expansion (1972b) is highly suggestive, but his perceptive linking of changes over time in public service expenditures to suburban population growth is convincing (1972a).

PROBLEMS WHICH LIMIT EMPIRICAL TESTS OF DYNAMIC THEORY

A problem that often plagues diachronic analysis is the lack of high-quality data over extended time periods for a large number of units of analysis. This difficulty, coupled with measurement problems, has led Davis (1976: 1) to conclude that, in sociology, "full-blown time series analysis is seldom appropriate." However, it may be possible to realize some of the benefits of temporal analyses in the absence of observations over numerous points in time. For example, Speare et al. (1975), in a study of residence histories of Rhode Island residents from 1955 to 1967, obtain N as the product of time intervals covered and the number of respondents. While possessing a definite appeal, this method appears to raise serious questions concerning the independence of observations (Frisbie, 1979).

Another strategy suggested by Lieberson and Hansen (1974) combines cross-sectional and longitudinal analyses in a way which takes into account the problem of lack of temporal depth while seeking to preserve the advantages of causal inference. The recommendation is for use of diachronic case studies "to examine the inferences drawn from cross-sectional results" (for which significantly larger amounts of data are apt to be available [1974: 539]). In this way inferences from data at one point in time may be checked against findings from time-series. This technique would seem especially relevant for urban research since there are a few major cities for which data of appropriate longitudinal depth are available—the analysis of which could be used to evaluate inferences derived from larger cross-sectional samples.

Although time-series data can provide much needed leverage in attempts to determine causal priorities, it is necessary to consider some of the methodological and statistical problems associated with it. A technique that at first glance appears especially promising involves the use of lagged correlations (Pelz and Andrews, 1964). However, in addition to demanding rather strong a priori assumptions regarding direction of causality (Duncan, 1969), the method requires a reasonable approximation, if not exact knowledge, of lag-time. Many researchers have found it improbable in most situations that one could have precise information on lag-time without knowledge of causal direction (Davis, 1976). Though notable advances in method have been made in this regard (Heise, 1970, 1975), one may still be faced with a lack of appropriate data at the intervals required.

Another issue that must be resolved is the determination of just what type of temporal relationship is of major interest. Here again, the close and inherent interplay of theory and research comes to the fore. One, for example, might be interested in how levels of X at t_1 affect levels of Y at t_2. Alternatively, the concern might be with the relationship between levels of X at t_1 and the *changes* in Y between t_1 and t_2, or how changes in X over an interval are associated with changes in Y over the same or a lagged interval. Each of these foci must be established theoretically before problems of estimation and statistical inference can be addressed. For example, problems may arise in correlations of type $r(X_{t_2} - X_{t_1})(Y_{t_2} - Y_{t_1})$ out of stability effects related to the correlation of Y with itself. Such a difficulty might be handled by partialing out the stability effect (Lieberson and Hansen, 1974), although "in some cases where the effect of X on Y is immediate and temporary," this method may result in the reversal of the direction of the true relationship (Miller, 1971: 291). In the event of immediate effects, cross-sectional data would allow an appropriate test, but the general issue must ultimately be resolved at the conceptual level.

Another difficulty when the dependent variable is operationalized in terms of change scores and the equation is estimated using change scores and/or end-of-period variables as predictors is that of simultaneity bias. If changes in Y engender changes in the independent variables, OLS single-equation estimates will be biased (Greenwood, 1975).

A further obstacle in arriving at causal inferences from time-series data is the frequent occurrence of serially correlated error terms, that is, autocorrelation (Blalock, 1969; Heise, 1970; Hibbs, 1974). Although employing OLS in the presence of autocorrelated disturbances will yield unbiased estimates of regression coefficients, underestimates of sampling variances and standard errors are likely (Johnston, 1972: 246), and values of R^2, t, and F will tend to be inflated (Hibbs, 1974: 257).

Among the techniques developed for dealing with nonindependent disturbances (see Nakamura et al., 1976, for a useful summary), perhaps the most common approach involves differencing and other transformations of data. However, "the rationale for the use of first differences" depends on the assumption that the coefficient of autocorrelation "is *close* to one" (Aigner, 1971: 132, emphasis in the original). Once again, the initial consideration is conceptual. In testing for the significance of a linear relationship of first differences of two series, "we are not testing exactly the same hypothesis as when we test for a linear relation between the two series themselves" (Nakamura et al., 1976: 218).

Perhaps the test for autocorrelation most familiar to sociologists is that developed by Durbin and Watson (1950, 1951). If autocorrelation is detected, the data may be transformed as: $(Y_t - r_2 Y_{t-1})$, $(X_t - r_2 X_{t-1})$, where r_2 is obtained "by regressing the simple least-squares residual on itself lagged one period." Subsequent residuals may then be tested for autocorrelation (Johnston, 1972: 262–63; Aigner, 1971).

Unfortunately, the Durbin–Watson test is not always conclusive (Theil and Nagar, 1961). Further, it has been pointed out that

> use of the Durbin–Watson statistic presumes a first-order regressive series, but it is certainly possible that higher-order processes are at work. Further, if lagged endogenous variables appear in the system, OLS no longer yields unbiased estimates (Hibbs, 1974: 290), and the Durbin–Watson statistic itself is *"biased against* finding serial correlation" (Aigner, 1971: 136, emphasis in the original; Frisbie, 1979).

Other methods which may offer assistance in these complex matters have been developed. Hannan and Young, for example, suggest conducting "separate analyses for each lag period" to "uncover changes in the causal structure over time" (1977: 57). If changes are not observed, a further alternative is the pooling of scores for several time periods, T, for all N units of analysis.

SUMMARY

Despite the dynamic quality of ecological theory and the existence of certain studies that have profitably carried out diachronic analyses, a review of the literature will disclose that urban ecologists have been no more likely than others (and perhaps less likely) to subject their hypotheses to dynamic tests (Hunter, 1971: 425). Although there are a fair number of investigations which deduce trends from comparisons of a sequence of cross-sectional data sets collected at two, or a few, points in time, sophisticated longitudinal analyses of time-series data at numerous points in time are few. In order to achieve realization of the dynamic potential of ecological theory and to demonstrate the full range of its applicability to urban phenomena, more attention must be paid to methods of handling data relevant to true longitudinal studies as well as to temporal sequences of cross-sectional comparisons.

As a final caveat, one should also beware of assuming that diachronic designs are always superior to cross-sectional ones. As Hannan and Tuma point out, cross-sectional analyses will be preferable "if confounding influences vary more over time than over units" (1979: 303).

Epilogue

The purpose of this discussion has been to identify certain gaps that prevent a close interface between urban ecological research and the theoretical models on which it is based. This evaluation has been made in terms of what urban ecology claims as its conceptual province, and little or no attention has been paid to criticisms suggesting that it ought to be something else. Hence, there has been no attempt to respond to critics who think urban ecology ought to devote greater attention to more policy relevant or applied research, to individual motives rather than to organized aggregates (Michelson, 1970), or to qualitative as opposed to quantitative adaptation (Micklin, 1973: 3–27).

There are of course other neglected theoretical and empirical issues in urban ecology not addressed here, but which fall easily within the conceptual boundaries of the field. It could easily be argued, for example, that the environment, both natural and man-made, has received little emphasis except as a nebulous background against which organizational form and process can be highlighted (Michelson, 1970: chap. 1; Micklin, 1973: 3–27).

Three general sources of the theory/research gap in urban ecology were explored: (1) the proclivity for overly descriptive analysis; (2) the incomplete conceptualization of size as an ecological variable; and (3) the frequent tests of dynamic theory with static measures. Specific illustrations of each were offered and progress made toward resolution of the problems was assessed. Whatever its failings, it remains clear that the theoretical potential of an ecological approach to urban form and development is well worth the expenditure in time and effort that will be required to bring our empirical grasp into closer alignment with our theoretical reach.

18

Convergencies Between Conflicting Theoretical Perspectives in National Development

Alejandro Portes

THE DEBATE BETWEEN modernization and dependency/world-systems perspectives on development has gone through a series of phases and seems to have run its course. It would thus be repetitious to restate the critique of modernity as a theory of development and the reasons that led to its replacement by views in the tradition of political economy. In essence, the emphasis on cultural values and ideological *leitmotifs* as determinants of economic growth has given way during the seventies to a vision of development and under-development as parts of an integral totality. This overarching unit simultaneously depends on and re-creates conditions of economic inequality worldwide. As a field of research, "development" seems to have abandoned the early theoretical debates and moved on to explore the implications and possibilities of the new structural perspectives.

In this context, we might well drop a now unneeded polemical stance and reconsider modernization in a less critical light. To pursue this alternative argument, we may consider three questions: First, did modernization theory represent a significant contribution in the intellectual context where it emerged? Second, is there anything lost with the current shift of attention toward the dynamics of international capitalism? Or, alternatively, what correctives do modernization themes provide for the apparent limitations of dependency and world-systems theories? Third, what convergencies can be found between the older and more recent perspectives? In particular, how has each been affected by its transformation into "testable hypotheses" for empirical research? These are the three questions which I would like to raise and briefly discuss in this presentation.

Modernization is a generic label for a number of different and frequently conflicting approaches. Seen in perspective, however, they share a basic emphasis on cultural themes—value orientations, religious and lay ideologies—as determinants of processes of social change. Modernization analyses center on the transition from the value legitimation of preindustrial social orders, that is, "tradition," to those supporting new political and economic structures consonant with the requirements of industrial society.

Taken as a whole, modernization theories are essentially the projection in the international comparative field of the more general culturalist paradigm dominant in U.S. social science during the post–World War II era. Modernization writings are thus closely intertwined with the general functionalist theory of social structure and with more specific culturalist perspectives in other subfields, such as the assimilation approach in the field of ethnic and racial minorities.

The concept of modernization has been employed in two different contexts. One is the century-and-a-half-old recapitulation of major processes of change which occurred in Europe beginning in the sixteenth century. The other is the more recent comparison between countries which are industrialized, wealthy, and technologically advanced and those that are at different stages of "underdevelopment." The first theme has generated a vast literature around the question: What were the forces which impelled Europe to evolve into industrial capitalism out of a rather conventional feudal order? The second has been concerned with the issue: What forces, present in some societies, have been absent in others and hence prevented their advance toward development? Extrapolation of insights and concepts generated by analyses of the first "historical" theme into the second "comparative" one has been one of the primary sources of criticism against this entire literature (Portes, 1976).

At the time of their emergence, however, modernization writings represented a progressive departure from earlier biologically grounded theories of evolution. For the latter, the existence of inequality among societies stemmed from biologically determined differences in ability among their inhabitants. Advanced societies were peopled by stronger-willed, abler races; backward societies lacked the capacity to innovate and thus their "development" had to proceed through imitation and at a slower pace than leading ones. Culturalist theories liberated sociological analysis of nonindustrial societies from the twin conceptual straitjackets of regarding "development" as a charted path along the same essential stages and of defining the speed at which different societies traversed it as a consequence of immutable racial differences.

This opened the way for serious analytical comparisons between advanced and underdeveloped societies and among different types of the latter. Levy (1955) examined political, economic, and ideological structures of China and Japan—two nonwhite, non-Western societies—as they led to widely different modernization paths. Bellah (1958) also studied the religious ideology of Japan as it contributed to the developmental push of the *Meiji* period and noted the significance of the lay ideology of nationalism in the "modernization" of Turkey under Ataturk. Apter (1967, 1970) compared different political–ideological systems in Africa and noted their functionality for different periods: autocracies legitimized by tradition during extended periods of stability and "mobilization systems" with nationalist or socialist overtones during major transitional periods in the process of modernization.

While many theoretical writings on modernization may fall into oblivion, it is likely that these and other historically grounded studies will stand the test of time. Their significance as studies of legitimation under particular historical conditions may well endure beyond the theoretical framework which they originally represented. More important, as the novelty of the newer perspectives wears off, recourse might be made to these studies as examples of an alternative and necessary standpoint on comparative international development.

This leads logically to the second question. The world-systems and dependency literature has concentrated on mechanisms of political domination and the consequent expansion of capitalist exchange relations around the globe. It has also emphasized the need to examine these processes as part of a single overarching unit—the international capitalist economy—rather than as purely national or regional phenomena (Hopkins and Wallerstein, 1977). In the process of overcoming the past orthodoxy, these writings have successfully criticized culturalistic explanations of development and the limitations of analyzing major processes of social change at the level of individual countries (Cardoso and Faletto, 1969; Wallerstein, 1976a).

These very features criticized by the new perspectives might represent the most significant shortcomings of research derived from them. Prominent members of both the dependency and world-systems schools (Cardoso, 1976; Wallerstein, 1976b) have recognized the importance of ideologies as vehicles of legitimation. Still, the emphasis on material interests and structures of political domination have relegated the study of ideology to a fairly obscure and yet undefined place. It is noteworthy that few comparative studies of ideology have been explicitly inscribed in the new structural perspectives and certainly none comparable to the best produced by modernization scholars.

Similarly, a worrisome trend in the derivative empirical literature is the use of world-capitalism or dependency as a *deus ex machina* for explaining poverty and inequality among countries. The basic thrust of the structural perspectives is to view political and economic events in the centers as conditioning the chances and the nature of development in the periphery. In essence, world-systems writings are concerned with the conditions leading to expansion of the capitalist core on a world scale; dependency writings concentrate, in turn, on the internal impact that this expansion has had on regions incorporated as periphery. In part, world-systems and dependency theorists have emphasized the need for a supranational perspective on development and underdevelopment as a consequence of their current polemic with the modernization orthodoxy. These features of the new theories have outlived, however, the earlier theoretical debates.

Wallerstein (1976c) and Hopkins and Wallerstein (1977) have asserted that the appropriate unit of analysis for major political and economic processes is the not the nation-state, but the world system. Interpreted as the need to incorporate an awareness of events in the world economy into national-level studies, the dictum cannot be more appropriate. As affirmation, however, that only global phenomena merit analysis and that national processes can be subsumed in all its essentials under the international system, it is unacceptable.

Major structural theorists are themselves aware, through their own field experience, of the significant differences among peripheral societies and the irreducibility of phenomena within these national units to international developments. In particular, they are aware of the role of the national state as a key actor in altering the conditions of insertion into the international system and even "promoting" their respective societies from peripheral to "semi-peripheral" or core status. Yet, other scholars, less familiar with the complexity and diversity embodied in the term "periphery" and who become acquainted with these theories as a received intellectual product, can easily turn them into a source of mechanistic explanations. A generalist concern with worldwide processes of economic and political interaction does away with significant variations in class structure and the concrete articulation of classes and the state within particular societies.

The problem is that there is little in the new structural perspectives that calls attention to sources of dynamism in the periphery and to the "degrees of freedom" available within the economic parameters of the world system. An example is the absence of a theory of the state in peripheral and semiperipheral nations. The state in these contexts is defined, even if by default, as a dependent entity, conditioned at every step by the needs and wishes of ruling classes in the centers. A vigorous historical literature on the state stemming from Europe and Latin America contradicts this impression (O'Donnell, 1978; Pinheiro, 1977; Torres Rivas, 1974; O'Brien, 1975). While world-systems advocates might readily concede the point, the issue is that there is little in the perspective, as currently formulated, to guide inquiry on the domestic determinants of state formation and the effect of state activities on national development. For this, we must go outside the pall of the new paradigms to find studies which, like Guillermo O'Donnell's (1977, 1978) recent writings on the "bureaucratic–authoritarian" state in Latin America, provide much more historically grounded insight into these processes.

The world system is definitely not the only valid unit of analysis for research on structural and historical processes. While a number of inquiries may be couched at this level, others require primary attention to the region or the nation-state as contexts of phenomena irreducible to external determinants. Modernization studies, justly criticized earlier on for their vision of societies as isolated entities, may emerge in a new guise as correctives to the exclusive external focus of the new perspectives. The internal class structure, its articulation with agencies of the state, and ideologies employed to legitimize the existing social order are examples of topics which require concrete historical knowledge and which cannot be deduced from global principles.

The third question had to do with possible convergences between culturalist and structuralist perspectives on development. Indeed, the two schools, as we know them today, had their beginnings in historical studies dealing with the origins and maturation of Western capitalism. As seen above, the gap between "modernism and tradition" is simply the latest version of similar antinomies developed since the nineteenth century in the effort to grasp the transition from feudalism to the modern industrial era. Historical concern with the European transition to capitalism was then followed by studies of the experience of former colonies, such as the United States, and by analyses of major non-Western societies such as China and Japan (Lipset, 1963; Bendix, 1966; Levy, 1966; Bellah, 1966; Eisenstadt, 1961).

Similarly, the dependency school had its origins in historical studies of the political and economic condition of peripheral regions, principally Latin America. These studies traced the evolution of underdeveloped countries primarily as a consequence of their changing insertion in world trade in response to the needs of the centers (Cardoso and Faletto, 1969; Sunkel and Paz, 1976; Dos Santos, 1970; Martins, 1975). Similarly, the more recent world-systems perspective derives its name from the effort to trace the origins and consolidation of European capitalism on a global scale (Wallerstein, 1974).

Early historical studies of modernization and then dependency and the capitalist world economy generated, each in its time, a series of insights which challenged the existing orthodoxy. It thus happened that the initial studies were transformed into "schools." Aside from their historical origins, what the two perspectives have in common is their evolution from a series of general theoretical questions posed to a vast corpus of qualitative data to sources of "testable hypotheses" for empirical research.

This transformation was undertaken by later scholars who endeavored to "discipline" intriguing but vague historical ideas by the canons of positivist science. Such efforts, aimed at testing the new ideas, had a dual character as an outgrowth of the enthusiasm awakened by the original insights and as exercises in career promotion. Their result was to transform historically grounded observation on the experience of particular countries or interrelationships among countries into measurable constructs applied, irrespective of the historical context, as quantitative predictors of development.

Studies of the transition toward societal modernization became translated into "modernity," a concept measured through various attitudinal scales and related "cross-nationally" to other individual-level variable. Similarly, a more recent literature has transformed "dependency" into an empirical predictor of such variables as GNP per capita and domestic economic inequality.

The fundamental flaw in this derivative empirical literature is the uncritical transformation of a *perspective* on international processes into a "variable." Dependency was not conceived in the original studies as a continuum from "more" to "less"; rather, it referred to a distinct situation or series of situations characterizing entire societies in the periphery. Given a *situation* of dependency, relationships between specific economic and political factors may have certain predictable outcomes (Gereffi, 1979). Similarly, modernization did not originally refer to individual-level attributes; instead, it attempted to identify a society-wide condition of change resulting from contact with hegemonic European political and economic institutions.

To the scholar sensitive to the nuances of history, the use of "modernity" or "dependency" in their empirical–variable form as predictors of national development appears ludicrous. There is, however, more objective evidence of the limitations of this forced march into quantifiable measurement. Seen in long-range perspective, it seems evident that the derivative empirical literature has not ultimately proven or disproven the original historical insights; it has rather "consumed" them (Cardoso, 1977). Important earlier ideas become increasingly hidden from view by a self-producing accumulation of contradictory and minute empirical "evidence." The collective outgrowth of all this travail has seldom answered the original theoretical questions or effectively challenged the conclusions reached by the more serious historical research.

Sorel's comment that Marxism had become prisoner of its own disciples may well apply to the conflicting perspectives on national development. In the context of twentieth-century American social science, they seem to have run almost parallel courses. Ironically, perhaps, challenges against the modernization orthodoxy were most convincingly made against its quantified "cross-national" variants—social–psychological theories of modernity, achievement motivation, and the like. Such challenges ultimately justified the emergence of new structural paradigms which have, in turn, spawned their own quantitatively oriented literature.

In synthesis, the advent of the new theoretical viewpoints emphasizing the interdependence and organic relationships of development and underdevelopment represent a welcome event. They provide an alternative to the culturalist paradigm and sensitize researchers to aspects obscured or not readily understood by the latter. Still, in the context of the past theoretical

debate, a series of convergencies and complementarities between the two approaches have been neglected. They are more clearly perceived if one focuses
attention on the major historical works sustaining each approach, rather than
on the derivative empirical literature.

Highlighting convergencies between these conflicting perspectives should
not be interpreted as a call to eclecticism. If there is a practical implication in
all the above, it would be a warning against the emergence of a new
orthodoxy. Specific areas of research, such as international labor migration,
world finance, and the multinational corporation will benefit from the general
framework advanced by world-systems and dependency writings; others, such
as investigations into national ideologies of development might fruitfully draw
from earlier works stemming from the modernization paradigm. While my
own inclination is in directions congruent with the world-systems approach, I
would deny that such a perspective is the only valid or useful one.

A more worthwhile endeavor in the field of development might be in a
common opposition to apparently rigorous cross-national "tests" of the different perspectives. Such studies are typically based on aggregate data from
nation-states defined as sample units; the analysis ignores historical differences
across these units, assuming that the operationalization of variables is not
only valid for the whole but valid equally for the different countries. Statistical
results are often at variance with painstakingly acquired knowledge of individual countries and are frequently interpreted in terms divorced from all
known reality (Gereffi, 1979). These studies, as a consequence of the extrapolation of survey research methodologies to complex structural problems,
seldom advance knowledge of peripheral and core societies and, much less, of
interrelationships among them.

Opposition to this type of research should not be understood as opposition
to quantitative analysis per se, but to what might be called "context-less"
quantification. To overcome the temptation of turning every new perspective
into a variable, scholars may keep in mind two facts: First, that historical data
are data and that no reason exists to exclude them from analysis which
employs quantitative aggregate figures. Second, that appropriate interpretation of statistical findings in this field demands prior knowledge of the national context in which measurements were taken. Without such knowledge,
the analyst is at the mercy of a wide array of errors—from faulty measurement, to computer malfunctions, to his or her own flights of interpretative
fancy. Since no scholar can be familiar with all national histories, a logical
corollary is the need for a more modest scope of analysis restricted to individual nation-states, interlocked groups of countries, or specific processes
cutting across the international system.

The position outlined in these comments is not one that necessarily leads
to a middle-of-the-road theoretical stance. Confrontation between conflicting
ideas is important and has led to significant advances in our understanding of
development and underdevelopment. Such advances have been produced,

however, by individuals who took the *problematique* of development seriously and endeavored to understand what actually took place in a particular society or regions, or at specific points in the expansion of the world economy. Regardless of the perspective from which they were written, these studies are likely to survive. While theory will continue to be an essential component of research on national development, neither knowledge of modernization nor of dependency or world-systems models will offer an acceptable substitute for firsthand familiarity with the subject matter. Such detailed knowledge, not theoretical orthodoxy, will remain the primary characteristic of serious research in this field.

19

Comparative Race and Ethnic Relations: Issues of Theory and Research

William Julius Wilson

IN THE PAST TWO DECADES, ethnic and racial antagonisms have sharply increased in various countries around the world—in Western Europe with the increasing hostilities directed against immigrants from Eastern Europe and northern Africa; in North America with the proliferation of ethnic rivalries and growing manifestations of ethnic pluralism; in the Middle East with the heightened Israeli and Arab confrontations; in southern Africa with the efforts of white minorities to maintain their racial domination in the face of intensified black opposition; in Latin America with the continued subjugation of Indian tribes; and in Southeast Asia with the growing conflicts among the Chinese, Indians, and other native peoples.

This apparent rise in ethnic conflicts caught many social scientists off-guard. The proliferation of ethnic antagonisms in North America and Western Europe—including countries such as Canada, the United States, Holland, Belgium, England, Switzerland, and France—were hardly anticipated. And very few ethnic relations analysts were initially able to explain adequately the explosions of ethnic hatred in Northern Ireland. The new ''tribalism'' in these countries, as Pierre van den Berghe (1978: xi–xii) put it, had shaken ''the complacency of social scientists on the supposedly vanishing role of ethnic and racial particularism, and exposed the variety of the conventional wisdom of the topic.''

What is particularly interesting from the viewpoint of the sociology of science was the way social analysts responded to these new expressions of ethnic antagonisms. On the one hand, there was an outpouring of studies in response to each ethnic crisis. Instead of presenting thoughtful sociological analyses of the fundamental bases of ethnic hostilities, many of these studies were essentially polemical in nature. Often social scientists would merely try to formalize issues made popular by politicians and activists and, consequently, trends in social science thinking reflected trends in political movements.

Although there were a number of policy-oriented studies that tended to be more scholarly than the polemical studies, they were in many respects just as topical in nature—studies prompted more by concerns and issues in the public domain than by concerns with fundamental sociological problems. The response to the ghetto riots in the United States in the late 1960s provides one of the clearest and most forceful illustrations of the type of scholarship I am trying to describe. Although hundreds of studies were published on the various dimensions and aspects of the riots, only a handful have had any lasting worth. The most ambitious, the *Report of the National Advisory Commission on Civil Disorders* (1968), was quickly judged to be a document with little substantive or theoretical import, and today it is hardly mentioned as a study that merits consideration by serious students of race and ethnic relations.[1]

On the other hand, the new manifestations of ethnic antagonism did help to generate a serious reexamination of our approaches to the study of race and ethnic relations. Many observers of intergroup relations began to question the explanatory and predictive import of our traditional models of race and ethnic relations. Long-standing studies of American race and ethnic relations bore the brunt of these criticisms because, as one author put it, they tended to reflect "a functionalist view of society and a definition of the race problem as one of integration and assimilation of minorities into the mainstream of a consensus-based society" (van den Berghe, 1978: 7). These studies focused very heavily on the problem of changing prejudicial attitudes and, therefore, presented a subtle psychological account of intergroup relations. Critical of this approach, R. A. Schermerhorn (1970: 6-7) eloquently stated, "If research has confirmed anything in this area it is that prejudice is a product of *situations,* historical situations, economic situations, political situations; it is not a little demon that emerges in people simply because they are depraved. This is not to deny that the subject of prejudice has genuine importance but only that it is not central to the explanation of ethnic and race relations."

It is not a coincidence that this observation was made by one of the leading students of comparative race and ethnic relations, because comparative sociologists, I believe, were the most forceful and persuasive critics of the use of "prejudice" as an independent variable in accounting for racial and ethnic hostilities.[2] It could even be said that the comparative approach

---

[1] For two good critiques of this report see Marx (1970b) and Tabb (1971).

[2] See, e.g,. Schermerhorn (1978); van den Berghe (1978); Cox (1948); Frazier (1953); and Noel (1972).

has had a greater impact on the intellectual development of race and ethnic relations than it has had on any other single field in sociology during the past two decades. Nonetheless, there are significant problems with this approach that range from those that are essentially methodological to those that are purely theoretical.

Research Problems in Comparative Studies

There are several basic features of the comparative approach to race and ethnic relations: (1) the analysis of group relations tends to be at a macro level that encompasses the study of entire societies; (2) the main explanatory focus tends to be on the economic and political relations among groups rather than on the psychodynamics of individuals or on the uniqueness of group cultural traits; (3) the subject matter tends both to include as many different societies as feasible and to focus on the historical evolution of group formation and interaction in these societies; and (4) the group relations and affiliations are seen as a product of a conjunction of objective and subjective factors (van den Berghe, 1978).

Although these basic features of the comparative approach to race and ethnic relations broaden the scope of theory and research, they also present a number of major methodological problems that should be addressed seriously. Indeed, as Schermerhorn (1970: 252) appropriately points out, "One dilemma, and perhaps the major one facing comparative research is that, at the very moment when social scientists need methods and conceptualizations that enable them to deal with larger wholes like total societies, their most effective research tools are, all too often, the very ones fitted for minuscule units of single societies."

The very nature of comparative studies precludes reaching the levels of reliability and validity typical of microstudies. Nonetheless, a distinctive methodology had developed that combines the use of aggregate data, documentation, and secondary analysis with the use of data gathered by field researchers in various societies. The basic problems associated with this methodology are common to all cross-cultural studies.[3]

There are problems of conceptual equivalence. For example, the concept of "ethnic stratification" provides a perfectly valid focus for the comparison of complex industrial states but (as the writings of Lloyd Fallers [1973] and Louis Dumont [1970] so clearly show) loses its meaning when the analysis shifts to tribal or other less complex social units or to societies that stress inequality among men as a central principle. Investigators have to be fully cognizant of whether their concepts and definitions have equivalent, though

---

[3] In much of the following discussion in this section, I am indebted to Warwich and Osherson (1973).

not necessarily identical, meanings in the various cultures under consideration.

There are also problems of equivalence in measurement. The use of aggregate data often does not allow for definitive cross-cultural comparisons because the units of analysis are often not the same. For example, the quality, validity, and reliability of census reports vary enormously in countries around the world. We have few works in comparative ethnic and race relations that display the rigorous cross-cultural measures of human behavior such as Donald Treiman's (1977) Standard International Prestige Scale, which makes it possible to measure occupational status and related status characteristics cross-culturally. Moreover, our heavy reliance on secondary analysis is a poor substitute for the use of primary data. Too often comparative experts in race and ethnic relations rely on published studies and either fail to question seriously the validity of these studies or are not readily in a position to do so. Errors of fact and judgment committed on the primary level continue to be perpetuated or reproduced on the secondary level.

In addition, we have the problem of linguistic equivalence that relates essentially to matters of translation. This difficulty is by no means unique to race and ethnic relations but has been a major obstacle in all aspects of cross-cultural research. In general, the problems of language are reduced if a concept is fairly close to the everyday life of a people. Questions that require little abstraction from familiar experiences (such as those about migration, housing construction, children, and indigenous occupations) present few problems, whereas those dealing with matters of public opinion, political relations, and international affairs present real problems of translation. Nonetheless, conceptual–linguistic equivalence can be increased by extensively pretesting the research instrument in the local cultural setting. The problem is that researchers have not uniformly relied on pretests.

Finally, there is the problem of sampling procedure. As in other fields, cross-cultural research in race and ethnic relations has suffered because of human considerations that influence research sites. Samples have often been skewed in the direction of the more wealthy countries because of matters of convenience such as accessibility, ease of transportation, availability of research sites, and quality of research facilities and living conditions. Considerations such as climate, general living conditions for both the researcher and his family, including housing, sanitation, schools and other social amenities, and even the political climate of the country may be factors in the choice of a research site. It is significant to note that ethnic relations research by sociologists has rarely been conducted in the less developed countries.[4]

Despite the research problems inherent in comparative studies, R. A. Schermerhorn (1978: 253) has argued that "the information received from such large-scale explorations has strong evidential value, more and more

---

[4] One of the rare exceptions is Pierre van den Berghe whose field research has been conducted in countries such as Brazil, Guatemala, Kenya, Nigeria, Mexico, and Peru.

refined by constant application of validity and reliability criteria. Some of these studies are carried out in the absence of direct field research by the investigator, others are supplemented by more extensive field experiences.'' Others have argued that the combined results of comparative research in race and ethnic relations have provided far more information on the total societal dynamic than those provided by the results of microstudies of units in single societies (van den Berghe, 1978; Wilson, 1973). Still others have suggested that the theoretical and empirical payoff of historical and cross-cultural research is greater because historical and cross-cultural studies provide a greater range of cases to satisfy the theoretical requirements of scope sampling (Barth and Noel, 1973). In other words, in testing the validity of theoretical assumptions (or of providing historical illustrations to support or question the explanatory import of certain theories), the important point is not that one has, for example, a representative national sample but that one is able to collect enough empirical cases that reflect the scope of the theory—that is, fitting conditions appropriate to the theoretical framework (Willer, 1967). Historical and cross-cultural studies, it is argued, are more likely to provide conditions to test or to determine the scope of a theory than, say, a cross-sectional study in a specific society.

Although the above claims are reasonable and persuasive, there are still lingering questions about the extent of our knowledge in comparative ethnic relations, especially when the contributions of theoretical approaches are considered.

Theoretical Issues in Comparative Race and Ethnic Relations

In considering the level of theoretical development in comparative ethnic relations, I am struck by how much of the work has been descriptive and typological in nature and how little of it incorporates basic theoretical propositions. There exist a number of theoretical orientations and frameworks that help to identify key variables or antecedent conditions of the emergence, stability, and change of systems of ethnic stratification, but there is a noticeable absence of logically interrelated explanatory systems that fully explain and interrelate these variables.[5] Indeed, one of the problems with theory development in comparative race and ethnic relations is that the attention devoted to considering the strengths, weaknesses, and ideological bases of competing theoretical models or frameworks overshadows the attention given to constructing systematic propositions. The frameworks most widely dis-

---

[5] One notable exception is Blalock's *Toward A Theory of Minority-Group Relations* (1967), which presents a number of systematically constructed propositions that could be applied in comparative research.

cussed are the various economic class models, the plural society and power conflict models, the internal colonial model, and the functionalist model. I shall neither summarize these approaches here nor discuss the all-too-familiar criticisms of their respective strengths and weaknesses; but I would like to consider the extent to which their combined contributions provide a basis for a comprehensive theory of comparative race and ethnic relations.

In many respects we can become so critical of a field of inquiry that we lose sight of the real contributions that have been made. Ethnic relations analysts have presented impressive studies in explaining the emergence of different patterns of ethnic stratification. We have useful general theoretical frameworks such as Stanley Lieberson's "A Societal Theory of Race and Ethnic Relations" (1961) and Donald Noel's "A Theory of the Origin of Ethnic Stratification" (1968). A number of more specific studies have explained the sequences of intergroup contact. For example, our understanding of the ethnic stratification that emerges from voluntary migration has been enhanced by the economic class analysts, including Edna Bonacich (1972), who developed the important split labor market theory of ethnic antagonism; and by the Marxist social scientists Stephen Castles and Godula Kosack (1973), and Manuel Castells (1975). The plural society analysts have made significant contributions to our understanding of colonization and ethnic stratification, including such scholars as Pierre van den Berghe (1970), Leo Kuper and M. G. Smith (1964), Leo A. Despres (1967), and Harry Hoetink (1967). Contributions have also been made by nonpluralists such as John Rex (1970), Philip Mason (1971), and Michael Banton (1967); and by Marxist scholars such as Celso Furtado (1970), Andre Gunder Frank (1967), and Michael Burawoy (1974). Some of the more unique problems of ethnic stratification resulting from territorial incorporation have recently been clarified by Michael Hechter's (1975) penetrating analysis of internal colonialism and the comprehensive comparative work of R. A. Schermerhorn (1970). Finally, the works of Wilson (1973), Harris (1964), and Blauner (1972a) have contributed to our understanding of involuntary migration and ethnic stratification.

However, the presence of these many competent and diverse studies on the emergence of ethnic stratification is also a reflection of one of the major problems of theory development in comparative ethnic relations—there is no single comprehensive framework that pulls together these disparate studies and approaches. What is needed, it seems to me, is a theory of ethnic stratification that would not only explain the emergence of ethnic stratification per se but would also account for both the emergence of *different forms* of ethnic stratification in the same society or in different societies and the way in which these forms persist and change over time. For example, ethnic stratification embodied in labor exploitation is substantially different in form and substance from ethnic stratification embodied in, say, job segregation designed to eliminate economic competition among workers. The importance of such differences is often obscured in the more general theoretical framework because of a tendency to think about theoretical issues in terms of "majority" versus "minority" or "dominant group" versus "subordinate group." More specifically, different forms of ethnic stratification are not only structured by different economic and political arrangements, they are also shaped by the participants within the interracial arena. Thus, it is often necessary to consider the ways in which different segments of the dominant group population interact with different segments of the minority group population in order to explain fully the form that ethnic stratification ultimately takes. And this becomes an especially important consideration in the more industrialized societies with their complex divisions of labor and elaborate class structures.

It is true that important intragroup variations are addressed by economic class theories of ethnic stratification, but such theories tend to be limited to ethnic conflicts that are derived from or associated with basic economic arrangements. Therefore, they do not have the scope to deal with the politically based aspects of ethnic antagonisms that are emphasized by, for example, the plural society analysts. Moreover, such theories often fail to consider the strength of ethnic differentiation, which may have been manipulated originally by a *dominant* class for economic gains but which becomes firmly institutionalized and persists in other parts of the social system—in the polity, educational institutions, and residential areas (See, 1979).

Toward a Holistic Approach to Theory Development

If there is a sociological problem of ethnic stratification that has not been adequately explained, it is the persistence of ethnic stratification. When we carefully examine questions concerning the stability or persistence of systems of ethnic stratification, it becomes clear that our knowledge has not progressed much beyond the fact that stability can be a function of either consensus, interdependence, or coercion (Barth and Noel, 1972).

A good deal of the attention that comparative sociologists have devoted to this problem has been in the form of debates concerning the importance of value consensus in maintaining systems of ethnic stratification. However, important questions about the role of ideology in generating consensus still remain despite the existence of some excellent studies such as Louis Dumont's *Homo Hierarchicus* (1970). And definitive statements that are made about consensus seem to be reduced to such truisms as "in general, consensus is probably the single most important and most efficient basis of maintaining ethnic patterns although it is never the only basis and in some societies it is of very little importance" (Barth and Noel, 1972: 340). Nonetheless, "as societies urbanize," Barth and Noel (1972: 339) remind us, "their stability does become increasingly based on interdependence with the result that the need for consensus between social units is greatly reduced. Thus, by stressing values to the exclusion of interdependence and coercive power, the consensus framework provides only a partial explanation of stability. Recent analyses of 'plural societies' clearly demonstrate that a high degree of consensus is not an essential basis of societal integration and persistence.''

Still, a comprehensive explanation of the persistence of systems of ethnic stratification remains elusive. Barth and Noel have correctly emphasized that, in complex societies, social groups are compelled to cooperate even in the absence of value consensus because they are heavily interdependent. This interdependence enhances multiple group commitments to the maintenance of order and thereby encourages social systems to ''be receptive to modifications to assure that they will not be destroyed by their own rigidity in the face of internal contradictions and environmental changes'' (1972: 340–41). This tendency often gives rise to an ordered process of change which is not disruptive to the social system.

Barth and Noel's conception of social system adaptation is related, although not identical, to Morris Janowitz's (1979: 6) interpretation of the classical meaning of ''social control'' defined as ''the capacity of a social group from the smallest primary group to the nation state and even the world community to effect an element of self regulation.'' This perspective of social control, not to be equated with the more contemporary meaning of conformity and repression, associates self-regulation with a set of goals, not simply a single goal, and therefore requires the researcher to explicate a fundamental value position.

However, ''social control does not rest on an exclusively normative conception of elements of social organization and society'' (Janowitz, 1975: 88). Indeed, the assumptions and variables of social control theory incorporate the economic, technological, ecological, and institutional dimensions of social organization. This systems approach requires a ''multivariate'' notion of causality. ''The goal is to account for the normative order which has emerged,'' states Janowitz, ''but this hardly dictates a 'normative' explanation or a normative 'theory of macrosociology.' On the contrary, in the classical formulation of macrosociology: (a) the point of entrance is to investigate the ecological—technological—economic structure of social organization and the resulting social stratification of the nation state; (b) the intermediate step is to explore the interactive processes which create societal institutions and institutionalized norms and values; and (c) the final step is the analysis of elites, power, and decision-making processes which are based on conscious efforts to intervene in and fashion patterns of political participation'' (1978: 18–19).

Thus, if we look at advanced industrial society, in contrast to preindustrial or even industrial society, we witness a period of ineffective and weakened social control and the alternative or even simultaneous outcome is disintegration and continued conflict. As Janowitz puts it, "Social disintegration implies a reduction in the ability of a group to control the behavior of its members and a decline in interaction and influence; social conflict implies an increase in interaction between groups on the basis of antagonistic means and goals" (1978: 30). Whereas Barth and Noel (1972: 340) argue that increased specialization and role differentiation have forced disparate groups and subsystems to cooperate with each other to "achieve a variety of goals which they cannot achieve alone," Janowitz (1978) maintains that despite these interdependencies, the capacity of a social group or a society to effect self-regulation consistent with a set of basic value principles is decreasing in advanced industrial society because of the difficulty of legislative institutions to mediate conflicting group interests and resolve social and economic conflicts.[6]

For the purpose of this chapter, the issue is not the effectiveness of social control in advanced industrial society; rather, the issue is whether the social control perspective could be helpful to race and ethnic analysts in our efforts not only to account theoretically for the persistence of systems of ethnic stratification but to explain changes in such systems as well. The concept of "social control" has broad generality for theoretical purposes because it suggests a holistic approach to social organization.

To be more specific, it suggests, first, the need to search for a set of overarching values to which all or most groups in society commit themselves at a given point in time (and these values need not pertain directly to the existing racial or ethnic stratification arrangement). Second, it suggests the need to consider carefully the way in which various institutions in society are arranged, and the way in which such institutional arrangements ultimately determine the nature of the overarching set of values. This calls for a detailed investigation of not only the political, economic, and other institutional dimensions of social organization but also of the ecological and technological dimensions. Third, it suggests that a detailed and careful investigation be made of the dimensions of social organization so that the role of what Janowitz calls "ordered social segments" in undermining or contributing to social control could be uncovered. These ordered social segments would not only include those groups organized or identified on the basis of racial or ethnic attachments, but also those organized on the basis of class, sex, age, and region. Thus, an investigation of the persistence or change of racial or ethnic inequality would of necessity be part of a larger investigation of the en-

---

[6] According to Janowitz (1978: 548), "The focal points of disarticulation are twofold: One set rests within and between the bureaucratic hierarchies—industrial and service—in which labor violence has been replaced to a large extent by 'manipulative' organizational authority and labor–management relations in the adversary model. The other nexus of disarticulation results from increased separation of place of work and community of residence; this serves to fragment social and political relations. The result is hardly the emergence of a population of 'isolated' persons and households but, rather, a complex of ordered social groups with striking primary group similarities."

tire social system—an investigation that would focus on an array of structural, institutional, and cultural variables.

Such a holistic approach, I believe, would mitigate against the tendency to view ethnic or racial problems from restricted or myopic perceptions, derived from prevailing and competing intellectual orientations or frameworks, that characterized theoretical approaches in this field. It would not only build on these frameworks; it would also integrate them into a more comprehensive scheme. This perspective could, in other words, incorporate and apply wherever appropriate (1) the ideas from plural society and power conflict theory with their emphasis on intergroup power balance, group dissensus, political fragmentation, and incompatibilities in beliefs, values, and interaction patterns; (2) the ideas of functionalist theory with their emphasis on value consensus as the fundamental mode of social organization; (3) the ideas of the economic class theories with their emphasis on the salience of class conflict derived from different modes of production; and (4) the ideas of the internal colonial theory and their emphasis on the effect of the cultural division of labor in separate core and peripheral areas of organization. Moreover, such a holistic approach would be entirely compatible with cross-cultural research conducted in a historical context.

This suggested approach for fruitful research and theory development in the field of comparative race and ethnic relations is not to imply that we do not currently have studies which reflect the holistic approach outlined above. One such study is Louis Dumont's *Homo Hierarchicus* (1970), a study that clearly shows how a common value system that relates to ethnic differentiation is determined by the mode of organization in society that includes structural, institutional, cultural, and ecological–technological variables. Focusing on early Indian society, Dumont demonstrates that the Indian caste system constitutes a perfect example of the principle of hierarchy, which he defines as "the principle by which the elements of a whole are ranked in relation to the whole" (1970: 66). Dumont points out that caste represents a specific mode of social organization that exemplifies the underlying principle of hierarchy common to traditional societies. He argues that whereas modern Western societies stress equality among men as a basic principle, traditional Indian society stressed inequality among men as a basic principle. Accordingly, the traditional Indian caste system represents not just simply a pattern of domination with explicit ideological support, it also embodies the hierarchical principle which had been abandoned by Western societies in the face of modernization. Hierarchy, in terms of a larger world view, demonstrates the important role of ideology in certain systems of ethnic differentiation—a role which contributes to the persistence of patterns of ethnic domination.

A central point in the works of both Janowitz and Dumont is that ideology, broadly defined in terms of a system of interrelated ideas and values, cannot be fully understood independently of the mode of organization. The importance of ideology at any given point in time is determined by the extent to which the "raw material which it orders and logically encompasses" (Dumont, 1970: 37) is actually explained by it. In other words, we often have to consider nonideological factors to account fully for the relations of political and economic phenomena, force, power, property, and territory. As Dumont notes (1970: 37), if ideology "reflected only the data, and reflected it completely, the system of ideas and values would cease to be capable of orienting action, it would cease to be itself." But the fact that ideology does orient action, sometimes in very fundamental ways, makes it a crucial phenomenon for investigation in any holistic explanation of the persistence and change of ethnic or race relations.

The Role of Ideology

It should be pointed out, however, that the role of ideology in systems of ethnic or racial inequality has received increasing attention from students of comparative ethnic relations, even though the concept has yet to be incorporated in a theory of ideology and inequality. And the most systematic discussions of ideology have had to do with the concept of "racism." In recent years, comparative sociologists have been systematically explicating the concept of racism as ideology so that, in the words of George Fredrickson (1976), "it can be used with some clarity, thereby making possible for the phenomenon to which it refers to be isolated, explained and placed in its sociohistorical context."[7] In these works, racism is treated as an ideology that legitimates patterns of racial domination and that may give rise, more or less independently, to new or more rigid patterns of domination. However, the major difficulty with these more systematic writings on racism is that definitional issues are discussed without the benefit of an explicit theory of ideology and inequality.

I would maintain, however, that we are all guided by an implicit theory—however vaguely articulated and however readily acknowledged—a theory that in effect assumes there is a meaningful relationship between ideology and power and ideology and social structure; a theory that furthermore assumes that the experiences of subordinated groups are affected differently by different structures of inequality; a theory that also assumes that deterministic ideologies applied to real or imagined racial groups have a qualitatively different effect on human behavior and social structure than nondeterministic ideologies; and a theory that assumes that real or imagined racial groups are affected differently by deterministic theories than are groups which are not so perceived.

[7] For systematic treatment of the concept of racism, see Noel (1972); van den Berghe (1978); Wilson (1973); Schermerhorn (1978); and Rex (1970).

Although studies of ideology and inequality have progressed to the point where ideology is not simply reduced to material forces but may be considered to have a life of its own in certain historical situations, there is still some confusion about the relationship between ideology and the problems of class relations as they affect ethnic stratification. Conventional wisdom associates the development of ideology of ethnic subordination with a dominant class. However, as Katherine O'Sullivan See has pointed out (1979: 10), "Ideological justifications acquire a prescriptive dimension over time, particularly as they are embodied in social institutions. Thus, the maintenance or further development of ethnic differentiation and stratification may be sustained, even when it is not necessarily in the economic interests of a dominant class." Indeed, in her study of ethnic antagonism in Northern Ireland, See persuasively reveals how the sectarian "orange" ideology, originally created by the dominant economic class, persisted even when its continued presence undermined the economic interests of that class.

The Social Control Perspective and Radical Social Change

The question of ideology as a part of a holistic theory of social control becomes less important when the matter of radical social change is considered. From the perspective of social control, radical social change implies a sharp increase in interaction between ethnic groups on the basis of incompatible means and goals. It is, in the words of Barth and Noel (1972: 346), "generally rooted in the clash of vested interests and altercation in the power balance. If the emergence of a powerful, organized group willing to use its power (procedurally, if possible, violently if necessary) against the entrenched establishment is not a prerequisite of radical change, it at least seems accurate to say that the use of such power is more effective than the appeal to legitimacy." Radical social change, in short, implies a period of ineffective and weakened social control. In order to account for radical social change a holistic theory not only has to explain the changing effect of the system of values and ideas and the various ecological, technological, and institutional dimensions of social organization on the intergroup arena, it also has to explain the responses of particular groups to these changes.

In this connection, it is generally accepted among comparative social scientists that the mobilization of minority resources against racial or ethnic inequality is inextricably related to basic societal changes—economic, political, and demographic. It is also understood that different systems of production, different arrangements of the state, and different shifts in the size and location of populations impose different constraints on intergroup interaction whereby intergroup relations are structured, ethnic antagonisms are channeled, and ethnic group access to rewards and privileges is differentiated. However, there does not exist an explicit theory of ethnic or racial change that would enable us to explain and predict variations in intergroup behavior based on structural shifts in any clear or precise way. Moreover, what is not readily understood, or in some situations even recognized, is that important changes in *intragroup* behavior accompany changes in the broader society. For example, in modern industrial society the economic class position of minority group members frequently shapes the way they perceive and define problems of racial inequality, determines the solutions they propose and support to eliminate the problems, and influences the way in which they select and mobilize resources to address the problems. The economic class position of minority members is also related to the benefits they receive from changes in a society's racial or ethnic policies. And the importance of minority economic class affiliation with respect to each of these matters increases as a society moves toward deracialization—a process in which racial or ethnic distinctions gradually lose their importance in determining individual minority mobility. I contend that in a society undergoing deracialization we cannot fully understand the timing of minority mobilization without considering how race and class intersect in the minority experience (Wilson, 1978a, 1978b).

Similar theoretical questions emerge in less industrialized societies undergoing decolonization, societies in which primordial attachments are based on tribal affiliation. As Gordon Chavunduka (1979) has pointed out, tribalism has tended to increase as historically colonized people attempt to cope with the problems created by political independence and modernization. Following independence, Africans undertook new responsibilities and competed for new wealth and power. For many African politicians, tribalism provides a base from which to participate in the competition for scarce resources and the struggle for political power. It has increasingly become "an ideological weapon in political conflict and economic competition" (Chavunduka, 1979: 2). In a number of African states, for example, tribal group tensions have erupted into massacres, murder, and civil war. Tribal pressures and tensions were in part responsible for the military takeover of the administration in Nigeria in 1966, for the Civil War in the Sudan, for the violent group conflicts in Angola and Zaire, and for the serious cleavages among political parties in countries such as Kenya and Zimbabwe, Rhodesia.[8]

Plural society, internal colonial, power conflict, and functionalist theorists have often been criticized for their tendency to ignore the significance of intraethnic relations and the conflicts of economic and political interests within groups. And even Marxist scholars have tended to treat subordinate groups as monolithic entities even though they fully recognize the significance of class divisions among dominant group members. A holistic theory of race and ethnic relations, if it is to be truly comprehensive, would have to acknowledge

[8] See also Sithole (1979) and Reader (1979).

and explain the importance of intragroup differences even among subordinate groups in certain historical contexts and situations.

Conclusion

In this chapter I have argued that despite the methodological and research problems inherent in comparative studies of race and ethnic relations, the major problems in this field have to do with theoretical development. I have contended that there are a number of theoretical orientations and frameworks that identify relevant variables or antecedent conditions of the emergence, stability, and change of systems of ethnic stratification but that our theoretical sophistication has not moved much beyond the typological stage, and that we seem to devote more time to debating the merit of a given theoretical orientation than to actual theory construction. Even more important, we are nowhere near developing a comprehensive theory of comparative race and ethnic relations from which more specific frameworks can be derived and organized. I have suggested that such a framework should not only account for the emergence of racial and ethnic systems, but should also be able to explain the persistence of and changes of such systems.

In this connection, I have drawn upon the social control metaphor to suggest the way in which such a perspective would be helpful to race and ethnic analysts in accounting for the dynamics and nature of different systems of ethnic stratification. The importance of the social control perspective, viewed in the classical sense of group self-regulation rather than the more contemporary interpretation of conformity and repression, is that it presents a holistic approach to social organization; an approach, if applied to comparative race and ethnic relations, in which the investigation of the emergence, persistence, and change of ethnic stratification would be treated not in isolation but in relation to the larger social system. Thus, cultural, economic, technological, structural, ecological, and intergroup variables that may impinge directly or indirectly on ethnic stratification would be examined. And even though the focus would be on social control, neither the question of stability nor the question of social change would be ignored.

This holistic approach would, I argue, mitigate against the tendency to view ethnic or racial problems through the prism of restricted theoretical orientations. In other words, the approach could, wherever appropriate, incorporate ideas from the plural society and power-conflict frameworks, the economic class theories, the functionalist model, and the internal colonial theory. Moreover, such a framework would enhance our sensitivity not only to intergroup differences in the interactive process, differences that help define and shape ethnic stratification, but to intragroup differences as well.

I believe that such an approach is ideally suited for research and theory development in comparative race and ethnic relations. It provides a comprehensive theoretical orientation which could be applied to specific case studies. And the results of empirical research from these studies could lead to specifications of relevant variables that might both facilitate the transformation of the framework to an explicit cross-cultural theory and specify the conditions under which a given theoretical proposition applies.

20

Structure and Process in Ethnic Relations: Increased Knowledge and Unanswered Questions

Robin M. Williams, Jr.

WITHIN THE AMERICAN sociology of ethnic relations during this century the first major development was a rejection of initial biologistic–racial assumptions; the second was to turn away from individual attitudes or prejudices, taken in themselves, as primary factors in racial or ethnic relations. An early preoccupation with assimilation gave way to a focus upon cultural pluralism, linked with economic and political integration; and this, in turn, was replaced by emphases upon institutionalized racism, ethnic distinctiveness and persistence, "nationalism" (Pinkney, 1976), conflict, and revolution. Such shifts in interests are sometimes regarded as changes in "theories," but they often represent preferences and ideologies at least as much as differences in explanatory schemes or empirical propositions.

The salience of ethnic differences in the modern world has been well documented. There are nearly nine hundred identified ethnic groupings within today's nation-states. Appreciable opposition, controversy, and conflict exist and will develop in many of these nations—Heisler (1977: 1) estimates "as many as one half," going on to claim that "ethnic differences are the single most important source of large-scale conflict within states, and they are frequently instrumental in wars between countries as well." Furthermore, and contrary to a once popular view that the political significance of ethnicity would decrease in modernized or industrialized societies, recent decades have shown both the persistence and the resurgence of ethnic politics in many societies around the world.

The "field of study" of ethnic and racial relations does not refer to an abstract analytical category such as "economic action" or "power," but rather to concrete types of social entities and relationships. Even so, the units—ethnic categories and collectivities—which are the starting points for inquiry typically do not have the sharp boundaries and tight internal connections of formal organizations or of small groups. And the diversity of topics that are studied under the umbrella of racial and ethnic relations is apparent. Evidently, then, what we have is an arena within which nearly any topic of sociological interest may be studied. Racial and cultural relations manifest all major social processes, from altruistic behavior and cooperation to total social conflict (Williams, 1975a, 1977), and connect with every kind of important social and cultural structure. Small wonder, then, that there are many nonobvious connections between ethnicity and other social and cultural phenomena (Yinger, 1977; Blalock, 1967).

The accumulation of empirical knowledge over the last thirty years or so has been great, and the advances in the scope and in the technical and theoretical sophistication of analysis has been impressive. It is important to emphasize these facts, for the field is marked also by enough intense disagreements and self-criticisms to obscure occasionally the extent of advancement of knowledge.

And even the most sober and cautious observers can be carried away by the momentary salience of large-scale social events. The result is a tendency for appraisals of the importance of this or that "factor" to shift rapidly from one historical period to another. Thus, we see overweening significance attributed to economic classes in the 1920s and 1930s, nations and ideologies in the 1930s and 1940s, the end of ideology in the 1950s, and ethnicity in the 1960s and 1970s. But societies and social relationships are multifactored and multidetermined, and the concrete causal role of one or another set of variables obviously changes from time to time and place to place. The enormous importance now attributed to ethnicity by many social scientists in the United States is historically conditioned and may be a transitory phenomenon. Of course, ethnicity today is a major factor in political events and social change in many societies; it will continue to be so for the foreseeable future. But nations, classes, economic interest groups, and status groupings based on sex and on age are and will be also highly significant social units and movements. Ethnicity is one among many bases of solidarity and cleavage.

The bulk of criticisms directed by workers in this field against the efforts of their peers fall into no less than fourteen major categories, ranging from the claim that important factors have not been included to the argument that the factors studied are not open to purposive manipulation (consequently, it is said, [1] clear causal imputations cannot be made, and [2] the work has limited relevance for social policy and practice), or to the assertion that the bulk of the studies deal with static constructs and cross-sectional data and therefore are unable to depict crucial processes and to demonstrate causal connections.

The mandate given by President Blalock to the Association's thematic sessions amounts to asking, "What is wrong with your field, if anything, and what can be done about it, if anything?" After the listing just reviewed, we may be tempted to answer the first part of the question with "Everything," and the second, with "Nothing." But a more careful appraisal will give grounds for greater, even if cautious, optimism.

This selection deals with the following topics: issues and progress in conceptualization, research methods, empirical generalizations, needed developments, and promising directions for further work. Such a broad survey runs the risk of becoming lost in a mass of details. Let us, therefore, state in advance a few central themes that run through the materials.

1. We see marked advancement in knowledge, but considerable divergencies in presuppositions and interpretations.
2. The main difficulties arise from use of unduly one-sided or narrow theoretical frameworks, resulting in many ad hoc or "ideological" interpretations that are not articulated closely with systematic comparative data.
3. Appropriate conceptual schemes and research methodologies are available and are being improved.
4. Out of many possibilities, we sketch a few broad lines of promising development.

Conceptualizations: Problems and Progress

The recent flood of writings concerning ethnic groupings and ethnicity presents numerous varying definitions of the central terms; but shows agreement on many characteristics, such as *cultural distinctiveness, group identity, solidarity and loyalty,* and *ethnic consciousness.* It seems evident, therefore, that the most useful definitions are likely to be enumerative or range definitions, which list a set of varying characteristics. In the perfect case or pure type, all will be present in marked degree; other "types" will have fewer of the attributes, and in less clear or developed forms. The extent to which the designated characteristics form an ordered set is an important empirical question. The meaning of ethnic group can be clarified by systematic comparisons of such sets with those identified as castes, estates, social classes, extended kinship groupings, and local communities. The result, happily, could be that we would have fewer discursive arguments about terms and more solid empirical generalizations and coherent theoretical linkages.

Although the several defining characteristics of ethnicity vary to some degree independently, they often are highly intercorrelated. "When, for example, there is a threat, real or perceived, to the unity or survival of the group, the salience of all variables will go up concurrently" (Schermerhorn, 1974: 2). Nevertheless, ethnicity varies greatly in its cultural, social, and psychological implications from place to place and time to time. For example, the New Ethnicity of the 1960s and 1970s has had a strongly self-conscious assertiveness and explicit cultural–political claims. In complex societies ethnic collectivities may emphasize different items among their potentially significant cultural traits at different times: language, religion, race, territory, national origin, occupational or economic position, political affiliations and ideologies, and so on (Das Gupta, 1974). The degree of fluidity in such rearrangements of the criteria and symbols of collective identity and organization depend upon varying combinations of two central conditions: (1) political, economic, and status *interests;* (2) *constraints and opportunities* defined by relationships with other ethnic and class groupings.

A growing emphasis is evident in the recent literature on the distinction between the *cultural content* of ethnicity and the *structural characteristics* of the congeries or collectivity carrying the culture. Two structural features receive increasing attention: (1) the definiteness of the group boundary; (2) the external structural constraints, such as political and economic inequalities and pressures.

The claim that ethnicity is primordial—"distinct from all the other multiple and secondary identities people acquire" (Isaacs, 1974: 15)—has been denied (Hechter, 1974) on the ground that ethnic solidarity in complex societies is primarily a response to structural discrimination. What Hechter's data indicate is that "status politics" rather than "class politics" seems most prevalent in those parts of Great Britain that have been relatively poor and culturally subordinated. From this finding, it is inferred that, with some exceptions, ethnicity becomes *politically salient* only when lines of cultural distinction coincide with or are used as the basis for social stratification (distribution of resources). The question of whether such outcomes depend upon the prior existence of "primordial," if latent, distinctions is not directly at issue in these conclusions.

The model or metaphor of internal colonialism has furnished a central mode of interpretation for several influential works (Blauner, 1972b; Hechter, 1975; Pinkney, 1976). The model focuses upon the routine functioning of dominant institutions as the pervasive base of categorical discrimination and prejudice. It achieves its evocative impact by vividly reminding us of similarities between the economic and political statuses of ethnic minorities and those of colonized societies. Some crucial conceptual problems lie in identifying, as well, the characteristics that differentiate between internal and external colonialism. As Hechter notes, a strict definition of colonialism should probably include a political (administrative) differentiation between "citizens" and "subjects" and should take into account territorial separation. Again, a range definition is needed, with specification of the ranges of variables within which the referent of the concept is to be found.

Throughout this field of study there is a clear need to move decisively away from ad hoc descriptions to the explicit, careful, and routine use of well defined variables that characterize *important types* of ethnic aggregates and collectivities and of the recurrent *situations* in which ethnically conditioned behavior occurs. The necessary empirical knowledge is available—much of it codified in critical summaries, in propositional inventories, and in proto-theorectical works. The nineteenth-century image of an ethnic group as a self-contained, culturally unique, firmly bounded, small "total society" is almost wholly outmoded as a basis for analyzing modern ethnicity.

One of the common sources of unresolved controversies in this field is precisely a failure to specify the context within which a given generalization can be expected to hold true. To take an obvious but striking case, the changing permeability of the boundaries of nation-states to ideas, persons, and weapons that affect internal ethnic relations is a fact of life that must be kept in the foreground in any analysis of a single national system. Failures of specification may occur with regard to place, historical period (high or low immigration; propserity or depression; war or peace, etc.), ethnic ecological concentration, length of residence, relationships among minorities, intragroup heterogeneity, and many other contextual variables (Yancey, Ericksen, and Juliani, 1976). Such lapses are simply special cases of the more general defect of treating variables as if they were constants. The most dangerous case is to assume that "ethnicity" (or "race") is a fixed condition, when in fact the meanings and causal significance of any particular ethnic or racial category are always changing.

In the ideal case, the process of developing an adequate explanation of a puzzling regularity in social behavior proceeds in a zigzag manner. Initial investigation produces a variable or set of variables that empirically covary with X and are theoretically connected with it. Other studies identify different independent variables, and competing models develop. Subsequent research pits the alternatives against one another—either in a "crucial test" case or in a cumulative pattern search—and the issue is tentatively resolved. Usually, it is found that each of the competing accounts is valid, but that the explanatory power of some is superior to that of others.

Examples of the process do exist. Thus, efforts to explain differences in political participation between whites and blacks in the United States have developed three main explanations: (1) *indirect effects,* (2) *isolation,* resulting from discrimination, (3) *ethnic community* cohesion and mobilization (Danigelis, 1977, 1978). Each of these hypothetical explanations is plausible and each is consistent with a substantial body of data. Yet the first account is clearly incomplete and the second and third explanations are partially contradictory. An obvious possible strategy is to seek to combine all three in a composite explanation which Danigelis (1978) calls a "political climate theory," that is, whether the total sociocultural setting is repressive/intolerant or indifferent or supportive of black political participation. The new explanation is appraised by means of multivariate analysis of data from six elections,

1952–72. Predictions supported by the data were (1) that white–black differences in political activity would change over time and in different ways in the North and in the South, and (2) that early "isolation" of blacks in the South would change to "ethnic community" mobilization in the mid-1960s. The data suggest that the relative importance of the three competing explanations varies with the type of political activity (e.g., whether it is visible and/or threatening to whites), varies over time (specific historical context), and differs as between North and South. The revised theory is more complex but also more specific and dynamic than any of the three explanatory accounts that it subsumes.

The possibilities for improved conceptualizations depend upon close attention to the developing body of empirical materials—for "detailed and precise knowledge of how the world works is the stuff of which genuine theories are made." At the same time, continuing critical review of existing schemes is indispensable. Such conceptual reexamination has disclosed, for example, the varying applicability of several major frameworks to ethnic relations in different total contexts. Thus, Barth and Noel (1972) have proposed that the "race-relations cycle" best fits the initial emergence of interethnic relations, "consensus" formulations are most suitable for problems of persistence, "structural interdependence formulations" for adaptive processes, and "conflict" (opposition, contradiction, incongruence) conceptualizations for hypotheses concerning change. Although there are unresolved problems in this proposal, it does illustrate the constructive possibilities for developing cumulative rather than topical, or faddish, interpretations.

Research Methods

As the preceding sections indicate, the recurrent calls for cross-cultural, comparative, or cross-national research are well founded: a necessary aim of a scientific sociology is to establish generalizations that transcend dated and localized descriptions and that are specified as to limits and necessary contexts, and these generalizations cannot be established or falsified solely on the basis of studies of a single culture or society.

The importance of somehow appropriately fitting the techniques and models to the conceptual schemes and hypotheses, and vice versa, is readily granted by nearly all investigators. But deciding in detail in specific cases just what is "appropriate" is a complex and often ambiguous problem and a fertile source of methodological controversy. For example, what underlies many sharp divergences in interpretation of such "factual" issues as recent changes in incomes of black and white families is the extent to which conclusions deal with highly aggregated or finely partitioned data. Furthermore, mistaken conclusions and diagnoses, when they do occur, often are strongly rooted in ideological distortions, both those that encourage wishful thinking and those that block off or minimize a whole range of factors or contexts while bringing others into the focus of attention. Clearly, any claim to scholarly objectivity and inclusiveness or to scientific generality must rest upon a comprehensive examination of all important types of actual historical cases. This assertion is trite, but it is neither empty nor irrelevant. For example, it is possible to pay attention only to conflict and competition, not to accommodation and cooperation. One may closely examine only the "winners" in ethnic struggles and transitions, failing to analyze the responses of the losers. Such selectivity may be unavoidable and proper in a single study; it is disastrous in a field as a whole. The total spectrum must be analyzed (Williams, 1977); peaceful processes of accommodation are no less worthy of attention than civil turmoil.

Development of Empirical Generalizations

Part of the necessary workload of research in this field is to make continuing inventories and appraisals of changes in the position of various ethnic categories in the social structure. Since change or the lack of it is a matter of theoretical importance and often has political and ideological significance, such appraisals are subject to immediate, and often heated, criticism. The indicators of change are numerous, the conditions indexed are quite complex, and the data vary greatly in reliability, validity, and generality. Disagreements concerning findings, accordingly, are frequent and typically generate at least as much heat as light.

For all these reasons, assessments of change and stability need to be methodologically sophisticated and theoretically and empirically well grounded. Fortunately, the level of skill and awareness in the best of such studies continues to rise. A first area of work that illustrates cumulative research is represented by those studies of changes in the economic and political position of blacks in the 1960s to 1970s that are careful to disaggregate the data for subgroupings (Farley, 1977). Thus, it has been shown that, overall, the gains of the 1960s were not lost in the 1970s—contrary to many public claims. The studies that illustrate encouraging technical progress have analyzed sources of racial and ethnic differences in education, employment, and income (Wilson, 1978b; Hogan and Featherman, 1977; Bonacich, 1976; Stolzenberg, 1975a).

A second important area of progress is in research on desegregation. In the early phases of school desegregation, the impassioned political threats and claims and the collective violence that characterized reactions of many whites in the South, and elsewhere, misled many "pop" sociology commentators into believing that hardening resistance would be the outcome of increased pressure to desegregate. It is salutary to remember that the Gallup Opinion

Index (1976: 9) showed that the proportion of white Southern parents who objected to sending their children to a school where a few of the children were black was 61 percent in 1963—and 15 percent in 1976. Further evidence that direct involvement in compliance with the law leads to favorable attitudes rather than to hardened resistance continues to accumulate. Thus in Milwaukee, before-and-after studies show that parents with children in public schools became more accepting, whereas persons without children in school became less accepting, and those with children in parochial schools became the most resistant of all to desegregation (Jacobson, 1978).

In an analysis of 1,600 schools in 50 districts of southern SMSAs, Giles (1978) investigated the relationship between proportion of blacks enrolled and changes in the enrollment of whites, *in particular schools* as well as in districts taken as wholes. The study found that changes in white enrollments subsequent to desegregation by districts were "substantively trivial" in size and concluded that "white withdrawals are not an inevitable result of desegregation" (p. 854). Detailed analyses showed that no set of variables explained more than 10 percent of the variance in white enrollments. In sum: "Despite the consistency of these findings, only a small percentage of the variance in white enrollment at the school level was explained by the percent black enrollment" (p. 863).

Simplistic views of effects of school or residential desegregation upon the movement of white populations to suburbs should be decisively rejected on the basis of accumulated critical work and new analyses (Frey, 1979).

A third set of cumulative empirical studies deals with ethnic mobilization and collective action. When mobilization is so continuous and pervasive that nearly all political struggle is conceived of and actually organized in ethnic terms one has a plural—rather than a pluralistic—society. Thus, the restructuring of politics along ethnic lines has occurred in many postcolonial nations once the common opponent of the metropolitan power had been overthrown or ejected. Also, resurgent ethnic "nationalisms" have appeared in highly industrialized Western democracies: French Canadians in Quebec; Walloons and Flemings in Belgium; Scots and Welsh in Great Britain; Blacks, Chicanos, Native Americans, and others in the United States; even in Switzerland, in the continuing Jura dispute in Bern. A notable feature of nearly all cases has been the rising levels of affluence, education, and political potential of the mobilizing minorities. In nearly all cases, the agitation for ethnic mobilization has been led by a "cultural elite" that emphasizes an ethnic distinctiveness that would redound to the benefit of members of that elite should it become the basis of political authority or influence. In a newly bilingual society, for example, an elite from the subordinate linguistic group is likely to reap many advantages in education, government, and business (Pill, 1974).

The internal characteristics of an ethnic collectivity will influence the ways in which its members seek the rewards they perceive in the larger society of which the collectivity is a part. For example:

1. Other things not counteracting the effect, any decrease in individualized competition (for extragroup rewards) among the members of a disadvantaged stratum or ethnic segment will reduce distrust among members of the stratum or grouping and will increase the likelihood of in-group solidarity.

2. The same effects will result from any decrease in individualized aggression against persons and property within the stratum or segment—for example, a reduction in intragroup crime will increase the level of social trust and facilitate in-group identification and cooperation.

3. The greater the extent to which the rewards and deprivations of individuals within a disadvantaged social formation are, in fact, categorically assigned by nonmembers on the basis of membership, the more likely is a sense of common fate and of fraternal deprivation.

The greater the degree to which the conditions described in the preceding propositions are found, the more likely it will be that attempts of individual members to enhance their own position will become collectivity oriented rather than individual oriented—for example, the greater will be the emphasis on political rather than economic means. Accordingly, social policies that categorically discriminate against all members of a minority will have the effect in the long run of increasing the cohesion and enhancing the power orientation of the minority and, especially, of its leaders.

Political processes are always more nearly understandable when we can see them in relation to the main types of interest substrata in the society. In the United States, such "latent interest groupings" are numerous and highly diverse: occupations, regions, sections, religious bodies and communities, prestige classes, ethnic groupings, ideological movements, and so on. The overt struggles and conflicts of the society do not always occur along the same lines of cleavage, but change from one historical period to another. It is enough to recognize that: (1) *every* major distinctive social formation is a potential partisan: (2) wherever decisions are made, there influence will be brought to bear. Alignments based on ethnic solidarity wax and wane. The present circumstances are not permanent, although ethnicity will be one important basis of political processes for the foreseeable future.

A fourth set of noteworthy studies deals with collective conflicts. Some estimate of the extent of ethnic and racial conflict is needed to place the matter in appropriate perspective, relative to other forms of social conflict. The available data are quite imprecise, but they are sufficient to show that ethnic conflicts are of major importance.

> One estimate suggests that worldwide 20 to 30 percent of all domestic violence in 1961–65 was between ethnic groups, and another source calculates that the sum of fatalities in ethnic hostilities during the 1945–70 period exceeded 10 million (Hewitt, 1977: 151).

A few illustrative generalizations follow:

1. Several important kinds of collective violence are distributed over time in a pattern that is consistent with instigating or reinforcing and inhibiting events—specifically, awareness of successful models versus knowledge of defeat, condemnation, and punishment (Pitcher, Hamblin, and Miller, 1978).

2. Where highly structured conflicts do emerge, ethnic clusterings become real social units—that is, collectivities or "organizations" rather than mere social categories or aggregates. Only when there is enough structure to allow mobilization of resources can diffuse aspirations and discontents be transformed into collective grievances, claims, protests, and conflicts.

3. Collective violence between ethnic groupings—or derived from ethnic relations—is not randomly or capriciously distributed among national societies. There are consistent and marked differences between societies that experience high levels of such violence and societies that have less frequent and less severe ethnic violence. Taking nineteen societies that have stable, clear, and salient ethnic cleavages between a majority and one or more minorities, Hewitt (1977) finds that the violent societies show great economic and political inequality, large minority groupings that are growing relative to the majority, and marked political differences concerning the constitution of the state (e.g., separatism, union with a "parent" society). Low-violence societies have demographic stability and approximate economic parity among ethnic segments and the minorities are politically well represented or have substantial autonomy under federalism.

Can useful implications be drawn from the kinds of studies just reviewed? Studies of conflict resolution and managment, once very rare in sociology, now appear in increasing numbers. Considerable help in this area comes from history and political science. To take only one of many recent examples, Levine points out (1977: 62) that although Calhoun's doctrine of the concurrent majority is overly simple it does formulate a basic principle for managing conflicts of regionalized subcultures:

> In societies with intense and politicized subcultural cleavages, institutional ar-
> rangements which guarantee minority access to decision making and provide
> effective modes of minority self-protection facilitate the handling of emotion-
> ally and symbolically loaded subcultural issues (such as schools, language use,
> abolition or extension of slavery) in a technical, incremental, and essentially
> negotiable fashion.

Needed Developments in Theory and Research

When we attempt to think of what is most needed to improve the generation of reliable knowledge, it is difficult to develop prescriptions that are either new or surprising. Several years ago we said:

> Further systematic mapping of . . . variables is essential for cumulation of research findings in a form suitable for building theories. Many of the inconclusive and contradictory results of past research derive from lack of clear specification of the triad of (a) concepts, (b) indicators of the conceptualized variables, and (c) hypothesized relationships among the selected variables linear or curvilinear, additive or multiplicative, etc. . . . . A mishmash of unordered ecological, psychological, social, and cultural factors no longer can be allowed to pass muster as the starting point for research. (Williams, 1975a: 127)

All these points have been touched upon in the present review. A few additional examples may be useful.

Studies of differences between white and black individuals and families have tended to focus either upon (1) ascribed status and associated socialization or "investments" (human capital factors of education, job experience, mobility and the like), or (2) structural factors such as occupational competition vs. segregation, or differing industry and area labor markets. It would be strange indeed were not both sets of factors influential in determining the socioeconomic positions of individuals (Parcel, 1979). The task is to *specify* the relative magnitudes of effects and the actual processes involved.

We now have a clearly articulated theoretical issue in the controversies about the empirical weight to be attached to the *content of the culture* of an ethnic group as over against *structural constraints and opportunities* that are hypothesized to account for stability or change of that content (Yancey, Ericksen, and Juliani, 1977; Williams, 1974). The most important structural conditions maintaining ethnic distinctiveness are said to include (1) intergroup conflict, (2) institutionalized discrimination, (3) ecological concentration and stability, (4) concentration in distinctive occupations, and (5) dependence upon common institutions and services. Efforts to measure variations in ethnicity in relation to variations in such conditions can produce significant new knowledge. It is not beyond our reach to gain some answers to what Richard Lambert calls "the most fundamental questions of all. [That is:] Why are ethnic groups and the conflicts they engender so difficult to categorize and analyze, yet so durable and pervasive? Why has the peculiar mixture of blood, religion, language, and territory been so lasting and so potent a force in our own and others' history?" (1977: viii).

An essential first step is to see that all major collectivities and larger social systems have *multiple* lines of social cleavage and cohesion, for example, age, sex, kinship, occupation, class, religion, region or locality, and ethnicity. One should *never* assume that ethnicity operates alone. Along with age, sex, and kinship and local community, ethnic collectivities and relationships are primary ascriptive bases of social organization. Further, ethnicity is likely to be strongly confounded with occupation, class, and religious affiliation. Every analysis that seeks to appraise the "importance" of ethnic factors, therefore, must be multivariate, contextual, and systemic.

Controversies continue concerning the relative causal importance of "race" or "ethnic origin" versus social class (as a position in the structure of economic production). Thus, Stolzenberg (1975a) estimates that incomes of blacks in nearly one-half of specific occupational categories represent rates of return to education higher than for whites—in seeming contradiction to several prior studies. Subsequently, Wright (1978), using national survey data, concludes that returns to education are essentially similar for whites and blacks within class positions (except for managerial positions); the study infers that "much of the commonly observed racial differences in returns to education is a consequence of the distribution of racial groups into class categories" (p. 1368). The complex and often "contradictory" effects of the interplay between racial/ethnic divisions and class/occupational cleavages are apparent.

Once again, detailed disaggregation of the data—as well as critical attention to the specific indicators and methods of analysis—is indispensable for valid appraisals.

Neither the concept of external nor of internal colonialism fits precisely the large-scale development of international migrant worker populations, now estimated to number 20 to 30 million in Western Europe alone. Such workers are recruited through government agreement, concentrated in low-income jobs and industries, subjected to strict legal control, and socially ostracized and discriminated against. This "proletariat on loan" can be called in when needed, sent back when not; the ghettos are located abroad, and the host society takes little or no responsibility for the workers in times of economic adversity (Bernard, 1978: 298–99). Cultural marginality and social disruption are apparently frequent. Marked differences in policies are found among the receiving nations, resulting in sharp divergencies in degree of stability and of cultural assimilation.

The tendency to deal in dichotomies of explanatory factors—class versus race, status versus power, primordial versus reactive ethnicity—is tempting, often productive of useful hypotheses and theories—and almost always ultimately erroneous or misleading. The fatal flaw emerges when each half of the pair is treated as if it were an exclusive or at least an overwhelmingly dominant explanation. Thus, the argument over whether Celtic sectionalism in Great Britain is due to class affinity (developmental) or status affinity (reactive ethnicity) is partly resolved by the finding that political behavior responds strongly to both factors (Ragin, 1977: 438).

There is every reason to expect sound contributions to systematic knowledge from policy-oriented research *if* it is designed to link into a dynamic social system model (Pettigrew, 1979). Thus, in analyses of political conflict management there is a crucial need for theory and research to join in specifying "what institutional arrangements and political practices at what stage of cleavage politicization are most effective in managing conflicts involving regional subcultures. Continued theoretical efforts combined with systematic empirical analysis of cases of conflict regulation success and failure are needed before truly adequate models are generated'' (Levine, 1977: 72).

One conceivable line of development that has many attractions would be to make the field of ''race and ethnic relations'' disappear—by analyzing all its structural units and relations into generic processes, for example, those common to all collectivities. Names, dates, and particular places would become irrelevant. This elegant scientific aspiration is unlikely to be realized in any future short enough to be of real interest to us. We are likely to retain many relatively concrete historical units and relationships and objects of study, although increasingly ethnic structures will be treated in combination with other structural units—for example, social classes.

Promising Directions for Further Work

Some of the dicta one feels impelled to state seem redundant, since they simply represent general sociological platitudes applied to the special area of ethnic studies. *Item 1:* All social relationships are (at the least) two-sided; hence, study of any relationship between two groupings should analyze the behavior toward, and influence on, each by the other, including the basic contingencies always generated by interaction. *Item 2:* Every single relationship between two social units is affected by relationships to other units; all relationships are embedded in networks. Hence, not just majority–minority relations but interminority relations must be analyzed. *Item 3:* All large collectivities and social categories are internally differentiated and heterogeneous; hence, no ethnic grouping should be treated as if it were a monolithic entity. *Item 4:* Ethnic categories and groupings often have boundaries that are vague or ambiguous or both and that change, sometimes quite rapidly, over time and from one situation to another.

It would seem evident that a suitable remedy for the artificial separation of ''macro'' and ''micro'' problems is the use of ''contextual models which retain the individual [or small group] as the unit of analysis while incorporating independent variables from both the individual and the ecological levels of analysis'' (Parcel, 1979: 264). Such models permit control of one set of variables while analyzing correlates or effects of the other.

As our examples suggest, we are recommending the explicit analysis of multivariate relationships within societies (and within other collectivities) that are specified as dynamic systems. This means that complex structural features will be identified, that attention will be given to both order and disorder, that both consensus and dissensus and conflict and harmony will be studied.

Because of the importance and salience of competition and conflict in interethnic relations, the study of racial and ethnic relations often must draw upon and contribute to more general analyses and theories concerning the sources and consequences of these fundamental social processes. We do find that some theory-building concerning ethnic relations draws upon game theory and interest-group concepts to develop rational–instrumental models; other models focus attention upon values, beliefs, and ideologies that are embedded in persisting collectivities and social relationships. Whether "interests" or "values" are treated as more central cross-cuts an "individual actor/collectivity" dichotomy. A third line of distinction appears between models that infer consequences directly from social structures and those that postulate a problematic intervening set of processes of collective awareness, mobilization, and organized action. A fourth component results from looking for explanatory variables in aggregated "tensions," that is, individual psychological states and processes (frustration, deprivation, envy, outrage) *versus* focusing upon power struggles, in which mass attitudes are seen as largely irrelevant.

The overlapping and crisscrossing of these four sets of distinctions is adequate to generate many complex and often ambiguous interpretations.

An "adequate" set of theoretical formulations will surely have to incorporate all of the perspectives just listed. The typical route by which the perspectives have developed is that after Model A has been presented, critics advance Model B as a contender to destroy Model A. Eventually, however, one of two things happens: either both views are incorporated in another formulation, Model C, *or* persisting "schools" engage in protracted controversy over the merits of their respective choices. If interest is maintained in explaining phenomena at the original level of complexity and organization, more and more concepts—and, hence, variables and their interrelationships—will have to be added to the total scheme in successive revisions. Presumably, there is no obvious or definitive point at which the process will stop.

Many discussions in this field thus bemoan the sorry state of "theory" or imply that there is no theory worthy of the name. The word "theory," of course, can be made to mean whatever we wish it to mean in any particular instance. But by the "customary and normal" understandings of what constitutes "theory" in contemporary sociology, the lamentations are misplaced and exaggerated. One should look for theory where theory-like formulations are being attempted, not in avowedly descriptive accounts, factual inventories, policy appraisals, ideological controversies, and other nontheoretical statements. When one does look for theoretical attempts, they are to be found. For example, E. K. Francis (1976) has presented a framework for analyzing, not "ethnicity," but ethnic *aspects* of social behavior by specifying some 59 central definitions that are used in over one hundred partially ordered, empirically based propositions. Such a comprehensive work paradoxically invites the charge that it is incomplete. Quite so, and necessarily. But there is no doubt that the work does represent the systematic building of theory.

In conclusion, let us for the sake of emphasis cite our summary appraisal of the state of the field in 1975—for the judgments then made have added urgency today.

The most effective attempts to explain ethnic relations have been both multivariate and systematically theoretical. . . .

Much of the contribution of past and current research has been the factual confrontations and logical criticisms that have debunked myths and stereotypes, refuted erroneous assumptions, and challenged superficial explanations. This critical activity is indispensable and must continue. But, in addition, we believe the time has come for greater pressure on work in this field to pose explanatory problems and to search for sufficient as well as necessary conditions. . . .

Full hospitality is recommended for data, methods, and concepts from other behavioral and social sciences. "Race and ethnic relations" are not respectful of academic boundaries. Of course, there is a distinctive sociological core, and within it emphasis rightly will remain on variables suggested by concepts of norms, institutions, power, and authority, statuses, social networks, social structures, and the like. The power of such variables in explaining large-scale social movements and conflicts of our time has never been clearer—thanks to some of the work here reviewed (Williams, 1975a).

21

Conceptual Problems in the Field
of Collective Behavior

Gary T. Marx

Two DECADES AGO, Herbert Blumer (1957: 151) wrote that the field of collective behavior "remains without a unifying conceptual scheme." He commented that he saw "not many signs of even tentative advances in this direction." This is even truer today with the weakening of the once dominant crisis-leads-to-collective behavior model and the diverse research that has grown out of the last decade's events.

A major impediment to a better understanding of collective behavior-social movement phenomena remains the failure adequately to define the nature of the field. There is little agreement about how (and even if) collective behavior differs from noncollective behavior. There is a similar lack of agreement about how major types of collective behavior differ from each other. The external and internal boundaries of the field are not clearly enough defined. Many of the definitions we have are either too broad or too narrow. This has a number of negative consequences:

- a less cumulative research tradition than is the case for many areas of sociology;
- conceptual categories and explanations which are not sufficiently inclusive of the range of collective behavior phenomena;
- conceptual categories and explanations which are too inclusive, lumping together phenomena best kept distinct;
- lack of attention to elements that may be shared by different types of collective behavior (such as crowds and social movements) relative to "traditional behavior" or "noncollective behavior" and which justify treating the former within the same area of inquiry;

258

- failure to study systematically the varied relationships that can exist between different types of collective behavior;
- undue attention to the origins and consequences of collective behavior at the expense of attention to the dynamics and to the collective behavior "episode" as an element worthy of analysis in its own right;
- lack of research on the short-term and diffuse elements of collective behavior and lack of attention to important psychological questions and processes studied by the earliest theorists of collective behavior and later students responding to European totalitarianism;
- the failure to develop paradigms capable of ordering the diversity of phenomena and relationships offered by the field;
- failure to note systematically how the field of collective behavior is differentiated from and yet related to areas of inquiry such as social change, organization, deviance, and political sociology.

In this chapter I wish to document these problems by review and critique of major conceptualization efforts. I will then suggest a conceptualization of the field which I think avoids many of the current problems and which contains the pieces that new paradigms should order.

If we take as our initial standard whether collective behavior and social movements are first differentiated from noncollective behavior and then whether systematic differentiation is made among types of collective behavior, we can identify three common conceptualization errors.

Type I errors involve the failure to differentiate collective behavior and social movements from traditional behavior. The field is made to disappear by arguing that there is nothing unique to it. *Type II errors involve only the failure to differentiate social movements from traditional behavior.* Social movements are made a part of the study of organizational or political behavior and split off from collective behavior. *Type III errors involve the failure to differentiate social movements and collective behavior from each other,* although both are differentiated from conventional behavior. But avoiding these errors does not insure adequate conceptualization. I will first illustrate the three common conceptualization errors. I will then critique some attempts that differentiate collective behavior and social movements from each other, but still leave something to be desired with respect to criteria such as systematic derivation, comprehensiveness, specificity, mutual exclusivity, and common sense (including keeping elements of classification distinct from explanation).

The Denial of Difference: Type I Errors

Among recent efforts to deny differences between collective and conventional behavior (type I errors) is the work of McPhail (1978) and Couch (1968, 1970). Rather than seeking to define a field and its internal boundaries, they have worked in the opposite direction denying that there is anything unique here with respect to either conceptualization or explanation. Taken to an extreme, this turns Ralph Turner's (1964: 384) speculation that research may ultimately suggest "no special set of principles is required to deal with this subject matter" into a statement of fact.

McPhail (1978: 5) offers a sweeping critique and a definition which "is a more precise step in the direction of merging collective and social organization behavior." He writes approvingly of Park's definition of all of sociology as the science of collective behavior.

McPhail attacks previous theorists for their general failure to provide a specification of what they are attempting to explain. Many definitions are seen to be negative, telling us what collective behavior is not (structured or organized behavior) rather than what it is. McPhail overcomes this problem, but at a cost of a highly general and inclusive definition which creates other problems.

In the most general terms, collective behavior refers "to what human beings are doing with and in relation to one another" (McPhail, 1978: 4–5). Collective behavior is then practically synonymous with interaction in the proximity of another person or persons. Thus, he has the opposite problem of some whom he criticizes. McPhail does not go far enough in telling us what collective behavior isn't. We are thus not in a position to analyze variation in the historical phenomena that have so long stimulated interest in this area. McPhail makes an important contribution in clearly defining and developing a methodology for the systematic study of some generally unstudied aspects of proximate group behavior. But I think little is gained by going in the face of well established convention in calling this "collective behavior," particularly when no new concepts are offered to deal with the themes of consistent interest to researchers over a sixty-year period.

The classification and understanding of collective behavior cannot be divorced from prior social structure and culture, or from its subsequent consequences. The meaning of this behavior to actors and others depends on its context.

A softer version that has contributed to the "no difference perspective" is Couch's (1968) article on the crowd, which is given the more general title "Collective Behavior: An Examination of Some Stereotypes."[1] Whatever his intent, Couch's article has contributed to efforts to deny or minimize differences between collective and noncollective behavior. In attempting to refute popular images of the crowd Couch argues that collective behavior is not pathological and bizarre (or at least no more so than noncollective behavior). But he does not tell us what collective behavior is.[2] In a later paper Couch (1970: 458) argues that "there are no activities, relationships or beliefs

---

[1] In a similar vein, see Currie and Skolnick (1970).

[2] There is an empirical and conceptual question here. My concern in this chapter is primarily with the latter. However, it would be useful to treat as hypotheses at least some of the beliefs about crowds that Couch identifies. These could profit from systematic empirical inquiry contrasting the extent of their presence in crowds and other collectivities.

unique to those situations commonly pointed to as instances of collective behavior.''

To the extent that the ''nondifference'' approach leads to demystifying phenomena undeservedly seen as exotic, more unified conceptual and explanatory approaches across sociology's subject matter, and efforts to discover through empirical inquiry commonalities among phenomena previously seen as separate, it is a positive development. To the extent that the nondifference approach leads to denying that the field treats phenomena that are different in at least some ways and which are not adequately or explicitly dealt with elsewhere, and refuses to treat the possibility of modal differences (or even nondifferences) between collective and noncollective behavior as hypotheses to be tested, then it is negative.[3]

Social Movements Yes, Collective Behavior No: Type II Errors

A second classification error can be seen on the part of those theorists who argue (in some cases implicitly) that the distinction between elementary collective behavior and social movements is so great as to warrant their being separate fields. The study of social movements is to merge with the study of organizations and political sociology, while collective behavior remains the province of the exotic, residual, and psychological.

Traugott (1978: 49), for example, argues that the study of social movements should be broken off from the psychological contamination of collective behavior, with which it has ''too long been locked in superficial and sterile association.'' He argues that they should be separated because social movements possess social solidarity and an anti-institutional orientation which collective behavior is said to lack. The field of social movements should ''concentrate its efforts upon social change accomplished by solidarity groups outside institutional channels'' (Traugott, 1978: 46).

It is certainly important to study such value- or power-oriented movements even if (short of armed revolution) most social change by social movements (when present) involves a mixture of institutional and noninstitutional channels. Yet beyond clouding the issue of actors' intentions as revealed in ideology versus the observed consequences, and limitations (to be noted) on social change as the defining criteria, I question whether his criteria empirically differentiate social movements from collective behavior. His distinction between social movements as anti-institutional and collective behavior as noninstitutional points up an important *conflict–oppositional* dimension of the phenomena. Yet this is not a dimension that can very clearly separate social movements from collective behavior. For example, social movements that seek to change persons rather than the social order (such as

---

[3] See also the critiques by Pfautz (1975), Zurcher (1979), and Aguirre and Quarantelli (1979).

many religious cults) or that seek to bolster and renew the existing society (such as moral rearmament) can hardly be said to be anti-institutional. In the same way, some short-lived collective behavior phenomena such as rumors, looting, or being unable to go to work because of a mysterious ailment, can be very anti-institutional in either intent or outcome.

McCarthy and Zald (1979), while not systematically differentiating social movements from collective behavior, seek to move the former away from social psychology and back into the mainstream of political sociology.

In focusing on resources available to create social movement actions they downplay attention to what was the heart of traditional collective behavior—mass responses (the demand side). Like the modern corporations studied by Galbraith (1968), skilled social movement organizations are thought to be in a position to create demand (grievances). McCarthy and Zald (1973: 523) hypothesize that "the definition of grievances will expand to meet the funds and support personnel available."

This work is important in showing how sociological approaches to conventional behavior can also help us to understand social movements. Recent social changes have contributed to the bureaucratization of social discontent and the increased prevalence of professional social movements. Their work has helped crystallize and structure much recent research and has weakened the strain-leads-to-collective-behavior model.[4]

Yet this emphasis can be taken too far. In focusing on social movements as organizations, resources, and rationality, attention to the special meaning, commitment, excitement, emergence, and fluidity that can surround a social movement (as other collective behavior phenomena) is likely dropped. It calls attention to structure rather than dynamics and environment rather than internal processes. Working for the NAACP is not strictly equivalent to working for General Motors. Nor is selling Krishna quite the same as selling Fuller brushes. There are likely to be differences in degree of routinization and ritualization and different bases of legitimacy. Social movements publicly present a component of disinterested moral superiority which justifies their claims and introduces contingencies on action.

Social movement participants can too easily be seen as only objects to be manipulated, or as wooden cost-benefit calculators, rather than as actors with a degree of autonomy responding to an environment often perceived as stressful. The market or demand for social movement actions must receive significant attention. It can generate a supply of social movement actions as well as the reverse.[5]

---

[4] Though it is well to note that it represents a difference in emphasis rather than a complete break with the past. A close reading of Turner and Killian, Smelser, and the Langs certainly shows some attention to resource mobilization variables and collective behavior as related to broader political and economic aspects of society.

[5] Some attention is given to this issue in McCarthy and Zald (1977). The question is one of relative emphasis.

How much, for example, could resource mobilization and cost-benefit analysis tell us about the actions of the Hungarian youth who threw rocks at Russian tanks during the Hungarian uprising or some of the spontaneous refusals to accept segregation that characterized parts of the early civil rights movement. I am also reminded of Berkeley FSM leader Mario Savio's "there is some shit we will not eat" speech. This was given to a large gathering of angry students that developed spontaneously in response to some particularly high-handed actions by the university administration. There is also an element of truth in the mid-1960s cartoon that showed a civil rights leader running behind a crowd of blacks and saying, "There go my people, I must lead them."

A strongly felt need may generate resources, as well as collective behavior. Having no tax-exempt foundations to turn to, Stalin robbed banks. A former IRA leader reports raising $500,000 over a several-year period through bank and hotel robberies, and that robberies were a major source of their money (*Boston Globe,* September 3, 1979). Conversely, abundant resources in the hands of entrepreneurs, whether on the part of Edsel or the Moon movement, is no guarantee of success when mass support is sought.

There are at least three reasons why social movements and collective behavior should remain within the same general field. First, the two are often intertwined in such a way that to understand adequately the social movement one must analyze mass responses and particular episodes. Indeed, a major part of some social movements is a series of collective behavior incidents. A number of common patterns of relation can be identified (e.g., crowd behavior eventually leading to a more organized social movement; the social movement's strategic use of crowds; a division of labor between social movement organizations such as the legalistic NAACP and direct action SCLC; and crowds arising [internally or externally] in opposition to the social movement). Masses and publics can also have major implications for a social movement. Beyond questions of support or opposition, one must also look to them to understand the diffuse effects of a social movement and what Gusfield (1968) refers to as the "undirected" phase of a movement. There is a need to contrast systematically movements based on the extent and form of their interrelations with other types of collective behavior.

Second, even if they are not intertwined, they may share (at least to a greater extent than is the case with traditional behavior) some similar characteristics with respect to the state of the social systems in which they appear, their organization, and psychological, cultural, and social processes.

Finally, the behaviors as such may also be conceptualized in a way that shows their analytical similarity, although the field has thus far failed to do this adequately. The similarity involves standing outside of conventional culture, though, as will be noted, in different ways. The field should not define away the stronger explanations which can emerge from including a wider range of phenomena.

Not Adequately Separating Social Movements from Collective Behavior: Type III Errors

Those arguing that social movements should be separated from the study of collective behavior generally start by criticizing conceptual efforts that lump them together. In so doing they identify what we can call type III errors. Herbert Blumer (1951) and his students, such as Turner and Killian (1972) and the Langs (1961), offer criteria for differentiating collective from noncollective behavior, but they tend to slide over (or at least do not give adequate systematic analytic attention to) the differentiating factors noted by McCarthy and Zald (1973) and Traugott (1978). Social movements and the other forms of collective behavior share some elements even while they may *differ* in important ways. Conceptualizing the field to deny either possibility restricts understanding. A conceptualization is needed which allows for both similarities and differences. Let us first consider Blumer's overall definition and then his subtypes.

For Blumer (1957: 130), collective behavior is beyond the area of "cultural prescription" and comes into existence and "develops along lines that are not laid out by preestablished social definitions." It involves organization and activity "formed or forged to meet undefined or unstructured situations." Whether we look at crowds, public opinion, fashion, shifts in popular interest in music, literature, entertainment, or the rise of a social movement, "the characteristic behavior of each such instance is not an expression of a pre-established prescription but is produced out of a forging process of inter-action."

Blumer's definition involves the coming together of specific values of two variables: (1) a group variable of an ecological nature—groups of large size;[6] and (2) a type of behavior that is outside cultural prescriptions "produced out of a forging process of interaction."

Having defined collective behavior, Blumer (1951) offers additional internal definitions. A social movement is a collective effort to establish a new life. He specifies four basic elementary forms of collective behavior: the acting crowd, expressive crowd, mass, and public

There are few, if any, other fields of sociology where a field definition has had such staying power. Blumer was instrumental in laying out the field and training of most of its major students for several decades. (See papers in his honor in T. Shibutani [1970].) He identified elements of which contemporary students must find a way to take account. His essay is rightfully a classic. Yet with the hindsight of almost forty years of research and history to draw on, a number of limitations of Blumer's pioneering effort can be noted.

[6] As Smelser (1962) notes, this actually bootlegs along variables involving feelings, communication, interaction, and forms of mobilization.

I will restrict my comments to the adequacy of his field definition rather than to his more frequently attacked causal mechanisms of circular reaction and contagion.

Blumer's definition of collective behavior as something limited to large groups rules out much activity that otherwise satisfies his other criteria of behavior outside of cultural prescriptions. Much collective behavior occurs in small groups. Indeed, given what we know about the importance of networks and interpersonal influence, the small group is a crucial place to look. For some purposes a distinction between large and small groups is worth making. However this should be as a variable whose consequences are to be explored, rather than as an initial criterion for classification. The latter results in excluding a vast amount of data.

For Blumer (1957: 130), collective behavior is partly defined in terms of what is thought to cause it. While not explicitly a part of his formal definition, the element of behavior "formed or forged to meet undefined or unstructured situations," in the context of the article, clearly enters as a definitional element. There is a latent causal model here. Here two elements (origins and the nature of the behavior) that must be kept empirically and analytically distinct are collapsed together. Questions of origin and motivation are important. However, the behavior to be explained cannot be defined in terms of what is thought to cause it.

The subtypes of collective behavior Blumer identifies are initially plausible and readily understandable because they stay so close to everyday language. Yet they do not lend themselves well to being operationally defined or to systematic inquiry. Nor are the interrelations among them specified. They are not very logically derived or analytically distinct.

Following Blumer, Turner and Killian (1972: 5) differentiate collective from noncollective behavior "according to the social norms that govern them." The groups wherein collective behavior occurs "are not guided in a straightforward fashion by the culture of the society." They lack defined procedures for selecting and identifying members and their "shared objective" is not defined in advance or arrived at by formal procedure. Popular language concepts such as crowds, fads, public and social movements are used to differentiate the field internally. "The same principles underlie the development of the various forms of collective behavior, and the same elementary processes are involved in all forms" (Turner and Killian, 1972: 101). While the search for what is shared by the various forms of collective behavior is important, so too is treatment of systematic difference. Emphasis on the absence of previously defined procedures and goals does not seem appropriate for the more enduring forms.

In a related fashion, the Langs (1961: 3–4) define collective dynamics as "transitory social phenomena." Such phenomena are "in a constant state of flux." They are "spontaneous and unstructured inasmuch as they are not organized and are not reducible to social structure." The Langs indicate that behavior having the characteristics of organization are to be excluded from their book, yet they end it with several chapters on social movements.

Not by Differentiation Alone: Other Conceptual Problems

Let us take Smelser and Weller and Quarantelli as examples of analysts who do attempt to separate collective from noncollective behavior and make analytical differentiations among the former.

Smelser (1963: 8–9) seeks to avoid certain of the problems faced by Blumer, while he still draws on some of Blumer's basic ideas. He extends Blumer's social movements as social change definition to all forms of collective behavior. The central definitional element is located in behavior which is mobilized on the "basis of a belief which redefines [changes] social action." The belief must be a generalized belief with special properties. Nor will any behavior growing out of a generalized belief about the need for change qualify as collective behavior. Smelser argues that the behavior must be noninstitutionalized and "to the degree to which it becomes institutionalized, it loses its distinctive (collective behavior) character." He follows Blumer's distinction between collective and culturally prescribed behavior in arguing that it is behavior "formed or forged to meet undefined or unstructured situations."

However, Smelser goes beyond Blumer in offering a more logical set of criteria for defining subtypes of collective behavior: these criteria, in turn, are related to his general definition of collective behavior. Applying Parsons' general delineation of the components of social action to differentiate among types of collective behavior on the basis of the levels at which change is sought yields five types: value- and norm-oriented social movements, hostile outbursts, crazes, and panics. His definition has the further advantage of being drawn from a general set of concepts that can also be applied to noncollective behavior.

Smelser's more systematic approach was a welcome addition to a loosely defined field. Yet he shares certain definitional problems with Blumer and also presents some new ones.

His definition is too restrictive in several ways. He combines elements that ought to be kept separate or used to form a typology. In requiring *both* a generalized belief and noninstitutionalized behavior, we are logically forced to *exclude* phenomena that most analysts would see as collective behavior. For example, (1) noninstitutionalized behavior (such as riotous behavior in victory or when social control is weakened) where a generalized belief is not present, and (2) situations where a generalized belief is present and where the behavior is institutionalized (e.g., groups such as the NAACP, whose major tactics are using the courts and lobbying, or the militant but law-abiding Socialist Workers' Party). It might be argued that these social movements qualify as collective behavior because the goals they seek are not institutionalized. Smelser is ambiguous here. A distinction between just what it is that is noninstitutionalized—means used or the future goals sought, or both—is needed.

This is related to the problem Blumer (1957: 130) faces in defining collective behavior as that which is "formed or forged to meet undefined or unstructured situations" and "not laid out by pre-established social definitions." Strict application of these criteria would require us to reject as collective behavior much social movement activity guided by competing (rather than new) social definitions. Much change-seeking behavior is thoroughly rooted in protest traditions and may be in response to situations that are all too clearly defined and structured. Further, a movement's origins, as the resource mobilization perspective notes, may be from external sources not experiencing the strains or problematic situations the movement seeks to redress.

There can be little disagreement over the frequent importance of the elements Smelser identifies. However, whether, when, and which ones are "determinants" (rather than being unnecessary) or themselves determined by collective behavior is a question for research. A generalized belief or strain may result from, as well as be a cause of, collective behavior. To the extent that we focus only on cases where a generalized belief is initially present, we are prevented from exploring alternative causal relations among these elements.

The notion of social change is important to the definitions of both Blumer and Smelser. Though not necessarily intended, this often leads to ignoring the role of collective behavior in blocking change through backlash, countermovements, and proregime collective behavior activities. But beyond this, much collective behavior does not in-and-of-itself represent social change or resistance to it, as the term is generally understood. For example, episodes of the June Bug (Kerckhoff and Back, 1968), windshield pitting (Medalia and Larsen, 1958), Madonna (Tumin and Feldman, 1955), or flying saucer sightings and phantom anesthetists (Johnson, 1945) represent things that happen to people and do not directly involve "social change," as the term is conventionally used in sociology. A broader definition is needed which can encompass such phenomena.

I think the most successful conceptualization thus far is that of Weller and Quarantelli (1973). They offer a broader view of the field that goes beyond popular language categories by overlaying a variable that relates to groups (whether the collectivity involved consists of enduring or emergent social relationships) onto the variable traditionally used to define collective behavior as such—whether the norms guiding behavior are institutionalized (enduring or emergent). The central variable is *emergence* of either new norms or new social relationships. This specification is important, and I will draw from it later in the chapter in suggesting six areas that I think should constitute the field.

However, I think there are drawbacks in using this typology to define the field, beyond the issues around institutionalization-emergence as the only behavioral criteria. The typology mixes elements of structure and behavior and classification and explanation. These elements are initially best kept separate (but kept). For example, they use a variable that describes group structure or type of collectivity (enduring or emergent social relations) as if it were a variable that also describes behavior.[7] The study of newly emerged groups engaged in *institutionalized activities* ought to be a part of this field, but their activities, strictly speaking, are not examples of collective *behavior*. In addition, combining variables of structure and behavior in a classification scheme may take attention away from examining causal relations between them. For example, enduring or emergent social relations are likely to condition the type of norms that are present. Also, while the social aspects they note are crucial, there are other important social, as well as psychological, dimensions.

Six Major Interest Areas of the Field of Collective Behavior

The most common response to the field's conceptual problems is simply to study things that are interesting without worrying about where they fit within some broader framework. Much research in this tradition emerges in an inductive and reactive manner in response to behavior seen by the analyst to be bizarre, curious, threatening, or exemplary. However, to the extent that sociology aspires to be a science and to develop cumulative knowledge rather than being only a humanistic undertaking, precise definitions and deductively guided research are necessary. If current field definitions are lacking how should the field be conceptualized? I think the field needs to be conceptualized more broadly and that it currently suffers from being defined primarily by reference to collective behavior as a unique type of behavior. My major concern is not to offer a more comprehensive definition of what collective behavior as a type of behavior is (though I will be unable to resist the temptation). Instead, it is to suggest that the field should consist of six subareas. These emerge partly out of analytical considerations and partly out of taking what it is that people who identify with the field actually study (regardless of their formal definition of collective behavior).

We must distinguish between the actions illogically called "collective

---

[7] For example, they note (1973: 676), "Figure 1 represents three types of collectivities that contrast with those engaged in institutional behavior." Yet, according to their typology, one of these (the upper left quadrant) is defined as involving institutionalized behavior. Their preliminary discussion indicates awareness of the collectivity–behavior distinction as they ask, "What are the social properties of the collectivities that engage in collective behavior?" (p. 669). Yet they then proceed to define collective behavior by the presence of one such collectivity.

behavior'' because of academic tradition, and the area or field of inquiry unfortunately also called collective behavior which involves much more than just the study of this type of behavior. In spite of its name, the field has had a strong interest in other areas that do not involve a focus on particular behavior as such. For some scholars, collective behavior has always been merely a vehicle for studying other phenomena such as social breakdown, types of interaction, symbolization, rumor, and social change. The greater integration of collective and noncollective behavior approaches and the great weakening of the field's dominant paradigm in recent decades has meant an uncoupling of elements previously treated as central parts of collective behavior as behavior.

We can identify six salient subareas of the field, only one of which involves the direct study of a type of behavior meeting the criteria of "collective behavior." How and the extent to which the other five areas relate to what sociologists have traditionally studied as collective (and noncollective) behavior is an important research question. But it cannot be decided a priori, nor is this the field's only question.

The six areas involve:

1. An interest in social systems which are in a pronounced state of breakdown, strain, malintegration, crisis, or disruption. This can be seen on a continuum from a well integrated social system with culture and resources adequate to goal attainment to a poorly integrated social system.[8]

2. An interest in a particular type of *group structure* which is either relatively undifferentiated *or* newly emerged (or both). These can be seen on continua from formally organized and/or well established groups with a complex division of labor and role specialization where it is known who belongs and who doesn't and who will play what roles to their opposites such as publics, masses, and some assemblies and new groups.

3. An interest in the cultural processes involved in the development and communication of collective definitions. This includes collective images, symbolization, ideology, and rumor. The mass and the public are central here but this area applies to other types of group structure as well.

4. An interest in a particular type of social influence and interaction which in Harold Pfautz' (1975) words is "direct, immediate, visual and thus highly involving . . . rather than indirect, mediate, conceptualized and thus relatively dissociating."

5. An interest in psychology states collectively experienced by individuals such as panic, hysteria, hypnotic states, visions, extreme suggestibility, and heightened emotion. This needs refinement and is clearly of a different level than the others. While it is fashionable to argue for the purity of a sociological approach uncontaminated by anything that hints of psychology, this area

---

[8] For the present, I wish to ignore the central and unresolved issue of how such "objective" states relate to perceptions of crisis, strain, and breakdown.

perhaps more than almost any other in sociology requires trying to integrate the social and the psychological. There is much for sociologists as sociologists to study here, given the collective character of these individual responses.

6. An interest in collective behavior as such.[9] The latter can be defined as group behavior outside of, or in a special relationship to, traditional culture in one or more of the following ways:

a. behavior not specifically defined in the traditional culture such as much fad behavior or innovative behavior in disasters. This ought to be seen on a continuum from behavior in situations where the culture offers almost no guidelines to situations that are highly structured and determined by culture. At the midpoint, showing elements of both collective and conventional behavior, are contexts that are culturally defined to have a high degree of indeterminacy and uncertainty with respect to development and specific outcome, such as contests. Contrast, for example, the relatively clear specifications about who will wear the crown in England with the use of an election for choosing rulers.

b. behavior defined in the culture but which is prohibited (e.g., looting during a blackout) or which has lost its cultural supports (e.g., collective defenses such as those studied by Wilsnack [1979]).

c. behavior directed toward institutionalizing alternative forms of action (irrespective or whether or not conventional means are used and how new the goals sought are to the culture). The study of social movements and responses to them is placed in this latter subcategory.

Past definitions (when not seeing collective behavior in terms of what is thought to cause it, a type of group structure, or the use of noninstitutionalized means) have used either the absence of traditional cultural patterns or change-seeking orientations. Both are needed. In addition, a component of culturally sanctioned indeterminacy must be added. I am aware that to extend the field of collective behavior to this residual area represents a considerable broadening and perhaps undue looseness. I do this hesitatingly and tentatively. But we need a way to deal with actions which are neither outside of culture nor seeking change. Aspects of political conventions (with their bandwagon effects) or sporting events (which are affected by team morale and home court audiences) are thus logically included.

At the most general level, collective behavior is group behavior which stands outside of, or in an indeterminate position with respect to, conventional culture and the institutionalized practices that flow from it—either

---

[9] This is the *behavior* as such that is commonly referred to as "collective behavior." This name is of course a distortion, as many observers have noted, since any group activity can logically be seen as "collective behavior," and as noted that field involves much more than the study of behavior as such. For reasons that might well be studied by students of collective behavior it is unlikely that this poorly named field will be renamed.

because the behavior is new to the culture, prohibited or not supported by it, seeks goals that are not institutionalized, or has a high degree of culturally sanctioned openness with respect to either (or both) specific means or outcomes.

The definition in (6) above may be a bit unwieldy and general. The first two elements include the point of view of the observer and the third that of the actor. Nevertheless, it offers one way to include the diverse phenomena studied by those identifying with the field. The definition differentiates collective behavior (including social movements) from traditional behavior. And it does offer one way of internally differentiating types of collective behavior (though [6c] may overlap with either [6a] or [6b]). But it does not do a very good job of this. Being able to label a type III error does not preclude one from committing it! There is a need to build in a number of crucial dimensions to classify types of collective behavior such as persistence in time, type of structure, and nature of the means used and goals sought.[10] The case remains to be made that popular language concepts such as crowds, fads, or panic are the best way to capture the field's internal variation.

I would prefer to work in a more deductive and then empirical fashion, listing and combining the major dimensions by which collective behavior may be contrasted and then seeing how and with what frequency the boxes get filled in. I think it is premature to foreclose on the basic types of collective behavior.

SOME IMPLICATIONS

I have suggested that this field should consist of six subareas with relatively autonomous status. It may seem heretical to suggest that the field of collective behavior should not have as its main (or only) concern the study of collective behavior as behavior. But if we look both at what it is that people who identify with the field or draw upon its traditions study and what they discover, the conclusion is hard to avoid.

I suggest a broadening of the field and an uncoupling of elements (particularly the system state, group structure, and behavior aspects) that until the later 1960s were thought by a majority of students to be empirically and temporally linked. There was a dominant paradigm in which I would include most of those in the Blumerian, as well as in the Parsonian, tradition. Simply stated, it assumed that breakdown or strain in the social system could lead to ideological critiques and certain types of group structures (publics, crowds) which might in turn give rise to more formally organized claims-making groups (social movements). These (crowds, social movements) were the group

[10] Another need is to indicate how the field overlaps with (and yet is distinct from) the study of social change, politics, deviance, sports, and social psychology. While the field shares elements with each of these it does not encompass them, or vice versa.

context within which activities not governed by traditional norms occur (collective behavior) and were a major mechanism of social change. Certain social and cultural processes (rumor, ideological short-circuiting) and psychological states (heightened suggestibility) were thought by many, though not by all observers, to be disproportionately present under such conditions.

This paradigm is no longer dominant. It has been shown to be a limiting case. While its elements may occur together in the sequence specified, there is increasing evidence of their independence and of alternative linkages. Thus while system breakdown, strain, or crisis may lead to collective behavior, they are neither necessary nor sufficient conditions. Much of the large-scale empirical work, such as that by Tilly and his students, has failed to find the expected relationships between strain and collective behavior. This is also true for much of the research on individual mobilization (McPhail, 1971; Heirich, 1977). Work on the professional social movement (McCarthy and Zald, 1973) and riots in victory (Marx, 1970) offers other examples of collective behavior without strain or crisis as they are usually defined. Nor is ideology a necessary condition. It may grow out of as well as precede collective behavior.

Beyond cases of collective behavior without crisis or ideology, we must take account of situations when causality goes in the opposite direction. For example, collective behavior such as a general strike, boycott, or civil disobedience may cause strain and breakdown instead of the reverse.[11] There may be another connection as well. To go back to an old idea from Durkheim, collective behavior and expressive actions may prevent breakdown and malintegration by offering a safety valve and a means of reaffirming shared standards. A major task for the field is to study alternative patterns that may exist among the six areas.

Furthermore, the elements specified may be joined in varying ways and degrees, but without the occurrence of "collective behavior" (as defined in area [6] above). Thus, in disaster situations we are likely to see systems in a state of crisis (area [1] and emergent groups area [2]), but we will not necessarily see widespread collective behavior. Quarantelli (1975) and other students of disaster have indicated the surprising degree to which behavior in disasters stays within conventional cultural bounds. But this is certainly not grounds for excluding disaster or crisis research from the field.

The study of assemblies (McPhail and Miller, 1973) is an important part of this field but only a small fraction of these result in collective behavior. Much more common, however, is the linkage with the social-psychological influence processes of area (4). For example, audience crying or laughing is culturally defined. Yet their release can be very much conditioned by the immediate presence and behavior of others. Contrast how much more one is

---

[11] Though if we adopt the longer term cyclical view inherent in the perspective of many classical theorists this becomes a dialectical chicken-and-egg problem. Thus, today's collective behavior solutions when successfully institutionalized over a long period of time can become dysfunctional. The resultant strains can lead to a new collective behavior aided solution, which in turn will eventually lead to new strains, and so on.

likely to laugh at a comedy when the theatre is full than when it is empty. The behavior seems to stem to a greater extent from heightened, immediate interpersonal influences than is the case of such behavior in more differentiated or established groups. Collective behavior processes are present in audience contexts, usually without collective behavior.

The specification of these six areas is partly a result of tradition. I think that they encompass most of what those identifying with the field study. Some of them are also residual, involving areas that do not have an adequate (or distinct) home elsewhere in sociology. Many of the specific topics, of course, reflect whatever happens to be newsworthy in a given time period. But I think there is a logic to defining the field this way that goes beyond tradition, the need to house homeless intellectual issues, or contemporary events. The tradition itself is not completely arbitrary. It has both logical and empirical sources.

As noted, collective behavior phenomena tend to stand in a special relation to conventional culture; and process and emergence, as well as institutionalization and routinization, are central cross-cutting analytical themes. They are often important elements in broader, and rather poorly understood, societal processes of breakdown and rejuvenation. Much institutionalized behavior becomes maladaptive over time. The collective behavior which may arise in response to it tends to become routinized and institutionalized.

Less abstractly, as the examples in the preceding paragraphs suggest, the six subareas are also likely to occur together empirically (though, to be sure, in varying combinations and rarely all together) to a greater extent than is the case of their opposites, or many other areas of sociology.

The reasons for this go much beyond any overlap in definition. Thus, in emergent and/or undifferentiated groups not bound by traditional standards, there is obviously more "room" for rumor, heightened interpersonal influence processes, and innovative behavior. As Le Bon and others have argued, the anonymity or sense of power of such groups in face-to-face contact may be conducive to acting contrary to conventional standards. Parallel or imitative behavior is made easier by the immediate presence of large numbers of others.

Chance elements play a more important role in affecting behavior. Restricted information and a sense of immediacy may give the behavior a cruder quality than is the case with groups that are more differentiated and have continuity. The pressure within social systems experiencing pronounced strain or breakdown can obviously help generate collective behavior (though the link between objective system states, perceptions, and collective behavior is one of the field's major unresolved questions).

I think the field's most pressing theoretical need is the development of new models beyond that of strain-collective behavior. The theoretical and research challenge ahead is to understand the variety of ways and conditions under which the six elements can relate.

While it is important to explore the extent of these links, the empirical phenomena of interest are nevertheless sufficiently complex and independent to warrant each area standing on its own.

In conclusion, I suggest that the field of collective behavior consist of studying the origins, dynamics, consequences, and interrelations of these six areas. Only one of these is an effort to understand collective behavior as such. I feel more confident of my critique of the field's internal and external definitional problems and of the need to uncouple the analytical elements from a single causal model, than I do with my suggested tentative solutions. Much conceptual work remains to be done with respect to elaboration of the subfields, relations with other areas of sociology, and development and documentation of the variety of causal paths that may be present. But, hopefully, several of the field's major problems have been documented and we have pointed toward one possible solution.

22

Theory of Collective Behavior: The Mainstream Revisited

Lewis M. Killian

IF A MODERN-DAY Gustave LeBon or Robert E. Park or even a Sigmund Freud were reviewing the events of the last ten or fifteen years he would exclaim with delight, "This is indeed the age of crowds!" LeBon would marvel at, but deplore, the spectacle of a crowd numbering in the millions crowding the streets of Teheran in a revolutionary assault on the Old Regime. Freud would lick his lips at the prospect of explaining the crowd leadership of "Daddy" Jim Jones. Park—and Herbert Blumer—would find in the battle—verbal, political, and physical—between prolife and prochoice forces examples of the three major types of collectivities: publics, social movements, and crowds.

The Collective Behavior Tradition

Of course these scholars could have and, indeed, did find collective behavior rampant at other times. So pervasive is what has been analyzed as collective behavior, by whatever definition, that it may well be reviewed as simply one facet of human social behavior, not as a discrete type. In short, the study of collective behavior should not be a field of sociology, but an approach which informs all of sociological analysis. From its earliest, immature formulations in the writings of Robert E. Park and Herbert Blumer, the concept of collective behavior has emphasized the continuity between conventional behavior and collective behavior and the recognition that they are both social in a truly human sense, not instinctive or individualistic.

PARK AND THE CROWD

Park made a point of distinguishing between the "animal" crowd and the human crowd and, in so doing, provided a warning of the individualistic bias that would come to characterize so many modern quantitative studies of collective behavior. He wrote:

> The organized crowd is controlled by a *common purpose* and acts to achieve, no matter how vaguely it is defined, a common end. The herd, on the other hand, has apparently no common purpose. Every sheep in the flock . . . behaves like every other. Action in a stampede, for example, is collective but it is not concerted. It is very difficult to understand how there can be concerted action in the herd or the flock unless it is on an instinctive basis. The crowd, however, responds to collective representations. (1921: 876)

BLUMER AND SOCIAL CHANGE

Herbert Blumer, in his first attempt to define the field, reflected another often neglected emphasis. Despite some current assertions that the founders of collective behavior were conservatives who were afraid of social change, Blumer clearly indicated that he regarded the field as being essentially the study of social change or the dynamic aspect of social life. Thus, in answer to his own question, "If practically all sociology is concerned with collective behavior, in what sense can one speak of the study of *collective behavior* as a separate division of sociology?", he replied:

> One may say that sociology in general is interested in studying the social order and its constituents (customs, rules, institutions, etc.) as they are; collective behavior is concerned in studying the ways by which the social order comes into existence, in the sense of the emergence and solidification of new forms of collective behavior. (1951: 168–169)

Caricatures and Critique of the Mainstream

If one takes seriously the efforts of these scholars to define the task of collective behavior, the stereotype of the "mainstream" or the "dominant tradition" in collective behavior which appeared during the 1960s is nothing less than a grotesque caricature. The clearest example of this uninformed and biased body of criticism is found in the flamboyant assertions of Currie and Skolnick:

Collective behavior theory has its roots in the anti-democratic theorists of nineteenth-century Europe, best represented by LeBon. In being transferred to American social science, the anti-democratic biases in "crowd" theory were modified but not abolished.

Perhaps the most fundamental of these biases is the implication that collective behavior is in some sense "irrational" behavior. This bias may be traced in LeBon's distaste for the mystical loss of individuality and civilized behavior in the "crowd," and reaffirmed in modern "riot control" manuals, as well as most social-scientific approaches. (1970: 35)

This polemical tour de force, which made collective behavior the scapegoat for all the conservative sins of sociology—even functionalism could be attacked through it since Neil Smelser is a Parsonian—fell on fertile soil. Gustave LeBon, elevated to the rank of god of collective behavior with Smelser as his prophet, was a devil-god to the self-styled radical sociologists. Little wonder that Weller and Quarantelli, in their 1971 survey of specialists in collective behavior, found that among classic writers in the field only LeBon received a majority listing, nearly twice as often as Park, leading them to conclude, "It is clear that many respondents were very hard pressed to name other important historical figures in the field of collective behavior once they went beyond LeBon" (1971: 60). This does not necessarily signify that most collective behavior theorists read only LeBon; it is more likely to reflect the fact that, giving a ritualistic kick to LeBon, the evil father, became the conventional way to start any discussion of collective behavior!

The politico-rationalistic critique of collective behavior did almost nothing to advance the state of theory, for it did not address itself to the actual mainstream of theory. The writings of Park and Blumer, and particularly the more recent work of the latter, were distorted to make them appear disciples of LeBon. LeBon, Everett Dean Martin, E. A. Ross, and Roger Brown, none of them central to the field and most of them not even sociologists, were treated as dominant theoretical influences. The work of Kurt and Gladys Lang, Joseph Gusfield, C. Wendell King, Tamotsu Shibutani, Rudolf Heberle, Richard LaPiere, Muzafer Sherif, S. E. Asch, Ralph Turner, Enrico Quarantelli, Joseph Zygmunt, and myself was ignored, misinterpreted, or cited only as adumbrating the "brilliant" discoveries of the current crop of revisionists. Neil Smelser came to be identified as the major theorist, and at the same time the chief offender, in presenting collective behavior as a defense of the status quo.

SMELSER AND HIS CRITICS

His book, *Theory of Collective Behavior,* is of central importance in my analysis, not because I agree with him, but because his critics have been as much in error as he has (1963). Critiques of collective behavior which treat his work as exemplary of the field have produced a conventionalized version which reflects a minor theme rather than the ideas of the major students in the field. In fact, most of Smelser's critics have committed the same error for which they attack him, that of assuming that human behavior can be sorted into neat, discrete piles of the "rational" and the "irrational."

There are apparently three reasons for the evaluation of Smelser's temporary digression into this field to the rank of the major theoretical contribution. The first is that he announced in his title that he was presenting a *theory* of collective behavior and his readers assumed that the work must therefore be portentous. Second, he offered a neat set of variables which were specific enough to be easily remembered but vague enough to be used in almost any way the user wanted. For example, most critics follow Currie and Skolnick in regarding his central variable, the generalized belief, as epitomizing the irrational bias of "collective behaviorists." Gary Marx, however, interprets the generalized belief as a reaction *against* characterizations of crowd action as irrational and "purposeless" since, in his words, it "identifies sources of strain and calls forth an appropriate response" (1970a: 24). He seems to regard it as equivalent to an ideology or a definition of the situation which would be a good meaning for "generalized belief" but is not Smelser's meaning! Third, and most important, the usual identification of "generalized belief" as short-circuited, impatient, exaggerated, and even paranoid made Smelser a prime target for the "politico-rationalistic" critique of collective behavior.

THE POLITICO-RATIONALISTIC CRITIQUE

This critique charges that theory of collective behavior has treated crowds and particularly social movements as dominated by irrational, extreme, and destructive impulses while treating conventional, organizational, or institutional behavior as rational, moderate, and hence "constructive" (Currie and Skolnick, 1970: 35). It is true that some theorists analyzing crowd behavior and social movements have implied such a contrast, but I have in mind such writers as Hans Toch, Eric Hoffer, Joost Merloo, and a variety of frustration-aggression theorists, not sociologists writing in the tradition of Park and Blumer. Such a model of irrational collective behavior incorporates three contrast conceptions. First, collective behavior is portrayed as impulsive action stemming from unconscious motives such as the frustration-aggression syndrome, alienation or even hallucinations caused by drugs, or alcohol or mass hypnosis—as allegedly practiced by such geniuses as Jim Jones. This contrasts with the calm cognitive decisions of "rational" actors who apparently follow an ethnomethod which corresponds to the logicoempirical method of social scientists, the most rational of all beings!

The next feature of collective behavior, according to this model, is the failure of the actors to note critical aspects of the situation and to select *valid lines of action* because their cognitive functioning is impaired by intense affect and the urgency of the problem they face. The calm, "rational" actor supposedly considers a much broader range of cues and alternatives, much the same ones that social scientists identify as significant in their post hoc analysis. Finally, and most important, there is the implication that the actor in collective behavior, if not acting with complete blindness and impulsiveness, as some people think is the case in panic, acts on a subjective, unrealistic definition of the situation which reflects fear, hostility, greed, anxiety, or other affective states. In the case of the "rational" actor, there is supposedly a good fit between the subjective definition of the situation and the objective situation—as discerned by the social scientist!

It is this sort of model of "irrational collective behavior" that the critics both created and attacked. Their critique had certain distinguishable features. One was primarily political, arguing that the definition of reality by participants in protest movements fit the objective situation better than did the definitions of the supposedly rational decision makers of the Establishment. This was evident because the definitions by the protestors of what was oppressive, undemocratic, or otherwise immoral corresponded to the definitions of the new radical breed of social scientists who had been, miraculously, liberated from the problems of bias in a way impossible for establishment sociologists. Like B. F. Skinner, exempt from the iron laws of behaviorism, they alone were free from the ideological constraints which participation in any type of political action imposes. The alleged restriction of attention of the protestors could be justified politically by denoting the oppressive nature of their situation. Since legitimate means of action were indeed closed to them because of the overweening power of the authorities, then resort to illegitimate means—and this must include terrorism—becomes rational. Yasir Arafat has made a more cogent and honest case for this position than has any social scientists I know of.

The illegitimate or short-circuiting actions of the authorities has not been subjected to the same kind of analysis. If a President circumvents congressional authority because of the very obvious fact that Congress typically acts slowly and indecisively, he is likely to be perceived as dishonest or immoral, rather than acting in a rational although authoritarian fashion because of oppressive constraints.

One of the most common means of refuting the irrational model of collective behavior has been the curious procedure of demonstrating that the actors were not the kind of people who would act irrationally, whether they were George Rudé's *menu peuple* of the French Revolution, Black rioters in the Detroit ghetto, or students in the FSM at Berkeley. Empirical data showing that they were not criminals, members of the lumpenproletariat, unemployed, unattached drifters, or "dumb" students who were on the verge of flunking out is taken as evidence that they could not have acted irrationally. This is a peculiar sort of revolutionary logic which holds that rationality is positively correlated with socioeconomic status! Of course, there are intervening psychological variables which are invoked to explain the collective behavior of what the conservatives call the "riffraff"—frustration or, more commonly for sociologists, alienation. That the protests of the alienated might make as good sense to them as the protests of the allegedly better adjusted but more socially conscious "upper-lowers" is not considered. That they have even more to protest about does not fit the prevailing conceptions of "structural strain" as a mysterious subjective variable.

The concept of relative deprivation has been acclaimed as valuable in explaining the paradox that those who, objectively, have less to protest about are more likely to engage in collective behavior, and that the time to revolt is when things are getting better, not when they are at their worst. This apparently irrational behavior can be seen as rational when we assume, with George Homans, that the search for distributive justice is not only more logical but more compelling as a motive than is hunger.

I hope it is clear that I am not defending the actions of the guardians of the existing social order as more rational or moral than those of protestors. I am merely pointing out what Gary Marx has expressed well when he said of "liberal-to-left" sociologists, "They rather naturally and correctly reject the Gustave LeBon-Ronald Reagan 'mad-dog' image of rioters, though in so doing there is a tendency to ignore variations and see all violent outbursts as 'rational,' 'intrinsically political' and 'instrumental and purposive' " (1970a: 35). But Marx still implies, in his concept of "issueless riots," that some collective behavior is more irrational than other types.

RATIONALITY-IRRATIONALITY REJECTED

I go further, rejecting entirely the utility of the rational-irrational distinction for the analysis of human behavior. This is not new. In both the 1957 and the 1972 editions of *Collective Behavior,* Turner and I stated as firmly as we could that the concepts of irrationality and emotionality were fallacious as distinguishing characteristics of collective behavior. We said first:

> Another recurring problem in collective behavior is the tendency to single out for study only those collective phenomena of which the observer disapproves and to depict the processes of collective behavior in value-laden terms. Alarm over the actions of destructive mobs, panics and revolutionary or totalitarian social movements is reflected in this tendency. On this basis collective behavior is often erroneously contrasted to "rational" behavior by being designated "irrational" or "emotional." (1957: 16)

We went on to say:

> Using internal criteria, behavior is irrational when the individual does not weigh all possible alternatives of which he can be aware in deciding his course of action. By this definition most institutional behavior is irrational since social

norms narrow the range of alternatives which the individual can effectively consider. While each of the major types of collective behavior has its own characteristic ways of so restricting attention within the range of potential alternatives, collective behavior is not different from other types of behavior in this respect. (1957: 17)

So, for what is the third time, I will assert, but in a somewhat different way, that the concepts "rational" and "irrational" are of no value whatever in the analysis of either group behavior or of most individual behavior. If we take seriously the principle derived from phenomenology and the sociology of knowledge that for the human actor reality is socially constructed, through a dialectic between "objective facticity and subjective meaning" (Berger and Luckmann, 1967: 60), then no human behavior can be classified as more or less rational in terms of the goodness of fit to some positivistically defined "reality." Only a psychotic individual totally out of communication with fellow human actors as they construct and reconstruct social reality could be classed as "irrational"—and R. D. Laing might challenge this!

THE OBJECTIVISTIC ERROR

Those approaches to collective behavior which utilize either the rational–irrational dimension or the politico–rationalistic critique involve two types of errors. One is an "objectivistic" and "positivistic" error which assumes, implicitly or explicitly, that the social science observer can identify an objective substructure of reality and thereby differentiate between rational generalized beliefs and irrational ideologies. This violates the fundamental canon of what Berger and Luckmann call the radical sociology of knowledge. They observe that while the man on the street takes reality for granted and the philosopher is obligated to deal with the epistemological question of ultimate reality, the sociologist is "stuck with the quotation marks" around the term "reality" (1967: 2). It is not only conservative positivists clinging to the myth of a value-free sociology who commit this error. It is equally true of those Marxists who, as Berger and Luckmann point out, interpret the substructure in a mechanistic manner as simply and totally the economic structure and thus fall into a posture of economic determinism. I suggest that one reason Marxist theorists must continually revise their theories is that, even when the workers read substantial fragments of Marx, they keep constructing versions of reality which do not fit the revealed truth of the theorists.

THE REDUCTIONIST ERROR

The second error is an individualistic or reductionist one. This consists of attempting to reconstruct the motivational context of both individual and collective acts by identifying individual psychological variables and then summing or averaging them. The psychoanalytically oriented researcher looks, as the British social psychologist Michael Billig (1976) has shown, for infantile and unconscious strivings, basic anger, interpersonal relations, and personal motivations. As Billig emphasizes, this prevents analysis of the social structure, the power relations, and the ideological context in which individuals act as members of collectivities. Sociologists who attempt to construct a dynamic model of group behavior by counting social characteristics—age, sex, education, income, occupation, class, and so on ad infinitum—commit the same reductionist error. So also do those who treat individual attitudes and opinions as motives and as the building blocks of ideology, rather than accepting the complexity of the "causes" of human action and the fact that an ideology, a collective belief system, a *Weltanschauung*, however denoted, is an essential part of the environment in which individual beliefs are formed.

What I am calling "the ideology" corresponds to what Turner and I have, perhaps unfortunately, sought to convey by the concept "norm." We have not been speaking of "norms" simply in the narrow sense of prescriptions for or prohibitions against specific actions, or as the motivational system of the oversocialized man. Norms may tell us what to do, but before that they tell us what the situation is. Hence we are talking in the broad sense of a socially constructed reality which, in collective behavior, undergoes reconstruction. A basic assumption of the emergent norm approach is that emergent norms, ideologies, world views, definitions of the situation, versions of reality, or typifications are constructed through a process of communication, not through the convergence of individual motives, attitudes, or impulses.

Superrationalistic Approaches

The politico–rationalistic critique enjoyed a brief and undeserved flurry of action and then suffered the usual fate of sociological fads—being referred to as conventional wisdom in introductory paragraphs or merely in footnotes. The newest direction being proposed for collective behavior may be termed the "rationalistic" approach, or, to distinguish it from the "politico–rationalistic," the "superrationalistic" approach.

THE GAMING APPROACH

There are two discrete lines of development of this approach, focusing on different forms of collective behavior. The "gaming approach" seeks to apply decision theory to crowds. Resource mobilization theory concentrates on social movements. Both avoid the radical but naive political bias of the politico–rationalistic critique, although this has led to charges that they have a conservative bias. They still, however, incorporate the objectivistic error and, particularly in the case of decision theory, an individualistic error.

Richard Berk has characterized gaming approaches to crowds as attempts to "delineate the theoretical mechanisms through which crowds respond to their environments and to each other. Resting heavily on Decision Theory, the gathering of a crowd is viewed as an *opportunity* in which individuals can experience certain rewards and certain costs. Each individual tries to maximize rewards and minimize costs" (1974: 67). Obviously, this theory substitutes a rational human actor for the impulsive, irrational creature ascribed by some to Turner and Killian. Crowd norms, while admitted as a factor, are seen simply as constraints which may increase or decrease the costs of an activity to the individual actor. Thus Berk cautions, "Remember that each crowd member seeks to gain a minimum outcome, and the payoffs for various possible actions are *fundamentally dependent on the actions of others gathered at the scene*" (1974: 69). Later, Berk treats action under a norm and collective decision making as complementary forms of action, the first being unconscious and the second rational and conscious.

Decision theory in collective behavior incorporates an objectivistic error, for it is based on a model of the human actor as both rational and hedonistic. Viewed from the perspective of phenomenology, game theory encounters the same problem as does reinforcement theory—how is what constitutes a reward and a cost for the individual decided except by the a priori definition of the scientific observer? Michael Billig cites a study by Tropper of an experimental game in which subjects participating in an auction behaved quite irrationally—they were willing to pay as much as three and a half dollars for a one-dollar bill! Billig presents Tropper's interpretation of his results along with his own conclusions as to the implications for game theory:

> Tropper interpreted his results as demonstrating that the subjects' main motivation was not to secure the best bargains possible in economic terms. It was to pursue victory over the other player, even if such victory is worth less financially than the effort expended in obtaining it. In Game Theory terms, Pyrrhic victories are defeats, but in psychological terms the victory itself seemed to be of prime value. (1976: 190–191)

We simply cannot understand collective behavior or any other form of social behavior unless we constantly remember that what may be a cost to one actor may be a reward to another if they act in different ideological frameworks—such as those of crowds or social movements. One actor's rationality is madness to another. Within the universe created in the isolated jungle community of Jonesville, some of the dying followers of Jim Jones could have cited with thousands of Christian martyrs before them, "O grave, where is thy victory? O Death, where is thy sting?"

EMERGENT NORM THEORY VERSUS
DECISION THEORY

Game theory falls into an individualistic error when it reduces emergent norms to rules, to prescriptions and proscriptions to which the individual responds as positive or negative reinforcers. The norm remains a mysterious, inexplicable part of the external environment to which the actor responds either as a rational calculator or as an oversocialized conformist, never as a complex actor building up the act in terms of a constructed definition of the situation. Careful reading of Ralph Turner's extended presentation of the emergent norm approach in the *Handbook of Modern Sociology* in 1964 should dispel any illusion that by "emergent norm" is meant simply a precise behavioral expectation (Turner, 1964). Perhaps the choice of the term was misleading, but Turner's discussion shows that it is meant to include an extensive complex of factors: rules applicable to a situation, explanations of the situation, evaluations of potential actors, and a "shared conviction of right, which constitutes a norm, sanctions behavior consistent with the norm, inhibits behavior contrary to it, justifies proselyting, and requires restraining action against those who dissent" (1964: 399). Let us boil this down by proposing that the emergent norm includes:

1. A definition of what the situation is—a collective definition, not a collective *decision*.
2. An indication of what sort of action is appropriate or inappropriate in this situation. This may include, but is not limited to, specific behaviors, including expressions of certain moods, as well as more broadly defined types of behavior which are perceived as consistent or inconsistent with the definition.
3. A set of justifications for both the constructed version of reality and of the actions defined as appropriate.
4. An evaluation of population segments—potential actors—in relation to the situation as defined.

A very important feature of the emergent norm so conceived is that it is not only constraining but is also permissive. While specific acts may be required or prohibited—such as displaying some minimal symbol of agreement with the emergent definition—latitude exists for a wide range of acts which are consistent with the norm. Not uniformity but differential expression and participation in which each member can "do his own thing" within the bounds of the emergent norm is the real source of the dynamic quality of collective behavior.

It permits the operation of individual personality variables, such as courage, without forcing us to look for a common psychological state; it is the basis for identifying a structure in the crowd which reflects differences in intensity and quality of participation; and it helps explain the shifts of crowd behavior as the result of interaction within the crowd and between the crowd and nonmembers, such as the authorities. In illustration of the difference between an emergent norm as a collective definition and a collective decision, we may consider looting during ghetto insurrections, as analyzed by Quarantelli and Dynes (1940: 168–82). They identify as the emergent norm in civil disorders not the requirement that everyone loot but rather open, collective support for looting. No observer has reported that everyone who might have looted did so during the riots. The collective definition was that looting, at least certain types, was justified and feasible in this situation, and that those who interfered with it were the enemy. Yet the only people who would be constrained to loot would be individuals who experienced small group pressure to demonstrate loyalty, macho, or even common sense by joining us.

Thus, even though we may be speaking only of a crowd, we may nevertheless classify the emergent norm in this case as a "riot ideology." It is the concept of the emergent norm as collective definition or ideology that permits us to subsume the crowd and the social movement under the same heading as "collectivities."

RESOURCE MOBILIZATION THEORY

Resource mobilization theory, as developed primarily by Zald (1977), McCarthy (1977), Oberschall (1973), and Tilly (1978b), addresses itself to social movements or, to be exact, to the "social movement industry" which is regarded as "the organizational analogue of a social movement" (McCarthy and Zald, 1977: 1219). Like game theory, this approach emphasizes "the importance of costs and rewards in explaining individual and organizational involvement in social movement activity" (McCarthy and Zald, 1977: 1216). It also stresses the significance of structure, in the form of social movement organizations as over against the "set of opinions and beliefs in a population which represents preferences for changing some elements of the social structure and/or reward distribution of a society," which is Zald and McCarthy's definition of a social movement (1977: 1217–18).

While criticizing the resource mobilization approach for its superrationality, I do not wish to detract from its valuable contributions. Zald and Ash's concept of the social movement organization (1966: 327–40), and Oberschall's (1973) notion of the mobilizing functions of groups intermediate between the elites and the atomized masses give greater substance to the general principle that "social movements do not develop out of a vacuum or a state of complete social disorganization" (Killian, 1964: 431), and that "for a social movement to develop there must not only be a vision of a different state of affairs but an enduring organization devoted to the attainment of this vision" (Killian, 1964: 433). In their concept of "social movement careers,"

Zald and McCarthy counter both the myths that social movements are dominated either by Eric Hoffer's psychopathological "true believers" or by the rational but enlightened zealots who existed in the mythology of radical sociologists. As did Turner and Killian in their concept of "the exploiter" as a participant in collective behavior, and as does Gary Marx in his examination of the agent provocateur (1974: 402-40), they emphasize the variety of rewards which may lead individuals into social movement activity. Finally, although they do not seem to recognize that Turner and Killian do not belong in the same camp as these others, they reject the "grass roots" approach represented in Gurr's relative deprivation theory and the structural strain theory of Smelser.

Whereas Turner and Killian begin their analysis with the creation of an emergent norm which constitutes "a sense of injustice," the resource mobilization theorists start with the social organizations which define a set of "target goals" consistent with the prevailing preference structures which to them constitute the social movement. How these preference structures arise and what their relationship to objective conditions in the society is appears to be unimportant. They are taken as constants, although it is pointed out that they may be "defined, created and manipulated by issue entrepreneurs and organizations" (McCarthy and Zald, 1977: 1215).

The critical independent variable in this theory is the perception by these structures or, by implication, by the decision makers within them, that the availability of resources which may be mobilized for the attainment of the target goals is great enough to make the rewards outweigh the costs. Hence, like a body of investment bankers, these decision makers commit themselves to investing in the social movement, to mobilizing the resources necessary for themselves and for other beneficiaries, and to "selling" the target goals to as large a number of constituents—not members—as possible. It is an important insight that, as in the case of any group, a social movement organization once formed operates as though organizational survival were the primary goal. This is better suited, however, for the explanation of the persistence of social movement organizations and the institutionalization of social movements than for understanding how they arise.

This model, admittedly paralleling the concept of industry in economics, obscures the dynamics of social movements by what it does to the emergent norm, to the cadre of decision makers in the movement, and to what others would call the members of the movement. Let us consider these in reverse order. By being treated as customers rather than members, the participants outside the charmed but faceless circle of decision makers are treated not as actors but as one class of resource to be mobilized and manipulated. They affect the career of the movement only insofar as the social movement organizations adjust their target goals to fit the consumer preferences.

This treatment of all but the cadre as passive constituents rather than active participants is most graphically illustrated in the case of individuals who might, in Orrin Klapp's terms, be called at the least "symbolic leaders" but who are treated instead as resources (1964). I quote McCarthy and Zald:

> Another technique advertisers utilize to appeal to isolated adherents is the linking of important people to the organization, thereby developing and maintaining an image of credibility. In the same way that famous actors, sports heroes, and retired politicians endorse consumer products, other well-known personalities are called upon to endorse SMO products: Jane Fonda and Dr. Spock were to the peace movement and Robert Redford is to the environmental movement what Joe Namath is to pantyhose and what William Miller is to American Express Company credit cards. (1977: 1231)

In like manner, the decision makers, pictured as manipulating heroic figures like hired hands in order to overcome consumer resistance of potential adherents who might "buy into" another social movement organization, emerge as coldly calculating, superrational economic men. Granting limited utility to the concept of resource mobilization by social movement leaders as well as by other entrepreneurs, I would prefer to use a military rather than an industrial analogy.

The resource mobilization model brings to mind Field Marshal Montgomery, cautiously weighing the resources available to support the strategy he preferred, beseeching Eisenhower for more resources, stubbornly insisting that the mission couldn't be accomplished without these resources. A social movement model suggests George Patton driving his armored units until they ran out of gas in the faith that he could get more resources by his boldness, that he would not be abandoned if he gambled on his vision of victory. Patton succeeded, but the model also recalls Robert E. Lee fighting for four heartbreaking years for a cause which he must have known was lost early in the struggle but which he supported out of loyalty, not as a result of cost analysis.

In citing these individuals' cases, I am not suggesting an individualistic, "Great Man" theory of social movements, but in recognizing organizational and strategic considerations we should not overlook the interaction between operational and charismatic leadership functions, and between strategy and ideology. Can we explain both the daring and the victory of the Iranian Revolution by viewing the Ayatollah Khomeini as merely a decision maker and resource manager, or even less as an advertisement put "out front" by a hidden cadre of decision makers?

Nor can we understand this or any other social movement simply in terms of either the charisma or the rationality of the decision makers. Michael Billig's statement concerning the relation of ideological presuppositions to bureaucratic decision making applies with equal force to social movements:

> The narrow cost-efficiency logic does not exist in some ideological vacuum— bureaucratic thinking implies the existence of a bureaucratic structure, whose social, political and economic functions can be analysed. (1976: 224)

Billig was criticizing the war-gamers and peace researchers who, in reducing strategic decisions concerning U.S. involvement in Vietnam to the level of interpersonal games and cost-efficiency analysis, failed to investigate the ideological roots of this kind of rationality. Similarly, to separate the analysis of the organizational behavior of social movements from the ideological bases is to mask the dynamics which make the social movement essentially a challenge to the existing order. It makes the daring gambles of both leaders and followers seem irrational, it treats Pyrrhic victories as truly defeats. The hope which, whatever the objective conditions may be, makes these conditions seem no longer inevitable and therefore unjust, is transformed into yet another shrewd, rational decision. Thus, I would extend Billig's judgment of "the ideology of order" as essentially conservative to resource mobilization theory. Returning to my original theme of the importance of a phenomenological analysis of collective behavior as against an objectivistic analysis, I again quote Billig:

> Social reality is a man-made construction and can be changed by the actions of men. If the hopes of dissidents outstrip the social realities, as defined for them by the forces of order, then it is those realities which they aim to change. It is the conservative who attempts to portray the existing social realities as immutable facts of nature, and who wishes to see the social structure, which has created those realities, remain untouched. Revolutionary ideology, on the other hand, does not aim at adjusting to the present realities and preserving their social basis—the crucial point about revolutionary ideology is that it aims to change reality. (1976: 171)

The Central Tasks of Collective Behavior Research

In the case of the social movement, as in the case of the crowd, the central tasks of collective behavior are to describe the socially constructed version of reality—the emergent norm—which makes what the participants are doing make sense to them, and to analyze the process of communication through which this definition is constructed. The most difficult aspect of this approach in the study of social movements is conceptualizing the dialectic between objective conditions, which we cannot arbitrarily dismiss as unimportant any more than we can claim to know them in a positivistic way, and the subjective processes through which the socially constructed reality which is all we can observe emerges. Charles Tilly is making a signal contribution to this task through his historical analyses of the objective side of revolutionary situations (1978b). It is the social construction of reality, not merely the substructure, which must remain the focus of attention, however.

The importance of this reality, this ideology, this world view, for social movements is that it defines for those who operate within it not only what is possible in terms of cost efficiency, but also what is inevitable, what is unbearable, what is worth sacrificing all lesser rewards for, and what is worth dying for. All other considerations of structure, of varieties of individual motivation, of the reactions of the authorities, the opposition, and the bystander public, must be secondary to this central feature of the social movement as a form of collective behavior.

23

Has Deviance a Future?

Paul Rock

ANY ATTEMPT TO SURVEY the present state or imagine the future of the sociology of deviance risks becoming entangled in the squabbles and problems of a most factious discipline. Instead of transcending or subduing argument, it is likely to be regarded as merely another contentious description of the development of thought. Sociologists of deviance have not passively awaited interpretation but have themselves vied to provide formal records of their own work (Downes, 1978). The legitimacy and tenability of their theorists have been at issue and much writing has offered a logic of historical justification to accompany a logic of analysis. Thus Nanette Davis, Lyn MacDonald, and Taylor, Walton, and Young take the culmination of intellectual endeavor to be radical criminology; Jeffery defines it as a grand synthesis of the different sciences; and Nettler and Hirschi take it to be control theory. It is evident that the process of diagnosis and anticipation is not wholly disinterested. Every projection tends to betray some sympathy with one of the warring schools.

Speculative difficulties are multiplied by the hazards of predicting an emergent process. Criminological prophecies have usually failed in the past. For example, the evolutionary narrative produced by Mannheim and his colleagues in 1960 (Mannheim, 1960) has been disowned by many of their successors in the 1970s. Lineages have now been plotted back to Husserl, Marx, and Hobbes. Haviland, Doe, Ray, and Maudsley are forgotten. If prophecies were wanting before, they are not necessarily more capable now. Not only is the discipline shaped internally by a dialectical form of reasoning which alters its materials in strange ways. It has also proceeded by absorbing "external" ideas and responding to crises in a seemingly indeterminate fashion. Very often it has been affected by the thought of marginal men whose work does not reflect normal sociological disciplines and organization.

The quest for novelty has continually imposed apparent discontinuities upon the sociological tradition. A perusal of ordinary criminological publications would not have encouraged one to foresee the influence exerted by Schutz, Gramsci, Mary Douglas, James Wilson, Oscar Newman, or Leslie Wilkins. There might well have been an expectation of the unexpected, but there could have been no certainty about which ideas would be embraced and which spurned. It is not always the case that interesting thinking *is* exploited. There is an abundance of potentially fertile thought which remains quite dormant. Its vitalization would seem to rest on a group existing or being in embryo, on that group being intellectually jaded or unemployed, and on some preparation to serve as a sponsor of the new. Very typically, that group will consist of younger sociologists who have no proprietorial claims to existing theory, little sunk intellectual capital, and an eagerness to make a mark on the world. Clearly, that group cannot be *too* young or inexperienced because the diffusion of its thought hinges on the active response of publishers and editors.

Theoretical movements do appear to have an adventitious character. Although the "normal science" of the sociology of deviance is pursued by a large mass of people, what passes for interesting work at any one time tends to be the creation of only a few. There are real limits set by the capacity of journals and publishers to promote innovation. There are other limits set by the construction of teaching timetables and bibliographies. There are further boundaries established by the rank inability of people to read and incorporate all that appears. Principles of selection emerge, mirroring the interplay between intellectual biographies and professional talk. Those principles, in turn, will restrict academic discussion to a rather narrow range of arguments and authors. The literate must have some acquaintance with that range if they are to retain authority. To be sure, the sociological profession is well populated and diverse. What is held to be an important innovation in London might not be acclaimed in Sheffield or San Francisco. But there is considerable concentration, bringing about a serial focusing of thought. Acknowledged creativity belongs to a small number, and the doings of that number will affect the progress of sociology for a while. Individual contingencies can accordingly become most important. An odd encounter with a novel or a work of anthropology may feed back into the discipline with surprising consequences. *The Dice Man,* an idiosyncratic essay on cybernetics, or a treatise on etiquette can mold more conventional analysis. The appropriation of such writing is palpably haphazard. It does not flow from the more purposive and orderly processes of study. Neither does it stem from the routine social organization of the university. Works apparently acquire significance at particular stages of one's education. There must be an affinity between personal schemes, the possibilities of an idea, and the larger world of sociology itself. Thus the writings of Lemert were relatively neglected for some years, only to be rediscovered in the 1960s. Similarly, there has been a recent return to the reflections of the first Bolshevik legal theorists.

The problem of prediction is quite deliberately compounded by a profession which courts the unpredictable and the novel. As I have remarked, academic work is distinguished by its search for the original and remarkable (Davis, 1971). It strains after the special which will enable its author to make something of himself. Universities and publishers work in concert to reward those who do not simply ape or apply the thoughts of others. Indeed, the sociology of deviance is replete with books which proclaim their utter newness. Instead of attempting to extend and amplify strands within the discipline, those books may claim to sever all ties by acts of intellectual revolution. There is a propensity to inflate slight differences of emphasis, to be jealous of intellectual property (Douglas, 1977: 51), and to change language and vocabulary. In many instances, there are appreciable problem shifts. In many instances, there are not. What is transparent, however, is the effort to move in extraordinary directions. The credibility and creditability of the extraordinary tend to be judged by fairly ordinary criteria. There are real penalties which can be inflicted on those who assume too great a license. They may remain unread, or may be dismissed as foolish or anachronistic. Yet the order and continuity maintained by those penalties have become weaker over time. Sociologists of deviance have progressively spread out into a loose network of factions and social worlds. They do require the support of employment, publications, and a cooperative circle. But once that support has been secured, they may become relatively independent of one another.

Intellectual prominence has become increasingly parochial: radical criminologists discuss each other's ideas, discounting the criticisms and works of outsiders as trivial and ideologically laden; interactionists may not embark on debate, being reluctant to trade on a metaphysical plane; applied criminologists may have no commerce with the fanciful and irrelevant abstractions of the theorists. Such a drift toward closure has insulated one schismatic group against its fellows, permitting diverse ideas to be aired without effective challenge. The result has been only the most superficially controlled growth, a growth which moves thought in very different ways and toward very different goals.

If there is any discernible structure to the evolution of the sociology of deviance, it tends to be marked by an erratic piling up of disconnected stages. Elsewhere, I observed that it might be helpful to recognize a division of academic labor within criminology (Rock, 1979). I traced a rudimentary divide between those who serve as innovators and those who perform a custodial role. Until recently, the bulk of criminological innovations was deposited by outsiders who had no great stake in the preservation and furtherance of the sociology of deviance. They touched on criminological problems in the pursuit of solutions to puzzles which had their chief relevance and roots elsewhere. Durkheim treated law as an index of solidarity and his analysis of crime revolved around a demonstration of the functionalist method and an exploration of social cohesion. Merton is not a professed criminologist. Neither was Marx, Schutz, Cicourel, or Kingsley Davis. Their interests were lodged in regions beyond criminology; their works were not devised to illuminate peculiarly criminological issues; and they did not return to repair all the muddles and perplexities which their ideas engendered. On the contrary, major innovators tend to retreat and to be silent about the difficulties which they create.

The business of synthesis, reconciliation, and exegesis is usually pursued by people who identify themselves with criminology proper. The writers of textbooks and the teachers of courses have tried to foist a unity and interconnectedness of thought on a collection of incomplete and fragmented analyses. Theirs has been a difficult task: the sociology of deviance has undergone no smooth or logical progression. It consists of a number of fitful leaps from one partially examined thesis to another. Like many other areas defined by a substance rather than by a theory, it has been constituted by those who have briefly passed through the discipline. The contexts, objectives, and analysis of its principal architects can be appreciated only be deserting deviance itself. Marxist ideas about crime cannot be elucidated with criminological materials alone. "Labeling" theory must be referred to the wider corpus of symbolic interactionism. And phenomenology must invoke Heidegger, Husserl, and Merleau-Ponty. In sum, criminological innovators generally refrain from settling disputes, criminological custodians lack the competence and commitment to undertake the work on their behalf, and the discipline is correspondingly somewhat vacant and inconclusive.

Superficially, it does seem that such a division of labor is beginning to disappear as radical, phenomenological, and other sociologists invade criminology. Yet their allegiance is frequently frail: efforts to build a systematically sociological criminology are prone to founder on the conflict between substantive and formal explanation. Any rigorous and schematic sociology displays a fondness for describing the forms of structure and life. There is a strain toward the discovery of logics or grammars which subtend all the phenomenal appearances of the social world. Phenomena are reduced to epiphenomena, mere illustrations of the workings of ultimately authentic and interesting causes. Deviance becomes no more than an exemplification of a profound order which manifests itself widely across the surface of society. Thus, the phenomenological flirtation with deviance was brief and led to no great consummation. Phenomenology is occupied with the constitutive processes which produce the objects of consciousness, not with those objects "themselves." At bottom, there is no intrinsic fascination in deviance. Any organization of social appearances would do as well. There is a divorce between the constituting and the constituted, and the prime business of phenomenology is with the first. It is a divorce that is well emphasized by an erstwhile sociologist of deviance:

> In thinking out of deviance . . . I would treat it as a theoretical imperative the very thrust of which would be to overcome it as a descriptor. In this way we

could then turn away from constitutive and arbitrary judgments of public rule breaking as deviance towards the concept of rule itself and the dialectical tension that ruling is a subject surely more central to the fundamental practice of sociology where men and sociological speakers are conceived as rule makers and followers. What is now the sociology of deviance might then be pushed to the margins of sociological discourse as a museum piece to be preserved perhaps as that antediluvian activity which sought to show oddities, curiosities, peccadilloes and villains as central to sociological reason. (Phillipson, 1974: 5-6)

Marxists are exposed to identical strain. They are repeatedly enjoined to attend to the fundamental dialectic of historical transformations, to the organized contradictions of capitalism, and to the social formations thrown up by political economy. Radical sociologists of deviance are reproached for discussing the peripheral and evanescent phenomena of bourgeois society. There is alleged to be an insurmountable barrier to the free deployment of Marxist techniques:

> Criminology and crime are not central disciplines for radicalism—indeed . . . a concern with criminology will fade as a radical analysis is achieved . . . the idea of a radical criminology is not possible in *principle*. . . . Marxism as a form of theoretical system specifies its own objects of analysis and . . . those objects are not crime or law, but the mode of production and the form of social formations in general. . . . Marxism, by the analysis of the relationship between and within social formations, includes and subsumes (logically and empirically) the analysis of crime and law in these more general concerns. (Bankowski et al., 1977: 45-46)

Well resolved and coherent theories, therefore, tend to encompass a metaphysics which defines commonplace phenomena as substantial. They do not commend a sustained analytical assault on deviance. On the contrary, their adherents are exposed to the seductive criticisms of those who discredit criminology as an enterprise. The examination of deviance will probably preoccupy them for no more than a short time. At some stage, there will have to be a decisive choice between a compromised and revisionist theory and an abandonment of the substantive. Only those who are phenomenalists or abstracted empiricists are liable to dwell on deviance for very long. They must either reveal some indifference to the ontological and epistemological recommendations of systematic theorizing or maintain a belief in the realities of appearance. The latter group are presumably represented by those innumerable criminologists who are housed in institutes of applied research and training: the otherworldly morass of abstract theory does not attract them; their work is tempered by the practical reasoning of policy making, and they are absorbed in worlds which are not dominated by the academy. The phenomenalists, by contrast, would observe that the mundane objects of common sense are authentic and irreducible. They would align themselves with Blumer, who asserted:

> The question remains whether human society or social action can be suc-
> cessfully analyzed by schemes which refuse to recognize human beings as they
> are, namely as persons constructing individual and collective action through an
> interpretation of the situations which confront them. (1969: 89)

Implications

I have argued that it would be unhelpful to portray the sociology of deviance as a simple march toward an ever greater intellectual mastery and certainty. On the contrary, it consists of a sequence of relatively disconnected
and underdeveloped analytical episodes. The work of the Chicago School did
not evolve to merge into the functionalist phase of criminology. Neither did
functionalism foster symbolic interactionism. Each style tended to dominate
debate for a time. Each style emerged from the parent discipline of sociology
and not from the workings of criminology itself. And each style was succeeded
by arguments which attempted to establish analysis on a new base. Typically,
the ideas received by criminology were those which seemed to have an immediate bearing on the explanation of crime, deviance, and control. Authors
and works which did not touch on substantive problems were cast off, leaving
an unrepresentative residue of observations and studies. Criminological
reviews of phenomenological work thereby ignore Kant, Bergson, and
Jaspers. The "labeling" approach is forwarded without allusion to Dewey,
Peirce, and James. Functionalism has been amputated from the writings of
Radcliffe-Brown.

The criminological refractions of sociology have been appropriately
deformed. Not only have they stripped context and theory away, leaving little
more than a husk behind. They have also been presented as if they were entire. It is as if symbolic interactionism were exhausted by the writings of
Schur, Becker, Scheff, and Erikson; functionalism by Bell, Davis, Coser, and
Merton; and anomie theory by Merton, Cloward and Ohlin, and Durkheim.
Such partial and incoherent versions can never become more than the
simulacrum of tenable theory. They are readily discredited and easily
superseded. Thus the criticisms of Liazos, Mankoff, and Akers can be cited as
authoritative refutations of interactionism. Quinney, Taylor, Walton, and
Young can overwhelm phenomenology by the assertion that it does not attend
to the problem of reality. Functionalism can be subjected to a form of argument described as "ideological critique."

The critique of theory has been accompanied by an occasional intellectual
impatience. Sociologists of deviance have often failed to exploit even those

remnants which they have imported into their discipline. Their work has sometimes been attended by an imperative to accomplish practical results. It has led to a precipitate abandoning of those ideas which do not seem to produce palpable social change. Some anomie theorists, for instance, jettisoned their thinking after the apparent reverses of Mobilization for Youth. There was much in the idea of anomie which remained unresolved, but resolution did not take place. Again, the search for intellectual distinctiveness and the rapid succession of academic generations have brought about a continual toying with the new. *Ex California semper aliquid novis.* The half-life of publicly discussed theoretical developments would now seem to be about five years: anomie theory, subcultural theory, interactionist theory, phenomenology, control theory, radical criminology have rapidly followed one another. Of course, exponents of a few of those stances have continued to pursue ideas after they have been partially displaced. But there does appear to be a collective appreciation of what is significant, a strain toward fashionableness, which shifts attention from theme to theme. Interactionists may flourish, but they are no longer in vogue.

One major consequence has been an organized deficiency of analytical effort. Ideas introduced into the sociology of deviance have rarely been fully exploded or explored. Perhaps that is why teaching courses tend continuously to resurrect old theories, revealing a reluctance to dismiss them finally. That is why recent works on the deviance of women or the sociology of law generally return to beginnings, unable to leave thoughts buried. Criminology might well have been created by Stoker, being populated by the undead. It has been marked by a cyclical disinterring of hypotheses and thoughts: for instance, anomie theory thrived in the eighteenth century, was revived at the end of the nineteenth, and rediscovered in the twentieth century; and ecological theory was developed in the mid-nineteenth century and redeployed at the beginning of this century, and it has reappeared in the 1970s.

To be sure, sociological reasoning may be regarded as a reservoir of ideas which can be drawn upon at will. The history of criminology can itself be transformed into a series of latent and active periods for different modes of analysis. It is unlikely that there will ever be a decisive arbitration between the principal schools. They are ultimately embedded in a metaphysics which resists final proof. In a modified guise, theories of deviance encapsulate all the diverse moral and political philosophies which have circulated in the West. Just as there has not been a definitive resolution of the debates between those philosophies, so particular forms of sociology cannot triumph without coercion. It is not the intrinsic merits of theory which stimulate acceptance on all occasions. Rather, theories present different opportunities for practical employment. Phenomenology might not guide the work of prison administrators, and functionalism could prove uncongenial to police officers. While needs and uses themselves stem from visions provided by theory, they also have independent sources. Until the sociology of deviance is dedicated to the pursuit of a single task or problem it will not be uniform, harmonious, or unilinear in its evolution. What remains evident, however, is the undeveloped quality of the different theories which are allowed to compete with one another.

I have advanced several reasons for the persistence of that quality: the tension between formal and substantive argument; the expectation of immediate effects; the leaning toward innovativeness; and the incorporation of deracinated and vulgarized borrowings from the wider universe of sociological thought. Most of the arguments composing the sociology of deviance deserve expansion and clarification. Anomie theory, for example, has been largely confined to an examination of the disjunction between the structure of means and ends. It could be redrafted into a provocative description of the relations between men and the collective representations, of the play between reified forms and local realities, and of the infirmities of symbolism. Indeed, Berger and McHugh have suggested how anomie might define some of the experiences which attend living in a socially constructed world.

Similarly, subcultural theory has not been subject to extensive amplification. Identified mainly with the writings of Cohen, Miller, and Cloward and Ohlin, it has lacked an adequate methodology and analysis of belief systems. Apart from Douglas and Lemert, few have ever inquired whether is *is* possible to catalogue the ideas of 200 million Americans or 50 million Britons. Descriptions have been reduced to simple lists of "values," but the distribution, structure, interrelations, and mapping of those values are tacitly taken to be too unproblematic to warrant argument. It is not even clear that there is a unified constellation of beliefs. If such a constellation exists, we offered no intelligent plans for surveying it. Quite characteristically, subcultural theory has been needlessly barren. It could well have been transformed into an extension of the sociology of knowledge, although I know of no attempt to investigate what might have come of that union. While David Matza, Stuart Hall, and Paul Willis have done something to repair the more obvious flaws of the approach, work has only just begun, and it has been generally restricted to a Marxist regeneration. It would be intriguing to acknowledge the implicit formalism of Finestone or Willis and bring it to a greater prominence.

Again, Weberian theory could aid the analysis of the emergent properties of deviant beliefs. Logical developments could be tracked over time, moving subcultural theory beyond an interest in static responses to structural strains. Mannheim, too, has prepared much that would lend itself to an understanding of changes in deviant styles over the generations: expressive rule-breaking is patently stratified chronologically and oppositionally. Mannheims's arguments might elucidate the cognitive structures of deviance which flow from different political commitments. They might illuminate the part played by competition. But it would seem that a sociologist of knowledge who refrains from criminology can have nothing to say to the criminologist. This process of addition and elaboration might be deplored as an instance of directionless scholasticism. Yet there is even less profit in a sociology which permits its theses to stay thoroughly uncultivated. Subcultural theory has apparently been discarded although it has never been tried.

The entire corpus of theories bearing on deviance is unresolved. There is only a slight promise that the position can ever change. What may be anticipated is a procession of archaeological expeditions to resuscitate the prematurely abandoned thinking of the past. What will also occur is a series of attempts to innovate by injecting the hitherto unused theories of sociology proper. Most developments in Marxism eventually work themselves into criminology. There is an endless scanning which prospects sociology for other sources of criminological inspiration. Structuralism has not yet been exploited except in a piecemeal fashion. Formalism has not been attempted apart from its mediated expression in symbolic interactionism. There are the first stirrings of an effort to construct a Weberian sociology of deviance, although none has been widely publicized so far. It may be presumed that these intellectual excursions will not give rise to schematic or sustained work. On the contrary, criminology will probably continue to evolve in a series of analytical flurries.

The Relations Between Theory and Empirical Work: The Possibility of Remedies

Prescriptions invariably mirror theoretical assumptions. There is no elevated platform from which universally legitimate decrees may be issued. I have argued that any intervention in a schismatic discipline is liable to be dismissed as one more example of partisanship. What may be conceived as a sensible reform will only be regarded as an attempt to direct thought away from its proper objectives. Proposed solutions tend to remold sociology, imposing an unwelcome entropy on an argumentative and torn enterprise.

A review of gaps and problems is almost certainly doomed to be inconsequential. Thus radical criminology might be reproached for its failure to undertake comparative work. It could be claimed that an insistent focus on the pathologies of capitalism forbids consideration of analytically strategic questions (Downes, 1979). It promotes false syllogisms and offers specious promises (Aron, 1979). A sensitive exploration of crime control in socialist, preindustrial, and capitalist societies could well disclose the presence of more extensive uniformities than the radical criminologists concede. It might make the radical manifesto problematic. It might reveal that "capitalism" is not an essence which is unchanging from place to place and from time to time. Yet some styles of Marxism ban the comparative method, proclaiming it mere "speculative empiricism" (Hirst, 1975a). An interest in the phenomenon is itself deprecated and devalued: it commits one to a serious appreciation of false consciousness; it diverts one from the true Marxist project; it fissures totality; reifies thought; and undermines any prospect of global diagnoses. It will be remembered that Lukács maintained that Marx would have been correct even if every single Marxist proposition had been falsified. The truth of Marxism resides in its method, not in its empirical demonstration. Radical criminologists disown the universe of appearances, substituting their own noumenal objects. Exhortations to be empirical will be met with the reply that empiricism is no more than a creature of ideology. Exhortations to examine troubling anomalies will be referred to a "real" world in which anomalies have been censored away. Marx himself may have occasionally resembled an empiricist. Many of his heirs do not. They would define an empiricist Marxism as an absurdity and no Marxism at all (Althusser, 1969).

Appeals to empiricism have substance only when there is some agreement about the constitution of the social world. It is more than obvious that functionalists, phenomenologists, interactionists, Marxists, and control theorists do not inhabit the "same" society. Their theories spawn the materials which are scrutinized by theory. Thus Marxists deny the facticity of common-sense constructions, refusing to defer to the objects ordered by lay consciousness. Their theory constitutes its *own* world. Similarly, functionalists discern an underlying machinery which alone possesses ontological reality. Durkheim echoed Marx when he announced that he considered "fruitful this idea that social life must be explained, not by the conception of it held by those who participate in it, but by profound causes which escape consciousness" (Durkheim, 1897: 648).

I suspect that there would be little response to a request for empirical exploration of certain functionalist hypotheses. Of course, the most impressive functionalist work on deviance, *Crime and Custom in Savage Society*, was based on ethnography. But sociological functionalists have long deserted ethnography: they refuse to recognize the authority of sensual evidence, they are unimpressed by the formulations offered by common sense (their business is with latent, not manifest, functions), and they tend to allude only to the unfoldings of their own a priori schemes. There is a good deal that is momentous in the functionalist sociology of deviance. However, its authority stems from pontifical judgment, not from the results of sensory investigation. Thus it has been alleged that the work of control serves to define moral boundaries, dramatize order, and promote solidarity. The argument pursues the dialectics of the medieval schoolmen, its persuasiveness resting on its affinity with the very logic by which we construct our sense of the social. Any venture beyond the demonstration by affinity would require a patient hunt for the diverse, complicated, and mediated effects of judicial and police activity. Unless one employs what Phillipson (1974) has called "verification by anecdote," there is little of the functionalist system that *can* be referred to normal empiricist procedure. How could one recognize a moral boundary or ascertain its condition? An unseen, unheard, untouched, unsmelled structure of profound causes cannot render itself open to the empiricist.

Versions of phenomenology and ethnomethodology are similarly protected from vulgar sensual visits. It will be recalled that Jack Douglas was reproved for the very suggestion that some meanings and processes might be "transsituational," that it was possible to transcend the awesome indexicality of the social world. It will also be recalled that attempts to establish statistical regularities are often dismissed as mere "number-crunching." The distribution of events in space and time cannot be charted by a discipline which borrows from Heraclitus. Empiricism necessarily violates aspects of the phenomenological charter: it propels one toward a gross clustering of unlike, situated phenomena, it imposes an alien logic of explanation, and it requires a denial of hermeneutics. After all, phenomenology stemmed from a rejection of the assumption that there is an objective world which can be inspected without the mischievous intervention of intelligence. It is to intelligence that phenomenologists turn, not to the materials which intelligence surveys. Descriptions of the inner topographies of the self can be quite compelling, but there can be no *proof* of the existence of those landscapes. Indeed, how could one choose between psychoanalytic, Jungian, and phenomenological models of subjectivity? The sole criterion must be a sense of plausibility and personal recognition. But that sense is itself nurtured and cultivated: the psychoanalyst would see himself reflected in a Freudian portrait, the phenomenologist in a Husserlian one. Gellner has identified this problem as the "scandal of undemonstrated privacy" (1975: 431).

Phenomenology cannot really lay itself open to any conventional empiricist strategy. For example, Garfinkel's (1967: chap. 5) Agnes furnishes a telling depiction of sexual typifications. Yet Garfinkel would presumably endorse no investigation of the typicality, distribution, interchanges, and stability of those typifications. It is uncertain whether Agnes is supposed to represent an incision into the moving totality of the American *Geist* or just one eccentric person in an unknown world. It is no more certain whether Sudnow's courtroom or Bittner's skidrow police officers are supposed to be contextually, temporally, and existentially unique, or instances of a general order. The ideographic strains of phenomenology do not encourge nomothetic reasoning. Taxed about nomothetic problems, some phenomenologists manifest a palpable lack of interest in the entire search for lawlike regularities and falsifying procedures (Hill and Crittenden, 1968). They are unhappy about the demand for systematic, comparative examinations of the scope and limitations of their claims.

It would seem to follow that a move toward "empirical study" is not a simple process. Many sociologists of deviance would protest that empiricism is itself suspect. Empiricism explores that which is made available to the senses. Major sociologists such as Adorno, Lukács, and Althusser distrust the senses. Their voices echo in criminology: Quinney, for example, extolled a critical consciousness which would reveal "conventional experience" for "what it is—a reification of an oppressive social order" (1975: 188). Empiricism is as much a special kind of epistemology as any of the theories which shun it. Its pursuit entails some compromising of a prioristic and essentializing theory, a willingness to defer to the obdurate qualities of a world outside theory. In turn, theory is required to become looser, more uncertain, and more tentative. Its constituent ideas must resemble Blumer's "sensitizing concepts": they do not create a world but merely point to one. A few principal theories have been so compromised and diluted, but the reasons for negotiation are not immediately apparent. One major possibility *does* occur when an analyst enters criminology with the intellectual perspectives of another discipline. For instance, English historians have typically subordinated the demands of theory to cautious and meticulous documentation. If they are Marxist, their Marxism is required to submit to empirical controls. One of the most consequential works on deviance has been Edward Thompson's *Whigs and Hunters* (1975), and it is a work which marries an allegiance to Marxism with historiographical rigor. He would not have accepted Paul Hirst's command that Marxism ignore crime (1975b: 204).

> I was like a parachutist coming down in unknown territory: at first knowing only a few yards of land around me, and gradually extending my explorations in each direction. . . . This might appear to be less "an experiment in historiography" than a way of muddling through. . . . Since I started with the experience of humble foresters and followed up, through sketchy contemporary evidence, the lines that connected them to power, there is a sense in which the sources themselves have forced me to see English society in 1723 as they themselves saw it, from "below." I have avoided, until late in this book, any general description of that society which could have come to me from the constructions of other historians. I cannot of course pretend to have approached the theme without prejudices and preconceptions: certainly I did not expect to find a society which was uncorrupt or wholly just. But the method and the sources have placed my preconceptions under some controls. (Thompson, 1975: 16)

It is crucial whether controls emanate from within or from without theory. The historiographic work of Thompson, Hobsbawn, and Rudè is a Marxism which is modified by the demands of a discipline somewhat removed from sociology. The intellectual parachutist tends to resemble the interactionist ethnographer, not the radical, functionalist, or phenomenological criminologist. The platform from which he leaps should probably remain uncontaminated by the more elevated forms of metaphysics. He might be a Solzhenitsyn (Horowitz, 1974) or a historian or an anthropologist like Schapera or Gluckman. He is unlikely to be one who has been nursed by sociology. If this is so, it appears inevitable that the sociology of deviance will continue to worry over the leavings of outsiders. Its composition will be largely dictated by those who do not wish to improve it.

Enduring revisionist sociologists of deviance are liable to be those who have been stranded after the passing of a particular wave of theory. Jack Douglas has retained his fascination with rule-breaking although most phenomenologists and ethnomethodologists have decamped. Kai Erikson has maintained some interest in Durkheimian problems of communities under threat despite the retreat of the functionalists. Irving Horowitz is an unusual radical, revealing considerable independence of doctrine. Their ideas tend to depart from orthodoxy, becoming alienated and idiosyncratic by conventional canons. It is such revisionists who will persist in their parachuting role, sustaining the intellectual momentum of the discipline. They will form part of a company with the phenomenalists who have been free of metaphysical encumbrances. Indeed, Erikson, Horowitz, and others have shown a remarkable capacity to work with interactionism and the interactionists.

The flight from empiricism characterizes many of the theories which have been imported into the sociology of deviance. Apart from the abstracted empiricists and the interactionists, there is little zeal for patient documentation of deviant processes. I have explained that flight as a requirement of the more metaphysical sociologies. But it must also be clear that empirical research on deviance is a most difficult and unrewarding enterprise. Deviant worlds rarely parade themselves for public inspection. Of course, there are political and expressive styles of rule-breaking which are explicitly intended to intrude on public situations. Most are not: they are structured by furtiveness and deviousness, by suspicion of the outsider, and by attempts to misrepresent systematically. Although sociologists have often been sanguine about the methodological difficulties of criminology (Polsky, 1967), the problems of chronicling deviance are probably more taxing than any others. It is likely that access will be limited, networks ill articulated, and activities concealed. Accusations can be leveled that sociologists were misled by formal accounts (Patrick, 1973) of behavior that is not amenable to direct surveillance. Few ethnographers have managed to enter the homes, families, and intimate settings of deviants. Their work has typically been confined to the streets and public places. Consideration has barred any extensive mapping of phenomena. In short, it may only be possible to assemble a few pieces of what Becker (1970: chap. 4) has called the "scientific mosaic." Such modest productivity is largely regarded as unbecoming: sociologists seek grander answers to basic problems. There is a strain toward an eschewing of unrewarding work. The claims of criminology would require substantial reduction if the limitations of empiricism were acknowledged. There could be no New Criminology or general theories of deviance.

Conclusion

Theories which touch on substantive areas seem to acquire special characteristics. Reasoning about deviance, in particular, has been somewhat perfunctory and inconclusive. There is an abiding conflict between schemes designed to achieve comprehensive understanding and the restrictions of a small and dimly known segment of the social world. The master models of society defy compression: they are unsuited to a sustained onslaught on rule-breaking alone. Instead, they are destined to carry their adherents on beyond the sociology of deviance. Few of their principal authors have been engrossed in criminology, theorizing being undertaken by representatives who are continually exposed to the invitation to quit deviance as an analytical object. There is a companion hostility to the demands of empiricism. If empiricism is conceived as the doctrine that scholars surrender some of the reach and power of theory, it is patent that the more firmly structured metaphysics of sociology do not lend themselves to empirical work. It is incumbent on the sociologist to depress his ambitions, embrace uncertainty, and prepare for conversion.

Deviance tends to be extraordinarily humbling as a topic: its opportunities for empiricism are unusually meager and they do not permit substantial generalization. It is only the sociologist who reduces theorizing to a subordinate position that can entertain the prospect of a career devoted to criminology. Plummer (1979) and Becker (1974), for instance, devalue theory as an accomplishment. The work which they espouse will probably persist. Its chief handicap is its modesty. Contrasted with the other contenders for sociological dominion, it has few pretensions to scope or finality. Emphasizing the indeterminacy and openness of speculation, it cannot reach lofty goals. Interactionism may encounter problems of recruitment, being dismissed as a less than robust and satisfying form of sociology. If those problems can be overcome, and if interactionism survives as a marginal but active expression of sociology, then the sociology of deviance will itself persist. Criminology will resemble what Arnold Rose defined as a "crescive" discipline, a slow accumulation of minor studies without overall design or claims to absolute truth.

24

Where Are the Streakers Now?

Jackson Toby

ABOUT FIVE YEARS AGO—when the streaking phenomenon was arousing wild enthusiasm on American campuses—a reporter from the Rutgers College radio station telephoned to ask whether I thought streaking was here to stay. "Yes," I replied, "streaking offers an almost cost-free opportunity for young people to defy adults and flout their rules." Within a few days streaking ceased, and, despite occasional reminders from me that it serves as symbolic rebellion, streaking has not reemerged.

The current whereabouts and behavior of the streakers of 1974 is not of great concern to the general public or even to deviance theorists. Drug abuse and armed robbery seem to pose more challenging causal questions. Yet the sudden appearance (and equally sudden disappearance) of streakers is as baffling as the onset of alcoholism or the variation of criminality by sex and age level. Furthermore, there is at least one intellectual advantage to thinking about the sociology of deviance from the perspective of an ephemeral phenomenon like streaking instead of traditional forms of *persistent* deviance like delinquency or prostitution. An explanation general enough to account for streaking has to appreciate the possibility that the connection between deviant behavior and motivation is loose. If persistent forms of deviance alone are regarded as worthy of causal analysis, one might erroneously infer that an isomorphic mapping can be made between deviant behavior and specific motivational tendencies within the personality system. It may well be useful to attempt the "rehabilitation" of some drug addicts, armed robbers, or prostitutes, but the patent foolishness involved in rehabilitation programs for streakers suggests that deviance can and does occur without specifically programmed personality roots.

More generally, we speak of the sociology of deviance as though our theories and our research dealt impartially with everything covered by the concept of deviance. In practice, however, we tend to think about deviant behavior in terms of traditional, albeit somewhat bizarre, types of deviance. We are likely to do research concerning juvenile delinquency or about sex offenses and to formulate theoretical propositions about deviance in general based on such research. We are less likely to design research projects concerning deviance in the family or on the job.[1] I propose to run counter to this tendency in my discussion of three unresolved issues in the sociology of deviance by utilizing streaking as a test of my provisional formulations.

Issue 1: Is the Extent to Which Deviant Behavior Is Denied Cultural Legitimation a Variable in the Genesis and Control of Deviant Motivation?

By definition, deviant behavior is *socially* disapproved behavior. In large-scale societies, social disapproval is formally organized through the criminal law and administered by the police and the criminal justice system. It sometimes seems that legal sanctions are independent of the shared moral sentiments of members of the society. In smaller social systems it is more obvious that a major basis for social disapproval is that deviant behavior is regarded as *wrong,* that is, as defying or evading cultural standards of legitimacy. Talcott Parsons spoke of the institutionalization of cultural standards to call attention to the interpenetration of social and cultural systems in an ongoing society. He did not mean by interpenetration, however, the absence of some independent variability between social and cultural systems, including the social and cultural aspects of deviance.

In the case of streaking, the social and legal norms were clear. Public nudity constituted "disorderly" behavior. The police could and in some cases did make arrests. But what happened in 1974—for a brief time, anyway—was a redefinition of public nudity under certain circumstances. Although the bodies of young people were totally uncovered as they ran, bicycled, jogged, and pranced through public streets, they were not defined as "exposing" themselves. A new term, "streaking," was coined to describe and evaluate the behavior. The behavior was partially legitimated in terms of temporary youthful playfulness. A positive label was applied to behavior that would in previous times have been negatively labeled. I am using the expressions, "positive label" and "negative label," with diabolical cunning—to call attention to the fact that "labeling" is a pejorative term. The more generic and less loaded term is "cultural definition." In this generic sense, Talcott Parsons was a labeling theorist; he constantly called attention to the necessity for

---

[1] Roethlisberger and Dickson (1939) wrote about deviance with respect to work expectations and the social-control mechanisms (e.g., "binging") used by fellow workers to reduce it. But this landmark study in industrial sociology is not usually cited in the deviance literature.

cultural definition to orient the individual and the society to otherwise in-determinate meanings of the situation.

Before March of 1974 the cultural system had evaluated public nudity as immoral because of the symbolic association between nudity and eroticism. But "streaking" was defined as a youthful lark having nothing to do with eroticism. This temporarily legitimated it in terms of cultural values and justified reducing the normative sanctions against it.

Parsons called attention to the possibility of cultural legitimation (or par-tial legitimation) of deviance in his discussion of the sick role. The sick in-dividual fails to fulfill his social obligations. To the extent that his failure is motivated, he is reprehensible.[2] But he gets partial legitimation for his failure to conform by placing himself in a special social status. As a sick person, he is not completely getting away with deviance because illness is culturally defined as undesirable. Furthermore, he agrees to cooperate with nondeviant per-sons—"health professionals"—in an effort to get well. The general point that Parsons was suggesting was that deviance is culturally defined and that this definition affects its attractiveness to members of the social system. The greater its legitimacy, the more likely will it be tried. Furthermore, the greater its legitimacy, the less likely will conforming members of the system react with moral indignation and thereby nip deviance in the bud. Thus, par-tial legitimation of deviance tends to increase the rate of deviance for two reasons: partial legitimation both increases the motivation to engage in it and reduces the motivation to control it. This does not mean that partial legitima-tion necessarily increases the disruptive consequences of the specific type of deviance. Although the rate tends to be higher, partial legitimation lessens the stigma to the deviant and thereby increases the likelihood of a quick return to conformity. Thus, partial legitimation led to a rapid spread of streaking and an equally rapid abandonment of it.

Exceedingly complex empirical questions are implied by this line of reasoning. Deviance theorists tend to assume that the greater the rate of de-viance from a norm in a population, the greater the threat to the viability of the norm. What Parsons did by introducing considerations of partial legitima-tion of deviance was to demonstrate that, under some conditions, the deviant from the norm remains bound to the norm and that consequently even a high rate of deviance does not threaten it. In a sense, the sick person is coöpted by society. In quite a different way, so were the streakers. Parsons spoke of this issue in terms of burning ideological bridges to society or of not burning them. Quite clearly, armed robbers and rapists burn their ideological bridges to society in ways that sick people do not. The political radical, even the ur-ban terrorist, also maintains ideological contact with society by claiming to

---

[2] Parsons was particularly interested in mental illness, such as depression, not in purely phys-iological ailments. Parsons insisted that deviance was *motivated* noncompliance but that the motivation was not necessarily conscious. This was the formula by which illness could qualify as deviance.

adhere to basic values that society, in its corruption, has abandoned. Thus, the urban terrorist, like the streaker, finds it relatively easy to return to conformity if he wishes to do so. These considerations bear on the issue of the effects of deviance but do not settle it. Ultimately, the extent of the threat to the social order of partially legitimated deviance is an empirical question of great complexity.

A special case of partial legitimation of deviance is subcultural legitimation. Although many examples of subcultural legitimation are to be found in the sociological literature, the clearest example is Miller's analysis of adolescent gang behavior in Roxbury, Massachusetts (1958). According to Miller, a sufficient explanation of the legal infractions committed by gang members was the lower-class cultural milieu, which required, or at least encouraged, the expression of "toughness," "smartness," and "excitement." Whether or not Miller's description of Roxbury was correct, it illustrates a special sort of partial legitimation: a subsystem of the larger society that has values different from those of the larger society. According to subsystem values, behavior deviant in terms of the values of the larger society may be quite justifiable. Hirschi (1969) found that subcultural legitimation could not explain much of the variation in delinquent behavior in data collected in Oakland, California. But this empirical result may have been due to the limited variation in subcultural values in the school population under study. It seems theoretically plausible that regional and ethnic subcultural versions of the value system of the society may serve to partially legitimate deviance.

To put the issue in general terms: Some moral standards are shared throughout the society; others are shared within smaller groupings contained in the larger society. Assessing the degree of subcultural legitimation of a presumably deviant act is complicated by the system reference of the act; in some systems it is less legitimate than in others. It may well be that streaking was temporarily legitimated fairly broadly throughout American society, but there were some subgroups in which it continued to arouse indignation. And on many college campuses it was legitimated to the point of religous fervor.

A striking instance of the system-reference problem of cultural standards occurred at Rutgers College in 1966. In retrospect, I think of it now as a pre-streaking innovation in the area of public nudity that did not catch on. It began late in the spring semester. One of the students in my criminology class—I shall call him Gary—telephoned me at home about 8:00 P.M. and asked me whether I could see him that evening. I suggested that I'd be glad to see him the next morning, but Gary said that the next day would be too late. He was scheduled for a disciplinary board hearing at 9:00 A.M.; he sounded very upset. He explained that my discussion of sexual deviance was the reason he was consulting me. "You see," Gary said, "I exposed myself." Drawn partly by sympathy and partly by curiosity, I hurried to my office, met Gary there, and listened to him. Gary was a member of a fraternity, and, several weeks before, about 60 brothers, formally dressed in jackets and ties, stood in the fraternity parking lot, being photographed for the annual edition of the college yearbook, *The Scarlet Letter*. Gary stood in the front row; another brother stood between him and the elderly housemother of the fraternity. Apparently, the various fraternities had developed a tradition of clowning for this rather stuffy formal photograph. One of the brothers would make an obscene gesture with his hand. Everyone had a good laugh when the picture appeared in *The Scarlet Letter,* and one fraternity's symbolic obscenities were compared with another's. Just as the photographer was preparing to snap the picture, Gary made an obscene gesture that topped them all. He unzipped his fly, took out his penis, and nonchalantly stared into the camera as the shutter clicked.

According to Gary, he anticipated that his prank would be discovered as soon as the photograph was developed; he was sure that his penis was conspicuous in the picture and would be airbrushed out. However, no one noticed a bare penis in a group portrait of 60 fraternity members and their housemother. Even after Gary told me what to look for in his copy of *The Scarlet Letter*, it took me a while to see it. A magnifying glass was necessary to confirm the dawning hypothesis that a penis had somehow gotten misplaced. Gary had managed to distribute (with the unwitting cooperation of the senior yearbook) more than two thousand copies of his penis not only to the Rutgers community but throughout the State of New Jersey. Although the misplaced penis took more than a week to reach the dean's eyes, when the dean did see it, he failed to realize that a few years later he would see hundreds of campus penises exposed to public view. He convened a disciplinary board. In his desperation, Gary asked me to come to the board and explain that he was a sexual deviant in need of rehabilitation.

I did not testify on Gary's behalf. The disciplinary board suspended him from Rutgers for a semester. What is theoretically interesting about the case is that Gary would probably not have been punished at all if knowledge of what he had done had not gotten beyond the fraternity system. In terms of the cognitive and evaluative definitions of his fraternity peers, "exposing" himself (as Gary described it to me) was playful competitiveness: an imaginative joke. But once the knowledge of Gary's lark seeped into the consciousness of the larger Rutgers community and even into the New Jersey environment (state legislators, newspaper editors, and groups containing parents of Rutgers students), fraternity members themselves reevaluated his action. After all, the fraternity system is not self-contained. Fraternity values are subcultural versions of university values, and university values are subcultural versions of New Jersey values. The definitions of the situation on the part of more inclusive entities tended to prevail. The disciplinary board's penalty was severe because the board was not responding socially in terms of the fraternity system's cultural definition of the situation; it was responding partly in terms of the definitions of the larger Rutgers community, including secretaries and coaches as well as professors and students, and partly in terms of its assessment of the likely definition of the situation by the social environment in which Rutgers is located.

To sum up issue 1: Deviance is defined and responded to in terms of shared criteria of partial legitimacy or illegitimacy. The greater the partial legitimacy of a deviant act within a social system, the more likely that sizeable proportions of the population will feel released from normative control. Thus, partial legitimation tends to increase the rate and expand the incidence of deviant behavior. But high rates of deviance do not necessarily mean that the deviant contagion will spread without limit. Legitimation increases the likelihood that deviance will only be temporary, that deviants continue to identify with the societal community, as Parsons called it (1977), and therefore return to conformity even without special rehabilitative pressures. Thus, the effect of partial legitimation for social control is a complex empirical question. A further complexity lies in the nesting of social and cultural systems within one another. What is partially legitimated in a small social and cultural system may not be legitimated in a more inclusive social and cultural system. Nevertheless, I believe that the best starting point for explaining the genesis and control of deviant behavior is sociocultural analysis. After sociocultural analysis has contributed as much as it can, the causal input of personality systems and behavioral systems may be able to add further insight.

Issue 2: IS DEVIANT MOTIVATION QUALITATIVELY DIFFERENT FROM CONFORMING MOTIVATION OR IS THERE CONTINUOUS VARIATION BETWEEN DEVIANCE AND CONFORMITY?

One of Bleuler's and Freud's contributions to personality theory was an insistence on ambivalent feelings rather than simple love or simple hostility (Bleuler, 1911). Parsons (1951) and Merton (1976) advanced a parallel insight with respect to motivated tendencies either to conform to social rules or to violate them. According to Parsons (1951: chap. 7), a socialized individual cannot violate previously internalized rules without ambivalence. Thus, deviant motivation is always ambivalent. What about conforming motivation? Parsons said that unambivalent conforming motivation is possible but that ambivalent conforming motivation occurs also; it arises from situations in which deviant motives and conforming motives are both present but in which the conforming motivations are stronger. Parsons did not estimate how frequently unambivalent conformity occurs. Probably it is rare, a limiting case. The usual situation is one that Parsons called "strain"—where the individual is simultaneously under pressure to conform and to deviate.

If indeed most conformity as well as most deviance is motivated ambivalently, the motivational difference between behavioral conformists and behavioral deviants can be quite small. What seems qualitatively different in behavioral terms turns out to be a matter of continuous variation in motivational terms. This proposition has implications for both deviance and conformity. If the behavioral deviant is motivationally ambivalent, he is not as firmly committed to his deviance as might appear. Similarly, if the behavioral conformist is also motivationally ambivalent, he is more vulnerable to a slip into deviance than might be supposed. The Parsonian approach assumes that both conformity and deviance are chronically unstable, thereby making it easier to explain deviance (because the seeds of deviance are present in outward conformists) and easier to explain the resocialization of deviants into behavioral conformity (because the motivational basis for conformity is present to some degree even in outward deviants).

Against this intellectual background, consider two problems posed by streaking: why streakers emerged so suddenly and why they disappeared equally quickly. In the course of socialization, young people internalized the social norm prohibiting public nudity—along with many other norms taught them by adult socializing agents. Presumably, some of these socialization experiences aroused resentment, psychological resistance to obeying the norm or obeying the norm-giver, or both. Young people had to do what they did not want to do because socializing agents put pressure on them. Ambivalence about rules and rule-givers stemming from these developmental experiences fed the motivation to streak, once the streaking pattern developed and was culturally defined as quasi-legitimate. That is to say, deviant motivation is, according to Parsons, widely distributed in a population. As soon as situations occur where social controls are weak and cultural definitions propitious, these deviant potentialities get harnessed; the outcome is behavioral deviance. On the other hand, it is possible for little or no overt expression of these deviant potentialities to occur. If social controls are strong and cultural definitions of the behavior deny it legitimacy, the personality predispositions toward deviance remain repressed potentialities rather than being carried out in actual behavior.

When streakers streaked, they did not thereby burn their motivational bridges to conventional dress. The prohibition against public nudity was temporarily suspended, not extinguished. As soon as the shared definition of the situation as a collective lark weakened, conventional reservations against public nudity reasserted themselves. The same individuals who enthusiastically ran naked in the streets returned happily to clothing. Possibly exstreakers subsequently patronized nude beaches more than nonstreakers of the same age and background. But Parsonian theory suggests that they didn't. When the compulsive rebellion that motivated streaking was reversed, there may have resulted an equally compulsive repudiation of public nudity. The outcome depends, of course, on the depth of the ambivalence of the average streaker, and that is an empirical question. The theoretical point is that streakers never lost touch emotionally with the conforming community, and, consequently, a return to conformity was not difficult. Ambivalence facilitates movement into and out of deviance.

By and large, Dennis Wrong was quite wrong about Parsons' alleged belief in an oversocialized conception of man (Wrong, 1961); but Wrong was right to suggest that Parsons regarded socialization as a crucial social process. Parsons believed that solidarity between the socializing agent and the socializee persists in the course of socialization even though the socializing agent pressed the socializee to learn a new role. Nevertheless, that solidarity is accompanied by feelings of ambivalence on the part of the socializee based on unconscious resistance to the pressure. Socialization simultaneously creates shared values and ambivalence. To paraphrase Cooley, for Parsons conformity and deviance are twin-born. Thus, the motivational similarity between behavioral conformists and behavioral deviants is no accident. It arises inevitably from the socialization process and helps to explain both the pervasiveness of deviance and the relative ease of the social control of deviance.

To sum up issue 2: If both conforming motivation and deviant motivation contain varying components of inclinations to conform to the rules and to violate them, most behavioral deviants are only slightly different from most behavioral conformists in the organization of their personality systems. This suggests that personality systems have only a limited role in the etiology of deviant *behavior*—even if they play a significant role in the genesis of deviant *motivation*.

Issue 3: How Important Is Motivation Derived from Personality Sources in the Production of Deviant Behavior?

Clearly, neither organismic changes nor personality changes in the American population explain the streaking epidemic of 1974. Only sociocultural changes can account for the sudden emergence and sudden disappearance of streakers. Yet streaking, like all behavior, deviant as well as conformist, was motivated. To what extent does the assertion of a loose connection (or no connection at all) between personality factors and streaking contradict the basic postulate that behavior is motivated? Not at all. Confusion tends to arise because "motivation" is used in two senses: it refers to the constellation of needs arising from the integration of drives within the psyche of the individual, and it also refers to the synthesis of organic, cultural, social, and personality strands of orientation so that integrated action occurs. The first meaning of motivation is summarized in the word "personality." The second meaning has no unambiguous verbal tag. Talcott Parsons used "general theory of action" to refer to this synthesis of four different motivational systems in concrete behavior. Parsons was calling attention to the empirical openness of behavior to influences from all four action systems.

When Parsons discussed "the genesis of deviant motivation" in Chapter 7 of *The Social System,* he was trying to explain why some actors developed the motivation to violate institutionalized rules or to defy authority figures. He devoted considerable space to the problem of the formation of deviant personality structures: compulsive dominance, compulsive enforcement, submission, ritualism, compulsive aggressiveness, incorrigibility, compulsive independence, compulsive evasion. But in a sense this was a side issue. These deviant personality trends were not the only road to deviant *behavior*. Nor did their development guarantee deviant *behavior* at all. Parsons went on to discuss the role of legitimacy (the cultural system) and of strain arising from the pressure of socializing agents (the social system) in producing deviant behavior.

In the case of streaking, a broader conception of motivation than one derived from personality alone is necessary in order to explain how motivation to defy the prohibition against public nudity appeared suddenly in 1974 and then disappeared. I have already discussed some of the main sources of the motivation to streak. Somehow a change occurred in the social expectation system faced by young people, including their expectations for themselves; or a change occurred in the system of the ideas that they shared; or in both. Although the details are not fully known, it seems likely that the change was predominantly cultural. For a brief period of time, young people developed a shared conception of public nudity (in the course of rapid motion) as funny and liberating: as a lark. Social networks transformed this idea into normative expectations. But considerable streaking occurred in direct response to the cultural definition transmitted through mass media rather than a response to the expectations of face-to-face groups. Social networks were directly implicated in some streaking, but they were not a necessary condition for streaking. This is the basis for the argument that cultural sources of motivation were the most important.

Cultural sources of motivation can explain forms of deviance less ephemeral than streaking. More than a generation ago Bales (1944) argued that the higher rate of alcoholism among the Irish as compared with the Jews could be explained by different cognitive, expressive, and evaluative associations made with alcoholic beverages in the two groups. Jews were taught to use alcohol in ritual contexts; the Irish learned more utilitarian and convivial uses of alcohol. Bales' argument was that a utilitarian orientation toward alcohol was much more compatible with alcoholism than a religious orientation. For an Orthodox Jew, wine was associated with the Sabbath, not with giving himself courage to face a difficult social situation. A utilitarian orientation toward alcohol did not necessarily lead to alcoholism, but without such an orientation alcoholism was almost impossible. The empirical difference in the alcoholism rates of the two ethnic groups reflected this orientational difference. Bales specifically rejected the notion that personality problems had a higher incidence among Irish than among Jews. Thus, in a different way from the examination of streaking, it is possible to demonstrate a predominantly cultural source of deviant behavior.

To sum up issue 3: If deviant motivation is defined broadly enough, it becomes tautological to distinguish between deviant motivation and deviant behavior. Deviant behavior is motivated, like all behavior; hence it springs inevitably from deviant motivation. But it is not tautological to consider the separate contributions of four strands of human motivation: the organic, the cultural, the social, and the personality. Within the skin of the individual, the four are synthesized so that integrated action occurs. The advantage of separating four strands of motivation rather than aggregating all motivation in one synthetic strand is that the relative weight of different motivational inputs into behavior can be assessed. Although Parsons devoted space and analytical skill to personality factors in deviance, he apparently believed that cultural and social factors were more closely related to deviant *behavior*.

Conclusion

Although I have discussed three separate issues in the sociology of deviance, they are closely interrelated. Legitimation or partial legitimation of the deviant act affects both sides of the interactional equilibrium. It justifies the expression of his or her deviant orientation to the potential behavioral deviant, and it undercuts the willingness of the conforming counterpart to disapprove and to visit immediate negative sanctions upon him or her. Pope John Paul was probably not under the influence of a Parsonian analysis of deviance when he said, ''The worst thing about terrorism is that it murders man's sense of sin,'' but he was conveying a similar perspective on the legitimation of deviance.

That legitimation should be relevant to deviant behavior follows from the omnipresence of deviant motivation—in the form of ambivalence—even in outward conformists. By raising the issue of continuous variation of personality tendencies toward deviance, Parsons suggested that social and cultural factors had great potential motivational input in deviant behavior and its control.

Finally, although the perspective of the general theory of action opens up the possibility of deviance being influenced by any of the four specific action systems—behavioral organism, personality system, social system, or cultural system—the fascinating empirical question is which action system predominates in explaining different types of deviant behavior. In the case of streaking, I am drawing on macroscopic observation rather than on systematic data, but my guess is that streaking can be explained predominantly in terms of cultural systems. In the explanation of other forms of deviance, the other action systems may have greater explanatory weight. Despite the empirical openness of this issue, the thrust of the Parsonian analysis is to downgrade the etiological importance of organismic and personality dimensions and to suggest strategies for examining the connections between social and cultural systems and deviant behavior.

25

A Fresh Look at Theories
of Secularization

Benton Johnson

A DECADE AGO secularization was a topic that occupied the attention of many of our most creative sociologists of religion. Bryan Wilson wrote about it, as did Peter Berger, Thomas Luckmann, David Martin, and even Talcott Parsons. Secularization was also a popular subject among theologians. *The Secular City,* Harvey Cox's best-seller of 1965, celebrated humanity's control over its destiny and called for a moratorium on God talk. Thomas J. J. Altizer announced that God had died in our time, and numerous other religious intellectuals declared the institutional church irrelevant and moribund. But then the mood changed. Perhaps the single most important reason for the change was the unexpected surge of interest in spiritual matters among many of the young people who had been involved in the counterculture. In the wake of this development Harvey Cox rediscovered the sacred. So did such men of science as Richard Alpert, John Lilly, and Carlos Castaneda. And so, in his own scholarly way, did Robert Bellah. By the early seventies, sociologists of religion were hard at work studying the new religious preoccupations of youth. Within a few years they had produced an enormous and detailed literature on the new religions. The sociological interest in secularization waned accordingly.

It has recently become apparent to some American sociologists that this lapse of interest was premature. In the early seventies, sociologists of religion were too busy with their research on the new religions to pay much attention to a problem that was already disturbing the officials of main-line denominations, namely, an unprecedented decline in membership and attendance. It is instructive to recall that the first serious attempt to document and explain this decline, Dean Kelley's *Why Conservative Churches Are Growing* (1972), was written by an ecclesiastic and not by a sociologist. Now, at last, a few sociologists are beginning to publish studies of some factors involved in the decline. One fact has become quite clear: *Apostasy,* not new forms of spirituality, has been the main new trend among youth since the mid-sixties. In fact, the decline in membership, attendance, and belief is more marked among young adults than it is among any other age group (Hoge and Roozen, 1979: 123–43, 315–33; Wuthnow, 1976). In their preoccupation with the more visible aspects of the youth culture, sociologists of religion failed to spot what in quantitative terms was the larger drift among the very cohort they were studying. This drift appears, on the surface at least, to have the earmarks of a process of secularization.

It seems appropriate, therefore, to take a fresh look at sociological theories of secularization. In doing so, I will concentrate on the works of contemporary sociologists rather than on the works of the classical theorists. Although I am indebted to others for many of the points I will make, I will try to be more systematic in my exposition and critique of these theories than many of the other critics have been, and I will try to be more programmatic than they in suggesting how sociologists can most usefully conceptualize and study secularization processes.

Perhaps the most striking fact about sociological theories of secularization is how little they agree with one another. The disagreement is reflected in an inability to achieve consensus on the very definition of the term itself as well as on the key issues of how and why secularization is occurring, or indeed whether it is occurring at all. Few fields in the sociology of religion are as plagued with such a bewildering variety of perspectives as secularization theory. Nor does the more recent theoretical literature help resolve the issues at stake. For example, Richard Fenn's book, published in 1978, is not only difficult to understand, it ignores many of the problems others have wrestled with. In short, the field is a mess.

Definitional Issues

The first unresolved issue in secularization theory is how the term itself should be defined. In 1967 Larry Shiner reviewed the literature in the field, isolating six different and not altogether compatible ways in which the term had been used. One of the most common definitions, the one used by Bryan Wilson, is the decline of religion. But, as Shiner argued, this definition requires the establishment of a religious norm or baseline against which decline can be measured. It requires that a religious "golden age" be identified. David Martin (1969: 48–57) has shown that very different conclusions concerning secularization can be reached depending on what golden age one selects. If one chooses a composite of characteristics associated with medieval Catholicism, then most varieties of Protestantism are examples of secularization, as are such recent Catholic innovations as the vernacular mass and the wearing of street clothes by clergy and religious. If one adopts a pre-Constantine baseline, as Harnack did, then the age of the supremacy of the Catholic Church itself is an example of secularization and Protestantism becomes a recovery of pristine religiosity. A special problem arises if the baseline is defined subjectively, that is, in terms of individual commitment to religious values, for it is difficult to determine what people's values were in the days before social scientists began studying them directly.

Not only is there little agreement on which religious baseline to use, there is disagreement over the very definition of religion itself. As is well known, some sociologists—for example, Peter Berger and Bryan Wilson—prefer what is usually called a "substantive" definition, whereas others—for example, Thomas Luckmann and J. Milton Yinger—prefer a "functional" definition. A substantive definition limits religion to systems of theory and practice that are supernaturally grounded, whereas a functional definition would consider any system of ultimate meaning to be religious. If one adopts a functional definition, then one cannot say that the rise of Marxism is a case of secularization. In fact, if it is assumed, as a handful do, that everyone subscribes to a system of ultimate meaning, then everyone is religious by definition and secularization is an impossibility.

According to Shiner, another very common definition of secularization is the tendency to conform to "worldly" ways. The problem with this definition is that it is hard to distinguish between what is worldly and what is not. Is it more worldly to serve God by practicing medicine than it is to serve him by mortifying the flesh? Are Judaism and Christianity, with their strong emphasis on ethical activity in this world, more secular than those religions of the Orient that emphasize the transformation of consciousness? Are changes within religious traditions which point in the direction of a greater concern with the conditions of life always to be ascribed to the intrusion of "secular," that is, worldly influences?

The difficulties involved with both these definitions can be traced to the fact that there are many different "religions" and many different "worlds." Consequently, what appears secular from one perspective may appear religious from another. Theorists of secularization rarely specify which "religions" or "worlds" they employ as baselines. Moreover, they rarely tackle the additional challenge of specifying the various facets or dimensions of secularization within the framework of their definition. They are therefore free to stress whichever aspect of secularization, or lack of it, that is congenial to their outlook. For example, when critics pointed out that Bryan Wilson assumed, but could not prove, that a golden age of Christian piety had existed prior to the industrial revolution, he considered it sufficient to reply that even if everyone in those times was not an orthodox Christian, scholars agreed that most people did believe in witchcraft and other superstitions (Wilson, 1979: 8). On the other hand, Wilson has no difficulty accepting the decline in church attendance and ordinations as proof that modern England is becoming secularized. Others, however, point to the persistence of Christian belief and the desire to retain religious instruction in state-supported schools as evidence to the contrary (Forster, 1972). Where such conceptual looseness is the rule, sociologists can justify almost any argument that suits them.

Is Secularization Occurring?

In view of the fact that sociologists of secularization cannot agree on how to define basic terms, it is not surprising that they also disagree on whether secularization is taking place at all. Three major theorists, Wilson, Luckmann, and Berger, are convinced that it *is,* and that it is a direct consequence of the processes of urbanization, industrialization, and bureaucratization that have been going on in many nations. In their view, there is a fundamental incompatibility between the "modern world" and the perspectives of historical Christianity. Each of the three has his own particular version of the sources of this incompatibility. Wilson (1966, 1979) believes modernization destroys the stable community ties that generate a sense of the sacred. Luckmann (1967) believes that modernization produces new institutional specializations whose norms are irrelevant to the old religious values. Berger (1967) agrees with Luckmann but also emphasizes the secularizing potential within historical Protestantism as well as the erosion of religious plausibility that modern pluralism produces. Although Berger (1974) has recently changed his mind about the inevitability of secularization, he has not changed his mind about what causes it. All three theorists agree that modernization gives the churches two options: either give in or decline.

There are many who do not agree with this analysis. A few deny that secularization is occurring at all. For example, Jan Lauwers (writing in French) dismisses secularization as "a magical reality, . . . a dream that vanishes with the daylight" (1973: 532). But he offers no general theory of the status of religion in modern society. Neither does David Martin (1969), though he challenges many of the arguments of those theorists who are certain that secularization is taking place. Andrew Greeley (1972a) shares Martin's skepticism about secularization. Greeley would agree with Martin that secularization is not "an irreversible master-trend" and that "most varieties of religion are compatible with industrialized societies" (Martin, 1969: 3, 28–29). Both men acknowledge that certain changes in the religious situation have occurred, but their chief emphasis is on the persistence, not the erosion, of religion.

The most ambitious theoretical alternative to secularization theory has been developed by Talcott Parsons (1960, 1967, 1974) and elaborated by his students, notably Robert Bellah (1964) and more recently Victor Lidz (1979).[1] Parsons and his followers admit that the status and character of religion have undergone important changes in the modern world, but they insist that these changes do not imply the disappearance of religion. For the Parsonians, religion remains very important. Their theory, which is based on a more general evolutionary theory of history, stresses the increasing differentiation of religious institutions from other institutions in both the organizational and the normative sense. In the process religious commitment becomes voluntary, and hence a private matter. Insofar as the Parsonians use the term "secularization" at all, they use it to mean this process of differentiation and privatization.

Both Luckmann and Berger would agree that such a process is taking place. They differ from the Parsonians, however, in insisting that it leads to the eradication of Christian influence on the institutional structures of modern society as well as to the diminished influence of a Christian perspective in people's private lives. Parsons, on the other hand, believes that values derived from and still grounded in Christianity continue to legitimate modern societies, and to govern their developmental course in the cybernetic sense. To be sure, as a byproduct of the process of differentiation, these values become exceedingly abstract so that they no longer prescribe the normative details of institutional life, but they continue to perform essential social functions. Moreover, the Parsonians insist that the individual need for a sense of overarching meaning of life has not diminished. In fact, they argue that the process of differentiation itself has put increasing pressure on individuals to develop an integrated sense of selfhood. Institutional religion, therefore, has the vital spiritual task of helping people find the meaning they need. Although in modern societies there is considerable leeway for variation in the particulars of personal meaning systems, these systems must be consonant with societal values, for the legitimation and hence the integration of society still depend on a goodness of fit between individual motivation and institutionalized norms. Victor Lidz sums up the Parsonian view by saying that "secularization has vastly affected the sociocultural environment of religious action. It has not necessarily affected the inner vitality of our diverse religious traditions" (1979: 213).

Evaluating Theories of Secularization

It is hard to assess the comparative merits of the various theories of secularization. For one thing, the fact that theorists define secularization in different ways makes it difficult to determine precisely how their theories differ. It seems likely that to some extent the various theorists are talking past

[1] For a succinct summary of Parsons' position see Porter (1973).

each other because they are addressing different phenomena. The task of assessment is complicated by the fact that little effort has been made to evaluate their empirical validity. None of the theories can claim to synthesize existing knowledge concerning changes in the religious situation in all those nations in which industrialization or the modern forms of structural differentiation have been occurring.[2] The theoretical literature on secularization rarely makes detailed comparisons of religious change in a variety of countries. To be sure, all theorists offer evidence in support of their arguments, but this evidence cannot be regarded as sufficient to establish the superiority of any one argument as a general explanation of religious change under conditions of modernization. Nor have students of secularization embarked on programs to test their theories in a rigorous or systematic manner by reviewing existing studies or by designing comparative and historical studies of their own.[3] All the major sociological theories of secularization are vulnerable to the criticism that they ignore or gloss over troublesome empirical or methodological problems. Let me illustrate this conception with several examples.

THE HERBERG PLOY

The first involves an uncritical reliance on Will Herberg's (1955) famous analysis of the American religious situation to prove that the United States is a thoroughly secularized nation. The Herberg ploy is used by three major theorists: Wilson, Luckmann, and Berger. It plays an important part in their argument about the decline of the Judeo-Christian tradition in industrialized nations, so important in fact that if Herberg is wrong then these three theorists of secularization are also wrong. Now there is plenty of evidence that various aspects of the Christian religion have been declining in most of the industrialized nations of Europe. Wilson (1966, 1979) documents the English decline in great detail. But the United States presents a problem. Almost all the conventionally used indicators show that the United States is more religious than England, Sweden, or France; that in fact it is one of the most religious of all the industrialized nations (*Washington Post,* 1976). And yet if the theories of decline are correct, the United States should be among the *least* religious of the Western nations by virtue of its very high degree of urbanization and industrialization. This is where Herberg proves useful. More than

---

[2] Hans Mol (1972) has edited a lengthy book containing valuable information on the religious situation in most of the Western nations. Unfortunately, much of the material cannot be systematically compared and the editor does not offer a detailed theoretical analysis. A much more promising attempt to discover general patterns in the bewildering array of materials concerning the religious situation in traditionally Christian nations has recently been made by David Martin (1978). Although his book contains many novel and arresting insights, it does not synthesize them well or use them as the basis for assessing the validity of existing secularization theories.

[3] Happily, there are some recent signs that this situation may soon be rectified. See Wuthnow (1977) and Rigney et al. (1978).

twenty years ago he argued that, despite surface appearances to the contrary, the real operating creed of most American religious bodies is a complex of "worldly" values which he referred to as The American Way of Life. Religion thrives in America because its *content* has become secularized.

The credibility of one school of thought concerning secularization hinges on the credibility of Herberg's analysis. Yet it is astonishing how little attention these theorists pay to examining Herberg's evidence. It is fair to say that Herberg's assessment of the American religious situation is not based on conclusive evidence and that the real picture is more complex than he painted it. For one thing, we now know that church participation is lower among those who belong to denominations whose theology Berger (1967) would describe as secular than it is among those who belong to denominations with a more transcendent theology (Stark and Glock, 1968: 81–107). These are also the denominations that have experienced membership losses during the past fifteen years (Kelley, 1972). Moreover, a necessary implication of the Herberg ploy is that European religion fails to retain its popularity because its content has *not* become secularized. Yet secularization theorists present no evidence that this is the case.

THE PRIVATIZATION THESIS

The second problem that secularization theorists face concerns some of the implications of the thesis that religion is becoming increasingly privatized and hence less relevant to any of the publicly debated issues of industrial societies. There are, as we have seen, disagreements among secularization theorists concerning the continuing relevance of religion in the public sphere of life. The Parsonians stress its relevance in providing the abstract value commitments that legitimate and guide social institutions, whereas others believe these institutions now guide and legitimate themselves and that religion has therefore become irrelevant to them. But there is general agreement that religion does not have much to do with the concrete, day-to-day operation of modern institutions and, by implication, that it is not involved in the concrete struggles and controversies surrounding them.

No one can deny that in most industrialized nations religious commitment is now formally voluntary and that traditional religious controls have been relaxed or abandoned in many spheres of life. But secularization theorists tend to overlook the fact that the concrete norms of religious communities continue to exert an influence on some of the public affairs of many nations. In certain European countries, many church people actively oppose efforts to make divorce or abortion a matter of individual choice. In doing so, they do not hesitate to involve themselves in politics. In the United States we have recently witnessed the emergence of a politically organized opposition to the Equal Rights Amendment, gay rights, and the use of public funds for abortion on the part of a consortium involving several religious communities.

Nor is religious involvement in public issues confined to questions of sexuality and the family. Studies of voting behavior in Europe have shown a clear and persisting relationship between religious commitment and general political preference (Glock and Stark, 1965: 185–226). Studies of the American clergy have repeatedly shown that there is a correlation, in many cases a strong one, between religious persuasion and a large array of attitudes and behaviors on public issues (Quinley, 1974). Twentieth-century Protestantism's principal internal rift—namely, the rift between theological liberals and traditionalists—involves not only a struggle over the interpretation of Genesis but a struggle over the character and destiny of the United States as a nation. Throughout this century, religious liberals have tried to identify Christian piety with the liberal thrust in politics and social action. Whether this development is itself a manifestation of secularization depends on how one defines the term, but if the term refers to the withdrawal of religious concern with public issues, then this shift is the opposite of secularization. It is true that the American laity as a whole has not responded with enthusiasm to most of the political war cries of either the liberal or the conservative clergy. But present reality could conceal a potential that only future circumstances will reveal. If a Marxist socialist movement should ever gain wide support in the United States, would it be absurd to expect organized opposition to surface among, say, the Mormons, Southern Baptists, and Roman Catholic traditionalists? Is it conceivable that the persistence of strong religious communities in the United States is one of the reasons why this country has never developed a mass-based Marxist movement?

Anyone who is familiar with the history of the religious situation in Western nations in recent centuries knows that in many instances the boundaries of religious and antireligious communities have coincided with national, ethnic, class, or status group lines. For the members of such communities, piety, politics, economic interests, and life style tend to form a unity which can often be differentiated only with difficulty. Consequently, controversies about religion have in many instances also been controversies about class or national interests. In Europe, in particular, what Marxists refer to as the "class struggle" has involved religious as well as economic and political issues. Yet one can read most theories of secularization and gain only the vaguest notion that it has anything at all to do with the projects of contending interest groups or that religious communities have often been deeply involved in public issues. Whatever its other merits, the privatization thesis as generally formulated obstructs a clear view of this aspect of historical reality.

THE CRITICISM OF RELIGION

There is another curious omission in secularization theories. They do not adequately deal with one other very important set of factors that has affected the religious situation in the West during the past two hundred years and that could well have played a causal role in whatever secularization has occurred.

In view of the fact that the effects of these factors have been especially marked among intellectuals, it is strange that sociologists of religion tend to neglect them. I refer to the criticism of religion, which emerged as an important intellectual and political force during the Enlightenment period and has persisted in varying forms and with varying degrees of intensity down to the present.

At the risk of simplification, I think it can be said that the criticism of religion reduces to two basic charges: First, that the historic teachings of the Christian churches are not true; and second, that many of the practices encouraged or tolerated by Christians are inimical to the welfare of humanity. Neither charge can be adequately understood without also understanding the important shift they embodied in the criteria for assessing the truth of propositions and the goodness of norms. The charge that religious teachings are not true embodied the application to religious doctrine of the new and more rigorous criteria for evaluating the validity of cognitive propositions which had already been developed and applied in philosophy and the new empirical sciences. The charge that religious practices are morally evil embodies a radical extension of the value standard of moral universalism, with all its fraternal and equalitarian implications. Both charges also implied that religious theory and practice must be judged by external criteria grounded not in revelation but in reason—in other words, that they must be judged by what many would call "secular" criteria.

Most sociologists of religion do not deny the existence of this landmark development or of the challenges it has posed to our religious traditions. But, with only a few exceptions, when they write about secularization they give little or no weight to the part which the criticism of religion may have played in bringing it about. As Colin Campbell has noted (1972: 7), secularization theories have little to say about the impact of irreligious movements. They also have surprisingly little to say about the impact of Marxism. In my opinion, a close study of history would reveal several kinds of impacts which the criticism of religion has had. One impact is the creation of new communities estranged from religion and united by a sense of intellectual or moral outrage against the theories or practices of ecclesiastics and their supporters. Another is on the course of change within certain religious bodies, especially those whose leaders or major constituents are in close and friendly touch with the modern intellectual community. This course of change is in the direction of modifying religious theory and practice so as to make it more palatable to this community.

Ideological Elements in Secularization Theories

The deficiencies of secularization theories cannot be attributed to lack of intellectual power on the part of their authors, for their authors include some influential and highly respected sociologists. Yet there is reason to believe that the work which they and others have produced on secularization does as much to mystify as to clarify the subject. As many have noted, including Parsons himself, distorted pictures of social phenomena are often the product of value commitments about the phenomena themselves. Insofar as value commitments interfere with scientific objectivity they can be called ideological. In the case of secularization theories, we must entertain the possibility that they contain ideological distortions and that some of the disagreements among the theorists are reflections of conflicting value commitments.

This is not a novel idea. Several years ago, Roland Robertson asserted that the debate about secularization "is a highly significant case of sociologists grounding their analyses in deeply held views about the *raison d'être* of human life" (1971: 300). On a more concrete level, David Martin has declared that the "whole concept" of secularization "appears as a tool of counter-religious ideologies" such as rationalism, Marxism, and existentialism (1969: 16). More recently, Berger has alleged that those who do not define religion the way he does aid and abet those with an ideological interest in denying the experience of the sacred (1974: 127–128). And, more recently still, Peter Glasner has spoken of secularization theories as demonstrating "the ubiquity of the ideology of progress in sociologists' views of the place of religion in society" (1977: 116).

I think it is important to identify the value perspectives informing secularization theories. Knowing what these perspectives are can enhance our understanding of the theories themselves by revealing an underlying aspect of their logic. It can also help pinpoint some possible sources of their shortcomings as theories. Although several sociologists (Robertson, 1971; Glasner, 1977) have attempted to identify the value perspectives underlying secularization theories, in my opinion none of them adequately discern these perspectives. Therefore, I would like to try my hand at identifying them and suggesting how they may have affected the intellectual content of these theories.

THE DEFENSE OF RELIGION

We can best begin the analysis by reminding ourselves that as sociologists of religion we deal with a subject which has been highly controversial in the recent intellectual and social history of the Western world. The question of the basic character of religion, its relation to other aspects of social life, its history and its destiny, have all been hotly debated. Moreover, as I have just noted, the "religious question" has been intertwined with other questions— for example, the "stratification question" and the "power and authority" question. These and other topics have been of more than academic interest in our recent history. Modern social science was born in the process of the debates about them. When we conceptualize the character and destiny of religion we continue to participate, if only indirectly, in these debates.

In unearthing the value elements in secularization theories, it is convenient to take as our intellectual reference point the criticism of religion discussed above. This criticism involved a forthright condemnation of traditional religion and was typically associated with the expectation that it would die out and be replaced by a theory and practice of life grounded in the exercise of reason. Although the criticism was initially associated with the spirit of liberalism, today its most confident, coherent, and influential expression is in Marxism. Despite a nervous curiosity among some Eastern European Marxists concerning the persistence of religion in their nations, and despite the fact that certain Western Marxists have discovered a few things to admire in Judaism and Christianity, by and large, Marxists have had few second thoughts about the criticism of religion. To them, secularization *is* the long-range trend and the sooner it is completed the better.

At this point it is important to observe that there are few Marxists among contemporary sociologists, and fewer still who have participated in the recent debates on secularization. Nor does our field contain many non-Marxists who are militant skeptics. If the situation were otherwise, the character of our debates would surely be different.

In spite of the fact that the discussion about secularization proceeds without the participation of Marxists and other overt skeptics, the legacy of the criticism of religion still exerts an influence over the character of the discussion. Let me try to show how it does. As I have argued elsewhere (Johnson, 1977), the general theoretical framework shared by most contemporary sociologists of religion is not only a scientific "analysis" of religion but also a *defense* of religion against the two basic criticisms which we have just reviewed. It is, however, a *veiled* defense, that is, one that does not present itself as a species of apologetics but rather as a purely scientific theory. This theory was devised by intellectuals for other intellectuals and those susceptible to their influence. Since much of the modern intellectual community has inherited the skepticism which the criticism of religion engendered in the first place, certain modes of defense are simply out of the question because they would never pass muster among today's intellectuals. It will not do, for example, to insist, in the arguments of the sixteenth century, that Roman Catholic doctrine is true and that everything the Church encourages is morally excellent. Moreover, though some sociologists of religion are believers, many are not. They tend to be friendly toward religion, but personally they are skeptics or they are uncertain about their religious commitments. What they write must also pass muster among themselves.

Modern general theory is based largely on the works of Pareto, Durkheim, and Weber, though Talcott Parsons deserves most of the credit for the interpretation, modification, and synthesis of their works that form the real core of the modern theory (1937, 1952, 1954). This theory contains two lines of defense against the criticism of religion. The first line of defense is methodological. It consists of arguments that dismiss the charge that religious teachings are untrue and religious practices are evil on the grounds that science is incapable of passing judgment on either theological or normative issues. They imply that these criticisms themselves are merely ideological and may be ignored by real scientists. All of us are familiar with these arguments. I believe they are seriously flawed (Johnson, 1977). They are, however, the primary line of defense against the criticism of religion.

The secondary line of defense consists of a set of empirical propositions which also bear on the truth and goodness of religion. As for the question of truth, these propositions minimize the part which cognitive interests play in religious commitment. As David Martin puts it, "The elements of information are not only subordinate but probably exercise little influence so far as man's religious commitments are concerned" (1969: 18). On the matter of religious truth, the first line of defense tells us that sociologists cannot judge the validity of religious teachings, and the second line of defense tells us that the question of religious truth is of small concern to people anyway.

As for the matter of the goodness of religion, modern theory first declares such questions off-limits to sociological inquiry and then, under the veil of value neutrality, offers a set of empirical propositions that plainly imply that religion is basically a good thing. These propositions tell us that religion supplies answers to the fundamental questions of human existence and that it provides the normative foundation needed for coherent and sustained group life. As Andrew Greeley has put it, religion offers both meaning and belonging (1972b: 30–65). General theory constrains us to look on the bright side of religion and to avoid a preoccupation with the moral issues thematized by its critics.

The implication of these two constraints of modern theory is that as sociologists we need not concern ourselves with the part that cognitive or moral *argumentation* may have played in the recent development of religions. I believe this disposition is the principal source of the failure of secularization theories to pay close attention to the influence which the criticism of religion itself may have had in the process of secularization. We should remember that the criticism has clearly had an effect on intellectuals. Perhaps it has had an effect on others as well.

THE SECULARIZATION CONTROVERSY

The disposition I have just described does not, however, account for all the ideological distortion which secularization theories may contain, for it explains what they have in common and not how they differ. There is a near consensus among sociologists of religion at the most abstract levels of general theory, but at lower, more concrete levels, there is much controversy. As far as value commitments are concerned, all we seem to have in common is that we are not Marxists and we are not actively hostile to religion. Otherwise, we are a heterogeneous lot whose predilections reflect the social fact that the modern friends of religion disagree on many issues. One of these issues is secularization.

In my opinion, divisions of opinion on the issue of secularization reflect religious and to some extent political predilections that vary along a continuum ranging from very conservative to very liberal. Those close to each extreme of this continuum tend to view current trends with alarm, though of course they are alarmed by different things. Those closer to the center tend to be much more sanguine in their assessment of the religious situation.

At the conservative extreme are Wilson (1966, 1979), Berger (1967), and, with certain qualifications, Luckmann (1967). They are not, as a few have alleged, in favor of secularization, nor are they devotees of the idea of "progress." Their analysis of recent religious change is not based on an Enlightment criticism of religion, but on a criticism of those forces in the modern world which are eroding traditional Christianity. These forces include not only industrialism, but religious leaders such as Harvey Cox and Bishop Robinson, who assist in the scuttling of their own traditions. Wilson's distaste for machine civilization is barely concealed, as is his admiration for the old Church of England and the sturdy nonconformists. The conservatism of Berger's critique of modernity is now as plain as day. It is the alarmed conservatives among secularization theorists who use the Herberg ploy to demonstrate the secularity, and hence the shallowness, of American religion. It is they who offer the version of the privatization thesis that in effect bemoans the loss of Christian influence over the large-scale institutions of modern life. Their theories of secularization are an elliptical plea to conservatives to stand up and fight before it is too late.

David Martin (1969) has a decidedly conservative temper both in religion and politics, but he is not an alarmist. He is relatively at ease in the modern world. He shares with the alarmed conservatives a fondness for traditional forms of faith, but he emphatically rejects their theories of secularization. Martin emphasizes the persistence of religion. So does Andrew Greeley (1972a), though his position is a shade more liberal than Martin's. Greeley shares the conservatives' distaste for ecclesiastics who cater to the secular intelligentsia. He admires the position which the conservative sociologist Robert Nisbet takes on social change and on history. But he describes himself as a liberal in political and ecclesiastical matters and he speaks of the need to reinterpret religious language in light of the fact that the older religious myths are "broken." He is guardedly sympathetic to Parsons' explanation of religious change.

To Greeley's left are those who are not partisans of older forms of Western religious or political consciousness. Although they do not believe that religion is dying out, they accept and in some cases encourage certain types of religious change. They make no snide remarks about Harvey Cox or Bishop Robinson. The Parsonians are in this camp, as is Yinger (1970), who identifies with the most liberal branches of Protestantism and with their humanistic allies outside the churches. Parsons has little patience with fundamentalists or other traditionalists who would impede the processes of structural differentiation and value generalization.[4] Those in this camp identify strongly with Western industrial societies. In the latter part of his career, Parsons (1977) constructed an evolutionary theory of history in which the United States is assigned the role of "lead society" of modern times. But just as conservatives are divided into those who are alarmed and those who are not, so too are the liberals. Thus, Parsons' works convey no sense that it is essential to take special steps to build a more humane social order or to fashion a new religious consciousness. On the other hand, Yinger (1970) thinks both tasks are essential. And recently, in his provocative book, *The Broken Covenant* (1975), Robert Bellah has taken a similar position.

On Value Commitments in Sociology

Not long ago the main disposition among sociologists who perceived ideological elements in the work of others was to insist on eradicating these elements in the interest of a value-free analysis. They assumed, of course, that their own work was value-free. I share, however, the opinion of an increasing number of sociologists that a completely value-free social science is impossible to achieve. It has long been recognized that value commitments direct our interests toward certain phenomena and toward certain questions about these phenomena. It is now widely acknowledged that these commitments may also play a part in framing the answers we find congenial, and hence credible. Moreover, the use of a formally "neutral" scientific language cannot prevent our values from affecting the answers we frame (Johnson, 1975: 57-59). As sociologists, we must live with the fact that we do have attitudes about what we study and that these attitudes can affect our work.[5]

The fact that value commitments influence our work need not mean that we cannot achieve an objective account of the phenomena we study. For one

---

[4] For a discussion of the value commitments in Parsons' work see Johnson (1975: 59-63).

[5] I make no claim that my own attitudes have not colored my critique of secularization theories. Religiously, I am a skeptic but not an atheist. I combine a rationalistic temper with a primal affinity for traditional forms of evangelical Protestantism, especially of the southern variety. I have never had an experience I would label "religious," but I would be pleased to have one, just as I would be pleased to hear a strong proof of a congenial system of religious propositions. I am a wayward Parsonian with a restrained interest in the Marxist tradition, though I suspect that there are more things on earth and perhaps in heaven than are dreamed of either by Parsonians or Marxists. Politically, I lean to the left but am wary of left fads and panaceas and I confess to a few conservative predilections. I leave it to my critics to discern precisely how these and other attitudes have affected the arguments in this chapter. Critics often do this better than the authors themselves.

thing, value commitments do not invariably lead to biased accounts. Although it is certainly true that they are a common source of distortion, as sociologists of knowledge have long maintained, it is entirely possible that in some cases they enable us to see aspects of reality that those with different commitments overlook. To put it another way, things are sometimes as we wish them to be and sometimes they are not. Identifying the value commitments in sociological work gives us a better grasp of its underlying logic and helps us locate it within a larger context of issues, thereby pinpointing possible sources of distortion, but it does not invalidate the empirical assertions which the work contains.

By now it should be clear that I strongly suspect that the absence of the critics of religion from our recent debates on secularization has made it possible to ignore some very real and very relevant aspects of this phenomenon which the friends of religion have found it hard to see. On the other hand, I also suspect that the optimistic friends of religion who emphasize its persistence, especially in the United States, see an aspect of reality more clearly than the conservative alarmists who are sure that religious decline always accompanies modernization. But I could be wrong. These are properly issues for empirical investigation. Happily, as sociologists, most of us share a commitment to a broadly scientific methodology for settling such issues. Despite our other value commitments, we like to think of ourselves as skeptics when it comes to social analysis—to use Andrew Greeley's description of himself (1972a: 6). The trick is to be skeptical enough of our own hypotheses to be able to modify or discard them when necessary.

We may take heart that now and then some value-laden issues in our field do get settled in the sense that the empirical evidence finally becomes so compelling that it is accepted even by those who find it uncongenial. Fifteen years ago, there was a sharp debate as to whether the so-called Weber thesis is applicable to contemporary North America. Now, largely as the result of empirical investigations, it is generally conceded that it is not applicable, at least not to the major religious communities and not in the forms in which it has been operationalized.

Some Proposals

In the case of secularization theory, it is not sufficient to call for an empirical investigation of all the issues at stake, for two of these issues are not empirical but conceptual, namely, the question of how the terms "religion" and "secularization" are to be defined. There are no empirical tests for definitional issues. I would, therefore, like to make some proposals that would have the effect of removing some of the tougher conceptual issues from our studies of secularization in the interest of achieving enough agreement on definitions to permit studies to be done that can be readily compared. My proposals are based on the assumption that, despite their many differences, students of secularization do, or can, agree on certain definitional matters. I believe there is more common ground than is generally recognized.

Let us begin by examining the definition of religion. Everyone agrees that it is proper to use the term "religion" to refer to meaning systems that rest on the notion that "beyond the visible world there lies an invisible one"—to use Clifford Geertz's phrase (1969: 97). No one—neither intellectuals nor the proverbial persons on the street—would argue that such a usage is improper. The issue we intellectuals debate is whether it is also proper to use the term "religion" to refer to meaning systems not grounded in supernatural notions. This is not a trivial issue, but it is one that cannot be resolved easily or soon. I think we can avoid it in our studies of secularization.

One reason we may be able to avoid it is that I think there is also greater latent agreement on what we mean by secularization than is commonly thought. First, everyone would agree that secularization refers to a certain kind of *change* in the religious situation within a specified milieu or tradition over a specified period of time. The definitional issue consists of the question, What kind of change? We will recall that Larry Shiner (1967) isolated six different ways modern scholars have defined it. After carefully rereading Shiner's article I am convinced that his six definitions can easily be reduced to two, and that the two can be melded into one. The disagreements are not as numerous as Shiner thought. Definition number five is, by his own admission, essentially a different version of number one. Number six is a general theory of social change and not a definition of secularization. Shiner does not consider it, and neither should we. Definitions three and four turn out to be specification of some of the processes which may be involved in numbers one and two.[6] We are left, then, with his first two definitions.

What are they? Number one is the "decline of religion." Shiner lists several difficulties with it, some of which were reviewed above, but they all boil down to the problem of how religion is to be defined. This leads us nowhere new. Definition number two is "conformity with this world." Shiner correctly notes that it also requires a definition of religion, for to be worldly is to fail to be religious. But, whereas his first definition is compatible with almost any definition of religion, the second is not, because those who use it ordinarily take worldliness to mean a loss of focus on the supernatural. This

---

[6] Shiner's third definition of secularization is the disengagement of society from religion, e.g., the shrinking of religious relevance to the private spheres of life. He considers this definition to be broadly compatible with Parsons' theory of differentiation. His fourth definition is the "transposition" of religious norms and orientations so that their content, though preserved to a certain extent, comes to be regarded as a "purely human creation." An example would be the eradication of the religious legitimations of the spirit of capitalism. In my opinion, these two definitions are on a lower level of generality than Shiner's other definitions. They can, therefore, be considered as possible *examples* of processes that can be subsumed under definitions one and two.

implies that they are using a definition of religion that includes a reference to Geertz's invisible world. Since everyone agrees that meaning systems referring to an invisible world are religions, then perhaps we can achieve a working agreement on the definition of secularization by melding Shiner's two definitions into one. The result is a definition of secularization as *a process of change that involves a decline of the supernatural element in systems of meaning.*

This is the definition I propose that we adopt. I believe it comes as close as any to capturing whatever agreement there may be in our field as to the meaning of the term. Even David Martin, who has carefully documented the difficulties involved in defining secularization, has no trouble at all labeling as secular what he calls "an exclusively rationalistic or empiricist framework" of thought—in other words, a framework that dispenses with any supernatural reference (1969: 52, 56). Regardless of their terminological preferences, surely all sociologists of religion will admit the possibility that a decline of the supernatural may have occurred somewhere sometime and that it would be legitimate to study it. Even Greeley, who emphasizes the persistence of religion, observes that "a considerable number of phenomena which once received a directly religious interpretation can now be explained by rational science." He notes with approval that Robert Nisbet, who believes that "fixity and persistence are more typical than change," perceives that a process has been occurring which involves "the kind of change that is associated with the rise of critical rationalism" (Greeley, 1972a: 14, 28, 50).

If we can agree on this definition of secularization, then I believe we can devise a number of methodological rules to help resolve some of the other problems that are closely associated with the definitional issues. I will review some of these problems and suggest rules for resolving them. My review will take the form of a series of questions and answers.

Q. What are the units of entities to which the term "secularization" might apply? *A.* Whatever units we wish to study—for example, the value commitments of individuals or the legitimations of various corporate bodies. Among the latter are the legitimations of ecclesiastical bodies. This means we can speak of the secularization of theology, as Berger has done.

Q. Are there various dimensions of secularization? *A.* Undoubtedly there are, just as there are various dimensions of religiosity itself. We should not assume that all these dimensions are correlated.

Q. Can we speak of degrees of secularization? *A.* Yes. There is no need to assume that the process is an "all-or-nothing" matter. For example, we might compare religious traditions for the degree to which they are secularized.

Q. In order to measure secularization, is it necessary for sociologists to identify a religious "golden age" or to specify what is "authentically" religious? *A.* No. All that is necessary is to establish some empirically verifiable baseline against which to measure change over time.

Q. Are religions that emphasize activities in "this world" more secular than those that do not? *A.* Not necessarily. It depends on the character of their legitimations.

Q. Is the decline of ecclesiastical control to be equated with secularization? *A.* Not unless it is also accompanied by an erosion of supernatural legitimations in the sectors of life involved.

Q. Is religious indifference to be equated with secularization? *A.* That depends. First one must specify the religious tradition, or aspects of it, to which people are indifferent. If indifference is accompanied by an acceptance of an alternative meaning system that is supernaturally grounded, the answer could be no. If it is not, the answer could be yes.

Q. Is secularization an irreversible process? *A.* This is an empirical question. We should guard against assuming that it is. We should be alert to processes of desecularization.

Q. Can secularization have religious sources? *A.* This is also an empirical question. It is conceivable that it can.

I am sure this analysis and those proposals will raise many new issues. It is my hope, however, that they will help settle some old ones and that the new issues they raise will be issues encountered on the road to understanding secularization a little better than we do now.

26

The Gap Between Theory and Research in the Sociology of Religion

Phillip E. Hammond

MORE THAN TWENTY YEARS AGO, Charles Glock (1959) noted that, while the sociology of religion had been an active discipline in the *early* decades of American sociology, it nearly disappeared after World War I, not to reappear until the 1950s, resurrected largely by the questions of whether the religious revival at the time was genuine—and whether, indeed, a revival was even taking place.

I doubt if those questions ever got answered, but in any case, though we have moved past those substantive questions to many, many more, the theoretical issues implied in those two questions remain with us. They still dominate the sociology of religion. They are the following—though, of course, different people will phrase them differently:

1. Where *is* the sacred in modern society?
2. What is the relationship of so-called religious organizations to the sacred?
3. How, and to what extent, are people conscious of the sacred, how do they manifest it, and with what effect?

These three issues, I would submit, are as far from resolution today as they were two decades ago.

Of course, during these past twenty years the sociology of religion has greatly expanded. In the United States, two journals devoted to its study were founded, and a third was transformed out of a general-duty predecessor. Other journals exist in Europe and Asia. Why, then, has little or no progress been made in our theoretical understanding? I decided to search the journals for some answers.

Any judgment about either theory or research in the sociology of religion is hard to make if one reads only the *American Sociological Review*. Only thirteen articles, or approximately 2½ percent of the ASR's output in this decade have dealt in any direct fashion with religion. And three or four of these thirteen were really methodological refinements.

I went, therefore, to the *Journal for the Scientific Study of Religion* for a close look at what has been published in its pages. I reread the first five years (1961–65) and the last five years (1974–78). And I did so with two general questions in mind: (1) What research strategies have been employed during the last two decades, and have they changed? (2) What theoretical domains have been investigated, and have *they* changed?

You will note the peculiar terms being used. I looked for research "strategies" rather than "techniques," because the technical changes in JSSR of course reflect those of sociology-at-large. It was not this information I sought, however, but some idea of the kinds of evidence being offered. Likewise, I looked for theoretical "domains" rather than "theories," because in fact few if any theories get examined in the sociology of religion. Rather, we have substantive areas we investigate. The second question is thus: What *are* these substantive areas, and have *they* changed in twenty years? Not until we answer this second question can we hope to understand why those same issues from the 1950s remain undeveloped. But, as I hope to show, the answer to this second question is significantly a function of the research strategies that have been employed.

I conceived of six kinds of research strategies. Boundaries between them can be ambiguous, it must be admitted, but generally I found it easy to classify each article, at least in terms of primary strategy. An example of each category will help convey this classification:

1. Programmatic: A statement of what *should* be studied or *how* it should be studied. For example, a piece on religious statistics in the United States, and the arguments for and against, including religious I.D. in the census.

2. Philosophic speculation: Not always philosophic in the narrow sense, this category includes articles where the critical terms are not empirically based, though the argument may have considerable relevance for the scientific study of religion. For example, an essay on the bearing of technical data banks for ethical theory.

3. Survey–reviews: Here the author assembles a great many studies or observations and renders a generalization from them. The significance here lies, however, in the assembling, not in the generalization. Whatever is found, in other words, is what is presented. Thus, for example, a report on the current religious practices of Russian citizens based on studies during a twenty-year period.

4. New applications of old ideas: In these pieces we find what might be called replications, except that seldom is a theory being tested under new circumstances. Instead, the author borrows the idea of someone else and shows that it works (or possibly does *not* work) in this new setting. Thus, a paper showing that New England fishermen have more taboos about high-risk than low-risk activities.

The remaining two categories are harder to differentiate because both are likely to involve quantified data, and both are likely to invoke the language of hypothesis testing. But in one—what I shall call the three-variable investigation—an explicit proposition is being examined: X causes Z because of Y, and we are given information about Y, therefore, as well as about X and Z. An example is seen in research showing that the differences in attitudes between Protestants and Catholics toward abortion can be explained almost entirely by differences in ideal family size.

In the sixth category, no idea is really being tested. Instead, whatever is found is presented. And it is presented as if it were as valuable theoretically as anything else that might have been found. We are given new information about the world, but no advance claim is made as to its significance. I call this category ''measurement or concept refinement,'' even though many variables may be involved. An example is seen in an article seeking to know what role definitions hospital chaplains have of themselves.

I trust it is clear that, so far at least, I am making no judgments about the relative value of these categories. They are called research strategies because they are depictions of the kind of evidence offered, combined with the major use to which that evidence is put. Generally speaking, therefore, category 5 stands to contribute most, but the theory to which it may speak so eloquently is possibly of utmost unimportance. Likewise, category 2 (philosophic speculation) or category 3 (survey–reviews) may be far removed from hypothesis testing and thus contribute least. But possibly that insight or those amassed observations provide just the link that was missing for somebody else. The lesson I want to draw, in any event, can be seen when we look at the distribution of cases, first in 1961–65—early in the period of resurrected interest in the sociology of religion—and then in 1974–78, the most recent years.

Several observations from the table seem warranted. First, survey-reviews and new applications of old ideas used to play a minuscule role in the published sociology of religion, and they still do. Second, programmatic statements, and especially philosophic speculations, while once a significant part of this literature, have now faded in significance. Third, the bulk of this scholarly work *was* and *is* quantitative, but the vast majority of the work (80% by count here) was and is also largely atheoretical. It consists overwhelmingly of research showing, for example, that religious beliefs can be factor-analyzed, that the result is 1, 4, or 5 factors, that old people exhibit the same

Categories of Articles Published in *JSSR*

	1961–65		1974–78	
	N =	% =	*N* =	% =
1. Programmatic	15	16	9	7
2. Philosophic speculation	16	17	0	0
3. Survey–reviews	2	2	4	3
4. New applications of old ideas	6	6	4	3
5. Three-variable investigations	6	6	25	20
6. Measurement or concept refinement	47	51	80	66
	92	100%	122	100%

dimensions, but only if they live in nursing homes, that one dimension alone explains 23 percent of the variance in answers to an index of civil libertarianism, which turns out to be differently related in its dimensions to religious orthodoxy, church attendance, and private devotionalism.

Somebody can be counted on to show, then, that for blacks and whites the situation is also different, except that black Catholics seem to resemble East European Jews more than either German Jews or Catholics from south Europe.

It is easy, of course, to poke fun at this kind of thing. Let me confess, therefore, that some of my own work got so classified in preparing this chapter. Perhaps that is all we should do, and all we need to do, to be reminded that science properly is the *reduction* of empiricism, not its endless elaboration. Perhaps we recognize that much of what we do—careful, elaborate, costly, and technically current as it might be—is nevertheless not very relevant to any theories we might be developing. And thus we learn not to take ourselves too seriously in the study of what Durkheim called the "serious life."

But now you can anticipate my next point. If the greater amount of the research in sociology of religion is atheoretical, what can this review of the past twenty years tell us about theory *development* in our discipline? The virtual disappearance of what I called philosophic speculation was seemingly replaced during the two decades by more data-dredging, the turning over of ever more stones. We seem to have eliminated the philosopher types in our midst, but where are the theorists to take their place? The answer, as we shall see, is by no means encouraging for the sociology of religion, although a possible beacon glimmers.

I returned to my two time periods and recoded all the empirical articles, that is, all except the programmatic and philosophic pieces. This was done in terms of four theory domains: (1) The administrative-bureaucratic domain, which includes studies of organizations: organizational leadership, innovation, response, shape, growth, decline, and so on. If we learn anything from articles in this domain, we learn it about organizations or groups, or roles within them. (2) The societal domain, which includes studies of movements or histories within entire societies. What we learn from these articles we learn about a whole society. What these two domains share is a concern for social structure, for culture, for institutions. Altogether, these two kinds of articles make up about one-quarter of all empirical articles in both periods—21 percent in the early sixties, 26 percent in the late seventies.

In substantive terms, the questions they pose and the answers they offer range all over the place. If Durkheim and Marx are the inspiration for studies viewing religion as a social product, or if Weber inspires those who view religion as movement or organization, it can be said that little accumulation is to be seen in either of these traditions. There are more facts, perhaps, but hardly more knowledge, and certainly less consensus, about church and sect, religion as opium, or the ritual integration of society.

What, then, of the other two theory domains that make up the other three-quarters of the empirical articles? These deal not with social phenomena but with individual psyches. What we learn from them is more about the mental operations of individual persons. I exaggerate, no doubt, since it is possible to learn things about society from amassing data about individuals. But this is why I am calling these "theory *domains*"—the logic of the inquiry presumes that the knowledge is being sought for some theoretical purpose. Even if the authors do not declare the purposes themselves, can we infer the *kind* of theory for which these data are most likely relevant? I am assuming we can, and that in this latter case, the theories are social–psychological, not sociological.

One more distinction needs to be made before I get off my coding kick, however. This distinction—between the third and fourth domains—I admit is fuzzy. But if it is valid at all, it provides the kind of clue that efforts like this one are supposed to provide—in closing the gap between research and theory in the sociology of religion.

This distinction is between a social psychological theory domain that is primarily rational and cognitive versus a social–psychological domain that is primarily arational and emotional. Again, the line is not always easy to draw, but perhaps some examples will help convince us that the line exists. Contrast studies of religious beliefs with studies of who has mystical experiences. Contrast an investigation of the relationship of age, SES, and church participation with an investigation of how people articulate a sense of injustice, suffering, and meaninglessness. Or contrast a study of the degree of orthodoxy with a study of what symbols, if any, people *do* invoke in a crisis.

The first halves in these comparisons suggest that persons are thoughtful and calculating, that the pieces of their lives fit together rationally or else distress is felt, and that we as sociologists can understand and predict their individual behaviors if *we* but know what *they* know.

In the second halves of the examples above, the assumption is made that persons respond to forces they apprehend only imperfectly, if at all; that these forces are often unwitting but certainly contradictory, and even if identified for participants, may not be "recognized" as influences in their behavior.

The first of these I am calling "rational" and "cognitive," the second "arational" and "emotional." I can indicate now that, in the two periods covered, the rational/cognitive outnumbered the arational/emotional by a sizeable amount—almost 4:1 in the earlier period, more like 2½:1 in the recent period. In that declining ratio may lie some hope, but still we need reminding that the majority of research in the sociology of religion falls into this social–psychological domain, and it presumes that what we should know is what individuals out there already know. Add to this fact that, while about 60 percent of *all* articles employ the research strategy we earlier called "measurement/concept refinement" (and therefore are largely atheoretical), fully 75 percent of these in the social–psychological, cognitive domain are of this type. In other words, the possibilities of theory development here are practically nonexistent, because the research bears on no issues that are posed theoretically. Whatever is found is what is reported. Often enough it is reported in the form of hypotheses, but instead of helping us understand the world better, it creates distinctions we don't make and can't use, it makes up in superficial precision what it lacks in relevance to any theory. If Weber, Simmel, Freud, and James are the inspirations here, it is probably the case that they would not even recognize this work as in their tradition.

I remind you that we are speaking of the gap between theory and research in a *collection* of articles. Many of these pieces are individually fine examples of social science, of course, and it may be that books, not journals, are the place to find continuity, accumulation, and consolidation. Nevertheless, seen together, these years of articles offer little in the way of theoretical development. We know little more now about the sacred than we did before.

The picture is not entirely gloomy, however. Because of the interest in "new religious movements," whole new arenas of investigation have been opened up: mysticism, astrology, symbolism, glossolalia, evangelical Protestantism, the charismatic movement, and so forth, in addition to assorted Eastern imports.

Along with these new substantive questions, however, has had to come an appreciation for the arational and emotional in religious behavior. Who would conceive a new Hare Krishna recruit in terms of orthodox Hindu beliefs, for example, and thereby try to explain his membership? Who would view the speaking in tongues as an individual psychic phenomenon, when it turns out that friendship is the major path into the charismatic movement?

Religion, it is being rediscovered, is a *social* fact, and, with Durkheim, we may be rediscovering also that society is a religious fact. Thus, from investigations into civil religions to the call for phenomenological research, from studies of religioethnic ties to the implications of symbolic realism, from new looks at the paranormal to the contributions of attribution theory, we are being forced to abandon the model borrowed from physics, the view that people are to be understood mechanically. Especially in the sociology of religion has this model been disastrously nonaccumulative, perhaps because religion deals exactly with the nonmechanical, the ineffable, the arational and emotional— in short, the sacred.

From a substantive interest in contemporary religious movements may be coming, then, a promising and more general shift—from a concentration on social psychological studies of the cognitive/rational sort to those of the emotional/arational sort. Possibly, too—there's a slight hint in the data I've assembled here—we will be seeing an increase of studies in the administrative/bureaucratic and societal domains.

Bryan Wilson (1979b), in a paper recently published in JSSR, reminds us that, while ten and fifteen years ago there were calls to abolish the category of "sacred," now we are told that the sacred has returned. Probably it was there all along, but we're just now getting smarter about how to study it. Charles Glock, twenty years ago, could look out at a sociology of religion that was reactivating after a quiescence of forty years. Twenty years later, the activity continues, but it has not accumulated very much yet. Perhaps we are on the brink of consolidating our heaps of data and stray hypotheses into commanding new theoretical perspectives.

27

Age and Aging: From Theory Generation to Theory Testing

Matilda White Riley

My CHAPTER CONCERNS two closely interrelated sociological concepts: the aging of individuals from birth to death (as all of us grow up and grow old as members of society); and age as a structural feature of society (as in every society both people and roles are stratified by age).

This topic lends itself to the theme of this book: the interplay between sociological theory and sociological research. Over the past dozen years, concepts pertinent to this topic have become clearer, research strategies have become more appropriate, and the gap between concepts and research procedures has been narrowing. I shall write about four recent phases in this interaction between theory and method: an empirical phase, a model-building phase, a phase of exploratory research, and a current phase of model specification and testing. I shall conclude with just a few of the issues and problems of this current phase—issues which can perhaps contribute to the new research agenda for sociologists concerned with individuals growing older within the changing age-stratified society.

I shall trace this intellectual history as a participant observer, as I myself have experienced it—together with colleagues at Rutgers, Bowdoin, Russell Sage Foundation, the Social Science Research Council, and last year at the Center for Advanced Study in the Behavioral Sciences. More generally, our

☐ This chapter was prepared while the author was a Fellow at the Center for Advanced Study in the Behavioral Sciences, with funding from the National Science Foundation and the National Institute on Aging. She is indebted for suggestions and criticism to John W. Riley, Jr., and Marilyn Johnson.

experience suggests a dynamic for the development of a new scientific specialty which, starting in a multidisciplinary area, requires empirical mapping and a discipline-free conceptual framework before valid theories in particular disciplines can be specified.

First, a word about the sociological tradition. Though I start my account with a recent phase of sheer empiricism, age and aging as social phenomena are venerable topics. Pertinent ideas and philosophies extend across all cultures and back into the remote past. In recent times, diverse strands of sociological thought had been variously concerned either with the aging of individuals or with the age structure of the changing society. For example, sociologists (Clausen, 1968; Brim, 1966) had dealt with socialization of individuals in early life and in adulthood. Portions of the life course had been traced through diaries and letters (as by Thomas and Znaniecki, 1918) or through panel studies (Lazarsfeld et al., 1944). Mannheim's seminal essay on the "The Problem of Generations" (1928, 1952), foreshadowed by Comte (1839) and subsequently amplified in the writings of Ryder (1965) and Cain (1964), had shown how each new cohort (or generation of individuals all starting their lives at a particular point in time) has unique characteristics because of the particular historical events undergone or the particular knowledge or attitudes acquired in childhood and adolescence.

Other sociologists (Parsons, 1942; Sorokin, 1941, 1947; Eisenstadt, 1956) had focused on the age structure of society, noting how both the people and the roles in society are stratified by age, much as they are stratified by sex or socioeconomic class. Thus *people* at varying ages differ in their motivations and capacities to perform key social roles, while age criteria govern access to these *roles* and to the associated role rewards (of power, wealth, influence). Such sociological theories have been enriched from other disciplines, notably psychology, psychiatry, anthropology, history.

However, prior to the phases I am about to review, there had been little integration of these diverse sociological strands. There was little clear formulation of how social structures, as they change, are composed of people who are aging. (Ryder's elegant "Process of Demographic Translation" [1964b] deals with populations, but not age role structures; and Homans [1964], in "bringing the men back in," does not deal with historical change.) Moreover, these sociological traditions had been almost entirely disregarded in the empirical phase with which I begin. This first phase was multidisciplinary. It transcended the theories available in any single discipline. Empirical mapping was first needed in order to generate a new overarching conceptual scheme.

Empirical Phase

The first phase, then, was experienced by us through the preparation of our first volume of *Aging and Society*. For me, this work was an interruption in our Rutgers research (with Anne Foner, Marilyn Johnson, and many other colleagues) on two sizeable cohorts of adolescents and young adults (and *their* mothers and fathers). Two foundations (Russell Sage and Ford) offered to fund these continuing cohort studies with the proviso that we would first put together an inventory of social science findings on the middle and later years. We were assured that this was a simple task—readily accomplished in maybe six months with the help of a couple of graduate assistants. (After all, several major handbooks on gerontology had already been published.)

Yet it was not until five years later that seven of us (aided by no less than seventy consultants) finally finished the volume (published in 1968 by Riley and Foner). The available handbooks in gerontology (much like those in child development) were indeed excellent, but they barely scratched the surface. We unearthed masses of studies—in books, journals, government documents here and abroad, fugitive manuscripts. Save for the largely ad hoc "theories" of disengagement versus activity (Cumming and Henry, 1961; Maddox, 1966), most studies were atheoretical. And the research methods were often severely flawed (by biased samples, inappropriate procedures of measurement or analysis, fallacious interpretations). Of the literally thousands of studies we examined (indeed, reanalyzed) for the inventory, only a few hundred met minimum criteria of empirical validity. It was difficult to avoid the *mis*information engendered by a whole series of *fallacies* that we began to identify (Riley, 1973), fallacies that still continue to plague much work in this area. For example, we defined:

- A *compositional* fallacy—where the kinds of people in a cohort changed over its life course as some survived longer than others, yet these aggregate changes were erroneously interpreted as a process of individual aging
- A fallacy of *cohortcentrism*—assuming that all cohorts will age in exactly the same fashion as our own
- A *life-course* fallacy—assuming that cross-sectional age differences refer to the process of aging

Of course, cross-sectional data refer to the structure of society; thus, they can rarely be used to demonstrate any process of individual aging. Yet this is such an important point that I want to make it crystal clear with an absurd example. When we look at cross-sectional data by age, older people have lower levels of education than younger people. But this obviously cannot be interpreted to mean that, as individuals grow older, the amount of schooling they have had declines!

Model-Building Phase

Second, the empirical phase was followed by a model-building phase. All these facts, however interpreted or misinterpreted, cried out for explanation.

We set out to develop a *conceptual model*—that is, a parsimonious set of broad concepts and postulated relationships—to be used as a guide for planning new research in this multidisciplinary area and for appropriate interpretation of existing research. For us, this phase of model building was marked by publication in 1972 of our theoretical and methodological volume of *Aging and Society* (Riley, Johnson, and Foner, 1972).

In this model, we view society as an *age stratification system* within which individuals are aging. Though familiar to many of you, I shall sketch five of its major emphases. These can be visualized schematically if (as in Figure 1) you think of a succession of diagonal bars within a social space that is bounded on its vertical axis by years of age (0 to 80 or 100), and bounded on its horizontal axis by dates (1900, 1980, 2,020).

1. Each diagonal bar suggests the life course of particular individuals (or a cohort of individuals born at the same time).

These individuals are *aging* over their life course.

They age socially as well as biologically and psychologically: that is, they move forward across time and upward through the age strata of society (social aging is one type of social mobility). They pass through sequences of roles, learning to play new roles and relinquish old ones, accumulating knowledge and attitudes and experiences, interacting with peers, parents, offspring who are all aging together.

2. The series of diagonal bars suggests how *new cohorts* of people are continually being born, aging over the life course, and moving through historical time.

Figure 1.   The Age Stratification System: A Schematic View

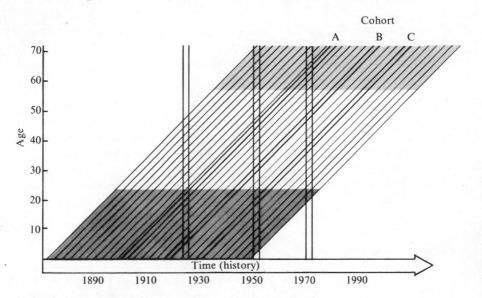

3. At any single moment of history, such as 1979 or 1929, a cross-sectional slice through the successive cohorts divides the *people* into *age strata* (the young, middle-aged, and old), who coexist and interact within and across age boundaries.

Equally important, each cross-sectional slice denotes the age structure of *roles*. (In every society there are customs and rules as to which roles are to be performed at different ages—getting into school, out of school, marrying, performing military service, retiring, etc.)

Comparison of such cross-sectional slices sequentially over time (e.g., 1929, 1949, 1979) can suggest how the age-stratified society is moving across time.

4. The *calendar year* axis suggests how the society itself is changing (or remaining stable) over historical time—in most ways subtly, but frequently in dramatic ways: wars, depressions, famines, revolutions.

5. Thus there is a *dynamic interplay* between two interdependent processes: individual aging and social change.

Now these five considerations lead inexorably to a general principle (clearly formulated by Ryder, 1964a: 461): because of social change, different cohorts cannot grow up and grow old in precisely the same way. Aging is not an immutable process. Just consider: cohorts of people born recently differ sharply from those born a century ago—in prenatal care, age of puberty, level of education, age of widowhood, retirement practices, average length of life.

Clearly, then, there have been enormous changes both in the age structure of society and in the process of aging. But how do such changes come about? How can we understand the dialectical relationship between individual aging and social change?

Exploratory Phase

How useful is such a model? Intentionally global enough to comprehend the multiple facets of age and aging, the model aims simply to alert investigators to the broad range of relevant concepts and their dynamic interconnectedness. It is designed for exploration. And indeed the model, with variations and amplifications, has been (and continues to be) used in guiding research in sociology and other social science disciplines in the third or exploratory phase of development of this approach. Many research strategies are used, but I shall run quickly through one example illustrating just one strategy—cohort analysis—which is a direct translation of key aspects of the model, and is exploratory (designed to suggest clues and possible explanations and to raise questions).

My example concerns rates of female participation in the labor force, which have been rising throughout this century in the United States. How does age enter in? Consider two sets of data (as presented in Kreps and Leaper, 1976: 66–69).

First, the traditional *cross-sectional* data refer to age as a structural feature of society. They show, by *age,* the proportions of women in the labor force at particular periods. For example, in 1950 there was a peak at age 20, then a dip, then a secondary peak at around age 45, followed by a gradual decline at the later ages. In 1960, when rates were higher at every age, these two pronounced peaks still appeared.

How can such cross-sectional data be interpreted? They are clearly important for understanding the *age structure* of the female labor force: the proportions of women actually working at various ages, the age-related match or mismatch between work roles available and women seeking work. Such cross-sectional data also suggest many interesting questions about the relations among age strata: for example, between middle-aged women who were working, their spouses, their elderly parents, their young unmarried daughters who were also likely to be in the labor force.

What these cross-sectional data to *not* describe directly is the work life of women. To make inferences from them about the aging process, about how women move in and out of work as they grow up and grow old, would constitute a life-course fallacy in this instance, as a cohort analysis shows.

The *second* set of data, rearranged by *cohorts,* does provide clues to the aging process. Here the data show the life-course patterns for a succession of cohorts. (Such cohort data on a variety of topics can be unearthed from the archives.) The data refer to some seven cohorts of women, ranging from those born in about 1880 (Riley and Foner, 1968: 45) to those born about 1940. For each cohort, a curve shows the life-course pattern of labor force participation. (Schematically, the cohort rearrangement corresponds to the diagonals in our conceptual model, Figure 1.)

These life-course curves are substantively interesting. For each more recent cohort, the entire curve is generally higher than its predecessor— reflecting the long-term rise in labor force participation. In addition, these curves *change shape* from one cohort to the next. The earliest cohort (1880) starts with a peak at age 20 and then shows a gradual decline with aging. The middle cohorts (born around 1920 and 1930) show a peak at age 20, then a dip at age 30 (when the children are little), followed by a steep rise. And the most recent cohorts (born around 1940) do not even show the dip around age 30 but tend to rise steadily from age 20 on. Thus, there has been a complete reversal in the shape of these life-course curves—from a general *de*crease in participation over the life course of early cohort members, to a general *in*crease in participation over the lives of more recent cohort members. There has been a veritable transformation over the century in the work life of women.

How can these cohort data be interpreted? What kinds of questions do they suggest for further study?

Looking at any *single* cohort, one can seek to explain one aspect of the process of aging. One can ask why, on the average, individual women tend to work at certain ages (e.g., while young and unmarried) or not to work at other ages (e.g., when they have little children, or when they have grown old).

But when the several cohorts are compared, how can the striking *cohort differences* in life-course patterns be interpreted? Such changes across cohorts raise macro-level questions as to how it is that many millions of women in one cohort have come to behave differently from many millions of women in another cohort, why the entire course of women's work life has altered, why the age criteria for entering or leaving the work role have shifted.

In answer to such questions, one can speculate about potentially related social changes, for example, about the breakdown of *employers'* resistance against hiring older married women—as the number of female-typed jobs expanded, and experience with older women showed they could perform after all. One can also speculate about why women as *employees* found it increasingly acceptable to work, learned to manage both work and family, came increasingly to seek added income—perhaps also to seek independence and self-fulfillment.

This example shows the character of this exploratory phase. It has been, and should continue to be, richly productive of descriptive findings, stimulating conceptual insights and questions, and pressing for theoretically appropriate methodologies.

The approach has alerted us to new fallacies and problems, such as:

- The fallacy we call "age reification," that is, treating chronological age in itself as a causal life-course variable (a person "becomes his own man" because he is 40, as in Levinson, 1978, for example).
- The fallacy of "reifying historical time," that is, failing to ask what *aspects* of historical change may be pertinent to understanding particular shifts in the aging process.

And the approach seems endlessly beset by the "identification problem" (Cohn, 1972), which seeks to determine the separate contributions of three equivocally defined terms, "cohort, age, and period." Conceptually, this problem overlooks the critical distinction between age and period as temporal dimensions and cohort as the research case, composed of people who are aging and moving through time. Methodologically, since only two pieces of information are used to measure the three concepts, the question, as Ryder (1979) has said recently, "is without an answer, and one that we should stop wasting our time on" (but see continuing discussions, as in Fienberg and Mason, 1979).

Apart from such difficulties, the exploratory approach remains global, designed to suggest theories and hypotheses, but not to test them. It has begun to raise, but not formulate or answer, the three kinds of specific questions I have just been illustrating: focused on the life course, on cohort differences in the life course, and on the age strata in society.

Phase of Specification and Testing

Exactly such questions are the concern of the current fourth phase, the phase of specification and testing of the model. The global approach of the exploratory phase is now being supplemented by a range of special approaches aimed—within the broad framework of the model—at specific objectives: to examine conditions under which particular variations occur, and to probe into particular postulated causal linkages. Many of the questions being raised and research strategies developed refer to one or another of the three foci I have been emphasizing, and I'll give just a few examples of each.

FOCUS ON THE LIFE COURSE

Questions focused on the life course no longer merely describe aging but ask, in effect, *why* does an individual age in a particular way? How to explain particular shapes of the life-course curve (or portions of it) (Uhlenberg, 1969; Winsborough, 1979)? For example:

- We used historical data to ask whether disengagement—allegedly *caused* by old age—might instead be associated with peculiar social conditions of old people today (reduced income, loss of function, lowered esteem). By examining *young* men who became unemployed during the Great Depression, we found all the same symptoms of disengagement—suggesting it was not age but joblessness that was operative (Riley et al., 1969).
- Other researchers are engaged in intervention research that manipulates the social conditions of old people, to see whether increased practice or heightened motivation might alleviate certain malfunctions associated with old age (Baltes and Danish, 1980).

All such studies are examining the relevance, not of age per se, but of specific age-related factors. (They are avoiding the fallacy of age reification.) Other studies penetrate still farther into the sequence (Hogan, 1978) or duration of events over the life course, often using causal modeling to examine such life-course sequences as: education and occupation in early life, labor force participation in later life, income and assets in old age (Henretta and Campbell, 1978; Featherman, 1980).

However, much of the longitudinal research on the life course still suffers from a static bias. It is not easy for us even to think processually. In data gathering, information on the timing and duration of life events is rarely obtained. And improved methods of analysis, though gradually developing, are surprisingly little utilized.

FOCUS ON COHORT DIFFERENCES IN THE LIFE COURSE

In addition to this life-course focus, other studies focus on cohort differences in the life course: on how it comes about that people in different cohorts age in different ways as society changes. Such studies aim to avoid reifying historical time by measuring relevant aspects of social change. For example, they ask questions about the relationship:

- between unemployment rates in the society and dropping out of high school by adolescents (Land and Felson, 1976)
- between economic changes in the society and fertility among young women (Ogburn and Thomas, 1927)
- between societal fluctuations in cohort size and life-course opportunities (Easterlin, 1979; Waring, 1975)

Such studies of cohort differences in the life course are also plagued with methodological problems: with the pervasive static bias, and with the difficulties of multilevel analysis—of interrelating macro-level societal characteristics with micro-level personal characteristics (Riley, 1963: unit 12; Riley and Nelson, 1971).

FOCUS ON AGE STRATA IN SOCIETY

Finally, questions focused on age stratification (Foner, 1979) concern many implications of particular configurations in the role structure and in the differing cohorts that coexist at particular times. For example:

- What is the impact on the middle-aged of long-term increases in the percentage of old people? (The percent 65 + rose from less than 3 percent in 1850 to 11 percent today to an estimated 18 percent in 2030—and recent estimates predict 40 percent of the federal budget going to care of the aged by 2030.)
- How are changing patterns of divorce and remarriage among young adults affecting other age strata (Furstenberg, 1979)?
- How does age segregation of little children (as in nursery school) affect the lives of their older siblings (Whiting, 1978)? Or residential segregation of old people affect the young—who have fewer models for their own later years (Rosow, 1967)?

- How will the hospice and the move toward old people's dying in the home affect the other family members?
- What consequences follow from older people's return to school? How do teachers interact with pupils who are older than they?
- Under what conditions does age conflict emerge (Foner, 1974)?
- To what extent is there a gradual loosening of the age boundaries separating the three boxes of school, work, and retirement?

So much for the third set of questions. By listing three such sets, I am reaching toward a new research agenda, one that is only partially under way (Elder, 1975; Neugarten and Hagestad, 1976; Maddox, 1979). In such an agenda the emphasis shifts from all-embracing exploratory research to detailed but interrelated studies of cumulating hypotheses—all within a broad conceptual framework necessary for designing research and phrasing interpretation.

Thus, many questions are being raised by our developing sociological approach to age and aging. But in the search for answers, I am bold enough to believe that important conceptual and methodological advances are taking place. That these advances will feed back into several disciplines. And that sociological understanding will be enriched in many areas: in stratification and social mobility, in socialization and intergenerational relationships, in social dynamics and social change, and in the sociology of age and aging.

28

The Life Cycle and Life Strains

Leonard I. Pearlin

THE RATHER DRAMATIC UPSURGE of interest in the life cycle and in various aspects of the aging process have been truly impressive. Indeed, the reasons for the expansion of attention to these areas are themselves deserving of study. As students of the sociology of knowledge, we can be sure that this intellectual movement is being guided not only by the power of its ideas, but also by the power of surrounding social conditions. If one were to try to identify some of these conditions, one would probably consider such factors as the development of sophisticated methodologies for the analysis of longitudinal data, the changing age composition of the society (and of its academicians), and the surfacing of fresh perspectives provided by disciplines—demography and history in particular—that previously had little or no interest in matters such as the life cycle. Whatever else may be contributing to the current interest in life-cycle issues, there is no doubt that a richer and more exciting body of knowledge is resulting.

But the body of knowledge that is developing has some rather fuzzy and ambiguous edges, a price paid by any field that is undergoing rapid growth and attracting scholars from a variety of disciplines. One reflection of this lies in the different meanings acquired by similar terms and by the proliferation of different terms to convey similar meanings. In this vein, I must confess to some blurred vision when I try to fix the boundaries and interfaces between such notions as life span, socialization, development, aging, and life cycle. Indeed, the idea of a cycle itself is rather confusing, for it evokes an image of something circular, a process that repeatedly leads back to where it initially began, only to take place over and over again. But, of course, the very nature of the life cycle is that of a process carrying people irreversibly through a succession of new circumstances, not one that is serially repeated. Whatever may be the intellectual rewards one discovers by working in the general domain of the life cycle, conceptual clarity is not among them. The presence of ambiguity and uncertainty, in turn, makes it somewhat difficult to appraise what the field really knows or to recognize the directions in which knowledge is moving.

My own understanding—and misunderstanding—of these subjects is not shaped by long years of research into the life course. Instead, I have found myself gradually drawn into the area through my studies of the social origins of stress. It had become apparent to me that in order to capture fully the sources of stress, it is necessary to observe life conditions both as they are structured at any moment in time and as they change over time. Clearly, the longitudinal study of social stress and adaptation is inseparable from the longitudinal study of the life course itself. It was inevitable, therefore, that the questions we were asking in our research about the emergence of stresses through time would eventually lead us to ask questions about aging and the life cycle. Since my selection will draw heavily from this research, a brief description of its aims and substance is useful.

Our investigations have as their general concern the identification of social circumstances that stimulate emotional stress and psychological disturbance. One such circumstance is represented by the relatively persistent frustrations and conflicts that are embedded in daily social roles. The rather ordinary problems encountered by ordinary people as they act as breadwinners and jobholders, spouses and parents, are of vital importance in shaping lives. Yet these typically low-key chronic problems have not received the same attention in research as the more dramatic precursors of stress. Therefore, in interviews with a large sample of people conducted in 1972, we gave particular emphasis to the distressful effects of a number of role strains—that is, the relatively structured and enduring problematic experiences that are woven into the fabric of people's lives.

Four years after the initial inquiry, we returned to our sample with a second interview. Many of the original questions were repeated in the follow-up interview, thus allowing us to detect any shift in role strains that might have occurred during the four-year interval. In addition, the second interview brought under study a host of life events. Many of these events involve role and status transitions closely associated with the life cycle: entering into and retiring from the labor force, getting married, having children, seeing children establish their own households, and becoming a widow or widower. Whereas the role strains—that is, the relatively chronic problems—focus on experiences within roles, these transitional events entail experiences stemming from movement between roles. Because most events of this sort are linked to the family cycle, one of their outstanding features is predictability. Although there is certainly some variation in the timing of life-cycle transitions, they can be viewed as the relatively scheduled and anticipated events of life.

In the follow-up interviews we also asked many questions about a second type of event, one markedly different from transitions tied to the life cycle. I refer, of course, to unexpected events, events that occasionally are eruptive and frequently disruptive. Some of these events—divorce and illness, for example—may be quite widely experienced; nevertheless, we don't plan on being divorced when we decide to marry, nor do we count on a chronic illness when we are in good health. There may be some general awareness that events of this sort can befall us, and there may be some forewarnings of their actual occurrence, but we do not schedule them into our lives as we do the life-cycle transitions.

We have, then, conceptually delineated three types of circumstances, in seeking to identify those forces that bear on the well-being of people and that contribute to changes in their psychological functioning: continuing strains embedded in daily roles; life events involving the scheduled, life-cycle transitions from one role or status to another, almost all of them within the context of family; and those life events that are nonscheduled. This distinction, which we have employed in prior data analyses (Pearlin and Lieberman, 1979), avoids the rather buckshot use of life-event inventories found in some early research (Holmes and Rahe, 1967; Myers et al., 1971). Nevertheless, although it is useful to distinguish these types of life conditions conceptually, it needs to be understood that, from the perspective of people moving across the life span, the different conditions of life flow together and are probably experienced as a unity. That is, the events that arise in the lives of people converge with the more persistent circumstances with which they have to contend, and together they shape the nature and direction of their life course. As I shall describe later, the particular manner in which these forces do come together can influence the effects that they jointly exert.

In addition to identifying some of the problems and events of life and their distressful consequences, there are other important ingredients of our research. Specifically, we have sought to take into account the conditions that mediate the impact of problematic experiences, that is, conditions that can either exacerbate or minimize the effects of such experiences (Pearlin and Radabaugh, 1976; Pearlin and Schooler, 1978). I refer to the coping responses of individuals, their psychological resources, and their access to and use of social support networks. People are not simply unreacting objects molded by whatever circumstances happen to prevail in their lives; instead, they actively attempt to deal with these circumstances through their coping repertoires and their uses of social and psychological resources. Essentially, their coping behavior and their active enlistment of resources represent people's efforts to intervene in behalf of their own interests. Consequently, what happens to people in the course of the aging process and in the twists and turns of the life cycle depends not only on changing circumstances, but on how these circumstances are met and dealt with as well. I shall have more to say about these matters below.

Life-Cycle Transitions as Turning Points

Let us turn directly to the question that will be pivotal to the remainder of this chapter: What are the effects of the various life-cycle transitions, to what extent do they constitute the turning points in the inner lives of people? The life cycles of individuals, of course, are closely intertwined with the movement of families through various stages. That is, as families progress through the life cycle, their individual members are presumably also undergoing some corresponding changes. The importance of some of these stages to the family is self-evident. Having a first-born or launching a last-born, for example, represent much more than the mere addition or subtraction of bodies from the household. Events of this sort have the capacity to transform the structure of the family and to rearrange profoundly the patterns of interaction within it. Because life-cycle transitions can so fundamentally alter family life, it seems quite reasonable to suppose that the same transitions have the capacity to penetrate and alter individuals' emotional lives as well. Indeed, there is considerable literature reporting on research efforts to establish the linkages between family transitions and their psychological effects (Burr, 1972; Dyer, 1963; Glenn, 1975; Hobbs, 1976; Russell, 1974; Spanier, 1975; Lopata, 1975). The overall results of these efforts, however, are somewhat mixed, and essentially leave unclear what the impact of life-cycle transitions may be beyond their obvious effects on family structure.

Our own results are less mixed: they consistently show that key transi-'
tional events—such as being married, having children, seeing children progress through the various levels of the educational system, having a child leave home, having a parent die, and becoming a grandparent—bring about little or no emotional changes that are sufficiently stable to be discerned. Nor can change be detected when appropriate events are further distinguished according to whether it is a first-born, middle, or last-born involved in the transition. Having one's youngest child leave home, for example, makes neither more nor less difference than seeing one's oldest child leave the nest. Such distinctions really don't matter, for in general family transitions leave in their wake no emotional changes of an appreciable magnitude.

These statements are based on the assessment of a number of indicators of psychological functioning, including depression, anxiety, and several measures of emotional distress within the context of such roles as occupation, marriage, parenthood, and breadwinning. All of our measures, I should further note, have been established by the use of maximum-likelihood confirmatory factor analysis. Essentially, this method enables us to identify and control measurement error, a desideratum in all research, but especially in that involving longitudinal data (Jöreskog, 1969; Jöreskog and van Thillo, 1972). To evaluate changes in the various dimensions of psychological functioning, we have simply regressed our time-two measures on those based on the first wave of interviewing. In effect, this procedure statistically controls for the initial level of functioning, leaving the differences between the two time periods attributable to the events being assessed in the regression equations.

Depression is of particular interest to me, for in previous work it has been shown to be quite sensitive to certain kinds of social circumstances (Pearlin, 1975; Pearlin and Johnson, 1977). Yet only a single family transition can be identified as raising depression to a higher level than that at which it was measured prior to the event: being widowed. With regard to anxiety, none of the transitional events, including widowhood, has any significant effect. Furthermore, on the reasonable assumption that marital relations, in particular, would mirror family transitions, an analysis was designed to determine if marital stress fluctuated with any of the life-cycle stages (Menaghan, 1978). Again, the results were the same. That is, the stresses that people experience in their marriages do not vary appreciably or consistently with the various stages of the family cycle. There is some decrease in marital discord that occurs with the emptying of the nest, but this effect is apparently temporary, for it exists only in families where departure of the last child has taken place within the preceding four-year span (Mullan, 1979). Where departure was longer ago than four years—and the empty nest presumably has had time to cool off—no change is detected in the level of marital stress. These findings suggest, therefore, that any marital harmony resulting from the departure of children may wear thin with the passing of time.

It needs to be underscored that I have been discussing a relatively limited range of possible consequences of life-cycle events. It is entirely conceivable that, outside the boundaries of our own concerns with emotional distress, there are potential effects worthy of examination. For example, there are probably many cognitive alterations prompted by family changes, very likely including our mental maps of where we stand in relation to our own eventual deaths (Kastenbaum, 1975). It is equally plausible that certain transitions act either as constraints or as liberating influences on elements of life style. Thus, having children and launching children will each have its impact on the availability and uses of economic resources, time, and energy. There is the further distinct possibility that as the life cycle progresses one's feelings and attitudes toward one's self undergo a change. The realm of self-attitudes is one that we do not have to speculate about, for we have longitudinal measures of two rather crucial aspects of self-concept, mastery and self-esteem. *Mastery* represents the extent to which people feel in control of the forces importantly affecting their lives and is assessed by a scale we developed for use in our research. *Self-esteem,* of course, refers to the positive or negative regard one has for one's self and is evaluated by the Rosenberg scale (Rosenberg, 1965). When we search for the possible effects that the various transitions might have on these dimensions of the self, we once again fail to find that movement through the life cycle makes any difference.

Why Don't Life-Cycle Transitions Matter?

Overall, then, there are no clear or strong connections between the transitions through which people pass and alterations in, first, their emotional states; second, the marital strains they experience; or, finally, the attitudes they hold toward themselves. In short, we find no evidence that life-cycle changes serve as points around which these aspects of psychological functioning turn. These findings are somewhat surprising, especially in view of the fact that a number of the transitions do result in a rather dramatic reordering of household composition and family structure. It seems entirely reasonable to expect that such important life changes would ultimately be reflected in a host of inner feelings and attitudes. It behooves us, I think, to ask why these expectations are not confirmed, and much of the remainder of this chapter will be devoted to some possible explanations.

ANTICIPATORY COPING

One such explanation that merits brief discussion concerns the distinctive character of transitional events and the equally distinctive coping behavior they allow. I refer here to the fact that the role transitions that are embedded in the life cycle can be predicted far in advance of the actual occurrence of the transitions themselves (Pearlin, 1980). Their very predictability, in turn, means that adjustment to these changes can begin to take place prior to the onset of the changes. The processes of anticipatory socialization for change are not clearly known, but it is likely that they rely heavily on such behavior as the rehearsal of future roles in our fantasies, on the selection and use of strategic role models, on the mass media, and so on.

In contrast to the anticipatory adjustments allowed by scheduled events, we typically have neither the inclination nor the lead time to prepare in advance for the more unscheduled and less expected changes. We are not socialized to being divorced as we are to being married; we don't go through training for being laid off as we do for a career; we can happily foresee our children establish their own households, but we're caught unprepared if they suffer a disabling illness. Thus, the coping mechanisms we employ when we confidently anticipate later scheduled transitions are not likely to be available for coping with the less foreseen, unscheduled events. Of course, what begins as an unexpected event can crystallize into a persistent condition; then other coping modes more appropriate to chronic problems presumably come into play. However, in dealing with the sheer change involved in a nonscheduled event, one probably employs quite different coping techniques from those called forth by other types of problems. Specifically, one may hypothesize that it is at the point where adverse circumstances unexpectedly surface in our lives—circumstances with which there is no prior experience—that we are particularly likely to fall back upon our confidants and social networks for help and support.

But as far as the transitional events are concerned, coping does not begin with the emergence of the event, but with its advance anticipation. How well prior learning actually prepares us for future changes depends, I would suppose, on how closely the anticipated experiences fit later demands. It is doubtful that the fit is ever perfect; because of ongoing social changes in complex societies, the conditions for which we prepare ourselves may be quite different from the conditions that prevail when we finally assume our new roles (Benedict, 1938). Regardless of preparation, it would seem that some readjustments are required at the time when future change becomes present reality.

As a general observation, I'd like to underscore the importance of coping as a factor influencing one's experience over the life course. To the extent that the life course is an ever changing blending of scheduled transitions, unscheduled events, and chronic role strains, one is constantly called upon to react and adjust. To understand one's emotional development and psychological functioning through time, we have to recognize not only the important external forces that people are confronting, but also how they negotiate these forces. The area of coping is currently one in which knowledge is lagging behind interest. As more is learned about it, I think we shall also be able to learn more about the psychological fates of people across the life span.

CHANGE: AN OVERRATED CAUSE OF DISTRESS

One possible reason, then, that changes tied to the life cycle have so little adverse impact on psychological functioning is because of the advanced adjustments that can be made to such change. As a second reason, I would like to propose that change itself is overrated as a source of distress. There is, I am suggesting, some theoretical exaggeration of the part played by change, such as that embodied in life-cycle events, as a force in the psychological well-being of people. From the important pioneering work of Seyle (1956) and others, many of us have acquired a perspective of the human organism as being host to a myriad of inner forces, among which there is normally a delicate balance or equilibrium. When the organism confronts an important change in its environment, according to this perspective, the dynamic forces within it are dislodged from its balance and it must then struggle to achieve a new equilibrium. During the effort to adjust to the altered environment and to reestablish a homeostasis, the organism is thought to be under stress. If the stress persists—that is, if the organism fails to make an adjustment to the new elements of its environment—it will suffer damage. The damage in which earlier scholars were primarily interested concerned physiological functioning and psychosomatic ailments, but the antecedents are the same for those whose stress is manifested in overt emotional disturbance.

Much of the current research into life events and their arousal of stress is intellectually rooted in these perspectives. The research was given some impetus by the development by Holmes and Rahe of the Social Readjustment Scale (1967) which, while methodologically flawed and conceptually crude (Brown, 1974; Rabkin and Streuning, 1976), succeeded in stimulating useful work by a number of investigators. Consistent with the established theoretical orientations that life changes are causes of stress, much of the research into the linkages between life events and psychological functioning has tended to assume that the intensity of disturbance is a function of the sheer amount of change one confronts. The more dislocations one faces in life, the greater is the presumed disequilibrium that the organism must strive to correct. Viewed from this perspective, the occurrence of events—even the transitions encountered in the normal course of the life cycle—thus have the capability of upsetting the delicate fine tuning among inner forces, and this, in turn, is reflected in the emotional states of people.

If we draw out the implications of these assumptions, we could reasonably conclude that advancing along the life cycle must indeed be a painful process, one that is bad for physical and mental health. The layering of transitional events would seem to make traversing the life course a cumulatively difficult process, for the farther one moves, the greater the number of changes one will necessarily have confronted. Add to this the fact that the more advanced our position is along the life course, the closer many of us come to dependency and the closer all of us come to death. Viewed from these kinds of perspectives, we are left with a rather gloomy picture of the life cycle as entailing an ever growing psychological burden imposed by relentless change and inexorable loss. If this picture is accurate, we should find that adults in the middle portion of the life cycle experience more distress than those at earlier stages, and that those at the upper reaches of the cycle should be even more distressed than those in the middle.

How well does this picture fit the reality? What we find is this: Emotional stress and the conditions of life that are most likely to produce it are found to be more prevalent among the young, those who are at the beginning portion of the adult life cycle. As we move to the older age brackets of our sample, the presence of these stress producing conditions is diminished. It needs to be emphasized that the upper limit of our sample extends only to 70 years, too soon for the severe problems of infirmity, health, and dependency to be as widespread as they undoubtedly will become later in life. Within this age limit, however, and even when widowhood is taken into account, it appears that adult life generates most distress for those who for the first time are beginning to engage independently in occupational, family, and economic institutions. Conversely, it is least distressful among those who, because of their advanced position in the life course, have progressed through a succession of transitions. In the work realm, particularly, young adults are more likely than those who are occupationally established to experience a number of strains and involuntary disruptions. Moreover, at the very time that they may be experiencing occupational insecurity, younger adults are also more vulnerable to severe economic strains, for it is the period of life when there is commonly a great disparity between rapidly escalating material needs and actual earnings.

Indeed, in no area that we are able to observe do we find support for any assumption that the cumulative changes experienced as one moves along the life course result in increased psychological burdens. On the contrary, those people who, by virtue of their comparatively young ages, have experienced least cumulative change are typically the most stressed. Clearly, it is erroneous to think of progression through the life cycle as entailing either a gradual increase in the burdens of change or a corresponding decline and emotional deterioration. Judging by our indicators and within the age limits of our sample, there is little in life-cycle change that can be considered as a challenge to psychological well-being.

THE CONDITIONS AND MEANING OF CHANGE

To this point, then, I have discussed two reasons why our emotional lives and our self-images are not particularly responsive to life-cycle events and transitions: first, change that is scheduled and predictable may be particularly innocuous because of the anticipatory coping it allows, and second, change by itself may be less of an unbalancing and stressful force than we often think of it as being. A third possibility, to which I would like to turn now, is suggested by the second. It is that life-cycle change can indeed be potent in leading to alterations in psychological functioning, but only among some people and under some conditions. Despite the evidence that by themselves transitional events have little impact, I am proposing that in combination with certain social and economic circumstances they may be capable of contributing to psychological distress. A few illustrations will clarify this process.

Earlier, I noted that having a first child and seeing a last child enter the school system are two of the several life-cycle transitions found to be unrelated to changes in emotional distress. Let us again observe the same events, this time distinguishing the effects they have on people of different backgrounds.

Thus, when we separately examine the influence of these transitions on mothers and fathers, we discover that they are not as lacking in impact as they initially appeared to be. We learn, instead, that both having a first-born and entering the last-born into school do affect the depressive states of parents. However, the directions of their effects on mothers and fathers are opposite, so that when the events are examined without regard to the sex of the parent, it spuriously seems that the events are without potency. In the case of having a first child, for example, it is apparent that the event is not an equal source of joy to mothers and fathers, for new mothers are likely to experience a slight increase in depression over the level measured four years earlier, while those who are fathers for the first time are apt to experience a reduction in depression, a reduction that is statistically significant. With regard to the last-born child entering into a school system, an event that presumably signals a first step toward autonomy on the part of the child and a corresponding easing of parental responsibilities, we find a similar but reversed set of relationships. In this instance we learn that fathers experience a slight increase in depression, but that mothers of last-born, school-bound children experience a significant decrease in depressive symptomatology.

It is not only around sex-role divisions that the effects of life-cycle events are likely to be differentiated; other socioeconomic characteristics of people also mediate the impact of certain events. Retirement provides us with a good example. By itself, retirement from work for reasons of age is among the transitions that was found to have no relationship to changes in psychological distress. However, this picture is changed quite dramatically by considering retirement in conjunction with people's economic resources. Specifically, when retirement is coupled with limited income it is likely to result in an increase in depressiveness; by contrast, the same event is likely to result in a decrease of depression among the more affluent retirees. Entry into the labor market provides still another illustration of how the effects of life events can be conditioned by economic circumstances. In this instance, relief from depressive symptomatology is most likely to be enjoyed by those who were economically deprived prior to their labor market entry, while among those who had relatively abundant resources, entry has no effect. Again in this example, then, we find that the same event can have quite different consequences for people, depending on their economic circumstances.

One circumstance is worth notice not because of its relevance to the outcome of transitional events, but in spite of its irrelevance. I refer to the modal timing of these events. Respondents were asked with regard to each transition through which they had gone whether they had experienced the event earlier, at about the same time, or later than most of the people they know who had experienced the same transition. Although studies have shown a surprising consensus among people regarding the age at which particular life-cycle transitions should optimally take place (Neugarten, 1965), the age at which it actually occurs is apparently unrelated to well-being or distress. It makes no difference to psychological functioning, for example, whether such events as marriage or starting a family took place before, after, or at the same age as one's reference figures. The timing of such transitions relative to perceived norms is apparently less significant than the quality of conditions that are experienced once these transitions are made. Timing may possibly have some importance in movement along occupational career lines, but we were unable to discern any consequences that it might have in family transitions.

From the few illustrations I have given, it should be evident that in those instances where the consequences of transitions can be detected they result not from change per se, but from the meanings of the change for people. Meanings, in turn, are shaped by the characteristics of people and by the social and economic contexts in which they are located. The sheer number and magnitude of life-cycle changes, therefore, appear to be far less important to emotional states than the manner in which these changes fit or conflict with the more structured features of social and economic life. It is not the passages that matter; it is, rather, the nature of the contexts from which we have departed and those that we discover at our destinations.

Conclusions and Implications

I think that the issues and findings I have reported here have some strategic implications for research into the life cycle. One implication, briefly stated, is the importance of incorporating into the research a comparative perspective. Specifically, studies should be designed in a fashion that brings under observation people possessing a diversity of social characteristics and experiencing a range of life conditions. Some research, particularly that which conceives of life as being organized around distinct stages, occasionally confines its subjects to those coming from quite similar backgrounds (Gould, 1972; Sheehy, 1976; Levinson, 1978). In doing this, there is at least the suggestion that the demands people experience as a result of their being at a particular stage of life are so powerful that they override social and economic differences, thus obviating the need for comparative analysis. However, any attempt to explain the fates of people solely in terms of the stages at which they are located, or in terms of their movements from one stage to another, are at best limited. Given the variety of ways in which different people respond to being at the same stage, any research that is worth its salt has to attend to the parts played by social and economic factors in creating and channeling the effects of life-cycle transitions. Understanding these effects is certain to be incomplete and likely to be distorted if attention is confined exclusively to men, for example, or to the privileged and highly placed, or to any other homogeneous group. In order to identify the conditions that influence people at a particular phase of the life cycle, it is essential that we compare people who are exposed to different conditions.

In addition to comparisons within life-cycle stages, research should also be designed to allow for comparison between the various stages. There is a fairly common practice of selecting for study groups located at particular arcs of the life span, rather than sampling from a range of such groups. Thus we frequently see investigations of the aged, or of new parents, or of people at the mid-portions of their occupational careers. Less frequently, we see studies that are constructed so that comparisons can be made among people at different stages of the life cycle. The strategy of studying separately the different segments of the life cycle has resulted in a substantial body of knowledge, but it is a strategy that has shortcomings, too.

Foremost among them is their failure to accumulate data and develop theories that have some general applicability to the whole of the life cycle, or even the adult portions of it. Whatever the processes are that might extend through the entirety of life, they are likely to be overlooked or to be difficult to recognize in segmental studies of the different life stages, for such studies typically address themselves to different issues, employ different conceptual frameworks, and search for conditions considered unique to a particular life-cycle stage rather than for those that may cross-cut different stages. Although the substance and salience of different life tasks undoubtedly varies with movement through the life cycle, in the absence of studies permitting cross-stage comparisons, there is no way either to determine reliably the nature and extent of such variation or to evaluate the relative effects of the different life-cycle tasks. It is tempting to assume that the particular group and the particular set of conditions we happen to be observing within a segment of the life cycle capture the most intense and the most dramatic of life's struggles; but these assumptions are best put to test in comparative analyses. Otherwise, we are left with a host of discrete studies whose findings are not additive, whose reliability may be limited, and whose relevance to more general concerns with the life course is ambiguous.

It would be useful, I believe, to direct a few final words to the viability and utility of the notion of the life cycle as a framework for understanding the life strains people experience through time. To the extent that it simply calls attention to a temporal pattern of changes and transitions that most people encounter during the course of their lives, its usefulness is limited. And, as I have been arguing, its limitations are even more severe when we focus on but one of these transitions and ignore the others. Nevertheless, when the life cycle and its transitions are viewed not alone, but in conjunction with the predispositions that have been imprinted by historical conditions, with the more durably structured elements of social and economic life, with events that can surface at nonscheduled intervals, with patterns of coping, and with the availability and use of social resources, then the life cycle takes on greater interest and added importance. The productivity of the concept, in short, depends on how it can be used with other concepts.

29

Some Current Issues in Medical Sociology

John A. Clausen

MEDICAL SOCIOLOGY CROSS-CUTS many other subfields. Many medical sociologists seek to bring sociological theory and methodology to bear on the assessment of health status, the maintenance of health, and the organization and utilization of health services. Others focus on the health professions and medical organization as segments of occupational and organizational sociology. Yet others focus on the interaction of individual and society, examining the influences of life chances, life styles, and the social situations and circumstances of the life course that tend to produce illness or that shape the individual's awareness of and readiness to use health services, or again those that mediate the responses of others to the ill person.

The definition of health and illness is itself socially patterned. All workers in the field must wrestle with this critical issue which will in one sense always remain unresolved and problematic, because it must be expected to vary by time and place. The definition of health and illness also takes us beyond the usual boundaries of sociology, as do many of the most important unresolved problems of the field. Perhaps this helps to explain why medical sociology is not rich in sociological theory. We borrow both from other subfields and from outside the discipline.

My own research in medical sociology has dealt largely with aspects of mental disorder and with the society–individual relationship. I shall limit my analysis here to topics with which I have some real familiarity and which are, I believe, sufficiently problematic to meet the guidelines laid down for the thematic sessions at the 1979 meetings.

☐ Preparation of this chapter was facilitated by Grant MH-19649 from the National Institute of Mental Health.

361

It did not require social science to establish that disease is differentially distributed in society. Nor were epidemiological studies required to reveal that there are close linkages between emotional well-being and physical well-being. But the nature of the linkages could only be examined systematically as we achieved adequate conceptualizations and classifications of states of physical health and disease, indices of emotional well-being, and conceptualizations of those aspects of social experience that appear to make a difference.

More than two generations ago, the effects of social class on longevity, infant mortality, and general health status were well recognized. Subsequently, we learned that class seems to make a difference in the distribution of schizophrenia and a far greater difference in the distribution of symptoms of emotional discomfort and anxiety (Hollingshead and Redlich, 1958; Srole et al., 1962). But we are still far from having spelled out at all adequately the nature of the linkages between social class and other social structural features and the prevalence and incidence of physical and mental disorders.

During the past decade the concept of stress has become the popular choice in seeking to link life conditions and health. There has been a great increase in the amount and sophistication of research on stressful life events, yet we have made only very modest progress toward an adequate formulation of the ways in which social stressors and life experiences that require adaptation interact with social supports, resources, and coping skills to influence current and future states of physical and mental health.

Life Stress, Social Supports, and Illness

Life events and persisting threats or tensions have been invoked as explaining a portion of the difference between the social classes in illness and/or illness behavior, but findings of various studies have frequently been contradictory. Equally important, the causal chains by which life events may influence physical and mental health have for the most part been disregarded or dealt with in simplistic or narrowly segmental ways. What elements need to be included in an adequate formulation? What conceptual problems need to be tackled? What practical problems of data collection need to be addressed more squarely?

Let me restate the basic question that I believe needs addressing: How does it come about that certain events and experiences that tend to be perceived as stressful seem to have deleterious effects on the health of some individuals and no discernible effects on the health of others? A large body of recent research suggests both that one person's stressor is another person's challenge, and that individuals differ greatly not only in their ability to cope with and master the experience of stress but in what they respond to as stressful (Hinckle, 1974).

Research on the physiological consequences of extremely stressful experiences has gone on for roughly half a century, and there is much evidence that both severe acute stress and long-continued stress can produce physical lesions and dysfunctions of many organ systems, most notably gastrointestinal and cardiovascular (Knapp, 1975). Loss of a spouse in the early or middle adult years greatly increases morbidity and mortality of the remaining spouse in the year after such loss (Parkes and Brown, 1972). Severe depression and feelings of guilt in survivors of disasters in which loved ones were lost have been linked to ulcerative colitis and other health problems of such survivors (Lindemann, 1944). Sustained, intense stresses are mediated by endocrine systems, but for less intense stress, physiological linkages are not well understood. We must assume that subtle linkages exist, but we shall have to look to physiologists and biochemists for their delineation. The task for sociologists would seem to be to focus upon the nature and meaning of stressful events in broader social contexts and in the light of the individual's life history.

ASSESSING STRESS

The involvement of sociologists in studying stressful life events was greatly stimulated by the development of a technique for scaling life-event items, the Holmes and Rahe (1967) Social Readjustment Rating Scale. For those unfamiliar with the technique, it is based upon the idea that changes in one's accustomed pattern of life, whether regarded as desirable or as undesirable, require a degree of readjustment which is inherently stressful. Holmes and Rahe attempt to establish ratings or scores delineating the degree of readjustment required by a large number of more or less expectable events, such as marriage, changing one's residence, taking a new job, losing a job, and so on. These ratings are utilized as weights to be assigned to event histories which are then summed up to assess the stressfulness of recent life experience as reported retrospectively by some group of respondents. Most often the respondents are selected on the basis of their presenting some health problem, and their stress ratings are then compared with those of a more or less comparable sample free of the health problem.

There have been many adaptations of the Holmes and Rahe scale and of the rating and weighting scheme. Some investigators argue that only events with negative connotations should be considered, others that positive and negative events should be weighted differently; some argue that all negative events should be weighted equally, and some argue that events should be weighted in terms of their meaning for an average person in a given set of social circumstances (Ross and Mirowsky, 1979). A most promising development has been the collection of life-event histories from cross-sections of the population at successive points in time, so that one can assess changes in health status as related to changes in the type and number of recent life events (Myers et al., 1974).

I shall not comment in detail on methodological issues, since many have been discussed at length by Mechanic, Brown, and Cobb in the excellent symposium which was organized and edited by the Dohrenwends some years ago (Dohrenwend and Dohrenwend, 1974). Many assumptions underlie the scale, but I shall limit my discussion to two of the more important ones. First, in applying the ratings to individuals, except in the work of Brown and his colleagues (Brown and Harris, 1978), it is assumed that the meaning of the event can be assessed without having to know anything about the individual's life space and life course. Birth of a first child, for example, is given the same weight whether it is the first child born to a couple that has long wanted children or whether it is the first child born to a woman who has just finished law school and has been looking forward to getting started in legal practice, and who has, moreover, a strong aversion to the idea of an abortion.

The second assumption to which I wish to call attention is that any relationship between reported life events and illness reflects a general relation in the phenomenal world. That is, it is assumed that the current health status of the reporting person does not influence the recall of events, and further, that the person's health problem, prior experiences, or characteristics that may have been implicated in the etiology of the health problem were not themselves causative agents in bringing about the life events that have recently occurred.

The neatness of having a scale whereby one can make a more or less objective assessment of life events as stressors is seductive. The theory underlying the effects of the events as posited by Holmes and Rahe is relatively simple: events require adaptation, and adaptation causes wear on the organism; life-change events lower bodily resistance through faulty adaptive efforts. But human behavior is to a large extent goal oriented, and pursuing goals may entail many self-selected events—getting married, having children, changing jobs—as well as unexpected events. Active people should presumably wear out more quickly than people who avoid new undertakings, if one were to take seriously the perspective that life events are ipso facto stressors. But there is little evidence that such is the case, and indeed some evidence that lack of change may be more stressful than change for active, effective persons (Antonovsky, 1974).

What kinds of adaptations are required by life events? The answer to that question will depend on the kinds of definitions that are imposed upon life changes that are selected or encountered by the individual. Although we are far from consensus on this point, the stressfulness of any event will depend on the meaning of the event for the individual, yet if we are to assess the effects of stress, subjective responses cannot be the primary criterion for assessing stressfulness. Responses to any given stressor may reflect peculiar vulnerabilities or pathologies. On the other hand, to ignore the total social context and individual history in which an event is embedded is to strip that event of its essential meaning. A particular event may either facilitate the attainment of the individual's long-range objectives or utterly blight the possibility of reaching the desired goal.

Much more thorough conceptual analysis and specification of critical dimensions is needed if we are to make substantial progress. Pearlin and Schooler (1978) have recently made a helpful contribution by seeking to formulate more explicitly the relationships between stressors, social supports, and coping modes. I would like to suggest a few further steps that seem worth taking. First of all, for events that are widely experienced as stressful, it would be helpful to know the concatenated changes that each event tends to entail for persons in specified life-goal and social context categories. Some events entail intense short-range stress, but with successful coping the effects of such stress may be quickly damped down. Other events such as bereavements continue to have reverberations for considerable periods, even when coping has been relatively effective. Some events entail changes in social networks and/or in basic routines of sleeping, eating, and habitual activities.

If we are going to formulate valid theories, we ought to have much more information on the behavioral and psychological ramifications of events, and not merely ratings of the assumed stressfulness of hypothetical events for which raters draw upon varied images of the event in context. Leonard Pearlin has reported that by and large expectable life transitions—events like leaving school, marriage, or taking a job—did not in his research appear to engender appreciable emotional distress. Unexpected events were far more threatening than expected events. This is certainly true in my own research experience in examining the life histories of mental patients and of participants in the long-term longitudinal studies that have been carried out at Berkeley. It is particularly those events that entail loss or role failure (or severe threat of failure) that seem to produce the greatest distress and have the longest reverberations.

But it is not enough to study stressors without considering the different materials that are under stress. How much stress comes from overreaction to trivial annoyances, for example? Some of us can get as worked up about a minor frustration or irritation as about a serious threat. Other persons manage to keep their cool. A study by Singer (1967) suggests that among persons with high blood pressure, those who blow up under stress do not thereby relieve tension but rather put a greater strain upon the organism, one that seems to account for higher mortality in this group.

Most of us are familiar with the formulation of type A and type B personalities and cardiac problems (Friedman and Rosenman, 1959). Personality encompasses coping strategies, and, in addition, more general aspects of reactivity which may act as buffers against or as triggers to encountering stress. Tension management can be an important aspect of personal organization. It is something that seems to be learned relatively early in life. A recent finding from the longitudinal research at Berkeley is that emotional blandness and control as rated in junior high school students in the 1930s was associated with superior health at ages 40 and 50, and for this group of persons, early personality assessments were better predictors of midlife health than were assessments of physical health in the early years.

SOCIAL SUPPORT SYSTEMS

The importance of social support systems has been verbalized for some time, and we are beginning to conceptualize the various facets of social supports as well as amassing evidence from systematic research on the extent to which such supports make a difference (Kaplan et al., 1977).

What are the significant components of what we call "social supports"? Durkheim focused on the importance of the individual's integration into the social fabric. Such integration may be indexed in a number of ways, but we have done less to make explicit the psychologically significant components of social integration. One such component is that we are tied to others, whether in dyads or in larger groups, who *matter* to us and to whom we matter. As Morris Rosenberg (1979) has noted, to matter to others is to have responsibilities which may at times entail stress, yet the fact that we matter to others affirms our self-worth. In Rosenberg's analyses, for example, an adolescent's feeling that his or her views really mattered to Mother and Father was associated both with high self-esteem and with fewer symptoms of psychological discomfort.

Social support entails involvement in social roles that offer a structure of expectations to guide the individual; uncertainties and doubts are diminished when one has such a structure and finds within it satisfactions through the demonstration of competence in meeting the expectations of self and others. At times, social support can derive from the simple understanding that one is in the same boat with others who share the same feelings. The boat may be in danger of foundering, but if one can recognize that others face the same problems and especially that others have learned to cope with the problems, this can be enormously heartening.

The availability of others as *resources* certainly constitutes another kind of social support. In some respects, resources should be considered as a distinct category, but having others with whom one can share experiences, or from whom one can receive information, assistance, and guidance, must certainly be considered an important component of social supports. Here, however, we must face the possibility that there may be optimal levels of support. The availability of others as resources is important, but if one habitually leans upon others rather than handling problems through one's own efforts, the use of supports can actually be counterproductive.

This may be true of other components in the total support system that any person has. Commitments to others are a crucial element in achieving a stable, positive self-image. But when do commitments cease to sustain the individual? When do they become burdens? In general, we need to look at supports and the processes they engender as closely as we need to look at stresses and their sequential effects over time. And here again, we need to look at them in the context of major aims, satisfactions, and activities that the individual pursues.

In much of our theorizing and research on stress, we have been as simplistic as we were several decades ago when social class was invoked as an explanation of particular health problems. We are far from having traced out the linkages among stress, social supports, and coping mechanisms, and research designs based upon incomplete and inadequate conceptualizations will produce incomplete and inadequate results.

Sociological Research on Schizophrenia

My second topic relates exclusively to the field of mental illness. There are perhaps still a few sociologists who think mental illness is a myth, though they may be willing to grant that madness has existed and been a problem for social control since earliest antiquity. What seems most difficult for some sociologists to accept is the claim of the medical profession that it can diagnose and classify mental disorders and deal with them therapeutically. I cannot resist the comment that when a family member is severely emotionally distressed or overtly psychotic, even the staunchest advocates of labeling theory and of the theme that mental illness is a myth are likely to seek the best psychiatric help they can obtain.

Many sociologists have been particularly interested in that most puzzling category of psychosis called schizophrenia. It is currently fashionable to refer to the schizophrenic syndrome, for it appears that there may be several different schizophrenias as well as different pathways for becoming schizophrenic (Cancro, 1979). There are, however, certain symptoms that are found in combination here, though most of them also occur in other conditions. When they are found together, and in the absence of depression, and especially when they include behavior such as hearing one's thoughts broadcast or spoken aloud, or feeling that others are controlling one's thoughts and behaviors, there is a high degree of consensus among research-trained psychiatrists in assigning a diagnosis of schizophrenia (Carpenter et al., 1974). But there are many patients who receive the diagnosis without presenting such symptoms, and it is in such instances that we most often find ourselves questioning the classification of schizophrenia, and, at times, doubting that we are dealing with psychosis at all.

It is now more than forty years since Faris and Dunham (1939) published their exciting study of the differential distribution of hospitalization for serious mental disorder within areas and population groups in several major cities. Looking at the conditions of life in the areas with highest rates of schizophrenia, and with a bow to Durkheim, they proposed that social isolation might explain the development of schizophrenia. We knew little then about how social background might influence psychiatric diagnoses or how persons presenting the kinds of behavioral difficulties labeled schizophrenia were sorted and sifted by existing social institutions. The Faris and Dunham formulation appeared extremely promising, especially to sociologists.

We know now that at least part of the greater expectation of schizophrenia in the lower working class is a resultant of sorting processes, but we are little closer now than we were in being able to delineate the relationship between sociocultural milieus and the incidence of schizophrenia. There is clearly a genetic linkage, but it does not explain more than perhaps half of the variance in the distribution of schizophrenia (Worden et al., 1976). Indeed, it appears that genetic vulnerability is not specifically a vulnerability to schizophrenia, since a variety of problems of self-control and social competence are found more frequently among offspring of schizophrenic mothers who have been adopted away early in life than they are among other adopted children (Heston and Denney, 1968).

Let me give an example of sorting processes which may themselves lead to a linkage between social status and vulnerability to schizophrenia and related problems. In a twenty-year follow-up of the families of patients hospitalized for schizophrenia in the 1950s, we have found that children in a family with a schizophrenic parent did not exceed the average of their parents in educational attainments (Clausen and Huffine, 1979). In general, adolescents of the 1960s and 1970s markedly exceeded the educational attainments of their parents; the failure of the children of a schizophrenic parent to do so constitutes a downward drift in the average status of children who themselves carry a high genetic risk for schizophrenia.

Perhaps genetics, coupled with intrauterine development, explains schizophrenia (Kinney and Jacobsen, 1978). This seems to me possible, but not so probable as to justify giving up attempts at identifying and specifying sociocultural features in the etiology of schizophrenia. Why have we not made more headway? First, there is the difficulty in our getting a handle on the genetic component, except through the follow-up of high-risk groups, such as the offspring of schizophrenic parents or the siblings of the schizophrenic. But even when one studies high-risk groups, it is impossible to know whether a given child carries whatever gene combination or combinations may be involved in vulnerability to schizophrenia. It is, therefore, very difficult to study gene–environment interaction.

Overreliance on a single dimension of classification—diagnosis—has also plagued much research in this area. A useful cross-cutting classification of schizophrenics is based on their social competence and interpersonal skills prior to the onset of psychopathology. Outcome in schizophrenia, for example, is highly related to demonstrated social competence and late, acute onset of the disorder. We have then the "process-reactive" distinction, with evidence that those who showed poor premorbid social competence are most likely both to become chronic patients and to have close relatives who are themselves schizophrenic (Phillips, 1953).

Although there has been much fascinating research on family patterns and particularly on communication deviance in the families of schizophrenics, one never knows whether one is dealing with patterns that are of etiological significance, are reflective of genetic loading, or are themselves the results of living with a schizophrenic (Goldstein and Rodnick, 1975). In general, socialization research has ignored the characteristics of the organism that is being socialized. Every parent who has several children learns that different techniques may be required for getting across the messages that socialization requires. Moreover, vulnerable or problematic children call forth quite different responses than do more normal siblings. But we have made little effort in our research to look for social types or patterns that have implications for the development of schizophrenia.

Melvin Kohn (1973) has suggested that social class differences are real and that certain features of working class life styles and value orientations may lead to greater proneness to the development of schizophrenia in vulnerable individuals. Until we have more adequate markers for genetic vulnerability, however, there is little prospect of our being able to test formulations of gene–environment interaction. Still, it would be desirable to learn much more about the distribution, by class and ethnic group, of those interaction and communication patterns that appear to characterize families with a schizophrenic patient. Such research would be perfectly feasible, though less glamorous than efforts to establish the etiology of schizophrenia by direct approach.

Perhaps the greatest promise at present comes from research less focused on etiology than on the course of schizophrenia. Whether or not sociocultural processes are involved in etiology, the importance of social response is now well documented. Labeling theorists have claimed far too much in attempting to explain "careers" of mental illness, with almost no data. As a consequence, we have wasted a lot of time and effort in arguing about the effects of labeling rather than specifying what labeling entails in various social contexts, what consequences it has for the person's immediate mental state, and how the longer term identity of the individual is influenced by subsequent recurrence of or freedom from symptoms. Can labeling an upset person "mentally ill" make that person mentally ill instead of merely upset? Very, very seldom, in my experience. A highly suggestible person may occasionally let go and decide that he or she might as well act crazy, but in roughly 150 families we have studied, there are only two or three such instances. Far more often, the patient is the first one to entertain the idea that he or she may be in need of psychiatric help, though usually not until after a period of upset behavior.

We have found, in the study of married patients, that sympathy is far more rare than anger or annoyance when a spouse manifests symptoms of psychosis or severe anxiety. And anger and annoyance—or contempt, as one sometimes finds—may be more devastating to the emotionally disturbed person than the suggestion that professional help is needed. One of the most promising developments in recent years has been the work of George Brown and his associates in England on "expressive emotion" (Brown et al., 1972). Brown's staff interviewed the closest relatives of schizophrenic patients in the period just before the patient's return home from the hospital. If there was high emotional involvement, with much critical comment, it was found that the patient was much more likely to be returned to the mental hospital within a relatively short period. However, patients were more likely to be retained in the community if they had limited contact (in terms of hours per week of exposure) with the persons who had expressed high emotional involvement, or, if the patient received a heavy dosage of tranquilizing drugs which would blunt emotional responsivity. Higher returns to the hospital were also associated with the number of prior admissions, and undoubtedly there is a gradual shift in the ability of significant others to accept the patient, as Greenley (1979) has recently documented. But, clearly, response to the patient does make a difference, whatever helps to explain that response.

Would it make any difference if we said that people have "problems of living" instead of "schizophrenia"? I don't think so. There would still be a need, in the face of psychotic behaviors, to get the patient out of the situation in which tensions become unbearable. Would it make any difference if parents and spouses could respond more sympathetically to disturbed children, husbands, or wives? I think it probably would.

There is a need for more intensive study of the processes of definition and response to mental illness, monitoring families, and perhaps coupling this with assistance. The problems of securing access to families at the critical time are formidable, but in my opinion such research can best be incorporated in long-term longitudinal studies of populations at high risk for mental disorder (Garmezy, 1974).

Socialization to Illness

Finally, let me return to an issue that has relevance for the field of medical sociology in general. We know that all illness entails social definitions as well as medical ones. Not everyone who has an illness chooses to take the sick role and secure relief from other role responsibilities; equally, we know that some people find the sick role and continued dependency a satisfying way of life, whether or not they are fully aware of this proclivity. Several decades ago, Zborowski (1952) illuminated our understanding of cultural differences in response to pain by examining rather globally parental responses to childhood risk taking and injuries in different cultures and the orientations given to children for dealing with pain and illness. He noted how such early teaching seemed to influence cultural differences in adult responses to pain.

How do small children learn what it is to be ill—how to label their feelings and how to deal with them? There have been a few studies in this area, such as the recent research of John Campbell (1975), but we lack an adequate theoretical formulation of the ways in which some children come to be preoccupied with questions of health and illness, while others remain much more casual about the topic. Some adults are major consumers of medical services, while others help keep the rates of medical insurance from being even more astronomical than they are now. To what extent, and how are such differences related to socialization experiences? In a sense, we have come full circle to an aspect of the topic with which I opened this chapter. The impact of stressful situations is likely to be different, depending on whether one is preoccupied with health or casual about it. Better conceptualization might be derived from intensive study of families with small children. I doubt that this problem can be handled by survey methods, but I suspect that one might learn a good deal by systematic observation. The selection of families in which to make observations would obviously be a crucial matter. One group that might be of interest to look at is families that take Christian Science very seriously and that reject the medical interpretation of illness. What are children taught, and how do they build up characterization of their feelings when ill? I do not think that the child's earliest experience with illness will in any sense *determine* his or her orientations later in life, but analysis of the formation of the earliest orientations and the social supports and emotional charges that go with them might help to improve our formulations of the circumstances under which the sick role is adopted in later life. Ideally, one might carry out short-term longitudinal research with overlapping age groups to assess shifts in orientation over time.

Is there any relationship between the way in which we learn about our bodies and their care and the extent to which we subsequently somatize our stresses? This is not, I think, a trivial question, and it is one that the medical profession is not likely to tackle without a good deal of help from social scientists.

Within the realm of my own particular interests, I find that a great many problems seem to require that we pay more attention to the organism as such and to the ways that the organism and its responses are shaped by the social environment. Real progress in this field is not likely to be made until our conceptualizations focus more sharply on the interactions between what is biologically given and the course of life experience. Sociologists know that an understanding of the history of any given human group is basic to an understanding of the orientations of the group at the present time. Similarly, an understanding of the history of the person is likely to be basic to significant advances in theoretical formulations bearing on a number of issues in the field of medical sociology. As we become better informed about human biology and more sophisticated in the sociological study of the life course, there is a promise of such advances in the decade ahead.

30

Medical Sociology: Theoretical Underdevelopment and Some Opportunities

Jack Elinson

MY ANSWER to Tad Blalock's first question, which he proposed as a guide for the thematic sessions, is that the most important unresolved issue in the field of medical sociology is understanding the relationship between the health of a population and what society does about it. Stated in these general terms, we are impelled to recognize the vagueness of the issue, and driven to see how far sociologists have gotten in more clearly defining the implied concepts on both sides of the equation, and in their operationalization and measurement.

Despite the apparent growth of medical sociology in the past quarter of a century—as documented by the three editions of Freeman, Levine, and Reeder in their sturdy *Handbook of Medical Sociology*—in the world of social science and social policy medical sociology must still be regarded as one of the less developed social sciences. As a particular discipline rooted in sociology, Eliot Freidson (1978) noted that medical sociology was "in decline," and might even "vanish."

Unlike medical economics and social medicine, there are few representatives of the discipline of medical sociology influencing social policy, especially on a national level. With few exceptions, such as Matilda Riley, David Mechanic, and Odin Anderson in this country, Margot Jefferys and Raymond Illsley in the United Kingdom, Robin Badgley in Canada, and Magdalena Sokolowska in Poland, we do not find leaders in medical sociology forcefully projecting the products of their theoretical concerns and empirical

investigations in the halls of policy. Even when the most courageous—
including most of the ones mentioned—venture into the policy arena, it is
usually on a short leash from the safe base of university tenure. There are no
sociological Karen Davises (health economics) or George Silvers (social
medicine) in the Office of the Secretary of Health of the Department of
Health, Education and Welfare.[1] Medical sociologists mainly work in their
own backyard, now and then producing concepts or insights or research
results suitable to be displayed before the larger society, but most often con-
served in the little-read hothouses, known as professional or scholarly journals. We tend to work for each other and, when we go public, to restrict
ourselves to the role of social critics, rarely daring to be playwrights.

An intellectually friendly physician, John Knowles (1979:xi), believed
that part of the reason for the lack of use of medical sociology in the formulation of public policy was that "health professionals . . . are ignorant of the
findings." That may be, but the discipline itself suffers both from a lack of
confidence in what it knows and from a feeling that the knowledge it does
have is insufficiently developed to form a basis for policy. This withdrawn,
schizophrenic-like behavior of sociology exhibits itself not only in the arena of
applied medical sociology, but also in other realms of social action as well.
Not so long ago, when the issue was being debated in the Congress,
sociologists were sharply divided on the question as to whether there even
ought to be a Council of Social Advisors to the President, as there is a Council
of Economic Advisors and a Council or Office of Science and Technology.
Like medicine before the nineteenth century, medical sociology today is
theoretically underdeveloped. As a consequence it has too little prestige, and
perhaps too little knowledge, to warrant the sustained and serious attention of
kings.

The absence of theoretical and empirical understanding of the relation
between health and social action is the most unresolved important question in
medical sociology. Recognition of this lack takes many forms and finds support in various respectable sociomedical quarters. For example, Odin Anderson (1979:i), chairman of a Committee on Organizational Consequences of
Varying National Programs for Providing Health Services, said:

> The persistence and continuing expansion of the personal health services must
> rest on a faith analogous to the persistence and support of churches and
> synagogues. Both presumably offer assurance, solace and relief from pain in
> coping with life's vicissitudes. The difference is that faith in the intrinsic value
> of churches and synagogues is not being questioned (except by a small minority
> of atheists and agnostics). The faith in the efficacy of health services in having

---

[1] Karen S. Davis, Ph.D., a medical economist, is (March 1980) Deputy Assistant Secretary for
Planning and Evaluation/Health. She was appointed to this high policy position by a former
presidential cabinet member, Joseph A. Califano, Secretary of the Department of Health,
Education and Welfare. George Silver, M.D., was special assistant to an earlier Secretary of
Health, Education and Welfare, John Gardner, Ph.D., a psychologist.

any impact on health levels is now, however, being questioned as costs of these
services continue to rise. [We need to] . . . shift from pure faith in the efficacy
of health services to some objective criteria of need in relation to services.

From a planning perspective, Tom Bice (1977:115) noted that "research
on the efficacy of interventions provides the planner with transition probabilities which measure the likelihood that their application will effect changes
in the health status of individuals to whom they are applied. . . . Assuming
that efficacious interventions exist, attention is directed toward determining
which processes and structures are the most effective, efficient and acceptable
means of making them available to the population."

And in a larger sense Sol Levine (1979:339) expressed the hope that "we
may . . . be able to relate factors in the larger economic and political order to
the more immediate behavior of the sick person."

Compared with some prominent medical economists, medical sociologists
have been relatively unwilling to take the best of the most readily available
statistics and adopt them as satisfactory indicators of the health of populations
for purposes of sociological analysis. Blalock, in this volume, tells us how in-
secure we are in data collection and in conceptualization of variables. It seems
that this particular self-characterization stands in the way of the introjection
of medical sociology in social policy.

Some years ago the social demographers Evelyn Kitagawa and Philip
Hauser (1972:180), in their in depth analysis of *Differential Mortality in the
United States,* arrived at the conclusion that "perhaps the most important next
gain in mortality reduction is to be achieved through improved social-
economic conditions rather than through increments to and application of
bio-medical knowledge." Taking this notion a step further the medical
economist, Victor Fuchs (1974:155), still relying on mortality as a measure of
population health, after noting that there was little relationship of mortality to
medical inputs of physicians, nurses, hospitals, and dollars for medical care,
concluded that the "marginal contribution of medical care to health is very
small in modern nations."

What has followed from this kind of conclusion reached and still maintained by Fuchs (1979) and other medical economists about the relation between health status of populations and medical care are the assumptions that
just about everyone in developed nations is getting all the medical care he or
she needs, and maybe more; that it is therefore unwise for the country to
allocate further scarce resources to the provision of medical care; that contain-
ment of medical care costs is a top priority; that since national health insurance is bound to raise expenditures for medical care it should be modified
severely in concept, that is, limited to the indigent and to catastrophic ex-
penses, deferred indefinitely, or abandoned altogether.

Now, while one's welfare philosophy may be in agreement with those
policies, the social data on which they are based consist of grossly inadequate

indicators of the health status of a population. Recently, in an editorial in the *American Journal of Public Health,* I called attention to the insensitivity of mortality as an indicator of population health status (Elinson, 1977). Except to undertakers, gravediggers, and vital statisticians, a doubling or a halving of mortality will do little to enlighten us about the health of living populations in economically developed countries. What affects a tiny proportion in any given year is unwarrantedly assumed to reflect the health status of the total population.

Mortality data, as Iwao Moriyama (1968) pointed out over a decade ago, are no longer adequate as measures of health of the population.

From his vantage point as director of the Office of Health Statistics Analysis of the National Center for Health Statistics, Moriyama argued that the relationship of mortality and morbidity is not clear. There are some highly prevalent disabling morbid conditions which contribute little to mortality.

Arthritis is one good example; schizophrenia is another. On the other side there are, among the leading causes of death, the violent causes—accidents, homicide, and suicide—whose morbid etiology, if any, is unknown. With the aging of the population and the corresponding increase in absolute prevalence of chronic disease, the interpretation of mortality statistics has become more difficult, particularly in cases of multiple, potentially fatal, chronic conditions. In one study the mean number of chronic, disabling, or potentially medically disabling conditions found among persons 65 years of age or over was six (Trussell and Elinson, 1959).

Mortality data for populations are the most readily available statistics on a national level and hence the most widely used in both popular and professional discussions of a nation's health. We are familiar with the ranking of countries by mortality, in general, and by infant mortality, in particular; and the ready, enormous, and unjustified leap to the conclusion that the lower the mortality, the healthier the country.

To Moriyama's soberly cogent observations, it is painful to feel the need to point out the obvious: that in economically developed countries the annual death rate is 1 percent or less; that 99 percent of the population alive on January 1 of a year are alive on December 31 of that year. During that year the living 99 percent are in various states of health which are *not* demonstrably indexed by the state of health of the 1 percent who die. Moriyama's observation that the relation between morbidity and mortality is unclear understates the case. Public health, Ernest Gruenberg (1979) noted, has paid too much attention to the first and last years of life and too little to the years in between. Medical economists and some medical sociologists following the fashion have done the same. Public attention is riveted to the traditional vital statistician's and demographer's view of public health as indexed primarily by countable births and deaths.

Early intrepid sociological explorers in the measurement of health status, such as Harold Dorn (1951), formulated a concept of health as a continuum from perfect health through sickness to death. In more recent years, a number of theoretical mathematical solutions have been proposed (Chiang [1965], Glasser [1977], and Linder [1966], the first head of the National Center for Health Statistics), combining morbidity and mortality into single indices purporting to represent the total health of a population—in imitation of the economists' use of the index of the GNP (Gross National Product). Unfortunately, from a theoretical and methodological perspective, no sociomedical scientist has been able to discover or invent, for this purpose, *units of health* which are similar to the monetary units available for computation of the GNP. We take due note, in passing, of the extraordinarily useful estimates of the monetary cost to society of various diseases that have been made by social economists, notably Dorothy Rice (1966, 1977), Anne Scitovsky (1976), and others.

I agree with Bice (1979:193) who observes that "quests for the single, global index of health status . . . raise conceptual and methodological difficulties that predispose unnecessary pessimism," and that these should be regarded as impediments to the end of developing sociomedical health indicators intended primarily to assist decision making. Posing the question of measurement of health status in a simplistically global way also inhibits the theoretical development of medical sociology.

The challenge that has faced sociologists ever since Parsons offered a sociological definition of health has been comprehensively appraised by Bloom and Wilson (1979) in their chapter on "Patient–Practitioner Relationships" in the *Handbook of Medical Sociology* and has been gracefully and succinctly reviewed by Sol Levine and Martin Kozloff (1978:339) in their recent assessment of the sick role in the *Annual Review of Sociology*. Levine and Kozloff concluded, "We . . . need to leave the Parsonian formulation in the background, to free ourselves of the limits of the paradigm, and to learn much more about the behavior of the sick person."

Containing as it does elements of common sense, Parsons' definition was operationalized by many sociomedical researchers and biostatisticians innocent of Parsons, like writers unknowingly writing prose. The best known of these efforts is the work of the National Center for Health Statistics through its Health Interview Survey, which has been depicting the health status of the living population in this country for over twenty years through such operationalized concepts of health as ability to carry out one's usual activities, as well as by reports of acute illness and injury medically attended or not, and reports of chronic conditions which have been medically diagnosed. Notably absent from the Health Interview Survey is that large and important class of morbidity consisting of asymptomatic chronic disease, potentially disabling and fatal, which has *not* been medically diagnosed. This latter class of morbid conditions—that is, present and diagnosable, but *not* diagnosed—is the Big Divide between research technologies which establish the prevalence of illness by household interviews and the prevalence of disease by clinical examinations, and leads to differing views of the elephant by sociologists and medical clinicians, with sometimes major consequences for both sociological theory and social policy. Following Parsons, sociologists have been limited in their view of health in its manifest aspects. Nonmanifest disease, preclinical and clinical—that is, free of symptoms and not yet interfering with social functioning, such as neoplasms, diabetes, and hypertension, and discoverable only through the arcane arts of medicine—is a biological fact which does not become a *social fact* until it is medically diagnosed. Failure to take account of biological facts before they become social facts is like donning sociological blinders, only to have them ripped off by medical scientists with concomitant disdain for theoretical musings of medical sociologists.[2]

Nevertheless, one should not downplay the impact of theoretically based sociological research or even social-philosophical writings of medical sociologists on social policy. There are numerous examples of influential pieces of medical sociological work which will not be reported here. Nor should one overlook the essential, steady stream of contributions of medical sociologists in government agencies such as in the National Center for Health Services Research, the National Center for Health Statistics, the Alcohol, Drug Abuse and Mental Health Administration, the National Institutes of Health, and other agencies of the Department of Health and Human Services; and in closely related strategic and prestigious bodies such as the Institute of Medicine in the National Academy of Sciences; in the various private, eleemosynary foundations; on presidential commissions; and in numerous committees in local as well as in national settings.

Sociomedical Health Measures

Blalock also posed for us the question: ''What are the most difficult problems of conceptualization and measurement in your field, and what steps can be taken to resolve them?''

Over the past decade some progress has been made in the clarification, operationalization, and measurement of the concepts of population health from a sociomedical viewpoint. In this effort, societal concerns with the effects of deviations from physiological status deemed desirable from a medical point of view have been guiding. Among the desiderata for sociomedical measures is that they be applicable and collectible from populations as well as in-

---

[2] It should be noted that the adjective ''medical'' for sociology is one adopted by *sociologists* to describe their field of inquiry. It is not bestowed by medicine upon sociology. That the adjective is welcome was demonstrated in a recent vote of the membership of the Section on Medical Sociology to reject a proposed change of name to the Sociology of Health, which some felt was more descriptive of the boundaries of the field.

dividuals, mainly by sample surveys which make generalization tenable. Wittingly or unwittingly, the best developed and most promising measures of health status reflect Parsonian notions of social functioning. These include the Health Status Index described by Patrick, Bush, and Chen (1973); the Function Status Index reported by Reynolds, Rushing, and Miles (1974); and the Sickness Impact Profile developed by the Gilsons, Marilyn Bergner (1975), and collaborators at the University of Washington. What all these function-based measures have in common conceptually is that they cut across the thousand and more disease entities labeled by the three- and four-digit numerals in the World Health Organization's International Classification of Diseases and Causes of Death (1969). What is more, these sociomedical measures take into account the impact of disease with respect to social and behavioral functioning. For older age groups and for persons with chronically disabling disease, even finer measures of functioning have been developed in terms of activities of daily living. For example, Katz and Akpom (1976) have devised a measure of primary sociobiological functioning for which they claim anthropological confirmation of the biological primacy of functions which comprise their index. Comparable measures have yet to be constructed for other age slices of the population. The most vigorous research along these lines is being done for adolescents (Brunswick, 1969), and investigated for younger children (Elinson and Guttmacher, 1979), and for outcomes of pregnancy (Muller et al., 1979).

Perhaps the most difficult problem has been raised by Donald Patrick (1979); and that is the problem of a social metric for sociomedical indicators of health status. At the level of natality and mortality the problem of metric appears to be resolved. To the vital statistician, at any rate, a birth equals a birth and a death equals a death; a mortality of 20/1,000 is twice as great as a mortality of 10/1,000. Patrick puts it as a problem in the binary 0/1 assumption of value: it is better to be alive than dead. But even with mortality the issue of *social metric* has been avoided. The death of a child, for example, has a different stress value from the death of a spouse, as the Dohrenwends (1978) have empirically demonstrated in a public opinion survey of a community. The characterization of morbidity as minor and major, a cold versus pneumonia, implicitly assumes social preferences. These characterizations are often nominal or, at best, ordinal systems used without explicit attention to the social weighting process.

As Patrick points out, the conceptual and measurement problem is how to incorporate social preference measures with respect to the various morbid states. Many approaches have been made toward constructing preference metrics; among them utility modeling, psychometric scaling, and empirical social decision evaluation. Constructing a metric based on preference for whatever factors are used to describe function status faces a complex and time-consuming data-collection problem. Judges, whether health professionals, patients, or representative samples of the public, are asked to state their preference for various conditions of dysfunction. The number of these, while not infinite, is extraordinarily large, taxing the attention of the most obedient respondent. Furthermore, many people are reluctant to express their choices in a research situation even though some of these choices, implicit or explicit, are at some time a special part of the lives of all of us, and part of the regular occupational life of many health professionals, in both individual clinical decisions and public health planning and allocation of resources.

Indirect psychometric scaling models such as the paired comparison technique have been found useful and practical in other fields besides medical sociology. One of the most notable examples was the use of paired comparisons in determining the point score for demobilization of the armed forces after World War II developed by Louis Guttman et al. (1966). Such a psychometric scaling model appears to be feasible, however, only when the number of factors in the choices is severely limited, probably to fewer than ten. When confronted with morbidity states, the task appears to be overwhelming, if not hopeless.

Another form of psychometric scaling, the so-called category scaling, proposed by S. S. Stevens, elicits numerical estimates of subjective feelings for stimuli. In medical sociology it has pioneeringly been successfully applied by Patrick to health conditions. In criminal sociology this method has been used in the effort to determine the extent to which it is possible to make the punishment quantitatively fit the crime. The method is efficient in that it requires minimal time on the part of the judges, and the decision process is no more threatening than an opinion poll or a household survey.

When empirical social decision valuations methods are used to construct a preference metric, quite a different set of problems are encountered. As described by Patrick (1979:79):

> Implicit values are assigned to various health conditions by a wide variety of social decisions. Health programs with alternative concerns, populations, and goals are allocated different amounts and types of resources by political leaders, health professionals and program administrators. The health budget of the U.S., for example, is distributed among competing agencies, disease categories, target populations and health activities. The courts compensate disability, disfigurement and abuse at different levels. Outside the public sector, life insurance companies and other risk agents use economic valuation to assign different dysfunction/disability rates. These empirical decisions might be used to construct social preference weights.

The use of monetary awards by the courts for disability/distress may overcome the criticism which relates to the social economists' (Dorothy Rice, 1977) computations of the economic value of human life, as in Dublin, *The Money Value of a Man* (1930). Imputation of economic values to housework only begins to recognize the social fact that "every mother is a working mother." The courts are "arenas for both sympathy and monetary exchange." The courts' decisions would appear to be one of reflection of social values. What the relations between court-determined valuations and other assessments are, are matters of both theoretical and empirical concern.

A sociomedical health metric that fairly represents society's preferences should be useful for social decisions. Such a metric would be expected to vary with developments in medical therapy. One of the most important ways of looking at the purposes of sociomedical health measures is to indicate the extent to which medical knowledge is being applied in a given society or to a specified population. This approach directs attention away from both the social and biological consequences of a disease and toward the discharge of social responsibility for the organization and delivery of health care (Elinson, 1973). The prevalence of disease varies independently from the provision of care. I have argued that the provision of care when needed is more easily recognized as a social responsibility in populations that have achieved a high rate of success in the prevention of preventable diseases. Whether medically needed care is provided then becomes the measure not so much of the health of a population, but rather the assessment of social capacity to care for the sick. Thus, it should be possible to state what proportion in a given population is receiving needed care. As Lu Ann Aday and Ronald Andersen and I have shown in different ways, populations can be compared with respect to degree of neglect (Aday and Andersen, 1975; Trussell and Elinson, 1959).

Preference for a particular health state may be expected to vary with the availability and efficacy of medical care. Adequate representation of society's preference for various states of well-being suggests probability sampling of community values. I have already referred to the Dohrenwends' community survey to establish assessments of stress values for life events. Similarly, this approach could be applied to obtaining quantitative assessments of preferences for various states of health. These could then be related to professional judgments of the prognosis and medical seriousness of conditions.

Economists have been accepted and successful as the appropriate philosophers to advise the kings in many areas of social policy, including the field of health. The monetary metric is readily understood. Some unorthodox economists, such as Mancur Olson (1972), have dared to question the adequacy of the market criterion. They are looking to sociologists to provide conceptualization and accounting of economically valuable social behavior which ultimately may be translatable into the monetary metrics that economists and the public at large are comfortable with. This unorthodox economic view has become the rationale and springboard for the social indicators movement (Sheldon and Moore, 1968; *Social Indicators, U.S.,* 1976). The camel's nose is in the tent. Medical sociologists in the past decade have been industriously conceptualizing and operationalizing sociomedical health indicators, meaningful from both the sociological and medical perspectives. Whether medical sociologists can carry this idea a step further and devise metrics for social values with respect to various states of health remains to be seen. It is a challenge. And one which is not limited to medical sociology.

References

Additional references are found beginning on page 433.

ADAY, LU ANN, and RONALD ANDERSEN
   1975 Development of Indices of Access to Medical Care. Ann Arbor, Mich.
   Health Administration Press.

AGUIRRE, B., and E. L. QUARANTELLI
   1979 "A critical evaluation of critiques of collective behavior as a field of inquiry."
   Unpublished paper.

AIGNER, D. J.
   1971 Basic Econometrics. Englewood Cliffs, N.J.: Prentice-Hall.

ALDOUS, JOAN
   1977 "Family interaction patterns." Pp. 105–35 in Alex Inkeles, James Coleman,
   and Neil Smelser (eds.), Annual Review of Sociology, Vol. 3. Palo Alto, Calif.:
   Annual Reviews.

ALDOUS, JOAN, THOMAS CONDON, REUBEN HILL, MURRAY A. STRAUS, and IRVING
TALLMAN (eds.)
   1971 Family Problem Solving. Hinsdale, Ill.: Dryden Press.

ALDRICH, HOWARD E.
   1979 Organizations and Environments. Englewood Cliffs, N.J.: Prentice-Hall.

ALEXANDER, KARL L., MARTHA COOK, and EDWARD L. McDILL
   1978 "Curriculum tracking and educational stratification: some further evidence." American Sociological Review 43: 47–66.

ALEXANDER, KARL L., and EDWARD L. McDILL
   1976 "Selection and allocation within schools: some causes and consequences of
   curriculum placement." American Sociological Review 41: 963–80.

ALTHUSSER, L.
   1969 For Marx. London: Allen Lane.

ALWIN, DUANE, and LUTHER B. OTTO
   1977 "High school context effects on aspirations." Sociology of Education 50:
   259–72.

383

AMINZADE, RONALD
    1977 "Breaking the chains of dependency: from patronage to politics, Toulouse, France 1940–1972." Journal of Urban History 3: 485–506.

ANDERSON, ODIN W.
    1979 "Foreword" in J. Elinson and A. E. Siegmann (eds.), Sociomedical Health Indicators. Farmingdale, N.Y.: Baywood Publishing Company.

ANTONOVSKY, A.
    1974 "Conceptual and methodological problems in the study of resistance resources and stressful life events." Pp. 245–58 in B. S. Dohrenwend and B. P. Dohrenwend (eds.), Stressful Life Events: Their Nature and Effects. New York: Wiley.

APTER, DAVID
    1967 The Politics of Modernization. Chicago: University of Chicago Press.
    1971 Choice and the Politics of Allocation. New Haven: Yale University Press.

ARIÈS, PHILLIPPE
    1962 Centuries of Childhood: A Social History of Family Life. New York: Knopf.

ARON, R.
    1979 "On liberalization." Government and Opposition 14: 37–65.

ARONOWITZ, STANLEY
    1973 False Promises: The Shaping of American Working Class Consciousness. New York: McGraw-Hill.

ASHBY, ERIC
    1966 Technology and the Academics: An Essay on Universities and the Scientific Revolution. New York: St. Martin's Press.

AUMANN, R. J.
    1967 "A survey of cooperative games without side payments." Pp. 3–27 in M. Shubik (ed.), Essays in Mathematical Economics in Honor of Oskar Morgenstern. Princeton, N.J.: Princeton University Press.

BABAD, ELISHA Y., and LIORA AMIR
    1978 "Bennis and Shepard's theory of group development: an empirical examination." Small Group Research 9(4): 477–92.

BAILES, KENDALL E.
    1978 Technology and Society Under Lenin and Stalin. Princeton, N.J.: Princeton University Press.

BAILYN, BERNARD
    1960 Education in the Forming of American Society. Chapel Hill: University of North Carolina Press.

BALDRIDGE, J. VICTOR, DAVID V. CURTIS, GEORGE ECKER, and GARY L. RILEY
    1978 Policy Making and Effective Leadership. San Francisco: Jossey-Bass.

BALDWIN, JOHN W., and RICHARD A. GOLDTHWAITE (eds.)
    1972 Universities in Politics: Case Studies from the Late Middle Ages and Early Modern Period. Baltimore: Johns Hopkins Press.

BALES, ROBERT F.
    1944 The "Fixation Factor" in Alcohol Addiction: An Hypothesis Derived from a Comparative Study of Irish and Jewish Social Norms. Unpublished doctoral dissertation, Harvard University.

1950 Interaction Process Analysis: A Method for the Study of Small Groups. Cambridge: Addison-Wesley.

BALTES, PAUL B., and S. J. DANISH
1980 "Intervention in life-span development and aging: issues and concepts." In R. R. Turner and H. W. Reese (eds.) Life-Span Developmental Psychology: Intervention. New York: Academic Press.

BANKOWSKI, Z., G. MUNGHAM, and P. YOUNG
1977 "Radical criminology or radical criminologist?" Contemporary Crises 1: 45–46.

BANTON, MICHAEL
1967 Race Relations. London: Tavistock.

BARBER, BERNARD
1970 L. J. Henderson on the Social System. Chicago: University of Chicago Press.

BARNES, J. A.
1954 "Class and committees in the Norwegian Island parish." Human Relations 7: 39–58.

BARRETT, J. C., and W. BRASS
1974 "Systematic and chance components in fertility measurement." Population Studies 28: 473–93.

BARTH, ERNEST A. T., and DONALD L. NOEL
1972 "Conceptual frameworks for the analysis of race relations." Social Forces 50: 333–48.

BAUMAN, ZYGMUNT
1972 Between Class and Elite. Manchester: Manchester University Press.

BEALE, C. L., and G. V. FUGUITT
1976 "The new pattern of nonmetropolitan population change." Working Paper 75–22. University of Wisconsin Center for Demography and Ecology.

BECK, E. M., PATRICK M. HORAN, and CHARLES M. TOLBERT, II
1978 "Stratification in a dual economy: a sectoral model of earnings determination." American Sociological Review 43: 704–20.

BECKER, HOWARD S.
1970 Sociological Work. Chicago: Aldine.
1974 "Labelling theory reconsidered." Pp. 41–66 in M. McIntosh and P. Rock (eds.), Deviance and Control. London: Tavistock.

BEIER, A. L.
1978 "Social problems in Elizabethan London." Journal of Interdisciplinary History 9: 203–21.

BELLAH, ROBERT N.
1958 "Religious aspects of modernization in Turkey and Japan." American Journal of Sociology 64: 1–5.
1964 "Religious evolution." American Sociological Review 29: 358–74.
1965 Religion and Progress in Modern Asia. New York: Free Press.
1966 "A case study in cultural and educational mobility: Japan and the Protestant ethic." Pp. 262–79 in N. J. Smelser and S. M. Lipset (eds.), Social Structure and Mobility in Economic Development. Chicago: Aldine.
1975 The Broken Covenant. New York: Seabury.

BEN-DAVID, JOSEPH
1968 "Universities." Pp. 191–99 in International Encyclopedia of the Social Sciences 16. New York: Macmillan and Free Press.
1971 The Scientist's Role in Society: A Comparative Study. Englewood Cliffs, N.J.: Prentice-Hall.
1977 Centers of Learning: Britain, France, Germany, United States. New York: McGraw-Hill.

BEN-DAVID, JOSEPH, and ABRAHAM ZLOCZOWER
1962 "Universities and academic systems in modern societies." European Journal of Sociology 3: 45–85.
1963–64 "Professions in the class systems of present-day societies." Current Sociology 12: 247–350.

BENDIX, REINHARD
1964 Nation Building and Citizenship. New York: Wiley.

BENEDICT, RUTH
1938 "Continuities and discontinuities in cultural conditioning." Psychiatry 2: 161–70.

BERG, BARBRO, and BERTIL OSTERGREN
1977 Innovations and Innovation Processes in Higher Education. Stockholm: National Board of Universities and Colleges.

BERGER, JOSEPH, THOMAS L. CONNER, and M. HAMIT FISEK (eds.)
1974 Expectation States Theory: A Theoretical Research Program. Cambridge: Winthrop.

BERGER, PETER L.
1967 The Sacred Canopy. Garden City, N.Y.: Doubleday.
1974"Second thoughts on defining religion." Journal for the Scientific Study of Religion 13: 126–33.

BERGER, PETER L., and THOMAS LUCKMANN
1967 The Social Construction of Reality. New York: Doubleday.

BERGNER, MARILYN, RUTH A. BOBBITT, SHIRLEY KRESSEL, WILLIAM E. POLLARD, BETTY S. GILSON, and JOANNE R. MORRIS
1979 "The sickness impact profile: conceptual formulation and methodology for the development of a health status measure." Pp. 9–31 in J. Elinson and A. E. Siegmann (eds.), Sociomedical Health Indicators. Farmingdale, N.Y.: Baywood Publishing Company.

BERK, RICHARD
1974 Collective Behavior. Dubuque, Iowa: Brown.

BERKOWITZ, LEONARD, and ELAINE WALSTER (EDS.)
1976 Advances in Experimental Social Psychology, Vol. 9. New York: Academic Press.

BERL, J. E., R. MCKELVEY, P. C. ORDESHOOK, and M. WINER
1976 "An experimental test of the core in a simple n-person nonsidepayment game." Journal of Conflict Resolution 20: 453–77.

BERNARD, CHERYL
1978 "Migrant workers and European democracy." Political Science Quarterly 93: 277–99.

BERNSTEIN, RICHARD J.
1976 The Restructuring of Social and Political Theory. New York: Harcourt Brace.

BERRY, BRIAN J. L.
1972 "Latent structure of the American urban system, with international comparisons." Pp. 11–60 in B. J. L. Berry (ed.), City Classification Handbook. New York: Wiley.

BERRY, BRIAN J. L., and JOHN D. KASARDA
1977 Contemporary Urban Ecology. New York: Macmillan.

BETZ, MICHAEL D.
1972 "The city as a system generating income equality." Social Forces 51: 192–98.

BIBB, ROBERT, and WILLIAM H. FORM
1977 "The effects of industrial, occupational, and sex stratification on wages in blue-collar markets." Social Forces 55: 974–96.

BICE, THOMAS W.
1979 "Comments on health indicators: methodological perspectives." Pp. 185–95 in J. Elinson and A. E. Siegmann (eds.), Sociomedical Health Indicators. Farmingdale, N.Y.: Baywood Publishing Company.

BICE, THOMAS W., and MARY JANE BUDENSTEIN
1977 "Methodological perspectives on health status indexes." Pp. 114–24 in J. Elinson, A. Mooney, and A. E. Siegmann (eds.), Health Goals and Health Indicators: Policy, Planning and Evaluation. American Association for the Advancement of Science Selected Symposium. 2. Boulder, Colo.: Westview Press.

BIDWELL, CHARLES
1965 "The school as a formal organization." Pp. 972–1022 in J. March (ed.), Handbook of Organizations. Chicago: Rand McNally.
1972 "Schooling and socialization for moral commitment." Interchange 3: 1–27.
1973 "The social psychology of teaching." Pp. 413–49 in R. M. W. Travers (ed.), Second Handbook of Research on Teaching. Chicago: Rand McNally.

BILLIG, MICHAEL
1976 Social Psychology and Intergroup Relations. New York: Academic Press.

BLALOCK, H. M.
1964 Causal Inferences in Nonexperimental Research. Chapel Hill: University of North Carolina Press.
1967 Toward a Theory of Minority-Group Relations. New York: Wiley.
1969 Theory Construction. Englewood Cliffs, N.J.: Prentice-Hall.
1979 "Dilemmas and strategies in theory construction." Pp. 119–35 in W. E. Snizek, E. R. Fuhrman, and M. K. Miller (eds.), Contemporary Issues in Theory and Research: A Metasociological Perspective. Westport, Conn.: Greenwood Press.

BLALOCK, H. M., and PAUL H. WILKEN
1979 Intergroup Processes: A Micro-Macro Approach. New York: Free Press.

BLAU, PETER M.
1973 The Organization of Academic Work. New York: Wiley.
1974 On the Nature of Organizations. New York: Wiley.

1977 Inequality and Heterogeneity: A Primitive Theory of Social Structure. New York: Free Press.

BLAU, PETER M., and OTIS DUDLEY DUNCAN
1967 The American Occupational Structure. New York: Wiley.

BLAU, PETER M., REBECCA Z. MARGULIES, and JOHN B. CULLEN
1979 "The professional and academic context of professional schools." Pp. 339–63 in R. K. Merton, J. S. Coleman, and P. H. Rossi (eds.), Qualitative and Quantitative Research in Sociology. New York: Free Press.

BLAU, PETER M., and RICHARD A. SCHOENHERR
1971 The Structure of Organizations. New York: Basic Books.

BLAUNER, ROBERT
1964 Alienation and Freedom: The Factory Worker and His Industry. Chicago: University of Chicago Press.
1972a "Colonized and immigrant minorities." Pp. 243–58 in P. Rose (ed.), Nation of Nations. New York: Random House.
1972b Racial Oppression in America. New York: Harper and Row.

BLUELER, EUGEN
1911 Dementia Praecox, oder Gruppe der Schizophrenien. Leipzig: Deuticke.

BLOCK, JACK, and NORMA HAAN
1971 Lives Through Time. Berkeley: Bancroft Books.

BLOOM, SAMUEL W., and ROBERT N. WILSON
1979 "Patient–practitioner relationships." Pp. 275–96 in S. Levine, H. Freeman, and L. Reeder (eds.), Handbook of Medical Sociology. Englewood Cliffs, N.J.: Prentice-Hall.

BLUMER, HERBERT
[1939] "Collective behavior." Pp. 167–98 in A. M. Lee (ed.).
1951 Principles of Sociology. New York: Barnes and Noble.
1957 "Collective behavior." Pp. 127–58 in J. B. Gittler (ed.), Review of Sociology: Analysis of a Decade. New York: Wiley.
1969 Symbolic Interactionism: Perspective and Method. Englewood Cliffs, N.J.: Prentice-Hall.

BONACICH, EDNA
1972 "A theory of ethnic antagonism: the split labor market." American Sociological Review 37: 547–59.
1976 "Advanced capitalism and black/white relations in the United States: a split labor market interpretation." American Sociological Review 41: 34–51.

BOOCOCK, SARANE
1972 An Introduction to the Sociology of Learning. New York: Houghton Mifflin.

BOSSERT, STEVEN T.
1979 Tasks and Social Relationships in Classrooms. Rose Monograph Series. New York: Cambridge University Press.

BOUDON, RAYMOND
1973 Mathematical Structures of Social Mobility. San Francisco: Jossey-Bass.

BOULDING, KENNETH E.
1953 "Toward a general theory of growth." Canadian Journal of Economics and Political Science 19: 326–40.

BOWER, J. L.
1965 "Group decision making: a report of an experimental study." Behavioral Science 10: 277–89.

BOWLES, SAMUEL, AND HERBERT GINTIS
1976 Schooling in Capitalist America: Educational Reform and the Contradictions of Economic Life. New York: Basic Books.

BRAVERMAN, HARRY
1974 Labor and Monopoly Capital. New York: Monthly Review Press.

BREIGER, RONALD L.
1974 "The duality of persons and groups." Social Forces 53: 181–90.

BRETON, RAYMOND
1972 Social and Academic Factors in the Career Decisions of Canadian Youth: A Study of Secondary School Students. Ottawa: Manpower and Immigration.

BRIM, ORVILLE G., JR.
1966 "Socialization through the life cycle." Pp. 1–49 in Orville G. Brim, Jr., and Stanton Wheeler (eds.), Socialization After Childhood: Two Essays. New York: Wiley.

BROWN, GEORGE W.
1974 "Meaning, measurement, and stress of life events." Pp. 217–43 in Barbara S. Dohrenwend and Bruce P. Dohrenwend (eds.), Stressful Life Events. New York: Wiley.

BROWN, G. W., J. L. T. BIRLEY, and J. K. WING
1972 "Influence of family life on the course of schizophrenic disorders: a replication." British Journal of Psychiatry 121: 241–58.

BROWN, G. W., and T. HARRIS
1978 Social Origins of Depression. New York: Free Press.

BROWN, RICHARD H.
1977 A Poetic for Sociology: Toward a Logic of Discovery for the Human Sciences. Cambridge: Cambridge University Press.

BRUNSWICK, ANN F.
1979 "Indicators of health status in adolescents." Pp. 109–26 in J. Elinson and A. E. Siegmann (eds.), Sociomedical Health Indicators. Farmingdale, N.Y.: Baywood Publishing Company.

BURAWOY, MICHAEL
1974 "Race, class and colonialism." Social and Economic Studies 23: 421–550.

BURKE, KENNETH
1941 The Philosophy of Literary Form. Baton Rouge: Louisiana State University Press.
1968 Language as Symbolic Action: Essays on Life, Literature, and Method. Berkeley: University of California Press.

BURR, W. R.
1972 "Role transitions: a reformulation of theory." Journal of Marriage and the Family 34: 407–16.

CAIN, LEONARD D.
1964 "Life course and social structure." Pp. 272–309 in Robert E. L. Faris (ed.), Handbook of Modern Sociology. Chicago: Rand McNally.

CAMPBELL, COLIN
1972 Toward a Sociology of Irreligion. New York: Herder and Herder.

CAMPBELL, D. T.
1963 "From description to experimentation: interpreting trends as quasi-experiments." Pp. 212–42 in C. W. Harris (ed.), Problems in Measuring Change. Madison: University of Wisconsin Press.

CAMPBELL, J.
1975 "Illness is a point of view: the development of children's concepts of illness." Child Development 46: 92–100.

CANCRO, R.
1979 "A selective history of the conceptualizations and treatment of the schizophrenic syndrome." Pp. 9–24 in R. Cancro, L. E. Shapiro, and M. Kesselman (eds.), Progress in the Functional Psychoses. New York: Spectrum.

CARDOSO, FERNANDO H.
1976 Ideologias de la Burguesia Industrial en Sociedades Dependientes. Mexico, D. F.: Siglo Veintiuno.
1977 "The consumption of dependency theory in the United States." Latin American Research Review 12: 7–24.

CARDOSO, FERNANDO H., and ENZO FALETTO
1969 Dependencia y Desarrollo en América Latina. Mexico, D. G.: Siglo Veintiuno.

CARPENTER, W. T., J. S. STRAUSS, and J. J. BATKO
1974 "Use of signs and symptoms for the identification of schizophrenic patients." Schizophrenia Bulletin 11: 37–49.

CARTWRIGHT, DORWIN, and ALVIN ZANDER (eds.)
1968 Group Dynamics. New York: Harper and Row.

CASTELLS, MANUEL
1975 "Immigrant workers and class struggle in advanced capitalism." Politics and Society 5: 33–66.

CASTLES, STEPHEN, and GODULA KOSACK
1973 Immigrant Workers and Class Structure in Western Europe. London: Oxford University Press.

CATHCART, ROBERT S., and LARRY A. SAMOVAR (eds.)
1970 Small Group Communication: A Reader. Dubuque, Iowa: Brown.

CHAVUNDUKA, GORDON
1979 "The tribal factor in African politics." Paper presented at National Affairs Association, Salisbury, Zimbabwe, Rhodesia.

CHEN, MARTIN K.
1979 "The gross national health product: a proposed population health index." U.S. Public Health Reports 94(2): 119–24.

CHIANG, C. L.
1965 An Index of Health: Mathematical Models. Washington, D.C.: U.S. Department of Health, Education and Welfare, Public Health Service.

CICOUREL, AARON
1973 Cognitive Sociology: Language and Meaning in Social Interaction. Harmondsworth: Penguin.

CLARK, BURTON R.
1962 Educating the Expert Society. San Francisco: Chandler.
1963 "Organizational adaptation to professionals." Pp. 283-91 in H. M. Vollmer and D. L. Mills (eds.), Professionalization. Englewood Cliffs, N.J.: Prentice-Hall.
1977a Academic Power in Italy: Bureaucracy and Oligarchy in a National University System. Chicago: University of Chicago Press.
1977b "Structures of post-secondary education." Yale Higher Education Program Working Paper No. 10. Also pp. 3968-79 in A. Knowles (ed.), International Encyclopedia of Higher Education, Vol. 8. San Francisco: Jossey-Bass.
1978 "Academic differentiation in national systems of higher education." Comparative Education Review 22: 242-58.
1979 "The many pathways of academic coordination." Higher Education 8: 251-67.

CLAUSEN, JOHN A.
1978 Socialization and Society. Boston: Little, Brown.

CLAUSEN, JOHN A., and C. L. HUFFINE
1979 "The impact of parental mental illness on children." Pp. 183-214 in R. G. Simmons (ed.), Research in Community and Mental Health. Greenwich, Conn.: JAI Press.

CLAVELIN, MAURICE
[1968] The Natural Philosophy of Galileo. Translated by A. J. Pomerans.
1974 Cambridge: Massachusetts Institute of Technology Press.

CLEMENTE, FRANK, and R. B. STURGIS
1972 "The division of labor in America: an ecological analysis." Social Forces 51: 176-82.

CLOWARD, RICHARD A., and LLOYD E. OHLIN
1960 Delinquency and Opportunity: A Theory of Delinquent Gangs. Glencoe, Ill.: Free Press.

COALE, ANSLEY J.
1973 "The demographic transition reconsidered." International Population Conference. Liége: International Union for the Scientific Study of Population.
1978 "T. R. Malthus and the population trends in his day and ours." University of Edinburgh, Encyclopaedia Britannica Lecture.

COHEN, YEHUDI
1975a "Schools and civilizational states." Pp. 103-40 in J. Fischer (ed.), The Social Sciences and the Comparative Study of Educational Systems. Scranton, Pa.: International Textbook.
1975b "The state system, schooling, and cognitive and motivational patterns." Pp. 103-40 in N. Shimohara and A. Scrupski (eds.), Social Forces and Schooling. New York: McKay.

COHN, RICHARD
1972 "On interpretation of cohort and period analyses: a mathematical note." Pp. 85-88 in Matilda White Riley, Marilyn Johnson, and Anne Foner (eds.), Aging and Society: A Sociology of Age Stratification, Vol. 3. New York: Russell Sage Foundation.

COLEMAN, JAMES S.
1975 "Social structure and a theory of action." Pp. 76-93 in Peter M. Blau (ed.), Approaches to the Study of Social Structure. New York: Free Press.

COLEMAN, JAMES S., E. Q. CAMPBELL, C. J. HOBSON, J. MCPARTLAND, A. M. MOOD, F. D. WEINFELD, and R. L. YORK
1966 Equality of Educational Opportunity. Washington, D.C.: U.S. Government Printing Office.

COLLINS, RANDALL
1971 "Functional and conflict theories of educational stratification." American Sociological Review 36: 1002-19.
1975 Conflict Sociology: Toward an Explanatory Science. New York: Academic Press.
1977 "Some comparative principles of educational stratification." Harvard Educational Review 47: 1-27.
1979 The Credential Society: A Historical Sociology of Education and Stratification. New York: Academic Press.

COMTE, AUGUSTE
1839 Cours de Philosophie Positive, 1830-42, Vol. 4, 51st Lesson. Paris: 635-39.

COOK, KAREN
1975 "Expectations, evaluations and equity." American Sociological Review 40: 372-88.

COOK, KAREN, and RICHARD M. EMERSON
1978 "Power, equity and commitment in exchange networks." American Sociological Reveiw 43: 721-39.

COOK, KAREN, and T. L. PARCEL
1977 "Equity theory: directions for future research." Sociological Inquiry 47: 75-88.

COOMBS, PHILIP
1968 The World Educational Crisis: A Systems Analysis. London: Oxford University Press.

COSER, LEWIS A.
1975 "Two methods in search of a substance." American Sociological Review 40: 691-700.

COUCH, C.
1968 "Collective behavior: an examination of some stereotypes." Social Problems 15: 310-22.
1970 "Dimensions of association in collective behavior episodes." Sociometry 33: 457-71.

COX, HARVEY
1965 The Secular City. New York: Macmillan.

COX, OLIVER CROMWELL
1948 Caste, Class and Race: A Study in Social Dynamics. Garden City, N.Y.: Doubleday.

CULLER, JONATHAN
1975 Structuralist Poetics: Structuralism, Linguistics and the Study of Literature. Ithaca, N.Y.: Cornell University Press.

CUMMING, ELAINE, and WILLIAM E. HENRY
1961 Growing Old: The Process of Disengagement. New York: Basic Books.

CUMMINGS, WILLIAM K., IKUO AMANO, and KAZUYUKI KITAMURA (eds.)
1979 Changes in the Japanese University: A Comparative Perspective. New York: Praeger.

CURRIE, ELLIOTT, and JEROME H. SKOLNICK
1970 "A critical note on conceptions of collective behavior." The Annals 391: 34–45.

CYERT, R. M., and J. G. MARCH
1963 A Behavioral Theory of the Firm. Englewood Cliffs, N.J.: Prentice-Hall.

DANIGELIS, NICHOLAS L.
1978 "Black political participation in the United States: some recent evidence." American Sociological Review 43: 756–71.

DAS GUPTA, J.
1974 "Ethnicity, language demands and national development." Ethnicity 1: 65–72.

DAVIES, MARGERY
1974 "Women's place is at the typewriter." Radical America 8: 1–28.

DAVIS, JAMES A.
1967 "Clustering and structural balance in graphs." Human Relations 20: 181–87.
1976 "Studying categorical data over time." Paper presented at the Conference on Strategies of Longitudinal Research on Drug Use, San Juan, Puerto Rico.

DAVIS, KINGSLEY
1949 Human Society. New York: Macmillan.

DAVIS, KINGSLEY, and WILBERT E. MOORE
1945 "Some principles of stratification." American Sociological Review 10: 242–49.

DAVIS, M.
1971 "That's interesting! towards a phenomenology of sociology and a sociology of phenomenology." Philosophy of the Social Sciences 1: 309–44.

DEMHOFF, G. WILLIAM
1967 Who Rules America? Englewood Cliffs, N.J.: Prentice-Hall.

DEMING, DONALD D.
1977 "Reevaluating the assembly line." Supervisory Management 22: 2–7.

DE SANTILLANA, GIORGIO
1955 The Crime of Galileo. Chicago: University of Chicago Press.

DESPRES, LEO A.
1967 Cultural Pluralism and Nationalist Politics in British Guiana. Chicago: Rand McNally.

DOHRENWEND, BARBARA S., LARRY KRASNOFF, ALEXANDER ASKENASY, and BRUCE P. DOHRENWEND
1978 "Exemplification of a method for scaling life events: the PERI life events scale." Journal of Health and Social Behavior 19: 205–29.

DOHRENWEND, BRUCE P., and BARBARA S. DOHRENWEND (eds.)
1974 Stressful Life Events: Their Nature and Effects. New York: Wiley.

DORE, RONALD P.
1976a "Human capital theory, the diversity of societies and the problem of quality in education." Higher Education 5: 79–102.
1976b The Diploma Disease: Education, Qualification and Development. Berkeley: University of California Press.

DORN, HAROLD
1951 "Methods of measuring incidence and prevalence of disease." American Journal of Public Health 41: 271–78.

DOS SANTOS, THEOTONIO
1970 "La crisis de la teoria del desarrollo y las relaciones de dependencia en América Latina." Pp. 147–87 in H. Jaguaribe et al., La dependencia politico-economica de América Latina. Mexico, D.F.: Siglo Veintiuno.

DOUGLAS, J.
1977 The Nude Beach. Beverly Hills: Sage.

DOWNES, D.
1978 "Promise and performance in British criminology." British Journal of Sociology 29: 483–502.
1979 "Praxis makes perfect." Pp. 1–16 in D. Downes and P. Rock (eds.), Deviant Interpretations. Oxford: Martin Robertson.

DUBLIN, LOUIS
1930 The Money Value of a Man. New York: Ronald Press.

DUMONT, LOUIS
1970 Homo Hierarchicus: The Caste System and Its Implications. Chicago: University of Chicago Press.

DUNCAN, BEVERLY, and STANLEY LIEBERSON
1970 Metropolis and Region in Transition. Beverly Hills: Sage.

DUNCAN, OTIS DUDLEY
1961 "A socio-economic index for all occupations." Pp. 109–38 in A. J. Reiss (ed.), Occupations and Social Status. New York: Free Press.
1968 "Social stratification and mobility." Pp. 675–719 in Eleanor Bernert Sheldon and Wilbert E. Moore (eds.), Indicators of Social Change. New York: Russell Sage Foundation.
1969 "Some linear models for two-wave, two-variable panel analysis." Psychological Bulletin 72: 177–82.

DUNCAN, OTIS DUDLEY, ROY P. CUZZORT, and BEVERLY DUNCAN
1961 Statistical Geography. Glencoe, Ill.: Free Press.

DUNCAN, OTIS DUDLEY, and ALBERT J. REISS
1956 Social Characteristics of Urban and Rural Communities, 1950. New York: Wiley.

DUNCAN, OTIS DUDLEY, R. W. SCOTT, S. LIEBERSON, B. DUNCAN, and H. H. WINSBOROUGH
1960 Metropolis and Region. Baltimore: Johns Hopkins Press.

DUNPHY, DEXTER C.
1972 The Primary Group. A Handbook for Analysis and Field Research. New York: Appleton-Century-Crofts.

DURBIN, J., and G. S. WATSON
1950 "Testing for serial correlation in least-squares regression." Biometrika 37: 409–28.
1951 "Testing for serial correlation in least-squares regression." Biometrika 38: 159–78.

DURKHEIM, EMILE
1888 "Cours de science sociale: leçon d'ouverture." Revue Internationale de l'Enseignement 15: 23–48.
1895 Les Règles de la Méthode Sociologique. Paris: Alcan.
1897 "Review of A. Labriola, Essais sur la conception materialist de l'histoire." Revue Philosophique 44: 648.
[1902] The Division of Labor in Society. Translated by George Simpson.
1966 Glencoe, Ill.: Free Press.
1912 Les Formes Elementaires de la Vie Religieuse: Le Systeme Totémique en Australie. Paris: Alcan.
[1922] Education and Sociology. Translated by S. D. Fox.
1956 Glencoe, Ill.: Free Press.
1961 Moral Education: A Study in the Theory and Application of the Sociology of Education. Edited by E. K. Wilson and H. Schnurer. New York: Free Press.

DURYEA, E. D.
1973 "Evolution of university organization." Pp. 15–37 in J. A. Perkins (ed.), The University as an Organization. New York: McGraw-Hill.

DYER, E. E.
1963 "Parenthood as crisis: a restudy." Journal of Marriage and the Family 25: 196–201.

DYER, J. S., and R. F. MILES
1976 "An actual application of collective choice theory to the selection of trajectories for the Mariner Jupiter/Saturn 1977 project." Operations Research 24: 220–24.

EASTERLIN, RICHARD A.
1978 "What will 1984 be like? socioeconomic implications of recent twist in age structure." Demography 15: 397–432.

EBERSTEIN, ISAAC W.
1979 Intercommunity Sustenance Flow and the Metropolitan Hierarchy. Unpublished doctoral dissertation, Department of Sociology, The University of Texas.

EDWARDS, ALBA M.
1938 A Social-Economic Grouping of the Gainful Workers of the United States, 1930. Washington, D.C.: U.S. Government Printing Office.
1943 Comparative Statistics for the United States, 1870 to 1940. U.S. Department of Commerce. Washington D.C.: U.S. Government Printing Office.

EISENSTADT, S. N.
1956 From Generation to Generation: Age Groups and Social Structure. Glencoe, Ill.: Free Press.
1961 Essays on Sociological Aspects of Political and Economic Development. The Hague: Mouton.

ELDER, GLEN H.
    1975 "Age differentiation in life course perspective." Annual Review of Sociology
    1: 165–90.

ELINSON, JACK
    1977 "Insensitive health statistics and the dilemma of the HSAs." American Jour-
    nal of Public Health 67: 417–18.

ELLIS, DONALD G., and B. AUBREY FISHER
    1975 "Phases of conflict in small group development: a Markov analysis."
    Human Communication Research 1: 195–212.

EMERSON, RICHARD M.
    1962 "Power-dependence relations." American Sociological Review 17: 31–41.

ESMAN, MILTON J. (ed.)
    1977 Ethnic Conflict in the Western World. Ithaca, N.Y.: Cornell University
    Press.

EVANS-PRITCHARD, E. E.
    1940 The Nuer. London: Oxford University Press.

FALK, G.
    1978 An Examination of Some Normative Effects of Unanimity and Majority
    Rules on the Quality of Solutions in Problem Solving Groups with Unequal
    Power. Unpublished doctoral dissertation, Graduate School of Business, Univer-
    sity of Chicago.

FALLERS, LLOYD A.
    1973 Inequality: Social Stratification Reconsidered. Chicago: University of
    Chicago Press.

FARIS, R. E. L., and H. W. DUNHAM
    1939 Mental Disorders in Urban Areas. Chicago: University of Chicago Press.

FARLEY, REYNOLDS
    1964 "Suburban Persistence." American Sociological Review 29: 38–47.
    1977 "Trends in racial inequalities: have the gains of the 1960s disappeared in the
    1970s?" American Sociological Review 42: 189–207.

FEATHERMAN, DAVID L.
    1980 "Schooling and occupational careers: constancy and change in wordly suc-
    cess." In Orville G. Brim, Jr., and Jerome Kagan (eds.), Constancy and Change
    in Human Development. Cambridge: Harvard University Press.

FEATHERMAN, DAVID L., and ROBERT M. HAUSER
    1978 Opportunity and Change. New York: Academic Press.

FENN, RICHARD K.
    1978 Toward a Theory of Secularization. Storrs, Conn.: Society for the Scientific
    Study of Religion.

FIEDLER, FRED E.
    1967 A Theory of Leadership Effectiveness. New York: McGraw-Hill.

FIELD, ALEXANDER
    1976 "Educational expansion in mid-nineteenth century Massachusetts." Har-
    vard Educational Review 46: 521–52.

FIENBERG, STEPHEN E., and William M. Mason
1979 "Identification and estimation of age-cohort models in the analysis of discrete archival data." Sociological Methodology 1979: 1–67.

FIORINA, M. P., and C. R. PLOTT
1978 "Committee decisions under majority rule: an experimental study." American Political Science Review 72: 575–98.

FIREBAUGH, GLENN
1978 "A rule for inferring individual-level relationships from aggregate data." American Sociological Review 43: 557–72.
1979 "Assessing group effects: a comparison of two methods." Sociological Methods and Research 4: 384–95.

FONER, ANNE
1974 "Age stratification and age conflict in political life." American Sociological Review 39: 187–96.
1979 "Ascribed and achieved bases of stratification." Annual Review of Sociology 5: 219–42.

FONER, PHILIP S.
1976 Labor and the American Revolution. Westport, Conn.: Greenwood Press.

FOOTE, NELSON
1953 "The professionalization of labor in Detroit." American Journal of Sociology 58: 371–80.

FORM, WILLIAM H.
1976a Blue-Collar Stratification. Princeton, N.J.: Princeton University Press.
1976b "Conflict within the working class: the skilled as a special interest group." Pp. 51–73 in Lewis A. Coser and Otto N. Larsen (eds.), The Uses of Controversy in Sociology. New York: Free Press.
1979 "Comparative industrial sociology and the convergence hypothesis." Annual Review of Sociology 5: 1–25.

FORSTER, PETER G.
1972 "Secularization in the English context: some conceptual and empirical problems." Sociological Review 20(N.S.): 153–68.

FRANCIS, E. K.
1976 Interethnic Relations: An Essay in Sociological Theory. New York: Elsevier.

FRANK, ANDRE GUNDER
1967 Capitalism and Underdevelopment in Latin America. New York: Monthly Review Press.

FRAZIER, E. FRANKLIN
1953 "Theoretical structure of sociology and sociological research." British Journal of Sociology 4: 292–311.

FREDRICKSON, GEORGE
1970 "Racism in concept and theory." Paper presented at Annual Meeting of Organization of American Historians, St. Louis.

FREEMAN, HOWARD E., SOL LEVINE, and LEO G. REEDER
1979 Handbook of Medical Sociology. Englewood Cliffs. N.J.: Prentice-Hall.

FREIDSON, ELIOT
1978 "Design by accident." Pp. 115–33 in R. H. Elling and M. Sokolowska (eds.), Medical Sociologists at Work. New Brunswick, N.J.: Transaction Books.

FREUD, SIGMUND
1960 Group Psychology and the Analysis of the Ego. London: Hogarth.

FREY, WILLIAM H.
1979 "Central city white flight: racial and nonracial causes." American Sociological Review 44: 425–48.

FRIEDMAN, M., and R. H. ROSENMAN
1959 "Association of specific overt behavior patterns with blood and cardiovascular findings." Journal of the American Medical Association 169: 1286–88.

FRIEND, K. E., J. D. LAING, and R. J. MORRISON
1977a "Bargaining processes and coalition outcomes: an integration." Journal of Conflict Resolution 21: 267–98.
1977b "Game-theoretic analysis of coalition behavior." Theory and Decision 8: 127–57.
1978 "Contending 'signals' in coalition choice." Journal of Mathematical Sociology 6: 23–46.

FRISBIE, W. PARKER
1980 "Data and methods in ecological analysis." In Michael Micklin and Harvey Choldin (eds.), Sociological Human Ecology: Contemporary Issues and Applications. New York: Academic Press.

FRISCH, ROSE E.
1978 "Population, food intake and fertility." Science 199: 22–30.

FUCHS, VICTOR
1974 Who Shall Live? Health, Economic and Social Choice. New York: Basic Books.
1979 Economics, Health and Post Industrial Society. New York: Milbank Memorial Fund Quarterly/Health and Society.

FUGUITT, G. V., and S. LIEBERSON
1974 "Correlation of ratios or difference scores having common terms." Pp. 128–44 in H. L. Costner (ed.), Sociological Methodology, 1973–1974. San Francisco: Jossey-Bass.

Furstenburg, Frank, Jr.
1979 "Remarriage and intergenerational relations." Unpublished paper.

FURTADO, CELSO
1970 Economic Development of Latin America. Cambridge: Cambridge University Press.

GALBRAITH, J.
1968 The New Industrial State. New York: New American Library.

GAMSON, W. A.
1961 "A theory of coalition formation." American Sociological Review 26: 373–82.

GARDEN, MAURICE
1975 Lyon et Les Lyonnais au XVIIIe Siècle. Paris: Flaumarion.

GARFINKEL, HAROLD
1967 Studies in Ethnomethodology. Englewood Cliffs, N.J.: Prentice-Hall. Chap. 5.

GARMEZY, N.
1974 "Children at risk: the search for the antecedents of schizophrenia." Part 1, Conceptual Models and Research Methods. Schizophrenia Bulletin 8: 14–90.

GEERTZ, CLIFFORD
1969 Island Observed. New Haven: Yale University Press.
1973 "Thick description: toward an interpretive theory of culture." Pp. 3–30 in his The Interpretation of Cultures. New York: Basic Books.

GELLNER, E.
1975 "Ethnomethodology: the re-enchantment industry or the Californian way of subjectivity." Philosophy of the Social Sciences 5: 431–50.

GEREFFI, GARY
1979 "A critical evaluation of quantitative, cross-national studies of dependency." Paper presented at the panel on "Dependency Theory" meetings of the International Studies Association, Toronto.

GERUSON, RICHARD T., and DENNIS MCGRATH
1977 Cities and Urbanization. New York: Praeger.

GIBBARD, GRAHAM S., JOHN D. HARTMAN, and RICHARD D. MANN (eds.)
1974 Analysis of Groups. San Francisco: Jossey-Bass.

GIBBS, JACK P., and HARLEY L. BROWNING
1966 "The division of labor, technology, and the organization of production in twelve countries." American Sociological Review 31: 81–92.

GIBBS, J. P., and D. L. POSTON, JR.
1975 "The division of labor: conceptualization and related measures." Social Forces 53: 468–76.

GIDDENS, ANTHONY
1973 The Class Structure of the Advanced Societies. New York: Harper and Row.
1976 New Rules of Sociological Method: A Positive Critique of Interpretative Sociology. London: Hutchinson.

GILES, MICHAEL W.
1978 "White enrollment stability and school desegregation: a two-level analysis." American Sociological Review 43: 848–64.

GLASNER, PETER E.
1977 The Sociology of Secularisation. London: Routledge and Kegan Paul.

GLASS, DAVID V.
1957 The University Teaching of Social Sciences: Demography. Paris: UNESCO.

GLASS, DAVID V., and D. E. C. EVERSLEY
1965 Population in History: Essays in Historical Demography. London: Arnold.

GLASSER, JAY, and PEARL FISHER
1977 "Applications of health indices related to demographic and probability bases

measures." Paper presented at the 2nd National Center for Health Statistics Conference, Seattle.

GLENN, N. D.
1975 "Psychological well-being in the postparental stage: some evidence from national surveys." Journal of Marriage and the Family 37: 105–12.

GLOCK, CHARLES Y.
1959 "The sociology of religion." Pp. 153–77 in R. K. Merton, L. Broom, and L. S. Cottrell, Jr. (eds.), Sociology Today. New York: Basic Books.

GLOCK, CHARLES Y., and RODNEY STARK
1965 Religion and Society in Tension. Chicago: Rand McNally.

GOFFMAN, ERVING
1967 "Where the action is." Pp. 149–270 in his Interaction Ritual: Essays on Face-To-Face Behavior. Garden City, N.Y.: Doubleday.

GOLDMAN, ROBERT B.
1976 A Work Experiment: Six Americans in a Swedish Plant. New York: Ford Foundation.

GOLDSTEIN, M. J., and E. H. RODNICK
1975 "The family's contribution to the etiology of schizophrenia: current status." Schizophrenia Bulletin 14: 48–63.

GOLEMBIEWSKI, ROBERT T.
1962 The Small Group: An Analysis of Research Concepts and Operations. Chicago: University of Chicago Press.

GOODE, WILLIAM J.
1978 The Celebration of Heroes: Prestige as a Control System. Berkeley: University of California Press.

GOULD, R.
1972 "The phases of adult life: a study of developmental psychology." American Journal of Psychiatry 129: 521–31.

GOULDNER, ALVIN W.
1973 "For sociology." Pp. 128–70 in his For Sociology: Renewal and Critique in Sociology Today. New York: Basic Books.

GRANOVETTER, MARK S.
1973 "The strength of weak ties." American Journal of Sociology 78: 1360–80.

GRAY, LOUIS N., JAMES T. RICHARDSON, and BRUCE H. MAYHEW, JR.
1968 "Influence attempts and effective power: a re-examination of an unsubstantiated hypothesis." Sociometry 31: 245–58.

GREELEY, ANDREW M.
1972a Unsecular Man. New York: Dell.
1972b The Denominational Society. Glenview, Ill.: Scott, Foresman.

GREENLEY, J. R.
1979 "Family symptom tolerance and rehospitalization experiences of psychiatric patients." Pp. 357–86 in Roberta Simmons (ed.), Research in Community and Mental Health. Greenwich, Conn.: JAI Press.

GREENWOOD, J. M.
1975 "Simultaneity bias in migration models: an empirical examination." Demography 12: 519–36.

GURALNICK, STANLEY M.
1975 Science and the Ante-Bellum American College. Philadelphia: American Philosophical Society.

GUSFIELD, J.
1968 "The study of social movements." Pp. 445–52 in D. L. Sills (ed.), International Encyclopedia of the Social Sciences. New York: Macmillan and Free Press.

GUTMAN, ROBERT
1960 "In defense of population theory." American Sociological Review 25: 325–33.

GUTTMACHER, SALLY, GAIL GARBOWSKI, and JACK ELINSON
1980 Toward the Development of a Child Health Profile. New York: Foundation for Child Development.

HADDEN, JEFFREY K., and EDGAR F. BORGATTA
1965 American Cities: Their Social Characteristics. Chicago: Rand McNally.

HAGGERTY, L. J.
1971 "Another look at the Burgess hypothesis: time as an important variable." American Journal of Sociology 76: 1084–93.

HALL, IVAN P.
1975 "Organizational paralysis: the case of Todai." Pp. 304–30 in E. F. Vogel (ed.), Modern Japanese Organization and Decision-Making. Berkeley: University of California Press.

HALL, J., and W. H. Watson
1970 "The effects of a normative intervention on group decision-making performance." Human Relations 23: 299–317.

HALL, J., and M. S. WILLIAMS
1966 "A comparison of decision-making performances in established and ad hoc groups." Journal of Personality and Social Psychology 3: 214–22.

HALLINAN, MAUREEN T.
1974 The Structure of Positive Sentiment. Amsterdam: Elsevier.

HALSEY, A. H.
1960 "The changing functions of universities in advanced industrial societies." Harvard Educational Review 30: 118–27.

HANNAN, MICHAEL T.
1971 Aggregation and Disaggregation in Sociology. Lexington, Mass.: Heath-Lexington.

HANNAN, MICHAEL T., and LEIGH BURSTEIN
1974 "Estimation from grouped observations." American Sociological Review 39: 374–92.

HANNAN, MICHAEL T., and JOHN FREEMAN
1977 "The population ecology of organizations." American Journal of Sociology 82: 929–64.

HANNAN, MICHAEL T., and NANCY TUMA
1979 "Methods for temporal analysis." Pp. 303–28 in Alex Inkeles, James Coleman, and Ralph H. Turner (eds.), Annual Review of Sociology, Vol. 5. Palo Alto, Calif.: Annual Review.

HANNAN, MICHAEL T., and ALICE A. YOUNG
  1977 "Estimation in panel models: results on pooling cross-sections and time
  series." Pp. 52–83 in D. R. Heise (ed.), Sociological Methodology, 1977. San
  Francisco: Jossey-Bass.

HARARY, FRANK, R. Z. NORMAN, and DORWIN CARTWRIGHT
  1965 Structural Models. New York: Wiley.

HARE, A. PAUL
  1962 Handbook of Small Group Research. New York: Free Press.

HARRÉ, ROMANO, and PAUL F. SECORD
  1972 The Explanation of Social Behaviour. Oxford: Blackwell.

HARRIS, CHAUNCEY D.
  1943 "A functional classification of cities in the United States." Geographical
  Review 33: 86–99.

HARRIS, MARVIN
  1964 Patterns of Race in the Americas. New York: Walker.

HARVARD UNIVERSITY PROGRAM ON TECHNOLOGY AND SOCIETY
  1969 Technology and Work. Research Review No. 2. Cambridge: Harvard
  University Press.

HASKINS, CHARLES HOMER
  1957 The Rise of Universities. Ithaca, N.Y.: Cornell University Press.

HATT, PAUL K.
  1950 "Occupation and social stratification." American Journal of Sociology 55:
  533–43.

HAUG, MARIE R.
  1977 "Measurement in social stratification." Annual Review of Sociology 3:
  51–77.

HAUSER, ROBERT M.
  1978 "A structural model of the mobility table." Social Forces 56: 919–53.

HAUSER, ROBERT M., PETER J. DICKINSON, HARRY P. TRAVIS, and JOHN N. KOFFEL
  1975 "Temporal change in occupational mobility: evidence for men in the United
  States." American Sociological Review 40: 279–97.

HAUSER, ROBERT M., and DAVID L. FEATHERMAN
  1977 The Process of Stratification: Trends and Analyses. New York: Academic
  Press.

HAUSER, ROBERT M., JOHN N. KOFFEL, HARRY P. TRAVIS, and PETER J. DICKINSON
  1975 "Structural changes in occupational mobility among men in the United
  States." American Sociological Review 40: 585–98.

HAUSER, ROBERT M., WILLIAM H. SEWELL, and DUANE ALWIN
  1976 "High school effects on achievement." Pp. 309–41 in W. H. Sewell, R. M.
  Hauser, and D. L. Featherman (eds.), Schooling and Achievement in American
  Society. New York: Academic Press.

HAWLEY, AMOS H.
  1944 "Ecology and human ecology." Social Forces 22: 398–405.
  1948 "Discussion of Hollingshead's 'community research: development and present condition.'" American Sociological Review 13: 153–56.

1950 Human Ecology. New York: Ronald.
1968 "Human ecology." Pp. 323–32 in D. L. Sills (ed.), International Encyclopedia of the Social Sciences. New York: Crowell, Collier and Macmillan.
1971 Urban Society. New York: Ronald.

HEATH, ANTHONY
1976 Rational Choice and Social Exchange: A Critique of Exchange Theory. Cambridge: Cambridge University Press.

HECHTER, MICHAEL
1974 "The political economy of ethnic change." American Journal of Sociology 79: 1151–78.
1975 Internal Colonialism: The Celtic Fringe in British National Development, 1536–1966. Berkeley and Los Angeles: University of California Press.

HEIRICH, M.
1977 "Change of heart: a test of some widely held theories about religious conversion." American Journal of Sociology 83: 653–79.

HEISE, D. R.
1970 "Causal inference from panel data." Pp. 3–27 in E. F. Borgatta and G. W. Bohrnstedt (eds.), Sociological Methodology, 1970. San Francisco: Jossey-Bass.
1975 Causal Analysis. New York: Wiley.

HEMPEL, CARL G.
1942 "The function of general laws in history." Journal of Philosophy 39: 35–48.

HENRETTA, JOHN C., and RICHARD T. CAMPBELL
1978 "Net worth as an aspect of status." American Journal of Sociology 83: 1204 23.

HERBERG, WILL
1955 Protestant—Catholic—Jew. Garden City, N.Y.: Doubleday.

HERN, FRANCIS
1978 "Rationality and bureaucracy: Maoist contributions to a Marxist theory of bureaucracy." Sociological Quarterly 19: 37–54.

HESSE, MARY
1974 The Structure of Scientific Inference. Berkeley: University of California Press.

HESTON, L. I., and D. DENNEY
1968 "Interactions between early life experience and biological factors in schizophrenia." Pp. 363–76 in D. Rosenthal and S. S. Kety (eds.), The Transmission of Schizophrenia. New York: Pergamon Press.

HEWITT, CHRISTOPHER
1977 "Majorities and minorities: a comparative survey of ethnic violence." The Annals 433: 150–60.

HEYNS, BARBARA
1974 "Social selection and stratification within schools." American Journal of Sociology 79: 1434–51.

HIBBS, D. A.
1974 "Problems of statistical estimation and causal inference in time-series regression models." Pp. 252–308 in H. L. Costner (ed.), Sociological Methodology, 1973-1974. San Francisco: Jossey-Bass.

HICKSON, D. J., C. R. HININGS, C. J. McMILLAN, and J. P. SCHWITTER
1974 "The culture-free context of organization structure." Sociology 8: 59–80.

HILL, R., and K. CRITTENDEN (eds.)
1968 Proceedings of the Purdue Symposium on Ethnomethodology. Institute for the Study of Social Change, Lafayette, Indiana.

HINCKLE, L.
1974 "The effect of exposure to culture change, social change and changes in interpersonal relationships on health." Pp. 9–44 in B. S. Dohrenwend and B. P. Dohrenwend (eds.), Stressful Life Events: Their Nature and Effects. New York: Wiley.

HIRSCH, SUSAN E.
1978 Roots of the American Working Class: The Industrialization of Crafts in Newark, 1800–1860. Philadelphia: University of Pennsylvania Press.

HIRSCHI, TRAVIS
1969 Causes of Delinquency. Berkeley: University of California Press.

HIRSCHMAN, ALBERT O.
1958 The Strategy of Economic Development. New Haven: Yale University Press.

HIRST, P.
1975a "Marx and Engels on law, crime and mortality." Pp. 203–32 in I. Taylor et al. (eds.), Critical Criminology. London: Routledge and Kegan Paul.
1975b "Review of P. Anderson, Passages from Antiquity to Feudalism and Lineages of the Absolutist State." Economy and Society 446–75.

HOBBS, D. F., JR., and S. P. COLE
1976 "Transition to parenthood: a decade replication." Journal of Marriage and the Family 38: 723–32.

HOETINK, HARRY
1967 Caribbean Race Relations: A Study of Two Variants. Chicago: Rand McNally.

HOFFMAN, L. R.
1961 "Conditions for creative problem solving." Journal of Psychology 52: 429–44.

HOFSTADTER, RICHARD
1963 Anti-Intellectualism in American Life. New York: Random House.

HOGAN, DENNIS P.
1978 "The variable order of events in the life course." American Sociological Review 43: 573–86.

HOGAN, DENNIS P., and DAVID L. FEATHERMAN
1977 "Racial stratification and socioeconomic change in the American North and South." American Journal of Sociology 83: 100–26.

HOGE, DEAN R., and DAVID A. ROOZEN (eds.)
1979 Understanding Church Growth and Decline, 1950–1978. New York: Pilgrim.

HOLLINGSHEAD, A. B., and F. C. REDLICH
1958 Social Class and Mental Illness: A Community Study. New York: Wiley.

HOLMES, F., and R. H. RAHE
1967 "Social readjustment rating scale." Journal of Psychosomatic Research 11: 213–18.

HOLSINGER, DONALD
1974 "The elementary school as modernizer: a Brazilian study." Pp. 24–46 in A. Inkeles and D. Holsinger (eds.), Education and Individual Modernity in Developing Countries. Leiden: Brill.

HOLTON, GERALD
1978 The Scientific Imagination: Case Studies. Cambridge: Cambridge University Press.

HOMANS, GEORGE C.
1958 "Social behavior as exchange." American Journal of Sociology 63: 597–606.
1964 "Bringing men back in." American Sociological Review 29: 809–18.
1967a "Fundamental social processes." Pp. 27–78 in Neil J. Smelser (ed.), Sociology: An Introduction. New York: Wiley.
1967b The Nature of Social Science. New York: Harcourt, Brace and World.
1974 Social Behavior: Its Elementary Forms (revised ed.). New York: Harcourt Brace Jovanovich.

HOPKINS, TERENCE K.
1964 The Exercise of Influence in Small Groups. Totowa, N.J.: Bedminster Press.

HOPKINS, TERENCE K., and IMMANUEL WALLERSTEIN
1977 "Patterns of development of the modern world-system." Review 1: 111–45.

HORAN, PATRICK M.
1978 "Is status attainment research atheoretical?" American Sociological Review 43: 534–41.

HOROWITZ, I.
1974 "The penal colony known as the USSR." Society 2: 22–26.

HUBBELL, CHARLES H.
1965 "An input–output approach to clique identification." Sociometry 28: 377–99.

HUNNIUS, GERRY, G. DAVID GARSON, and JOHN CASE (eds.)
1973 Workers' Control. New York: Vintage.

HUNTER, ALBERT
1971 "The ecology of Chicago: persistence and change, 1930–1960." American Journal of Sociology 77: 425–44.

IRWIN, LAURA, and ALLAN J. LICHTMAN
1976 "Across the great divide: inferring individual level behavior from aggregate data." Political Methodology 3: 411–39.

ISAACS, HAROLD R.
1974 "Basic group identity: the idols of the tribe." Ethnicity 1: 15–44.

JACKSON, D. D.
1965 "The study of the family." Family Process 4: 1–20.

JACOBSON, CARDELL K.
1978 "Desegregation rulings and public attitude changes: white resistance or resignation?" American Journal of Sociology 84: 698–705.

JANOWITZ, MORRIS
1975 "Sociological theory and social control." American Journal of Sociology 81: 82–108.

1978 The Last Half Century: Societal Change and Politics in America. Chicago: University of Chicago Press.

1979 "Social control and the study of political regimes." Paper presented at Annual Meeting of the American Sociological Association, Boston.

JAQUES, ELLIOT
1956 The Measurement of Responsibility. Cambridge: Harvard University Press.

JENCKS, CHRISTOPHER, M. SMITH, H. ACLAND, M. J. BANE, D. COHEN, H. GINTIS, B. HEYNS, and S. MICHELSON
1972 Inequality: A Reassessment of the Effect of Family and Schooling in America. New York: Basic Books.

JOHNSON, BENTON
1975 Functionalism in Modern Sociology: Understanding Talcott Parsons. Morristown, N.J.: General Learning.

1977 "Sociological theory and religious truth." Sociological Analysis 38: 368–88.

JOHNSON, D.
1945 "The phantom anesthesiologist of Matoon: a field study of mass hysteria." Journal of Abnormal and Social Psychology 40: 175–86.

JOHNSTON, J.
1972 Econometric Methods. New York: McGraw-Hill.

JÖRESKOG, KARL G.
1969 "A general approach to confirmatory maximum likelihood factor analysis." Psychometrika 34: 183–202.

JÖRESKOG, KARL G., and MARIELLE VAN THILLO
1972 "LISREL: a general computer program for estimating a linear structural equation system involving mutliple indicators of unmeasured variables." Research Bulletin 72-56. Princeton, N.J.: Educational Testing Service.

KAESTLE, CARL, and MARIS VINOVSKIS
1979 Education and Social Change in Nineteenth Century Massachusetts. New York: Cambridge University Press.

KALLEBERG, ARNE L., and LARRY J. GRIFFIN
1978 "Positional sources of inequality in job satisfaction." Sociology of Work and Occupations 5: 371–400.

1980 "Class, occupation, and inequality in job rewards." American Journal of Sociology 85: 731–68.

KAPLAN, B. H., J. C. CASSELL, and S. GORE
1977 "Social support and health." Medical Care 15: 47–58.

KASARDA, JOHN D.
1972a "The impact of suburban population growth on central city service functions." American Journal of Sociology 77: 1111–24.

1972b "The theory of ecological expansion: an empirical test." Social Forces 51: 165–75.

1974 "The structural implications of system size: a three-level analysis." American Sociological Review 39: 19–28.

KASARDA, JOHN D., and PATRICK D. NOLAN
1979 "Ratio measurement and theoretical inference in social research." Social Forces 58: 212–27.

KASS, ROY
1973 "A functional classification of metropolitan communities." Demography 10: 427–45.
1977 "Community structure and the metropolitan division of labor." Social Forces 56: 218–39.

KASTENBAUM, ROBERT
1975 "Is death a life crisis? On the confrontation with death in theory and practice." Pp. 19–50 in Nancy Datan and Leon H. Ginsberg (eds.), Life-Span Development Psychology: Normative Life Crises. New York: Academic Press.

KATZ, LEO
1953 "A new status index derived from sociometric analysis." Psychometrika 18: 39–43.

KATZ, MICHAEL
1968 The Irony of Early School Reform: Educational Innovation in Mid-Nineteenth Century Massachusetts. Cambridge: Harvard University Press.

KATZ, S., and C. A. APKOM
1976 "A measure of primary socio-biological functions." International Journal of Health Services 6: 493–508.

KELLEY, DEAN
1972 Why Conservative Churches Are Growing. New York: Harper and Row.

KELLEY, HAROLD H., and JOHN W. THIBAUT
1978 Interpersonal Relations: A Theory of Interdependence. New York: Wiley.

KEMPER, THEODORE D.
1972 "The division of labor: a post–Durkheimian analytical view." American Sociological Review 37: 739–53.

KERCKHOFF, A. C., and K. W. BACK
1968 The June Bug: A Study of Hysterical Contagion. New York: Appleton-Century-Crofts.

KERR, CLARK
1963 The Uses of the University. Cambridge: Harvard University Press.

KEYFITZ, NATHAN
1971 "Models." Demography 8: 571–80.
1975 "How do we know the facts of demography?" Population and Development Review 1: 267–88.
1979 "Causes and consequences of population change." Pp. 76–95 in Amos H. Hawley (ed.), The Forms of Societal Growth. New York: Free Press.

KEYNES, JOHN MAYNARD
1936 The General Theory of Unemployment, Interest, and Money. London: Macmillan.

KILLIAN, LEWIS M.
1964 "Social movements." Pp. 426–55 in R. E. L. Faris (ed.), Handbook of Modern Sociology. Chicago: Rand McNally.

KINNEY, D. K., and B. JACOBSEN
1978 "Environmental factors in schizophrenia: new adoption study evidence." Pp. 38–51 in L. C. Wynne (ed.), The Nature of Schizophrenia. New York: Wiley.

KIRK, DUDLEY
1971 "A new demographic transition." Pp. 123–47 in National Academy of

Sciences, Rapid Population Growth: Consequences and Policy Implications. Baltimore: Johns Hopkins University Press.

KLAPP, ORRIN E.
1962 Heroes, Villains, and Fools: The Changing American Character. Englewood Cliffs, N.J.: Prentice-Hall.
1964 Symbolic Leaders: Public Dramas and Public Men. Chicago: Aldine.

KLAUSNER, S. F.
1971 On Man in This Environment. San Francisco: Jossey-Bass.

KNAPP, P. H.
1975 "Current theoretical concepts in psychophysiological medicine." Pp. 1631-37 in A. M. Freedman, H. I. Kaplan, and B. J. Sadock (ed.), Comprehensive Textbook of Psychiatry (2nd ed.). Baltimore: Williams and Wilkins.

KOHN, MELVIN L.
1971 "Bureaucratic man." American Sociological Review 36: 461-74.
1973 "Social class and schizophrenia: a critical review and a reformulation." Schizophrenia Bulletin 7: 60-79.

KOMORITA, S. S., and J. M. CHERTKOFF
1973 "A bargaining theory of coalition formation." Psychological Review 80: 149-62.

KREPS, JUANITA M., and R. JOHN LEAPER
1976 "Home work, market work, and the allocation of time." Pp. 61-81 in Juanita M. Kreps (ed.), Women and the American Economy. Englewood Cliffs, N.J.: Prentice-Hall.

KUHN, THOMAS S.
[1962] The Structure of Scientific Revolutions (revised ed.).
1970 Chicago: University of Chicago Press.

KUNSTADTER, PETER
1979 "Demographic transition theory: requiescat in pace?" Family Planning Perspective 11: 71-72.

KUPER, LEO, and M. G. SMITH
1964 Pluralism and Africa. Berkeley: University of California Press.

LAING, J. D., and R. J. MORRISON
1973 "Coalitions and payoffs in three person sequential games of status: initial tests of two formal models." Journal of Mathematical Sociology 3: 3-26.
1974 "Sequential games of status." Behavioral Science 19: 177-96.

LAING, J. D., and S. OLMSTED
1978 "Policy-making by committees: an experimental and game-theoretic study." Pp. 215-81 in P. C. Ordeshook (ed.), Game Theory and Political Science. New York: New York University Press.

LAING, J. D., and P. C. ORDESHOOK
In Preparation   Game Theoretic Analysis.

LAMBERT, RICHARD D.
1977 Preface. The Annals 433: vii-viii.

LAMPARD, ERIC E.
1965 "Historical aspects of urbanization." Pp. 519-54 in Philip M. Hauser and Leo F. Schnore (eds.), The Study of Urbanization. New York: Wiley.

LAND, KENNETH C.
1970 "Mathematical formalization of Durkheim's theory of the division of labor."
Pp. 227–82 in Edgar Borgatta and George Bohrnstedt (eds.), Sociological Methodology, 1970. San Francisco: Jossey-Bass.

LAND, KENNETH C., and MARCUS FELSON
1976 "A general framework for building dynamic macro social indicator models: including an analysis of changes in crime rates and police expenditures." American Journal of Sociology 82: 565–604.

LANDES, D. S.
1969 The Unbound Prometheus. London: Cambridge University Press.

LANE, DAVID, and FELICITY O'DELL
1978 The Soviet Industrial Worker. New York: St. Martin's Press.

LANG, K., and G. LANG
1961 Collective Dynamics. New York: Crowell.

LANGBEIN, LAURA IRWIN, and ALLAN J. LICHTMAN
1978 Ecological Inference. Beverly Hills: Sage.

LAUWERS, JAN
1973 "Les théories sociologiques concernant la sécularisation—typologie et critique." Social Compass 20: 523–33.

LAZARSFELD, PAUL F., BERNARD BERELSON, and HAZEL GAUDET
[1944] The People's Choice. New York: Columbia University Press. 1960.

LEIK, ROBERT K., SHEILA A. LEIK, BRUCE MORTON, R. BROCK BEARDSLEY, and MARGARET E. HARDY
1975 "The emergence and change of stratification in social exchange systems." Social Science Research 4: 17–40.

LENNARD, H. L., and ARNOLD BERNSTEIN
1969 Patterns in Human Interaction. San Francisco: Jossey-Bass.

LÉVI-STRAUSS, CLAUDE
1967 The Elementary Structures of Kinship. Translated by James H. Bell, John R. Von Sturmer, and Rodney Needham. London: Eyre and Spottiswode.

LEVINE, MARC V.
1977 "Institution design and the separatist impulse: Quebec and the Antebellum American South." The Annals 433: 60–72.

LEVINE, SOL, and MARTIN A. KOZLOFF
1978 "The sick role: assessment and overview." Annual Review of Sociology 4: 317–43.

LEVINSON, DANIEL J., CHARLOTTE N. DARROW, EDWARD B. KLEIN, MARIA H. LEVINSON, and BRANTON McKEE
1978 The Seasons of a Man's Life. New York: Knopf.

LEVY, MARION J.
1955 "Contrasting factors in the modernization of China and Japan." Pp. 496–536 in S. Kuznets (ed.), Economic Growth: Brazil, India, and Japan. Durham: Duke University Press.

LEWIN, KURT
1951 Field Theory in Social Science: Selected Papers (of Kurt Lewin). Edited by Dorwin Cartwright. New York: Harper and Row.

LIDZ, VICTOR
1979 "Secularization, ethical life, and religion in modern societies." Sociological Inquiry 49: 191–217.

LIEBERSON, STANLEY
1961 "A societal theory of race and ethnic relations." American Sociological Review 26: 902–10.

LIEBERSON, STANLEY, and L. K. HANSEN
1974 "National development, mother tongue diversity, and the comparative study of nations." American Sociological Review 39: 523–41.

LINCOLN, JAMES R.
1979 "Organizational differentiation in urban communities: a study in organizational ecology." Social Forces 57: 915–30.

LINDBLOM, CHARLES E.
1977 Politics and Markets: The World's Political–Economic Systems. New York: Basic Books.

LINDEMANN, E.
1944 "Symptomatology and the management of acute grief." American Journal of Psychiatry 101: 141–48.

LINDER, FORREST E.
1966 "The health of the American people." Scientific American 214: 21–29.

LIPSET, SEYMOUR MARTIN
1960 Political Man: The Social Bases of Politics. Garden City, N.Y.: Doubleday.
1963 The First New Nation. New York: Basic Books.

LIPSET, SEYMOUR MARTIN, and REINHARD BENDIX
1959 Social Mobility in Industrial Society. Berkeley: University of California Press.

LONG, NORTON E.
1949 "Power and administration." Public Administration Review 9: 257–64.

LOPATA, HELEN ZNANIECKI
1975 "Widowhood: societal factors in life-span disruptions and alternatives." Pp. 217–36 in Nancy Datan and Leon H. Ginsberg (eds.), Life-Span Developmental Psychology: Normative Life Crises. New York: Academic Press.

LUCE, R. D., and H. RAIFFA
1957 Games and Decisions. New York: Wiley.

LUCKMANN, THOMAS
1967 The Invisible Religion. New York: Macmillan.

LYND, ROBERT S., and HELEN M. LYND
1929 Middletown. New York: Harcourt.

MABRY, EDWARD A.
1975 "Exploratory analysis of a developmental model for task-oriented small groups." Human Communication Research 2: 67–74.

MACHLUP, FRITZ
1962 The Production and Distribution of Knowledge in the United States. Princeton, N.J.: Princeton University Press.

MacMillan, Alexander, and Richard L. Daft
1979 "Administrative intensity and ratio variables: the case against definitional dependency." Social Forces 58: 228-48.

Maddox, George L.
1966 "Persistence of life style among the elderly: a longitudinal study of patterns of social activity in relation to life satisfaction." Proceedings, Seventh International Congress of Gerontology 6: 309-11.
1979 "Sociology of later life." Annual Review of Sociology 5: 113-35.

Main, Jackson T.
1966 "The class structure of revolutionary America." Pp. 111-21 in Reinhard Bendix and Seymour Martin Lipset (eds.), Class, Status, and Power. New York: Free Press.

Mannheim, H. (ed.)
1960 Pioneers in Criminology. London: Stevens.

Mannheim, Karl
[1928] "The problem of generations." Pp. 276-322 in Paul Kecskemeti
1952 (ed.), Essays on the Sociology of Knowledge. London: Routledge and Kegan Paul.

March, James G., and Johan Olsen
1976 Ambiguity and Choice in Organizations. Bergen: Universitetsforlaget.

March, James G., and Herbert A. Simon
1958 Organizations. New York: Wiley.

Marglin, Stephen A.
1974 "What do bosses do? the origins of hierarchy in capitalist production." Review of Radical Political Economics 4: 60-112.

Martin, David
1969 The Religious and the Secular. New York: Schocken.
1978 A General Theory of Secularization. New York: Harper.

Martins, Luciano
1975 Nação e Corporacao Multinacional, a Politica das Empresas no Brasil e na America Latina. São Paulo: Paz e Terra.

Marx, Gary T.
1970a "Issueless riots." The Annals 391: 21-33.
1970b "Two cheers for the National Riot Commission." Pp. 78-96 in J. Szwed (ed.), Black Americans. New York: Basic Books.
1974 "Thoughts on a neglected category of social movement participant: the agent provocateur and the informant." American Journal of Sociology 80: 402-40.

Marx, Karl
1963 Early Writings. Translated and edited by T. B. Bottomore. New York: McGraw-Hill.

Mason, Philip
1971 Patterns of Dominance. New York: Oxford University Press.

Matthews, Fred H.
1977 Quest for an American Sociology: Robert E. Park and the Chicago School. Montreal: McGill-Queen's University Press.

McCarthy, J. D., and Mayer N. Zald

1973 The Trends of Social Movements in America: Professionalization and Resource Mobilization. Morristown, N.J.: General Learning Press.

1977 "Resource mobilization and social movements: a partial theory." American Journal of Sociology 82: 1212-39.

1979 The Dynamics of Social Movements. Cambridge: Winthrop.

McClendon, McKee J.

1976 "The occupational status attainment processes of males and females." American Sociological Review 41: 52-64.

1977 "Structural and exchange components of vertical mobility." American Sociological Review 42: 56-74.

McConnell, Grant

1966 Private Power and American Democracy. New York: Knopf.

In press "Vote trading: an experimental study." Public Choice.

McKelvey, R. D., and P. C. Ordeshook

1978 "Competitive coalition theory." Pp. 1-37 in P. C. Ordeshook (ed.), Game Theory and Political Science. New York: New York University Press.

McKelvey, R. D., P. C. Ordeshook, and M. D. Winer

1978 "The competitive solution for n-person games without transferable utility, with an application to committee games." American Political Science Review 72: 598-615.

McKelvey, R. D., and H. Rosenthal

1978 "Coalition formation, policy distance, and the theory of games without side-payments: an application to the French apparentement system." Pp. 405-50 in P. C. Ordeshook (ed.), Game Theory and Political Science. New York: New York University Press.

McLaughlin, Steven D.

1978 "Occupational sex identification and the assessment of male and female earnings inequality." American Sociological Review 43: 909-21.

McPhail, C.

1971 "Civil disorder participation: a critical examination of recent research." American Sociological Review 36:1058-73.

1978 "Toward a theory of collective behavior." Paper presented at Symposium of Symbolic Interaction, University of South Carolina, Columbia.

McPhail, C., and D. Miller

1973 "The assembling process: a theoretical and empirical examination." American Sociological Review 38: 721-35.

McPherson, J. Miller

1980 "Voluntary affiliation." In P. M. Blau and R. K. Merton (eds.), Continuities in Structural Inquiry. London: Sage.

Mead, George H.

1934 Mind, Self, and Society. Chicago: University of Chicago Press.

Medalia, N., and O. Larsen

1958 "Diffusion and belief in a collective delusion: the Seattle windshield pitting epidemic." American Sociological Review 23: 180-86.

MEEKER, B. F.
1971 "Decisions and exchange." American Sociological Review 36: 485-95.

MENAGHAN, ELIZABETH G.
1978 The Effect of Family Transitions on Marital Experience. Unpublished doctoral dissertation, University of Chicago.

MERTON, ROBERT K.
1967 "On sociological theories of the middle range." Pp. 39-72 in his On Theoretical Sociology: Five Essays, Old and New. New York: Free Press.
[1949] Social Theory and Social Structure. New York: Free Press.
1968
1976 Sociological Ambivalence and Other Essays. New York: Free Press.

MEYER, JOHN
1977 "The effects of education as an institution." American Journal of Sociology 83: 55-77.

MEYER, JOHN, FRANCISCO RAMIREZ, RICHARD RUBINSON, and JOHN BOLI-BENNET
1977 "The world educational revolution, 1950-1970." Sociology of Education 50: 242-58.

MEYER, JOHN, and BRIAN ROWAN
1978 "The structure of educational organizations." Pp. 78-109 in M. Meyer et al. (eds.), Environments and Organizations. San Francisco: Jossey-Bass.

MEYER, JOHN W., RICHARD SCOTT, and TERRENCE DEAL
1979 "Institutional and technical sources of organizational structure: explaining the structure of educational organizations." Conference on Human Service Organizations. Stanford, Calif.: Center for Advanced Study in the Behavioral Sciences.

MEYER, JOHN, DAVID TYACK, JOANE NAGEL, and AUDRI GORDON
1979 "Public education as a nation builder in America." American Journal of Sociology 85: 591-613.

MICHELSON, WILLIAM
1970 Man and His Urban Environment: A Sociological Approach. Reading, Mass.: Addison-Wesley.

MICKLIN, MICHAEL
1973 "Introduction: a framework for the study of human ecology." Pp. 3-27 in Michael Micklin (ed.), Population, Environment, and Social Organizations: Current Issues in Human Ecology. Hinsdale, Ill.: Dryden

MILLER, ALDEN A.
1971 "Logic of causal analysis: from experimental to nonexperimental designs." Pp. 273-94 in H. M. Blalock (ed.), Causal Models in the Social Sciences. Chicago: Aldine-Atherton.

MILLER, SEYMOUR M.
1960 "Comparative social mobility: a trend report and bibliography." Current Sociology 9: 1-89.

MILLER, WALTER B.
1958 "Lower-class culture as a generating milieu of gang delinquency." Journal of Social Issues 14: 5-19.

MILLS, THEODORE M.
1967 The Sociology of Small Groups. Englewood Cliffs, N.J.: Prentice-Hall.

MINUCHIN, SALVADOR
1974 Families and Family Therapy. Cambridge: Harvard University Press.

MITCHELL, J. CLYDE
1969 Social Networks and Urban Situations. Manchester: Manchester University Press.

MITCHELL, JACK N.
1978 Social Exchange, Dramaturgy, and Ethnomethodology: Toward a Paradigmatic Synthesis. New York: Elsevier, North Holland.

MOCH, LESLIE PAGE
1979 Migrants in the City: Newcomers in Nîmes, France at the Turn of the Century. Doctoral dissertation, University of Michigan.

MOL, HANS
1972 Western Religion: A Country by Country Analysis. The Hague: Mouton.

MONTAGNA, PAUL D.
1977 Occupations and Society. New York: Wiley.

MOODIE, GRAEME C., and ROWLAND EUSTACE
1974 Power and Authority in British Universities. London: Allen and Unwin.

MOORE, BARRINGTON, JR.
1966 Social Origins of Dictatorship and Democracy: Lord and Peasant in the Making of the Modern World. Boston: Beacon.

MOORE, WILBERT E.
1963 "But some are more equal than others." American Sociological Review 28: 13–18.
1966 "Changes in the occupational structure." Pp. 194–212 in Neil J. Smelser and Seymour Martin Lipset (eds.), Social Structure and Mobility in Economic Development. Chicago: Aldine.
1969 "Occupational socialization." Pp. 861–83 in David A. Goslin (ed.), Handbook of Socialization Theory and Research. Chicago: Rand McNally.
1970 The Professions: Roles and Rules. New York: Russell Sage Foundation.
1978 "Functionalism." Pp. 326–61 in Tom Bottomore and Robert Nisbet (eds.), A History of Sociological Analysis. New York: Basic Books.
1979 World Modernization: The Limits of Convergence. New York: Elsevier.

MORENO, JACOB L.
1934 Who Shall Survive? Washington, D.C.: Nervous and Mental Disease Publishing Company.

MORIYAMA, IWAO M.
1968 "Problems in the measurement of health status." Pp. 573–600 in E. B. Sheldon and W. E. Moore (eds.), Indicators of Social Change. New York: Russell Sage Foundation.

MUELLER, EVA, with JUDITH HYBELS, JAY SCHMIEDESKAMP, JOHN SONQUIST, and CHARLES STAELIN
1969 Technological Advance in an Expanding Economy. Ann Arbor, Mich.: Braun-Brumfield.

MULLAN, JOSEPH T.
1979 Changes in Marital Happiness and the Transition to the Empty Nest. Unpublished doctoral dissertation, University of Chicago.

MULLER, CHARLOTTE, FREDERICK S. JAFFE, and MARY GRACE KOVAR
1979 "Reproductive efficiency as a social indicator." Pp. 89–108 in J. Elinson and A. E. Siegmann (eds.), Sociomedical Health Indicators. Farmingdale, N.Y.: Baywood Publishing Company.

MULLINS, CAROLYN J.
1973 Theories and Theory Groups in Contemporary American Sociology, chap. 5. New York: Harper and Row.

MUMFORD, LEWIS
1938 The Culture of Cities. New York: Harcourt, Brace.

MURNANE, RICHARD J.
1975 The Impact of School Resources on the Learning of Inner City Children. Cambridge, Mass.: Ballinger.

MYERS, JEROME K., J. J. LINDENTHAL, and M. P. PEPPER
1971 "Life events and psychological impairment." Journal of Nervous and Mental Disease 152: 149–57.
1974 "Social class, life events, and psychiatric symptoms." Pp. 191–206 in B. S. Dohrenwend and B. P. Dohrenwend (eds.), Stressful Life Events: Their Nature and Effects. New York: Wiley.

NAKAMURA, A. O., M. NAKAMURA, and G. H. ORCUTT
1976 "Testing for relationships between time series." Journal of the American Statistical Association 71: 214–22.

NARITA, KATSUYA
1978 Systems of Higher Education: Japan. New York: International Council for Educational Development.

NASH, J. F.
1953 "Two-person cooperative games." Econometrica 21: 128–40.
1968 Report of the National Advisory Commission on Civil Disorders. National Advisory Commission on Civil Disorders. New York: Bantam Books.

NEIDERT, LISA J.
1978 The City as a System Generating Equality. A Replication and Extension. Unpublished MA thesis, University of Texas, Austin.
1979 "Industrial diversification, industrial composition, and income inequality among Anglos, Blacks, and Mexican Americans in the southwestern United States, 1970." University of Texas Population Research Center mimeo, Austin.

NEUGARTEN, BERNICE L., AND GUNHILD O. HAGESTAD
1976 "Age and the life course." Pp. 35–55 in Robert H. Binstock and Ethel Shanas (eds.), Handbook of Aging and the Social Sciences. New York: Van Nostrand-Reinhold.

NEUGARTEN, BERNICE L., JOAN MOORE, and JOHN C. LOWE
1965 "Age norms, age constraints, and adult socialization." American Journal of Sociology 70: 710–17.

NEWELL, A., and H. A. SIMON
1972 Human Problem Solving. Englewood Cliffs, N.J.: Prentice-Hall.

NISBET, ROBERT
1976 Sociology as an Art Form. New York: Oxford University Press.

NIXON, HOWARD L., II
1979 The Small Group. Englewood Cliffs, N.J.: Prentice-Hall.

Noble, D. F.
1978 Social Choice in Machine Design: Case Studies in the Labor Process. New York: Monthly Review Press.

NOEL, DONALD
1968 "A theory of the origin of ethnic stratification." Social Forces 16: 157–72.
1972 The Origins of American Slavery and Racism. Columbus, Ohio: Charles E. Merrill.

NORTH, D., and W. WEISSERT
1973 Immigrants and the American Labor Market. Washington, D.C.: Trans-Century.

NOTESTEIN, FRANK W.
1945 "Population—the long view." Pp. 36–57 in Theodore W. Schultz (ed.), Food for the World. Chicago: University of Chicago Press.
1953 "Economic problems of population change." Proceedings of the Eighth International Conference of Agricultural Economists: 13–31.

OBERSCHALL, ANTHONY
1973 Social Conflict and Social Movements. Englewood Cliffs, N.J.: Prentice-Hall.

O'BRIEN, PHILIP
1975 "A critique of Latin American theories of dependency." Pp. 7–27 in Ivar Oxaal, Tony Barnett, and David Booth (eds.), Beyond the Sociology of Development: Economy and Society in Latin America and Africa. London: Routledge and Kegan Paul.

O'DONNELL, GUILLERMO
1977 "Estado e alianças na Argentina, 1956–1976." Pp. 15–57 in Paulo Sergio Pinheiro (ed.), O Estado na America Latina. São Paulo: Coediçoes Paz e Terra.
1978 "Reflections on the patterns of change in the bureaucratic–authoritarian state." Latin American Research Review 13: 3–38.

OGBURN, WILLIAM F., and OTIS D. DUNCAN
1964 "City size as a sociological variable." Pp. 129–47 in E. W. Burgess and Donald J. Bogue (eds.), Contributions to Urban Sociology. Chicago: University of Chicago Press.

OGBURN, WILLIAM F., and DOROTHY S. THOMAS
1927 "The influence of the business cycle on certain social conditions." Pp. 53–74 in Dorothy S. Thomas (ed.), Social Aspects of the Business Cycle. New York: Knopf.

OKOCHI, KAZUO, BERNARD KARSH, and SOLOMON B. LEVINE (EDS.)
1974 Workers and Employers in Japan. Princeton, N.J.: Princeton University Press.

OLSON, DAVID H. L.
1976 Treating Relationships. Lake Mills, Iowa: The Graphic Publishing Company.

OLSON, MANCUR
1972 "Unidentified educational costs in university teaching hospitals: initial study." Journal of Medical Education 47: 243-53.

OPP, KARL-DIETER
1979 Individualistische Sozialwissenschaft. Stuttgart: Ferdinand Enke Verlag.

OTTO, LUTHER B., and ARCHIBALD O. HALLER
1979 "Evidence for a social psychological view of the status attainment process." Social Forces 57: 887-914.

PAMPEL, FRED C., KENNETH C. LAND, and MARCUS FELSON
1977 "A social indicator model of changes in the occupational structure of the United States: 1947-1974." American Sociological Review 42: 951-64.

PARCEL, TOBY L.
1979 "Race, regional labor markets and earnings." American Sociological Review 44: 262-79.

PARK, ROBERT E., and ERNEST W. BURGESS
1921 Introduction to the Science of Sociology. Chicago: University of Chicago Press.

PARKES, C. M., and R. J. BROWN
1972 "Health after bereavement." Psychosomatic Medicine 34: 449-61.

PARSONS, TALCOTT
1937 The Structure of Social Action. New York: Macmillan.
1940 "An analytic approach to the theory of social stratification." American Journal of Sociology 45: 841-62.
[1942] "Age and sex in the social structure of the United States."
1949 Pp. 89-103 in Talcott Parsons (ed.), Essays in Sociological Theory, Pure and Applied. Glencoe, Ill.: Free Press.
1951 The Social System. Glencoe, Ill.: Free Press.
1952 "Religious perspectives of college teaching: sociology and social psychology." Pp. 286-337 in Hoxie N. Fairchild (ed.), Religious Perspectives of College Teaching. New York: Ronald.
1954 "The theoretical development of the sociology of religion." Pp. 197-211 in Essays in Sociological Theory. Glencoe, Ill.: Free Press.
1960 "Some comments on the pattern of religious organization in the United States." Pp. 295-321 in Structure and Process in Modern Societies. Glencoe, Ill.: Free Press.
1967 "Christianity and modern industrial society." Pp. 385-421 in Sociological Theory and Moden Society. New York: Free Press.
1968 "Professions." Pp. 536-47 in David L. Sills (ed.), International Encyclopedia of the Social Sciences, 12. New York: Macmillan and Free Press.
1977 The Evolution of Societies. Englewood Cliffs, N.J.: Prentice-Hall.

PARSONS, TALCOTT, and R. F. BALES
1955 Family, Socialization and Interaction Process. Glencoe, Ill.: Free Press.

PARSONS, TALCOTT, and GERALD M. PLATT
1973 The American University. Cambridge: Harvard University Press.

Parsons, Talcott, and Neil J. Smelser
1956 Economy and Society: A Study in the Integration of Economic and Social Theory. Glencoe, Ill.: Free Press.

Patrick, Donald L.
1979 "Constructing social metrics for health status indexes." Pp. 75–85 in J. Elinson and A. E. Siegmann (eds.), Sociomedical Health Indicators. Farmingdale, N.Y.: Baywood Publishing Company.

Patrick, J.
1973 A Glasgow Gang Observed. London: Eyre Methuen.

Pearlin, Leonard I.
1975 "Sex roles and depression." Pp. 191–207 in Nancy Datan and Leon Ginsberg (eds.), Life-Span Developmental Psychology: Normative Life Crises. New York: Academic Press.
1980 "Life-strains and psychological distress among adults: a conceptual overview." Pp. 174–92 in Neil J. Smelser and Erik H. Erikson (eds.), Themes of Love and Work in Adulthood. Cambridge: Harvard University Press.

Pearlin, Leonard I., and Joyce S. Johnson
1977 "Marital status, life-strains and depression." American Sociological Review 42: 704–15.

Pearlin, Leonard I., and Morton A. Lieberman
1979 "Social sources of emotional distress." Pp. 217–48 in Roberta Simmons (ed.), Research in Community and Mental Health. Greenwich, Conn.: JAI Press.

Pearlin, Leonard I., and Clarice Radabaugh
1976 "Economic strains and the coping functions of alcohol." American Journal of Sociology 82: 652–63.

Pearlin, Leonard I., and Carmi Schooler
1978 "The structure of coping." Journal of Health and Social Behavior 19: 2–21.

Pelz, D. C., and F. M. Andrews
1964 "Detecting causal priorities in panel study data." American Sociological Review 29: 836–48.

Pennings, Johannes M.
1975 "The relevance of the structural contingency model for organizational effectiveness." Administrative Science Quarterly 20: 393–410.

Perkin, Harold
1969 Key Profession. New York: Augustus M. Kelley.

Perrow, Charles
1979 Complex Organizations. Glenview, Ill.: Scott, Foresman.

Pettigrew, Thomas F.
1979 "Racial change and social policy." The Annals 441: 114–31.

Pfautz, H. W.
1975 "Collective behavior and its critics: an uncritical mass." Unpublished paper.

Phillips, L.
1953 "Case history data and prognosis in schizophrenia." Journal of Nervous and Mental Disease 117: 515–25.

Phillipson, M.
1974 "Thinking out of deviance." Unpublished paper.

PILL, ROISIN
1974 "Social implications of a bilingual policy, with particular reference to Wales." British Journal of Sociology 25: 94–107.

PINHEIRO, PAULO SERGIO
1977 O Estado na America Latina. São Paulo: Co-ediçoes Paz e Terra.

PINKNEY, ALPHONSO
1976 Red, Black, and Green. Black Nationalism in the United States. New York and London: Cambridge University Press.

PIRENNE, HENRI
1934 "Guilds: European." Pp. 209–14 in Encyclopedia of the Social Sciences, 11. New York: Macmillan.

PITCHER, BRIAN L., ROBERT L. HAMBLIN, and JERRY L. L. MILLER
1978 "The diffusion of collective violence." American Sociological Review 43: 23–35.

PLOTT, C. R.
1967 "A notion of equilibrium and its possibility under majority rule." American Economic Review 57: 787–806.

PLUMMER, K.
1979 "Misunderstanding labelling perspectives." Pp. 85–121 in D. Downes and P. Rock (eds.), Deviant Interpretations. Oxford: Martin Robertson.

POLSKY, N.
1967 Hustlers, Beats and Others. Chicago: Aldine.

PORTER, JUDITH R.
1973 "Secularization, differentiation, and the function of religious value orientations." Sociological Inquiry 43: 67–74.

PORTES, ALEJANDRO
1976 "On the sociology of national development: theories and issues." American Journal of Sociology 82: 55–85.

POTTER, DAVID M.
1954 People of Plenty. Chicago: University of Chicago Press.

PUGH, D. S., D. J. HICKSON, C. R. HININGS, AND C. TURNER
1968 "Dimensions of organization structure." Administrative Science Quarterly 13: 65–105.

PURCELL, VICTOR
1966 The Chinese in Southeast Asia (2nd ed.). London: Oxford University Press.

QUARANTELLI, E. L.
1975 "Panic behavior: some empirical observations." Unpublished paper.

QUARANTELLI, E. L., and RUSSELL R. DYNES
1940 "Property norms and looting: their patterns in community crises." Phylon 31: 168–82.

QUINLEY, HAROLD E.
1974 The Prophetic Clergy. New York: Wiley.

QUINNEY, R.
1975 "Crime control in capitalist society." Pp. 181–202 in I. Taylor, P. Walton, and J. Young (eds.), Critical Criminology. London: Routledge and Kegan Paul.

RABKIN, JUDITH G., and ELMER L. STRUENING
1976 "Life events, stress and illness." Science 194: 1013-20.

RAGIN, CHARLES
1977 "Class, status, and 'reactive ethnic cleavages.'" American Sociological Review 42: 438-50.

RAMIREZ, FRANCISCO, and RICHARD RUBINSON
1979 "Creating members: the political incorporation and expansion of public education." Pp. 72-82 in J. Meyer and M. Hannan (eds.), National Development and the World System. Chicago: University of Chicago Press.

RAPOPORT, A.
1970 N-Person Game Theory: Concepts and Applications. Ann Arbor: University of Michigan Press.

RASHDALL, HASTINGS
1936 The Universities of Europe in the Middle Ages, Vols. 1, 2, 3. Oxford: Oxford University Press.

RAUSH, H. L., W. A. BARRY, R. K. HERTEL, and M. A. SWAIN
1974 Communication, Conflict and Marriage. San Francisco: Jossey-Bass.

RAWLS, JOHN
1971 A Theory of Justice. Cambridge: Harvard University Press.

READER, JOHN
1979 "Microcosm of a continental force: tribalism in Kenya." Smithsonian 10: 40-50.

REEVES, MARJORIE
1970 "The European university from medieval times." Pp. 61-84 in W. R. Niblett (ed.), Higher Education: Demand and Response. San Francisco: Jossey-Bass.

REISNER, E. H.
1927 Nationalism and Education Since 1789. New York: Macmillan.

REISS, ALBERT J., JR.
1961 Occupations and Social Status. New York: Free Press.

REX, JOHN
1970 Race Relations in Sociological Theory. New York: Schocken.

RICE, DOROTHY P.
1966 Estimating the Cost of Illness. Washington, D.C.: U.S. Department of Health, Education and Welfare, Public Health Service.

RICE, DOROTHY P., JACOB K. FELDMAN, and KERR A. WHITE
1977 The Current Burden of Illness. Washington, D.C.: Institute of Medicine.

RICHMOND, MARIE L.
1976 "Beyond resource theory: another look at factors enabling women to affect family interaction." Journal of Marriage and the Family 38: 257-66.

RIGNEY, DANIEL, RICHARD MACHALEK, and JERRY D. GOODMAN
1978 "Is secularization a discontinuous process?" Journal for the Scientific Study of Religion 17: 381-87.

RILEY, MATILDA WHITE
1963 Sociological Research. New York: Harcourt, Brace and World.

1973 "Aging and cohort succession: interpretations and misinterpretations." Public Opinion Quarterly 37: 35–49.

RILEY, MATILDA WHITE, ANNE FONER, BETH HESS, and MARCIA L. TOBY
1969 "Socialization for the middle and later years." Pp. 951–82 in David Goslin (ed.), Handbook of Socialization Theory and Research. Chicago: Rand McNally.

RILEY, MATILDA WHITE, ANNE FONER, MARY E. MOORE, BETH HESS, and BARBARA K. ROTH
1968 Aging and Society: An Inventory of Research Findings. Vol. 1. New York: Russell Sage Foundation.

RILEY, MATILDA WHITE, MARILYN JOHNSON, and ANNE FONER
1972 Aging and Society: A Sociology of Age Stratification. Vol. 3. New York: Russell Sage Foundation.

RILEY, MATILDA WHITE, and EDWARD E. NELSON
1971 "Research on stability and change in social systems." Pp. 407–49 in Bernard Barber and Alex Inkeles (eds.), Stability and Social Change. Boston: Little, Brown.

ROBERTSON, ROLAND
1971 "Sociologists and secularization." Sociology 5: 297–312.

ROBINSON, ROBERT V.
1979 "Ownership of the means of production and authority in the workplace: a cross-national study of class mobility." Yale Series of Working Papers in Sociology.

ROBINSON, ROBERT V., and JONATHAN KELLEY
1979 "Class as conceived by Marx and Dahrendorf." American Sociological Review 44: 38–58.

ROCK, P.
1979 "The sociology of crime, symbolic interactionism, and some problematic qualities of radical criminology." Pp. 52–84 in D. Downes and P. Rock (eds.), Deviant Interpretations. Oxford: Martin Robertson.

ROETHLISBERGER, FRITZ R., and WILLIAM J. DICKSON
1939 Management and the Worker. Cambridge: Harvard University Press.

ROGOFF, NATALIE
1953a Occupational Mobility. Glencoe, Ill.: Free Press.
1953b Recent Trends in Occupational Mobility. New York: Free Press.

ROSENBAUM, JAMES E.
1976 Making Inequality: The Hidden Curriculum of High School Tracking. New York: Wiley.

ROSENBERG, MORRIS
1965 Society and the Adolescent Self-Image. Princeton, N.J.: Princeton University Press.

ROSENBERG, MORRIS, and C. B. McCULLOUGH
1979 "Mattering: inferred significance and mental health." Paper presented at the Annual Meeting of the American Sociological Association, Boston.

ROSOW, IRVING
1967 Social Integration of the Aged. New York: Free Press.

Ross, C. E., and J. Mirowsky, II
  1979 "A comparison of life-event weighting schemes: change, undesirability and effect-proportional indices." Journal of Health and Social Behavior 20: 166–77.

Rueschemeyer, Dietrich
  1977 "Structural differentiation, efficiency, and power." American Journal of Sociology 83: 1–25.

Russell, C. S.
  1974 "Transition to parenthood: problems and gratifications." Journal of Marriage and the Family 36: 294–303.

Rutter, Michael, Barbara Maughan, Peter Mortimore, and Janet Ouston
  1979 Fifteen Thousand Hours: Secondary Schools and Their Effects. Cambridge: Harvard University Press.

Ryder, Norman B.
  1964a "Notes on the concept of a population." American Journal of Sociology 69: 447–63.
  1964b "The process of demographic translation." Demography 1: 74–82.
  1965 "The cohort as a concept in the study of social change." American Sociological Review 30: 843–61.
  1979 "Commentary on cohorts, periods and ages." Unpublished paper.

Schelling, Thomas C.
  1978 Micromotives and Macrobehavior. New York: Norton.

Schermerhorn, R. A.
  1970 Comparative Ethnic Relations: A Framework for Theory and Research. Chicago: University of Chicago Press.
  1974 "Ethnicity in the perspective of the sociology of knowledge." Ethnicity 1: 1–14.

Schnore, Leo F.
  1963 "The socio-economic status of cities and suburbs." American Sociological Review 28: 76–85.
  1965 The Urban Scene. New York: Free Press.
  1969 "The statistical measurement of urbanization and economic development." Pp. 91–106 in W. A. Faunce and W. H. Form (eds.), Comparative Perspectives on Industrial Society. Boston: Little, Brown.

Schnore, Leo F., and Hal H. Winsborough
  1972 "Functional classification and the residential location of social classes." Pp. 124–51 in B. J. L. Berry (ed.), City Classification Handbook. New York: Wiley.

Schuessler, Karl
  1973 "Ratio variables and path models." In A. S. Goldberger and O. D. Duncan (eds.), Structural Equation Models in the Social Sciences. New York: Seminar.

Schultz, Beatrice
  1978 "Predicting emergent leaders: an exploratory study of the salience of communicative functions." Small Group Research 9: 477–92.

Schwirian, K. P.
  1974 "Some recent trends and methodological problems in urban ecological research." Pp. 3–31 in K. P. Schwirian (ed.), Comparative Urban Structure. Lexington, Mass.: Heath.

SCITOVSKY, ANNE A.
1976 "A method of estimating physician requirements." Millbank Memorial Fund Quarterly 54: 299–320.

SEE, KATHERINE O'SULLIVAN
1979 "The dialectic of ethnicity and class in Northern Ireland." Paper presented at Workshop in Comparative Macrosociology, University of Chicago.

SEIDMAN, HAROLD
1970 Politics, Position and Power: The Dynamics of Federal Organization. New York: Oxford University Press.

SEYLE, HANS
1956 The Stress of Life. New York: McGraw-Hill.

SHAVER, KELLEY G.
1975 An Introduction to Attribution Processes. Cambridge: Winthrop.

SHAW, MARVIN E.
1976 Group Dynamics: The Psychology of Small Group Behavior (2nd ed.). New York: McGraw-Hill.

SHEEHY, GAIL
1976 Passages: Predictable Crises of Adult Life. New York: Dutton.

SHELDON, ELEANOR B., and WILBERT E. MOORE
1968 Indicators of Social Change. New York: Russell Sage Foundation.

SHEPARD, JON M.
1971 Automation and Alienation. Cambridge: Massachusetts Institute of Technology Press.

SHEPS, MINDEL C., and JANE A. MENKEN
1973 Mathematical Models of Conception and Birth. Chicago: University of Chicago Press.

SHERIF, MUZAFER
1936 The Psychology of Social Norms. New York: Harper and Row.

SHEVKY, E., and W. BELL
1955 Social Area Analysis. Stanford, Calif.: Stanford University Press.

SHIBA, SHOJI
1973 A Cross-National Comparison of Labor Management with Reference to Technology Transfer. Tokyo: Institute of Developing Economies.

SHIBUTANI, T.
1970 Human Nature and Collective Behavior. Englewood Cliffs, N.J.: Prentice-Hall.

SHINER, LARRY
1967 "The concept of secularization in empirical research." Journal for the Scientific Study of Religion 6: 207–20.

SHORT, JAMES F., JR., and FRED L. STRODTBECK
1963 "The response of gang leaders to status threats: an observation on group process and delinquent behavior." American Journal of Sociology 68: 571–79.

SHUBIK, M.
1971 "Games of status." Behavioral Science 16: 117–29.

SIEGEL, PAUL M., ROBERT W. HODGE, and PETER H. ROSSI
1974 Occupational Prestige in the United States. New York: The Academic Press.

SIMMEL, GEORG
1950 Sociology of Georg Simmel. Translated by K. H. Wolff. Glencoe, Ill.: Free Press.

SIMON, HERBERT A.
1962 "The Architecture of complexity." Proceedings of the American Philosophical Society 106: 467–82.

SINGER, M. T.
1967 "Enduring personality styles and responses to stress." Transactions of the Association of Life Insurance Medical Directors 51: 150–66.

SITHOLE, MASIPULA
1979 Zimbabwe Struggles Within the Struggle. Salisbury: Rujeko.

SLATER, PHILIP E.
1966 Microcosm: Structural, Psychological, and Religious Evolution in Groups. New York: Wiley.

SLOSS, J.
1973 "Stable outcomes in majority voting games." Public Choice 15: 19–48.

SMELSER, NEIL J.
1963 Theory of Collective Behavior. New York: Free Press.
1970 "Two critics in search of a bias; a response to Currie and Skolnick." Annals 391: 46–55.
1974 "Growth, structural change, and conflict in California public higher education, 1950–1970." Pp. 9–141 in N. J. Smelser and G. Almond (eds.), Public Higher Education in California. Berkeley: University of California Press.

SMELSER, NEIL J., and SEYMOUR MARTIN LIPSET
1966a Social Structure and Mobility in Economic Development. Chicago: Aldine.
1966b "Social structure, mobility and development." Pp. 1–50 in Smelser and Lipset (eds.), Social Structure and Mobility in Economic Development. Chicago: Aldine.

SMELSER, NEIL J., and R. STEPHEN WARNER
1976 Sociological Theory: Historical and Formal. Morristown, N.J.: General Learning Press.

SMITH, ADAM
[1776] An Inquiry into the Nature and Causes of the Wealth of Nations.
1937 New York: Modern Library.

SMITH, DAVID L., and R. E. SNOW
1976 "The division of labor: conceptual and methodological issues." Social Forces 55: 520–28.

SMITH, RICHARD A., and ROBERT H. WELLER
1977 "Growth and structure of the metropolitan community." Pp. 76–149 in Kent P. Schwirian (ed.), Contemporary Topics in Urban Sociology. Morristown, N.J.: General Learning Press.

SMITH, ROBERT T. H.
1965 "Method and purpose in functional town classification." Annals of the Association of American Geographers 55: 539–48.

SNYDER, DAVID, MARK D. HAYWARD, and PAULA M. HUDIS
1978 "The location of change in the sexual structure of occupations, 1950–1970."
American Journal of Sociology 84: 706–17.

SNYDER, DAVID, and EDWARD L. KICK
1979 "Structural position in the world system and economic growth, 1955–70."
American Journal of Sociology 84: 1096–1126.

SOROKIN, PITIRIM A.
1927 Social Mobility. New York: Harper.
1941 Social and Cultural Dynamics: Basic Problems, Principles, and Methods,
Vol. 4. New York: American Book.
1947 Society, Culture and Personality. New York: Harper.

SOUTH, SCOTT J., and DUDLEY L. POSTON, JR.
1979 "Stability and change in the U.S. metropolitan system: 1950–1970." Paper
1.020. Austin: University of Texas Population Center.

SPAETH, JOE L.
1979 "Vertical differentiation among occupations." American Sociological
Review 44: 746–62.

SPANIER, G. B., R. A. LEWIS, and C. L. COLE
1975 "Marital adjustment over the family life cycle: the issue of curvilinearity."
Journal of Marriage and the Family 37: 263–75.

SPEARE, A., JR., S. GOLDSTEIN, and W. H. FREY
1975 Residential Mobility, Migration and Metropolitan Change. Cambridge:
Ballinger.

SPENNER, KENNETH I.
1979 "Temporal changes in work content." American Sociological Review 44:
968–75.

SPILERMAN, SEYMOUR
1977 "Careers, labor market structure, and socioeconomic achievement." American Journal of Sociology 83: 551–93.

SROLE, L., T. S. LANGNER, S. T. MICHAEL, M. K. OPLER, and T. A. C. RENNIE
1962 Mental Health in the Metropolis: The Midtown Manhattan Study. New
York: McGraw-Hill.

STARK, RODNEY, and CHARLES Y. GLOCK
1968 American Piety. Berkeley: University of California Press.

STEINER, IVAN D.
1972 Group Process and Productivity. New York: Academic Press.

STERN, ROBERT N., and OMER R. GALLE
1978 "Industrial conflict and the inter-metropolitan structure of production."
Social Science Quarterly 59: 257–73.

STINCHCOMBE, ARTHUR L.
1965 "Social structure and organizations." Pp. 142–93 in J. March (ed.), Handbook of Organizations. Chicago: Rand McNally.
1968 Constructing Social Theories. New York: Harcourt, Brace and World.

STOLZENBERG, ROSS M.
1975a "Black/white differences in occupation, education, and wages." American
Journal of Sociology 81: 299–323.

1975b "Occupations, labor markets, and the process of wage attainment." American Sociological Review 40: 645-65.

1978 "Bringing the boss back in: employer size, employee schooling, and socioeconomic achievement." American Sociological Review 43: 813-28.

STONE, KATHERINE
1974 "The origins of job structures in the steel industry." Review of Radical Political Economics 6: 113-73.

STOUFFER, SAMUEL
1966 Measurement and Prediction. Magnolia, Mass.: Petersmith.

STRAWSON, P. F.
1959 Individuals: An Essay in Descriptive Metaphysics. London: Methuen.

STRODTBECK, FRED L.
1951 "Husband-wife interaction over revealed differences." American Sociological Review 16: 468-73.

STURMTHAL, ADOLPH
1964 Workers' Councils. Cambridge: Harvard University Press.

SUMMERS, ANITA A., and BARBARA L. WOLFE
1974 "Equality of educational opportunity quantified: a production function approach." Unpublished manuscript. Federal Reserve Bank of Philadelphia, Philadelphia.

1977 "Do schools make a difference?" American Economic Review 67: 639-52.

SUMNER, WILLIAM G., and ALBERT G. KELLER
1927-28 The Science of Society. 4 Vols. New Haven: Yale University Press.

SUNKEL, OSVALDO, and PEDRO PAZ
1976 El Subdesarrollo Latinoamericano y la Teoria del Desarrollo. Mexico, D.F.: Siglo Veintiuno.

SUSSMANN, LEILA
1977 Tales Out of School: Implementing Organizational Change in the Elementary Grades. Philadelphia: Temple University Press.

SWANSON, GUY E.
1965 "On explanation of social interaction." Sociometry 28: 101-23.

1967 Religion and Regime: A Sociological Account of the Reformation. Ann Arbor: University of Michigan Press.

1968 "On sharing social psychology." Pp. 20-52 in Sven Lundstedt (ed.), Higher Education in Social Psychology. Cleveland: Case-Western Reserve University Press.

1969 "Rules of descent: studies in the sociology of parentage." Anthropological Papers No. 39. Museum of Anthropology, University of Michigan.

1970 "Toward corporate action: a reconstruction of elementary collective processes." Pp. 124-44 in Tamotsu Shibutani (ed.), Human Nature and Collective Behavior. Englewood Cliffs, N.J.: Prentice-Hall.

1971 "An organizational analysis of collectivities." American Sociological Review 36: 607-24.

1974a "Family structure and the reflective intelligence of children." Sociometry 37: 459-90.

1974b "The primary process of groups: its systematics and representation." Journal for the Theory of Social Behavior 4: 53–70.

1976 "Orpheus and star husband: meaning and the structure of myths." Ethnology 15: 115–33.

1978a "Trance and possession: studies of charismatic influence." Review of Religious Research 19: 253–75.

1978b "Travels through inner space." American Journal of Sociology 83: 890–919.

1979 "Ego defenses and the legitimation of behavior." Mimeographed, Department of Sociology, University of California, Berkeley.

SZTOMPKA, PIOTR
1974 System and Function: Toward a Theory of Society. New York: Academic Press.

SZYMANSKI, ALBERT J.
1978 "Braverman as a neo-Luddite." Insurgent Sociologist 8: 45–50.

TABB, WILLIAM
1971 "Race relations models and social change." Social Problems 18: 431–44.

TAYLOR, HOWARD F.
1970 Balance in Small Groups. New York: Van Nostrand–Reinhold.

TEITELBAUM, MICHAEL S.
1975 "Relevance of demographic transition theory for developing countries." Science 188: 420–25.

TEMME, LLOYD V.
1975 Occupation: Meanings and Measures. Washington, D.C.: Bureau of Social Science Research.

THEIL, H., and A. L. NAGAR
1961 "Testing the independence of regression disturbances." Journal of the American Statistical Association 56: 793–806.

THERNSTROM, STEPHAN
1964 Poverty and Progress. Cambridge: Harvard University Press.

THIBAUT, JOHN, and LAURENS WALKER
1975 Procedural Justice: A Psychological Analysis. New York: Halsted.

THOMAS, WILLIAM I., and FLORIAN ZNANIEKI
1918 The Polish Peasant in Europe and America. Chicago: University of Chicago Press.

THOMLINSON, RALPH
1969 Urban Structure: The Social and Spatial Character of Cities. New York: Random House.

THOMPSON, E. P.
1978 The Poverty of Theory and Other Essays. London: Merlin Press.

THOMPSON, E.
1975 Whigs and Hunters. London: Allen Lane.

THOMPSON, EDGAR
1939 Race Relations and the Race Problem: Durham, N.C.: Duke University Press.

THOMPSON, JAMES D.
1967 Organizations in Action. New York: McGraw-Hill.

THRASHER, FREDERIC M.
1927 The Gang. Chicago: University of Chicago Press.

TILLY, CHARLES
1978a "Introduction." Historical Studies of Changing Fertility. Princeton, N.J.: Princeton University Press.
1978b From Mobilization to Revolution. Reading, Mass.: Addison-Wesley.

TILLY, LOUISE A.
1977 "Urban growth, industrialization, and women's employment in Milan, Italy, 1881-1911." Journal of Urban History 3: 485-506.

TORRES RIVAS, EDELBERTO
1974 "Poder nacional y sociedad dependiente: notas sobre las clases y el estado en Centroamerica." Revista Paraguaya de Sociologia 29: 179-210.

TRAUGOTT, M.
1978 "Reconceiving social movements." Social Problems 26: 38-49.

TREIMAN, DONALD J.
1977 Occupational Prestige in Comparative Perspective. New York: Academic Press.

TREIMAN, DONALD J., and KERMIT TERRELL
1975 "Sex and the process of status attainment: a comparison of working women and men." American Sociological Review 40: 174-200.

TROW, MARTIN
1977 "Departments as contexts for teaching and learning." Pp. 12-33 in D. E. McHenry et al. (eds.), Academic Departments. San Francisco: Jossey-Bass.

TRUSSEL, RAY, and JACK ELINSON
1959 Chronic Illness in a Rural Area: The Hunterdon Study. Commission on Chronic Illness, Commonwealth Fund. Cambridge: Harvard University Press.

TUMIN, M., and A. FELDMAN
1955 "The miracle at sabena grande." Public Opinion Quarterly 19: 124-39.

TURNER, R. STEVEN
1971 "The growth of professorial research in Prussia, 1818 to 1848—causes and context." History Studies in the Physical Sciences 3: 137-82.

TURNER, RALPH H.
1964 "Collective behavior." Pp. 382-425 in R. E. L. Faris (ed.), Handbook of Modern Sociology. Chicago: Rand McNally.
1970 Family Interaction. New York: Wiley.

TURNER, RALPH H., and LEWIS M. KILLIAN
[1957] Collective Behavior. Englewood Cliffs, N.J.: Prentice-Hall.
1972

TYACK, DAVID
1974 The One Best System: A History of American Urban Education. Cambridge: Harvard University Press.

TYREE, ANDREA, and BILLY G. SMITH
1978 "Occupational hierarchy in the United States: 1789-1969." Social Forces 56: 881-99.

UDY, STANLEY H., JR.
1970 Work in Traditional and Modern Society. Englewood Cliffs, N.J.: Prentice-Hall.

UHLENBERG, PETER I.
1969 "A study of cohort life cycles: cohorts of native born Massachusetts women, 1830–1920." Population Studies 23: 407–20.

U.S. BUREAU OF THE CENSUS
1975 Historical Statistics of the United States, Colonial Times to 1970. Bicentennial Edition, Part 1. Washington, D.C.: U.S. Government Printing Office.

U.S. DEPARTMENT OF LABOR
1965 Dictionary of Occupational Titles. Vol. 1, Definition of Titles. Washington, D.C.: U.S. Government Printing Office.

USHIOGI, MORIKAZU
1979 "The Japanese student and the labor market." Pp. 107–26 in W.K. Cummings, I. Amano, and K. Kitamura (eds.), Changes in the Japanese University: A Comparative Perspective. New York: Praeger.

VAN DE GRAAFF, JOHN H., BURTON R. CLARK, DOROTEA FURTH, DIETRICH GOLDSCHMIDT, and DONALD F. WHEELER
1978 Academic Power: Patterns of Authority in Seven National Systems of Higher Education. New York: Praeger.

VAN DEN BERGHE, PIERRE
1970 Race and Ethnicity: Essays in Comparative Sociology. New York: Basic Books.
1978 Race and Racism (2nd ed.). New York: Wiley.

VANBERG, VIKTOR
1975 Die Zwei Soziologien. Tübingen: J. C. B. Mohr.

VANNEMAN, REEVE, and FRED C. PAMPEL
1977 "The American perception of class and status." American Sociological Review 42: 422–37.

VINACKE, W. E.
1962 "Power, strategy and the formation of coalitions in triads under four incentive conditions." Office of Naval Research NONR 3748(02), Technical Report No. 1, University of Hawaii.

VON NEUMANN, J., and O. MORGENSTERN
1947 Theory of Games and Economic Behavior (2nd. ed.). Princeton, N.J.: Princeton University Press.

WALLACE, WALTER L.
1971 The Logic of Science in Sociology. Chicago: Aldine-Atherton.
1979 "Hierarchic structure in social phenomena." In P. M. Blau and R. K. Merton (eds.), Continuities in Structural Inquiry. London: Sage.

WALLERSTEIN, IMMANUEL
1974 The Modern World System: Capitalist Agriculture and the Origins of European World-Economy in the Sixteenth Century. New York: Academic Press.
1976a "Modernization: requiescat in pace." Pp. 131–35 in Lewis A. Coser and Otto N. Larsen (eds.), The Uses of Controversy in Sociology. New York: Free Press.

1976b "Semi-peripheral countries and the contemporary world crisis." Theory and Society 3: 461–83.

1976c "A world system perspective on the social sciences." British Journal of Sociology 27: 343–52.

WANNER, RICHARD A.
1977 "The dimensionality of the urban functional system." Demography 13: 519–37.

WARD, LESTER
1883 Dynamic Sociology. Boston: Appleton.

WARING, JOAN M.
1975 "Social replenishment and social change: the problem of disordered cohort flow." Pp. 237–56 in Anne Foner (ed.), Age in Society. American Behavioral Scientist, 19.

WARWICH, DONALD P., and SAMUEL OSHERSON
1973 "Comparative analysis in the social sciences." Pp. 3–41 in D. P. Warwich and S. Osherson (eds.), Comparative Research Methods. Englewood Cliffs, N.J.: Prentice-Hall.

WASHINGTON POST
1976 "The American public is extraordinarily religious." July 23.

WATZLAWICK, PAUL, JOHN H. WEAKLAND, and RICHARD FISCH
1974 Change: Principles of Problem Formation and Problem Resolution. New York: Norton.

WEBER, MAX
[1921] Economy and Society. Edited by G. Roth and C. Wittich. New York: Bedminster.
1968
1947 The Theory of Social and Economic Organization. Translated by A. M. Henderson and T. Parsons. New York: Free Press.

WEICK, KARL
1976 "Educational organizations as loosely coupled systems." Administrative Science Quarterly 21: 1–19.

WELLER, J. M., and E. L. QUARANTELLI
1973 "Neglected characteristics of collective behavior." American Journal of Sociology 79: 665–85.
1974 "The structural problem of a sociological specialty: collective behavior's lack of a critical mass." American Sociologist 9: 59–68.

WELLER, ROBERT H.
1967 "An empirical examination of megalopolitan structure." Demography 4: 734–43.

WHEELER, DONALD F.
1978 "Japan." Pp. 124–44 in John H. Van de Graaff, Burton R. Clark, Dorotea Furth, Dietrich Goldschmidt, and Donald F. Wheeler (eds.), Academic Power: Patterns of Authority in Seven National Systems of Higher Education. New York: Praeger.

WHELPTON, P. K.
1954 Cohort Fertility: Native White Women in the United States. Princeton, N.J.: Princeton University Press.

WHITE, HARRISON C., SCOTT A. BOORMAN, and RONALD L. BREIGER
1976 "Social structure from multiple networks, I." American Journal of Sociology 81: 730-80.

WHITEHEAD, ALFRED N.
1949 The Aims of Education and Other Essays. New York: Mentor Books.

WHITING, BEATRICE B.
1978 "The dependency hangup and experiments in alternative life-styles." Pp. 217-26 in J. Milton Yinger and Stephen J. Cutler (eds.), Major Social Issues: A Multidisciplinary View. New York: Free Press.

WHYTE, MARTIN KING
1973 "Bureaucracy and modernization in China: the Maoist critique." American Sociological Review 38: 149-63.

WHYTE, WILLIAM FOOTE
1943 Street Corner Society. Chicago: University of Chicago Press.

WILENSKY, HAROLD L.
1964 "The professionalization of everyone?" American Journal of Sociology 70: 137-58.

WILENSKY, HAROLD L., and ANNE T. LAWRENCE
1979 "Job assignment in modern societies: a re-examination of the ascription-achievement hypothesis." Pp. 202-48 in Amos H. Hawley (ed.), Societal Growth: Processes and Implications. New York: Free Press.

WILKINSON, RICHARD G.
1973 Poverty and Progress: An Ecological Perspective on Economic Development. New York: Praeger.

WILLER, DAVID
1967 Scientific Sociology: Theory and Method. Englewood Cliffs, N.J.: Prentice-Hall.

WILLIAMS, J. A., NICHOLAS BABCHUK, and D. R. JOHNSON
1973 "Voluntary associations and minority status." American Sociological Review 38: 637-46.

WILLIAMS, ROBIN M., JR.
1974 "Attitudes and behavior towards immigrants and ethnic groups." Pp. 13-25 in William S. Bernard and Judith Herman (eds.), The New Immigration and the New Ethnicity: Social Policy and Social Theory in the 1970's. New York: American Immigration and Citizenship Conference.
1975a "Race and ethnic relations." Pp. 125-64 in Alex Inkeles, Neil Smelser, and James S. Coleman (eds.), Annual Review of Sociology, Vol. 1. Palo Alto, Calif.: Annual Reviews.
1975b "Relative deprivation." Pp. 355-78 in Lewis A. Coser (ed.), The Idea of Social Structure: Papers in Honor of Robert K. Merton. New York: Harcourt Brace Jovanovich.
1977 Mutual Accommodation, Ethnic Conflict and Cooperation. Minneapolis: University of Minnesota Press.

WILSNACK, R.
1979 "Counterfads: episode of collective disbelief." Paper presented to American Sociological Association meetings, Boston.

WILSON, BRYAN
   1966 Religion in Secular Society. London: Watts.
   1979a Contemporary Transformations of Religion. Oxford: Clarendon.
   1979b "The return of the sacred." Journal for the Scientific Study of Religion 18:
   268–80.

WILSON, KENNETH L.
   1978 "Toward an improved explanation of income attainment." American Journal of Sociology 84: 684–97.

WILSON, R.
   1971 "Stable coalition proposals in majority-rule voting." Journal of Economic
   Theory 3: 254–71.

WILSON, STEPHEN
   1978 Informal Groups: An Introduction. Englewood Cliffs, N.J.: Prentice-Hall.

WILSON, WILLIAM J.
   1973 Power, Racism and Privilege: Race Relations in Theoretical and Sociohistorical Perspectives. New York: Free Press.
   1978a "Deracialization and minority mobilization: color class issues in antidis-
   crimination movements." Paper presented at Indo–U.S. Seminar on Ethnicity
   and Social Change, New York.
   1978b The Declining Significance of Race: Blacks and Changing American Institutions. Chicago: University of Chicago Press.

WINSBOROUGH, HALLIMAN H.
   1979 "Changes in the transition to adulthood." Pp. 137–52 in Matilda White
   Riley (ed.), Aging from Birth to Death: Interdisciplinary Perspectives. Boulder,
   Colo.: Westview Press.

WISH, MYRON, and SUSAN J. KAPLAN
   1977 "Toward an implicit theory of interpersonal communication." Sociometry
   40: 234–46.

WOLF, WENDY C., and RACHEL ROSENFELD
   1978 "Sex structure of occupations and job mobility." Social Forces 56: 823–44.

WOLF, WENDY C., and NEIL D. FLIGSTEIN
   1979 "Sex and authority in the workplace: the causes of sexual inequality."
   American Sociological Review 44: 235–52.

WORDEN, F. G., B. CHILDS, S. MATTHYSSE, and E. C. GERSHON
   1976 Frontiers of Psychiatric Genetics. Neurosciences Research Program Bulletin,
   14.

WORLD HEALTH ORGANIZATION
   1969 International Classification of Diseases and Causes of Death. Geneva: World
   Health Organization.

WRIGHT, ERIK OLIN
   1976 "Class boundaries in advanced capitalist societies." New Left Review 98:
   3–41.
   1978 "Race, class, and income inequality." American Journal of Sociology 83:
   1368–97.

WRIGHT, ERIK OLIN, and LUCA PERRONE
   1977 "Marxist class categories and income inequality." American Sociological
   Review 42: 32–55.

WRONG, DENNIS
1961 "The oversocialized conception of man in modern sociology." American Sociological Review 25: 183-93.

WUTHNOW, ROBERT
1976 "Recent patterns of secularization: a problem of generations?" American Sociological Review 41: 850-67.
1977 "A longitudinal cross-national indicator of societal religious commitment." Journal for the Scientific Study of Religion 16: 87-99.

YANCEY, WILLIAM L., EUGENE P. ERICKSEN, and RICHARD N. JULIANI
1976 "Emergent ethnicity: a review and reformulation." American Sociological Review 41: 391-403.

YINGER, J. MILTON
1970 The Scientific Study of Religion. New York: Macmillan.
1977 "Countercultures and social change." American Sociological Review 42: 833-53.

ZALD, MAYER N., and ROBERTA ASH
1966 "Social movement organizations: growth, decay and change." Social Forces 44: 327-40.

ZBOROWSKI, M.
1952 "Cultural components in responses to pain." Journal of Social Issues 8: 16-30.

ZEITLIN, MAURICE
1974 "Corporate ownership and control." American Journal of Sociology 79: 1073-1119.

ZELDITCH, MORRIS, JR.
1969 "Can you really study an army in the laboratory?" Pp. 528-39 in Amitai Etzioni (ed.), A Sociological Reader on Complex Organizations (2nd ed.). New York: Holt, Rinehart and Winston.

ZURCHER, L.
1979 "Collective behavior: from static psychology to static sociology?" Paper presented at Pacific Sociological Association meetings, Anaheim, Cal.

Additional References

AUMANN, R. J., and M. MASCHLER
1964 "The bargaining set for cooperative games." Pp. 443-76 in M. Dresher, L. S. Shapley, and A. W. Tucker (eds.), Advances in Game Theory. Princeton, N.J.: Princeton University Press.

BOCHNER, ARTHUR P.
1976 "Conceptual frontiers in the study of communication in families: an introduction to the literature." Human Communications Research 2: 381-97.

DERBER, MILTON
1963 "Worker participation in Israeli management." Industrial Relations 3: 51-72.

HEISLER, MARTIN O.
1977 "Ethnic conflict in the world today: an introduction." The Annals 433: 1-5.

KNAPP, VINCENT
   1976 Europe in the Era of Social Transformation. Englewood Cliffs, N.J.:
   Prentice-Hall.

PARKER, RICHARD
   1972 The Myth of the Middle Class. New York: Harper and Row.

PATRICK, DONALD, JAMES BUSH, and MARTIN CHEN
   1973 "Toward an operational definition of health." Journal of Health and Social
   Behavior 14: 6-23.

REYNOLDS, W., WILLIAM RUSHING, and DAVID MILES
   1974 "The validation of a function status index." Journal of Health and Social
   Behavior 15: 271-78.

Name Index

Subject Index